D0212992

Bohemian Fifths

An Autobiography

HANS WERNER HENZE

Translated by Stewart Spencer

PRINCETON UNIVERSITY PRESS
PRINCETON, NEW JERSEY

Published in 1999 in the United States of America by
Princeton University Press, 41 William Street, Princeton, New Jersey 08540

This translation first published in Great Britain in 1998
by Faber and Faber Limited
3 Queen Square London WC1N 3AU
Originally published in German in 1996
by S. Fischer Verlag GmbH, Frankfurt am Main

Typeset by Faber and Faber Ltd
Printed in England by Clays Ltd, St Ives plc

The publication of this work has been subsidized by Inter Nationes, Bonn

Stewart Spencer is hereby identified as translator of this
work in accordance with Section 77 of the Copyright,
Designs and Patents Act 1988

ISBN 0–691–00683–0

http://pup.princeton.edu

2 4 6 8 10 9 7 5 3 1

Contents

List of Illustrations

19 Gustav Rudolf Sellner (producer of *Die Bassariden*), W. H. Auden, HWH, Salzburg, 1966. Photo by Hilde Köster.
20 HWH with the cast of the world première of *Pollicino*, Montepulciano, 1980.
21 Peter Maxwell Davies, HWH, Harrison Birtwistle. London.
22 HWH and Simon Rattle, rehearsing with the CBSO, Aldeburgh, 1986. Photo by Nigel Luckhurst.
23 HWH and Oliver Knussen, 1997. Photo by Clive Barda.

The photographs are from the private collection of Hans Werner Henze, unless otherwise stated.

Translator's Foreword

No text of such cultural complexity as the present one can be translated single-handedly, and I am grateful to the following friends and colleagues for answering individual queries: Peter Adam, Germana Cantoni, Andrew Clements, Alexander Goehr, Sally Groves, Helga Harman, Jitka Ludvová, Barry Millington, Ulrike Müller, Jeffery Pike, Mavis Sacher, Mayumi Shimizu, John Sidgwick and Jeremy Spencer. Particular thanks are due to Oliver Knussen for reading through the whole typescript and making many invaluable suggestions and to Eva Zöllner for promptly and good-humouredly dealing with countless queries about German life and letters.

No translator could wish for a more inspiring collaborator than Hans Werner Henze, who has worked through the whole of the translation with me and brought to bear on it his remarkable grasp of English nuance and keen ear for metrical sentence structures. At the same time he has taken the opportunity to make a number of changes to the German original, correcting a handful of errors and bringing the text up to date. Although any translation must inevitably be a pale reflection of the original, it is hoped that it may still retain something of Hans Werner Henze's style and character, most notably his use of irony, his virtuoso command of a wide range of shifting stylistic registers from diaristic terseness to the rhetorical set piece and his mercurial and protean ability to assume any number of different personalities, while at the same time remaining uniquely and engagingly himself.

Stewart Spencer

per il Moretto di Berardone

I

Do you think the ancient fiddler
Whose universal fiddle makes
The very constellations dance
Will play our earthly lives again
From start to finish once those lives
Are done, but higher, at the fifth?

Nikolaus Lenau, 'Der Steirertanz'

In October 1986 I returned home to my birthplace at Gütersloh in Westphalia, my first visit to the town in more than fifty years. Although I had been only four when I had last seen the place, I thought I could recognize certain things – houses, streams and clouds. The house in the Brunnenstraße where I had been born was, and still is, an attractive little building in a kind of rustic *Jugendstil*, dating from 1901. (I recognized it from photographs.) After more than half a century, I had been invited to take tea with its present inhabitants, who filled me in on the house's history, informing me, for example, that in the wake of the Second World War it had served as a mess for British NCOs and that it was the victorious British army that had had the bathroom installed. Here, on the upper floor, was the apartment that my newly wed Protestant parents – Franz and Margarete Adele Henze née Geldmacher – had moved into in 1926, in order that I myself might first see the light of the world there.

I spent a whole week in Gütersloh during that Indian summer of 1986, fêted with lavish concerts, lectures and opera performances to mark my sixtieth birthday. I was moved and even a little proud. And grateful that there were no importunate souls to monopolize my attention. I was simply left in peace. I had arrived in Gütersloh by train with Michael Vyner, the then director of the London Sinfonietta, in whose memory I wrote my *Requiem* between 1990 and 1992, and, such was my curiosity, had immediately set

off on a tour of inspection of the attractive little town, in the course of which we stumbled across a huge menhir-like object with a golden menorah and an inscription, in German, hewn into the rock. A little apprehensively, Michael, who was Jewish, asked me to translate it for him. It said:

> To the memory of the Jewish community of Gütersloh
> and its synagogue, which stood not far from this place
> and which was destroyed by townspeople on 9 November 1938.
> As a warning to us all.

So even here, in my own home town, there had been murderers and madmen! We hurried away from the scene of the crime, and I hid myself away in my hotel room, feeling ashamed and hurt.

Three years later I returned to Gütersloh and this time stayed a whole month, running a summer school – a workshop not only for young English singers and instrumentalists but also for young directors from various countries – and preparing for a production of my comic opera, *The English Cat*. The town had placed an apartment at my disposal and, since it contained a grand piano, I was also able to spend a certain period each day working on the two closing scenes of my opera, *Das verratene Meer*.

I wanted to capture in my music the light of this particular part of eastern Westphalia, which has a certain silent melancholy to it: there is never the sort of dazzling brightness that I find at home in central Italy, for instance. It is a completely different sort of light that produces a wholly different kind of music and also, of course, a different way of thinking. On my way to rehearsals at the theatre in Gütersloh I would sometimes bump into people on their way to church, wrapped in grey raincoats, wearing severely styled hats and carrying umbrellas, all with the same expression on their faces, as though they had been summoned to appear before their local tax inspector. Yet they were going to hear the word of God, an act which, for Protestants, I imagine is largely one of penance – or so I assume on the strength of my admittedly limited knowledge of the subject: Protestant sermons somehow always seem more like a warning or a reprimand. It occurred to me that very few young sinners would choose to hear such a homily. Often the bells must peal in vain. Those in the Martin-Luther-Kirche, where I myself was baptized, are now electrically operated and are in C minor – just like the final bars of *Das verratene Meer*, when Noboru and his schoolfriends prepare to execute his stepfather, the merchant navy officer, Ryuji Tsukazaki, whom they have communally condemned to death.

The feeling of flatness that overcomes me whenever I spend any length of time in an area like that around Münster – in other words, the absence of anything to break up this flatness, the lack of valleys, hills and gullies – has left a remarkable, but by no means disagreeable, impression upon me. Eternity either stops or starts where you can see the last row of poplars: endless simplicity goes on and on like this, in the most beautiful and unobtrusive way imaginable. It is not far from Gütersloh that the Teutoburger Wald begins, at first barely perceptibly, like a kind of sand dune, then a further hollow in which nestle towns like Bünde, Detmold, Herford and Salzuflen, where my mother died in 1976. According to Tacitus and Kleist, it was here that a terrible battle was fought in AD 9, in the course of which a loose confederation of Germanic tribes under the Cheruscan leader, Hermann, defeated the Roman armies under Varus. The site is marked by a monument to Hermann, the life's work of the patriotic sculptor, Ernst von Bandel, and a popular destination for classes of schoolchildren. Even today, I am told, it is possible to climb up into the head of the statue and, from a vertiginous height, peer out through the hero's nostrils over the fields of potatoes and grain that stretch as far as the eye can see across the Vale of Ravensberg, a generally sandy area that is otherwise overgrown with heather and juniper and pine trees, together with the odd turnip field, and that reminds me of the Brandenburg Marches. Heine described the people who lived here or who came from these parts with a few deft strokes of his pen in his satirical epic, *Deutschland, ein Wintermärchen*:

Those dear old friends of the Göttingen days!
How we drank while we were able,
And then how we fell on each other's hearts,
And sank beneath the table!
[...]
They can fight, they can drink, and, when hand-clasps seal
Love's bond, their spirit mellows
And they weep; they are sentimental oaks,
And the rarest of good fellows.

(trans. Margaret Armour)

We are, indeed, phlegmatic as a people, tending towards melancholy and pessimism, mentally lazy and, at the same time, amiable by nature. The language spoken in Westphalia is Low German, which sounds almost like Dutch at its most attractive, although we were not allowed to speak it as children. Another of our parents' rules was that we were not allowed to talk to those of our classmates whose mothers made cigars at home on a piece-rate basis. We were told that they all had tuberculosis. Needless to say, we were also told never to set foot inside the smallholdings where these large but indigent families lived and which invariably smelt of tobacco leaves. As a result, the only local traditions with which I and my brothers and sisters ever came into contact were woollen socks and the wooden clogs known as 'Mülheim boats'. A pair of them lasted years and, as in Japan, had to be left outside when you entered the house. In our own case, this meant walking in woollen socks on wooden floors that our mother had polished until her face was reflected in them, inviting us to slip and crack open the back of our heads.

I was a sorry sight during this early period, when I was four or five years old. Starting at the bottom, I remember that my feet pointed inwards and tended to fall over each other. Taken together with the fact that my left leg was – and still is – eight millimetres shorter than my right, this later led to all manner of complications, not least with NCOs and sergeant-majors, who thought I was just being bloody-minded in refusing to stand up straight. The upper half of my body was nothing to write home about either. I suffered from a squint which took years to correct with the help of a black eyepatch. I also wore a fringe that today's punks would have loved, and my general appearance was hardly helped by the fact that, as the result of an unfortunate fall from our kitchen cupboard, I sustained a deep cut between my upper lip and nose that looked for all the world like a harelip and left a permanent scar clearly visible to this day. My eyes were greener then than they are now, but even at that time the pupils could contract to form two vertical slits in order to register censure. It is also true to say that even then I already had a foul temper and would fly into a rage if I did not get my way. As a child I would scream my head off, lying on the floor and pummelling it with my fists, shouting 'Leave me alone, leave me alone!' as loudly as I could, till Father came and gently placed a blanket over me. The luxurious darkness must have comforted me, since I invariably quietened down. And so I got my way in the end and was left alone. Physical punishment was frowned upon. Instead, we were not allowed to go out or read and were deprived of our parents' love, a form of emotional torment that consisted of their refusal to speak to their refractory offspring for hours on end. It seemed to last an eternity – we never knew if it was to be for ever or for only a short space of time. It may well be that the reasons for my life-long attempts to achieve perfection as an artist lie with all these old physical defects and personal accidents and illnesses. Perhaps there is some instinctive urge at work here, aimed at drawing a contrast between failure in life and success at work and thus bringing the one into line with the other, somewhat in the manner of such hard-working artists as Michelangelo, Jacopo da Pontormo and Caravaggio, all of whom sensibly and admirably achieved forgiveness for their private sins in the here and now on earth.

Like all loving parents at that time, my own forced their left-handed first-born child to write with his right hand. Not wanting others to see that their offspring was possessed by the devil, such parents caused their pitiful charges severe psychological and physical damage, confusing their minds and preventing them from using their limbs and intellectual abilities both freely and uninhibitedly. Westphalia was briefly a kingdom under Jérôme Bonaparte, after which it became part of Prussia, which perhaps explains why such Prussian characteristics as discipline, militarism and a strict sense of duty are all second nature to us Westphalians. It may have been this that prompted my father to write to me in 1944, barely a year before the end of the war, to say that, in spite of my repeated complaints about the unspeakable awfulness of my life as a soldier, I would soon come to regard my straw mattress as my best friend and imagine nothing finer than to fight and die for our fatherland and the final victory. It was the summer of 1944 and we could already hear the thunder of the heavy guns on the various fronts along which the Allied armies were steadily advancing; every night, more and more towns and cities were bombed or 'rubbed out', as Hitler would say, and thousands of civilians killed.

But my early childhood was peaceful, and all still seemed well with the world. My parents were young, and I could sense that they were in love: it rubbed off on me. They both came from what is called a 'simple background'; young, intelligent people filled with expectations of all that life had to offer them. My father was from the Hanover area. His mother – our grandmother – was born Helene Meinecke in Berlin and had once been to Weimar, where a friend of hers had had piano lessons with Liszt, since which date she had always worn silk in token of her gentility. Her husband, Karl, whom I never knew personally, worked first for the Hanoverian railways and later, following Hanover's annexation by Prussia, for the Prussian railways. My grandmother would always give me a biscuit or two for posting the countless letters that she wrote every day. Her silver-grey hair was parted down the middle and tied in a knot with a deaconess's genteel simplicity. She often read the Bible and was completely unmusical – not that that prevented her from singing in the local church choir and filling God's house with her fervently strident wrong notes. I can still hear her in my mind's ear. She smelt pleasantly of lavender. But she so annoyed us children with her constant reminders and reproaches that we called her 'Grandma Pericolosa'.

One of her many sons was my father, Franz, who, like most of his brothers, became a primary schoolteacher. Gütersloh was his first post. He was born in 1898 and saw active service in the First World War. He was wounded at Verdun – I think it was a head wound. A thin bespectacled man, 1.70 metres tall, with thinning hair, which he always combed back, he liked animals and, to our mother's dismay and in spite of her many protests, kept huge Great Danes and borzois (I still have photographs of them) and also bred ringdoves, which would take off from his hand, fly round in circles and then land on his head or the back of his hand. In Gütersloh and the surrounding area, however, he was known less as a zoologist than as 'Henze the musician', since he had made a name for himself as an accordionist. He played at weddings and similar occasions, including the wedding of the parents of the philosopher Jens Brockmeier, with whom I later became very friendly. I have another photograph, this time showing my father surrounded by members of the Gütersloh football team, including Brockmeier senior, all of them wearing football boots, shorts and shirts sporting their team colours. A third photograph shows them, unsurprisingly, wearing brown Nazi uniforms.

Before she married, my mother worked as a shorthand typist for the publishing house of Bertelsmann. (The firm existed even at that time, although it was then much smaller than now.) She was born at Witten in 1907. Photographs from 1928 and later show her as a young woman, with or without her high-wheeled pram, dressed in the fashion of the late 1920s, which included, of course, bobbed hair, high heels and a cloche hat à la Pola Negri. She later told us that her father once hit her for coming home with rouge on her cheeks. 'Grete, stay as you are!' he had said to her at the time (she was still in her teens), although it remains unclear what he meant by that. Be that as it may, Grete heeded his advice and from that day forth never once wore make-up, obedient but unpainted to the last. We children were immensely fond of her: she inspired us, and, because we knew how sensitive she was, we were always painfully anxious to avoid anything that might upset her.

She often told us about the difficult winter of 1917, when the war was at its height, German children went hungry and she herself was sent to stay with a Dutch family in Scheveningen in order to recover her health. She retained the happiest memories of the kindness and compassion she was shown there. We children learnt that the Dutch were a very special people and that they were kindness itself, as I later had occasion to discover for myself. Our mother would recite nonsense poems and had a fund of surreal stories with which she used to amuse us. And she also helped me, patiently and lovingly, with my maths homework and guided my right hand with her own as I wrote out my very first letters of the German alphabet with old-fashioned pen and ink.

I was fortunate enough to have known her father, Karl Geldmacher, a miner from the Ruhr. Every year he would move on from one mine to the next and, as was usual at that time, pile his family, with its increasing complement of daughters, furniture and household possessions, into a handcart and take them with him. Miners invariably tried to sell their labour to the highest bidder and obtain the best conditions for their families. I found him imposing and awe-inspiring, with his wildly threatening and unsmiling eyes and his long grey beard, which was yellow with tobacco stains around the corners of his mouth. I can still smell the tobacco in his long pipe whenever I think of him. Its porcelain bowl reached down to the ground, and his grandchildren, kneeling in front of him, were periodically allowed to fill it and light it for him. The women of the household – in other words, our grandmother on our mother's side and her daughters – went in fear of their lives under the iron rule of this patriarchal figure, who was always quick to lash out. They dared not raise their voices in his presence, and when they did so in his absence, it was to speak in tearful tones that reminded me of keening, the despondency of which is so deeply ingrained in my memory that it may almost certainly be heard here and there in my scores. 'Kommt, ihr Töchter, helft mir klagen.' I have a photograph of Grandpa Geldmacher taken one Sunday, showing him with a walking stick over his arm and his beard extending beyond the lower edge of the picture. He has a sprig of heather in his hand and some kind of medal in his buttonhole. He had fought against France in 1871 and so played an active role in the emergence of the German Empire, a process from which the world has still not recovered, even today.

One of our mother's many sisters, Aunt Else, was married to Uncle Hugo, who suffered from tuberculosis and liked Tchaikovsky. Somehow the two went together. In our living room at home, a black-framed oil painting hung over the black piano, showing a young girl with close-cropped hair playing a black piano, while several people listen raptly. A gaunt man with sunken cheeks leans against the door-frame, his head lowered, his hands in his pockets: this, for me, was my consumptive Uncle Hugo.

My parents and I left Gütersloh in the spring of 1930 and moved to the nearby town of Bielefeld, where my father had got a job teaching, first in an ordinary school and later in a more progressive type of comprehensive. I have seen the minutes of the meetings of the town council from the early months of 1933, which show that the school was closed down by ministerial decree and on the orders of the local NSDAP on the grounds that it was disseminating Marxist ideas. The Social Democrat headmaster of the school, Artur Ladebeck, was incarcerated in a concentration camp and not released until 1945, when he was installed as Bielefeld's mayor by the British military government, a task he performed with distinction for many years to come.

My father and the other young teachers from the disbanded comprehensive were exiled to the tiniest villages, no doubt to punish them for their pedagogical ambitions. Their salaries were cut, and they suffered discrimination. It was at this time that my father became more and more of a Nazi sympathizer, a change of heart undoubtedly due as much to fear for his livelihood as it was to intimidation. I observed the way in which, within a matter of years, he was persuaded – for the most part by his new colleagues, all of whom were Nazis – to abandon his existing attitudes and join the party. One of his reasons for yielding to such pressure was the fact that he one day incurred the suspicion and displeasure not only of his colleagues but of others in the area. I still remember the day. It was 23 March 1934. My brother Jochen had just been born in the local hospital, and my mother had asked my father to go into town and buy some baby's nappies. He was photographed leaving the local haberdashery, and the photograph appeared in the daily paper the next morning with the caption: 'This man buys from Jews.' I suppose he then had no choice but to try to rehabilitate himself in whatever way he could.

In the autumn of 1933 he was given a job at the primary school at Dünne, a village at the north-western edge of the Vale of Ravensberg, in the foothills of the Wiehengebirge, not far from the old Roman frontier. Life was not easy for him or for the other four members of his family (the latest addition was my sister Elisabeth, who was now three years old). It was particularly difficult for me: for the last two years I had attended school in Bielefeld, where I had a wonderful teacher, Frau Bohnstedt, and some fantastic fellow pupils. I also had to give up my piano lessons and Fräulein Seewöster's enthusiastic attempts to foster my interest in music in general.

It was a time of farewells not only for us children but also for our parents. My father was unable to continue playing the viola in the Bielefeld Chamber Orchestra, our social lives came to an end, as did membership of the local Teetotallers' Association and the town's Brass Band and Choral Society, to say nothing of cabinet-making, modern ideas and our beautiful ground-floor flat in the Zastrowstraße. Here, in a room with a bay window, the ceiling of which my father had painted in an art deco design, had stood a grand piano. It was unplayable – it had no strings, so that the keys merely clattered emptily – but Franz Henze was a craftsman (a gift that I have unfortunately not inherited) and had planned to restore the instrument himself. During the winter he and his colleagues from the Free School went tobogganing in the Teutoburger Wald on an eight-man bobsleigh that he himself had built, only for the toboggan and several of his team-members' bones to shatter on their very first trip.

One Christmas, when we were still in the Zastrowstraße, I remember peering through the keyhole into the living room, where the tree was already decorated, and, together with my younger brother, Gerhard, seeing our parents helping Father Christmas to arrange our presents on a table. Among these presents were two glove puppets, but, as a result of our being naughty, they were no longer a surprise, so that when we opened them that evening, we had to feign surprise, although our delight was none the less quite genuine. Father had made the puppets himself and had also built a theatre with a curtain and all the other accessories, while Mother had made the costumes. It was a great success. My brother and I immediately put the theatre into operation, painting scenery and writing plays. It followed us into exile in Dünne, only to fall into neglect, since we had no new puppets and no new ideas. Instead, I began writing monologues and performing them for the neighbours' children, dancing and waving my arms around, while swathed in sheets and tablecloths. The subject matter was generally taken from the numerous cheap paperbacks in Father's collection of classics, which I discovered in a trunk in the attic and which included Schiller's *Wilhelm Tell*, Lessing's *Emilia Galotti*, Grabbe's *Scherz, Satire, Ironie und tiefere Bedeutung* and even Theodor Körner's *Zriny*.

Among my other memories are two that date back to my childhood even before I was old enough to go to school. I remember walking one Sunday in the Teutoburger Wald with my parents, who were still deeply in love at that time. The oak trees were all bare, and the dry November leaves crackled noisily beneath our feet. Gerhard and I collected acorns, which we took back home with us, feeling a warm glow not only from so much walking and running, but also from our sense of inner harmony and love, so it was a matter of total indifference that our apartment was unheated. We had no money to pay for coal. Our parents made us a veritable menagerie of the most delightful bipeds and quadrupeds out of matchsticks and acorns.

Our first home in Bielefeld was only a few minutes away from a wood, which I often think about even now. The trees were a mixture of deciduous and coniferous, with bracken, brambles and other bushes at its edges. It contained a huge beech, the roots of which were so large that they formed a cave in which we boys could hide. This ancient beech had firm, broad boughs, and when we clambered up it, we felt as though the tree itself were helping us, like a mother or elder brother. It was possible to live in it and become one with it. At its foot ran a forest path leading to a clearing in which stood a little rustic house, from which never a soul emerged and which never a soul was seen to enter. It was an enchanted house, a house with a secret. Later, when I heard the *Kindertotenlieder* for the first time, I immediately saw this deathly silent house in my mind's eye, and its image returns whenever I hear the mournful strains of Gustav Mahler's music.

But now we were in Dünne, and everything changed, both at home and at school. I no longer had to bow stiffly when greeting grown-ups, no longer had to say hello to people. We now had to do as the children of Father's new colleagues did, clicking the heels of our clogs together and saluting the unspeakable Führer. We joined the Hitler Youth, and Gerhard and I only narrowly avoided having to obey the written injunction of its leader, Baldur von Schirach, that hung framed on the wall in our room and that invited all young Germans to get down on their knees every morning and thank God for giving them the Führer. I noticed books by Jewish and Christian writers disappearing from Father's bookcase and being replaced by *Mein Kampf*, by Rosenberg's *Myth of the 20th Century*, Karl Schenzinger's novel, *Hitlerjunge Quex*, and by other anti-Semitic, anti-Communist and National Socialist literature. Grandma Pericolosa was furious. The Ministry of Education's guidelines were now regularly to be found on Father's desk. We were no longer taught religion and no longer attended confirmation classes. It was not until much later that I got to know the Bible – or parts of it – through Bach's Passions, but all that I know of the Ten Commandments is that they are forever being broken, at least by the present writer.

My mother, a miner's daughter, regarded all this with the critical eyes of her class, but behaved as befitted a German wife and mother – obediently and with only the gentlest of sighs. After all, she had sworn, in the eyes of God and the law, to obey her husband in all things. My father, too, seemed initially embarrassed by his change of attitude, especially towards his genteel mother, who was now living under our roof in the country, where she died in 1941, never having believed in the final victory. A Pietist and a supporter of the anti-Fascist pastor, Martin Niemöller, she regarded developments within our household with feelings of deep dismay, shaking her head and expressing her concern and disapproval even in our presence. With the passing years, we children – and by 1944 there were six of us – came to regard these developments, including our parents' estrangement, like a daily dose of poison. In the end we forgot what it was to laugh.

Yet I cannot claim that we knew only sorrow and worry. Although many years have passed since then, I can still recall a handful of pleasant memories – looking for mushrooms on early mornings in late summer, discovering a hedgehog in the garden hedge, gorging ourselves, in secret and unpunished, on cherries while hidden high in dense foliage, improvising at the black piano in our parents' living room (the instrument looked for all the world like a child's coffin), and music lessons in general, lessons that began again when I was nine or ten: once a week a certain Herr Albrecht Hüing would shut up his cigar shop in the nearby town of Bünde and cycle over to Dünne to give piano lessons to me and the children of some of the other teachers. It was Herr Hüing who gave me my first insights into harmony, and every Wednesday evening I was allowed to turn the pages for this sullen and taciturn man when he played classical trios at Dr Butenuth's house in one of the neighbouring villages. The doctor himself played the violin and a baroness from a nearby castle played the cello. They would begin with a trio by Haydn or Mozart, then one by Beethoven, followed by a break for tea and biscuits, after which they would turn with resolution to what they termed a 'modern' composer, by which they meant Niels Gade, Smetana or Dvořák. Were they any good? I remember only that Herr Hüing used a good deal of pedal. But they always got through the piece and never had to stop or rehearse or correct what they had played. Oddly enough, they never discussed the piece in question. And a dark secret shrouded the whole affair: as a non-Aryan, Frau Butenuth was in constant danger, protected perhaps only by the fact that her husband was an important and well-respected local doctor. The beautiful music that I was privileged to hear, year in, year out, in this cultured middle-class household that was threatened by sinister forces undoubtedly taught me a very great deal and confirmed me in my belief that the true home of art is in the world of those who are persecuted, among people whose feelings and exceptional qualities are bound to cut them off for ever from the vast majority of so-called normal people.

In 1940 French prisoners of war arrived in the village and were quartered in an empty cottage surrounded by barbed wire. During the daytime they helped the local farmers in the fields. They had a relatively easy time: they were well treated and took their midday and evening meals with the family. I got to know one of them at our neighbours' house. I liked him a lot. He had dark flashing eyes and dazzling white teeth. I had never seen such beauty in a fellow human being. How could I have forgotten his name! I gave him cigars and tobacco, which I regularly siphoned off from Father's supplies at home. I would run out into the fields to be with him whenever I could and tried to engage him in broken English. One day he took me into his confidence and showed me a photograph of his fiancée in Paris, and I realized from the vague but painful shock in the pit of my stomach, like some momentary miniature earthquake, that I felt something akin to jealousy. But Jean, or François, or whatever he was called, did not notice. And of course I continued to help him learn German, since he wanted to escape back to France, to his Aimée or Madeleine and Marshal Pétain, and I myself would have to assist him.

Strange things happened at these old Westphalian farmhouses, among the oak trees, behind the walls. Every farm had its resident clairvoyant, people who saw ghosts, who had second sight and who always had some new horror to prophesy – horrors that almost always came to pass. It was said that these people were 'not right in the head', but they were left in peace, they were respected, they were part of the family, members of the household. One of these remarkable figures was old Fräulein Ilsabein, a gaunt and spectral woman who lived at the beautiful farm directly opposite and who spent all the hours of daylight wandering among the oak trees, between the stables, wringing her hands and hopping from leg to leg. She never left the protective confines of the farmyard walls yet seemed afflicted by the cruelties of the whole world, with her furrowed face, grey clothes and grey hair, the unkempt strands of which resisted every attempt to comb them into submission. Whenever she saw me, she would beckon me over. I did not have the heart to ignore her. Anxiously glancing round and talking in a rapid whisper, she would confide in me all the terrible, sinister, conspiratorial and dangerous things that had happened in the meantime either to her own immediate family or on the farm or in the surrounding area and beyond. Murder and discord lurked in every recess of her imagination, tormenting her troubled mind. Perhaps everything she told me was true. Perhaps I simply did not understand. I never really listened. After all, I was as prejudiced as the rest of the village and knew that, unlike me, Fräulein Ilsabein was not quite right in the head.

But the imaginative world of us children, too, was filled with sinister figures, with monsters, fears and troubles. Children have secrets that they share with no one and about which they are unable to speak. And there were certain aspects of this world of the emotions that could in any case never be explained in words but articulated only through music. I mean the anxieties that stem from an ill-defined sense of existential fear: where have I come from? What is to become of me? Where is this journey leading? And then there is the daily worry of whether one's mother still loves one or not. It was this uncertainty that tormented me above all else, settling over my life like some dank fog. Children suffer constantly from deprivations and unintelligible rules, and yet they enjoy the good things of life with hedonistic delight. They have a festive view of the world, a world that is full of secrets and mystery but that is slowly destroyed by their elders, by monsters sprung from the sleep of reason. And there is something profoundly spiritual about their links with the animal kingdom, for the latter constitutes a different kind of reality familiar in the first instance, of course, to those children who have grown up in the country among wild and domesticated animals and who have stared into the unfathomable eyes of goat and barn owl, cow and fox and toad, behind which the Great Mystery lies hidden.

Once, while we were still living in Bielefeld, we found a stray kitten, but we children were not allowed to keep it. It was sick, our parents told us, and had to be given away, whereupon my brother and I, infected by the pain of parting, were struck down by a high fever and for days talked ramblingly about nothing else. It was also about this time that a circus of midgets visited the town. We children were allowed to go and see it, and were able to watch the hideous dwarfs, with their ancient, careworn faces and tiny arms and hands, performing their tricks as jugglers and acrobats in brightly coloured costumes. They lived in tiny dolls' houses, where the gadgets, furniture and utensils were all correspondingly small. It was like Ravel's house – like *L'enfant et les sortilèges* in reverse. For me, it was proof that dwarfs existed. Later I was to be introduced to giants, angels, demons and magicians, too. Our Hanoverian grandmother had read

Grimms' fairy-tales to us, with all their curious mythical figures, both evil and good, such as Snow White, Rapunzel and Thousandfurs, where pennies fall from heaven, frogs turn into princes, and princes into frogs. Many of the characters from the magical world of the Brothers Grimm's fairy-tales, with their wicked, cruel and pernicious imagery, I later met in real life, so I can also claim to have made the acquaintance of cannibals, heroes and elves, as well as murderers and poisoners, to say nothing of brave little tailors and lads who have successfully set forth to learn the meaning of fear.

As children, we were unable to form a clear picture of our father, since we knew nothing at all about him. He told us nothing, so we did not know whether he had had a happy childhood in and around Hanover at the turn of the century or whether it had been a terrible time for him. He had been born in 1898. Had he screamed as a baby? When did he have his first girlfriend? Or was our mother, nine years younger than he, his first? Just as Father was probably *her* first boyfriend. They were decent, God-fearing folk, then. For Franz and Grete, life could have gone on as normal, quietly and agreeably, but the little happiness and peace that they might so easily have been allowed was not, in fact, to be granted them, at least not in the longer term.

I still recall an incident that took place during my first year at school, since it was my first experience of music as a means of expression: our teacher, Frau Bohnstedt, whom I liked a lot and whom I was always anxious to impress, wanted us to rehearse a round. In German, the words were 'Unser Hans hat Hosen an, und die sind ihm zu klein. Horch, wie der Wind weht, horch, wie der Hahn kräht!' (Our Hans is wearing trousers, and they are too small from him. Listen to the wind blowing, listen to the cockerel crowing!) I have forgotten the rest, although I think there was something about a cold wind whistling over a high mountain. The other children in the class were unable to manage the minor third on the fifth syllable, 'Ho . . .', but invariably produced a banal major third. I was the only one who had no difficulty with this passage and with the deeply felt diminished interval of its gypsy scale, and I sang the achingly painful minor third, effortlessly and full-throatedly, identifying fully with my freezing namesake on Calvary, where the wind whistles and the cock crows thrice.

One Christmas – I must have been seven or eight at the time – my father gave me a copy of Collodi's *Pinocchio* in Otto Julius Bierbaum's German translation. The book was beautifully bound and superbly illustrated (I no longer remember the name of the illustrator), it smelt wonderful and felt somehow precious in my hands. I read it again and again, hanging on every word and feeling each and every one of Pinocchio's fears and predicaments as though it were my own: how often did I later fall into the hands of knaves and rogues like the Cat and Fox! How rarely was I rescued by a Good Fairy! Initially I took it all at face value, as though it were perfectly true, including even Pinocchio's death and resurrection and his reunion with Gepetto inside the whale, a scene that regularly moved me to tears. Among my other favourites were *Doctor Dolittle's Circus* and *Doctor Dolittle's Zoo* by Hugh Lofting. Here, I particularly liked the story of an Elysian rest home for old horses in the countryside near Bristol, where there was enough shade and enough green grass and all the other amenities needed to brighten the twilight years of these ancient working animals. And then there was Kipling's *Jungle Book*, which I must have been given when I was a little older. It left a lasting impression on me, and for a long time I became completely bound up in the world of Mowgli and Rikki-Tikki-Tavi, the mongoose that could kill a poisonous snake with a single bite of his powerful jaws. But I was bitterly disappointed to discover that at the end Mowgli returns to live among human beings. I wanted him to spend the rest of his life with Bagheera and to remain cradled in the black panther's arms day and night. This was a scenario which, given my propensity for identifying with these characters, seemed to me infinitely preferable. Although based for the most part on Indian fairy-tales, my opera *König Hirsch* contains a number of elements related to those in *The Jungle Book*, and I now know that vestigial memories of my boyhood dreams and fantasies were taken over, subliminally and unconsciously, into the sound world of this opera.

My father must have followed my literary and musical activities with a certain pedagogical interest and may even have helped to guide them in a particular direction, even though, to my regret, we never spoke about books or music or, indeed, about anything else. I never discovered the reason for this lack of understanding and coldness between us, but I remember that another of the presents that he gave me one Christmas – the time of year when, as a rule, something like a truce breaks out in families in general – was a copy of Anna Magdalena Bach's *Clavierbüchlein*, again in a particularly fine edition. Once I could play all the pieces in it and had memorized them all, the road to Bach lay open. Whenever I heard the sounds of organ music issuing from any of the churches in Bünde, Bielefeld or Herford, I would slip inside and listen to the organist practising. Even composers such as Buxtehude and Pachelbel I came to admire for their severe and searing austerity, but it was Bach's music above all that was like a light that filled the gloom of my life at that time with a feeling of great solemnity but, at the same time, a very real optimism: it was an expression of righteousness and truth, of rightness and consolation; it was the voice, in short, of salvation. It was no accident that I studied Protestant church music, especially Bach, when the war was over. When I was younger and practised regularly, I could play a fair number of Bach's keyboard pieces on the piano. Even today, whenever I am composing, I generally start the day with something by Bach in order to play myself in, as it were, and put myself in the right frame of mind.

Bach's music speaks of a quite specific culture, of the nascent German burgher class, of Gothic art and what were then the modern Italians: it speaks with the tongues of angels of Lutheran Christianity, of the malaise bound up with this type of Christianity and of the bitterness and spirit of self-sacrifice with which suffering can and must be borne and endured. A good Christian, I learnt, must regard life as a time of perpetual suffering and deprivation, a time of physical abstinence. Everything is forbidden, from parallel fifths to polygamy, from clairvoyance to contact with people with different ideas. None of this, thank God, is found in the case of that man of God, Johann Sebastian Bach.

I must report two murders that disturbed me profoundly at this time (I must have been around ten years old), one in the forest near Dünne, the other in the garden attached to the flat that came with Father's job. In the forest, someone had discovered a vixen's den and, unable to keep his mouth shut, had broadcast the news far and wide. The place in question was in the middle of a length of piping that ran beneath a forest path. A small crowd gathered, young and old alike. The pipe was long and pitch-dark inside, and the cunning little vixen refused to be flushed out, but remained inside with her cubs. But the butchers were nothing if not resourceful and, with the help of a tin plate, which they pushed along the inside of the pipe by means of long poles, they drove the poor animal and her two cubs out into the open and into the jaws of death. Tally-ho! As soon as the vixen came within his sights, making her desperate dash for freedom, the huntsman fired. I ran to my father and begged him to let me adopt the two bewitching cubs, but the answer was no. I was not surprised. I expect that there was a law forbidding Prussian civil servants from housing wild animals in their living rooms.

As if that was not bad enough, my father had a wonderful cage in our garden that was home to a family of squirrels. When you entered it, the red furry creatures would scamper across, run up your legs and scour your trouser pockets in search of something to eat. Who can describe the horror that I felt when I discovered them all dead one morning on the floor of the cage, clearly bludgeoned to death! There they lay in their own blood. Someone must have killed them out of revenge or purely out of bloodlust. Perhaps they had wanted to hurt my father, or perhaps it was a political gesture. Perhaps the father of one of the children at school had wanted to avenge himself on my own father for the treatment meted out to his son. My brother and I had no enemies, so it must have been aimed at the old man, but if this brutal murder and all that it symbolized affected him in any way, he did not let it show. The tiny bodies were buried without a word. The cage remained empty from that day forth.

Some twenty years ago I wrote a piece on a school outing to the Roman frontier. It runs as follows:

> School trips were something to be feared, although we were grateful to them for the fact that there were no lessons on such days. They recalled nothing so much as forced marches, making it impossible to stop for even a moment, still less to lie down in the grass or have a good look round. On one such excursion – in my memory they all took place in the autumn – I came across a genuine salamander. It was the only time in my life I had ever seen one. He would have made a delightful companion, and I only wish I could have taken him home, but I expect that he preferred it here in the wood, living a life of freedom, under the moss and close to a grotto with its rivulets of water. Also, I had to run to catch up with the rest of the class, which, implacable in its progress, had marched on ahead without me. The whole of Germany was marching at that time, increasingly implacably, beneath the whip hand of the capital's high-ranking slave-drivers.
>
> The leaves were not always damp, as they were on the day I encountered my salamander. The ground could also be hard and dry, crackling and crunching beneath the boots of us children. The boles of the lofty beech trees could also be silver, instead of black, and the light in the leafless treetops would sometimes be blue and gold.
>
> Panting. My heart beats loudly, I've a stitch in my side, and my feet are hurting. I'd like to sink to the ground and never get up again. My clothes, which won't be changed again until next Saturday, are soaked with sweat. My sandwiches have all been eaten, and there's no more raspberry juice in my canteen. We're on our way to the northernmost

frontier of the Roman Empire. We've already been given a detailed account of the arch-enemy's cowardly and degenerate characteristics and even sung a song on the subject. And we've seen a performance of *Hermann, Prince of the Cherusci* at the open-air theatre in Nettelstedt, a play in which the emperor Varus and his mistresses and legionaries cut sorry figures indeed. They didn't stand a chance against the decorous Hermann and his loyal supporters – our own forebears – who always appeared on horseback and whose cause was clearly just. All this had in fact served only to diminish our interest in the Roman frontier, although we still expected to feel a certain sense of awe and emotion as, flaxen- and ginger-haired, we pressed on through the rustling leaves, often sinking in to our knees. It would, we felt, be a great moment – it could not be otherwise after all that effort, all the sufferings and complaints! Such a long walk to see only a bump in the ground? We could not believe it when we finally stood there. It was just like any other bump in the ground, indistinguishable from all the rest, except that it may perhaps have extended further on either side. A bump in the ground on top of another bump in the ground, not far from the main town of the area, Lübbecke im Wiehengebirge.

I think how boring it must have been here for the olive-skinned youths from Rome and North Africa, and also how cold it must have been for them (I would later learn that Virgil had expressed similar concerns in his eclogue, 'Alpinas, a! Dura nives et frigora Rheni'), but it is difficult to imagine anything in the face of this bleak bump in the ground, covered by autumn leaves that have accumulated over the years. Were there once any fortifications here? Shelters? Trenches? Hot food, swimming baths? Was it dangerous to keep watch here? Did the Roman soldiers have to be on their guard day and night against the barbarian hordes? Did they have passwords? Were those who were sent to this desolate outpost felons? Ugly, unpopular, recalcitrant, unwanted, fit only to stare into space at the Empire's northernmost boundary, at the back of the beyond? No hares, no deer or squirrels to play with, but only an embarrassed silence weighing on this scene of desolation. Even the trees would like to leave. The children are silent, each one thinking to him- or herself: our teacher has taken us for a ride, or else he himself is uncertain whether or not this really is the Roman frontier. (No plaque indicates that it might be here, no inscription, be it ever so fragmentary.) A few of the children feel something like pity for their teacher, and the swots among them ask questions in their piping voices, as though they have just been vouchsafed some Damascene experience. I am not one of those who would like do something to please him: I am thinking of the way home and of the maths lesson tomorrow morning. I have nothing to look forward to. I feel only immense impatience and contempt for the age in which I live and the conditions that now prevail. I find everything inadequate and live only from day to day, waiting for better times that will come when I am bigger. Then I'll do only the things that I want to do.

Meanwhile the children are peeing along the silent frontier, one child to each beech tree, before preparing for the journey home. There is a clatter of metal pots and pans, empty haversacks hang down behind bare knees. We stumble over roots, slither and slide down into the Vale of Ravensberg, which welcomes us with a blast of cold air and the smell of newly ploughed fields, wisps of autumn mist and the smoke from fires made from dried potato leaves that glow red in the distance as evening falls and the air grows damp; and as it gets darker, so my inquisitiveness grows and, with it, my hunger and toothache and sense of impatience.

I am trying to reconstruct and recapture the Hans Henze of that time in as true to life a manner as I can, trying to observe myself as a cameraman might (admittedly one who unfortunately knows a little too much about his subject), on my way to school, practising the piano, walking through the forest initially on my own and then, from some indeterminate moment onwards, no longer on my own but swathed in autumn mist or wandering through the bracken on a summer afternoon (bracken that grew so high that it closed over our heads as we passed), calling out the names of the flowers in the fields and attempting our first awkward kisses in the shadow of the trees, silently yielding to the feelings that welled up inside us and that we were neither able nor willing to explain, while black and white storm clouds gathered above us like threatening fists. As we grow older, memories of our childhood and youth reassert themselves, borne along by clouds that are not the ones we once knew: I am thinking of the moods, the smells and colours, this lasting, ineffable sadness, the sense of loss and disillusionment, the sort of loneliness, so typical of puberty, that everyone knows, but that finds adequate artistic expression only very rarely – Cherubino's music in *Le nozze di Figaro* comes to mind as the finest example, although Wedekind, in *Spring Awakening*, also captures something of this disquieting sense of melancholy. And the mournful pride and mysterious reserve that stare back at the observer from the convex mirror in Il Parmigianino's self-portrait also seem to me to have something to do with the secrets and fathomless mysteries of this period in our lives. Was loneliness a source of pain and nothing more? After all, one wanted to be alone. One needed every moment – as much time as possible to get to know and understand oneself, to get used to leading a life of introspection and to guarding one's secrets and dreams and longings from hostile interference, while simultaneously cultivating them and allowing them to develop. I wanted to build a citadel within myself, to shut myself away in it and regard the resultant state of siege as permanent, preferring not to know if it would ever end.

My brother and I had to cycle ten kilometres to school every day, a journey we had to make even in winter when it was often insanely cold – as low as minus 25°C. There was something quite wretched about it all. Since then I have always hated having to get up and leave the house in the dark. It did not start to grow light until we arrived in Bünde. One day, as we were approaching the town, I saw the pale sky lit up by fires and blackened by smoke. It was 9 November 1938 – *Reichskristallnacht*. In Bünde as in Gütersloh and every other German town and city, Jewish houses and synagogues had all been set on fire. From our schoolroom window we could look down into the small Jewish cemetery and see where the trees had been cut down and the tombstones knocked over and daubed with anti-Semitic slogans and swastikas. No one said a word about it, not even our teacher, who was there to teach us German. We all pretended that nothing had happened. And no one asked after the taciturn, dark-haired boy who never returned to the school from that day onwards. Not even I myself asked what had become of him – at least not in so many words. It had become clear to me by now that not even this terrible and fateful event would ever be mentioned in our parents' house. Our world had grown cold and tight-lipped.

Throughout the entire war my poor brother and I had to wear the hideously practical Hitler Youth uniforms – a sort of black skiing outfit – every single day in winter. Although we had nothing else to wear, I sometimes wonder whether it was not part of a secret plan on my father's part to induct us into a paramilitary regime. By contrast, our classmates – especially those from well-to-do families (and there were many of them, mostly the sons of cigar manufacturers) – flaunted their clean new clothes every day, thus leaving us with a gnawing feeling of shame and neglect.

Even during my second year at school, Frau Bohnstedt had repeatedly advised my parents to send me away to the coast to recuperate during the summer, since I was a nervous, fidgety child, but her wishes were never met. Throughout my entire childhood I never once went away on holiday: we always had to stay at home – out of poverty, I assume, rather than to atone for some transgression or merely out of thoughtlessness. During the holidays we had to help out in the garden and, during the harvest, to lend the farmers a helping hand for five marks a day. In the evenings, if we found the courage to do so, we would ask Father's permission to cycle over to the swimming pool, where swarms of mosquitoes would dance in the light of the sun, which was already low in the sky, and where the prevailing smell was a mixture of piss and chlorine. We would arrive in time for the last fifteen minutes, when most of the others had already left. When we returned to school at the end of the summer holidays, our teacher would ask: 'Well, Georg, where did you go for your holidays?' 'My parents took me to Venice,' Georg would reply. 'I was in Switzerland, in the Alps,' Wilfried would say, and one of the class had even been to England – fantastic! Unlike the children of other impoverished parents, who could go on holiday at the state's expense, we Henzes were never once able to say that we had had a wonderful holiday. The most that we could report was that we had been on a couple of terrible camping holidays or gone on excursions with other members of the Hitler Youth to the Porta Westfalica near Minden on the Weser, but on every occasion I had found some inglorious excuse to come home early, much to my father's annoyance.

Meanwhile war had broken out. Father returned home from the Polish campaign after only a few weeks with a newly inflicted head wound and was able to devote himself once more to married life and to educating adolescents. We acquired a radio, so that the Henze family, too, could cluster round it at supper-time, listening *en famille* to the rabble-rousing rhetoric, to news of German victories and to Hans Fritzsche's comments thereon. We young ones were amused by the extent to which our grandmother was exercised by Fritzsche and allowed herself to get worked up by his demagogic drivel. She could simply have switched off, we thought. During the daytime the radio was not used, so that on Sunday mornings and afternoons and all weekday afternoons (in winter in an unheated room) I was able to listen to classical music. For the first time in my life I heard the sound of a western orchestra, albeit somewhat brassily distorted. All Mozart's works were broadcast during these years, and as frost patterns formed on the window, untouched by the warmth of my breath, I eagerly devoured his messages of joy and promises of love. I heard for the first time of a south German, Bohemian and Austrian world of sun and pleasure, a world where saints and gods did not strike fear in one's heart and where sins were forgiven without further ado, as in the fifth movement of Mahler's Third Symphony:

> **Peter** And should I not weep, you merciful God?
> **Women's Chorus** You shall not weep! No, you shall not weep!
> **Peter** I have broken the Ten Commandments.
> **Women's Chorus** You shall not weep! No, you shall not weep!

And silvery children's voices sing 'ding-dong' as they tell of heavenly joys.

Listening to Mozart, I was immediately struck by the link between artistry and simplicity. It seemed to me as though here was a composer who, lovingly and knowingly, had evolved beyond the music that typified his time and country. The songs and contredanses, the serenades and alleluias had become entirely his. Here, I thought (or at least I think so today), is an archetypal landscape of the soul inhabited by innocent Catholic children who, delighting in their senses, amuse themselves to their hearts' content, here are Alpine kings, misanthropists and philanthropists of the liveliest intelligence, urbanity and candour. Against the cultural background of his age, Mozart opened up a whole new world of emotion in which Kleist's *liebliche Gefühle* – feelings such as femininity and desire, tenderness and love – are just as important as frivolousness and danger, risk-taking, death and despair in the form of aggression and masculinity. In Mozart's works, everything is exceptional, even though they contain no substantial technical innovations and even though a vocabulary is used and rules applied that other musicians of his age were using. Yet whenever Mozart put pen to paper, the result was something that rose above its age as though of its own accord, soaring aloft to the furthest Olympian heights.

With Mozart, thinking about music went hand in hand with the compositional process itself: the action of thinking was indistinguishable from that of felicitously and self-confidently noting down the ideas that inspired him. It is all just like the theatre, I thought, as, wrapped in a blanket and with chattering teeth, I listened to the *Gran Partita*, K361. It is music of and for humanity, consisting of operatic scenes, dance numbers and solo arias, while the stage works themselves contain real characters drawn from everyday life, lawyers and countryfolk, elegant women, sensuous and seducible – and the same is true of the men. And the Masonic pieces! To my ears, *Brüder, reicht die Hand zum Bunde* K623a, is one of the most beautiful of all choral works, testimony to a wonderful and mature awareness of life. Towards the end of his life, Mozart's music became increasingly beautiful and warm, more earthly and inwardly lit by a generous, humanistic view of the world. Its naturalness has something of the mysterious perfection of plants and the musculature of beautiful animals, or else it reminds one of particularly perfect examples of Apollonian beauty in humans.

Needless to say, I knew all this on only an instinctive, intuitive level at this time, as I listened to my parents' wartime radio and Mozart stirred my frozen heart with his messages from another world and age. The trumpets and timpani invariably entered at just the right moment, I found, but on each occasion it came as a huge surprise, for the most part proclaiming the advent of saviours and archangels, bringing recovery, promising peace and joy and telling of a better and more real reality. This music was the only thing I had in the world at that time. It gave me the courage to brave the difficulties of my little life and to set off into the big, wide world all alone. My goal was Mozart, beauty, perfection, a new form of truth – a truth that pays no heed to the Zeitgeist and that triumphs over death itself.

2

In August 1942 I was removed from the rolls of the Bielefeld Grammar School and despatched to the State School of Music in Braunschweig. I had been attending the former since the April of that year, when my father had been transferred to the Senne, an area of fenland to the north of Paderborn, and I would like to have stayed there longer – I enjoyed the casual atmosphere and soon made lots of friends – but a plan was already forming in my mind: I would sit my school-leaving exam, for only then would I be able to study at the Cologne Academy of Music and attend a course in composition with Wilhelm Maler. Rosemarie Lütkemeyer, the sweet and chubby-faced daughter of a teacher in one of the neighbouring villages, who had studied music in Cologne and with whose long-legged cellist sister, Erika, I was flirting at that time (we would break our journey home from school and cycle to some secret assignation), had once shown Professor Maler a little piece of mine – something for Rosemarie, for cello and piano, and his response had been so positive that I felt encouraged to continue with my attempts at composition and prepare myself mentally for a period of serious, systematic study in Cologne. But my teachers in Bielefeld had warned my father that, even by repeating a year, I would still have no chance of achieving my objective. I was simply not up to the mark in Latin, maths, physics, chemistry, geography and sport; only in German, English, art and music could I begin to hold my own.

I had started to take an interest in composition at Dünne during the twelve months following Grandma Henze's death, when, out of respect for her memory, my parents had stopped me from having piano lessons. We were not allowed to play music. But music was something that interested me more than anything else – even more than painting and natural science. Following our move to the Senne I was further encouraged by a number of my more musical classmates (among whom were two or three of my contemporaries from primary school), so that I now devoted myself to practical music-making and composition with a single-mindedness that simply left no time for ordinary schoolwork. It was hardly surprising, therefore, that my teachers and parents were at their wits' end. I spent every afternoon in the town, making music with schoolfriends and composing for our chamber group, which met at the home of Theo Waupke, the freckled, red-haired son of a local pharmacist. The house was surrounded by lilac trees and contained not only a music room but even a harpsichord, which came complete with another young female cellist by the name of Tütchen Breithaupt and a pianist called Gundula Kaiser. Together with Theo Waupke, who displayed a ready wit and who played the violin, and a Swabian flautist, Hans-Theo Woernle, who was secretly but hopelessly in love with Tütchen, the two girls would perform Bach's Fifth Brandenburg Concerto at least once a week under my own direction, without ever once suggesting that we might stop to practise certain difficult passages that invariably went awry. The ripieno, too, was made up of classmates, though I no longer recall their names, only that I was much taken with them all. Their social backgrounds were very different from my own. Bielefeld also offered me my first opportunities to go to concerts and to hear and see operas – *Orfeo ed Euridice*, *Ariadne auf Naxos*, *Carmen* and even a novelty, Wolf-Ferrari's *La dama boba*. I came to regard the house in the Senne that was placed at our disposal by my father's school and where my parents led increasingly taciturn lives merely as an occasional place to eat and sleep. And when it became clear that I would leave school at Easter with no qualifications, my teachers – who were basically decent types – stopped demanding anything from me in terms of homework and even my physical presence. For that I should like to thank them belatedly, though they must all be dead by now.

An important book came my way at this time. It was Hans Mersmann's *Music of Today*, which Rosemarie had borrowed for me from her father's library and which seemed to me a mine of information. Not only was it well written, it also included illustrations and musical examples, ranging widely from Mahler to Webern and from Debussy to Stravinsky. By studying this book, I was able to imagine what these works – all of which were banned and which I knew only from hearsay – must have sounded like in reality. It made me curious about the future, when there would no longer be any censorship and artists and their art would be free to develop in whatever way they wished.

One of the most stimulating friendships of these teenage years was with Adalbert Rang, who was the same age as me and whom I wanted to become a poet. He duly applied himself to this task and I even set some of his poems. His father, Bernhard, ran the Bielefeld Public Library. We saw each other almost every day during the holidays and I was sometimes invited to dine at his house. On one occasion I remember having partridge – a rare treat in those days. As his mother was carving the beast, she announced: 'Hanswerner is our guest, and so he shall have the heart.' Fortunately, I managed to manoeuvre the bird's vital organ off my plate and into my trouser pocket without being seen, since even at that early date I already felt disgusted and disturbed by the sight and taste of dead meat.

Adalbert had managed to purloin his father's key to what was known as the 'Poison Cabinet' in the Public Library, in other words, the cupboard containing the books which, on racist or ideological grounds, were to remain inaccessible to readers in eastern Westphalia eager to improve their minds: the authors concerned were Jakob Wassermann, Stefan Zweig, Lion Feuchtwanger, Ernst Toller, Thomas and Heinrich Mann, Franz Werfel, Hugo von Hofmannsthal, Frank Wedekind, Bertolt Brecht and all the Expressionists – everything, in short, that the Nazis deemed degenerate. For a long time – perhaps even years – we enjoyed this forbidden literary fruit, secretly and undisturbed, our heads in a constant whirl, and began to think and feel and speak like Moritz Stiefel and Melchior Gabor in *Spring Awakening*. The voices of decay and decline that entered German poetry through Georg Trakl's lyric verse struck a chord within us: our evenings passed in a haze of blue; crystalline tears would fall from our eyelids, shed for a bitter world. Shivering bluely, the night wind swept down the hillside like a mother's dark lament, only to die away again, and for a moment we glimpsed the blackness at the centre of our hearts, whole minutes of shimmering silence. We lived completely bound up in this world of forbidden pleasures.

It was only to be expected, therefore, that my own dear father would discover the whole conspiracy and telephone Adi's old man and thus put an end to this educational journey of ours, with all its wonders and excitements. As always, there was no argument and no discussion: not a single word was exchanged between us. But we had already had the experience: no one could take that away from us. On another occasion, my mother must have said something disturbing to my father about my private life – a life, be it added, that was as discreet as it was innocent and solitary. To this day it remains unclear to me what she could have meant, but the result was that my father – a qualified teacher – summoned me into his presence and told me that 'people like me' belonged in concentration camps. I shall never forget his words. I was forbidden to write any music and for three weeks had to spend two hours every afternoon chopping wood instead of practising the piano. With this mortifying insult our family idyll's already crumbling edifice developed a further crack.

At that time I knew of concentration camps only from rumour and hearsay. Perhaps I should have asked my father for more concrete information, in order to find out what I had done to merit such a punishment and what went on in such places. But as chance would have it, I gained a fairly direct insight into the matter during the autumn holidays a year or two later: it was at a reception following the wedding of the daughter of one of our neighbours, a veritable fair maid of the mill. Night was already falling as several of the menfolk, including not only Jürgen, the groom, but also my father and other party members wandered off into the forest distinctly the worse for drink, bawling Nazi songs to celebrate Jürgen's farewell to his youth (I can still hear their raucous voices in my mind's ear as I write these lines), leaving me alone in the house with the bride. Over wedding cake and real coffee, she told me that her Jürgen – a sexy, blond SS man with the most perfect profile – had difficulty sleeping at night because of his job as a concentration-camp guard. It had become a problem for him. He was too sensitive, she said, and could not bear the sight of the prisoners, who would run out of their huts at night and clutch the electrified barbed-wire fence in order to end their misery. He had already asked for a transfer, she said. This was the first time that I had heard about this terrible alternative reality. A little later, in Braunschweig in 1943, I learnt about mass executions and extermination camps in Poland and Russia from wounded soldiers who had returned to the school from the front.

I was soon to gain a first-hand impression of our country's humanitarianism: the parlour of Father's house in the Senne (the room with the black piano and coloured print of Tchaikovsky) overlooked a forest path that ran alongside our garden fence. Here, in the evening, Soviet prisoners of war who had spent the day doing forced labour were rounded up under strict supervision before returning to their camp. I have never seen men looking so deathly ill. They could scarcely stand. It was said that they lived in holes in the ground, that they were given nothing to eat but raw turnips and that large numbers of them had died of typhoid fever, pneumonia and hunger. Civilians were forbidden on pain of punishment to talk to them, still less to give them a crust of bread. After all, Hitler had described these prisoners of war as subhuman Bolsheviks and now made sure that they were treated as such. No one did anything about it. It was as though the conscience of the German nation had simply been switched off and disconnected.

A year or so before I left the Bielefeld Grammar School, my by now thoroughly Nazified father sank to new depths in my sight by deciding – again without any discussion – to send me to a school of music run by the Waffen-SS (such institutions did indeed exist). There, he must have told himself, I would not only learn to play military marches and medleys on an ophicleide or sousaphone but would also play in an orchestra once a week, even if only as a violist. But what must really have attracted him to the idea, of course, was the thought that such studies would also involve square-bashing, the only proper preparation for war in one of the Führer's crack regiments. There my fancy ideas would soon be beaten out of me, he must have said to himself, and I would become a proper German before it was too late. More than that, I would be trained as part of the nation's new aristocracy. The idea was obscene and came to nothing, although it seemed as though it would be realized until only a few weeks before I was due to be packed off to this cadet school for the artistically impaired. My music teacher in Bielefeld happened to ask me what I was going to do when I left school, and when I told him, he wrote at once to my father, urging him to renounce his insane decision and find some more suitable, less drastic solution. This was the first time in my life that I had been rescued by a stranger. Six months later I sat the entrance examination for the Braunschweig State School of Music (formerly the local conservatory). It lasted a mere five minutes. I was immediately awarded a grant and since that date have never cost my parents a single additional penny.

In Braunschweig I studied the piano as my main subject, with percussion and harmony as subsidiary subjects. I boarded at the school and also took my meals there. We practised in other buildings. The dormitory held twenty-five beds arranged on top of and beside each other. There I slept with musicians of my own age, representatives of a particularly curious type of person, all of whom had to practise assiduously in order that one day they might be able to live by their art and pour out their wrath and grief in operas and cantatas. It was a wonderful time, in spite of all the privations, in spite of the lack of any private life and in spite of the fact that I was separated from Hans-Theo Woernle and Adi Rang in Bielefeld – although I now began a lively correspondence with them both. It was at this time that postcodes were first introduced into Germany, and I remember returning home one holiday to be greeted by my easily shockable mother: 'You gave me quite a turn, my boy! When I saw the number on the back of your letter, I thought you'd been sent to a concentration camp after all.'

It was not only important to be taught at last by professional musicians, it was also immensely stimulating. Best of all were my piano lessons with Ernst Schacht, who was so polite and considerate that I made every effort to please him. I worked on Haydn with him – pieces that I can still play today – and also Schumann, Mozart and Brahms. Although I never learnt to play the piano sufficiently well to get beyond a certain level of technical proficiency, not least because I was further handicapped by the fact that I am left-handed, I did at least take a few steps in the direction of becoming a professional pianist. Professor Brandt was responsible for teaching us the theory of musical forms. He was a surly and unshaven individual, with a mass of unkempt hair, who would grin at us through decaying teeth and contemptuously draw our attention to the superficial modulation at the beginning of the development section in the final movement of Mozart's G minor Symphony, K550. The rhythm class, in which I would sometimes take part out of sheer curiosity and which seemed inspired by Émile Jaques-Dalcroze, was run by Frau Gottschalk-Wegmann, an oldish, sylphlike creature with bobbed hair, culottes and a rather piping voice that sounded as though she was sighing whenever she exhaled. I particularly enjoyed her class, even though I found it rather funny and often had difficulty keeping a straight face as we hopped around in a circle to the sound of her tambourine. I soon became friendly with a number of my fellow students. For the violinist, Kurt Stier, who was later to become leader of the Bavarian State Orchestra in Munich, I wrote a brief concerto of which he still has the original manuscript. He showed it to me in Munich not so very long ago, so I know what an unspeakable piece it is. It was played only once, under my own direction, by Kurt and some of our fellow students in our wash-room during a lunch break and left all concerned, myself included, distinctly cold. I was still almost wholly lacking in self-awareness as a composer at that time. Hindemith's was the only modern music that could then be obtained – under the counter – and that could be studied and played in private. I knew most of his piano pieces and took them as my point of reference. Their influence could be detected in my music for many years to come, even in the actual appearance of the notes on the written page.

In 1943 Braunschweigers heard the German première of Frank Martin's *Le vin herbé*, a chamber oratorio based on Joseph Bédier's modern retelling of the medieval Tristan legend. Conducted by the town's general music director, Ewald Lindemann, it was an event of some cultural significance for local middle-class music lovers, since it represented a risk, a secret act of resistance, analogous to the sale of Ernst Jünger's allegorical and anti-totalitarian novel, *Auf den Marmorklippen*, which was likewise regarded as a work of protest. The score was published by Universal Edition of Vienna and I was able to attend the rehearsals and follow their progress with the help of a copy that someone had lent me. So that's what twelve-note music sounds like, I thought. So beautiful and so tender! Such ravishing sounds! And it was all produced without *Stufengänge* (to borrow Schenker's expression), without Hindemithian fourths and fifths. No wonder that it found so little favour in the eyes of our martial dictators. This concert was an exception. I wondered whether the music of Schoenberg, Berg and Webern sounded as beautiful as this. I was curious, perhaps because I already suspected that there were other fruits that were even more forbidden. But I was unable to get to know their music until 1946 or 1947. I could find virtually no secondary literature on the subject, and the scores of 'degenerate' works were nowhere to be had. It was as though they had never existed.

My subsidiary subject in Braunschweig was percussion. My teacher, an elderly, white-haired emeritus professor, who always wore a beautiful tie beneath his elegant wing collar, told me about his glorious past under Nikisch in Leipzig and Berlin. After a while, I was allowed to play the timpani in the school orchestra, which enabled me to learn some of the traditional repertory, including Haydn's *The Seasons*, Beethoven, the *Peer Gynt* Suite (which I hated) and the Prelude to *Die Meistersinger* (which struck me as deeply unpleasant), and to do so, moreover, from the standpoint of its lowest frequencies. From my position behind the double basses and tubas, it was barely possible to hear the violins on the other side of the orchestra, and the day came when one simply gave up paying them any attention and concentrated instead on the cosy world of one's own imagination within the walls and palisades provided by the bass instruments. The rehearsals were taken by Rudolf Hartung, who was one of the conductors at the Staatstheater in the town, a local man, jovial, spirited, no longer in his first flush of youth and invariably good-natured. It was he who taught me theory – the theory of Ludwig Thuille of the New German (Munich) School. He also composed, though his works were rarely performed, perhaps because he was no Nazi. He had the most wonderful calligraphy. On one occasion I remember him showing me the score of his opera, *Der Kammersänger*, based on the play by Wedekind. Needless to say, it, too, was unperformed, since – he informed me – Wedekind's works were banned. In spite of such confidences, nay, almost complicities, I never dared show him any of my own attempts at composition, attempts that were likewise written in a style that was outlawed, influenced, as they were, by Hindemith and, more recently, by Frank Martin, too. I knew that he was dismissive of Hindemith, a position that he may have felt obliged to adopt not only as a representative of the traditionalist post-Thuille school but also as a loyal and obedient servant of the state.

I lost count of the number of times that I saw *Figaros Hochzeit* (operas were regularly given in German in those days) during my years in Braunschweig, generally standing at the back of the gallery. When the curtain went up on the garden scene in the final act, the white papier-mâché bushes onstage always seemed to give off an overpowering scent of lilac, so evocative was the music. And I have never known anything more beautiful in the whole of my life than the electrifying second-act finale, with its exquisite blend of sympathy, wit and compassion and its changes of tempo and key signature, changes which, however well one knew them, always came as a total surprise and yet always seemed so satisfyingly right.

Visits to the theatre and concert hall were no longer a luxury but part of my course. As a result, I scarcely missed a single concert and saw virtually every play and opera in the Braunschweig repertory. Everything was new to me. I heard not only the standard classics but also unknown masterpieces such as Humperdinck's *Königskinder* and a number of modern works, including operas, that were considered not too extreme. One such opera was Leo Justinus Kauffmann's *Die Geschichte vom schönen Annerl*, which had received its first performance in Strasbourg in 1942. I earned a little pocket money by turning the pages at chamber concerts and accompanying fellow students, as well as by singing in the cathedral choir, where our repertory included Handel's *Alexander's Feast* and a cappella works by older and newer composers. The cathedral conductor, Wolfgang Auler, would glance at me gratefully whenever I helped to reinforce the bass or tenor line, since male voices were in short supply at a time of increasing wartime austerity, and my voice had a range of over three octaves, a compass that I was more than happy to put to such good use.

On Wednesday afternoons I would see my maiden aunt, Leni Bünger, who was a half-sister of my father and who worked as a shorthand typist at the camera manufacturers, Voigtländer's. The fact that she lived in Braunschweig was no doubt why the town had been considered a suitable place for me to study. We always met at the same café. On Sundays, however, she deigned to invite me to lunch, after which we would go for a walk together and then, at around five or six o'clock, listen to one of the Philharmonic concerts that were broadcast on the radio from Berlin, after which I had to return to the dormitory. During the holidays I would always return to the Senne and, more often than not, see my friends back in Bielefeld. I was working at the time on an opera, *Die Leier des Palamedes*, based on a play written in Greek metres by Erich Jüngst, the son of Hans Jüngst, who had just scored a major success with his morale-boosting play, *Achill unter den Weibern*, at the Schiller-Theater in Berlin, with Horst Caspar in the title role. His son, my librettist – whose first teacher had been my own dear father – had just been killed in action. Through Hans Jüngst's good offices, the finished score was sent to the publisher Ludwig Strecker at Schott's in Mainz and soon returned with a few kind words designed to spare my feelings but leaving its rejection in no doubt – and a good thing too, one must add. It was the work of a greenhorn and, although it survived the war, it has happily since been lost, together with various other youthful transgressions, all of which went missing in the course of one of my many removals.

The new artistic impressions that fired my imagination during my years of study in Braunschweig undoubtedly left their mark on my developing style in a whole series of different ways. Many of them became fixtures, caught up in the network of memory and acquiring a life of their own. Whenever one sets to work on a new composition, all one's past experiences have to be put behind one and repressed: unless one bids farewell to the past and forgets it, it is impossible to create new images. The man who wants to write music must behave on each occasion as though he has not yet produced anything, he must be like a traveller in no man's land. By which I do not mean that map and compass would not be of some assistance in one's voyages of discovery through this uncharted terrain. Rather, one's approach to the composers of the past and to one's own particular experiences must always remain an integral part of some dialectic, living process.

As with Mozart and Wagner, chamber music and the symphony were, so to speak, the doors through which I approached what really mattered, the theatre and opera, where all one's creative energies have to be mobilized and all five senses brought to bear on the task in hand. Opera is a highly artificial art form in which nothing corresponds to the facts as we know them and the music has to answer for the credibility of the oddest and most exceptional states of mind. It must bewitch its listeners, enchant them, startle them, entreat them, seduce them, entertain them, take them by the hand and introduce them to magic moonlit gardens or thrust them into the dazzling light of day. A theatre composer must be able to depict in music every human emotion, from the happiest to the saddest, and do so, moreover, in a way that can be grasped by the senses. He must draw on the archetypes of his culture, for only by reference to their presence can he make it clear in what way his own music diverges from that of other composers of his own generation and of the past. The composer who wants to express pain must also have to hand the language needed to express its opposite – namely, the absence of pain, or joy – and he must speak that language as fluently as he handles the metaphors meant to represent pain. Only through his depiction of contrasts can things begin to speak and persuade the listener to agree with him and understand what he is saying.

Such considerations were as yet unfamiliar to me in Braunschweig, where I was still trying to find my feet in a novel world of musical sounds in which all the individual notes, with their various characteristics, are linked together and interrelated, a world, in short, that fascinated and stirred me and made me more and more curious. Thuille's theory of harmony, by contrast, was of no particular interest to me, since it seemed to me to have little to do with the more modern approach to composition and the emancipation of the dissonance. There was also a class in counterpoint, but it was really only later that I studied the subject seriously with Wolfgang Fortner in Heidelberg. I would, in fact, encourage all young composers to study Fuxian counterpoint, since it contains an essential idea that is of profound significance today, more especially against the background of free tonality. I am thinking here of the degrees of tension that arise when two or more lines converge, a tension that can be increased or decreased by means of part-writing. At the same time, I would be the first to concede that, in order to be truly inventive, the composer must also develop an appreciation of the subtleties and emotional upheavals that can be grasped on only a musical level and that demand to be heard in a process full of friction and tension – as in the music of Bach, for example, and especially in his church cantatas, those monuments to waywardness and experimentation.

This, they say, is no longer done today, it seems to have become obsolete and anachronistic. But, I reply, I cannot imagine that this is so, and so I continue to write polyphonically, following the ancient rules, even when I violate them for artistic reasons. As I often do. Clusters – dissonant bundles of notes that modernist composers put into circulation in the course of the 1970s like so many inflationary banknotes and that I, too, have used – have now become combinations of notes in my scores that can be followed not only on the printed page but also by the listener, fixed points in musical lines that overlap to such a degree that the impression of a cluster may momentarily arise, even though we are dealing here with nothing more than a massive overlap between lines and layers in a state of constant flux. They land on the manuscript paper, moving from left to right, passing from past into future and forever creating new contrapuntal, harmonic and emotional relationships. I am tempted to use a conceptual construct such as 'psychopolyphony' to describe my present technique, which I have spent half a century developing. But I also value the old rules simply because, without them, I should feel distinctly uneasy. I should soon discover that my writing was not turning out properly and that the music bore no relation to what I had intended. I write in the only way I can, on the basis of the harmonic and polyphonic way of thinking to which I have grown accustomed, although, plagued by self-doubts, I have repeatedly tried to break away from it. It is simply not possible for me to do it in any other way.

But let us return to Braunschweig and January 1944. A year earlier than the nation's grammar-school pupils and her future academics, all the non-academic boys who had been born in 1926 (skilled manual workers, showmen, musicians and members of similar professions) were abruptly called up to do three months' paramilitary service, followed automatically by regular military service. I still vividly recall being herded into the train for a journey lasting several days that finally ended in the Polish town of Sepólno Krajeńskie and a parade ground just outside that was surrounded by administrative buildings, barracks, a field hospital and an open-air latrine. Wherever one looked, there was snow. Here, in temperatures of between minus 20° and minus 30°C, the young men of Germany, the sons of ashen-faced mothers, had some sense knocked into them – to use the then current euphemism. From dawn till dusk we were drilled in the use of spades. The days were spent in a torrent of insults, abuse and punishments hurled and inflicted by company sergeant-majors and their seconds-in-command. We began to think ourselves almost as idiotic as these oppressive idiots themselves. It amazed me that, at a time when everyone knew that the war had already been lost, this hare-brained Prussian square-bashing was still being practised and clearly considered a proven means of raising to new heights of intensity not only our deeply unremarkable patriotism, but also our fighting spirit and delight in self-sacrifice. There were times when I imagined taking my spade and laying into our company commander, or whatever the bastard was called, and rearranging his slavering Nazi features. I made a note of the names of some of our sergeant-majors and their subordinates and even today would still be happy to punch them in the mouth to repay them for the insults and humiliations that we were made to suffer at that time. I was later able to track some of them down and punish them for what they did. While people like me, with no academic qualifications, were being introduced to the spirit of the age by having to clean the barracks steps with our toothbrushes and crawl across the snowy wastes in a forlorn attempt to ensure the final victory, the grammar-school pupils remained at home at their desks, although they admittedly often had to get up in the night and help to man the anti-aircraft guns that were aimed in vain at the Allied bomber squadrons which every day, and especially at night, discharged their fatal cargoes on German towns and cities, generally completely unchecked. During one particularly heavy air raid on Bielefeld, my Uncle Fritz – the brother-in-law of my consumptive Uncle Hugo – was burnt to a cinder by napalm. In the philistine camp at Sępólno Krajeńskie, where one of my fellow students from Braunschweig, Kurt Stier, had also been posted and where he, too, learnt to feel the same burning anger as I, the best thing that ever happened to me was a bout of influenza that put me in hospital for two or three days. It helped me to recover. From there I wrote a mildly despairing letter to my mother, telling her that I felt homesick, to which she replied, as kind as ever, and told me what my younger brothers and sisters were doing. It was in response to this same letter that my father wrote recommending that I regard my straw mattress as my one true friend in life.

What was more important was that it was here, while square-bashing or digging trenches (which meant breaking up ground that was frozen as hard as concrete), that I first learnt to live in a world of my own devising, concentrating on my art, hearing progressions of dissonant chords in my head, creating tension and delaying its resolution. It was here, in short, that I really began to compose. Today I can plan whole works in my head, passing them in review, fully orchestrated, before my mind's ear. At the end of 1944 I sent my parents a cycle of Christmas poems that I had written and that were modelled on Rilke, Weinheber and Manfred Hausmann. My mother kept them. They contain lines such as

A thousand stars stand shining in the sky,
A thousand true believers hurry by
To see the Son of God, the Nazarene

and

We walk together hand in hand,
Our silent tread the only sound
That echoes through what seems the heart
And epicentre of this round.

These poems had the effect of encouraging my father to write to me from the eastern front to say that I really would have to stop sprinkling my lyrical effusions with Jewish concepts such as Bethlehem, Christ and the Three Wise Men. It was the last letter that we ever exchanged. Three months later my father was killed, fighting for his fatherland. For years afterwards, long after the war was over, I still found it hard to forgive him for this – and for other things besides. I suspected that he had volunteered. I felt that, when it came to it, he should have defended his family not on the eastern front but at home. Once, in a dream, I managed to forgive him for a few seconds: Franz, the former lance-corporal, returned home from a Russian prisoner-of-war camp, long after the war had ended, dressed in rags and as gaunt as the Russian labourers from the camps in the Senne, wearing the bilious green and purple that I associated with the hungry and dying, sadder than ever before, beaten, a footnote to history. It was as though a weight had been lifted from my shoulders: I could embrace him effortlessly, the poor broken man, my prodigal father, and could rejoice for a moment in the sense of well-being that invariably comes with forgiveness.

After three wasted months of snow and ineradicable anger at all that I was expected to do for this band of common soldiers (who still failed to make a soldier of me, in spite of all their bullying), a thaw set in at Sepólno Krajeńskie and by the end of March it was finally possible to tell that spring was in the air, bringing with it a feeling of freedom. I returned home, where I was able to rest a little, see friends, despondently pick out a few old sonatas on the piano and visit those of my fellow students in Braunschweig with whom I had grown very close and to whom a couple of females had attached themselves in the meantime – two delightful students of acting who struck me as chic and *mondaine*. Every day new orders might arrive, posting me to some other far-off place. Every day the sentence could be carried out. I would rather be dead, I thought, than repeat what I had already been through at Sepólno Krajeńskie. It was impossible to flee the country: I had discovered that the whole of Europe was occupied by our people and that the Swiss were even sending back Jews who had crossed into the country illegally. When my call-up papers arrived a few weeks later, I broke down and howled my head off, but the very next morning reported for duty, dry-eyed and as instructed, at the Seeckt Barracks in Magdeburg, a building situated on the Elbe, which is edged hereabouts by lines of tall, white poplars. On the eve of my departure I went with some friends to a concert in Bielefeld – a performance of Beethoven's Seventh that was like some ultimate message of freedom and beauty and that could so easily have been the last concert I ever attended. By way of a farewell present, Adi Rang, who was now working part-time as an anti-aircraft auxiliary, gave me a copy of Trakl's poems that he himself had made. I said goodbye to my parents – a wretched occasion at which none of us attempted to wish the others well. As always, no words came. Something had snapped and was broken beyond repair. We were already drifting apart.

In the wake of total war, my father, already twice invalided out of the army, had been called up for what was to prove the final time on 16 September 1943. Before being sent to the front for the third time in his life, he and my mother visited me in Magdeburg one Sunday afternoon in early summer. It was their final visit. Because of it, I had exceptionally been granted a three-hour pass: I was, after all, a recruit. The three of us sat on the banks of the Elbe, on the steeply sloping embankment, overhead the poplars rustled and, as always, no one spoke. We fortified ourselves on sandwiches and raspberry juice. Then Mother suddenly started to cry, as if she knew that her husband and eldest son would never see each other again, but Father could not abide such expressions of tender-heartedness, and so we relapsed into our usual silence, until, some time before my pass was due to expire, I returned – not ungladly – to barracks.

Here I trained as a radio operator in the panzer division. In selecting recruits, they had clearly chosen people who knew something about shorthand, languages or, in my own case, signalling and the art of listening. We learnt to handle classified information and to encrypt radio messages using codes that changed every day, so that they could not be understood by an enemy receiver. For this we used an encoding machine and, at a later stage in our training, an ingenious system that had only just been invented and that involved an astonishingly simple trick that the Allies, we were assured, had still failed to solve by the end of the war. Or had they? And we learnt to transmit these signals – ideograms in sound, each representing a different letter – and to make contact with unknown transmitters and receivers elsewhere by means of the monotonously bleeping rhythms of dots and dashes that had something intensely exciting about them – these codes, after all, were a matter of life and death. We learnt to write down the signals as we received them, so that hearing and recognition – the auditive and cognitive tasks – became indistinguishable (the process of simultaneously writing them down was a third element). This was something that I liked doing, something that interested me. It was better than fatigues, better than cleaning my gun, better than doing guard duty.

We were trained in the use of this secret language by Arthur Zimmermann, an NCO who in civilian life worked at a bank in Frankfurt. I soon became the fastest student in the class and was the only one who could still write down the instructor's signals as they passed the 100 mark and started to diverge more and more from officialese: on one occasion, I remember, he signalled the four letters of my first name at breakneck speed. I looked up. He looked away. Out of gratitude for the fact that he had noticed me, I gave him the cigars that I used to bring back from the clearing-up operations for which we were detailed after every air raid on Magdeburg. Apart from the bodies, we also brought out books and other useful objects such as tobacco and bottles of brandy that had survived the wholesale destruction. Once I found a copy of Ferdinand Lion's libretto to Hindemith's opera *Cardillac* among the rubble. NCO Zimmermann and I occasionally met for walks when off duty or would dine together in the evening in the comfort of his NCO's room. He was either unaware of, or chose to ignore, the fact that I belonged to a secret club for antimilitarists that had been constituted among the young cannon fodder in the company dormitories. Among other members of the club were Achim Streubel, who later became well known as a stage designer, the artist Walter Kremser, a passionately imaginative and animated individual, and Dieter Schojan, a romantic lead. If I remember aright, the violinist Kurt Stier was also a member. Be that as it may, it was an impressive little group of nonconformists that was drilled hard on the meadows along the Elbe one Saturday afternoon in the burning heat of summer with a particularly brutal form of punishment drill involving old and impossibly heavy machine-guns and gas masks, the airtightness of which was constantly checked by our institutional tormentors. We were herded into the Elbe and driven out again in an attempt to beat a sense of blind obedience into us teenage softies in a way we should not soon forget. But it made not the slightest difference. Our military training was not yet over, I could still not hold my rifle correctly, still could not take it apart, clean it, put it back together again and use it and still had not learnt to assemble our signalling equipment when, late one summer morning, all our equipment was destroyed by Allied bombs that fell on our barracks and stables. Twenty-four of the officers' horses were blown to bits in the blast.

A few days later a number of officers arrived at the barracks. Perhaps they looked a little too nice and their dress was a little too *soigné*. At all events, they selected a group of young lads, almost all of whom, as it happened, belonged to the Antimilitarist Club which, in spite of being persecuted, continued to lead an underground existence. We had to give our written undertaking that we would not say a word about the mission for which we had all been chosen, a curious and in some ways disturbing request. I said goodbye to my NCO, and we set off into the unknown, wearing the brand-new black uniforms of our armoured division and carrying our stupid rifles. There was no moon that night. It was dawn when our bus reached Ostenholz, an attractive little village on the Lüneburger Heide, where we were billeted on the somewhat uncomfortable dance floor of the place's only pub. Again there were no private rooms. In the days that followed we were to discover why we had been brought here, but one thing was clear straightaway from the casual atmosphere that obtained here: our former army lives were over, at least for now. Here there was no punishment drill, no training in the use of machine-guns, not even the morning alarm call, the nauseating shriek of which had woken us at Seeckt. The only thing that I missed were the Wednesday evenings spent at Walter Kremser's house in Magdeburg while his parents were in Paris and where we were able to enjoy the *specialités de la maison*, including a cellar that was stocked with French wines representing the spoils of war. Unfortunately, Walter himself had not come to Ostenholz, perhaps because he was not considered sufficiently photogenic. Only a few weeks before our secret transfer, we had had to go on manoeuvres to the Harz Mountains, where, overcome by tiredness, I had fallen asleep on guard duty one night in the forest and slumped to the ground, only to be kicked awake and haled before my superior officers. Had the case been serious, I would have faced the death penalty, but in this particular instance the sentence consisted of only six night watches in a row. Fortunately, I had to share the watch with Walter, so we were able to keep awake by maintaining a stream of antimilitary invective and other seditious nonsense.

Among other memorable incidents that took place while we were in Magdeburg, I remember on one occasion a fellow soldier being dragged before his whole unit, branded an enemy of the people and sentenced to close arrest for having caught a dose of the clap at a brothel. I have still not forgotten the pallor of his expression, from which all trace of life had been extinguished by his sense of humiliation. I felt his shame as though it was my own. This was a case that was discussed at length at the secret sessions of the Antimilitarist Club, where our superior officers and their pedagogical and ethical views came off very badly. Sometimes, however, there was cause for celebration. One such occasion was 6 June 1944. We were confined to barracks and unable to meet at Walter Kremser's apartment, so we repaired instead to a dugout in the furthest corner of the barrack yard, where we drank his parents' looted Medoc and toasted the Allies, our saviours, who had landed on the Continent that morning and whom we all wished Godspeed. The news had been broadcast on the barracks' radio that morning and relayed on the tannoy while we were all outside, vainly going through our drill with our ancient rifles, and we had found it difficult to show no reaction, still less not to throw down our weapons and dance for joy or weep for sheer delight – or both.

Six weeks later, on the evening of 20 July 1944 – that historic day on which, true patriot that he was, Claus von Stauffenberg planted a bomb beneath the table of the General Staff in the Führer's headquarters at Rastenburg – the alarm was sounded in our barracks and five minutes later we all reported for duty, armed to the teeth, just as we had been trained. We were loaded into lorries and sent off in the direction of Berlin. It later transpired that our own particular armoured division was among the contingent of troops rallied by the insurgents, something I have always considered a special honour. On this occasion, therefore, our night-time's excitement turned out not to be a simple field exercise in the course of which we would comb the woods for non-existent partisans. This time it was serious: we sensed that there was something in the air. After we had been on the road for a few hours, however, the convoy stopped, turned round and returned the way it had come. By dawn we and the other units were back in Magdeburg and our hateful barracks. The insurrection in Berlin had been put down: the news was relayed over the same radio in the barrack yard as the one that six weeks earlier had announced the Allies' landing. That same evening we antimilitarists had to take part in a torchlight procession through the streets of Magdeburg with hundreds of Nazis and other uniformed men and women. We passed between bomb-ravaged house fronts to the square in front of the town hall, where we heard the local gauleiter, Rudolf Jordan, deliver himself of a fatuous speech that inevitably mentioned Providence and held up to public ridicule the traitors from the old and decadent aristocratic caste. A new set of scapegoats had been found now that the other enemies of the state had all been exhausted both physically and in the press. Many officers were hounded out of the army, including Ludwig of Hesse-Darmstadt, with whom I later became very friendly. The military salute was abolished and replaced by the Nazi salute. For common soldiers like me, square-bashing and technical training continued, the only difference being that it was becoming increasingly obvious that we would now be posted to the front sooner rather than later. But suddenly these angels had arrived at our barracks in the guise of smartly dressed officers and taken us off on a secret mission to the Lüneburger Heide. The aim of our new deployment, it now turned out, was to play at being soldiers.

It beggars belief. We were part of a contingent of soldiers and officers from Berlin, who in their private lives worked in the film industry and whose job was now to make educational and propaganda films purporting to show life on the front and intended to be shown in cinemas and used as teaching material for the next generation of privates. As soldiers, we were to play the part of soldiers. We were made up by professional make-up artists and filmed by professional cameramen, while professional scriptwriters placed words in our callow mouths. The director, who specialized in battle scenes, experimented with a whole range of dramatic shots, showing us attacking and engaged in hand-to-hand fighting with genuine Russian soldiers who, just like us, were instructed to be themselves – which explains why their Slav appearance was emphasized by our inventive friends in the make-up department, making them look like Tartars and thus suggesting subhuman characteristics. One day we filmed a scene in which we had to storm a hill. The scene was rehearsed several times, during which it was borne in upon us that on no account must we step off the paths that the director had marked out in white sand. The clapperboard announced the first take and the cameras started to roll: a handsome lieutenant stormed up the hill to the sound of apparently authentic explosions that rang out, according to plan, using the sort of theatrical explosive that was always employed for such purposes and that was ignited by a technician from a central control. But there were so many that the black earth thrown up by them covered the white marks in the sand, with the result that our lieutenant stepped on one of the mines and was blown to a thousand pieces. I saw the bits of his body flying through the air and buried myself in the sand in my horror, hiding my face, incapable of any movement.

The battle scene was aborted, and filming was not resumed until several days later, by which time the lieutenant had been given a decent burial by his beautiful wife and by ourselves and our Russian colleagues. The script may then have been slightly altered. The Russian officers, who played the part of subhuman creatures, were quartered very close to us. The star among them, in my own eyes at least, was the charming Victor, whom I got to know while we were peeling potatoes in the mess. One day he asked if, when I was on guard duty at night, I would allow him to slip through the barbed-wire fence surrounding the building where he slept and fraternize for a couple of hours with his blonde German village girl who lived diagonally opposite. He hugged me warmly when, proudly and happily, I assured him of my vigilance. We had lots of time between takes and so I used the opportunity to compose, setting a number of Trakl poems for voice and organ. The tenor soloist was a member of our crew, one Walter Sklarek from Duisburg, and I myself played the organ in the village church, where it was exceptionally cold in November 1944 – as cold as the unheated room in the neighbouring house, where a wonderful Steinway piano had survived the hail of bombs that had descended upon the capital. Even at that time, I invariably took not only my books with me on my travels, but also eau de Cologne, music and manuscript paper. Here I could spend an hour every evening, practising pieces by Hindemith, Beethoven and Schumann (the *Kinderszenen*), playing until my fingers grew stiff with the cold and making the same mistakes at the very same point every time. The neighbours were always extremely grateful when I stopped and returned to quarters.

When the day's filming was over, Achim Streubel and I would sometimes wander off across the heath to a nearby cottage that was similarly surrounded by barbed wire and where French Jewish officers were interned. Here we would remove our make-up and wash, or fetch water. Among the officers were the actor Jacques Huth and the conductor François Jaroschy, whom I met on several later occasions in Paris and New York. Here in captivity, he asked me about Pfitzner's new cello concerto which, according to a report in an old newspaper that he had just read, had recently received its first performance in Berlin, but I had heard nothing to that effect. At the end of November, shortly before our film crew was ordered to leave for Prague, Achim and I visited him again in order to say goodbye. When he heard that we were going to Prague, he asked us to call on his brother, who owned a factory manufacturing pharmaceutical products, and give him a letter, since they had not heard from each other for some time. Immediately on our arrival in Prague we did as he had asked us and made our way to a third-floor apartment in a house in the Soukenická, one of the streets leading off the Revoluční. The door was opened by a fine-featured, aristocratic woman dressed in dark clothes, who gave a start when she saw us, but whom we were quickly able to reassure when we explained the reason for our visit. Fear haunted her tearful eyes: her husband, she said, had been arrested a few days earlier in Na příkopě, where people wearing Jewish stars were forbidden to loiter. On alighting from his tram, instead of moving smartly on, he had stopped on the pavement to clean his glasses, which, she said, had steamed up. All that she knew was that he was now at Theresienstadt. We saw Frau Jaroschy as often as possible and, wearing our black uniforms (in the seams of which the common louse – *Pediculus vestimenti* – had now taken up permanent residence), joined her and her two children for Midnight Mass, including organ music by Janáček. By the time that the service was over, the last train had already left, and so, braving partisan fire, we walked back to the film studios at Hostivař along the deserted railway tracks. The moon was especially bright that night.

On one occasion we attended a concert given by the Czech Philharmonic under Václav Smetáček, at which all Dvořák's Slavonic Dances were patriotically applauded by an elegantly dressed and exclusively Czech city audience. On another occasion – this time without the Jaroschys – we heard the Duisburg Orchestra, which had been evacuated to Prague, but its performance of a Bruckner symphony under Joseph Keilberth left me unimpressed. At Hostivař, where we were also living, part of the Lüneburger Heide had been reconstructed in one of the local studios. As before, we had time on our hands, sitting around for days on end in our make-up and waiting for the scenes in which we were due to appear. According to the script, my big moment – and, if the truth be told, my only moment – was to be the lines, 'Well, Paul, were there any letters for you? What's your mummy got to say?' But the scene was never filmed, since the project fell victim to the deepening political and military crisis. By January 1945 we had the impression that our production managers had gone into slow motion, making all progress impossible, so that we actors would slope off to the neighbouring studio, where Willi Forst was making a film, *Wiener Mädeln*, with a number of other Viennese film stars. Whenever we were not ogling one or other of these darlings of the public, we would spend the time hunting for lice in our battledress. The whole army was riddled with the creatures, with the result that once a month the entire clothes of the whole German army had to be steam-cleaned – as if that made any difference to the vermin. It was not until the introduction of the highly effective Anglo-American insecticide DDT, which entered the world of German hygiene only after the final victory, that we saw the last of these lice. For that alone we would have had every reason to be grateful to the Allies.

Our Prague idyll ended suddenly but not unexpectedly in the wake of the new wave of hostility towards those who had stayed at home behind the lines, a hostility sparked by the Russian winter offensive and to which the few theatres and orchestras that were still functioning fell victim in turn. *Rien n'allait plus*. Willy-nilly we were ordered back to Magdeburg by unseen forces. The train passed through Dresden on the morning of 14 February 1945 – the night after the city had been razed to the ground in two raids by the RAF, leaving thirty thousand dead among the still burning rubble. We arrived unharmed in Berlin the following morning and were given twenty-four hours' leave, which I spent at the Streubels, where I was given a bath, fresh rolls and clean underwear and where we were visited that evening by family friends with a taste in light music and not a single good word to say for the Nazis. We had arrived at the Zoo Station very early in the morning and emerged on to the Kurfürstendamm to see the roof trusses of the houses on fire and the sky filled with soot. The sun looked like the palest of moons. The country's collapse was assuming increasingly apocalyptic dimensions. I shall never forget the impression left by that night of bombing, when the city's zoo was hit, and reptiles, elephants and beasts of prey broke out and roamed through the burning metropolis. It was just like Sodom and Gomorrah.

The next day we reached Magdeburg and the Seeckt Barracks. The conduct and spiteful remarks of the staff sergeant – a particularly uncivilized brute – left us in no doubt that they knew we had spent the last few months shirking the war, even though there was nothing that any of us could have done about it: it was simply a duty, just like any other, nothing more nor less. NCO Zimmermann and I resumed our walks, and the poplars along the Elbe continued to rustle, just as they had done before. Spring and the Allies were drawing closer. It was clear that we would soon be sent to the front as part of an armoured division. Our training was intensified: we had to learn how to keep in contact by radio-telephone with the radio operators in neighbouring tanks and how to coordinate our actions with whoever was in charge of the battle. Magdeburg suffered more bombing raids. Whenever we were not on guard duty and had to remain in the open, we would sit in the air-raid shelter, where we were able to see the youngest soldiers, mere boys of barely sixteen, sitting there, pale and silent, their steel helmets on their heads and their carbines clutched in their tiny hands, listening to the whistle of the bombs and feeling the shelter shake with each explosion. We older privates felt quite sorry for them. We watched as the mortar trickled down on a Bavarian NCO, one of the brutes responsible for drilling the latest intake of youngsters and preparing them to fight for the fatherland and the final victory, who now crumpled to his knees, praying in a loud voice and invoking the names of Catholic saints. In vain.

I had now been assigned to the radio post that had been set up in the shelter and from where our own division remained in contact with other divisions and with company headquarters. I was placed on night duty by the soldier in charge, so I could sleep in the booth by day and make myself as inconspicuous as possible. I was able to read while on duty at night, which meant that I sometimes failed to hear the signals on my radio. Since they had to be recorded in the book provided and could afterwards be checked, these lapses could have resulted in my arrest. Finally the signals would impinge upon my consciousness and recall me from Rilke's *Malte Laurids Brigge* or whatever I happened to be reading, and I would receive and decode some new military secrets, which I would then deliver, without delay and in keeping with my instructions, to the officer on duty and sometimes even to the company commander in person. The Magdeburg Stadttheater closed its doors with a performance of *Figaros Hochzeit*, and it was clear from our radio that it was not a moment too soon. The head of the US Ninth Army reached the edge of the town on 18 April 1945, and everything on two legs that was still in the barracks was hurriedly loaded into lorries and evacuated. They were the same vehicles as those that should have taken us to Berlin nine months earlier, when we had hoped to defeat the tyrant. Now they were taking us, rattling and clattering, in the same direction, but in order for us to save him. The Magdeburg barracks were evacuated so abruptly that I was forced to abandon my trunk of books and music, which was left behind in the cellar. And I became separated from my NCO.

I found myself with total strangers and was thrown back on my own resources. We were divided into groups, each consisting of five radio operators, and sent to Krampnitz, just outside Potsdam, where we spent some time in the local barracks under permanent attack from British hedge-hoppers, which had now started to shoot civilians, including farmers in their fields. The end was not far off. Potsdam had been destroyed only a few days earlier, on the night of 14/15 April, and once again we had to help with the clearing-up operations. Fellow students whose families lived in Berlin disappeared, but not everyone managed to escape. Deserters and defeatists were strung up from lamp-posts in Charlottenburg and Wilmersdorf. On one occasion, an officers' clerk and a motorcyclist from our own division were shot in our barrack yard as soon as they had recovered sufficiently from their injuries to stand up or lean against the wall. They had tried to escape from the present hell by fleeing westwards in a service vehicle using forged papers, but had collided with an anti-tank obstacle. Every radio team had to send two of its members to the execution as witnesses, and when they came back, they told us all about it. I covered my ears, clutching my dearest friend, my straw mattress, and whispering into it: 'Keep calm, old tom-cat, keep calm.' (I should add that, at school, I was known as Hinze, after the tom-cat in Tieck's play about Puss-in-Boots.) In a word, I behaved like the Thinker in Brecht's *Lehrstück* by lying as flat on the ground as possible, making myself as small as I could and keeping a look-out. We had to leave the barracks and were quartered in forest bunkers on the lakeside, with only a single armoured scout car, no fuel, no ammunition, no radio equipment, and only our guns and a few bazookas and grenades. I can still recall Goebbels' speech to mark the Führer's birthday on 20 April, which we were forced to listen to on the radio together, effortlessly comparing the truth of his claims with the reality that we could see all around us.

It was only a matter of time before the Soviet army reached the eastern edge of Berlin and our groups of radio operators, each equipped with its own set of travel documents, were sent off, on foot, in the direction of Flensburg, where we were to report to one of the regional headquarters before joining the German troops that were stationed in Scandinavia and that were to attack the Allies from the north and relieve Berlin and the rest of the Reich – a plan that notoriously came to nothing. The next few days were extremely difficult for us. The road to Flensburg looked like a battlefield. Although I have often spoken and written about this period in my life, I have still not managed to adopt a balanced and objective view of it. Our various forms of transport included not only military vehicles but also farm carts filled with refugees and the wounded, who were being passed from one overcrowded hospital to another. We were under constant attack from low-flying aircraft, whose bursts of fire would hit drivers and passengers the moment they came into sight from behind a wood or elevation. Two members of our group were so terrified by these aircraft that on the very first day they leapt down from the moving lorry and, abandoning their knapsacks and weapons, disappeared into the surrounding countryside, never to be seen again. Whenever an aircraft came into sight, the lorry or cart would veer from its path, and soldiers and civilians alike would hurl themselves into the ditch at the side of the road, often enough being hit as they did so by the bursts of deadly gunfire. On one occasion I saw a group of nurses sitting in a farm cart, their heads shot off by machine-gunfire. On another occasion, a convertible full of party officials in yellow uniforms overtook us, hooting peremptorily. Hours later, we passed it in turn, now a blackened ruin in the ditch, its occupants' charred remains still sitting in their seats.

It was evening when we arrived in Schwerin. The three of us who were all that remained of our group of signallers happened to be occupying a farm cart that a couple of peasant women had allowed us to share with them and that was now directed by members of the SS into a barracks, where many others like us had already been rounded up. On the adjacent parade ground, soldiers of all ages, together with civilians who, like us, had been caught in the Nazi net while fleeing northwards, were once again being drilled in Prussian military discipline, ready to be deployed against the Bolshevik arch-enemy and used as cannon fodder in the decisive offensive against the plutocratic invaders. We had already heard of this arrangement, which was like the press-gangs of old. We joined the lengthy queue inside the barracks yard and watched these training exercises while waiting to register our names and receive our new instructions and assignments. But the peasant women, who had followed events from their cart and who must have felt sorry for us three boys, surreptitiously helped us to clamber back into the cart, where these angelic creatures hid us under empty potato sacks, before driving on. Rescued by their ministering hands, we continued our effortful journey northwards, eventually reaching Flensburg, where everywhere was deserted and deathly quiet, a silence broken only by the sound of enemy aircraft circling high above us. I spent a day at the command post on the front, where we tried to clean ourselves up and recover our strength. A train – which, no doubt because of the danger of guerrillas, kept stopping – took us by night to Jutland, where we found refuge in the classroom of a primary school in a tiny village near Esbjerg and where other German soldiers, both old and very young, were already being quartered. Here there was no more square-bashing, no more rounds of duty, no more rifle inspections: we sat around, waiting, playing cards, listening quite openly to the British and American military radios and reconstructing on the blackboard the course of the war as reported by them. Bielefeld and my parents' house, for instance, must have been overrun by American units in early April. The postal service had long since broken down, and it was not until after the war that I heard from the Jaroschys in Prague and discovered that their father had been taken from Theresienstadt to Auschwitz, from where he had not returned.

I went to see the pastor in the little Jutland village and asked if I could play the organ in his church. He gave me his permission, then sat down below me in one of the pews and listened to me playing. Afterwards he invited me to have supper with him, where I was allowed to share a table with his delightful children and imposing figure of a wife. I now knew how and where I would spend the time until the next troop displacement. Then, late one evening, as we privates were lying on our straw mattresses in the classroom, we heard Siegfried's Funeral March on the radio and knew at once that something important had happened. And, sure enough, the German people received the historic news that Hitler had killed himself in Berlin. Excited, even radiant, we sat round the table, lit a candle and celebrated with an impromptu banquet made up of the alcoholic and culinary treats that each of us had saved for this occasion. A short time later, at a ceremony in Reims on 7 May, General Jodl put his signature to Germany's unconditional surrender, and during the night of 8/9 May Field Marshal Keitel signed a similar undertaking at Karlshorst on the outskirts of Berlin. Hitler's successor, Admiral Dönitz, was finally arrested, together with the remnant of his government, on 23 May. I no longer remember what day of the week it was, but I had just set out for a midday stroll with one of my comrades, the lilac was in blossom, the cereal crops were beginning to show, larks were singing and the earth smelt sweetly beneath the warm spring sun, when the church bells started to peal and one of the local farmers cycled past us, calling out to us in German from a distance: 'The war's over!' We trotted back to the village. The German soldiers fired rounds of ammunition into the air in sheer delight, much to the disapproval of their company commander, who was unable to prevent them. The good-natured Danes came out of their houses and held out their hands to us with the words: 'Let's be friends once again.'

I spent the evening with my pastor and his family. He took me to a barn behind his house and showed me what he had hidden beneath the straw: an armoured scout car belonging to the Danish Resistance. A few days later I took my leave of the family. It was a touching occasion. As in the Grimms' fairy-tale, I wanted to give my gun to their youngest child, but the pastor – and the rules of war – would unfortunately not allow it. Then, in the wake of the exodus of German troops from Denmark, we set out on foot for the Eiderstedt peninsula, an extraordinarily exhausting trek destined to take us back to German soil. I can no longer remember how long it took, but it seemed to me to be endless. The spirit of history must have looked down on the little fair-haired youth from eastern Westphalia, bathed in sweat, a strained expression on his face, still weighed down by his knapsack, gas mask and rifle and hobbling southwards in one of the endless columns of beaten soldiers with bloodied feet, heading towards a new age and a freedom that promised no easy solutions. Local women, filled with pity, stood by the side of the road, first in Denmark itself, later in Holstein, and offered us cooling water to drink. By now we were back on German soil and allowed to throw away our carbines. The pile of them was as high as a mountain. A stern-eyed British officer watched as the mountain grew, while others took photographs, at least one of which must show little Henze, smoking his first Player's and happily conscious, it seems, of his role as a loser. He is thinking (then or perhaps only later): 'Maybe this snapshot will one day find its way into a family album in Leicestershire, Buckinghamshire or Wales. That would be nice.'

I now had to spend several months as a prisoner of war in a tent in a field in Schleswig-Holstein. Time seemed to stand still, a sensation that I relished. And I enjoyed myself, too, playing the organ in village churches filled to overflowing: every Sunday the Lutheran divisional padre would clamber on to his motorbike, with me as his pillion passenger, and together we would comb the peninsula's churches, where I would improvise and produce appalling dissonances on instruments through which the North Sea wind howled and which had clearly not been tuned or repaired for decades. I have still not forgotten the sound of these instruments and I evoke it in my music whenever I want to suggest a mood of wistfulness, melancholy, want and the post-war years in general. On one occasion – I think it must have been while we were being moved as prisoners – I remember passing along a treeless coastline and through a deserted Husum and seeing the beautiful old streets and dark and rickety houses and thinking that if the old tom-cat were lucky and survived, he might one day try to get a job as organist in this grey seaside town; he would perform his duties rigorously and conscientiously and, at the same time, lead a totally private life of which no one would know any details – not even I myself. I would carry my secret around with me like some Hoffmannesque violin case beneath a scrawny arm. It would always be a little too cold for me, the winds blowing off the North Sea would penetrate my threadbare jacket, and few visitors would be admitted to the badly heated apartment that came with my appointment, an apartment looked after by a humourless and sexless housekeeper. An air of tragedy would play around my sunken cheeks. Later I would become completely hunchbacked and acquire second sight, but my secret, about which I myself still had no very clear ideas, would accompany me to the grave. Thus I imagined the future and dreamt what my life would be like. The present situation meant that my expectations were not especially high.

On one occasion during these months of internment some professional artists and I walked miles along one of the many dykes that dominate the area, since we had heard a vague rumour to the effect that it was possible to buy sauerkraut in St Peter. It would have made a welcome change from our starvation rations, but we arrived too late. Yet we had enjoyed our walk and had chatted at length about art. I shall not mention the minimal bread rations doled out to us from the empty cupboards of the German army, since I kept reminding myself that they were more than Dr Jaroschy was getting at Theresienstadt and more than had been given to the Soviet prisoners of war in the Senne outside Bielefeld. For years I had regularly traded my meat rations for cigarettes, but here in the fields of Schleswig-Holstein there were neither. Instead, we took courses in English and French or listened to our elders, who could tell us about a free world that must once have existed before totalitarianism took hold and the dead hand of middle-class values descended upon us all. We listened while our elders talked among themselves about modernism and about other, better, democratic forms of government. We asked them about art at the time of the Weimar Republic, about theatrical highlights and operatic premières in Berlin, about Brecht, Weill and Eisler, about *Wozzeck* under Kleiber, the Kroll Opera and men like Piscator, Ebert, Reinhardt, Klemperer, Schoenberg, Walter, Hindemith and Furtwängler. I thought: 'The more I hear about these things, the clearer it becomes where and how the thread must be taken up again.' Among artists from the pre-Fascist era who were with us in the camp was an oboist from the Dresden Staatskapelle, Willy Meyer. Not only was it from his lips that I first heard the expression 'dictatorship of the proletariat', he also told me many new and astonishing things about people and music, all from the perspective of the practising musician and concert performer, a perspective that I knew from my time at music school. To mark the end of my eighteenth year on 1 July 1945 Willy Meyer honoured me by giving me his iron ration. It was a touching gesture, and in return I wrote one oboe piece after another on manuscript paper that I myself had made – a quartet, perhaps also a trio, a quintet for four instrumentalists and a singer that he later performed on Cologne Radio without my permission and, finally, following my return home, an oboe concerto. He was a good friend to me and a great collector, and his heirs still own all the manuscripts of these various pieces. Shortly after his release he became principal oboist with the West German Radio Orchestra in Cologne and also founded a wind quintet for which Stockhausen wrote not only *Zeitmaße* but also *Adieu*, a threnody to Meyer's son, who had been killed in a car accident while visiting Italy.

We were released from the internment camp at Eiderstedt in groups: first, all those who were needed to bring in the harvest, then those who were required in the mines (which sparked off a rumour that this was a trap on the part of the victorious powers and that all who reported for duty would be set to work within days in the mines in Siberia or Yorkshire) and, finally, in August, all the academics and those involved in administration and the law. Artists were never mentioned. It was clear that they were not needed. I reported for duty with the academics and so it must have been towards the end of August that I found myself in the release camp with a group of lawyers, doctors and professors. I lost count of the number of times that we had to fall in, strip to the waist and stretch out our arms in order to help the British military police in identifying members of the SS, who, it was well known, had indelible tatoos under their arms revealing their blood groups and now betraying their owners' barbarous past. I thought of Father's idea of sending me to an SS-school for musical cadets – if my music teacher in Bielefeld had not intervened, I would now either be dead or accused of being part of a criminal organization. English lorries dropped us privates some distance from our homes, equipping us with our release papers and three days' rations and setting us down on the road to freedom. I was left to hitch-hike the twenty or so kilometres back to my parents' home in the Senne.

3

> Et la mère est assise, en costume de deuil,
> Et la mère est assise auprès d'une fenêtre.
>
> Jean Cocteau, *Le fils de l'air*, 1935

Mother was sitting by the window, sewing, when her eldest son appeared, unarmed, outside his father's house late one afternoon. She would sit by the window, sewing, for hours on end every day, looking out for my father – the main road ran directly past the house – but he showed no sign of emerging from the endless stream of soldiers returning home from the war, and so she had to make do with me instead. Yet she seemed pleased enough to see me. Better than nothing, she no doubt thought. Exactly a year had passed since that sombre Sunday on the banks of the Elbe. We had not seen each other during that time and had not even had any contact since Westphalia had fallen to the Allies in the spring of 1945. The Allied troops had met with little resistance when their armoured cars had rumbled through the Senne and the flags that hung from the windows no longer bore the swastika, but were the white flags of defeat and unconditional surrender.

Suspected – quite rightly – of being infested with vermin, my army clothes and boots were immediately burnt. With nothing to eat and no money, times were very hard. I applied successfully to work for the victorious powers and for several months earned German money and English cigarettes helping to load munitions crates and other heavy objects into lorries, a monotonous and tedious task that I sought to make less monotonous by engaging in more useful pursuits such as practising my English and scrounging for Player's Navy Cut, a make whose stubs were unblushingly scavenged by addicts and dealers on autobahns that no longer served the final victory but that were instrumental, rather, in the country's defeat. The place where I worked was at the far end of the Detmolder Straße in Bielefeld and could be reached on foot, a journey that took me through the local woods and over hill and dale. After I had finished work for the day and on days when I was not required, I worked on a cycle of six post-Hindemithian sonatas and read voraciously. My brother Gerhard also returned unharmed from the war. At home, Mother made swede bread, swede syrup and swede coffee. It took her a long time to overcome her scruples and beg a little bread and other farmhouse produce from the local farmers for us children.

In Bielefeld the British military governor had put up a sign over the entrance to the town hall: 'Informers not admitted.' The crimes committed in the concentration camps were now being talked about more or less openly, resulting in a growing sense of shame and horror. No one had known a thing. Everyone had always been against it. The men and women of the occupying armies looked disbelievingly at us Germans, or their eyes were filled with loathing. Ever since then I have felt ashamed of our country and of my fellow Germans and our people. Wherever my travels have taken me, my origins – my nationality – have always caused me problems, even in Italy. Nor is it any wonder, since the devils who dragged us into this war did such unforgivable and unforgettable things to our neighbours, especially in Rome, not only in their persecution of the Jews but also following Mussolini's fall from power and during the subsequent partisan struggles. Close friends such as Elsa Morante, Luchino Visconti and Pier Paolo Pasolini had all known victims of the German occupation among members of their own families. The Germans are still hated in Europe, still the object of contempt and mistrust. More time is needed: at least two more generations must come and go before the Germans' reputation is more or less restored and the events of 1933 to 1945 are mercifully forgotten. Like some latter-day Battle of the Huns, this evil raged across the whole of Europe, leaving some sixty million dead and revealing how fragile is the mask of civilization behind which such barbarous features lie concealed. All things German fell into disrepute, and every German was affected by it. For me, German art – especially the middle-class, nationalistic art of the nineteenth and early twentieth centuries – became insufferable and suspect. For a time I was unable and unwilling to take any interest in it, unable to contemplate the German forests or hear any mention of the German soul – the depraved German soul. Something had happened that could not be made good any longer.

Rationing, coal shortages, famine and epidemics and questions of public order: these were some of the problems that Field Marshal Montgomery sought to address with his orders of the day. Newspapers and radio stations were soon up and running again, in both cases operated by German licensees authorized and supervised by the occupying powers. Many leading Nazis had been arrested, others escaped abroad, mostly to Latin America; a number had changed their identities in Italian monasteries, others, finally, had taken their own lives. Many lesser Nazis, too, fell into the hands of the authorities and were brought before the courts, and preparations were already under way for the country's leading war criminals to be brought to book in Nuremberg.

The Bielefeld Stadttheater reopened its doors in the late autumn of 1945, its choice inevitably falling on *Fidelio*. Its music director, Hans Hoffmann, offered me a contract as an unpaid volunteer, the terms of which I fulfilled until almost the end of the season, while at the same time working in the evening as a pianist in military casinos and accompanying operetta songs in order to earn the money that my family so urgently needed. I was on duty from morning till evening and would spend the midday break waiting in the local coffee house for the afternoon rehearsals to start. When there were no rehearsals, I would practise the piano in the theatre. My duties ranged from onstage conducting (I cued in the invisible trumpeter's entry in the Dungeon Scene in *Fidelio* and conducted the offstage flautist in *Die Zauberflöte*) to playing the piano not only for chorus rehearsals for *Iphigénie en Aulide* but also, unfortunately, for the dance scenes in the operettas in our repertory. Old operettas were revived in new productions. 'Glücklich ist, wer vergißt, was nicht mehr zu ändern ist' – 'Happy who forgets what can no longer be changed,' the soloists sang as they linked arms and swayed from side to side in the heady triple-time rhythms of the first-act finale of *Die Fledermaus*, while trying to make us forget the ruins all around us. And then there was the brisk duple-time chorus from Kálmán's *Gypsy Princess*: 'Those fascinating, captivating, devastating, scintillating, pretty little ladies of the chorus. Such pretty little, witty little, sporty little, naughty little, perfect little ladies of the chorus.' It was my job to play the piano in the ballet rehearsal room and, hour after hour, to help seven or eight women of different ages and sizes to go over and over the same ritornellos and dance routines that accompanied these ghastly songs.

It is entirely possible that my aversion to this kind of music dates from the winter of 1945/6. I have never forgotten these schmaltzy numbers and cancans and since then have invariably used them as metaphors for mendaciousness and vulgar tomfoolery within my own musical vocabulary. Operetta music – especially the sparkling, witty and saccharine sort associated with Vienna – always makes me think of hangovers and bouts of deep depression. I know people who like this kind of thing and who, as it were, think and feel in the language of operetta. They are the same people who link hands at carnival time, Bacchic postmen brought up to bawl out choruses and army songs by rote. The noise that they make is both brutal and threatening. From a distance it reminds one of the roar of the masses whenever Hitler spoke. One thinks: 'Any moment now, and the whole thing may change – light music can turn into something deadly serious.'

Those who are in a minority must always be on their guard.

The German folk-song – to remain with 'light' music for a moment – suffered badly at the hands of war. It fell silent, perhaps as a result of the injuries that it had sustained, or it developed into dirty jokes or racist kitsch, or else it returned to its roots. Perhaps it continues to lead a secret, sublimated existence in unknown, inaccessible regions and hearts. My own music contains the odd folk-song quoted from childhood memories, generally disguised as an inner voice, as in Machaut or Heinrich Isaac. My earliest musical experiences were, on the one hand, the folk-songs and Schubert *lieder* that our mother used to sing to herself while doing the housework and, on the other, Salvation Army tunes, brass-band music and male-voice choirs in the local beer garden. It is no doubt as a result of this that 'classical' music – in other words, the music of the first Viennese School and the *ottocento* and the Russian, English and Austrian music of the twentieth century – does not strike me as belonging to the past, as something that we have put behind us and that no longer concerns us today. Rather, it is important to me for its intellectuality, its ability to make us more sentient beings. Here is a way of life and a way of thinking which, not originally my own and never intended for my own social class, I have had to acquire for myself. No less important to me are the aesthetic ideas of the young German bourgeoisie of the early nineteenth century, with its discoveries concerning not only the language of music and the music of language, but also the significance of our folk-tales and myths and the soulscapes that they conceal, since it seems to me that such ideas may help us to escape from our benighted state of spiritual underdevelopment and into the light and lucidity of classical culture.

Like any other artist who wants to be able to express himself freely and individually, I have – over the decades – developed my own technique, a technique that I am still at pains to improve in order to refine its expressive potential. I have evolved a concept of beauty nurtured by experiences both terrible and wonderful, a concept that may be explained in terms of the fact that music was once effectively beyond my reach, something to which I had to gain access by cunning and self-denial in order that I could one day say, without fear of being misunderstood, what motivates me, what I understand by art and what initially persuaded me to raise my voice in the hope of being heard. With my dissonances I stress the distance between the modern world and Mozartian reality. Dissonance is not an empirical fact of life but an expression of pain. It is, as it were, a gauge that registers the absence of the potential for beauty and of the living presence and impact that I find in Mozart's restful, free and songlike composure and in his sense of human scale.

By this, I do not mean that my music is no more than a perpetual lament on the loss not only of this kind of light but also of a corresponding sense of Apollonian well-being. It is not as simple as that. My music draws what strength it has from its inherent contradictions. It is like a thorny thicket full of barbs and other unpleasant things. It is as poisonous as any serpent's sting. Its embraces may be dangerous, they may turn out to be a form of betrayal and frustrate one's expectations. People may feel repelled by its often garish colours and the infernal din that it seems constrained to produce – often enough they run away in droves. My music has an emotional dimension that is unfashionable, an emotional untimeliness. And lovers of old New Music – at least, what is normally understood by 'New Music' – will certainly feel short-changed by it. I operate with old structures – the expert shakes his head: on a purely conceptual level, my music cannot be understood in terms of modern techniques, in which it claims no expertise and which it finds useful only in part. My own music is traditional in that it operates on a horizontal plane, with the vertical plane related to it both dramaturgically and harmonically. The traditional principle, whereby the dissonance has to be resolved, remains valid in my writing. One could say that it is music that uses the dissonance for its own dramaturgical ends, its composer seeking feverishly to end the conflict, to expunge the sense of guilt, to forgive the mortal sins, to resolve the dissonance and reduce the pain. I am not concerned to create a sense of obsolete grammatical order but to deal inventively with these hundreds and thousands of different shades of dissonance as one of the most eloquent and multifaceted means of expression available to living, modern music in all its baroque opulence.

Here and there in my music are a few seemingly successful passages, moments where, for an instant, there appears to be the sense of an impending cadence, of resolution or redemption. But running counter to this is a second level of understanding that I can describe only as an expression of my better judgement, so that in the course of my development, my works have become more and more multilayered. There are almost always several things going on at once. Figures and vehicles for ideas people the theatre of my imagination, contrasting starkly and irreconcilably with other such figures, before complementing each other in accordance with musical, dramaturgical and structural rules, even if it be only to produce a fleeting compromise, a kind of anti-doctrinal democracy. It is as though we are dealing with illusions and Utopias. The artificiality of the whole exercise is meant to strike the spectator or listener as such and to be obvious to him or her. Superimposed layers of music should be seen and heard as precisely that, with all their comings and goings, their appearances and disappearances, the increase and decrease in their presence and density producing a constant fluctuation in intensity and light and thereby ensuring excitement, surprise and variety.

I am writing these lines in the spring of 1991 while working on my *Requiem* for Michael Vyner, a piece which, scored for thirty-three instruments, consists of nine 'sacred concertos'. (I mentioned Michael in my opening chapter and shall have more to say about him when we come to the early 1960s.) It represents a highly personal approach to the Catholic liturgy and its Latin words (a point to which I shall likewise return in due course) and is an example of absolute music full of imagery and metaphor. Lasting some seventy minutes, it also involves what, for me, is a new and freer approach to chromaticism that sometimes suggests a return to the harmonic world of Wagner's *Tristan und Isolde*. I use this harmonic language much as a poet integrates a particular foreign idiom into his personal style for his own specific ends. I evoke feelings that are familiar not only to myself but also to my listeners as a result of our shared but solitary experience of Wagner's chromatic language. I work with brief quotations often consisting of no more than a couple of syllables or, rather, of a few notes that are capable of directing the thoughts of my more knowledgeable listeners in the direction that I desire, affording them the best possible opportunities to draw all necessary comparisons and, hence and above all else, allowing them to experience the interconnections for themselves. This is why I have increasingly chosen to call up harmonic (and melodic) gestures from German Romanticism in my own more recent music – not because I am a Romantic composer, but because I adopt a specific, modern approach to the expressive language of nineteenth-century music and do so, moreover, from an analytical standpoint. It is as though I were introducing words from earlier centuries into my spoken language: one recalls them, even though they are no longer used. They mean something – but precisely what that meaning is seems to have slipped from our grasp. We have to descend into the depths of oblivion in order to find the answer. I work with the echoes left in my psyche by all that is German, especially German folk-tales. The result is sounds and images, an interplay of light, all of which I bring to the surface, effortfully but with the best of intentions, in order to place them within my own poetic context. They help me to tell my story.

Shortly after the end of the war, I found myself confronted by a type of music about which people like me knew virtually nothing at that time. It had never really been able to gain a foothold in Germany, not least because its composer, Gustav Mahler, had been one of the first to be proscribed in 1933. It was music that moved me deeply, allowing me access to a mode of expression and a world of emotion of which I had previously had no notion. The first of Mahler's pieces that I heard were his *Kindertotenlieder* and Ninth Symphony. Over the years, I was able to get to know the rest of his works as well (occasionally as a conductor, too), and they naturally influenced my writing. The same thing happened to me later, during the 1970s, when I encountered the music of Monteverdi and was able to penetrate deep inside his world of late Renaissance and early Baroque imagery while freely elaborating the continuo part in *Il ritorno d'Ulisse in patria*, a detailed preoccupation with his way of thinking and composing that affected my own style of writing, clarifying, ordering and moulding it. Before I got to know Mahler, it was Stravinsky whose aesthetic outlook and understanding of art fascinated, preoccupied and influenced me profoundly for many years. Even today his music, especially that of his neoclassical period, continues to inspire me. Thanks to my work on Monteverdi, I became curious about the effect of simple chords in root position, which I now use uninhibitedly but wholly consciously. Once I have come to terms with Wagner and am through with him, too, I shall be left alone with my own music, without pre-existing models of any description. I can well imagine that this will not be particularly amusing. Indeed, it may even mark the end: death comes when one no longer has anything to love, when there is no longer any music that one would give anything to hear and sing and play once again.

I spent the autumn of 1945 unremuneratively rehearsing the Bielefeld Stadttheater *corps de ballet* and growing out of my student clothes, with the result that, in the absence of any alternative, I was obliged to wear my father's clothes and hats. No doubt I looked a sight, but there was a certain symbolic rightness to it all, since I had now taken his place as the head of the family. It was about this time that we got to know some new neighbours in the Senne, Walter Trenkler and his wife, Regina, who had fled from Berlin during the war and ended up in our neighbourhood. He was a doctor by profession and currently trying to establish a practice in the area. We became friends. His wife was a pianist and would practise for hours every day, chain-smoking as she did so. By way of a change, and to my own great good fortune, she also gave me piano lessons in addition to cigarettes and tea, her teaching methods not entirely uninfluenced by those of her own teacher, Wladimir Horbowski, whom she idolized to the point of distraction. And I learnt more about Berlin's wonderful musical scene, what it had been like before 1933 and what had become of it since. Legends came to life. She could still recall Hindemith's *Neues vom Tage* at the Kroll Opera (she had been a young girl at the time and had asked the composer for his autograph) and told me amazing things about the Philharmonic and about Furtwängler and various famous soloists. Members of the orchestra, including the violinist Fritz Peppermöller, were on friendly terms with the Trenklers. They also knew the pianist Helmut Roloff, who had been active in the anti-Fascist Resistance, and were acquainted with a young conductor from the Berlin Academy who evidently had a great future ahead of him – one Sergiu Celibidache.

As a result of all these anecdotes, I came to regard Berlin more than ever as the place where ability and the quality of one's work were judged by the highest standards: to be accepted in Berlin meant you had finally made it. It was Regina Trenkler who helped me at this time to escape from the confines that allowed my ambitions no chance to unfold. My work at the theatre was a torment. It was getting me nowhere and was taking up too much time and energy. I was unable to practise the piano as much as I needed and had no time at all to compose. Provincial life, poverty and the lack of any prospects gnawed away at me till I felt that I was being completely destroyed. It was time to find ways and means of packing in my work at the theatre and surviving without the need to rely on third-rate operettas. My contribution to the household budget had now been officially sorted out, so my support was no longer as vitally necessary as it had been hitherto.

The Trenklers assumed responsibility for my future, and it was decided that I should go to Berlin and continue my studies there. I was advised to take composition lessons with Boris Blacher, one of whose jauntier works I already knew from the radio. In order for me to obtain a letter of recommendation for him, it was resolved that Regina and I would travel to Tübingen, where I would play for the now elderly Wladimir Horbowski, who would in turn write to Blacher. In the spring of 1946, therefore, Regina and I set out for Tübingen, illegally crossing the border between the English and American zones in Kassel, spending the night in the open air and, again illegally, crossing into the French zone, where we were nabbed by the French border guards and banged up for eight days in an internment camp. The men were detailed to various duties, I myself spending most of the week dismantling a large factory for woven goods, in the course of which Father's powder-grey Sunday suit acquired several nasty oil stains. On the Saturday my travelling companion and I were haled before a military tribunal, sentenced to the eight days' detention that we had already served and immediately deported to the American zone. Foreigners were evidently unwelcome.

Fortunately, the affair now took a happier turn. We arrived in Heidelberg, where Regina looked up some old friends from Berlin. Among them was a young medical student by the name of Melchior Bengen, an admirer of Stefan George, who drew our attention to the fact that there was a widely respected teacher in Heidelberg in the person of the still relatively youthful composer, Wolfgang Fortner. I had already heard of him. He had been born in Leipzig, had studied with Hermann Grabner and decades later was also to teach the likes of Bose and Rihm. We telephoned him and arranged to meet. It was a glorious Whit Sunday when we called on him. Regina played him some of my piano pieces that she knew by heart, and I showed him some of my most recent compositions, prominent among which were my six Hindemithian sonatas that I had completed in the course of the previous year in the teeth of adversity, hunger and exhaustion. On the strength of this visit, Fortner accepted me as his composition pupil and I was allowed to enrol at Heidelberg's Institute of Evangelical Church Music, where Fortner taught harmony, counterpoint and score-reading and where students were required to sing in the choir, in addition to being taught how to read old clefs and to play from full orchestral scores on the piano – scores that were notated in a bewildering variety of different clefs and among which Bach's church music figured particularly prominently.

It was also arranged that I would earn my keep as a private tutor to a family in Heidelberg: the Schüles' three children, Verena, Franziska and

Gottfried, were to receive extra coaching in Latin, English, German and maths and also learn to play the piano. (They would later say that they learnt next to nothing from me, not even how to play the piano, but that they never again had such a good time with any of their tutors.) Frau Trenkler and I returned to the British zone and the Senne. I eagerly packed my belongings, ignoring the air of general disapproval exuded by my mother and by my brothers and sisters, and prepared for the journey to Heidelberg. I still remember getting up at dawn and, together with my mother, books and music, taking a rickety handcart to the station at Kracks. An embarrassed silence filled the morning air. 'There's no alternative,' I told her. 'But it's so far away,' she replied. Within twenty-four hours I was back in Heidelberg, this time legally. The Schüles, who turned out to be a thoroughly charming couple, put me up in their chauffeur's room, which it was impossible to heat. Frau Annemarie Schüle took charge of my food-ration card and from now on I joined the family for lunch, which made my life much easier.

And so, after two years' interruption, I resumed my music studies. Fortner had time on his hands, since, like so many other Germans at that time, he was waiting to be denazified and to be given a clean bill of health. He had had virtually nothing to do with the regime, but, having been declared unfit for active service on account of his poor eyesight, he had responded to an official invitation from the authorities and toured the front lines with his Heidelberg Chamber Orchestra – a harmless enough exercise, if ever there was one. And that, I think, was all. He soon received his denazification papers. And I had private lessons with him almost every day. Initially it was largely early counterpoint, which I found extremely difficult. I could see the logic and even the beauty and naturalness of these basic laws, but it took a lot of effort before I could operate confidently and intelligently within the limits that were set. After a number of months we then began lessons in what my teacher termed 'free counterpoint' and which, for me, was to be a preparation for a more modern approach to the dissonance. It became clear that music has a past, a present and a future and that observing the basic rules has nothing to do with faith or style. No, these basic rules are nothing more nor less than the alphabet of our music, rules without which we will ultimately produce only tentative stammerings and nonsense.

My whole life now lay ahead of me, and it depended entirely on me as to what I chose to make of it. It was a time of discoveries and new ideas, a time of catching up, of encountering new people and concepts and of getting to know them in greater detail – in short, it was one vast learning process. Sometimes it was all a bit too much for me, and I suffered two breakdowns, I was so unused to such hard work, and there seemed no end to it all. I earned a little extra by preparing a piano reduction of Fortner's Violin Concerto, which he had just written for the violinist Gerhard Taschner, and I also gave music lessons to two GIs and was happy to accept Chesterfields as a means of payment, not least because, ever since my days in the army, I had become addicted to the weed. A pleasant diversion from counterpoint and dreary harmony was provided by my relatively frequent – not to say, daily – visits to the fleapit in the Hauptstraße (it still exists today), where there was a different American film showing every day, always with the original soundtrack. One of the films I saw at this time was *Destry Rides Again* with Marlene Dietrich – my first encounter with her in the cinema. Not until later did I see the great films that she had made at an earlier stage in her career and hear the songs from *The Blue Angel.*

It was during the summer of 1946 that the first International Summer School for New Music was held at Kranichstein just outside Darmstadt – and it was on this occasion that my Chamber Concerto Op. 1 received its first performance. It had been written under Fortner's aegis and was introduced by the flautist Kurt Redel, the pianist Carl Seemann and the strings of the Darmstadt Municipal Orchestra under Fritz Straub's direction. On Fortner's recommendation I was immediately offered a contract with Schott of Mainz, the result of which was a lifelong partnership with the firm in the person, initially, of Willy Strecker. The friend and publisher of Falla, Hindemith and Stravinsky, Strecker was a witty and affable individual then in his sixty-third year. A native of Mainz, he had an Argentinian passport and a house in Wiesbaden, which, off limits to American soldiers, contained some of the finest Picassos, Klees and Braques. Without the trust that Strecker placed in me from the outset, everything would have been much harder and many things would simply have been impossible – notably my later move to Italy, to say nothing of my freelance status.

We got to know each other at the concert in Darmstadt, when, at the end of my own piece, he handed me his copy of the programme with the words 'Schott's publishing house' entered beside the title. My mother had travelled to Darmstadt for the performance and heard nice things said about her eldest son. Although we were able to hear a whole series of new or hitherto inaccessible scores at Kranichstein, the arrangements were still very modest during this first summer, and it was not until later that these courses attracted visitors from abroad and clear contrasts started to emerge between the different schools. Serialism had not yet arrived. Among the many subjects of lively discussion was Hindemith's setting of Brecht's *Badener Lehrstück vom Einverständnis*, which I remember having to conduct. (I have only a vague recollection of the performance, but I believe it was pretty awful.) Willing colleagues played through one or other of my pre-Fortner sonatas so that I could at least hear what they sounded like and be quite certain that they were deficient as compositions. Curiously enough, I have absolutely no recollection of these pieces, all of which were lost when I moved to Italy or possibly even earlier. It might perhaps amuse me now to take another look at them.

Among the other visitors to Darmstadt in 1946 were the Berlin critics, Hans Heinz Stuckenschmidt and Josef Rufer, both of whom were familiar with the music of the Second Viennese School and its principal practitioners. Stuckenschmidt's wife, Margot Hinnenberg-Lefèvre, was well known as a Schoenberg singer, while Rufer, who hailed from Vienna, had been Schoenberg's assistant between the latter's arrival in Berlin in 1923 and his shameful expulsion and emigration in 1933. (It was Rufer, too, who took charge of Schoenberg's estate following the latter's death.) During my own years in Berlin I was to have contact with both men, especially with Rufer, from whom I also learnt – at first hand – a whole series of serial ideas and other secrets of the trade.

A number of other people with an interest in music came to Kranichstein in 1946. Among them was Ken Bartlett, an English cultural officer who later became dramaturge at the Hamburg Opera, after which he ran the concert and theatre section at Schott's in Mainz for many years. He was accompanied by two other captains, Bill Frederick and Ronald Crichton. Crichton later became ballet critic of the *Daily Telegraph* and was kind enough to introduce me to Frederick Ashton after he had seen how enthusiastic I was when the Sadler's Wells Ballet visited Hamburg for a week-long series of guest performances in December 1948. Also present was the literary scholar Hans Mayer, who was then in charge of radio and press in Frankfurt, a position he was to lose shortly afterwards as a result, I believe, of the McCarthy purges, whereupon he returned to civilian life and was elected to a chair at Leipzig University. Adorno, too, turned up and delivered some wonderful lectures on Alban Berg, while the music critic of one of the Frankfurt evening papers, who was implacably opposed to the modernist movement, snored throughout it all. I think his name was Göttig. The Darmstadt composer Hermann Heiß, who had links with Josef

Matthias Hauer and his school, also put in an appearance, as did many students of my own age, all of them interesting people full of ideas, good intentions and dreams.

The second summer school was attended by the conductor Hermann Scherchen and the composer Karl Amadeus Hartmann and proposed a completely different sort of aesthetic agenda from the one with which I had been familiar until now: in their world, music was regarded as a specifically human means of expression that posited moral and political commitment. This encounter was to have a profound influence on my own philosophy of music.

The more I think about this period, the more other memories come flooding back, as individuals, scenes and images awaken from the slumber of oblivion. Often enough these visions assume the guise of visitations: creditors reappear, people whom I thought were dead, ghosts, memories of all those moments – alas too numerous! – when I was ungrateful, condescending and rude. Even now, I cannot help screaming with shame and remorse when I remember certain incidents. My incomplete schooling, the years I spent as a boarder in Braunschweig and my period in the army may all be reasons, if not an excuse, for my social insecurity. Even today I am still terribly afraid of people, a feeling that sometimes finds expression as an entirely reasonable reserve. (I still find it difficult to go into a bar on my own, to pass between the rows of drinkers, find an empty seat and order a drink for myself.) I would listen carefully when people talked about life and their fellow creatures, but I could say nothing conclusive or coherent myself – another reason for my being so shy: I was afraid of stuttering and drying up, afraid of scorn and contempt. I was also painfully aware of the embarrassing nature of poverty, although I never let it show. And since I had to cover it up, I occasionally ran up debts with friends and acquaintances, debts that I did not always repay.

To these failings and insecurities was added the fact that, no matter what I did, I somehow failed to fall in love with a girl like everyone else. I had felt a certain fondness for a number of young women, notably the cellist Heike Bultmann from Marburg, whom I met at Darmstadt in 1946, and there were two or three of my female fellow students in Heidelberg whom I thought I liked, but it was really only as people rather than as objects of desire and because they were attractive and intelligent. At the same time, there wasn't a man in sight who might have engaged my interest. Also, there was so much to learn, so much homework to do that there was simply no time to amuse myself. But these combined insecurities turned me into a bundle of nerves and I would react to the slightest insult with immoderate, almost blind rage.

And there was something else. Was it certain, after all, that I really *was* an artist – might I not have spent my whole life as a con man, a fraud, a kind of Felix Krull? Someone who merely stage-managed everything – his compositions, himself, his surroundings and everything that happened to him – since there was otherwise nothing to see or hear? Dressed in the emperor's new clothes. Just play-acting. Always just pretending. What I really wanted was for the world to realize that it was dealing with me as a *person*, with HWH, and to do so, moreover, unequivocally and in good time – and ideally even sooner and more unequivocally than I myself. Recognition was a pressing concern. My works were written with the aim of ensuring that people granted me the respect that alone would confirm that I really existed. From the outset, my music has sought truth in perfection. It strives to recapture the unattainable ideals of beauty that existed in classical Greece. It yearns to restore these ideals, since it needs to act as a surrogate for all that human existence is itself incapable of offering us in its utterly unfathomable grief. And it does so by transforming it into art.

Nothing has changed in this respect, except that it was far harder and worse for me then. After all, I was so incredibly voracious for life at that time, so that every disappointment, every rejection meant deep, unforgivable pain. It is easier for me now to be unforgiving or to break off a relationship with X or Y, effortlessly and for ever, even if for no better reason than the fact that I no longer derive any pleasure from the relationship or because a particular person bores me or simply because I want to be left in peace. But to snub influential people and not even say hello to them, when they themselves were disposed to be friendly, simply because I was angry with them, was a luxury that I could really not afford at that time. On one occasion – it is now more than thirty years ago – I remember refusing to acknowledge Hermann Scherchen when I found myself sitting at a neighbouring table in a London restaurant in order to punish him for the disfiguring cuts that he had made to the score of *König Hirsch* when he had conducted its first performance in Berlin in 1956. My old resentment resurfaced: it was easier to ignore the fellow than to pretend that I liked him or that I had forgiven him. I can now see that it was simply bad manners. He even wrote to me and asked me the reason for my rudeness, and I think I recall that, in my reply, I apologized to him or spelt out the reasons, or both. I also pretended not to see the director Helmut Käutner in theatre foyers in Berlin in order to bring home to him the fact that he had annoyed me with what was generally acknowledged to be an unspeakably awful production of my opera *Der Prinz von Homburg*, which he staged for the first time in Hamburg in 1960. In the late 1950s I also withdrew my favours from Heinrich Strobel, the leading light of modern German music, and refused to acknowledge him simply because I considered him – entirely correctly – the most terrible trendy, a loutish, cold-hearted snob. I wrote to him from Naples in 1958 in response to one of his many attempts to curry favour with me (an attempt which, as always, was accompanied with the lure of a new commission), announcing that I would accept no further commissions from him nor return to Donaueschingen. I kept my word.

Many years later, during the 1970s, I stopped speaking to Paolo Grassi. He was running RAI in Rome at the time and had failed to obtain the money that had been promised me for Montepulciano, a failure that led to immense difficulties for the 1979 workshop. And after a meeting of the Montepulciano town council in the autumn of 1979 I had to be forcibly restrained from publicly attacking the mayor, Francesco Colajanni, first verbally and later physically, since I felt that he had tricked me. I refrained from doing so only when told that there were people from the Christian Democrat opposition looking on in the square. Hours later I felt worn out, exhausted and utterly miserable at having hit the ceiling yet again. It was the same every time.

All these horrors – and the reader will have no difficulty in realizing that this lack of self-control was repeated in my private life, in my teaching and in my work as a creative artist – had a common cause: the feeling of disappointment. Disappointment at the fact that people had not taken enough trouble over me and my music. I felt a lack of understanding, an absence of solidarity. The ground very soon started to rock beneath my feet, I began to lose faith in myself, I lost my grip on myself, lost my composure, felt a sudden weakness, could no longer maintain a hold on myself, was no longer in control. It was as though someone else had taken over, someone who needed to be taken out of circulation, transported home, put to bed and left alone to recover.

Now I am much older. Nowadays no one can insult me without my permission, even if I sometimes still feel a certain unpleasant sensation in the region of my solar plexus. When I look back, I am – as I say – appalled at how badly I behaved at that time. But I *had* to be ill-mannered, it seemed. An evil spirit or an unknown law or mere force of circumstances willed it so. I had to make life difficult for myself, make it more difficult than it was. I had to cause myself pain and injury. Whenever things were going well, when the dissonances threatened to resolve into pure well-tempered harmony and love was smiling upon me, I immediately destroyed it all. After all, one can never have enough of the pain of parting that burns with such searing intensity. Also, it is a well-known fact that it is forbidden to be happy: happiness is unseemly, tasteless and middle-class. Whoever wants such a thing?

With the first of the Darmstadt summer schools over, I returned to my studies in Heidelberg. Fortner's composition class grew in size, and we pupils spent an exciting time, discovering the works that had been written outside Germany during the last fifteen years – works as surprising as they were inspiring. I travelled to Mannheim to see and hear the first production in Germany of Britten's *Peter Grimes*, the most successful work in the whole history of music theatre after 1945. I was spellbound, and even now still find it a beautiful and impressive piece. They also staged Stravinsky's *The Soldier's Tale* in Mannheim and I attended every performance (we took the tram from Heidelberg), unable to get enough of this electrifying, irresistibly diabolical music that continues to fascinate me even today. There was plenty to do. I had my first commissions to complete, including a piano concertino with winds, a cheerful little number, playful in style and consciously soulless, as prescribed by Fashion in the person of Heinrich Strobel, who was then controller of music at Baden-Baden Radio. Frigid inhumanity was now the flavour of the month, a vogue directed not only against the emotionally charged music of Beethoven and the Romantics but also against conductors like Furtwängler and their metaphysical leanings – as if *they* were to blame for the German dilemma. By contrast, French music by composers such as Poulenc, Milhaud and Satie was held up as an alternative model that we Germans were encouraged to imitate. Yet this fashion, too, had passed by 1948, when the French composer René Leibowitz came to Darmstadt and introduced us to Schoenberg's idea of the note row and we heard the first of Messiaen's works. Tonal composers were now left standing once again, with the result that Strobel and his cronies had to hurry to clamber aboard the latest bandwagon if they were not to lose their advantage, for however short a time.

Among the new faces at Kranichstein that year were Thomas Baldner, the son of the cellist Max Baldner, who was a member of the Klingler Quartet, and Hans Zehden. Both men were from Berlin and both now enrolled in Fortner's class. They had survived the Nazi years in the capital, in Zehden's case hidden by friends. They also brought a young lady with them, a Fräulein Häusler from Königs Wusterhausen, a composer herself, who would shake like a leaf with emotion. From Hans, I not only learnt important details about Germany's persecution of the Jews and the terrible stories bound up with that particular episode in our country's past, I also got to know a large number of Berlin cabaret songs from the 1920s, among which my particular favourites were those by Friedrich Hollaender. Zehden sang all these songs, including those associated with Fritzi Massary and Curt Bois, accompanying himself at the piano with both elegance and irony. His sister, Totta, was a popular tennis star. Zehden was much older than I and had led a totally different life from me, a life that had been lived in wholly different social circles, in a city rather than in the country, and in a totally different environment. The differences between us were those of class and history and could be bridged only by our common interest in music, by our discussions about art and our shared encounters with new forms of music, literature and the visual arts. For the official opening of an exhibition of works by Willi Baumeister in Heidelberg in 1947 or 1948, the two of us gave the first German performance of Stravinsky's Sonata for two pianos, which we were able to practise at the home of the famous psychoanalyst, Alexander Mitscherlich, where there were two instruments in the music room. My First Violin Concerto, which dates from this time, includes a quotation from one of Zehden's piano pieces in the form of three intervals of a fifth followed by a D flat major triplet that appears in the fourth movement's final section, first as a kind of calm arioso for solo violin and then, in the stretta, as a three-part canon in the trumpets, festive and triumphant, in memory of our wonderful friendship.

Through Annemarie Schüle, Willy Strecker and Fortner himself, I got to know a whole series of interesting people, including Karl Jaspers, Ferdinand Lion, Ricarda Huch and the celebrated pianist, Frieda Kwast-Hodapp, who was the widow of the Berlin piano teacher, James Kwast. She had been decorated by the tsar for the work she had done in bringing Skriabin's name to the attention of a wider public and was also widely known for her performances of Max Reger's Piano Concerto, a piece that was dedicated to her by its composer. She accepted me into her class, where I was allowed to spend one or two mornings a week with would-be virtuosos of my own age and to hear and see for myself how one can – and must – breathe, sing and phrase when playing the piano. Even at that time it was clear to me that the now elderly but regal Frau Kwast-Hodapp was one of the last representatives of an already outdated aesthetic outlook that was presumably also responsible for the great agogic liberties that she encouraged me to adopt when playing Schumann's G minor Sonata Op. 22, for example, and which she herself used to excess whenever she played us anything. She liked me and sometimes invited me to her private soirées, on one occasion performing some of the piano pieces that I had written for her. Her relatively conservative audience was not a little surprised when, a short time later, she included Stravinsky's 1924 Sonata alongside Schumann and Reger at a public recital that she gave in Heidelberg.

I was less and less able to carry out my duties as private tutor to the Schüle children, and we finally parted company with feelings of sadness but relief, although I remained a frequent visitor, not least on account of Annemarie Schüle, to whom I had grown very close. I now lived near the main railway station in a garret that could be heated only by means of a tiny electric stove. It was here, during the bitterly cold winter of 1947/8, that I completed my Violin Concerto, a piece that tells – among other things – of my recent encounters with the concertos of Bartók and Alban Berg. But it also tells of my attempts to put behind me the formalism that had still bedevilled my early Heidelberg pieces and to achieve a form of expression more independent of my previous models. My Chamber Concerto for flute, piano and strings of 1946 had been followed by other works in a similar vein, although I can no longer recall the order in which these pieces were written. Only two of them were published: a Fortner-like sonatina for flute and piano and a violin sonata. Inevitably, the imaginative world of the six amateur sonatas of 1945 was re-explored here, but this time on a quasi-professional basis. I went further and set some of François Villon's poems for chamber choir and small ensemble, the rough-hewn, tender songs of a wayfaring journeyman; and after several false starts I set about writing my first string quartet. Here, too, one finds traces of older and newer models, the linguistic gestures are still unconscious, unclear, tentative, even conventional – one senses that I was still searching and experimenting, in spite of the fact that I had already planned several such pieces, all of which I regarded as failures and accordingly cast aside.

It must have been in mid-1947 that, still without any formal instruction, I first began to explore the world of twelve-note music in my Chamber Sonata for violin, cello and piano. I have already mentioned my Concertino for piano and winds, a piece that still draws for its inspiration on traditional tonality and functional harmony. But dodecaphony and polytonality both loom large in my *Chor gefangener Trojer* from *Faust*, Part Two, which received its first performance on 6 February 1949 with the Bielefeld Musikverein and Bielefeld Municipal Orchestra under my former music director, Hans Hoffmann. It was a great evening for me. By then I had already begun work on a musical setting of Büchner's *Leonce und Lena*, but got no further than a handful of sketches. Time and again, I – and others – have tried to imagine music for this piece, but it is a play that resists all attempts to set it to music since it already contains within itself every conceivable sound, melody and emotion. In 1947 I found a dramatic poem, *Das Opfer*, in a volume of poetry by Franz Werfel published under the title *Wir sind*, but here, too, I was finally forced to abandon my attempts to set it to music. Yet, in spite of such defeats, a few melodic and harmonic phrases that were already distinctively my own were gradually beginning to stand out, causing an indescribable feeling of well-being inside me each time that it happened. To be able to present oneself as a plausible individual is the aim and hope – the arrogant hope – of every artist, but is possible only when one has discovered a little more about oneself. It is an insane delight to which one must be willing to sacrifice everything – love, health, reputation and personal happiness.

Among my very first works was my First Symphony. Written before my interest in dodecaphony, it is a four-movement piece scored for a relatively large chamber orchestra and should have received its first performance in Darmstadt in 1947 under the direction of Hermann Scherchen. I had written out the orchestral parts myself in Indian ink on tracing paper and left them at a small shop on the American side of the Rhine Bridge at Mainz, since the town itself and Schott's offices on the Weihergarten, which had been badly damaged during the war, were in the French zone. One of the firm's errand boys was authorized by the French military police to bring over music to our own side of the river and to take it back to Mainz. The parts were duly photocopied in Mainz and a few days later I took collection of them from the little shop on the American side. At the very first read-through with the Darmstadt Landesorchester it immediately became clear that they were almost completely illegible: the ink that I had used had been watered down and as a result was pervious to light. Together with Heike Bultmann, Helga Häusler and Thomas Baldner, I sat up all night, inking in the parts, but at the next day's rehearsal further problems arose, as the parts still proved difficult to decipher, with the result that Scherchen decided to play only the second, slow movement, in order not to lose any more rehearsal time.

I heard the whole symphony a year later, on 25 August 1948, at a festival at Bad Pyrmont in northern Germany, where Wolfgang Fortner included it in a concert programme which, if my memory serves me, also included Beethoven's Seventh. Not until the early sixties did I revise the work, and it was this new version that I conducted with the Berlin Philharmonic on 9 April 1964. The revised score retains a number of rhythmic, harmonic and melodic cells from the original version, and the slow movement is largely unaltered, but otherwise everything is not only new, but different and better. The themes are now more clear-cut, the exposition involves a greater sense of contrast and the Scherzo has been incorporated into the variations of the final movement. I conducted the work again with the Berlin Philharmonic on 2 October 1991 and used the occasion to introduce further retouchings and to make some additional improvements.

Other works, too, from this period were similarly much revised, initially as part of a purge that took place during the summer of 1963 and, later, while I was engaged in compiling a new and complete work-list between 1993 and 1996, a list that includes first editions, reissues, revisions and various other corrections. From time to time one puts one's house in order, and certain things such as the cantata *Der Vorwurf* (1947), the *Concerto per il Marigny* (1956) and the ballet *Die schlafende Prinzessin* (1951) get thrown away; other works resurface, eliciting amazement and reviving memories: articles of faith and hopes that had long been forgotten and definitively abandoned all come flooding back on occasions such as these.

My standard of living showed no signs of improving. On two occasions I remember travelling to Stuttgart for first nights at the opera (among the works I saw at this time were my first *Pelléas*, *Mathis der Maler* and Carl Orff's *Die Bernauerin*) and having to spend the night sleeping rough in the Schloßgarten, since I had no money left for a hotel room. Fortunately, it was warm at that time of the year. On other occasions I stowed away on the train from Stuttgart to Heidelberg or hitch-hiked by road, an equally illegal activity at that time. In Stuttgart I would sometimes look up another of Horbowski's pupils, the pianist Lieselotte Gierth, to whom I dedicated my Concertino. It was at one of the first Darmstadt summer schools that I was introduced to the local intendant, Walter Jockisch, and his wife, the writer Grete Weil. We soon became friends and in 1949/50 they wrote the scenario and libretto for my first opera, *Boulevard Solitude*. Also in Heidelberg I met the brilliant stage designer Rouben Ter-Arutunian, who had arrived in the town from Berlin with his elegant Armenian mother. They were both waiting for their papers in order to go first to Paris and then to New York, where a great career awaited him and where he was often to work with George Balanchine. Although his style was clearly influenced by some of Berlin's greatest designers such as Traugott Müller, Caspar Neher and Lothar Schenck von Trapp, the new visual ideas and aesthetic trends that typified New York's non-doctrinaire world at that time also fired his imagination. A wiry, energetic and boyish individual with sharply etched Armenian features and large Levantine eyes, he never seemed to stop working and soon became very famous. Whenever I was in New York, we used to meet and go out together in the evening. Rouben always knew the newest and most attractive bars. We worked together on two occasions, once on a production of *The Bassarids* at Sante Fe in 1968 and a few years later on my television opera, *La Cubana*. He died in 1992 from an Aids-related illness at his apartment on New York's East Side. Back in 1947/8 he and his dear mother would sometimes invite me to dine with them in Heidelberg, which gave me a chance to eat cooked meals. It was not until many years later that I was able to repay them for all their kindnesses. All my hopes at that time were pinned on my Violin Concerto, on which I had been working intensively and which I hoped would help me escape from my teachers and various models. It had been commissioned by Berlin Radio and was due to be given its first performance in the city in the autumn of 1948, but the Berlin Blockade put paid to these plans, and it was premièred instead in Baden-Baden on 12 December 1948, when the conductor was Ernest Bour and the soloist Heinz Stanske. I continued to visit Baden-Baden as often as I could, since it was here that some of Stravinsky's wonderful later pieces received their German premières. In particular, I remember the ballet *Orpheus* conducted by Hans Rosbaud and the Symphony in Three Movements under Roger Désormière. It was possible to borrow the scores from the local radio station and listen to the same recording over and over again in a soundproof booth, following the music and trying to retain as much of it as possible in one's head.

The controller of South-West Radio was Pierre Ponnelle, and it was he who brought these and other scores, including many French pieces, with him from Paris. I became a friend of the family, used their guest room whenever I visited Baden-Baden and got to know their son, Jean-Pierre, who was studying in Paris and who made his début as a stage designer in 1950 at the Wiesbaden Staatstheater with my ballet, *Jack Pudding*. His sets consisted of painted backcloths and flats, together with a frontcloth, and, as I recall, looked extremely good. They were an extension of his contemporary style in painting, a style that had been praised by no less a figure than Olivier Messiaen. Jean-Pierre painted all the flats himself by hand, without any technical assistance. But I am getting ahead of myself. Let us return to the winter of 1947/8 and the bitterly cold student room in Heidelberg, a room too small to house a piano, where I sat crouched over the sketches of my Violin Concerto, coughing, freezing and hungry.

In March 1948 I sat my examinations at the Institute of Evangelical Church Music, duly received my diploma and in consequence became eligible to teach. I hoped that I would never have to make use of that right, though my prospects at that time were far from rosy. My situation became decidedly precarious with the imminence of the Currency Reform of 20 June 1948. I gave up my room, left behind a heavy chest containing music (presumably also the six sonatas) and my father's winter clothing and returned home on 11 June, remaining there for several weeks in the temporary accommodation – a wooden shack at the edge of the forest – that had been offered my family as a home now that we had lost our entitlement to the house that had come with my father's job. From here I travelled to Darmstadt for the third summer school and, on my return, followed up the lessons that I had learnt from René Leibowitz and worked on a set of piano variations intended to reflect these new preoccupations. It was a beautiful, quiet summer. It emerges from letters that I wrote to one of my fellow students in Frankfurt, Peter Cahn, not only that I used to bathe in a sandpit with my youngest brother, Jürgen, but, more especially, that these weeks and months found me struggling to come to terms with all the experiences that I had gleaned in the course of the third Darmstadt summer school. Among the works that had been performed there was my cantata *Der Vorwurf* for baritone soloist, obbligato trumpet and orchestra, a setting of Franz Werfel's poem of the same name sung by Heinz Rehfuss and conducted by Wolfgang Fortner.

> Do you think I'd be lacking in understanding,
> You understanding fool,
> Because you do not understand me?

And so it went on. Old Testament invectives against a philistine culminated in the trumpet call of a 'terrible reveille' so that the accused – this philistine, critic, sceptic or whatever – no longer knew whether he was coming or going.

My Chamber Sonata for violin, cello and piano did not receive its first performance until 16 March 1950. I was unable to attend the concert in Cologne, and so it was not until many years later that I finally heard the piece. Although it contains twelve-note sets and textures, these are not essential elements but merely flutter into occasional view like Mörike's blue ribbons in spring. It was clear that things were moving and that new possibilities were constantly coming into sight.

The great event of the third Darmstadt summer school was the visit by René Leibowitz. Born in 1913, Leibowitz came to Darmstadt preceded by the reputation of having studied as a very young man with Schoenberg in Berlin, with Webern in Vienna, with Ravel in Paris and with Victor de Sabata in Milan. He spoke with ultimate authority. We awaited him with excited awe and awe-struck excitement. The man whom we saw before us was an uncommonly energetic, friendly individual with intelligent eyes and a delightful smile, who conveyed the not entirely false impression of a product of modern French existentialism, an impression due to his appearance, to the sobriety of his opinions and to the precision of his analyses – especially those of the classics of the Second Viennese School, chief of which was, of course, Schoenberg, whose Variations for Orchestra Op. 31 were the main subject of his lectures. As with Hans Zehden, I was impressed by his self-assured composure and authority, qualities which, characteristic of city-dwellers, are always so sadly lacking in provincials, as no one knew better than I. With all the courage I could muster, I showed him the score of my recently completed Violin Concerto and was able to place my own, unfavourable, gloss on his laconic, but polite, reaction to it. None the less, I was immensely proud of my achievement, not least because Herr Fortner had said such nice things to my mother about her son and his new piece. By the time it was all over and Leibowitz had returned to Paris at the end of a fascinating summer school that had changed the course of our lives, leaving not only me but others, too, enthusiastic, there was no longer any doubt in my mind: serial technique was the logical extension of western music and of the habit of thinking in motifs and their development. It allows us to discover new connections, making us listen more carefully and enabling us to create new concepts of freedom and beauty. It was exactly what I needed, I felt. On 11 August 1948 I wrote to Peter Cahn from our wooden shack in the Senne:

> everyone is amazed how quiet i am. i'm really not looking forward to Pyrmont. i think i'm in a state of change triggered by my meeting with Leibowitz, which is why i've nothing to say and why i'm so unapproachable.

And to Leibowitz himself I wrote from Heidelberg:

dear herr leibowitz,

zehden and i were very sad to discover that you had left so suddenly on friday. we were hoping to accompany you to the station – when we heard you'd already left, we resolved to write to you at once, but never got round to it, and now we've both returned home, each preoccupied with his own particular concerns. i was lucky enough to earn some money and am now spending a few days at a little guest house outside the town, where i'm resting and thinking. i've already written some brief twelve-note studies but there's nothing one can say about them. i must say rightaway, however, that with exercises like these that are intended to have a certain artistic merit (settings of poems by georg trakl) it is clear how much zehden and i will miss you during the coming year. i'd like to have learnt much more. but even the little that we heard and saw during these 14 days is already so much that we simply can't thank you enough for it. for myself, i see before me a year of doubts and dissatisfaction with my compositions. but i intend to send you what I write so that you can judge it for yourself, and if it contains anything that has turned out a success and if you like it, i'd like to dedicate it to you out of gratitude and also out of my great sense of affinity. the last two days at kranichstein were marked by a feeling that the party was already breaking up, on the saturday stadlen and roloff played piano music by schoenberg, webern and apostel (i didn't particularly care for the last piece, although it seems to be well written). i like stadlen very much, also the way he plays the piano, he's so cultured, sensitive and refined. i hope he'll soon return to germany. [. . .] in the evening [. . .] stadlen and i went for a walk with a girl. well, this won't be of any interest to you, since you've returned to your friends and are now completely bound up with music and the big city. if ever you think of us, don't forget that we'd like to see you again soon and would prefer you to stay with us here for ever. in two or three years from now, when things have improved here, it may be a matter of indifference to you where you live, and you may then even prefer it here to a large, noisy city. or if you want to recuperate in germany (for example, after you've given a concert or whatever), you could stay here as my guest, by then i'm certain that i'll have money etc. there's really not a lot i can say in this letter, no doubt because you've not been long gone, and, having had to use our brains for 14 days, we now feel only a great sense of emptiness. and nothing of any note has happened since you left. but please write to me again, perhaps there is something you want or something you would like to tell me. – a very good pianist asked me about a new concerto that she wanted to study. i said she should wait until you've recommended something and sent it to me. as far as i know, there's one by nigg. and what sort of piano music can you recommend to me? a friend of mine would like to have some new pieces. the local conductor is unfortunately in berlin at present, i've already tried to speak to him about the schoenberg concerto and to interest him in your own works and those of your pupils. all the best. we are all immensely grateful to you and think of you always. – hans werner henze – 5.viii.48

4

On the evening of 25 August 1948 all four movements of my First Symphony were introduced by Wolfgang Fortner at the Kursaal in Bad Pyrmont. Throughout the rehearsals I had become more conscious than ever of the weaknesses and inadequacies of this frivolous, infantile and ill-considered composition and even then had already decided what its future was to be. During the fourth movement, which was cast in the form of a theme and variations, my former teacher had to break off between one or other of the variations in order to wipe his glasses and rearrange the seat of his trousers, thereby adding to the impression of disunity. But none of this mattered in the slightest, I really could not have cared less, since I could think of only one thing: I had a date. I had met my first love in the festival canteen at lunchtime and now had eyes and ears for nothing else. I was completely and utterly convinced that everything would change now, that life was at last worth living, and so indeed it proved. I would learn the boundless joy that comes from emotional tenderness. And, feeling only love and gratitude for my redeemer, who had stirred me into life, teaching me tenderness and giving me an idea of what is meant by erotic love, I suddenly knew where my true home was, knew where I belonged, in whose society I would feel at ease and in whose I would not. I had become a human being, become a man. I began to see how I must lead my life. One after another, decisions were taken of their own accord. I felt pride, certainty and a kind of inner satisfaction: for the first time in my life I was truly happy.

Life, in short, began anew for me on the day of this encounter. I felt what it was like to be free or, rather, what I had wanted such freedom to feel like and what I expected of it. I was twenty-two. How, where and on what I was to live – these were all questions to which I had no answer for the present. For now, I had no hesitation in moving in with Heinz Poll, a silently smiling, freckled and red-headed spirit of the air who had studied ballet under Kurt Jooss at the Folkwangschule in Essen and who now lived in Göttingen, where he was a soloist with the Göttingen Stadttheater ballet. I was a kept man. Ken Bartlett sent me food parcels from Hamburg, including narcotics in the form of coffee, tea, gin and nicotine (Player's Navy Cut), all courtesy of the British Army, thus helping to make it a little less embarrassing to be as poor as I was. I started to compose again and wrote *Das Wundertheater*, a setting of one of Cervantes' innumerable intermezzos that had been drawn to my attention by a graduate of theatre studies in Göttingen. Within six months the piece had been staged in Heidelberg, where it received its first performance on 7 May 1949 in a production entrusted to the local intendant, Heinrich Köhler-Helffrich. I called it an 'opera for actors' – I had problems at this time with opera singers, whom I found to be physically ungainly and intellectually uninteresting, so that, in writing for the theatre, I much preferred working with actors and, most of all, with dancers. The Munich dancer and choreographer Marcel Luipart was also involved in the show, and it must have been at around this time that we dreamt up the insane idea of forming a small ballet company of our own in order to try out new works. But I am getting ahead of myself.

From my base in Göttingen I undertook all manner of excursions and on several occasions visited Karl and Elisabeth Hartmann in Munich, each time taking with me some newly finished piece and asking for their advice and constructive criticism. In Munich I also called on the painter Werner Gilles, to whom I had been introduced by Annemarie Schüle. I shall later have occasion to return to both Hartmann and Gilles, two father-figures who gave me their friendly advice, but for the moment it is enough to mention that here were two new influences of immense artistic importance to me, comparable to the inspiration that I had received from René Leibowitz, to whom I later dedicated my harpsichord concerto, *Apollo et Hyazinthus*, a piece that I worked on in overcrowded trains, sitting on suitcases, with the music on my knees, while shaken from side to side. Listeners so inclined may hear a sudden change in this score from the provisional, impersonal and derivative style of the past to something entirely new. (I myself conducted its first performance at the Frankfurt Festival on 26 June 1949 with the harpsichordist Edith Picht-Axenfeld and, in the final section of the work, which is a setting of words by Georg Trakl, the mezzo-soprano Hetty Plümacher.)

During the late autumn of 1948 I spent a week in Hamburg at the invitation of the British cultural officers mentioned in my previous chapter. Each evening I went to the theatre, where the Sadler's Wells Ballet was giving a series of guest performances, while daylight hours were spent at the British Council, listening to modern music on gramophone records and following the works with the relevant scores. The curtain rose on the company's opening night to the radiant brass and woodwind chords of Stravinsky's *Scènes de ballet*, revealing André Beaurepaire's painted backdrop and, in front of it, a group of dancers – a handful of elegant youths and a young woman as delicate as a meadow saffron. Her name was Margot Fonteyn. What followed was a rare example of interaction between the music in the orchestra and the dancers' movements on stage, a veritable interplay between them, a true exchange of ideas. The music seemed to dance, the dancers seemed to make music. I sat there completely enchanted. At each reacquaintance with this ravishing staging and with the other works in the company's week-long programme I was able to discover yet further surprising and fascinating aspects of the relationship between music, movement and space. For the most part, they were the work of that great neo-classical choreographer, Frederick Ashton. I was introduced to a magical poetry of which I had previously had no inkling and began to understand the thaumaturgic, sensual links between musical ideas and the gestures, positions and attempts to fly on the part of traditional ballet, with its cool and calculated, readily intelligible rules. There was something about it that spoke to me directly, although at that time I did not realize it: it was not yet clear to me that, as a result of this experience, I would spend the rest of my life attempting to grapple with the dialectical complexities of modern music theatre.

On my return to Göttingen I made straight for my desk and tried to translate into music the experiences gleaned in Hamburg. The result, of course, was a dance score, which I proceeded to title *Ballet Variations*, giving the individual variations movement headings of the kind I had seen in the score of *Scènes de ballet*, namely, 'Entrée', 'Variation', 'Pas de deux' and so on. I became quite silly about it all, so that the score contains a whole series of greater or lesser reminders of Hamburg, all of them more or less unconscious. Most were inspired by Ashton's *Symphonic Variations*, which he had choreographed to César Franck's *Variations symphoniques*, hence the presence of two piano solos in the finale of my own piece. A concert performance was given in Düsseldorf by the Cologne Radio Orchestra under the direction of Ljubomir Romansky on 3 October 1949, enabling me to make a shellac recording of it (there were still no tape cassettes or anything similar at this time). Encouraged by my English friends, I sent this recording to Frederick Ashton in London, together with a fan letter, and in this way initiated a correspondence that was to culminate ten years later, on 27 October 1958, with the London première of my ballet *Ondine*, an event that was to fill me with feelings of immoderate pride.

Other memories of Göttingen during the winter of 1948/9 include long walks along its mist-enshrouded ramparts as the last remaining leaves on the chestnut trees fell to the cold, wet ground. The day's activities were carefully planned, with lots of reading (Heine, Kafka, Mann, Gide, Balzac and Hemingway, in no particular order) and several hours' composition – at least as many as Heinz Poll had to spend exercising, rehearsing and performing at the theatre. I had no piano at my disposal but had unlimited opportunities to hear my music in my mind's ear and to write it down without the aid of an instrument. I led a quiet life, living from day to day, and for my own part could have gone on like that for ever. But I really had to find a job without any further delay.

As a result of the currency reform, the fees that I earned from my commissions were not even enough for me to be able to pay a regular monthly rent or to afford even slightly better clothes. I can no longer remember exactly when and how this problem was solved, but a solution there was, and it came through the good offices of Jan Schlubach, the set designer to the famous theatre director Heinz Hilpert, who had been in charge of the Deutsches Theater in Berlin until 1944. A resident composer was needed at Hilpert's new Deutsches Theater in Konstanz. I was more than willing to accept the offer, which arrived very quickly, and I wasted no time in suggesting to my new boss that we should also engage a small group of dancers in order for my artistic abilities to be exploited to the full. Hilpert was much taken by the suggestion and was finally able to realize a long-standing dream of his and stage Molière's *George Dandin* as a *comédie-ballet* with danced *intermèdes*. Marcel Luipart, with whom I had already hoped to found such a company, was engaged to run the ensemble, and three female and two male dancers, all handpicked by Luipart himself, began work in the autumn of 1949. Heinz Poll cancelled the contract he had just signed with the Stuttgart Opera and joined our little band.

We wanted to start with a short programme, and for this we had to settle for solo works from the present repertory and limit ourselves to a piano accompaniment. Meanwhile, the company's in-house composer got to work on the *intermèdes* for *George Dandin*, on which he made good progress whenever he did not have to appear in the theatre or on tour, conducting Beethoven's incidental music to *Egmont*, and whenever he was not required to provide incidental music of his own for Shakespeare, Kommerell, American marital comedies and whatever else it occurred to the management to put on, all of which required urgent last-minute preparations. I enjoyed watching Hilpert rehearsing: he adopted a deeply thoughtful approach to his work, discussing everything with his actors and in that way allowing fully rounded characters to emerge, a master magician with cunning pastor's eyes behind metal-rimmed glasses who, smiling good-naturedly, transformed his actors – all of whom were first-rate yet who hung on his every word – into princes and whores, gentlefolk and scoundrels, knaves and rogues, fools and senile old men, virgins and saints. It was all just an act, but what an act! Hilpert liked to take his meals with us 'children', and we felt at ease in his company (and in that of his two wives), as happy as in the friendly warmth of a large, extended family. We did not mind being criticized – after all, he was always right and we still had so much to learn, including even the way we conducted our lives: in the final analysis, we were all provincials and really quite impossible, so unpunctual and nervous and thoughtless – no wonder we could not cope with the outside world and gropingly sought our director's helping hand.

The only subjects that we were allowed to discuss at table were work, the present production and the way in which it was developing, together with danger areas and future trends. Hilpert's productions of Shakespeare's comedies may have been inelegant and rough-edged but, at the same time, they were filled with wit and melancholy, with pensiveness and, indeed, with the love and warmth that characterized him in real life. The season began in the autumn and initially all went well, by which I mean that we still had decent audiences. But this was a time when, armed with convertible currency, people in general – not just the good people of Konstanz – became rather more interested in motorbikes, washing machines, brand-name watches and Paris fashion shows and had less and less time for our beautiful new production of *As You Like It* or for Goethe or Kleist or the Municipal Orchestra, which was threatened with disbandment. Full department stores meant empty theatres; only operetta and musical comedy were still capable of luring the odd local couple into the theatre. But it would never have occurred to Hilpert to modify his plans. In consultation with the management, it was decided that, instead of being paid a contractual salary, we would share the box-office receipts. The consequences were all too predictable, with the youngest members of the company, those who were unmarried and who had no children to support, naturally receiving the least.

Commissioned by Stuttgart Radio, my Second Symphony was first performed in that city on 1 December 1949, when the Stuttgart Radio Orchestra was conducted by Hans Müller-Kray. I had started the piece in Heidelberg and completed it in the spring of 1949. Written with far more seriousness than my playful First Symphony, it has never been revised. It is music for a winter's day, utterly grey and gloomy. It is as though the experience of war had begun to demand an answer in my music. In January 1950 – I can no longer remember the exact date – I travelled to Munich with Hilpert to direct some incidental music that I had written for a play that he was producing on the radio. I have also forgotten the name of the play, though I recall that one of the actresses involved in the production was Maria Wimmer, whom I saw again the next morning on the plane to Berlin, where on successive days I attended the final dress rehearsal and first night of *Das Wundertheater* at the Städtische Oper in the Kantstraße. Unfortunately, I hated the production and stupidly said so to a local journalist. I had no idea what I had done. The intendant, Heinz Tietjen, was shocked and offended, and the whole house was against me. It snowed throughout my entire stay in Berlin, and on top of everything I received a telegram from Konstanz announcing that we were bankrupt and that the theatre had closed. It was not even worth my while returning to Konstanz; Heinz Poll would come to Berlin and bring my belongings with him. (He too would not otherwise have known where to go, since none of us felt like returning home.)

On the morning of the première, shortly after the telegram had arrived and only hours before the first performance of *Das Wundertheater*, I was introduced to Tatjana Gsovsky in the opera-house foyer. A tall, slim woman in a fur coat, she peered down at me from her keen, dark, slanting, Tartar eyes. She must, I think, have already heard of me. At all events, she invited me to have tea with her at five o'clock that afternoon at her apartment in the Fasanenstraße. She was then the principal choreographer at the Berlin State Opera, where examples of her work had already been much admired. (The company was currently performing at the Admiralspalast in the Friedrichstraße following the war-time destruction of its house on Unter den Linden.) The dancers had virtually all been trained by her, thereby ensuring a sense of stylistic unity. Her style lay somewhere between the continuing Classical tradition and a free gesturality derived from the German *Ausdruckstanz* and unrelated to the *rigueurs* of the older form of ballet. What she produced was 'theatrical dance', or perhaps it would be more true to say that for every piece she devised a choreography which, drawing on all the available styles, was uniquely suited to the work in question. Curious to get to know this already legendary figure, I turned up on time at the rear of the house at 68 Fasanenstraße, where she lived until her death, blind and deaf, in 1993. Her private ballet school, run by her daughter Ljena, had been accommodated at the front of the building until only a short time before. It was said that the bodies of German soldiers were buried in the rear courtyard. Her rooms were very Russian, I thought, from the icons to the gloomy lighting (a gloominess due to the heavy, red silk *abat-jours*), and from the *chaises-longues* to the samovar. She spoke eloquently and picturesquely in a Berlin dialect tinged with a Russian accent and with a few delightful grammatical mistakes.

We seemed to get on very well. (I was still inordinately bashful at that time and scarcely dared open my mouth.) At all events, when I left the Gsovsky apartments two hours later, it was with a whole new outlook on life: I would remain in Berlin and move into one of Tatjana's guest rooms. There I would complete my Third Symphony and then write the music for a ballet on the Icarus myth with which she was already preoccupied at that time. It was intended for Peter van Dyk, one of the young principal dancers at the State Opera. Tatjana also wanted to engage me at the State Opera, where I would conduct the ballet. New hopes! I wondered how she knew that I could conduct (I could barely do so) and whether she really considered the music of *Das Wundertheater* as adequate proof of my abilities. I moved into her guest room in the Fasanenstraße the very next day. Heinz arrived from Konstanz a few days later, bringing with him my books and music. Tatjana found accommodation for him, too, and it was not long before she had also found a place for him with her dancers at the State Opera. I resumed work on my Third Symphony. My room was small and impossible to heat. As there was no desk, I sat on the edge of the bed, with the music on my knees, working away with frozen fingers at the opening movement, an 'Invocation of Apollo' (or was it already the second movement, a 'Dithyramb', or even the final movement, a 'Dance of Conjuration'?), while the same unvarying sounds of the ballet school's répétiteur tinkling at his piano could be heard every day from ten in the morning till one in the afternoon and again from two until six, as the ballet pupils opposite exercised at the barre, a form of exquisite torment designed to polish their technique.

Whenever I left the house, it was to explore post-war Berlin. The city seemed like some badly injured beast of prey. Would it bleed to death or recover? It was necessary, I felt, to start all over again or at least to go back to 1918 to achieve a conceptual and creative *tabula rasa*. I had seen Berlin ablaze in February 1945 and been utterly fascinated by this apocalyptic twilight of the gods. Now only the rubble remained. A ruined landscape stretched out before one for miles around, a scene of desolation dotted by fire walls that had survived the appalling inferno, by the skeletons of houses and piles of abandoned debris. Slum kids emerged from their basement flats and congregated at the notorious bars and nightclubs to which I felt drawn as though by some magical force. Never before had I seen such places. It was said that all those members of Berlin's *demi-monde* who had survived the twelve years of Nazi terror and avoided being blown to bits by bombs or not fallen in their fatherland's defence were now celebrating their return, nay, resurrection, on a new and grander scale. Foremost among them was Prince Kropotkin, around whom everyone seemed to gravitate in the fashionable salons not only of the *demi-monde* but also of the underworld and the twilight zone between them. I longed to be accepted by this alternative Germany, this aggressively anti-bourgeois, bohemian world of misfits that existed on the very fringes of polite society.

But I never entirely succeeded. I expect I lacked the resolve. I was ultimately always a little afraid of the very thing that I wanted most of all, afraid of sinking and disappearing without trace. I was always prevented by something or some*one* – someone like Walter Jockisch and Grete Weil, who had come to Berlin in order for Walter to stage Stravinsky's *Histoire du soldat* at the Tribüne am Knie, a hugely popular production that was sold out for months and that starred Maria Fris as the Princess and Rudi Geske as the Soldier, two particularly talented dancers from the Gsovsky stables. The Jockisches took me under their wing and introduced me to the composer Paul Dessau, a meeting that resulted in a lifelong friendship. On Gilles's recommendation, I looked up the painter Werner Heldt, a simple soul, the son of a Brandenburg pastor, whose imagination, like that of Gilles himself, was haunted by ghosts and the spirit world and whose paintings of Berlin – cityscapes of boundless desolation with no trace of a living thing – continue, even today, to cut me to the quick whenever I see them. I recall joint expeditions by night to Wedding and Kreuzburg, both of which were a wonderland and *terra incognita* to me at that time. Just off the Kurfürstendamm, Valeska Gert, an exponent of expressionistic modern dance, had opened a cabaret known as the 'Witches' Kitchen', which I often used to visit and where I especially enjoyed her rather daring entertainments and those of her somewhat amateurish entourage. Sometimes I would stay till the end and be allowed to help Valeska into her unkempt fur coat and take her home. I also liked attending the parties given by the artist Katja Meirowsky, whose husband, a handsome fellow by the name of Karl, worked for the Americans, which I assumed was why the two of them were able to afford such a large house on a lake at Dahlem. Their home was a meeting place for all Berlin's modern artists: Alexander Camaro and Heinz Trökes, as well as Werner Heldt and many others, met there to plan the shows that they presented at the 'Badewanne' in the Nürnberger Straße on Saturday evenings, modern avant-garde pieces influenced by surrealism, Dada, Schwitters and Picasso, insanely funny and often of an *enfance* that was calculatedly *terrible*. I once had the privilege of contributing to them myself, an involvement I owed to the good offices of the group's resident composer, Theo Goldmann. How stupid of me to have wanted to use a pseudonym! I called myself John Davisson-Nepomuk. The piece I wrote was a short ballet entitled *Le tombeau d'Orphée* to which I gave the opus number 99, with Alexander Camaro – amazingly – in the dual role of hero and designer. By the time it was performed, I was unfortunately no longer in Berlin.

Paul Dessau was at that time resident composer at the Deutsches Theater in Berlin, where he had an enormous office, one corner of which, with a table and chair, he allowed me to use and where I was able to work on the fair copy of my Third Symphony better than in the Fasanenstraße. He took me to eat with him at the 'Möve' and introduced me to various artists and writers who, like himself, had returned from war-time exile. One such writer was Bertolt Brecht, who allowed me to sit in on the rehearsals of his adaptation of Jakob Lenz's *Der Hofmeister*. Dessau dressed like Brecht, in a plain grey tunic, like a kind of boiler suit, that was fastened beneath the chin, and both wore their hair brushed forward. Dessau was immensely lively and spoke with passion about the cares and hopes of all the men and women of our time. Everything affected him and moved him, making him happy or sad. My impression of Brecht rehearsing was of people speaking quietly and calmly: entrances, gestures, volume levels – everything was discussed and patiently examined with regard to its validity and rightness. The overriding mood was one of friendliness and democracy. Even the stage crew were asked for their views on the staging. Caspar Neher's sets mirrored the cool, didactic, comedic character of the piece, lending just the right tone to the production's detailed intimacy. I also attended the first night, which was tumultuously hailed as one of the truly great moments of Brechtian theatre.

By the time that spring arrived I had already completed my Third

Symphony (it received its first performance at Donaueschingen on 7 October 1951 under the direction of Hans Rosbaud) and set to work on a new piece, which had been commissioned by Ferenc Fricsay, the conductor of the Berlin RIAS Orchestra and the latest star conductor not only of Berlin itself but also of Deutsche Grammophon. The piece in question was a ballet score inspired by Paul Klee's painting, *The Vocal Fabric of the Singer Rosa Silber*, from which it also took its title. The fee helped me to survive the next few weeks and months. During the early nineties I subjected the work to a thoroughgoing revision and also altered the title somewhat, with the aim of clarifying the piece's meaning, form and status. It now has a subtitle, 'Exercise with Stravinsky on a Painting by Paul Klee', and is related to Klee's gouache in that it is a set of variations on the French nursery rhyme, 'C'est le mai, c'est le mai, c'est le joli mois de mai', which remains clearly recognizable throughout the entire work, its notes representing the initials R. S. that appear in the upper middle section of Klee's canvas. As with Klee, more and more particles and variations splinter off, squares of differing sizes, delicate blue splashes of the most disparate density, tiny areas of deviation that create a sense of nearness and remoteness, warmth or coldness, dissolution or stasis. After looking at it for some time, the observer has the feeling of entering a magic garden, a park in springtime – the tenderest moods arise, all is light and cheerful. The music tries to reflect all this in its own particular way by means of timbre, ideas and atmosphere.

By now I had moved out of my room in the Fasanenstraße and, on the Jockisches' recommendation, was living with Renate Brausewetter, the sister of the actor, Hans Brausewetter, who had died towards the end of the war. It was at about this time that I read, with great fascination, Eisler's (and Adorno's) treatise, *Composing for the Films*, which Henschel had recently published. The conducting post at the State Opera had come to nothing, and Tatjana had informed me, as gently as she could, that the Soviet cultural authorities had rejected my music as a product of western decadence and that the Icarus ballet was no longer wanted – at least not from me. In fact, I did not believe her claims about the Soviet cultural officers, not least because the latter had always left the most favourable impression on me and struck me as more intelligent than their colleagues from the other three victorious nations whenever I had seen them together at first nights. (Or maybe they had attended the dire production of *Das Wundertheater* in the Kantstraße and drawn their own conclusions, but I really cannot imagine that that was so.) Having to bear such a double disappointment, I slowly began to find that Berlin was getting me down. At the same time, I had met a large number of people who were more than ready to help me and who included not only the diminutive and wittily anti-dodecaphonic Boris Blacher (to whom I dedicated *Rosa Silber*) but also the immensely thoughtful poet, Heinz von Cramer, and the composers Rudolf Wagner-Régeny and Gottfried von Einem. Frau von Wedelstedt, who ran the British Council in Berlin, and her widowed Romanian daughter-in-law, Marietta, also did what they could to help me, while I myself made further attempts to gain a foothold in the city or at least to find some means of survival.

On one occasion – as always, it was snowing – I remember an early morning meeting with the then principal conductor of the Berlin Philharmonic, the young Sergiu Celibidache, at his home in the Königsallee at Grunewald. He greeted me gruffly, sporting a long grey bathrobe and a shock of unkempt hair. I showed him the scores of my Second Symphony and Violin Concerto, but he regarded the presence of note rows as an act of shameless provocation on my part and ventured the suspicion not only that I was not in the least bit serious as a composer but that I could not even write. He would not be able to form a proper opinion, he said, until he had seen something tonal from my pen, something like five two-part piano pieces in G major. I was to return with these five pieces in two weeks' time. Two weeks later I duly returned to the Königsallee and rang the great man's bell, my five two-part piano pieces in G major under my arm, all neatly written out in red and black ink on deckle-edged, handmade paper from the Wedelstedt household. I rang and rang, but no one answered. Finally, I decided to waste no more time, but stuffed my original manuscript under the door and pushed off into the blizzard. That was the last I ever saw of these pieces.

Not that this was any great cause for anguish, but I was slowly beginning to feel that I was just not equal to Berlin, there was too much concrete, too much rubble, coldness and snow. It was because of this that I had split up with Heinz Poll – but also, no doubt, because of a kind of cold-hearted promiscuity that I had started to feel more and more. I was beginning to lose my bearings. I had nothing more to hold on to, something that friends like the Wedelstedts, Jockisches, Rufers and Dessaus, however kind and concerned they were, were powerless to prevent, since the difficulties that I faced were to be found not in *their* world but in my own. It must have been in a moment of particular emotional exhaustion and depression, a feeling compounded by the pain and defiance of parting.

Perhaps I had received too many pieces of bad news, suffered too many personal problems for which I no longer knew a solution, perhaps I could see no light at the end of the tunnel. Whatever the reason, I took an overdose one Sunday morning in order – as I hoped – to end it all. Twenty-four hours later I woke up in Berlin's Westend Hospital, where Renate Brausewetter, who had discovered me and saved my life, was sitting at my bedside, wiping away her tears. Engulfed by the city and overthrown! Forced to my knees by debility alone! Paul Dessau came to visit me every day from Zeuthen in his ancient Horch, bringing fruit and tea and showing the kindest concern for his mad young colleague. Never once did he ask the reasons for my wretched deed, never once did he moralize about it. I respected him for that. Other visitors included Wolfgang Fortner, the Jockisches and Trenklers; only my family was kept in the dark as a precaution. And then, following my discharge from hospital and resumption of my dissolute life, Annemarie Schüle arrived in Berlin, packed together my few belongings with barely a word between us, took me under her arm and flew back with me to Heidelberg, where she put me up under the same roof as herself in the Mozartstraße, not on this occasion to teach her children (or *not* to teach them) but to play croquet with them in the garden, to be nursed back to health and restored to a sense of calm and inner composure. I set Walt Whitman's *Whispers from Heavenly Death* for soprano and piano and, immediately afterwards, produced a version for idiophones such as the vibraphone and marimbaphone that had just entered the world of modern music ('squawkingly and complainingly', as Ingeborg Bachmann would say).

During these early summer months I continued to see the Jockisches, just as I had been doing for the whole of the previous year, in order to work on the libretto of *Manon Lescaut* – for so we called our opera until enough people had come forward and said that we were mad and asking for trouble in choosing a subject that had already been successfully set by Auber, Massenet and Puccini. It was a subject that had suggested itself to me not only as a result of Henri-Georges Clouzot's recent film, which was set at the time of the French Resistance and starred Cécile Aubry, but also by my own particular experiences. I especially liked the name, Manon Lescaut – Prévost's short novel was as unfamiliar to me as its three existing settings. To be on the safe side, therefore, we decided to call our piece *Boulevard Solitude* instead. It was to Walter Jockisch and to his knowledge of the theatre, especially his experience of the music theatre of the late 1920s, that Grete Weil and I owed the clear-cut, flawless outline of the whole. I tossed off my First Piano Concerto and during the summer began work on the score of the opera at Grete Weil's house in Rottach-Egern, while she herself was still writing the final scenes. Hans Zehden looked in on me and showed me his String Trio, on which he was working at that time. I also learnt to play a little tennis and discovered how to deal with sudden gusts of wind when sailing on the Bavarian lakes – or, rather, I discovered that everyone else dealt with them differently and more successfully than I, who was always caught off balance.

Walter Jockisch was a gaunt, anthroposophical pedagogue and man of the theatre. He had known Grete Dispeker-Weil from an early age and had been friendly with the first love of her life, Edgar Weil. All three had belonged to the Munich circle of Klaus and Erika Mann. Edgar had perished at Auschwitz, Klaus Mann had taken his own life on 21 May 1949 and the remaining members of the group had been separated by whole continents. The bond between Walter and Grete was like that which exists between survivors who, held in tight embrace, grieve to the end of their days for the loved ones whom they have lost and whom they can never forget, lamenting the sense of irrevocable emptiness that they have felt around them throughout their lives. Grete Weil had been strikingly beautiful as a young woman, a Sulamith, a Rachel at the Well, a Susanna at Her Bath. Even today, as an old woman, she still creates the impression of an Old Testament princess with her charismatic appearance and large oriental almond-shaped eyes, which have grown harsher and more reproachful with the passing years. Yet she is a native of Munich, hails from a large middle-class family, went to school in Munich and witnessed much that was good and more that was bad in the city, including the rise of the Nazis. She told me all about Thomas Mann's lecture, 'The Sufferings and Greatness of Richard Wagner', that passionately sensible and masterly apology directed at the outside world that Mann delivered at Munich University in February 1933 and in which he not only drew fascinating parallels with Tolstoy and Baudelaire but protested in vehement terms at the composer's appropriation by *völkisch* elements. Mann's lecture is reprinted in his collected works and has twice been translated into English. It precipitated a 'Protest from Richard Wagner's Own City of Munich' signed, unbelievably, by the likes of Hans Pfitzner, Richard Strauss and Hans Knappertsbusch, in addition to the city's honorary cultural dignitaries, all of whom objected to the 'disparagement of our great German musical genius'. Fortunately, Mann and his wife were abroad at the time, since this Teutonic howl of antediluvian protest would otherwise have led to an order for their arrest, and Mann would have been dragged off to Dachau. It does not bear thinking about. It was stories of this kind, all of which were true, that inevitably meant my view of Germany was once again growing more sombre by the hour. The day finally came when one was no longer surprised at anything any longer.

Grete Weil repeatedly wrote of the horrors of her age, which are reflected in her writings as though in some *speculum mundi*. Walter died many years ago, and Grete now spends most of her time at her retreat in Ticino, unwilling to breathe the same air as skinheads and reactionaries, quite apart from which Munich suffers from the Föhn, which is bad for us old people. The best thing about Walter and Grete was that you could tell them absolutely everything and complain about everything you wanted. They spoilt you and let you be as rude as you liked. Either they did not feel justified in trying to teach me better manners or they regarded me as a hopeless case – which was precisely why I regarded them both so highly.

I particularly remember the 1950 Darmstadt summer school since it was the first time that I really began to feel bored there. My only other memory of the occasion was a visit by Luigi Nono, a man of marmoreal beauty for whom I spontaneously felt great sympathy and whose very nature I came to love in spite of all the difficulties involved, since I not only felt but *knew* that he had great music in him. We wrote lots of letters to one another and, for better and (unfortunately also) for worse, were often in contact during the years that followed.

I had written to Heinrich Köhler-Helffrich, who had recently moved from Heidelberg and taken up a new appointment as Staatsintendant in Wiesbaden, suggesting that he might like to engage me, so that I could continue my work in the dance theatre, work that had been interrupted when the theatre at Konstanz had gone bankrupt. He agreed at once, and so it came about that from the autumn of 1950 I had a new sphere of influence, as well as a regular income. I found a room in Wiesbaden, where I was allowed to install a piano, and the 1950/1 season started.

Shortly before that, I had written a brief chamber ballet, *Labyrinth*, inspired by André Gide's last novel, *Thésée*, which had prompted me to take an interest in this compelling theme, with its treatment of the Minoan labyrinth and its mysterious inhabitant, who brings with him the threat of cannibalism. The music turned out to be very cool, its composer no doubt having thought that this was the best way of catching Gide's light, ironical tone, and, somewhat comically, also contained elements of American jazz, which was popular at that time and which was soon to be found again in my first opera, *Boulevard Solitude.* As a ballet score, the piece was much too short and in consequence unusable. It was really no more than a sketch. Not until decades later did an opportunity present itself to return to the music and subject matter, not least as a result of my later encounters with Minoan art, and to produce a new scenario in collaboration with the New Zealand choreographer, Mark Baldwin. The new work was premièred in Schwetzingen on 24 May 1997. Thematic elements from the old score were now treated like the themes of a set of variations and developed and elaborated along the lines of my most recent style.

We accompany Theseus into the heart of the labyrinth and get to know the Minotaur, a beast from the deepest recesses of our imagination, a thick blot of the blackest ink on our waking consciousness. But there is no need to be afraid: even in this later version, a kind of danced divertissement, the mood is carefree and jovial, and it turns out that our Minotaur is really quite a decent chap who grows bored beneath his terrifying exterior and whose bad reputation irks him and leaves a bitter taste in his mouth.

Under the terms of my Wiesbaden contract, I had to provide the music for plays and ballets at the smaller and newer of the company's two theatres, which was just on the point of opening. Effectively, this meant writing much of the music myself. The first two pieces that I composed in this context were my Symphonic Variations for chamber ensemble, with which the Kleines Haus was officially to be opened, and some dance songs, duets and incidental music – some sixty numbers in all – for a production of Beaumarchais' *La folle journée*, given, of course, in German. Although the Symphonic Variations are quite an effective piece and had been well rehearsed, they were prevented from making their proper impression at the gala opening by the actions of the Wiesbaden borough treasurer, Heinrich Roos (whose name I have noted down for citation at the Last Judgement). Late in the afternoon, after the final rehearsal had already taken place, Herr Roos had inspected the festively decorated little theatre and high-handedly ordered the removal of two of the instruments required for the performance. Because there was too little space for them in the pit, a grand piano and a harp had had to be accommodated to the left and right of the proscenium arch. Their place was now taken by municipal laurel shrubs, something I discovered only at the very last moment. I ran to the intendant, who was already standing at the main entrance, beaming seraphically at the gathering dignitaries, and tugged at his sleeve. 'Can't you see I'm busy?' he retorted. 'Go and get on with your job.'

It was a sad beginning to the evening's entertainment. What must people have thought? And the Beaumarchais was not much better. The director, Heinz Dietrich Kenter, wanted to stage the play as a proletarian, pre-revolutionary, popular piece, he told me. He saw it as a work of protest. It should already be possible to hear the tumbrels rolling. Well, I armed myself with an encyclopaedia of Spanish folk music, from which I borrowed rhythms and motifs that seemed to me appropriate if I was to meet my director's demands. There was a lot of work involved. But the biggest problem was that my Susanna and Figaro, played by Gardy Granass and Claus Biederstaedt, were utterly incapable of learning their little songs and duets. No matter what I did, I was unable to drum the simple metres and intervals into their actors' heads. Perhaps I was not particularly astute as a répétiteur and lacked the requisite skills, perhaps I was too ready to abandon all hope that they might ever be equal to the challenge. But that was not all, for it soon became clear that the set designer and costume designer had either not known of the director's concept or, if they had, had thought very little of it, since their staging, far from resembling a revolutionary drama, looked just like any other Mozart production of the time, with its pink and silver frocks. Each rehearsal saw another of my numbers cut on the grounds that it was unsingable or unsuitable. The whole of my work was really a waste of time. The only pieces that could not be cut were the interludes, which were needed to fill in the time while the sets were changed.

For one of the scene-changes I had asked Hans Zehden to write a set of variations on the final Tempo di Minuet from Haydn's E flat major Keyboard Sonata No. 59, Hob. XVI:49, a request that Zehden was happy to meet, since he otherwise had few opportunities to hear his works performed. Here was such an opportunity. His variations (= revolutionary music) were a systematic exploration of the gradual dismemberment and collapse of the *ancien régime* (= Haydn). The music pursued its shrill and desperate course and lasted far longer than was necessary, since the sets had long been changed, and the audience was growing restless and even seditious. At the end of the performance I drove all round Wiesbaden in my first car, an ancient Panhard, looking for Zehden, who had disappeared without trace, in order to assure him that what had happened was of no matter to me and that I was not in the least bit angry. He could scarcely believe his ears. Under the terms of my contract I had to conduct the remnants of my score at every performance of Beaumarchais' piece, and unfortunately there were lots of them, since the production remained in the repertory for what seemed like an eternity. After the performance, I would go off to the pub and join the locals for a glass of cider in order to make up for lost time. It was here that I had my only experience of some of the local customs and heard the Wiesbaden dialect, a mellifluous form of the language spoken on the other side of the Rhine in Mainz. Otherwise – that is, during the daytime – it was generally only old ladies with equally ancient hats and poodles that one ever saw in Wiesbaden.

I have more cheerful memories of the first performance of my ballet, *Jack Pudding*, which was given for the first time on the smaller stage on 30 December 1950 and which marked Jean-Pierre Ponnelle's début as a stage designer. For the first time I spent Christmas not with my mother and brothers and sisters, but with Gottfried and Tutti Bermann Fischer in Frankfurt. During dinner an elderly woman, who turned out to be the widow of the great publisher Samuel Fischer, read out Christmas greetings from Thomas Mann, Hermann Hesse and other writers whose works had been published by her husband. My few free days and evenings in Wiesbaden were spent working on *Boulevard Solitude* – often enough I also had to work on the score at night. But it was a wonderful and exciting time: I was finally part of a company that produced music all the time and was able to sit in on opera rehearsals and performances as often as I liked. I particularly enjoyed *Les contes d'Hoffmann*, with its crystal-clear, graphic and psychologically apposite dramaturgy, far more than the half-baked *Tannhäuser*. I would talk to the orchestral players in the canteen and learn about valves and frets and about bowing and breathing techniques, grateful for every piece of advice, every new lesson learnt.

The music for *Jack Pudding* had originally been conceived as incidental music for Heinz Hilpert's production of *George Dandin* in Konstanz (a production which, it will be recalled, had not, in fact, taken place). It remained as sketchy as ever, since I simply had no time to rewrite it. Not until forty years later did I take out the score again and revise it for the summer festival at Montepulciano – a revision undertaken for the Neapolitan actor, Sergio Sivori, who specialized in the part of Pulcinella – but, like its predecessor, this version too was fated to remain unstaged. Finally, I was inspired and moved by a visit to the wonderful city of Naples in October 1995 to undertake a thorough revision of the score (just as I had done in the early sixties with my First Symphony and as I did in the early nineties with a fragmentary work for chamber orchestra then titled *Concerto per il Marigny*). I transferred the action of Molière's play to Naples, turned Pierrot into Pulcinella and drew on my own experiences to work in the Neapolitan climate and the city's world of colour and emotion, while imagining myself as the protagonist and narrator: *Pulcinella alla ricerca della fortuna per le strade di Napoli.* I brought out the glowing, phosphorescent quality of the city beneath the moon's cold light, emphasizing the idea of northern dreams and yearnings, of pleasure and obsessions, changing the storyline and bringing it closer to my decades of personal experience and my present way of thinking. The piece is now called *Le disperazioni del Signor Pulcinella.*

Following the première of *Jack Pudding*, which was produced by the company's resident choreographer, Edgar von Pelchrzim, I was given a few weeks' leave of absence and travelled with the Fischers to Paris, where I worked on the second act of *Boulevard Solitude* and met Jean-Pierre as often as I could. (He was then studying law at the Sorbonne in addition to painting.)

I need hardly add that I liked Paris, liked the absence of piles of rubble, liked its metropolitan, self-celebratory architecture, its people and, above all, of course, the students in the Latin Quarter, the pace of life, its big-city appeal, the absence of all things German. Jean-Pierre and I talked about nothing but art, heard lots of concerts, went to the Palais Garnier to see Vyroubova and Lifar in their greatest roles in ballets such as Balanchine's *Palais de cristal* and Lifar's *Les mirages* and *Icare*, and discovered the surrealists in painting and literature, including Artaud and Genet. The vast panorama of modern painting opened up before us. Every morning I would work on the score of *Boulevard Solitude* in a first-floor room at the Café Flore and within a few weeks had completed it. (In the final children's chorus I wickedly worked into the score the name of the titular hero of Genet's *Notre-Dame-des-Fleurs.*) Other composers and writers worked here, too, while a waitor would tiptoe in, bringing fresh coffee and emptying the generally overflowing ashtrays. There was total silence, as in a college library.

Sartre lived just round the corner to the left (we raised our eyes in awe as we passed his windows), while round the corner to the right, Thelonious Monk performed in the evenings and Juliette Gréco sang. Tutti Fischer and Goffi Bermann introduced me to their friend Thomas Harlan, the son of the anti-Semitic film-maker, Veit Harlan, and the actress Hilde Körber. Thomas was studying in Paris, I forget exactly what; he was delicately built and painfully thin, with violet-blue eyes, an ethereal lift boy with a gentle bass voice in which he was able to murmur seductively in an impressive array of languages. He spent his whole life feeling ashamed of his father and consumed with anger at the Nazis, feelings that left him no peace but tormented him perpetually. After the Fischers had returned to Germany, I moved into a room at the Hotel Gît-le-cœur, a tiny hotel in a narrow little street of the same name not far from the Place St-Michel, where the painter, Wols, had spent his final years. It was here that I met another young German, Klaus Geitel from Berlin, who wanted to become an art historian and who was working on a dissertation on fifteenth-century French miniatures, with the result that he was generally to be found in the Bibliothèque Nationale or at the Château de Chantilly, hunting down his sources. He had just developed a fanatical love of ballet and already knew the subject in some detail. He, too, was not particularly interested in opera at this time. He joined our little group and visited museums and theatres with us, including the Théâtre de Marigny, the then home of the Ballets de Paris, where some of the finest French dancers, choreographers and designers of the age were gathered and where we were able to admire Renée Jeanmaire and Roland Petit acting, dancing and singing in a ballet by the name of *La croqueuse de diamants*. A friend of Geitel's, Peter Adam, arrived from Berlin by rail, bearing a single red rose. He was on his way south and could stay only briefly. Many years later I met him again in London and the two of us became good friends, a friendship which, like many friendships, has grown in importance and mutual trust with the passage of time.

Annette Bermann Fischer, one of the Fischers' three daughters who was studying in Paris, wrote countless cheques in an attempt to help Jean-Pierre and me keep our heads above water – but our money invariably disappeared with magical speed on theatre, cinema and concert tickets. I still have a photograph, taken by Klaus Geitel, of Nedi Bermann Fischer sitting at a little table outside the Café Mabillon and writing out one of these cheques, while Jean-Pierre and I can be seen standing next to her, watching. In order to save money or whenever the buses and metro were on strike, as they often were at that time, we would walk from St-Germain to the Opéra and the Palais de Chaillot and back, along the banks of the Seine. We avoided speaking German in public. Once, on leaving a cinema where we had just seen *Roma, città aperta*, I am convinced that Klaus Geitel and I would have been beaten up by the angry crowd if they had known that we were fellow countrymen of the vulgar, perverse SS men in the film that had just been shown, smart and dashing Huns who only a few years earlier had made the Italian capital such a dangerous place to be, murdering in cold blood, destroying everything in their insane attempt to change the world – the world of other people – and wrecking civilization by trying to impose a permanent state of siege upon the whole of our continent.

I looked up René Leibowitz and accompanied him to rehearsals for a gramophone recording of Mozart's *Zaide*. He was pleased with my harpsichord concerto and its dedication, but there was no real question of any systematic teaching, even though this was something that I needed more than anything. On the other hand, I was now less willing to accept the teachings of others – not because I wrongly thought that I now knew all the tricks. No, it was something quite different: I now wanted to go my own way, to belong to no particular school or group, but to be my own group, my own school. From now on I had to teach myself, and, indeed, was most keen to do so. I got to know Pierre Schaeffer and Pierre Henry, two composers (and sound engineers) at French Radio, who had just managed to produce their first electro-acoustic montages of sounds and noises drawn largely from everyday life and described by themselves as *musique concrète*. I was particularly impressed by their *Orphée*, a vast symphonic treatise that explores the depths, the inner world, of sound. When my leave of absence was over and I had to return to Germany, I brought taped copies of these works back with me and played them to my friends. Yet however much I was fascinated by this novel approach to sound, it was insufficient to divert me from my chosen path, a path whose direction was slowly becoming clearer.

On my return to Wiesbaden I set about preparing for my second season at the theatre. At my instigation, eight dancers from Berlin, mainly from the State Opera, had been engaged, so I now had a small company at my disposal. The project that I had dreamt up in Konstanz was finally to be realized. Most of the works would be choreographed by Peter van Dyk and his sister, Eva-Inge. We already had a schedule of performances. I had now gone up in the world and was described as 'artistic director'.

During the summer of 1951 the Jockisches took me with them to Italy. We met at Chiasso, and by midday I was already exploring Milan's Galleria, where I had my first Italian breakfast, after which we set off in the direction of Genoa. Shortly before reaching the city I had my first glimpse of the Tyrrhenian Sea stretching out far below me, a strip of blue water bathed in golden sunlight. The following morning we reached Pisa, which glowed in the distance like some precious jewel, and the next evening arrived at Rome. That night I slept through a performance of *Andrea Chénier* at the Baths of Caracalla, waking up only at the end when the soprano, Maria Caniglia, let out a piercing scream and I was just in time to make out someone in the distance being dragged off to the scaffold in a cart drawn by real live horses. The heat was intense, but, eager to learn and hungry for art, I visited all the museums on our journey, inspecting collections of Greek and Roman sculptures and admiring the beautiful artefacts in the private collection of the Borghese family and also in the Vatican. My feet began to hurt. Then, late one afternoon, we drove out to Castel Gandolfo, toured the Castelli and found the house where Goethe had spent a few autumnal days in amusing company (including Angelika Kauffmann and probably also Tischbein) and where he fell hopelessly in love with a local girl and wrote nothing but gazed out into the countryside and painted. I, too, looked out across the countryside as it fell away towards the sea and scanned the sea itself, in which the sun was reflected, and felt that at any moment Neptune or Venus or even Jupiter in person would rise up from beneath its golden, sparkling, glittering surface. The sight of Rome and its environs filled me with feelings of religious veneration. We spent the evening at a trattoria in Frascati, sitting outside, as the sun went down. The freshening breeze that blew across the Castelli caressed our burning bodies, and the air was filled with the friendly voices of people who seemed to converse good-humouredly in a kind of Sprechgesang that could, it seemed, have turned at any moment into some operatic aria. And as this gentle, relaxed and calming confusion of voices mixed with the call of the swallows and the sun sank at last beneath the horizon, so it slowly grew cooler, luring the local couples back indoors from their evening strolls and swathing Rome in a bluish twilight as it lay stretched out on the plain beneath us, suffusing me with a sense of contentment, a feeling of glorious well-being.

There was, after all, a better world! It was something intangible and yet, at the same time, was plain for all to see: the people here were more friendly than they were at home in Germany. That evening I fell head over heels in love with the Italian people. Early the next morning we set off along the Appian Way via Terracina and Capua to Naples and, thence, by fishing boat to the island of Ischia and the tiny port of Sant'Angelo. On my first attempt to swim in the Mediterranean I stepped on a sea urchin, which drove me back to my desk rather sooner than I had planned – the piece in question was *Die schlafende Prinzessin*, a take on Tchaikovsky's *The Sleeping Beauty* to a libretto by Hans Zehden that we hoped to perform in Wiesbaden during the coming season. Hans himself now arrived from Germany and, after the Jockisches had left to continue their journey alone, he and I rented a whole floor in a beautiful Moorish house in a luxuriant Mediterranean garden in the kasbah at Forio. Hans was also working on his ballet, *Les chansons*, which was similarly planned for the 1952 spring season at Wiesbaden. Needless to say, we went swimming every day, and in the evening we would go for walks in keeping with local custom, ending up at the Café Maria Internazionale in the town's piazza. On a couple of occasions I visited Gilles at Sant'Angelo. He was feeling a little put out that I was staying some distance away and could not, therefore, commune with the ghosts and cyclops that peopled the gorges along the Marina dei Maronti and that he captured every day in watercolour upon watercolour. I could have meditated there and weaned myself away from metropolitan Forio with its luxury and seductions. He would have taught me not to wave my arms around so wildly, unconsciously conducting, whenever I went out walking and thought about music. (Even today, I can still be guilty of doing this in the street and in buses.) He felt that artists' lives and thoughts should always be turned in on themselves: whatever else they did, they should not be identifiable as artists but must learn the art of mimicry. Gilles was a tall, sloppily dressed and slippered peasant from the Lower Rhineland, with snow-white tousled hair, jolly eyes and a red wine-drinker's nose, a craftsman with a pipe that was constantly lit. He had only two books that he always took with him on his travels, the New Testament and Rimbaud's *Le bateau ivre*. In keeping with ancient custom he had crossed the Brenner Pass as a wayfaring journeyman while still a young man and explored the whole of Italy over the following years, stopping now and then to earn his viaticum by helping to paint stained-glass windows for churches. Since the end of the war he had spent the summer months at Sant'Angelo, moving to Munich for the winter and reproducing his Ischian watercolours in larger formats. He belonged to a group of Bauhaus disciples who, hailing from the North, worshipped Italy and, with the canvases of Mondrian, Klee and Matisse at the back of their minds, never tired of extolling in their own work the beauty of the Italian people and Italian landscapes and the light of the Mediterranean, in order at least to evoke the secret of this light and all its magic, a secret which, even if they could never fathom it, they still conjured up in their art. Other members of this loosely constituted group included Max Peiffer-Watenphul, Kurt Krämer, Hans Purrmann and Eduard Bargheer.

In March 1951 a bilingual edition of W. H. Auden's *The Age of Anxiety: A Baroque Eclogue* appeared in Wiesbaden and left a deep impression not only on me but on others, too, not least because I and others like me had hitherto had little or no idea of the existence of such verse. Auden had collaborated with Chester Kallman on the libretto of Stravinsky's opera, *The Rake's Progress*, which had received its first performance at the Teatro La Fenice in Venice on 11 September 1951, after which the two librettists had come to Forio d'Ischia, where they were to spend the summer and early autumn months every year till the end of the 1950s, returning to New York for the winter and earning the money they needed to spend the summer in Europe; later they gave up Italy in favour of Kirchstetten near Vienna and Christ Church, Oxford. I can no longer remember how we got to know each other – ambitious as I was, I no doubt overcame my shyness and simply introduced myself. But I do recall that in 1951 I was once or twice granted the honour of sitting at Auden's regular table at the Café Maria Internazionale and listening to him expatiate on his favourite subject, opera, in a form of Oxford English which, with its distorted vowels and New York stresses, struck the foreigner as almost unintelligible, not least as a result of the speed with which he spoke and his recondite choice of vocabulary. It was all so fascinating that I was sorry when the clock at San Vito's struck eleven, for that was the hour at which the poet stood up and, without another word or salutation, set off on his way back home, casting huge and slightly swaying shadows on the houses' whitewashed walls.

Our time on Ischia drew to an end, our wonderful holidays were almost over (I have no idea whether I finished *Die schlafende Prinzessin* there or whether it was not completed until I got back home), for I had to return to Wiesbaden for the start of the new season. My first task was an evening of ballet in the main house, with which I was to introduce the new company to local audiences. The programme was choreographed by Peter van Dyk and consisted of my own *Invocation to Apollo* in sets and costumes by Jean-Pierre Ponnelle (the music, it will be recalled, was drawn from my Third Symphony), a *pas de trois* designed by Katja Meirowsky to original music by Giselher Klebe and, finally, Schoenberg's *Pelleas und Melisande* in sets and costumes by Rudolf Küfner. I recall that in the case of *Pelleas und Melisande* I liked neither the music nor the sets nor the dancing: it was all as stilted and pedestrian as the score itself. Jean-Pierre's scenery for my own piece consisted of several sails of different shapes and colours stretched over and alongside each other and, as I recall, looked extremely attractive. All involved in the production helped to create a sense of radiant unity made up of musical textures, colour, form and movement. Composer, choreographer and designer, I should add, had all worked closely together. With this highly successful first night behind us, we then set to work on a second programme, this time for the smaller stage. It comprised Hans Zehden's *Les chansons*, on which Hans worked closely with the choreographer Eva-Inge van Dyk, and my own *Die schafende Prinzessin*, of which – curiously enough – I have not the faintest recollection. It may well be that the moral disintegration of the company had already started even before we had begun rehearsals not only for my own piece but also for the European première of Stravinsky's *Danses concertantes*, for which I prepared a – playable! – vocal score not least for my own edification but also to help the rehearsal pianist. (The score was unfortunately lost in the Wiesbaden Opera archives or perhaps elsewhere.) I expect we were all far too young and foolish to deal with questions of competence, to say nothing of intrigues among the ballerinas and all the rivalries and petty jealousies that broke out in our midst: we were simply unable to prevent things from escalating and delaying completion of our work on the production. For my own part, I found myself incapable of reasoning with the van Dyks, who refused, for example, to accept that Eva-Inge, who was as tall and thin as a beanpole, was much less suited to the role of Melisande than our enchanting, albeit somewhat stunted Maria Fris, who had in the meantime embarked on an affair with Jean-Pierre, causing all manner of passions to ignite. The van Dyks had unfortunately also brought their mother with them, a miserable old so-and-so from Berlin who had never learnt to smile and who one day strung up a washing-line in my office in order to dry her offspring's dripping leotards. What sort of a theatre was this, I wondered.

On one occasion – it was a Sunday morning – I managed to persuade Serge Lifar to come over from Mainz, where he and his *étoiles* were entertaining the troops, and take one of our coaching sessions. No one who was present will forget this unheralded visit. But, for my own part, I found myself increasingly losing interest in the company or, rather, I was becoming increasingly absorbed in my own compositional activities. On 19 November 1951 a recording of my radio opera, *Ein Landarzt*, was played in the studios of Hamburg Radio in the Rothenbaumchaussee. A word-for-word setting of Kafka's short story of the same title, it had been commissioned by North-West German Radio and was produced and conducted by Harry Hermann Spitz. The station's newly appointed controller, Ernst Schnabel, had been expected to give an inaugural speech, but instead he introduced my opera. An ebullient ex-sailor with flashing eyes, a deeply furrowed face and a booming, monochromatic voice, Schnabel was something of a daredevil who, after the war, had amused himself as a pilot by flying into the teeth of Caribbean storms but who was also a gifted writer with a somewhat circumstantial style and way of thinking. He received me in his office the following morning, offered me a gin and tonic and commissioned another radio opera from me, the result of which was *Das Ende einer Welt*, to a libretto based on one of Wolfgang Hildesheimer's *Lieblose Legenden*. By the time that it was first broadcast by North-West German Radio on 4 December 1953, with the Hamburg Radio Orchestra again under Harry Hermann Spitz, I was already in Italy. I had in fact visited Hamburg a whole year before the performance of *Ein Landarzt* and played sections of *Boulevard Solitude* to the local intendant, Günther Rennert. He appeared to accept the piece, an impression shared by my publisher, but when the new season was announced, there was no mention at all of the work, so I offered it to Hanover, where it was accepted with pleasure and alacrity by the general music director, Johannes Schüler, and pencilled in for February 1952. My suggestion that Walter Jockisch and Jean-Pierre Ponnelle be invited to work on the production was likewise accepted with enthusiasm. The rehearsals and performances took place at the very time that we were supposed to be preparing for our second evening of ballet in Wiesbaden, which unsurprisingly failed to engage my full attention. I am all the more sorry about this in that I am certain that our second evening could have been an important artistic event. I had taken a lot of trouble to build up this excellent little group, which now started to fall apart. If the performance did not in the end take place, it was not because I did not attend as many rehearsals as I had done at the outset (or perhaps it was precisely because of this?) or because I was unable to keep a close enough eye on the way that things were proceeding, but simply because we (who? my colleagues or I myself?) had forgotten to book the smaller of the two stages for the spring. There was no room for us, no dates left, all the remaining slots having already been filled with other productions.

This appalling piece of news had not yet broken when, beside ourselves with happiness, the Jockisches, Jean-Pierre Ponnelle and I were greeted by the ovations of a packed and, I think, favourably impressed house at the first performance of *Boulevard Solitude* in Hanover on 17 February 1952. Of course, there were also a number of boos. At that time I still could not know that my ears would have to get used to their sound for many years to come and that my sensitivities would have to find ways and means of not taking offence at such things. In fact, the few cries of protest in Hanover were no more than a harmless prelude to the later scenes of battle. In

Hanover, I should add, I also saw myself obliged to prosecute a hack for defamation. The judge sentenced him to a fine, which the man was unable to pay, so that I then had to decide whether he should be banged up for six days instead or whether it was enough for him to publish an apology in his rag. In the presence of a hostilely howling mob in the crowded public gallery, I played the Emperor Titus and, for reasons of pure prestige, decided to be lenient – with the all too predictable result that the newspaper never printed the apology ordered by the court. But the man had compared me with the apostle Judas who, as we know, betrayed our Lord Jesus for thirty pieces of silver, whereas I was said to have demanded 500 marks (the fee for *Boulevard Solitude*) in order to betray German art with my music. This, I felt, was going a bit too far. Not only the trial itself, which dragged on tiresomely until it was time for me to leave for Italy, but its whole ridiculous outcome taught me to avoid journalists and, as far as possible, to ignore their goings-on. Don't react! Never mix with them, in good times or in bad. It is a precept which, with a mere handful of exceptions that are not worth mentioning but which include my experience in Hanover, I have stuck to all my life. Also, never read what they say about you, especially when it is well meant. Better to remain in the dark and not know exactly what others may think and say, not know with what they attempt to surprise not only the public at large but also even themselves.

All our souvenir snapshots from this period have faded, events have started to overlap and to become confused and blurred. Among odd memories are long journeys by night through snow and rain between Wiesbaden and Hanover (often on country roads) in my unheated Panhard, which was always breaking down; a private party in Hanover thronged by amusing people, including Jean-Pierre's *maman*; and the general music director, Johannes Schüler, proudly showing me a handwritten letter that he had received from Arnold Schoenberg while he was working in Oldenburg in the early thirties, asking if, following the local success of *Wozzeck* by his pupil, Alban Berg, he – Schüler – might now consider staging his three one-acters, *Erwartung*, *Die glückliche Hand* and *Von heute auf morgen*, a question that the young Schüler had never thought needed a reply. Among the guests at the first-night party after *Boulevard Solitude* were Ernst Schnabel and Luigi Nono. Nono asked me why the score was partly dodecaphonic and partly heptatonic instead of only dodecaphonic (as he felt that it ought to have been). I explained the reason why. During that period Hanover Radio allowed us to listen repeatedly to a taped recording of his first orchestral work, *Composizione*, which had just been performed in Hamburg. I remember being deeply impressed by it (I later wrote about it in Alfred Andersch's Frankfurt-based periodical, *Texte und Zeichen*), without feeling any need to follow my friend, musically or conceptually, down the road that he himself had chosen – it was not, after all, *my* road. None the less, a remarkable number of Nonoesque features and other expressive devices have left an audible trace in my works. Jürgen Eggebrecht of North-West German Radio in Hanover was completely besotted with me and *Boulevard Solitude* and invited Jean-Pierre and me to have coffee and cakes with him. Hans Heinz Stuckenschmidt wrote something flattering, as he invariably would – unfortunately always a little wide of the mark, not really understanding what I was trying to say, missing the point and misquoting me or, rather, only half quoting me. *Boulevard Solitude* was revived the very next season and has never been out of the repertory since, with some twenty-six productions to date.

Within days of the Hanover première Jean-Pierre had signed a contract for five new productions with Karlheinz Stroux at the Düsseldorf Schauspielhaus. Back in Wiesbaden, I received a visit from Tatjana Gsovsky, who needed music for her ballet–pantomime, *Der Idiot*, at that September's Berlin Festival. This more or less coincided with a commission for a ballet from her ex-husband, Victor Gsovsky, for the 1952 Munich Opera Festival. I had to work harder than ever. It would never have occurred to me to turn down invitations of the kind that were now coming in. I think that by then I only ever set foot in the Wiesbaden Staatstheater in order to collect my pay packet. When I also recall that I was simultaneously working on my Second (strictly serial) String Quartet, I find it hard to imagine how I managed to produce what I did. I had to work very hard and had little time to relax. My latest room in Wiesbaden – my third – looked out on an inner courtyard, from where every conceivable kind of music came wafting towards me through open windows from a score or more of wirelesses. The company was disbanded. The dancers had fortunately all signed lucrative contracts with other leading houses: van Dyk went to the Paris Opéra, Maria Fris to Hamburg, where many years later she jumped to her death, plunging from the lighting gantry on to the empty stage of the State Opera.

I moved to Munich, intending to use the city as a base camp prior to my assault on Italy: in other words, I would learn Italian, pay off all my old debts, including the remaining instalments on my new Ford, and bid farewell to Germany. In Munich I wrote a wind quintet, began my cello concerto, *Ode to the West Wind*, and completed my radio opera, *Das*

Ende einer Welt. In this way I got to know Wolfgang Hildesheimer, who worked up one of his short stories for me as the libretto for this last-named piece. And it was Hildesheimer who took me with him to a meeting of the Gruppe 47, an anti-Establishment group of writers that met at Berlepsch near Göttingen at the end of October 1952. Among the many foremost minds of their day who had gathered here, virtually all of whom were men, were Ernst Schnabel, Heinrich Böll, Alfred Andersch, Hans Werner Richter, Peter Weiss, Milo Dor and Martin Walser. But also present was an elfin creature with large and beautiful eyes, tremulous eyelids and wonderful hands, a woman of grace and charm who exuded sensitivity, a daughter of the nightingale. Here, I felt, I was in the presence of someone exceptional. During the first coffee break, I asked her whether she, too, was a writer or whether, like me, she was merely there as an observer. No, she said, she was a writer, mainly of romantic novels with regional settings – which was only to be expected, she added, since she came from Carinthia. Hence her rejection of the sort of modern literature that was being touted here and that she dismissed as *Asphaltliteratur*, a term that had been used by the Nazis to denigrate non-Nazi art. She said that she felt as though she was there by mistake – Vienna Radio had sent her to report on the proceedings. It was clear she was making fun of me, not least because I could tell from the way that she spoke and her whole demeanour, including her Viennese tailored suit, that it was impossible to think of her in the same breath as romantic fiction and the heady atmosphere of Alpine pastures. What she actually wrote was to become clear to me very soon.

I can no longer recall whether it was that same evening or the following morning that I first heard Ingeborg Bachmann read her poems. As far as I remember, virtually none had appeared in print at that time. But what I do recall as vividly as though it were yesterday is the impact of her delivery and the hesitant, extraordinarily bashful way in which she expressed her ideas and images, as though whispering to herself. I felt as though she was looking at me and secretly taking my hand, like an elder sister trying to calm me down and taking me to the Slovene woods of her childhood, where it was dark beneath the tall fir trees and where fern and foxglove grew. The odd dry twig would crack beneath our feet and startled birds would call. Salamanders and beetles, owls and snakes, badgers, hedgehogs and foxes gathered there, the moon and stars were our friends and companions – without them, we would never have dared return home. She was six days older than I, but her knowledge of the world, of people and of art so far exceeded my own that she could have been my elder by two thousand years or more. I leant on her for support, her spirit helped sustain me in my infirmity.

We met again soon afterwards in Munich, and during the following spring often went for short drives together, along the Rhine, through ruined German landscapes. In Munich I introduced her to Karl Amadeus and Elisabeth Hartmann, who by now had become close friends of mine. I remember one particular Sunday at Schleißheim with the Hartmanns and Ingeborg. The lilac was in blossom, everything was peaceful, all seemed well with the world. The Germans, meanwhile, were working away at their hard-won affluence and burying guilt and atonement like Mafia corpses in the concrete blocks of their brand-new banks and department stores. People spoke of the need to restore the German soldier's lost honour and of a new and universal compulsory military service. (All the men of my own age were to be called up to serve in the Bundeswehr, but I had already deserted my post.) We were scandalized and, given our recent and appalling experiences, were in any case disinclined to place ourselves at our country's disposal. After all, we were pacifists and anti-Fascists. It was terrible to watch this new development in Germany, a development which, as we now know, impeded our country's chances of becoming emancipated and more humane.

I admired Ingeborg unreservedly and was very keen to please her – to impress her was not necessary – and so I chose to play the part of a joker so that she would always have something to laugh at. She found me genuinely funny, but also silly, old-fashioned and still immaturely obsessed with petty-bourgeois morality. None the less, a kind of bond developed between us, a sense of brotherhood, an elective affinity. At the Gruppe 47's next meeting in Mainz in May 1953, which I again attended as an observer, Ingeborg was awarded the annual prize. I could not believe it: so other people, too, had noticed her abilities. She now decided to give up her job with Austrian Radio, where she had worked for many years, editing and writing radio plays, and where she had come to hate Vienna. Like me, she decided to move to Italy. Her plan – which she also managed to put into practice – was to spend part of the summer on Ischia and in the autumn to start work in Rome as foreign correspondent of the *Westdeutsche Allgemeine Zeitung* and Bremen Radio, while at the same time devoting herself to her writing. In this way we were able to keep in contact when I was finally able to leave for Italy at the end of May 1953. My landlady at 6 Jakob-Klar-Straße, Frau Pröschl, locked away my suitcases on the day I planned to leave in order to stop me from trying to escape her clutches without paying my final month's rent – a last reminder of my fatherland. Yet things had been going well for me in Munich and elsewhere: my publisher, Willy Strecker, had decided to offer me advances on works still to be written and even provided me with a genuine letter of credit so that I would have sufficient funds at my disposal to be able to devote myself solely to composition without having to fall back on hack work in the theatre. Also, the regional arts council in Münster had awarded me a small grant for a period of three years from 1953, enabling me to pay the rental on my little house on Ischia and to continue to send money every month to my family in the Senne. I believe that I owe this award to the recommendation of my father's former headmaster, Artur Ladebeck, who, as mentioned in an earlier chapter, had survived internment in a concentration camp, joined the Social Democrats and, as Bielefeld's mayor, successfully managed the town's local fortunes from 1946 to 1952 and again from 1954 to 1961.

On 1 September 1952 Tatjana Gsovsky's production of her ballet–pantomime, *Der Idiot*, loosely based on Dostoevsky's novel and with music by myself, had proved a huge success when staged at the Hebbel-Theater in Berlin. But I shall never forget the anxieties, troubles and annoyances caused by the rehearsals of this piece, in the course of which Tatjana rearranged the order of the musical numbers and swapped around the roles, thereby robbing them of their dramaturgical significance. I complained to Tietjen, her boss at the Städtische Oper (she had in the meantime moved to the West, presumably because her work was now felt to be too modern for East Berlin, or perhaps it had something to do with convertible currency), but it did no good, of course. I got annoyed and carried on like nobody's business.

Young composers! Avoid making the same stupid mistake! Don't get worked up, remain aloof, don't get involved, leave the theatre to the experts. It makes not a scrap of difference. I could just as well say: get annoyed and put up a fight, defend your work and protect your rights with the very last drop of your blood. Tatjana had assembled a brilliant company of young dancers, and even today I can still see these lissom monsters prowling around the stage, demonic and sexy in Jean-Pierre's designs, each and every one of them glowing and gleaming with talent and energy. Klaus Kinski as Prince Myshkin was, of course, incredible. He roared and whimpered and spat out the lines that Tatjana had cobbled together, effectively if sacrilegiously, from the Bible and Dostoevsky, so that the very walls shook. Following the utterly chaotic dress rehearsal, which I attended with

Josef Rufer (at the end he turned to me and said: 'Poor Hans, you always have such bad luck in Berlin'), more rehearsals were arranged and a further *pas de trois* was added, with the result that the evening's performance finally started three quarters of an hour late, during which time the audience waited patiently, refusing to get worked up – Tatjana, after all, was a hugely popular figure. At last the curtain went up, and suddenly everything worked and made sense. The music – played by members of the Berlin Philharmonic under Rudolf Alberth – came across clearly and effectively, and the strikingly successful staging contained some veritable *coups de théâtre*: there were no *longueurs*, no dull or weak moments. Jean-Pierre's images created a vaguely poster-like impression in keeping with Tatjana's wishes. The piece made a powerful overall impression, the audience was enthralled and there were scenes of jubilation at the end. Two weeks later we revived the piece at La Fenice as part of the Venice Biennale. Between these two performances I had to rush off to Düsseldorf to conduct the first performance of my First Piano Concerto with the Australian pianist, Noel Mewton-Wood, on 14 September. The recipient of the previous year's Robert Schumann Prize, the piece had been clandestinely improved and expanded in the meantime.

In Düsseldorf, where I stayed with a delightful local couple, I suffered a particularly bad attack of sinusitis that had still not cleared up properly when, armed with a special visa provided by the Italian consulate in Cologne, I set off by train for Venice. On arriving in La Serenissima, I hired a gondola at Santa Lucia Station and had myself ferried to La Fenice – unaware that there were other, public, means of transport in the city that would have cost far less than the arm and a leg demanded by my gondolier. I left my suitcases at the stage door and went up into the theatre, where I found Jean-Pierre and Tatjana working on the lighting plot. I was given a room in which to change, then hurried off to the performance, which passed off like a dream – virtually without my involvement. I was completely bewitched by Venice and its setting and could scarcely believe my eyes. The lights were already being dimmed in La Fenice's beautiful auditorium, which was full of elegant people, all of them looking distinguished and self-assured (in those days people still wore something special whenever they went out in the evening). They thought that they all looked good, with the result that they sometimes did.

The performance on stage made much the same impression as it had done in Berlin and ended with thunderous applause – we could scarcely believe it, so much had gone wrong in the course of the evening: sets had got stuck, and flats had wobbled and swung to and fro. Perhaps it looked as if it was meant to be like that – German neo-expressionism. Kinski saved the show by running back and forth at the end between iron rods that had been lowered by mistake, howling in a loud voice and showering the audience with blood, snot and tears. We had succeeded in carving out a tiny niche for ourselves in Italy. An internationalist glimmer of hope surreptitiously lit up little Candide's life, making him think that Venice and La Fenice were just the place to perform his second opera, to which his thoughts were already beginning to turn. After the performance, the festival director, Alessandro Piovesan, introduced Tatjana, Jean-Pierre and me – my head quite swollen with pride – to Giorgio Strehler and the conductor Nino Sanzogno. It was rumoured that the great Luchino Visconti had been present at the performance.

The first-night party was held at the 'Colomba', where we were handsomely entertained, but the very next morning Jean-Pierre and I had to catch the early train to Frankfurt, from where we were to fly back to Berlin, where Karlheinz Stroux was expecting us both for the following day's rehearsal of Giraudoux's *Sodom und Gomorrha* at the Schloßparktheater. In order for us to be able to catch the train, Jean-Pierre had hired a motorboat from the Lido, where we were staying, to Santa Lucia Station, with the result that he, too, was now completely broke. We had to run and throw first our luggage and then ourselves on to the train, which was already starting to pull out of the station. Our only chance was to find someone on the train from whom we could borrow some money. We were in luck: among the first-class passengers were Nastasya Filippovna and her wealthy boyfriend. We were saved. Provided with fresh reserves of ready money, we duly reached Frankfurt but had barely taken off on our night flight to Berlin, when the aircraft caught fire and we had to return to a fog-bound Frankfurt, where the aircraft was smothered in foam. Not until the next day did we reach Berlin and immediately hurried to the Schloßparktheater, where we were given a lengthy, loud and, it has to be said, entirely justified dressing-down by Stroux, who treated us like two naughty schoolboys. There was one sentence in particular in his tirade of abuse of which I made a mental note in order to be able to use it again myself if the occasion ever arose.

I liked Berlin so much that I remained behind for some time after the first night of the Giraudoux. (Prior to my trip to the West, I had spent several nights in a recording studio preparing a soundtrack for the play, a highly effective *musique concrète* score that helped to restore me to

Stroux's good books.) I had had a string of successes and so I was now accepted. I attended every first night and every festival party. And I often saw Paul Dessau, who, kindness itself, was as lively as ever. On Sundays I would take tea in their garden with the Rufers, who told me all about Schoenberg and his teachings, about their remarkably non-doctrinaire application and also about the older composer's approach to tradition and modernism. I stayed with the actress Ruth Hellberg, whom I knew from Wiesbaden, where she had been one of our ballet company groupies and dazzled audiences as Blanche Dubois in *A Streetcar Named Desire*. Sadler's Wells Ballet paid a visit to Berlin, and I was able to scrounge a ticket to the first night of *Giselle*, with Margot Fonteyn in the title role. And, to my immense delight, I was finally able to meet Frederick Ashton face to face. He was forty-eight, affected a nonchalant elegance and was something of a dandy, but not a snob. Beneath his cool, even anthropophobic and reserved exterior, all the great English passions lay hidden, together with a wonderful sense of humour, a rare appreciation of art and a real understanding of people. He had time for me. We met almost every day during the company's visit – I think I must have attended every performance – and he came with me to a party at Katja Meirowsky's, where he tried to teach me to dance. He was successful, but only as long as he led – as soon as I was left on my own or when I danced with other people, I became as stiff and untalented as before. We never discussed artistic plans but spoke only about art in general, about music, painting, literature and people. I was wary of offering him my services as a composer, much as I would have liked to have done so. My earlier approach, when I had sent him the shellac pressings of my *Ballet Variations*, had already been a bold enough gesture. I still had so much to learn. I wanted to become an Englishman like Ashton, wanted my life to be based on a different set of cultural values and, most of all, I wanted to get away from Germany. Now at the very pinnacle of his career, Ashton was a sensitive individualist who, in aesthetic matters, came from a totally different background from anything we knew about in Germany – what did the likes of us know about Ruskin and Whistler, Beardsley, Fedorovitch, Bérard, Craxton and the Sitwells? And I? I was just a beginner, an inquisitive tearaway thirsting for glory, wild and cold-hearted, arrogant and naïve. 'A precious bird', I was described a few years later by someone else (not English), reproachfully but not entirely inaccurately. But there must have been something about what I said and did that amused and interested Ashton. As a young man he had danced in Pavlova's *corps de ballet*, had seen some of the great performances of Diaghilev's later seasons and then, like every artist inspired by the Ballets Russes, had gradually built up his own creative world, with an aesthetic sustained by English culture and English artistic traditions. At that time – the 1930s – his principal musical adviser was the conductor and composer Constant Lambert, a friend and mentor of the young William Walton, whose *Façade* had been Ashton's first great success when he had choreographed it for the Camargo Society in 1931. By the early 1950s he was artistic director of the Sadler's Wells Ballet and could delight in the triumphs of his company and his principal dancers.

During the final months of my time in Germany I returned to Berlin to work with Heinz von Cramer on an operatic project that involved rewriting Carlo Gozzi's baroque fairy-tale about King Stag (or perhaps it would be more accurate to call it a cross between an Indian and a Venetian myth) and turning it into a vast, surreal and circuslike spectacle. Cramer felt the same longing for Italy as I did and had already gained an insight into modern Italian art, including the modern Italian cinema. For him, too, Venice had surpassed all his expectations and he, too, was on the point of fleeing the Kurfürstendamm and settling on the island of Procida in the Gulf of Naples. His libretto is full of images that would be inconceivable without the colours of a place like Procida, with its tuffaceous rock formations, its smells and vegetation. A new Venetia was to be created in the middle of the Tyrrhenian Sea, with the different dialects merging together. The same is true of the music, of which more in due course. My thoughts are already racing ahead to the day on which I crossed the frontier into Italy, a red-letter day, the happiest day of my life. But we have not quite reached that point.

My happiest memories of Munich during the 1952/3 season were in the field of music. Karl Amadeus Hartmann's musica viva concerts, virtually all of which I heard at this time, probably did more for my musical education and development than all the courses I ever attended at Darmstadt. I shall never forget Berg's concert aria, *Der Wein*, Dallapiccola's *Cori di Michelangelo*, Scherchen's evening of works by Webern, Berg and Schoenberg in February 1953 and Messiaen's *Turangalîla* Symphony. Among conductors, I particularly remember Kleiber, Markevich and Mitropoulos.

There is no doubt that the care that I now lavish on orchestral timbre and that is found in all my works from the *Ode to the West Wind* onwards is the result of my encounter with Hartmann and his music. In much the same way, the freedom, exuberance and diffuseness of *König Hirsch*, which I went on to write on Ischia with the sound of the musica viva concerts still ringing in my ears, are due to the impressions and insights into the raw material of sound, as well as into the palette of colour available to the modern orchestra and into the concept of large-scale symphonic form vouchsafed to me by Hartmann and the other composers whose works were featured in his musica viva programmes. At the same time, I became a close friend of the Hartmanns, a friendship that had in fact begun as long ago as 1947, but at that time we had met only relatively infrequently, during my occasional visits to Munich, whereas now we were able to see each other almost every day since we were living fairly close to one another. I have rarely met such a kind and utterly unbourgeois couple. They loved one another and cared for each other, yet still found time for others. Whenever I returned from Italy to Munich in later years, not least to conduct the odd musica viva concert myself, there was invariably a warm welcome waiting for me at the Hartmanns'. One summer they visited me on Ischia and attended the celebrations accompanying the Feast of Saint Roch in the little village of Monterone, a festival attended by fireworks and brass-band music and remarkable for the fact that it was organized by the Communist villagers without the blessing and involvement of the Church. As a result, there was no procession, no saints, no incense – thus the clergy had its revenge. But there was dancing, music and food aplenty. Karl developed a curious fear that the volcano Epomeo might suddenly start to erupt again and insisted on returning to the mainland with Elisabeth as quickly as possible. I declined to go with them. Fortunately, I had already been able to show him a whole section of the score of *König Hirsch*, some of which he had pronounced to be bristling with thirds, which was certainly true (even though the thirds run in dissonant contrary motion), but on the whole his remarks were highly encouraging.

On 13 December 1963, eight days after Karl Amadeus's death, I conducted excerpts from his First Symphony in his memory at a musica viva concert. I had already performed his music on other, earlier occasions, so I may be said to be familiar with it and to feel an inner attachment to it. Elisabeth Hartmann never fully got over her husband's tragically early death, a loss that affected not just her but the rest of us, too, and often felt, as we all did, that Karl was still alive and might enter the room at any moment, where the music of the piece on which he was working when he died still lay open on the piano, with all his writing equipment neatly laid out beside a bowl of dried rose petals. At any moment, his loud and cheerful voice might ring out as he called high-spiritedly for Elisabeth or for their son, Richard, or greeted some newly arrived visitor in that effusive manner of his. Elisabeth continues to take a great interest in performances of her husband's works, which can now be heard all over the world, attending the most important of them and following closely – as Karl would have done – the works of a new generation of composers at the Munich Biennale and the musica viva concerts, concerts which, with the passage of time, have naturally changed in terms of both form and content but which continue, as before, to attract the best local audiences, a circle of listeners which, well versed in music, is above all eager to learn new things – *novarum rerum cupidus*.

Marino, 1991. While an autumn storm rages outside and my recollections of these years in Wiesbaden and Munich return like ghosts to haunt me, other images jostle for attention, memories of occasions, both happy and sad, that had long since been forgotten. I suddenly remember a Sunday afternoon in the Taunus, when Jean-Pierre and I sat in my car, sheltering from the rain and, profoundly moved, listened to some music on the radio that we had never heard before and that turned out to be Mahler's Ninth. Or the meeting at the Paris Opéra, arranged through Jean-Pierre, with Serge Lifar who, like Stravinsky, was to send us his best wishes for our first ballet evening in Wiesbaden. Or the winter of 1952/3 in Munich, with its endless snowfalls, a complicated operation on my sinuses and the first problems with my hearing, when my doctor recommended a stay in a warmer, drier climate. Then there was the Italian Film Festival at Wiesbaden, when I particularly remember *Shoeshine*, *Bicycle Thieves* and *A Sunday in August*. So that's what Italy and the Italians are like, I thought. If only I could live among such people – and sooner rather than later!

Also in Wiesbaden I wrote some incidental music for Giraudoux's *Judith*, which Gustav Rudolf Sellner staged in Darmstadt. Scherchen conducted my Second Symphony at the 1952 Darmstadt summer school – I remember having to enter a lot of accents, breath marks and performance markings in the orchestral parts, which proved a salutary experience. I noticed that the maestro was fond of ignoring the composer's tempo markings in order to be able to introduce undesirable expressionist distortions. Everything was always too slow or too fast, or both.

American soldiers everywhere. Adenauer. A woman in Konstanz complained about the presence of gays at the Deutsches Theater. I fell in love with the *Kindertotenlieder*. In Munich I gave private lessons to a young

American, who on one occasion returned from a study trip to the northern provinces and, beaming with pleasure, announced that he had got to know a certain Herr Stockhausen in Cologne and that the latter had taught him a novel compositional trick, but only on condition that he did not pass it on to me.

Who was this Stockhausen? He had not yet put in an appearance at Darmstadt nor made his mark in any other context. No, that was not quite true: Herbert Hübner, who, as controller of music at Hamburg, had organized a series of concerts under the title 'das neue werk', had recently told me that Stockhausen had dropped in on him, leafed through one of his contemporaries' scores and sighed: 'One can't write like that any more today.' That had impressed the modernist Herr Hübner. I wondered whether this remark portended some new doctrine. Were we again to be given guidelines? What did 'today' mean in questions of art? Who was meant by 'one'? And what did these hostilities portend? I would find out soon enough. It seemed to me strange, not to say absurd, that composers, as messengers of a higher spirituality, should want to make life difficult for one another in a way that now became quite common, taking away each other's livelihood, fighting each other like business managers and forming cliques and lobby groups. I found it repulsive, unethical and inartistic – another reason for preferring to remain alone and refusing to conform. The new arbiters of German music, who were really no more than jumped-up officials and civil servants like the grotesque Heinrich Strobel, the insipid Wolfgang Steinecke in Darmstadt and the foolishly garrulous Herbert Hübner in Hamburg, were all people I found profoundly unsympathetic. Their sharp-tongued menopausal spouses were invariably piqued when they noticed that other men did not find them desirable and pursed their lips as they drooled with middle-class malice and laughed uproariously whenever their menfolk regaled them with obscene rhymes that would not have disgraced a rugby-club dinner. A number of my colleagues thought it politic to dedicate their works 'in friendship' to these people, on whose grace and favour they appeared to depend, as though they were personal friends or members of the aristocracy, not interchangeable officials. They all had one thing in common – the heady feeling that comes with power and that was pursued with particular resolve by Heinrich Strobel, who, in his desire to steer music in his chosen direction, finally managed to have himself elected chairman of the International Society for New Music in order to be able to control that process from the top, a move that ended with his forced retirement when representatives of the smaller countries rebelled against the new German dictator. These were developments that I would follow only from a distance or, preferably, ignore altogether. In retrospect I can say without any exaggeration that I avoided this struggle between rival factions and consciously absented myself from Ars Nova's bloody battlefield.

I spent Easter 1953 on a lightning tour of Italy, gathering information and inspecting the lie of the land. I also heard a performance of *Boulevard Solitude* in the RAI concert hall in Milan – very beautifully sung in Italian and conducted by Nino Sanzogno. The orchestral pianist was my close contemporary, Luciano Berio. I then travelled by train to Sicily, planning to stay there anonymously and without knowing a soul – perhaps in Syracuse, which sounded promising, being both Greek *and* Shakespearian. I arrived in Catania, my southernmost point, on Easter Saturday and presented myself at the stage door of the Teatro Bellini during a break in the morning's rehearsals, hoping to speak to the players, to try out my newly acquired Italian (I had been having lessons three times a week for almost a year) and to discover how to set about renting a small house at Acireale or Aci Trezza, where Polyphemus had dwelt and Visconti had made his film, *La terra trema*. My colleagues thought I would do best to go to an agency. But it was Easter, I could not stay any longer, and my money was running out – it simply slipped through my fingers like water. As a result, Sicily came to nothing and I realized that I would have to settle for Ischia by way of a compromise. According to Gilles, Ischia was in danger of becoming the 'in' place, which was just what we wanted to avoid. Hardly anyone could have imagined then that the island would one day be owned by foreigners and that every last inch would be filled with pseudo-Moorish villas. At that date Ischia did not even have its own supply of drinking water.

But before I go any further, I must stop for a moment to recall a few other memories from this time, chief of which is of a dear friend of mine from Munich, the photographer Felicitas Timpe, a well-known figure on the city's arts scene between the end of the war and the present, a period of which she must have the most complete photographic record in existence. During the winter of 1952/3 she regularly invited a number of her friends, including myself, to have lunch with her. It was just like being at home, so for a whole winter we were spared the indignities of a guest house. I also cultivated the company of the young Princess Anne and Prince Heinrich of Bavaria. Anne de Lustrac was a disconcertingly beautiful, slightly mad woman who once drove me to Stuttgart, where I had to rehearse a suite from my ballet *Pas d'action* with the Stuttgart Radio

Orchestra. It did not go very well, since it was never long before I was brought up against the limits of my abilities as a conductor: the orchestra's principal conductor, Hans Müller-Kray, and the players were kindness itself and helped me as best they could, but I was ashamed of my own ineptitude and not at all happy with myself.

I have only a vague recollection of the staged performance of *Pas d'action*, which was given at the Prinzregententheater on 22 July 1952. The main problem was the interminable scene changes, most of which lasted longer than the scenes on either side of them, with the result that action and music fell completely apart. I was furious, but, to judge from the photographs that show Victor Gsovsky, Jean-Pierre and me beaming at the applause of Bavaria's balletomanes, the audience must have liked it. The scenario was by Otto Herbst, a friend of the Jockisches, though I seem to recall that Jean-Pierre and I changed it quite extensively and adapted it to suit our current Anglo-French tastes in our desire to turn it into the basis for a strictly classical ballet – for we would accept no other type at this time. It looked delightful, as one can tell from the photographs, since it was then all still fresh and new. The music was conducted by Kurt Eichhorn, one of the assistant conductors at the Bavarian State Opera, who observed the performance markings to the letter, while at the same time bringing out all the colours in the score. I withdrew the piece almost immediately afterwards and later rewrote it for Rudolf Nureyev, who staged the revised version in Vienna on 14 May 1966 with a new title, *Tancredi*, and a new scenario by Peter Csobádi. Nureyev himself danced the title role.

By the late spring of 1953 I had finally begun to sever my last remaining links with Munich, with the result that I can now set about describing the first day of my journey south. Yet once again a handful of memories emerges from the gloom, like carnival revellers in the morning mist. How could I ever forget dear old Schwabing? Even then, it was said to be no longer the place that it once had been. Schwabing was home to the painters Bele Bachem and Jo von Kalckreuth, to the surrealist and mannerist storyteller, Fabius von Gugel, the beau Kai Molvig and the actor Hubert Hilten, to say nothing of Manni Kortner and her husband, the actor Wolfried Lier, and the photographer Herbert List, who also collected old etchings. Have I forgotten anyone? Yes, of course, there was also Maxi Scheler, the son of the philosopher of religion. He, too, was a photographer, an art he had learnt from Herbert List. Here, in this élite, bohemian world, there was still a feeling amounting to sheer enthusiasm for the things of art; these people felt at home in Munich (and, for the most part, were indeed at home there), enjoying the city's amenities. I liked them all very much, and the times we spent together were always amusing and interesting and frank. All, moreover, were talented artists. For their sake and for the Hartmanns', I could have stayed in Munich.

Yet I had a constant nagging feeling, something that would not leave me in peace but demanded that I should get away from Germany. I was on the point of succumbing to the seductions of the commissions that kept pouring in, with the result that I now began to feel a sense of disquiet and mistrust. What did people want of me? I still had to finish my studies! And I needed time, needed air, fresh air! I was still a total novice. I wanted to investigate the origins of music, wanted to get to the bottom of things and begin at the very beginning. What I was trying to escape from was not so much post-war Germany as the musical avant-garde in Germany and/or avant-garde music in general. I needed to be on my own in order to live like a hermit and discover what music meant to me as an individual, how it is bound up with our lives, what it must mean to us and what is the cultural role that the composer fulfils within human society.

Ingeborg thought that Ludwig Wittgenstein would most certainly have approved of and respected my decision, and that – as far as I was concerned – was the main thing: I felt spiritually protected. And there was nothing more for me to hold on to: I sold my books and scores, including a number of particularly beautiful items, so that my luggage weighed virtually nothing when I retrieved it from the redoubtable Frau Pröschl one Monday morning in return for a lump sum in cash. I rushed away, not stopping until I had reached the part of South Tyrol where the people speak only Italian and had my first glass of Merlot in front of me. At last I felt able to breathe again, to breathe deeply and savour the feeling of happiness. 'All my old wrongs I forsake,' I thought and, like so many Germans before me, soaked up the sense of *italianità*. Sitting at the wheel of my car, I thought up some music for Hugo von Hofmannsthal's youthful *Reiselied*:

Overwhelmed by weltering breakers,
Crushed by cliffs that tower, immense,
Borne aloft on mighty pinions,
Birds have come to bear us hence.

But beneath us lies a land,
Whose fruits forever glisten
In its ageless lakes below.

Marble fane and fountain stand
On flowery earth. O listen
As the gentle breezes blow.

Meanwhile, my eyes were filled with Venetia's natural and architectural beauties. By late that same evening I was already walking on the *zattere* with Gigi Nono and telling him about *König Hirsch*. I called on the Biennale's artistic director, Alessandro Piovesan, and awakened his interest in the first performance of this piece, not a note of which had yet been written. But I stayed only a few days, so keen was I to reach my new home, where all my desires were to find fulfilment. I drove from Bologna to Florence via the Passo di Futa. It was already very warm, the air trembled, choruses of cicadas chirruped in the valleys and in the groves of olive trees. The desert landscape of Tuscany surrounded me like some heavy mantle that was none the less soft to the touch. The Via Cassia, narrow and winding, takes the traveller to settlements whose architectural elegance is a further source of wonder, their harmony reflecting the cultural awareness of their architects and inhabitants. One day I would be able to get to know Italian art and learn to understand it – already I was in love with it. I was glad to have been able to enter this other world, a world so totally alien to my own existing culture but one that filled me with the same kind of anticipatory joy and curiosity, the same feeling of deep happiness that I had already sensed two years previously on that summer evening in Frascati.

There is little doubt that my feelings were not unrelated to my insatiable need to be alone and to emerge from my chrysalis state. I spent only a single night in Rome, continuing southwards along the Appian Way the very next morning. I had to stop several times while crossing the Pontine Marshes in order to clean my windscreen, on which a thick film of squashed mosquitoes would regularly form. Eventually the traveller reaches San Felice Circeo, where Odysseus is said to have had trouble with the Sirens and his crew had to bind him firmly to his mast to prevent him from falling prey to the power of music. The Vatican State ends at the fortress of Gaeta, where the SS mass murderer, Herbert Kappler, served out his life sentence, breeding canaries and geraniums, and the Kingdom of the Two Sicilies begins. You notice the change straightaway: the houses now become Spanish and baroque (and the buildings that have only just been completed look even worse than in Latium), agaves grow everywhere, as does a kind of cactus known in these parts as the 'Indian fig' that sprouts from ancient stonework. With every kilometre the southbound traveller plunges a little deeper into the ancient world, though there is nothing specific to see: classical antiquity is underground, grown over with hops and vines, with olive trees and fruit plantations and meadows grazed by African water buffalo imported by Il Duce that stand out black against a grey sky, offset by the pink of the peach blossom. But as we leave Caserta behind us and approach Naples from the north, we notice how the streets and roads are lined with more and more large, old buildings, often in a state of advanced decay. Eyes and feelings become attuned to urban features. The predominant impression is that of the *settecento*, the age of the Bourbons, who left their architectural traces everywhere, but without ever succeeding in overshadowing the landmarks left by long years of Angevin rule.

Yet the most tenacious of all traditions in Naples is that of the Greeks, a tradition that survives in the people, in their customs and social intercourse. It can be observed in the classical grace of the younger generation and in the respect and deference accorded them by their elders.

It was evening when I arrived in the city. A fair had been set up along the whole length of the Via Caracciolo and the Posillipo, with drums and pipes and tarantellas. Later on there was a huge firework display over the entire gulf – I had not seen anything as spectacular since the night-time bombing raids of the early forties. I learnt that lightning and thunderbolts do not always have to be harbingers of death but may also be part of an incantatory ritual designed to drive away demons and exorcize ill fortune. I felt at my ease, entirely alone, anonymous and free among thousands of free and anonymous strangers. I did everything properly, slept peacefully in my little hotel room near the station and the next morning drove down to the harbour and on to a wooden boat, where my car was secured with ropes and brake blocks, and we soon set off, chugging out into the Gulf of Naples, the waters of which are generally quite choppy between Capo Miseno and Ischia. Needless to say, we arrived without any mishaps, and I drove at once to Forio.

After only a few days I found what I was looking for: a little Moorish farmhouse, half in ruins, hidden behind high walls, with a little vineyard and an ancient lemon tree. It had a flat roof, which was reached by a flight of stairs, and on it figs had been laid out to dry on basketwork. Each day they were sprinkled with sea water to keep them disinfected. An ancient *nonna* sat on these stairs. The first thing she asked me was whether the Germans were Christian. My landlady, Lucia Capuano, was a gaunt Arab woman whose husband and two eldest sons lived in Canada, where they worked as lumberjacks and from time to time would send her what they had saved, while Lucia remained at home and looked after their three younger sons, Peppino, Aniello and Mariolino. She lived in the neighbouring building with her sons and the old woman. Lucia saw to my needs and kept my house in order. It consisted of an entrance hall, a study (lit only by a small window some three metres up the wall) and a bedroom, from which double doors led out on to a small, semicircular terrace. From there I could look out over vineyards and the sea, with the old Saracen fort of Forio in the background. The furniture included a good, old-fashioned bed, a solid table and a couple of simple wickerwork chairs. The floor and walls were whitewashed and I left them unadorned throughout all the years I was there. Outside was a well fed by an underground spring and by rainwater and kept clean by an old eel that lived at the very bottom, where it led a comparatively monotonous existence. How silent it all was here! And how quickly I slipped off the shackles of the past!

5

It was pleasantly cool within these solid, protective walls, with their Arab vaultings and slanting rays of light. The deserter threw himself to the floor and pressed his ear against it, listening to the volcano as it bubbled and rumbled and sang of the onshore breeze brushing lightly and gently across it. Day and night he heeded the sea's susurration and slowly learnt to breathe in time to its uniform rhythms, feeling that this country would never hand him over. Himmler had vowed to 'root out all degenerate elements' and 'treat them as enemies of the state', but in my case his orders could no longer be carried out. His henchmen had come too late. And Hilde Strobel's strident jokes about gays would henceforth pass me by. My sickening experiences of petty-bourgeois provincialism, of firing squads and colleagues' spite and envy had all been left behind, beyond the Brenner Pass, from where their disgusting smells were already wafting back towards the German provinces.

During these early weeks I began, with some hesitation, to try out a new way of working and, once it had proved its worth, stuck to it from then on, maintaining it to the present day and suffering untold agonies whenever I am prevented from putting it into practice. My aim was to work on *König Hirsch* from sunrise until late morning (the clock in the tower at San Francesco's marked the passing hours with its hollow, metallic chimes). With the waxing moon I would compose amidst the deafening chorus of cicadas, and with the waning moon I would sort through all that I had written and work on the orchestral score. On the stroke of twelve I went for an hour's swim at one of the nearby beaches, which at that time was still deserted; then I prepared a light meal for myself in my tiny kitchen at home, had a siesta and then returned to my work, examining, revising and elaborating all that I had written that morning. In the evening I sat on the roof and read an Italian grammar with a carafe of chilled wine beside me, taking in the volcano of Monte Epomeo, the long fluting notes of the crickets and the movements of the stars. It was the first time in my life that I had discovered true tranquillity. I was almost thirty years old. There was little mail, and what little there was I was reluctant to read. Ghosts from the past! To be on my own and remain so! Here was a chance to do things differently and better than before – it seemed to me the greatest imaginable stroke of good fortune. Even today I can still recall my emotion at that time.

First of all, I had to calm down inside myself and develop a new sense of time, had to measure, grasp and *feel* my new sense of freedom. It was wonderful that everything was now directed to the future and that the past could be forgotten. I learnt to dispense with all that was unnecessary and to bring rigour and purity to my life. I had no difficulty identifying with my music, the usual schizophrenia notwithstanding. I had come to realize that I would spend my whole life promoting a concept of beauty that had something to do with the notion of truth – inner truth, one's own private truth – and that would be beholden to no other thinking except my own but that would also encompass the civil disobedience to which I lay claim for myself.

The first music that I wrote for Act One of *König Hirsch* was the duet between the girl and the young king: 'What can we do? The air was full of open cages. Our glances grew wings and, birdlike, flew away.' It was diatonic music that seemed to me to issue from the heart of this enchanted land that held me in its embrace and from the undergrowth where the peasants picked prickly pears, from the pomegranate trees and from inside the agaves, from which a slender shoot, a metre in length, develops every seven years, ending in a mass of flowers, at which point plant and flowers die. Flotsam and jetsam, tree stumps bleached white by the sun, sharks' jaws and seashells in which could be heard the eternally echoing song of lost mermaids.

There was no piano, but that did not matter – I had long since learnt to listen with my inner ear, so that I was not at a loss now. I learnt to concentrate for longer periods – for hours, not just for minutes, as had been the case hitherto – so that I could follow the musical argument in my head, carefully and patiently, before jotting down the notes on paper more or less intact. When I won the Premio della Radio Italiana in Palermo in the autumn of 1953, I not only bought myself some of the finest Italian clothes I could find, I also acquired a dilapidated piano and from now on was able to try out my different combinations of notes straightaway.

> Les souvenirs sont cors de chasse,
> dont meurt le bruit parmi le vent,

Apollinaire writes somewhere in his *oeuvre*, a passage that I quote in the hunt music in Act Two of *König Hirsch*. At that time, both my librettist, Heinz von Cramer, and I were especially interested in surrealism. I was also attracted to Max Ernst and to the sort of distortions that one finds in his paintings, distortions which, chameleon-like and kaleidoscopic, alarming and terrifying by turns, unfathomable, comically strange and strangely comical, I now wanted to translate into my music so that they would become part of my technique and help me to realize Leonardo da Vinci's idea that music should represent *le cose che non se vedono*.

Among the new faces I met in Forio d'Ischia were the artist Margherita Utescher, a voluptuous beauty from Munich, and her husband, the classical scholar, Carlo Ferdinando Russo. A deeply serious woman who was self-critical to a fault, Margherita painted motifs from the island on huge, coarse canvases until the images had acquired the intended harshness and feeling of menace. Her husband, an acerbic but witty man, with a great love of life and propensity for irony and sarcasm, had succeeded his father as editor of *Belfagor*, an important literary journal that continues to be published in Bari. Never before had I heard such polished Italian as spoken by Ferdinando Russo. It sparkled and rattled along, sounding for all the world like the reed stops of an organ. Among the Russos' visitors were the art historian Cesare Brandi and Natalia Ginzburg and her husband, the English scholar and Shakespeare translator, Gabriele Baldini. Even by this date, Forio already boasted a respectable artists' colony and was no longer a total wasteland. The American poet Anthony Hecht was another artist who spent some time here, as did several Italian painters, including Vittorio Verga and the great Leonardo Cremonini. I remember one evening sitting with Auden and Kallman at their regular table at the Café Maria Internazionale and seeing the actor and director Gustaf Gründgens at another of the tables, relaxing with his host, Eduard Bargheer. Gründgens had been officially married to Erika Mann from 1926 to 1929, and Wystan had later gone through an equally sham ceremony with her at a registry office in England in order for her to obtain a British passport. On leaving the café, Wystan walked past Mephisto's table and said in his heavily accented German: 'We really ought to get to know each other, after all we have the same wife.' To which Gründgens answered, coolly and dismissively: 'That's your problem now, Herr Orden.'

And now we were joined by Ingeborg Bachmann. She arrived one Sunday, the day of the great Forian Feast of Saint Vitus. I collected her from the port and took her to the small Saracen house that I had rented for her beside my own. She liked it. From her terrace she could look out over the flowering vineyards as far as the ravines and sheer slopes of the beautiful Monte Epomeo. We spent our first evening together on the flat roof of my own house, eating fresh figs and goat's cheese and drinking Lucia's wine. From here we had a spectacular view of the colourfully illuminated flotilla of boats in the Gulf of Forio and could hear scraps of what sounded like operatic music drifting up towards us, as the bishop blessed the fishermen and their catch. The whole scene was bathed in the yellow, red and golden light of torches. Lucia's house, too, was lit in the same festive manner. People stood on the roofs of neighbouring houses, gazing in amazement at the moonlit scene before them. And now there began one of those Neapolitan firework displays that leave one speechless with astonishment and that, formally speaking, remind me of baroque overtures. Lucia explained to us why the Feast of Saint Vitus always lasted three whole days (he is the village's principal saint), and when Ingeborg expressed her concern that these firework displays might place a crippling financial burden upon her fellow villagers, she exclaimed: 'Not at all! Once a year the feast *must* come!' This sentence was later repeated in the opening line of a processional dance song in Ingeborg's *Lieder von einer Insel*, which I set to music in the early sixties for small choir and a handful of instruments, including a positive organ.

The impressions left by her first evening on the island had led Ingeborg to believe that processions of boats and firework displays were a nightly occurrence on Ischia, but she now adapted to the quotidian round without a word of complaint: in the morning she worked on her poems, while I got on with my music next door; at midday I would collect her and we would go swimming together, after which I would cook some lunch for us both (at least during the first few weeks, after which Lucia took pity on us and, with all the skills of her rustic upbringing, assumed responsibility for our meals); and then, as the afternoon air began to shimmer, it was time to take a siesta. On some days, Auden would brave the unbearable heat and, sweating profusely, beat at my door, ask for some water, sit down briefly in the shade, then leap to his feet and disappear once again. The shadows were starting to lengthen as a further round of work began. Ingeborg would later drop by and we would talk or go for a walk together and tell each other all about ourselves: we were still almost total strangers. Her father, Matthias, had spent a year in Italy as a young man, travelling around the country on foot. He spoke Italian and Slovenian. The people from his part of the world are known as 'Wends' and are neither Slovenes nor Italians nor Austrians by extraction but have their own history and their own distinctive national character. And they always long for another land. Inge was currently working on her Myshkin monologues for a revised version of Tatjana Gsovsky's *Der Idiot*. We managed to get hold of a small gramophone and spent the evenings listening raptly to our first LPs: we had *La traviata* and *La sonnambula* with Callas, Mozart's *Requiem* under Victor de Sabata, Toscanini's recording of *Falstaff* and Bach's *Well-Tempered Clavier* with Madame Landowska, whose playing reminded me somewhat of crocheting.

We kept very much to ourselves. Inge in particular did not like to share her time with others. When autumn came and she had to leave to take up her job in Rome, we parted as brother and sister. But we still had so much to say to each other that we continued to write long letters. In the course of the foregoing weeks we had only just begun to exchange the most basic information, so we knew, for example, that Ingeborg was six days older than I, which gave her a certain right to boss me around, a right that I was determined she should continue to enjoy to the full. I could tell her everything and did so, too. If I asked her questions, she would answer, wisely and kindly, but she hardly ever asked me anything, nor did she always tell me everything. Why should she? After all, I did not want to know everything. Later it turned out that she had the curious habit of leading several lives at once or at least of pretending to do so. At that time our only concern was not to violate each other's privacy, an unwritten rule that meant that certain questions could not be asked and certain things not said. Perhaps our strict observance of this convention was the key to our friendship, which was based on the firmest of foundations. It also allowed a certain playfulness in our dealings with each other: we were able to laugh and fool around, generally putting on an act – comedy, by preference. I admired her not only for the wonderful things she was able to write and say, but also for her integrity and imperturbability. She exuded certainty, reliability and a very real sense of authority. She was very important in my life, but I do not know, and have never known, to what extent I was really important to *her*.

The mailboat steamed out of the tiny harbour of Porto d'Ischia, with Ingeborg on board, on its way to Naples. It was raining again – autumn drizzle – as I made my way home to *König Hirsch* and lit a wood fire in my little clay stove. The days were now even calmer than before, and I felt only one desire: that my piece should be a success. Towards five o'clock one afternoon, I heard a violent knocking at my door. I already knew the signal. It was the Waltons, who had come to take me for a walk. I had got to know them a few weeks earlier at Auden's. Prior to that I had seen them only in the distance – the famous composer enthroned in the back of his monumental Bentley, while his wife, the straight-backed, raven-haired Lady Walton, his junior by some thirty years, skilfully negotiated the narrow, winding country lanes between the island's vineyard walls. I already knew Heifetz's recording of his Violin Concerto. At the time it was said that, within a single year, more girls had been laid to the sounds of this music in the United States alone than in the whole of the previous half century.

The Waltons lived in a former Franciscan monastery. Ah, what fun it was to spend an evening in an elegant villa instead of a fisherman's hut! How different and how special to sit at a table with damask tablecloths, porcelain and silver, instead of oilcloth, stoneware and aluminium. Landlady Walton (as Auden wittily called her with reference to her property speculations on Ischia) treated me with exquisite Anglo-Argentine courtesy – whether from good sense, intelligence or simply because Sir William had told her to do so, I was never able to establish. On occasions she was even quite nice to me. One incident, in particular, I have never forgotten: it was in the spring of 1954, I had to go to Rome and, quite by chance, bumped into her at the bank one morning. She must have noticed that something was wrong: my monthly cheque had failed to arrive. An hour later I found an envelope at home containing what I needed – Susana had dropped by and pushed it under my door.

William Walton was born in 1902 and, like me, came from what is generally called a 'humble background', with the result that he derived all the greater pleasure from his present affluence, which he owed to the worldwide success of his music and to the support of his friends and sympathizers. He had written two coronation marches for George VI and Elizabeth II, film scores including *First of the Few* and Olivier's *Henry V*, a *Coronation Te Deum*, his famous oratorio, *Belshazzar's Feast*, a Viola Concerto, two symphonies (of which Walton himself had just recorded the first for Decca) and a number of overtures, all in a style which, for all its Elgarian Englishness, was more brilliant, flamboyant and exuberant than anything Elgar wrote and that I found somewhat alien and that struck me as somewhat strange. I simply did not know where to place this music in my own imaginative world. Our walks would sometimes end with tea or whisky in his study, where he showed me the score of his opera, *Troilus and Cressida*, on which he was currently working. He wrote at the piano, which invariably seemed to supply him with the same musical gestures, melismas and chord progressions. I showed him how to write music using twelve notes ('which are related only to one another'), but he was not especially interested. I had the feeling that he was a little lonely here, where there was so little going on, certainly no musical life, none of the glamour of London, no colleagues, orchestras, pubs and, above all, none of his old friends. Visitors had become increasingly infrequent, and not even the Sitwells, who had introduced him to England's astonished literary and artistic world, came to see him any longer. He was a little too young for the older generation among which he had grown up and a little too old for the younger generation that was now making all the running. He was particularly pained by Britten's meteoric rise to fame and by the first performance of *Peter Grimes*, which had been hailed as the birth of modern English opera when unveiled in 1945. The English press had begun to dismiss his music as old-fashioned – all this must have left him embittered and disappointed. He had no time for the political and cultural changes that were taking place in the world, even improvements he found uncongenial. *The Times* would always arrive on the island several days late. Three topics of conversation had to be carefully avoided: twelve-note music, homosexuality and Communism. In order to help my dear, older colleague relax a little, I took him with me to the Venice Biennale in the autumn of 1954. It was devoted to modern music, and I was surprised to see how much he enjoyed himself. There was nothing chic about the occasion, only much that was modern and interesting. He met Luigi Nono and other, even younger people, who welcomed him warmly and without a trace of condescension. He was put out when I completed *König Hirsch* and left Ischia in 1956: from now on we were to see each other far less often. He scarcely ever came to London, and his beautiful house, Lowndes Cottage in Lowndes Place, was put up for sale, its proceeds enabling the Waltons to acquire a large plot of land on Ischia.

The Ischian winter was cold and damp, but that did not matter. Whenever I was not invited to spend the evening with the Waltons, I would visit Margherita and Lallo. Lallo was working on an Italian translation of *Boulevard Solitude* for a new production of the piece at the Teatro San Carlo in Naples, and we would sit together, hour after hour, our brains on fire, tapping out rhythms, declaiming the text and humming or muttering the words to ourselves, a process that allowed me to understand and speak Italian rather better than before. Lallo was also my first Italian Communist, and he it was who first introduced me to the humanitarian rationale behind the world of Marxist ideas as expounded by Antonio Gramsci. And so I spent the whole of this winter gadding backwards and forwards between progressive left-wing evenings and liberal soirées of a much more conservative hue. I listened closely, paid attention to all that was said and weighed the one against the other. Often, however, I was on my own, sometimes a little too often. There were a few unpleasant moments that even today I do not care to recall and that were often to be repeated, even later in life, abroad, in foreign places, especially in large cities. It had nothing to do with homesickness (something I have never felt), but was the indescribable feeling of being completely alone, a sense of abandonment that would sometimes provoke a very real kind of panic, fear at my own temerity at having moved so far away from everything, from everything that was my own, and taken up residence in a totally different country, exchanging one culture for another and doing so, moreover, out of defiance, contempt and pride, this inexplicable, overwhelming need to turn tail and run, to be on my own and to be able to withdraw into myself and listen to the crystalline sounds of a solitary life, *le languide arie della vita solitaria*. As a result, it was no bad thing that I would soon be going to the mainland and spending some time among people, away from my work as a composer.

The world had run me to ground again. It was no doubt the success of *Der Idiot* in Venice and *Boulevard Solitude* in Milan, to say nothing of the radio award, that was to blame for this state of affairs. Be that as it may, no fewer than two new productions of *Boulevard Solitude* were now being planned, one in Naples in March 1954, the other the following May at the Teatro dell'Opera in Rome, where the piece would be staged as part of a festival of twentieth-century music. Having seen a number of unspeakably old-fashioned stagings of Italian works directed in a style altogether unsuited to my own piece, I asked to direct both productions myself, so convinced was I that *Boulevard Solitude* demanded a new style of theatre. In consequence, I kept having to return to the mainland in order to seek out singers and confer with theatre workshops, including costume departments, technical draughtsmen and choreographers. I had invited Margherita Utescher to design the sets and costumes for the Naples production, and since Rome insisted on different designs and singers from those in Naples, I asked Jean-Pierre Ponnelle to take charge of the Rome production.

During the previous autumn I had met a number of young music lovers in Naples, including Federico Forquet and Prince Francesco d'Avalos, together with their friends, Isabella Mosca Ducrot, the Giovagnonis, Annamaria and Gianni Eminente, Giulio di Majo and the various female members of the Balzo di Presenzano family, who hailed from the Kingdom of the Two Sicilies, the collapse of which in 1860/1 neither their parents nor they themselves had ever really accepted. My journeys to the mainland often took me to Rome, where Ingeborg was now living in the beautiful Palazzo Spada, the high vaulted rooms of which would echo to the sounds of her Olivetti 22. As soon as she had completed her daily reports for whichever paper or radio station she happened to be working for, she would return to her radio play, *Die Zikaden*, a commission from North-West German Radio in Hamburg, for which I later wrote some music – it must have been during the winter of 1955/6 or perhaps even slightly earlier.

We saw each other on a daily basis in Rome, and, needless to say, she came to the first night of *Boulevard Solitude* in Naples in March 1954, which was all that one imagines a gala evening should be. The performance was genuinely beautiful, quite exceptional, by no means provocative but, by the same token, not conventional, perhaps even a little strange and dreamlike. The Neapolitans are an intelligent people and had splashed out, showing themselves in agreement with every curious detail and applauding both themselves and me. I should perhaps add that a few days earlier I had agreed a handsome fee with the *capo della claque*, one Commendatore Spizzica, to ensure that his *ragazzi* would burst into spontaneous applause at just the right points in the performance, whenever they received a secret sign from him. The final orchestral interlude unfortunately had to be cut, either because the conductor was incapable of coping with the changing metres or because the players themselves were unable to follow his beat – a pity, since in the eyes of its composer this interlude was the opera's dramatic high point. Federico Forquet's parents gave a wonderful first-night party in their villa on the Posillipo, and at dawn the next morning I drove to Cuma with Ingeborg in order to greet the sun as it rose over the Lago d'Averno.

Soon it was time for me to go to Rome and start work on *Boulevard Solitude* at the city's Teatro dell'Opera. I stayed in the Via Sistina, it was spring and – I was finally forced to admit it, in spite of my enthusiasm for Naples – Rome was a wonderful place. But things were not easy at the Opera.

The Festival of Twentieth-Century Music, which was already under way, was a major event in the cultural calendar. The Accademia Americana held a reception for Stravinsky, to which I, too, was invited.

The whole of Rome was there, as were many foreigners, both musical and unmusical. The great man sat enthroned at the farthest end of the room, I could see him in the distance. The festival director, the composer Nicolas Nabokov, came over to me and said: 'Come on, Stravinsky would like to meet you.' For the first (and last) time in my life, I knew beyond a shadow of a doubt that I was in the presence of a living legend, a figure of mythic status. I was privileged to sit beside the composer of *The Rite of Spring*, *Les noces* and the Ebony Concerto. The hand that had written *Le rossignol* and *The Rake's Progress* touched mine. The simplicity and directness with which Stravinsky expressed himself and that is so characteristic of all great men and women could not fail to make its effect: I liked him enormously. He wanted to speak German, but I answered in English and so we stuck to English. His German sounded a little Baltic but was otherwise excellent – as I was later to have other occasions to remark. The first thing he wanted to know was what I thought of twelve-note composition. He himself was not entirely sure what to make of it at that time, although, if anything, he tended towards scepticism. I did not dare ask him what he himself was working on, but, since he insisted on knowing, I told him about the opera on which I myself was currently engaged and about the twelve-note and serial techniques that I had chosen to use in it. I should like to have told him about my Saracen fortress and about my unsociable and insular life – as if that would have interested him in the slightest! We arranged to meet the next evening, at the first night of *Boulevard Solitude*.

Stravinsky and Vera duly appeared in the main entrance of the Rome Opera on the stroke of nine, but the liveried doormen refused to admit them – Stravinsky was not wearing a dinner jacket. (He said it had smelt of mothballs.) Such rotten luck. The incident made headline news, and the Minister for Tourism and the Arts sent a letter of apology to the Hassler Hotel, where they were staying, with flowers for Madame. Stravinsky turned up for the second performance, this time the only person to wear a dinner jacket, since there was no requirement to wear formal dress for the later performances. Once again, therefore, he was inappositely attired. He came with our mutual publisher, Willy Strecker, who later enticed him into writing a few words of praise for my piece. What he had missed was the first-night fiasco that had broken out the previous evening within moments of the start of the opera – a passage on *pianissimo* percussion. Initially I had sat in the green room with Jean-Pierre, listening to the voices of protest and to the murmurings and laughter relayed via the theatre intercom, as they settled over the music like some miasma or fetid fog. Only now did it occur to me that no *capo della claque* had presented himself in advance of the performance – perhaps someone else had engaged him before me? It was clear that the disruption in the house was well organized, even though the rumblings were also coming from the stalls, where the most expensive seats were located. I could bear it no longer and left the theatre, spending the whole performance prowling around the immediate vicinity, wandering from bar to bar, from the Piazza Esedra to the Church of Santa Maria Maggiore, though I made no attempt to pray. I returned to the Opera in time for the final scene. The stage-door keeper ignored me. I found the dancers in tears on the steps – unable to follow the music, they had got out of time, the audience had bawled so loudly. I could hear it myself from the wings: it really was the most hellish din. The singers, too, were terrorized, with every high note, every solo ridiculed until they scarcely dared open their mouths any longer. But they finally made it to the end, and when I appeared before the curtain, hand in hand with poor Jean-Pierre, the fury on the part of the chicly dressed audience knew no bounds. Some of them even ran down to the front of the stalls and shook their fists at us threateningly: 'Viziati! Andate a Capocotta!' (Capocotta was a place where it was alleged that cocaine-snorting Roman playboys had recently bumped off a girl by the name of Wilma Montesi by means of a massive overdose.)

Even two days previously, after the final dress rehearsal, which had been open to the general public, everyone had been so taken by the piece and the directors of the festival so confident that they had a success on their hands that an Austrian aristocrat had spontaneously decided to throw a huge party in order to fête both me and my piece and what they were convinced would be its *grande successo*. We agreed to meet on stage and then go off together . . . but no princess arrived, only the Stuckenschmidts, with whom I went to a trattoria, the 'Re degli Amici'. Ingeborg had fainted during the performance, which she had attended with the Austrian cultural attaché, and was taken straight home. Luchino Visconti had asked his neighbours in the stalls to make less noise, whereupon he had been roundly abused and called every name under the sun.

At the stage door, a young man seized my hand and said that he had liked the piece enormously and that I should not for a moment imagine that the whole house had been against me. Not until several years later did I discover that my admirer was the classical philologist and cultural philosopher, Franco Serpa, a music lover whom I was to get to know properly in 1961/2, when he was secretary of the Accademia Filarmonica. We are still friends several decades later. In 1966 he helped me to set the Latin fragments of Virgil that I published under the title *Die Musen Siziliens* by teaching me how the lines should be stressed in keeping with their underlying rhythms. He is also the author of one of the finest essays on the myth of Orpheus and Eurydice.

The next morning's papers were uniformly devastating in their critiques, or so I was assured. I felt like a leper and lacked the confidence to attend any concerts or festival parties. I remained for only a couple more days in the city (on the evening of the second performance I dined at the home of the musicologist, Luigi Magnani, and only during the dessert did one of the servants confide to me in a whisper that the Opera had telephoned to say that everything had gone smoothly). I saw and heard nothing, but suffered a kind of breakdown and returned, ashen-faced, to Ischia. Thanks to the media, Lucia had learnt of my Roman débâcle and said that it was best if I avoided big cities in future and simply stayed with her at 5 Via Cesotta, with the old eel in the well, with her mother, who was dying and who groaned loudly day and night, with her sons and with my music. There was no doubt that I was overjoyed to be back. Spring had come, and I could begin work on Act Two of *König Hirsch*. Among the letters that were forwarded to me from Rome was a brief note:

> Thursday, 366 Via Salaria, Rome
> Dear Henze,
> In spite of the audience's boorish behaviour, I heard your opera yesterday evening and did so, moreover, with great interest. I already knew your ballet, *Der Idiot*, which was staged in Venice two years ago – and now I have found in *Boulevard Solitude* the same consistency of approach and fidelity to your principles that constitute your true artistic nature. I cannot say that I am in total agreement with all that you are aiming to achieve, but I assure you of my interest in your work and hope to make your personal acquaintance, if possible here in Rome or else on Ischia. Please accept my thanks. Sincere good wishes, Luchino Visconti.

I no longer remember whether or not I replied to these lines, but I do know that from the moment that I received them I kept hoping that, unannounced, Visconti would turn up on Ischia and that I then would get to know him. I harboured this hope for years. I did not even know what he looked like. But it was good to know that Italy's greatest man of the theatre was on my side and that he had time for me or, rather, for my work as a composer.

The first act of *König Hirsch* lasts around ninety minutes and had turned out rather rustic and gauche, a little ungainly, over-orchestrated and full of ups and downs and of absurdities and quotations from Ischian folk music and Neapolitan *opera buffa*. The second act, by contrast, was to be an example of large-scale form, a single, stylistically unified paragraph. I had found my old work rhythm, ensuring that no sentimental attachments disturbed my private life and drawing a line under anything that could come between me and my work. Day in, day out, I worked at the same steady rhythm over the coming weeks and months for the whole of the rest of the year. In September, as I have already reported, I visited Venice with Walton. We broke the journey at Bologna, so that he could initiate me into the delights of *fonduta di tartufi bianchi* at the world-famous Pappagallo. A few hours later we were just entering St Mark's Square in Venice, followed by a *facchino* with our luggage, when who should I see but the director Carl Ebert, who was then intendant of the Städtische Oper, Berlin, walking up and down in conversation with his business manager. I already knew that they had come to Venice to ask me to entrust them with the world-première production of *König Hirsch*, but since our meeting was not due to take place until the following morning, I left Ebert in peace and retired for the night – I think it was to the Hotel alla Fenice. The following morning the four of us – the director of the Venice Biennale, Alessandro Piovesan, the two Berliners and I – met at Piovesan's offices and agreed on a co-production between Venice and Berlin.

At the end of November I travelled to London for the first night of Walton's *Troilus and Cressida*. On the ferry from Calais to Dover I was cross-examined by a British customs official. How much money did I have on me, he wanted to know (very little, far too little), and where did I plan to stay? I told him. Finally he asked me whether I liked Walton's music, and – just to be on the safe side – I said that I did. In *Behind the Façade*, Susana reports that the authorities telephoned her in London in order to check the truth of what I had said. I do not think she was making it up. The Waltons' Bentley was parked opposite the platform at Victoria Station, where the two of them were waiting to collect me. In her book, Susana says that I stayed with them at Lowndes Cottage, but that is not true. I had a small room in a guest house at 19 Ovington Gardens, SW3, with a coin-operated gas fire and a wall-mounted payphone in an unheated corridor. But none of this mattered. I was in good spirits and enjoyed London enormously. Needless to say, I saw Ashton – and it may well be that it was during this visit that we first discussed the possibility of working together, but I cannot be sure any longer. And I also saw the former British cultural officers, all of whom had now returned home to civvy street and were working as publishers, concert and theatre agents, art critics and members of the British Council. Every evening I went to the theatre or opera. On one occasion – oddly enough – I remember seeing Thornton Wilder's *The Matchmaker* at the Old Vic with the wife of Igor Markevich and her sister. On another occasion I saw a highly entertaining new musical, *The Boy Friend*, at Wyndham's Theatre, just off Leicester Square.

I was often the guest of the Waltons and each time would find myself introduced to virtuosos, conductors, fellow composers and managers. If only all successful composers behaved as cordially and selflessly towards their younger colleagues! Needless to say, I attended the final rehearsals and first night of *Troilus and Cressida* and also returned for the third performance. I had certain difficulties with the piece (perhaps the libretto is at fault?), there was something that struck me as not quite right, even though (or perhaps because?) it is all so brilliantly orchestrated. I could not explain it even to myself, and, of course, I took care not to show my perplexity. There was a holiday atmosphere at Lowndes Cottage, and rightly so. There had been enough trouble at the rehearsals, and all involved had been forced to suffer untold agonies – the piece itself, with all its years of work and the doubts bound up with it, seemed to be in jeopardy. But, in the event, it all went well: Flash Harry – Sir Malcolm Sargent – finally managed to master the score, and the first night ended on a note of triumph. A few days later I travelled on to Paris and stayed until early January in the Faubourg St-Germain with the musicologist and Mahler biographer, Henry-Louis de La Grange, completing Act Two of *König Hirsch* and sending the score in the German Embassy's diplomatic bag to Mainz. Then, with Paris still in the grip of winter, I returned to Ischia and to my life of seclusion in order to attack Act Three. I now had a date for the first performances in Venice and Berlin: September 1956. So I still had more than a year in which to complete the piece.

Was it during the early summer of 1955 that I went to Darmstadt to run a composition course with Boulez and Maderna? Yes, it must have been then, and a depressing experience it turned out to be: young composers who preferred to express themselves in a musical language that dated back to the days before Webern were simply refused admittance. Maderna and I had to comfort and calm the students, and I myself got dreadfully bored. It was clear from all that I saw and heard that summer, including the person of Karlheinz Stockhausen, just how remote I had grown from the national musical scene. I was no longer a part of it, and in fact had never really been part of it, never even wanted to be a part of it. It was absurd to accuse me of betraying the cause of modern music, as I was accused of doing at least from the time of the first performance of *König Hirsch*, since I was – and remain – ignorant of modernism's most basic tenets. It is impossible, after all, to betray something to which one has never laid any claim. Stokowski conducted the first performance of my *Quattro poemi* in Frankfurt on 31 May. I arrived too late for the final rehearsal, to which latecomers were not admitted, and I was shut out from the evening's performance, too, since it had already begun when I arrived, and Stokowski would not allow anyone to be admitted until the interval. As a result I did not hear my piece at that time or get to know its conductor. I was happy to be able to return to Italy at the earliest possible moment and complete my opera there. The certainty that I would never return to Darmstadt had something reassuring and cheering about it, it was a cause for celebration.

Unless my memory plays me false, I completed the opera during the early autumn and then rented an apartment in Naples in the Via Bernardo Cavallino high on a hill in the old quarter of Vomero, beneath the monastery of Camaldoli, with an amazing view of the harbour, including Vesuvius in the background. I also spent part of the autumn at the Waltons' house on Ischia, where I stayed with Luigi Nono and Nuria Nono Schoenberg, who were there on their honeymoon. Nuria was a pretty young woman with a tiny snub nose. Brought up in the Viennese tradition, she was Californian by adoption and thought that Italy looked just like California. There was a general feeling of depression, and I found it hard to compose. After the rank excesses of *König Hirsch*, I resolved on a stricter regimen and prescribed for myself a sporadic cycle of strict serial compositions by way of exercise and self-examination and was currently working on my Three Symphonic Studies in addition to some guitar music for Ernst Schnabel's radio play, *Der sechste Gesang*. I occupied the Waltons' part of the house, while the Nonos took the guest room. We shared the common drawing room, with its much-needed open fire. As civilized human beings, all three of us were keen to keep the house clean and tidy, and so when Landlady Walton maintains in *Behind the Façade* that, on their return, they found the villa in ruins, that their marriage bed had 'collapsed' (much to my regret I had slept in it all on my own – and I then weighed a pitiful fifty kilos) and that the fridge and lavatory had been 'smashed', one is bound to wonder how anyone could invent such terrible tales. Did the name of her guests conjure up in her mind the seamier aspects of cultural bolshevism? Perhaps, but such an interpretation would throw an extremely curious light on my old friend's state of mind. William, at all events, would not have been amused. In *Behind the Façade*, Lady Walton also allows herself to repeat the most frightful gossip about Chester Kallman, stories that some obsequious factotum must have retailed to her. She also claims that Stravinsky visited Auden on Ischia, but Stravinsky never set foot on the island. If the meeting took place at all, it can only have been when Auden was in New York, at 77 St Mark's Place in Greenwich Village. Her whole account is like something out of *What the Butler Saw*. And while we are on the subject of factual accuracy: in chapter seventeen of her book ('Guests, Tenants, and Friends'), she says that on one occasion I took to my bed – *chez elle* – when I discovered that Baldur von Schirach, the erstwhile head of the Hitler Youth movement and Gauleiter of Vienna under the Third Reich, was staying as a paying guest under the very same roof, albeit after twenty years in Spandau and on the recommendation of a German baroness. The truth of the matter is that Fausto and I left the house at once. It was my final visit, as the gentle reader may well understand. It was infinitely sad.

Inge and I were now living in Naples, where we had a whole floor to ourselves, with plenty of space and light. What we had not considered was the question of heating: there wasn't any. And this was one of the coldest winters of the century. We made do with little electric fires. The furniture was frightful, the drawing room decorated in light blue damask. None the less, it was here that my godson, Pierre-Dominique Ponnelle, was conceived in the spring of 1956. But for the present it was still winter, bitterly cold and with lots of snow. Wolves prowled the suburbs. I wrote my *Fünf neapolitanische Lieder*, my fingers frozen with the cold, while Ingeborg worked on her *Lieder auf der Flucht*. I can still see her shovelling snow outside the front door, still see the huge camellia in the inner courtyard, its mass of red flowers covered with snow. We remained here until the following year, when, by a happy accident, I discovered another apartment, centrally located and much more attractive. It was even possible to heat it.

My mother visited me during the spring of 1956 and was pleased to meet Fräulein Bachmann. We showed her the city (the delights of which somehow escaped her) and drove with her out into the Campagna. One day – it was a Sunday, and Ingeborg had just finished typing out a fair copy of her *Anrufung des Großen Bären*, which was due at her publisher's the following morning – the three of us drove along the Amalfi coast towards Ravello. It was a beautiful day, the sort of day that makes you feel glad to be alive. But disaster awaited us on our return in the evening: Rufus, our black tom-cat, who had been given to us by the German consul, had been left alone in the apartment, and, whether from pique or simply to pass the time, had ripped the typescript into a thousand shreds. Mother said to me later how much she admired Ingeborg's equanimity and her ability to make light of the matter, though it must have caused her a great deal of mental anguish. She needed a week or more to retype the whole of the manuscript.

We often went to the cinema and, together with the rest of Naples's younger generation, became fans of Marilyn Monroe and James Dean. We read American thrillers in terrible Italian translations, which at least had the advantage of often employing the imperfect tense, so that we were able to practise its use in this way. For the most part, we spoke Italian together.

We finally met Visconti in Milan in the late autumn of 1955 – or was it, as Ingeborg claims in her notes to *Der junge Lord*, in January 1956? The very next day we were allowed to sit in on his rehearsals for a revival of his production of *La traviata*, with Callas as Violetta and Giulini as the conductor. The incredibly beautiful sets and costumes were by Lila de Nobili, to whom we were likewise introduced at this time. After each rehearsal we would accompany Visconti back to his hotel. I thought he looked wonderful, like a jet-black raven, and was captivated by his charm, his bass voice and by his harsh Milanese accent, with its uvular 'r'. On a couple of evenings we went out with him and his friends. Milan was dark, wet and foggy. Ingeborg wrote:

> During the dress rehearsal of *La traviata* [. . .], in a cold, creaking box, for a few short hours a rainbow must have arched high above a rain-swept Milan since it was then that Italian opera was convincingly reborn and my view of opera – a view that extended, I fear, from condescension to blank indifference – began to waver and I suddenly felt a fanatical interest in this art form.

The following week I attended a party at Visconti's house in Rome, but I found the cultural differences between the other guests and me depressing in the extreme: these people, for the most part Italian film-makers, actors, dandies and scriptwriters with whom Visconti regularly consorted, were all so self-confident, eloquent, witty and totally lacking in hang-ups – the very opposite of me. I was so intimidated by their glamour and arrogance that I forgot what little Italian I knew and, terrified of making a fool of myself, ended up saying nothing. Later that same evening, instead of returning to my hotel, I fled the Eternal City and drove back to Naples at high speed through the fog and rain and by the next morning was back at home with Ingeborg, who had hurried on ahead of me. Here I was on safe ground, here I had no problems about who I was, and did not feel awkward and provincial.

Visconti visited me in Naples and we also wrote delightful letters to one another, all of which I have kept. Hidden beneath the gruff exterior of his mercilessly caustic wit and the imperious gestures of a prince from Lombardy was a friendly, sensitive man. It annoyed him that I liked Mahler's music and he felt that he would really have to wean me away from the whole of this *pesantezza tedesca*. In February 1956 he wrote to me from Milan to say that he had just staged a kind of ballet–pantomime at La Scala, *Mario e il mago*, with Jean Babilée in the title role. On more than one occasion during the rehearsals (or it might have been during the later performances), Luchino had taken Babilée with him into the city's suburbs to show him the sort of dance marathons that were then all the rage in Italy. Babilée was to soak up the atmosphere that Visconti wanted to recreate in a *spettacolo* that he had promised to stage for the dancer and his Ballets Jean Babilée, a new company that was currently being set up in Paris. It was to be called *Maratona di danza* and would open in the early autumn. Would I provide the music for it? I wrote to tell Visconti that I was worried about the lack of time, but he reassured me, saying merely that I would manage. I set to work as soon as the scenario arrived. (As I later discovered, the story was surprisingly similar to that of Horace McCoy's 1935 novel, *They Shoot Horses, Don't They?*, which Sydney Pollack made into a film in 1969.) It required a neo-realist score, since Visconti's variant was set in a hangar in the suburbs of Rome, where young people take part in these endurance contests until they collapse with exhaustion. It was a crude enough story evoked in a series of scenes that resembled nothing so much as flashlight photographs of a barely acknowledged reality and, together with the garish colours of the young local painter, Renzo Vespignani, was meant to create a picture of social misery and cultural impoverishment. Two dance bands on stage alternate with each other and with a cheap gramophone, which plays at certain hours of the morning and night. The sounds that emanate from the orchestra pit are emphatically baroque in character, recalling Gluck and the *St Matthew Passion*, in order to ensure the most glaring contrast between the ideal nobility and Olympian neo-classicism that find expression in the pit and the bitter reality depicted on stage.

On 14 May, with the score still far from finished, I set off from Naples, intending to drive to Paris for the initial stage rehearsals, but first of all I called in at Ascoli Piceno to see our delightful Sardinian friend, Gigi Timo, who was doing his military service there, not leaving him until early on the Monday morning. By late afternoon I was driving along a country road near Lodi when my car – a brand new Fiat with customized bodywork – hit a milk cart, smashing the car and breaking my right collarbone, so that I ended up in hospital, where my arm and thorax were cased in plaster of Paris, as was customary at that time. Even though a good friend of mine in Milan, the composer Vittorio Fellegara, continued to work on the score of *Maratona*, acting as my amanuensis, there was still so much of it missing that in the end I gave up the unequal struggle. As a result, the Ballets Babilée had the most appalling gap in their inaugural programme, a gap which, at this late stage, could be filled only with makeweight items. Visconti's staging of *Maratona*, the evening's principal attraction, not to say, its *raison d'être*, had to be abandoned, and the fault was entirely mine. Luchino was very sweet about it all and sent me a sympathetic telegram, consoling me on my misfortune, but he made no attempt to visit me in hospital when he came to Milan to cast his vote. Perhaps he had no time. I felt terrible at this failure and desperately ashamed at the damage that I had done. I have no idea whether I was ever really forgiven.

The plaster cast was finally removed six weeks later and I immediately returned to Forio, where I spent the whole of August. Ashton had rented a large Moorish house by the harbour, with large, high-ceilinged, empty rooms, where we worked every day on the scenario for *Ondine*, which was loosely based on Friedrich de la Motte Fouqué's novella. It was Ashton's idea to write it in the style of a traditional *ballet d'action*, as Petipa and Tchaikovsky had done with *Swan Lake*, for example. And so we adopted a narrative method that required the composer to submit, unprotestingly and unconditionally, to the choreographer's timing. If I remember aright, the timing was all worked out during these weeks in Forio and did not need to be altered later. I should have preferred it if the ballet had been a little less conventional. On the other hand, Ashton allowed me to transfer the original's German Romantic setting, with its mossy banks and freshwater torrents, to my new, stonily classical maritime home, with the result that the score contains the odd reminiscence of Neapolitan folk-songs. The knight Huldbrand became Prince Palemon, his wicked German paramour,

Bertalda, was renamed Beatrice and the water sprite, Kühleborn, became Tirrenio, the Mediterranean's saltwater king. Ashton had no objection to all this, not least because an earlier version of *Ondine* had already been danced at Covent Garden by a certain Miss Frampton at Easter 1844, 'the Music selected from the Popular French Ballet of the same name'. Here, too, the action had been moved to southern climes.

The sets by Lila de Nobili depicted Nordic, neo-Gothic castles and forests, but also elements of a southern coastal landscape: as was later to become clear, this indecision was to lead to fairly blatant incompatibilities between music and stage picture. Needless to say, I attempted to adapt my music to reflect my colleagues' stylistic approach – a sophisticatedly imitative, reconstructive approach – but it never really worked. For sets such as these, one would really have needed a different sort of music – a nineteenth-century score by Weber or Mendelssohn or even Cesare Pugni (whose own setting of the Ondine legend was seen in London in 1843 and later revived in St Petersburg). But we could not have known all this as we sat together in Forio in the summer of 1956, hotly debating our piece's form and content. In the evening we would go down to the Café Maria Internazionale on the piazza, and I would sometimes gaze longingly at Auden's old table: perhaps he and/or Kallman would have had a few good ideas. But Fred refused to hear of any outside interference. He wanted to create his *opus maximum* without any help from others and without any other English influence apart from his own. It was to be a simple, popular but, at the same time, original and irresistible piece and, moreover, the first great ballet for his star pupil, Margot Fonteyn, whom he himself had created. Covent Garden advised me to score the piece lightly for reduced forces and ensure that it could be sight-read, so that the work could be performed in smaller theatres on tour and quickly learnt by provincial orchestras with a minimum of rehearsals. Later, when it had become famous, this production of *Ondine* was twice seen at the Met, as well as at the Bolshoi and the Kirov in St Petersburg. But it never reached the English provinces. In large houses the music sounds a little thin – one day I should like to add a few wind instruments, especially in the darker registers.

Our last few days on Ischia were overshadowed by a certain disquiet caused by a series of telegrams from Jean-Pierre Ponnelle in Berlin. Each proved more urgent than the last: the conductor, Hermann Scherchen, had starting rehearsing *König Hirsch* and, red pencil in hand, had set about cutting one aria after another. I was to come to Berlin immediately in order to rescue my piece. And so I went to Berlin, where I found that Jean-Pierre had not been exaggerating. Almost speechless with anger, I demanded to see the gentleman in question and received his now proverbial reply: 'But, my dear, we don't write arias today.' 'Who are "we"?' I asked. 'Oh, forgive me,' he retorted. From now on we fought over every bar of every aria – the arias, after all, were the best part of the opera, certainly its most interesting feature, since it was here that I had experimented in my attempt to achieve a sense of symmetry and to invent a new concept of beauty. Scherchen also pulled around the tempi of the remaining music and was either too fast or too slow, always on the look-out for ways of imposing his presence on the music and discovering things in it that were not there and that it was never intended to contain.

While Scherchen was attempting to galvanize some signs of twitching life into a torso in the orchestra pit, the lack of a firm director's hand was all too clearly felt on stage. Leonard Steckel, who had been engaged for this purpose, began rehearsals at ten on the dot each morning, but by five past one he was already on his way by taxi to Babelsberg, where he spent the rest of the day at the film studios, starring as Aristide Briand. It was impossible for any of us to talk to him, either to express our concerns or to discuss anything related to the piece. Helga Pilarczyk, who was playing the part of Costanza, would burst into tears and sob uncontrollably, since she was receiving no direction. The first night finally brought everything to a head. Much has been written and said about this performance. *Pianissimo* passages were drowned out by mocking laughter, and there was constant howling and whistling. This time it was not Ingeborg who fainted, but my mother. Tatjana Gsovsky climbed up into the gods and gave the trouble-makers a piece of her mind, but it did no good, the noise continued as before. Scherchen, who was verbally abused in the course of the evening, skilfully steered the rolling wreck through the home straits, and the curtain finally closed, allowing the *cori spezzati* of boos and bravos to break loose with all its force. It seemed to go on for ever, and lasted at least half an hour. I cannot claim that it gave me any satisfaction. Everything had turned out so differently from what I had hoped and imagined. We were not in Venice at the Fenice, but in Berlin, in the Kantstraße, within a stone's throw of the Zoo Station. A fair number of my arias had not been heard, and instead of a new work cast in classical metres that might possibly have marked the beginning of a new way of thinking about music, all that had been heard was a grotesque and distorted travesty. The production team, too, had remained indifferent to the innovative possibilities on offer or, more likely, had not even noticed them. A few days later I set off back to Naples and managed to write off my recently repaired Fiat just outside Karlsruhe. Among the casualties was a crate of wonderful Burgundy from Beaune, a first-night present from Jean-Pierre's father. Rarely can the asphalt of an autobahn have soaked up a nobler vintage.

Meanwhile, back in Naples, our workmen had made precious little progress on our new flat and only one room was usable, but fortunately I did not have to stay there for long – at the end of a few miserable weeks I left for London, where I spent the whole of the winter, working on the music for *Ondine* in almost daily contact with the master himself. I had a room in the house of Alexander Grant, who was dancing the part of Tirrenio. It was in Battersea, not far from the Thames, with its paper mills and power station, from which thick, black coal dust poured, seeping through the cracks in the windows and leaving marks on my manuscript paper. Ashton insisted that my piece contain 'tunes', by which he meant clearly recognizable melodies that could be identified as such. The dancers needed them for their *airs de danse*, I could see that. I went to the opera house every evening to watch them at their work and to see how they reacted physically to music. It was a sort of life class, allowing me to grasp what music can do and what it may not do, so that the dancers can leap into the air and cover the width and depth of the stage unhindered.

The best thing I saw that winter was the Royal Ballet's new production of *The Firebird*, lovingly reconstructed and directed by several of the people who had been actively involved in the first production in 1910 and who could still remember what it had been like. Among those involved on this occasion were the designer Nathalia Goncharova and the ballet master Serge Grigoriev and his wife Lubov Tchernicheva. And Margot Fonteyn, who was dancing the Firebird in the new production, had studied the role with her predecessor in the part, Tamara Karsavina, for whom the role had originally been choreographed by Fokine. There was a palpable – and heart-warming – sense of authenticity about the performance, as though this magical work had just been created. Virtually none of the dancing was classical: the Princesses danced barefoot in the style of Isadora Duncan, while Kashchey and his Demons recalled the world of Russian folklore. Prince Ivan was purely mimed, with only the Firebird herself dancing in the classical manner. It was a brilliant idea that worked wonderfully well as a dramaturgical device. The music systematically and unambiguously underscored this tripartite division. It was one of the most intelligent productions I have ever seen in the theatre. Even today I still recall it with immense enthusiasm and cannot get over the perfect rapport between music and gesture and the extent to which the music is clearly laid out along narrative lines. It is as though Fokine, Stravinsky and Diaghilev were all children, joking like children while telling each other – and us – this tale.

I got to know some of Ashton's other ballets. One was the three-act *Sylvia*, with music by Léo Delibes, which was fairly saccharine and camp. Another was a bright and modern *Daphnis and Chloe* designed by John Craxton and based on the original libretto for Ravel's *symphonie chorégraphique*. Uncut and in its proper setting and original function, the music seemed to me far more attractive than in the suites that one hears in the concert hall.

London was far gloomier then than it is now and still revealed numerous traces of the devastation caused by German bombs and missiles. Apart from the damp and the yellow smog, there was also the dense mist in which it was perfectly possible to get completely lost and, if not rescued in time, never be seen again. You could hear the taxis rattling by, close at hand or in the distance, but could never see them, not even their headlights. You stumbled and groped in the direction of the noise or heard steps that grew faster the closer you got to them. You might finally reach an underground station only to find it was closed. I urgently needed human company. Ingeborg was away on business. I felt sad and embittered from the previous autumn, the pain of parting still had to be worked out of my system. Instead, I had to get on with my work, in this cold and damp foreign land. One evening the fog seeped in through the draughty scenery doors that are all that separates the Covent Garden stage from Floral Street and, slowly growing denser, filled the orchestra pit until the players could no longer see the conductor or their music and, one by one, stopped playing. On the Thames the royal swans choked to death on motor oil, ships' sirens wailed continuously and swarms of starlings blackened the skies above Trafalgar Square or squawked in the leafless trees. The pubs were all crowded with people.

Whenever I wanted a break from composing, I would play works by my favourite classical composers on the piano that Covent Garden had placed at my disposal and that filled most of Tirrenio's drawing room. One day the housekeeper, Mrs Griggs, heard me playing Schubert, and when Alex and Fred looked in on me that evening, she announced that 'Mr Henze has written some wonderful music today'. All my fellow lodgers gathered to hear this miracle of modern music and, of course, I played what I had written in the course of the day, not what Mrs Griggs had heard while polishing or making coffee that afternoon. I noticed the look of dismay that flitted across my audience's faces, especially that of Mrs Griggs herself, and accepted it as an omen. But otherwise Ashton was perfectly satisfied with all that I was producing. The first night was now scheduled for the autumn of 1957, which unfortunately meant that I had to hurry. My publisher, too, was putting me under pressure.

The first act was already orchestrated and the second completed in short score when news reached me in London that our new apartment in Naples was ready, and so Ingeborg and I headed back to the South and to our beautiful rooms on the top floor of 6 Via Generale Parisi on the Piazzetta Nunziatella, which took their respective names from the eponymous military academy and its accompanying church. Pompeian red and Spanish Baroque mixed with the sound of trumpets and the cries of street vendors, while beneath us lay an overgrown orange grove, in which nightingales would cease their carolling at dawn, indignant at being disturbed by the earthly aubades of concupiscent cats. Beneath us was the old English embassy, where Goethe and William Beckford had once been guests of the Hamiltons. The Riviera di Chiaia and, in the other direction, Santa Lucia, the Teatro San Carlo and the Via Toledo were all only a few minutes' walk away. We acquired our furniture, *poco a poco*, from local junk shops, each item stretching our parlous finances to breaking point. At that time I was not only writing music but also arts features, including articles on the Neapolitan canzona and Visconti and even a radio play for the 'Radio Essay' slot on South German Radio in Stuttgart. (The station was then being run by Alfred Andersch, with the young Hans Magnus Enzensberger and Helmut Heißenbüttel as his assistants.) The piece – *The Revolt at San Nazzaro: Opera for Sicilian Marionettes* – was broadcast at half past ten at night on 24 May 1957, using music by Jimmy Giuffre and Chico Hamilton. The producer was Wilfried Willemzig and the cast included actors of the stature of Elisabeth Flickenschildt and Charles Regnier.

Ingeborg had arrived, followed in swift succession by spring and summer, and *Ondine* had been completed. The third act contained not only a *grand pas de six*, so that the company's solo dancers who were not otherwise needed in the piece would have a few variations for themselves, but also a divertissement for the younger dancers, especially the brilliant Brian Shaw, who were playing Pulcinella and other characters from Neapolitan *commedia dell'arte* and who then, at a word from Kühleborn/Tirrenio, were turned into water sprites and ghosts, destroying the palace of the faithless Palemon. For this, I wrote a set of variations for piano and orchestra on Scarlatti's 'Cat's Fugue', delightful dance music and, as such, a declaration of my love for Naples. I later expanded the piano part and added a cadenza to produce a new piece for the concert hall, *Jeux des Tritons*. In London there were difficulties at the rehearsals. I am not sure if they stemmed from the piano reduction, which may not have been an accurate transcription of the orchestral part, or whether they were due to the pianist, who, according to Freddy, played 'with her tits'. The music never got a look-in, everything sounded the same. And Ashton injured himself, so that work on the production was delayed. Meanwhile, I had managed to record the whole of the score with Hesse Radio, and when they heard it in London and heard how much the sound of the full orchestra differed from that of the cottage piano in the rehearsal room at Baron's Court, it was decided to postpone the première until the following autumn and to make a fresh start on the choreography. It was suddenly possible to hear the orchestral textures. Ashton wrote to me at this time:

> Dearest Hans,
>
> Your music is wonderful and I am thrilled with it. And I must say you have really done a wonderful job. But it is very difficult and on the tape it is very different from the piano. It is all so much more sustained and intense. The result of all this is that I have had to revise all the work I had done before in the light of the orchestration and bring it all much more 'au point' and I work both from the tape and the piano. Well, all this is a slow and very thorough process as I want to really interpret your music and get out of it all the inherent richness. Both Michael and Fonteyn are now working with a real love and concentration, but we work slowly and calmly and give everything we have to it. I am completely absorbed. I never go out and live a nun's existence. So I really don't think it will be ready till about November. I will not let it go out till I am satisfied with every detail as it must be the biggest thing of my career whether it is liked or not and it is a new music, written for me and I must give to it my life blood and all my experience and craft and pray to God for inspiration on top of all that. The 2nd Act is magnificent, better than Tristan [!], but it requires a new approach choreographically to anything I have ever done before. My only complaint is that it is fiendishly difficult. But that must be overcome somehow, and that the 3rd Act is too long. You must be pre-

> pared to cut. When I know it better I will have my suggestions. But on 1st hearing I think the pas de 16 is too long. You exceeded the minutage by 10 minutes which is grave. I will not cut anything in the 1st Act and the 2nd which is a jewel of luminosity. I love you more than ever for your great efforts on my behalf. Your music is distinguished, romantic and intense and should point to the future.

The previous year, on 26 May 1956, Dietrich Fischer-Dieskau had given the first performance of my *Fünf neapolitanische Lieder* in Frankfurt, but I did not attend the performance. Nor had I been present in Bielefeld in April 1954 to hear the first performance of my *Ode to the West Wind*, and did not hear *Die schlafende Prinzessin* in Essen in the June of that year or the Symphonic Studies in Hamburg in February 1956. It was as though I was slowly sloughing off old skins. But where was I really heading? Did I mean to sink without trace into Naples's cultural pessimism and never be seen or heard of again? Or was I still bent on creating a world of my own, a theatre in which to live out my dreams and desires, a bucolic scenario with shepherds and satyrs and heaven knows what to replace the ashen quotidian world of radio controllers and music advisers? I think that that is how it must have been: there was still an element of evasiveness, a sense of flight, not into work and music but into the world of fairy-tales and masks. In the spring of 1957 I wrote *Nachtstücke und Arien*, a setting of Ingeborg's 'Freies Geleit' and 'Im Gewitter der Rosen'. The latter initially consisted simply of a four-line stanza:

> Wherever we turn in the tempest of roses,
> The night is still lit by thorns, and the thunder
> Of leaves, once so muted within the bushes,
> Now follows us hard on our heels.

But for reasons of symmetry Ingeborg wrote four more lines for me, lines that make the poem even more beautiful:

> Wherever the roses' fire is doused,
> Rain washes us into the river. O night yet more distant!
> But a leaf that once struck us now floats on the billows
> And follows us down to the mouth of the river.

These lines more or less sum up the dominant mood of the *Nachtstücke und Arien*, even if the other 'aria' is a choral hymn to a beautiful future when the atom bomb no longer exists. These sentiments continue to reverberate throughout the instrumental finale, at the heart of which are a handful of notes from the epilogue to *Ondine*.

With this score I had reached a position that could hardly have been further removed from that of the so-called Darmstadt School, so it is scarcely surprising that at its first performance at Donaueschingen on 20 October 1957, under Hans Rosbaud's outstanding direction, three representatives of the other wing – Boulez, my friend Gigi Nono and Stockhausen – leapt to their feet after only the first few bars and pointedly left the hall, eschewing the beauties of my latest endeavours. Throughout the evening, heads continued to be shaken at my cultural *faux pas*, and Ingeborg and I suddenly found ourselves cold-shouldered by people who actually knew us, foremost among whom was Herr Dr Heinrich Strobel. There was a sense of indignation throughout the building, no doubt made worse by the fact that the audience had acclaimed our piece in the liveliest manner, and I found myself suffering a kind of excommunication – the very thing, in fact, that I wanted most of all. The impression arose that the whole of the world of music had turned against me, a situation that was really quite comical, but also somewhat disturbing from an ethical point of view: for what had become of artistic freedom? Who had the right to confuse moral and aesthetic criteria? Teddy Adorno? After all, *Nachtstücke* is a beautiful piece. As he was saying goodbye to me at the end of the evening, Alfred Andersch sighed: 'Ah, what's to be done? Next time, write something less pastel-coloured, then everything will be fine.' It was as simple as that. A few years later, on 23 and 25 September 1961, *Nachtstücke und Arien* was chosen to open the Berlin Festival. Karl Böhm conducted the Berlin Philharmonic, and the soloist was Gloria Davy, who had also given the first performance in Donaueschingen.

On 24 September 1957, a month before this novel experience in Donaueschingen, the Städtische Oper in Berlin had staged the first performance of *Maratona di danza*. I have retained only the most diffuse recollections of this period: I can still see Klaus Geitel's flat in Wilmersdorf, with its grand piano and with sketches of my *Sonata per archi* lying open on the music rest. (I remember having difficulty writing at this time and not knowing how things could continue, perhaps I had never been able to write properly, and the Neapolitan sun was now forcing me to see that.) It was here that the *Maratona* team met in the evenings: Jean Babilée, a warm-hearted, witty man with clean-cut features, eyes as bright as a panther's, the body of an athlete and immense charisma on stage; the Dutch choreographer,

Dick Sanders; the young Renzo Vespignani, a man of the people who single-handedly painted all the sets himself (as was usual in certain circles at that time – Lila did so, too; it gave the whole production a very special quality, I have never seen it done better); and Luchino with his assistants from Rome. Dick had already rehearsed all the dances before the maestro arrived. Luchino now proceeded to pick them all to pieces, one by one, and to turn drama and dramatic dance into the theatre of realism. He did so, moreover, without moving from his seat: in the manner of all film directors, he remained at his desk in the stalls, issuing instructions to his assistants who, as though stung by a tarantula, would leap up on to the stage, where they would harangue the people in question, repositioning them, sending them away or inviting them to remain. I was impressed by the composure, not to say condescension, that Visconti radiated both at work and in daily life, and impressed, too, by the ease with which he cast his spell on all around him. I, too, was one of these people and, from an emotional point of view, was in his immediate line of fire. On one occasion – it was at a stage rehearsal at which the orchestra was also present – I gave what he thought were opposite instructions to his own for lowering the main curtain, with the result that for days he refused to speak to me. It affected me so badly that I developed a fever and he had to come and visit me and forgive me before I could get up again and continue to work on the production.

The show looked wonderful, bilious and aggressive, provocative and somewhat stranger than anything that had been seen in Berlin for a very long time. It was the exact opposite of what was then in vogue and, as such, an exotic arrival on the city's current arts scene. During these weeks in Berlin, those of us who were involved in the production would often go to the theatre to see other plays that were on. I had to sit on Luchino's right and translate for him, since he was deaf in his left ear, which had been damaged while he was being interrogated during the war in Rome. We saw several Brecht productions at the Schiffbauerdamm and also Fritz Kortner's production of *Hamlet* at the Schiller-Theater, which Visconti enjoyed so much that he wrote to Kortner to say so. Both during and after the première of *Maratona* on 24 September, there were again demonstrations in the audience. At one point in the piece, I remember hearing a man shout across to Berlin's Minister for the Arts in a resounding voice: 'Tiburtius, is this your cup of tea?' People howled. I felt somewhat embarrassed on account of my foreign colleagues, but Luchino thought it was fine as it was: it was all very interesting, he said. I was sad that these wonderful weeks in Berlin with all my delightful friends were now over. I could have gone on working with them for ever.

I returned to Naples and set about scoring the *Sonata per archi* that I had started in Berlin. It is a piece that clearly reflects the aesthetic and compositional problems that exercised me at that time. In spite of my recent professional excursion into the world of neo-realism, my main concern was a spiritual examination of the different forms of German, English and Italian Romanticism – or what is commonly described as 'Romanticism'. I was permanently preoccupied with dreamers and nymphs, spirits and monsters, artificial psychoses and genuine neuroses, but without seeing myself as a Romantic. During my time in Berlin, Visconti had spoken to me more than once of his desire that I should set *Der Prinz von Homburg*. I had consistently refused. He had read Kleist only in Italian or French translations and could not know that, for a German, Kleist's language is itself already music, music that sounds like a vast storm-tossed orchestra. Curiously enough, he could not imagine *Der Prinz von Homburg* as a play: for him, the piece made sense only in the form of an opera. My reservations annoyed him and he threatened to end our friendship, with the result that I finally relented. I still have a photograph of him inscribed with the words 'Le Prince de Hombourg pour notre amitié', which he gave me as a souvenir to keep me constantly reminded of the day on which we had made our peace or, rather, when I had finally capitulated. I hurried back to Naples to confess my sins to Ingeborg and report upon my failure. As soon as she had recovered from the shock, she threw on her armour like some latterday Joan of Arc, sharpened her quill and wrote the most beautiful and intelligent libretto for *Der Prinz von Homburg*, thereby safeguarding me against all possible shame. I was now confronted by the task of having to depict two totally different worlds, the world of dreams and that of reason. Or that of frenzy and enthusiasm in stark contrast to that of sobriety and reflection. Sometimes I also thought of the idea of artistic freedom in contrast to the idea of servility and subservience to laws and rules and conventions. But I still had to face up to the dialectical problems of the music to *Der Prinz von Homburg*. I was still engaged in the preliminary skirmishes.

The String Sonata was finally performed in Zurich on 21 March 1958, when Paul Sacher conducted the Collegium Musicum. Sacher was kind enough to invite me to conduct one of the Collegium's concerts the following year, when I remember giving *Apollo et Hyazinthus* and *Rosa Silber*, together with Schubert's Fifth Symphony. I had difficulties with my stick technique, especially in the Schubert, and turned for advice to Hans Rosbaud, who was living in Zurich at that time. Throughout the whole week of the rehearsals he would come to my hotel first thing in the morning and give me lessons. He also came with me to a number of the rehearsals, when Sacher also offered his support. I think this is the only real training I have ever had in conducting; in everything else I have had to rely upon trial and error. In fact, I never had much opportunity to practise the art of conducting – not that this prevented me from putting myself forward as conductor of the London première of *Ondine*, the date of which had now been fixed for 27 October 1958.

The year 1958 was to prove a particularly peaceful one. Together with a couple of our friends, Klaus Geitel and I spent May and June touring the Balkan States and Greece by car. At that time there were still no tourists, and every trip was a voyage of discovery. Among my various memories are a veritable feast in a beautiful old hotel in Zagreb, huge turtles ambling across the motorway between Zagreb and Belgrade that had been built by German prisoners of war, and resting in the shade one Sunday afternoon, while boys and girls cycled past singing Mahlerian folk-songs. In Macedonia Muslim children threw mud at Klaus Geitel's Mercedes. In Skopje I carried on in an authoritarian manner and not only impressed my travelling companions but also ensured that I got the only room in the hotel with a bath. (It was reserved for a party official.) Most of the roads were unpaved, there was dust everywhere, and it was hot. One day we managed only sixty kilometres. In the first little town that we came to in northern Greece, the *hôtelière* offered to have sex with us, which gave us our first impression of the Hellenes' famed hospitality. And then there was Meteora, storks' nests and a cow in calf on a country road. We had ourselves hauled up in baskets by rope to a monastery, where we admired the ancient mosaics and peered out through tiny windows to see eagles circling the tower and staring back at us, a serious but somewhat absent-minded expression in their eyes. One evening we arrived at a ford – most of the bridges were still destroyed – where a group of young lads were washing horses. They came over to say hello. Clouds of Hölderlinian light, choruses of cicadas. One of the boys looked for all the world as though he had just descended from the Elysian Fields in an ocean of flames: dark burning eyes, ivory and ebony, I hardly dared look, it was a numinous sight, a Damascene experience, as I realized that the gods were still alive and in our midst.

This majestic and magical encounter by the river had a lasting effect on us all, and none of us felt like talking or fooling around for the whole of the rest of the day. In the distance we saw Olympus thrusting upwards into the cosmos. Later we came to Parnassus and saw the Temple of Apollo at Delphi. We sat down on the steps of the theatre that command an impressive view of the valley below and sat there in silence, sunk deep in thought. In Athens one night I drank tapwater, which made me extremely ill. In Návplion, where I slowly recovered, I worked in desultory fashion on the sketches of my *Kammermusik*, a setting for tenor, three wind instruments, guitar and string quintet of Hölderlin's late hymn, 'In lieblicher Bläue'. The guitar had long fascinated me as an instrument, not least because it had started life among the common people and could trace back its origins to the very beginnings of music but had now developed to the point where it had become supremely sophisticated. It was to play an important role in the present piece and accompany the more intimate, monological sections of the poem. From Návplion it was not difficult to reach Mycenae, where it seemed as though all the myths had only just been created. The very stones started to sing. I felt that at any moment Electra might rush through the Lion Gate, ashes upon her head, and throw herself into the arms of her brother, Orestes.

On Sunday the main square at Návplion was filled with church-goers in their Sunday best, and we watched them as, kindness itself, they greeted and kissed one another in their Greek Orthodox fashion, taking an evident delight in each other's company, apparently happy and contented with life. On the ship back from Patras to Brindisi it was so hot below, in our cabins, that we slept on deck in the company of some Greeks, dozing fitfully until an island suddenly loomed into sight in the grey mists of dawn. The boat glided past it, some distance away. All was at peace with the world. My neighbour, an old fisherman, was not asleep and so I nudged him gently and politely with my elbow, pointing to the island's rocky outline with a questioning look in my eyes.

'Ithaca,' he replied.

6

Inside, your feet are never on the move,
Already they have reached my velvet lands.
Inside, your bones are silv'ry bright-toned flutes
From which I can entice such magic sounds
That death itself will be ensnared by them.

Ingeborg Bachmann, *Lieder auf der Flucht*

The audience that foregathered at Covent Garden for the first performance of my three-act ballet, *Ondine*, on 27 October 1958 was the usual first-night crowd – diplomats and aristocrats, personalities from the world of art and members of the Establishment. In the royal box sat HM Queen Elizabeth II, together with the Queen Mother and Princess Margaret – at that time still a slip of a girl a few years younger than me. The whole of the audience rose to its feet as the little schoolteacher's son from eastern Westphalia signalled to the percussionist to begin a rousing *fortissimo* roll on the side drum that lasted until the conductor down there in the mystic abyss felt that all 2,156 patrons were standing up nice and straight, at which point he solemnly gave the downbeat for the national anthem to start. The orchestra played it standing. I conducted it with a certain emotion: quite apart from the fact that it is a baroque composition (the London Bach wrote a set of variations on it), it was, above all, a private expression of gratitude and praise, a hymn of thanksgiving addressed to my saviour, the Queen, a woman whose father's armies had thwarted the grand designs of the head of the Waffen-SS and stopped people like me from being exterminated or gassed or shot while trying to escape. The British monarch's soldiers and artists had come to liberate me, bringing democracy to me and the Germans and now inviting me over to their own country and to the safety of the spiritual home of men like Shakespeare, Purcell, Oscar Wilde, Francis Bacon and Freddy Ashton. God save the Queen!

The audience sat down again and the orchestra briefly retuned, then an expectant hush fell over the house, and I began the performance, outwardly placid but trembling violently inside. The delicately textured opening chords that anticipate Ondine's recurrent call had already died away, as, too, had the score's first raptly inchoate melodies, when the curtain rose on the opening act to the strains of early Romantic, oceanic horns. The sets were wonderfully lit and showed a Gothic fountain in front of a mossy Anglo-Saxon wood replete with ferns and belladonna in tastefully matching shades of green. Norwegian trolls, faunlike creatures and southern Italian Tritons emerged from the wood one by one. The second act, by contrast, was set in Naples, a setting clear not only from the colours, with their many different shades of red – carrot and coral, pink and carmine, the red of brick and terracotta – but also from the phantasmagorical costumes. Yet what we saw was not Naples as it exists in real life but a world of Neapolitan fairy-tales and dreams, a place transformed and translated, no longer the real world but a scene of art and artifice. At the lighting rehearsals I had watched with a kind of childlike astonishment as Lila de Nobili had managed to conjure up a tempest and shipwreck in this second act, producing stylish and spectacular effects by using techniques from old Italian opera houses that had fallen into virtually total oblivion. The third act seemed to be set in the great hall of the neo-Gothic Fonthill Abbey, which William Beckford had built between 1799 and 1807 in the little Wiltshire village of Fonthill Gifford, not far from Salisbury, but which was now no more than a ruin. Into this princely world come, first, proud wedding guests, who witness Palemon's new-Gothic and neurotic breach of faith, and then, disguised as Neapolitan jesters and led by Tirrenio, the fauns and Tritons and water sprites from the opening act, who rush in bent on revenge, bringing havoc and despair in their wake. And now Ondine rises out of the fountain and a chaconne begins, a ground over which the strings soar aloft in an ever more passionate lament, like some operatic aria: Ondine appears and implants her kiss of death on Palemon's thin-lipped, hapless, loveless and deceitful mouth.

I was too distracted by my conducting to be able to pay as much attention to the production as I should have liked, and it was not until the work was revived on 10 May 1988 that I was finally able to enjoy it – a thirty-year wait occasioned by the fact that not until then had a ballerina been found who could stand comparison with Margot Fonteyn. Only then did I see how intelligent and masterly the choreography was, not only in the solo scenes but especially in the passages involving the *corps de ballet*.

There was a constant sense of flowing movement. Yet even in 1958 I had been intensely aware of the drama from my position in the pit and had even helped to shape it. I shall never forget being so close to the great ballerina and to her huge green eyes that stared in astonishment and seemed to fill the whole stage, nor can I ever forget the way in which she identified with her role and the music, merging the two to form a single entity. How lucky I was! I breathed with her, and when the music grew tender again with its sylphlike strains – as it does in Act One at the start of the great *pas de deux* that follows the breathless chase that placed such huge physical demands on her and her partner – I would make the orchestra play louder so that listeners in the stalls could not hear to what extent this spirit of the air and waves was audibly out of breath.

Ondine was Fonteyn's favourite ballet, or so she said. There is a statue of her in her home town of Reigate that depicts her in this role. She and Ashton regarded it as the culmination of their work together. All her expressive gifts were pressed into service here and I, who was responsible for the music, gave everything that I had at that time in order to create an appropriate world of sound for her, to strike the right note and find ways of flattering and transcending her corporeal incorporeality. I conducted a total of six performances spaced over the next three weeks but by the third week of November had to return to the Continent. When she heard that I was leaving, Fonteyn declared herself incapable of dancing Ondine without me (a claim that turned out in due course to be mistaken). She appeared in the role some fifty-nine times in all between 1958 and 1966. The ballet was filmed and has enjoyed over fifty further productions to date. A few years later Ashton wrote to me, half pleased, half hurt:

> Dearest Hans, [. . .] I hear that Undine is being done in Munchen, Leipzig and West Berlin, Wippen Tal, Stuttgart, Hamburg, Kaiserslautern and that an open-air performance is being planned on lake Titisee. What I want to know is why did not all these people commission something from you before. Why did they all wait for me and then grab, however I am glad I brought you luck. [. . .] Love, Frederick.
>
> P.S. I am trying to sell Undine to Yugoslavia!

A number of my Neapolitan friends, including young Giulio di Majo and Inge, came to London for the first night. At first I failed to recognize Inge who, God knows how and where, had turned herself into a mermaid and looked indescribably beautiful: her clothes and hair sparkled and glittered with jewels and seaweed. Who knows how – perhaps through the kiss of some thin-lipped, hapless and loveless traitor – but the child of a Wendish peasant had been transformed into a mythical, ethereal creature.

Yet she always knew exactly who she was, even if she was sometimes – and increasingly – no longer entirely aware of all the things that were happening to her. But on that evening at Covent Garden she seemed to me the most beautiful woman in the world, notwithstanding the fact that among the other women who graced the house with their presence were Lauren Bacall, Diana Cooper, Florence Montague, Iris Tree and Cheryl Weatherfrog-Dobbs. She was admired by all, especially by me, while Ashton's feelings amounted to love – they had got to know each other during our weeks together on Ischia, when not even the *poetessa*, as Ashton liked to call her, was allowed a glimpse of the *Ondine* scenario on which the two of us were then working.

On later occasions, too, Ingeborg would always make the most incredible effort at our joint premières. When we did *Der Prinz von Homburg* in Hamburg in 1960, we appeared together before the curtain to be greeted by whistles and boos from a small but radical minority that was said to have come from Berlin for the occasion, and she trembled like a leaf. In 1966 she joined me in Salzburg for *Die Bassariden*, and on 7 April 1965 we naturally sat together, hand in hand, in Sellner's box at the Deutsche Oper in Berlin, delighted with the success of *Der junge Lord*, a production whose charm and elegance owed much to the character and artistry of Filippo Sanjust, a friend of ours from Rome, whose family hailed from Sardinia, who had worked with Visconti and whose career as a designer in Germany was launched that evening in Berlin. During our stay in London, I remember on one occasion being absorbed in my work and saying to Inge, unthinkingly, 'Fonteyn is a genius', a remark that brought down on my head a severe reprimand that I have never forgotten, a reproach of which I took good care to make a mental note: one should be wary of using the expression 'genius', Dr Bachmann advised me. Performing artists, people who do not create works of art but merely reproduce them, be they conductors, prima donnas, ballerinas, directors or whatever, may be brilliant and stunningly professional, but the term 'genius' can be applied only to those creative and inventive people who themselves bring new works into the world – and even then, she argued, one should always be careful when using the expression.

I wish I could have stayed longer in London, basking in the success of

Ondine, although I should have preferred to do without the stage fright that I suffered twice a week and that began on the morning of each performance, leaving me terribly isolated. In spite of these contractual obligations, however, I still had enough time to see a little of London (and also to record my *Sonata per archi* for the BBC with the Philharmonia Orchestra). I was splendidly accommodated in rooms that I had rented from the balletomane and novelist, Richard Buckle, in Henrietta Street at the heart of what was then Covent Garden's fruit and vegetable market (the first lorries of fresh carrots and cabbage were unloaded at three in the morning to the most infernal din). The whole area around the opera house (which, baton in hand, I could reach in three minutes on foot) had an immense charm to it, a wonderful architectural magic, especially St Paul's Church, a beautiful example of Inigo Jones's work dating from 1638 and built at the very heart of a market that once served this city of several million. On anyone coming from the country it was bound to leave an impression.

And so, I was not especially pleased to have to pack my bags and leave Alcina's isle, even if other pleasures were awaiting me on the Continent, including the rehearsals and first performance – on 26 November 1958 – of my *Kammermusik 1958*. Introduced by two English artists, the tenor Peter Pears and the guitarist Julian Bream, it was dedicated to Benjamin Britten, whose music I admired so much at that time that the results of that admiration may be heard at various points in my own music and nowhere more so than in the present piece. I had got to know Britten and Pears through the art historian Ludwig of Hesse and his half-Scottish, half-Irish wife, Margaret Geddes ('Aunt Peg'), at the latters' country house at Wolfsgarten near Darmstadt in 1956 or 1957. They were immensely fond of Britten and accompanied him on his concert tours and helped him to develop and organize the Aldeburgh Festival.

Kammermusik 1958 was completed soon after my return from Greece, which is why it always seems to me to reflect my impressions and memories of that country. Its twelve movements may be divided into three sections for voice, clarinet, horn, bassoon, string quintet and guitar, three for instrumental septet alone (without guitar), three for tenor and guitar and three for guitar alone. These last three movements were in fact taken over from my incidental music to Ernst Schnabel's radio play, *Der sechste Gesang* (from the *Odyssey*), and had also been used, in part, in *Maratona*. Under the title Three Tentos, they feature in the repertory of virtually every professional guitarist who considers himself worthy of the name. Like the other sections of the score, these three tientos or ricercares sound much as I imagine Greek music must have sounded and are characterized by the interplay of thematic structures and harmonic textures found throughout the piece as a whole: each of them functions as a nucleus that provides material for the rest of the piece. And I think it is true to say that they contain something of what I think of as Hellenism whenever I hear Stravinsky's orchestral music or his melodrama *Persephone*. It is as though this music – music which, whenever it deals with themes from classical antiquity, invariably recalls the Baroque or Monteverdi or the Renaissance – were a gateway through which one must pass in order to establish or maintain a living relationship with classical Greece, a link with our roots, with all that is most essential in our lives, with the art of metaphor and with tragedy.

Kammermusik 1958 received its first performance in North German Radio's Kleiner Sendesaal in Hamburg. The following day my Three Dithyrambs were premièred in the main studio of West German Radio in Cologne. Scored for chamber orchestra and written as a tribute to my first publisher and patron, Willy Strecker, whom those of us who were left would sorely miss, they were conducted by Hans Rosbaud, but I have virtually no recollection of their performance, only perhaps of the actual sound of these pieces, with their pentatonic street cries and outbursts, their lyricism and their tendency to resort to serial techniques once again. For several years to come I was to display a certain constructivist rigour in my writing, in conscious contrast to my past, with its stag kings, pastorales and mermaids.

My next work for the theatre, *Der Prinz von Homburg*, very much cried out for this contrast between dodecaphony and what – with a pinch of salt – might be termed traditional harmony: the dialectics of the law and its violation, of dreams and reality, of mendaciousness and truth. This dualism was now to become a part of my life as both man and artist and would remain an essential element of it right up to the present day, impinging on my consciousness and engaging my attention on countless subsequent occasions. It is curious to think that it was only now, at the end of 1958, that I hit upon the idea of seriously examining the phenomena of contradictions through the medium of my music.

Throughout the time that I was working on the opera and more especially in its immediate aftermath, I produced a whole series of strict, self-mortifying studies, all of which – I am bound to admit – sound extremely good. *Antifone*, for example, is scored for between four- and sixteen-part instrumental groups that make sounds intended to remind listeners of cries of protestation on the part of caged songbirds and birds of prey. Here I was at pains to avoid the clichés of modernist composers of the period or at least to do so to the extent that the serial material allowed it. Even the rhythms were serially ordered and circumscribed, in the manner of early Flemish isorhythm. I continued to explore the world of polychoral polyphony, while ensuring that, in spite of my being hampered by self-imposed restrictions of every kind, the work as a whole still sounded like music or, at any rate, like *my* music. This was certainly true of *Antifone*, which Karajan conducted with the Berlin Philharmonic at a series of subscription concerts between 20 and 24 January 1962, when both he and I were booed by his subscribers each time the piece was given. A few years earlier Karajan had given a wonderful performance of my *Sonata per archi* in Berlin, but on that occasion these very same listeners had not disrupted the proceedings. I have already described this earlier occasion in Peter Csobádi's book on Karajan, which was published in Germany in 1988:

> The first of my works to be conducted by Herbert von Karajan was *Sonata per archi*, which he gave with his Philharmonic players in Berlin in 1959. (The piece is dedicated to Paul Sacher, who had given its first performance in Zurich in 1958.) He did not stick to the small chamber orchestra resources for which the piece is actually intended, but, just as he had done a few years previously with Strauss's *Metamorphosen*, used the entire string section of the Berlin Philharmonic. The effect was overwhelming. But my fondest memory is of Herr von Karajan inviting me to attend all his rehearsals. He rehearsed each individual part for hours on end and did not give up until phrasing, intonation and build-up of tension were exactly as he wanted them or, rather, exactly as *I* wanted them, since time and again he would ask me: is it right like that? Loud enough? Quiet enough? Do you want more crescendo here, or less? And where should the crescendo end? During the midday break I was privileged to accompany him and Herr von Mattoni on their walk through the Grunewald (his official car followed us at a respectful distance, ready to take us back at any time), after which we returned to the rehearsal room and resumed our work on the piece. As each part and each line was rehearsed, the other players would listen and follow their own

part in the score in order to be able to grasp its tonal, contrapuntal relationship with the others. What we had by the end was a serious piece of music, the first part of which roared and raged, while the thirty-two brief and varied variations of the second were like a single dithyramb on which the conductor imposed an overall structure. Yet there was no sorcery involved here, only profound professionalism, knowledge of the material and an ability to identify formal patterns, which the conductor proceeded to translate into real terms, leaving nothing open or wanting. In this way the young Henze's *Sonata* became the work of a great conductor and belonged to him and his orchestra. This all happened a long time ago, yet I am still occasionally bound to think of it and to speak of it as an artistic experience that taught me to understand and respect Herr von Karajan as a conductor.

Once again I have anticipated events and need to retrace my steps to the spring of 1959, when I was still in Naples, working on the full score of *Der Prinz von Homburg*. Ingeborg stood over me, keeping an eye on this product of my newly espoused New Rigour, criticizing, losing heart, demanding yet greater rigour and, at the same time, working on a volume of stories of her own, *Das dreißigste Jahr*. With the exception of only a handful of diversions, I spent the summer of 1959 crouched over the score of *Der Prinz von Homburg*, the first night of which had already been fixed for 22 May 1960.

I must have started work on the piece during the autumn or summer of the previous year, otherwise it is hard to imagine how I could have finished it in time. During the 1959 Spoleto Festival, the Hamburg intendant, Rolf Liebermann, was kind enough to come to Naples and see Visconti's production of *Il duca d'Alba* (which he did not understand) and to discuss the Hamburg staging of *Der Prinz von Homburg*, which it was also planned to take to Spoleto. As a result, I had one of Visconti's most incandescent productions in my mind's eye and ear as I worked on the score of my opera. It inspired me in no small way. Unfortunately, I saw very little of Luchino and was all on my own in Naples. No, that is not strictly true: my youngest brother, Jürgen, had moved in with me, helping in his own small way to replace Ingeborg, who was often away on business. The day finally came when she did not return at all or, rather, she looked in only briefly in order to pack her belongings and move out of our flat in Naples and in with Max Frisch in Zurich. My brother Jürgen, a highly musical, timid and taciturn youth, had had enough of Bielefeld and its grammar school and pleaded with me to rescue him. How well I understood him! And how glad I was to assist him! He enrolled at the Naples Academy and learnt classical drawing, the Italian language and Neapolitan culture, later working as Heinz Wendel's assistant in Wuppertal. Prior to that – or possibly afterwards – he spent several terms in the stage-design class at the Kunsthochschule in Berlin, but on account of his lengthy absences left little impression on his teachers. He then returned to Italy and assisted Lila de Nobili, whose style and technique he made his own, reinterpreting it as and when he wanted for his own work in the theatre and in films. For me, he designed *Undine* in Hamburg, *König Hirsch* in Bielefeld and the London première of *We Come to the River*.

It was some time during the spring that Luchino telephoned to report that work on his film, *Rocco and his Brothers*, had been delayed by at least nine weeks. Although he bore one of the most eminent names in all Lombardy, the city of Milan had refused him permission to film the final scenes from *Rocco* there: according to the filmscript, they should have been shot in Idroscalo, a limbo where all the city's sewage plants and lowest forms of vice and prostitution are to be found. Presumably the city authorities had no particular desire to see such an image of Milan immortalized on celluloid, as a result of which Visconti had to recreate the whole of Idroscalo somewhere south of Rome in order for the film to be finished at all. He had already spoken to Liebermann, who now telephoned me in turn to say that Visconti had had to withdraw from the production of *Der Prinz von Homburg*. It was difficult to know what to do as I sat at my desk in Naples, unable to think of a replacement. Although the whole affair had now lost much of its appeal for me as a result of Luchino's defection and although I was disappointed at not being able to notch up a success in Italy with him and my music for *Homburg*, I still had no wish for the Hamburg State Opera to forgo its planned appearance in Spoleto. But it was now a matter of total indifference to me who would take over as director. Life, once again, had decided to be difficult.

And that was by no means the end of our disappointments. In our search for another director, Liebermann and I had finally alighted on Helmut Käutner, whose film version of *Hamlet* had just caused something of a stir in modernist circles. He had the time and was happy to work with Liebermann's head of design in Hamburg, Alfred Siercke, who was still owed a further production that season. I attended the first stage rehearsals, when the picture that I saw unfolding was one of Prussian affectation. The scenery was flat and cold and uniformly grey in its stiff conventionality. I had imagined completely different colours while composing the music. We had been rehearsing for a week when our Homburg, Hermann Prey, fell ill and, according to his doctor, would not be fit again until well after the first night. Prey was still a young man at this time, little more than a boy, and had already given so much of himself in rehearsal that we knew he would have scored a considerable personal triumph in the part. He was replaced by the Croatian baritone Vladimir Ruzdak, a stolid and phlegmatic, if pleasant enough member of the Hamburg ensemble with a round face, dark hair that fell low over his brow and sad, dark, Levantine eyes ill suited to flashing with anger. But he sang very beautifully, as indeed did the whole of the cast. The only trouble was that it all came out the same: even the great *fortissimo* passages sounded as soft as velvet. There was no radiance and little colour – or, rather, only one colour. Is it possible for an audience to grasp what is going on when a singer does not fully understand the words that he is singing? I also had problems with the conductor, Leopold Ludwig, who ignored all my suggestions regarding tempi, balance and so on. Meanwhile, I had to go to Trieste to rehearse the local opera orchestra, which I would be conducting in place of the Hamburg Staatskapelle in Spoleto later that summer, and it was not until the day of the dress rehearsal that I was able to return to Hamburg. Among the first-night audience were my mother, my brother Jürgen, Ingeborg and Ludwig and Margaret of Hesse (who were descended from the opera's eponymous hero). Rolf Liebermann and his wife Göndi were kindness itself. The music sounded fine, although, all in all, I might have wished for more translucency and a greater sense of contrast: *c'era una certa pesantezza nella lettura*. But the singers clearly liked the music.

In 1992 I heard *Der Prinz von Homburg* at the Cuvilliés-Theater in Munich, conducted by Wolfgang Sawallisch and intelligently and musically staged by Nikolaus Lehnhoff. It was the first time that I had heard the piece for many years, and the whole score suddenly acquired a very real immediacy, sounding fresh, inspired and sinewy, as sharp as a razor and as sparkling as crystal, but also soft-hued, silky, rapt and both visceral and soulful.

What a shame that Inge was no longer there to hear it. Our piece sounded just as we had imagined it would sound in the late 1950s. In the second act, with its suite of solo scenes, the music becomes austerely formal and contrapuntal, shedding light on Kleist in a way that ensures that each and every word is understood. The essence of Kleist's drama has been sympathetically captured in this piece and so, too, has what the poet tells us about himself through his characters. It is this, I think, that best explains the emotional range of the music in a work that I now see as a product of the final years of my youth. Every bar reveals Verdi's influence as a music dramatist, and it is impossible not to notice passages, especially in the great first-act finale, where the music could and should have inspired the operatic grandeur and emotional intensity associated with Visconti.

Later that summer we took the Hamburg production to Spoleto as agreed. It rained, I conducted and we played to empty houses, a sad and cheerless ending to a dream. There were the usual parties attended by arrogant Romans (they were all so fickle, superior and chic, and I continued to feel intimidated by their insolence, which they had inherited from their rich papas), but although I enjoyed myself exploring Umbria in my new and powerful car, a stylish Giulietta Sprint, it was no good. Luchino came on stage after the performance and embraced me without a word – it was not his fault after all! – after which we went for a meal with two young film stars who knew not a note of my music.

Following the first night in Hamburg, I travelled to Cologne for a festival arranged by the International Society for New Music. The local Academy of Music had also invited me to give a course in composition at nearby Schloß Brühl, but very few people showed any interest. I got bored and reproached myself for ever having accepted the offer. But I was more than compensated by the chance to hear a couple of interesting concerts in Cologne. Stockhausen's *Kontakte* on 11 June left a deep impression on me. I think it must have been the first of his pieces that I heard. Here were some genuinely novel ideas, new sounds and a total rejection of the patterns that had been customary until that time. The close link between instrumental music (piano and percussion) and electronics (which must have had something to do with delayed tapes) seemed to me both plausible and convincing. I watched as the room, which, at a solemn sign from the composer at his sound mixer, was plunged into operatic darkness at the start of the piece, slowly fell under the spell of this organistic hypnosis, producing a mood of almost religious devotion to which listeners were famously obliged to submit and which they could understand fully only if they suspended all rational thought processes. A no less powerful impression was left by Stockhausen's *Momente*, with the radiant Martina Arroyo as soloist, which I heard on another occasion. Here, too, modern music – modernity *tout court* – enters the present-day world, fit as a fiddle, all systems firing and completely self-assured. The music sparkles and roars and rattles along, forward-looking, futuristic, wholly convinced of its own validity and utterly self-affirming. Who knows, perhaps I should have accepted Stockhausen's invitation to go to Cologne in 1954 or whenever it was (I had only just settled in Italy) and collaborated with him there, just as he had suggested. Perhaps I should then have acquired a taste for it and done things differently. But that was something I really did not want to do, so that all that remained was to express my admiration and astonishment at a distance. And no one can claim that I know Karlheinz's works.

From Cologne I also took away happy memories of Kagel's *Anagrama*: here, too, was that powerful, aggressively virile *élan vital* that makes me think of people like Buñuel, Almodóvar and Arrabal. It must be something to do with the language, something to do with Catholicism and the Inquisition, with Dada and Kagel and pop art. Also in Cologne, Boulez performed a new piece, the beginning of which he himself played on the piano. It was no doubt from a work in progress, but I have forgotten what it was. There was nothing to take away and think about here – the only remarkable thing about the whole festival was the fact that I was forced once again to realize that I was on my own and that I would have to get used to the idea of journeying alone, a journey which – I had to admit – might well have set out from a wholly misguided starting point. But at least I knew the goal towards which I was working, and it was during the late fifties and early sixties that I first began to give it a name – my aim was now to create works of classical beauty. I knew what I wanted, and it was very simple: I wanted to write all the works that I missed in music, works conspicuous by their absence, works that did not yet exist.

If my narrative is to retain any sense of precision and clarity, I shall now have to wind back the film once again to December 1958, when I wrote to Auden in New York, asking him in all humility whether he might possibly be prepared, with or without Chester Kallman, to work for me. He replied as follows:

> New York, 6 January, 1959. Dear Hans: Delighted to get your letter. Chester & I would love to collaborate with you on an opera, provided we can earn some money thereby. – What would you say to this idea? A reincarnation of the Daphnis–Chloe story, set in an imaginary Forio in about 1910. One of them would have been brought up by grape-growing contadini, the other by pescatori. Gnatho, the rich queen, would be a version of Norman Douglas, the anti-Christian romantic 'Pagan'. L (our copy of the novel is in Kirchstetten, and I have forgot-

> ten her name), who teaches Daphnis the arts of love, a German Baronin from San Angelo, etc, etc. Though one wouldn't need a proper chorus, we think we should need a quartette of Forian Gossips at the side of the stage throughout, who would amorally comment upon the action and invariably get everything wrong, ie. They would think that X & B, Y & A were having affairs when in fact it was X & Y, A & B, they would predict that N won't marry M when they do, or that K will marry L when he doesn't, etc. A straight romantic love story with a buffo background. – Chester gets back to Kirchstetten in April; I have to go first to Oxford and will get out in the middle of June. I am enchanted with the place. As regards the Mezzogiorno, I am getting too old for the strange: the Krauts can be monsters like Hitler, or idiots like H. H. Stuckenschmidt, but I understand them in a way that I shall never understand Wops. – Let us know your reaction, and *please* come to see us in Niederösterreich. – Love – Wystan

With Auden's letter came the fulfilment of a great dream, one that I had scarcely even dared think possible. Over the years I had read everything that Auden had written, studying each new work and unreservedly admiring and worshipping this incredible man, both as a private individual and as a poet: although he had already turned fifty, he still looked like an Oxford graduate, a giant with huge hands, the face of a tortoise, a beer gut, carpet slippers and wonderfully sad and gentle eyes that reminded me of a dog's. I know someone who, as a young man, would sit in Auden's regular café in Oxford, gazing across at him from a distance and longing to have a face like his and to share his furrowed features. Auden himself thought his face resembled a wedding cake that had been left out in the rain for three days. We had become friends during our years together on Ischia, when I had been able to gain a certain insight into the way in which he and Kallman functioned as librettists. In writing their librettos, they would discuss everything as intellectual equals, a discussion that lasted all day, in the course of which they would jot down odd words and phrases. It was fascinating to be present on such occasions and listen to them at work. Kallman was from Brooklyn, as could clearly be heard each time that he opened his mouth, but he had Polish ancestors. He was a strange young man, a sensitive, acerbic poet with a booming bass voice and bad posture. Although he suffered badly under Auden's dominant, overbearing and leonine personality, he was unable to live without it. He also had to endure the premature (and permanent) loss of his once sensational, ever-so-slightly over-the-top East-Coast good looks. He died in Athens on 17 January 1975, some fifteen months after Auden, from cirrhosis of the liver and a feeling of total abandonment.

For Auden and Kallman, writing the libretto for *Elegy for Young Lovers* was like some playful competition: which of the two was the wittier, which was better at striking the note they were aiming for? Who could offer a quicker or better solution to the question of how the story should continue? Who would find the most suitable rhyme? Auden had moved to Austria with the help of an Italian literary prize and had bought a small farmhouse at Kirchstetten near St Pölten. It was a move that produced his great poem *Goodbye to the Mezzogiorno*, a strange and sad, somewhat pensive work, and that he himself had justified by arguing that the Vienna Opera was better than the San Carlo and the tickets cheaper. Here in the depths of the Lower Austrian countryside, surrounded by wheatfields and vegetables, at the edge of a wood where foxgloves glinted, we met in the summer of 1959 so that I could give them both an idea of what I imagined this chamber opera would be like. I told them I wanted a small group of singers, rather like the one in *Così fan tutte*, and a small instrumental ensemble comprising no more than twenty players. These instruments might perhaps play a role within the piece's dramaturgical structure by being identified with particular characters. I told them that I would like the work to be a psychological drama, a chamber drama that would deal in the most general terms with questions of guilt and atonement, in other words, with subtle and complex issues, and not with the all too pastoral and affected bucolicisms with which they had tried to fob me off in their letter of acceptance.

Our work in Kirchstetten began with endless discussions that resembled nothing so much as the verbal equivalent of an extended game of ping-pong for three, but which were interrupted by far too many extravagances such as the meals that Chester would lovingly prepare, closeted in the kitchen for hours on end, and that always turned out a disaster. Each, moreover, would be prefaced by far too many aperitifs that were always the same Beefeater Martini on the rocks (three drops of Martini in neat gin). We made only slow progress, but by the end of a week during which I was pleased to see how seriously they took my requirements and the description of the music that I could hear in my own mind's ear, we had a basic outline. This now had to be slowly filled in by the two poets. I once had in my possession the initial synopsis that they must have sent to me from Kirchstetten soon afterwards and that was really a quite marvellous document, but unfortunately I have lost it. I was delighted with this draft and even while reading it could already hear the artificial air of the Hammerhorn buzzing in my ears and could make out the voice of the mad and visionary old woman who for forty years has sung in metres from *Lucia di Lammermoor*, a modern Penelope who sits on the mountainside throughout the whole of the piece with her obbligato flute. I could already hear the first notes of the music for the two lovers, delicate flowers, meadow saffron and violets, and the grotesque, Wotanesque huffing and puffing of Gregor Mittenhofer, the cold-hearted poet who offers up human sacrifices to his Muse, the tragic, exhausted, Munch-like figure of the pitiful Countess Kirchstetten, who is associated with the sound of the English horn and whom we know one day will come to a sorry end – and at whom we can still poke fun, just as we can at the other characters, at least until such time as the laughter dies on our lips, a sensation that we are meant to feel time and time again in this piece. These people are real people, modern men and women, with their weaknesses and strengths, mortals, not gods or heroes or any other kind of supernatural being.

I did not have long to wait: within a matter of weeks the finished libretto had plopped through my Parthenopean letter box. Rarely had I received so generous a gift, and I started work on the music straightaway. Once again I had allowed others to take advantage of me, though I would far rather have done nothing at all for the foreseeable future. But a date had already been set for the première: 20 May 1961 – almost a year to the day after *Der Prinz von Homburg*. The Bavarian State Opera would make the piece available to the Schwetzingen Festival, and it was there that the first performance would be given – in German. The fee would be paid by South German Radio. The work would then be revived in June as part of the Munich Opera Festival, with myself conducting. So now it was all go. I decided that I had had enough of Naples, where a number of sources of social friction had in any case emerged in the course of my months in the city, not least of which was the noisy demolition of the old English embassy diagonally opposite and the erection in its place of a palatial telegraph office that cut off the view from my window. But I had already had enough of Naples and wanted to get away from the place: it was always so hot, and I felt a desire and a need to break free from my fellow creatures who were always so possessive and who took up so much of my time. Above all, I had to find a modern musical city as soon as possible and remain there until *Elegie für junge Liebende* – as it was now to be called –

was finished. I was still only half-way through Act One. I had to find somewhere where there were assistants, creature comforts, a fast and reliable postal service, where people were punctual and I could abandon myself undisturbed to the folly of this commission and to the race against time that it entailed. I moved to Berlin and stayed in a studio at the Academy of Arts, moving a few weeks later into a suite of rooms in a small hotel in the Grunewald, where I was able to redouble my efforts, aided by a greater degree of comfort which, above all else, helped to save me so much time.

I drove from Naples to Berlin, breaking my journey in Kirchstetten, where I regaled my poets with all that I had written so far, croaking out the vocal parts and accompanying myself at the piano. It seemed that they liked what they heard. They had imagined that there would be spoken dialogue, as is normal in Singspiels, but I preferred to set virtually all the spoken passages, specifying the rhythms and notating approximate pitches, since, almost without exception, singers are prevented by their foreign or regional accents from pronouncing a poet's words correctly if those words are unaccompanied. Minor adjustments and a number of cuts were made to the libretto, but otherwise there was nothing that needed to be changed any longer.

In Munich a meeting had been arranged at the Opera involving myself (as producer), Peter Kehm, the programme director of both South German Radio and the Schwetzingen Festival, and the intendant of the Bavarian State Opera, Rudolf Hartmann. Our brief was to discuss the production. Hartmann began by reading out a letter from my publisher, Ludwig Strecker, who wrote librettos in his spare time and who fancied himself as an expert on Goethe. It was effectively a demand that Hartmann reject the perverse libretto, with its cast of neurotics and lunatics, in order to prevent me from setting it to music. Hartmann said indignantly that he refused to discuss the matter further until this misunderstanding had been cleared up. I told him that I was ready to do so right away, since I fully intended to write the piece come what may and that I considered the libretto to be a masterpiece. I let it be known that I expected an apology from my publishers in Mainz, but was then asked to forget it, not least because I was assured that Schott's would produce the full score, vocal score and orchestral parts for the piece with exceptional speed and care. I duly sent off the opera, piecemeal, to Mainz, with the German translation already included. It was immediately copied and the vocal score gradually assembled. Of my two assistants in Berlin, one was the conductor Harold Byrns, who produced a fair copy of my short score with a kindness and professionalism that he was to show me on several subsequent occasions, while the other was the stage designer Werner Schachteli, a highly articulate and witty individual who had time to work through the score with me and to produce a German version of the text that came as close as possible to the English original: since this latter had already been set, the rhythms were already fixed. It was an extraordinarily difficult job. Our starting point was a translation by Ludwig Landgraf (Ludwig of Hesse) that followed the metres of Auden's and Kallman's original and that Hans Magnus Enzensberger had kindly cast an eye over, but, as it stood, the German only rarely fit my music. Schachteli and I would sometimes spend hours working on a single sentence until we had found something that more or less fitted the sense and style of the original. How much simpler if we had given the opera in English!

These unspeakable exertions occupied the whole of the winter, which passed very slowly and yet still far too quickly. The music rehearsals had already started in Munich, and the snow was beginning to melt in the Grunewald, where I was still struggling with Act Three: it was sheer madness. On one occasion I flew to Munich to inspect Helmut Jürgens' set designs, only to discover that he had long since realized them without thinking of consulting me. Unfortunately, he had mistranslated the terms 'upstage' and 'downstage' in the libretto, with the result that the whole set was back to front, so that at the first performance at Schwetzingen (and at later performances in Munich) the terrace of 'Der schwarze Adler', on which important scenes take place, was right at the back of the stage, where it was almost impossible to see and hear the singers. At this late juncture there was nothing to be done. I found Jürgens a talented individual, but pig-headed (not for nothing was he from Westphalia!), unapproachable, inadequate and something of a know-all. My trip to Munich was a waste of time and, annoyed, I returned to Berlin, where, cursing audibly to myself, I immersed myself in my score once again.

It should not be imagined, however, that the whole affair brought nothing but torment and trouble. I was immensely fond of Berlin (at that date it was still possible to travel freely between the eastern and western parts of the city, which meant, above all, that I was free to visit Paul Dessau and Ruth Berghaus). I enjoyed my freedom and discovered energies that I did not know I possessed. I retain many fond and delightful memories of this time, including those of my very dear, patient, generous and mad friend and drinking companion, the film producer Wenzel Lüdecke. He maintained a kind of salon at his home on the unspoilt Hundekehlensee, where

I soon became a regular visitor. Among his close friends were the actor Horst Buchholz and his actress wife, Miriam Bru. Other regulars were the producer Atze Brauner, the Socialist director Wolfgang Staudte (known as Uncle Pelle) and Toni Mackeben, the widow of the film composer, who now worked as a theatre agent. During the years that followed, I often occupied a floor in Wenzel's huge house, which was built in a post-war Scandinavian style, and which I remember for his dog Piefke and for its pine trees, wild boar and squirrels, for its picture windows and its private pathway down to the lake. During these years Wenzel's guest book would also contain such names as Stravinsky, Karajan, García Márquez, Enzensberger, Dessau, Bachmann, Schnabel, Dutschke, Grass, Sellner, Moroni, Salvatore, Sanjust, Craft, Dohnányi and many many more. On one occasion the Stuckenschmidts, Teddy Adorno and I had lunch in a private room in the Börsenstuben in the Hardenbergstraße (unfortunately the establishment no longer exists), and the conversation turned to Benjamin Britten. The Stuckenschmidts begged the great thinker at least to concede that . . . but for him there was nothing to concede. As always he was consistent in his intransigency and could not be persuaded to commute his sentence of death. I listened and found it hard to conceal my disbelief.

Later that same winter there was another, far better production of *Der Prinz von Homburg* in Frankfurt, where I met Adorno again. During the second interval he told me that he liked what he had heard so far, but that it was not sufficiently chaotic for him. New music had to be chaotic, he said. Well well, I thought. I really could not abide him, especially since the day he had insisted on singing some of his *lieder* to me, accompanying himself at the piano, in his flat in Frankfurt, where the furnishings were dominated by crochet-work covers. His songs had sounded like a clever forgery, certainly not like the work of an artist or composer. Teddy was a queer bird, I did not like him, there was something about him that I found disagreeable.

It was at the Börsenstuben in Berlin that Luigi Dallapiccola once explained to me the Gothic structures and musical techniques in Proust's *A la recherche du temps perdu*, an explanation that left a deep impression on me, persuading me to acquire the Gallimard edition and to set about reading the work for myself.

I also remember the city's night life – the disreputable sort, rough but *gemütlich*, and alcoholic binges designed to help me take a break from composing, if only briefly. My composing machine was in overdrive. Prairie oysters and black velvet (Guinness and champagne) on Sunday mornings at the Kempinski. With Karajan to see Felsenstein's *Othello*. Lots of Philharmonic concerts, which at that time were still held in the Hardenbergstraße. The orchestral sound had a veritable sheen to it and was rich in a thousand nuances, with immaculate balance between the different departments. I can still hear it to this day.

I felt an insane thirst for life yet, for all my sociability, still felt utterly alone, still felt a sense of desolation that nothing could console. But no! As though on cue, the desired diversion arrived in the shape of a flaxen-headed romantic lead from the Max Reinhardt School, a delightfully cheeky young actor with aspirations to rather more heroic roles, finely etched features, high cheekbones, an adorable mouth and large, brown, slightly slanting, giraffe-like eyes that looked down at one in amazement and incomprehension. His name was Folker.

Folker was keen to be acknowledged as the proud possessor of what Shakespeare calls a 'mannerly hearted mind', and his efforts in this direction were both touching and successful. His struggle to achieve this virtuous state and to gain possession of new and similar territories continues to this day. He was an amusing fellow, childlike, vulnerable and irascible. He suffered from migraines and took a great interest in life and its manifold manifestations, not least of which was vice. He had just enjoyed an early success as an actor, having played one of the three youths in Bernhard Wicki's *The Bridge*, and was now waiting for his second film. He spent the time restlessly driving round Berlin in his old Volkswagen, attending to its faulty carburettor, or else he would hang around in bars, in one of which he met me, his elder by several years, following me to the next bar in order to be able to continue our conversation. I sent him a letter, the contents of which are unprintable, but the result of which was a telephone call only a few hours later, announcing that he was on his way and that he needed only to change a tyre. I had hardly replaced the receiver when he came bounding up the stairs to my second-floor rooms, clutching a bunch of flowers.

During the weeks and months that followed I began to consider the idea of living together, but Folker resisted it with all he was worth. As a result I had my hands full each time I broke off from composing. Now there was not a single boring moment in my life. By the following spring I was already putting the finishing touches to my piece (a piece animated by my new zest for life and by my desire for a little peace and quiet at last), just as my friendship with Folker was beginning. I sent off the final scene to Mainz, after which we headed south by a series of forced marches, pausing briefly to regain our breath on Capri, then moving out of my rooms in Naples to a far less interesting flat in the Via Bruno Buozzi on the Parioli in Rome. I had rented it earlier that year, while giving a concert in Rome. It had been a Sunday morning, and I had either not noticed or not realized that on weekdays the road, which was on a slope, would be crawling with traffic and the source of the most frightful noise. And so it proved. But there was no time to brood on the problem, since we had to return to Munich, where the blocking rehearsals for *Elegie* were beginning, with myself as director. The conductor was the young Heinrich Bender, who was not a little astonished at this unexpected score.

Staging the work was a source of some pleasure for me, and the result was a decent production, concentrated and music-based, that also found favour with Wystan and Chester, although they could not see the reason for the overemphasis on *Jugendstil* elements in the sets. I am still attached to this work, so much so, in fact, that I revised it around ten years ago and took the opportunity to remove an artistic miscalculation that consisted of too many metallic sounds in the music, too many bells and gongs that were merely intended to evoke an Alpine atmosphere and suggest a sense of artificiality but which ultimately led not only to a certain conceptional confusion but also to a feeling of tedium on the listener's part. Now that I have revised the score, the whole piece sounds less top-heavy and, instead, a little more varied.

Following the final dress rehearsal in Schwetzingen on 18 May 1961, the two librettists treated the whole of the cast to a meal at the Europäischer Hof in Heidelberg – such kindness cannot have been lavished on our singers for a very long time. Auden felt that the male members of the first-night audience should wear tails, and so the male members of the first-night audience duly wore tails (Stuckenschmidt too, just imagine!), while the women wore long dresses. It was hot in the small rococo theatre on the evening of 20 May, and patrons would have been happy to escape from the auditorium after the first act to enjoy the fresh, if somewhat humid, air outside and to smell the wild garlic and overbred lilac that grew in the palace grounds. But Professor Jürgens had decreed that the first two acts should be played without a break, so the audience had to remain on their deeply uncomfortable stools for more than two hours. (This was put right by the second performance, and from now on there were two intervals.) For me, it was a wretched first night. I later had to call the hotel doctor, since I was suffering from the most terrible colic and felt violently sick. It was my nerves, he said, and no wonder, in view of all the stress. He gave me an injection. Folker and I then set off for Glyndebourne (we flew from Le Touquet to Folkestone, taking our car with us) in order to attend the final rehearsals of the British première of *Elegy*. It was immediately clear that the collaboration between Günther Rennert and Lila de Nobili was not working, there had been a breakdown of communication, and the director barely knew where to begin with the libretto. His reaction was the same as that of my publisher in Mainz, resulting in animosity between him and Auden and Kallman, who were simply on a different intellectual level. The part of Elizabeth was taken by Elisabeth Söderström, that of the Countess Kirchstetten by Kerstin Meyer, two charming and gifted Swedish girls whom I have always held in the greatest affection. John Pritchard conducted, ably and committedly. I took over from him after the fifth performance.

The piece caused consternation among Glyndebourne's first-night audience. At the beginning of the long interval, I had to pass through the packed foyer on my way to the private dining room of the festival director, John Christie, who had made no secret of the fact that he could not abide the opera, and it was impossible not to overhear a number of rude remarks about the work. 'We must warn poor Gwendolyn' was one of the comments that I caught in passing. At Christie's huge dining table there was not a single person I knew. I think they must all have been my host's neighbours, members of the landed gentry, bankers, sponsors or whatever. Be that as it may, not one of them addressed a single word to me throughout the entire seventy-minute interval. (Seventy minutes is the minimum time thought necessary for Glyndebourne's regular patrons to settle down on the damp lawns and open their Fortnum & Mason picnic hampers or broach a bottle of champagne or claret diluted by the light drizzle that is regarded as part of the experience.) But where were Wystan and Chester? Who would have thought that I would ever miss them so badly? The three-minute bell was already ringing when I finally found the former, lounging against a foyer wall and poring over the *Times* crossword. He was wearing a dinner jacket, but no shoes.

The *Evening News* of 14 July included a cartoon with the caption 'Conversation after the performance at Glyndebourne last night' and showed two women in evening dress returning to London in their limousine. 'Who was the composer of to-night's opera, dear?' asked one of them. 'Mozart, of course, it's always Mozart here.' 'Then he must have been very young – before he learned to write those pretty tunes.'

Chester Kallman wrote the words of a cantata for Elisabeth Söderström and Kerstin Meyer, but unfortunately I never found time to set it to music.

> *The Solitudes*
> A little Cantata for Elisabeth Söderström and Kerstin Meyer

Here is a brief extract:

> Nothing flew over the garden;
> Nobody slipped from the house:
> Glittering sands
> In an hour-glass
> Held in his eloquent white hands
> Gave nothing a voice.
>
> Telegram, telephone, letter
> Dropped into silence's ear;
> Over the sky
> Lay a bright blur
> Noting how safely and how high
> Nobody lived there.

In his review of the opera, the playwright Peter Shaffer spoke of 'W. H. Auden's self-accusations, accompanied by exotic music'. At the end of the run, while I was staying at John Pritchard's flat in London, I was again violently sick and in terrible pain, just as I had been in Schwetzingen. Our good neighbour from Seaford, who was also a doctor, discovered a problem with my appendix that had been left untreated for far too long. He ordered me to rest for a few days, then Folker drove me via Paris (where Claude and Georgette Rostand managed to persuade us to abandon our planned holiday in Provence) to the Schwabing Hospital in Munich, where I was immediately operated on. Since things had been allowed to drag on, it was a complicated operation, with the result that the healing process took longer than usual. Meanwhile, the day of the Munich revival of *Elegie* was drawing inexorably closer, and I was still not even allowed to get out of bed. But I was determined to conduct the performance. The senior consultant finally allowed me to leave the hospital but refused to accept responsibility for the consequences of my actions. I took a two-and-a-half-hour ensemble rehearsal during the morning and conducted the first performance later that same evening, when a whole series of things went wrong as a result of my nervousness (compounded by the fact that I was heavily sedated). Thanks to a false entry on my part, poor Fidi – Dietrich Fischer-Dieskau – suffered a lapse of memory in the second-act finale, something he otherwise never did. I have only unhappy memories of this evening, of which I had had such high expectations. Lassitude, the feeling of incompetence, weakness, inadequacy, paralysis, everything that constitutes a bad performance. It was like a dream in which your legs give way beneath you and you cannot escape from your approaching pursuers.

It was not until a few days later that I discovered that by the middle of the first act Luigi Nono had had enough and that he and Nuria had forced a whole row of people in the stalls to struggle to their feet in order that they themselves could leave as quickly as possible. It transpired that at a lunch given by Karl Amadeus Hartmann the local critic and writer on music, Ulrich Dibelius, had asked Gigi why he had left in the middle of the act and not waited until the interval. Instead of answering the question, Gigi had overturned the dinner table, reducing the Meissen porcelain from Elisabeth's dowry to smithereens. Carl Orff, too, was said to have left during the performance (*les extrêmes se touchaient donc*), albeit in a less ostentatious fashion. According to Karl Amadeus, Orff had come across a score of *König Hirsch* at his – Karl's – home some time before and, having cast an eye inside it, was said to have exclaimed: 'But he's still writing developments!' According to Orff, the notion that ideas, even if only musical ideas, had to be developed in order to be worthy of the name was absurd beyond belief and quite hopelessly out of date.

As for Gigi, I could not help wondering what was the reason for his sudden anger, his rejection of me and my works, not to say his hatred. In all my later dealings with him, I invariably pretended that I knew nothing of the affair with Elisabeth's Meissen. He always suffered from an irascible temper, there was always something or someone to upset him, and there was nothing that anyone could do about it. It was a kind of *Weltschmerz*. And he was always unspeakably rude to women, especially those he had ogled. What a remarkable character he was, and what a difficult life he led! In Darmstadt he booed Stravinsky's Mass (at the previous summer's concerts I myself had cuffed a youth for booing one of Nono's pieces, an act that I now consider unspeakable). It grieved me deeply that he refused to acknowledge me and, instead, let me feel his contempt, especially towards the end of his life. Yet he always knew the line I was taking, knew the person I was, so that he really should not have been surprised by the course of events. Surely he can't have been jealous? After all, he was well-to-do, one of the wealthiest men in La Serenissima, it was said, and highly regarded not only as a composer but in other respects as well.

Ten years previously I had successfully recommended Luigi Nono to

Schott's and I conducted his works on many occasions, including my conducting début in New York in 1971, when I introduced his *Per Bastiana: Tai-Yang Cheng* to local audiences. (The other work on the programme was my own Sixth Symphony, which I had recently conducted for the first time in Havana and which was now receiving its North American première.) My New York agent, Sheldon Soffer, had on his desk a copy of a letter from the BMI president, Oliver Daniel, to the American Symphony Orchestra, in which he drew the attention of the orchestra's board of directors to the fact that my entire programme was Communist in character. Was it merely a point of information? A warning? A reproach? Whatever the answer, Leopold Stokowski, now in his ninetieth year, drove in specially from his house in the country to show his solidarity, welcoming me, introducing me to the orchestra and remaining for the first rehearsal of Nono's *Tai-Yang Cheng*, a kind of orchestral fantasia on the notes of the Chinese battle hymn, *The East is Red*. The concert took place in Carnegie Hall and was a huge success with an audience largely made up of young people, at least half of whom were Latin Americans. It is also worth mentioning in this context that for a number of years during the mid-sixties I was artistic director of an all-night radio station run by North German Radio, during which time I broadcast all Gigi's works. Almost forty years ago, I remember going to Frankfurt for a performance of his setting of García Lorca's fragmentary *Romance de la guardia civil española* and taking him to see *Così fan tutte* under Solti with Christa Ludwig, who had just sung his Lorca setting. I spent the whole performance nudging him gently in the ribs at all the ravishingly beautiful passages in the score, not least of which, of course, is Fiordiligi's almost Webern-like aria, 'Per pietà', and still recall his forced smile and feeling that he had merely been humouring me. I loved and admired Nono and his music, especially his vocal works, and would have been very happy if I could at some point and in some way have gained his attention and respect – but I waited in vain.

He did not put in an appearance at the first performance of my cantata, *Novae de infinito laudes*, at La Fenice in April 1963, although, unless I am much mistaken, he was a member of the Biennale's team of directors at that time. Indeed, I can still see him striding through the La Fenice foyer clutching his briefcase. And I have a further sad and curious memory of him: in the summer of 1973 I attended the International Youth Festival in East Berlin as artistic director of the West German contribution, *Streik bei Mannesmann*, a piece of music theatre produced by a collective of largely West German composers and comprising a kind of sung report on the first spontaneous strike in the Federal Republic. Our piece had been written and prepared without any kind of public grant and was to be staged at the Theater am Schiffbauerdamm, where the intendant, Ruth Berghaus, helped with the get-in and lighting. Gigi was in Moscow but sent a twelve-note unison chorus, a setting of an Italian text that he himself had written and that dealt with the victory of Vietnam. Unfortunately, it was impossible to find anyone to sing it. Ruth had wrung her hands in despair and left no stone unturned in her attempts to find anyone to perform it, but there was not a single choir nor even an individual singer that felt able to take it on. It was an embarrassing situation, and as a result Gigi's twelve-note chorus – a distinctive expression of a great cultural leap forward – was not heard, as Gigi had intended, broadcast from all the public-address systems at Schönefeld Airport and on all the capital's thoroughfares. Instead, the masses were regaled by a new song by Paul Dessau in an ebullient C major, a turn of events that must have left Gigi, who had by now arrived as guest of honour, feeling not a little disgruntled and tense throughout the whole festival. And on top of everything, he had to put up with *me*, since we were staying at the same hotel. But at least he had a chauffeur-driven car of his own, whereas I myself was left to use the underground.

One evening at the Dessaus' home at Zeuthen, the GDR composer Friedrich Goldmann was subjected to an interrogation presided over by Gigi. I sat there, aghast, as a socio-political observer. Among those present were public prosecutors and two holders of national awards, including Hermann Henselmann, who had built the East Berlin Television Tower, as well as Paul and Ruth. Have I forgotten anyone? The accused was defended by Maxim Dessau who, like his father, had never really got on with the system. A couple of neighbours, pleasant enough comrades in leather jackets, looked in. Goldmann, whose works were deemed unacceptable in the Democratic Republic and, therefore, never performed there, now stood accused of the crime of performing those selfsame works in the West, at Donaueschingen, for example. Well, it was true, Goldmann had indeed done so, and a bad thing it was too, since it made an unfortunate impression on the outside world. What was needed, they said, was a basic discussion of first principles, and they tried to make it clear to Goldmann that, if he wanted to be a success in the Democratic Republic, he would have to write a different kind of music, music that genuinely served the people, in other words, conformed to the expectations of the Central Committee. With the cry of 'But what am I supposed to do?' the accused broke down, sobbing, whereupon Maxim and Paul began to argue, with the latter retiring insulted and without a word, so that this whole delightful evening ended on a note of discord.

The following evening witnessed the first performance of our own *Streik bei Mannesmann*, the musical side of which was placed in the hands of the Hamburg-based instrumental ensemble Hinz & Kunst, who were later to rename themselves L'Art pour L'Art and with whom I was to work on many subsequent occasions. The theatre – the home of the Berliner Ensemble – was packed to the rafters, with a palpable sense of intense excitement and interest in our piece. Following the tumultuous final applause, the East Germans in the auditorium spontaneously joined hands with the West Germans on stage and struck up one old German workers' song after another. There was an exceptional and overwhelming feeling of unity and solidarity. Apart from *Brüder in Zechen und Gruben*, I myself knew hardly any of these songs, most of which had originated in my own homeland. Fortunately, my grandfather, a miner and foreman, was no longer alive to share my embarrassment. We all felt a warm glow of satisfaction. With tears in his eyes, Paul said it was the most wonderful evening of his life (I hope he had more wonderful ones). Everyone was happy; everyone, that is, except for Gigi, who stood in a corner, tight-lipped and pale. I asked him in all innocence whether it had not been a great evening. He said nothing, but merely raised the index finger of his left hand and waved it to and fro a number of times. How well I knew what he meant, and so I refrained from asking him any more questions, assuming, quite rightly, that it would have entailed a basic aesthetic discussion, and for that I really had no inclination just then.

We left the Theater am Schiffbauerdamm and, with it, the eastern sector, the capital of the GDR and, for a time at least, Luigi Nono, my dear and difficult Gigi Nono. The scene now shifts back once again to Munich's Franz-Joseph-Straße. It has just struck twelve, and the Hartmanns' cleaning lady is still sweeping up the shards of Meissen tableware. It is the summer of 1961. And now I am back in my cold and noisy apartment in torrid Rome, starting work on my new cantata, *Novae de infinito laudes*. I soon discovered that I would never get used to the street noise, and so I drove up into the Alban Hills, where I straightway stumbled on a quite frightful little house overlooking Castel Gandolfo. Built of inferior materials, it was almost impossible to heat but at least it was perfectly quiet, with its own little vineyard and a terrace from which it was possible to see not only the Cyclops-like eye of the Lago di Albano glinting far below me but also the golden-blue strip of the Tyrrhenian Sea stretched out on the western horizon beyond the outlines of the Pope's summer residence. At night the moon and stars would be reflected in the Lago di Albano, a blue-green freshwater lake in an old volcanic crater, on the upper edge of which I was to spend the next five years. Sometimes little white clouds would obscure my view, especially in winter, when the stars looked cold and pale, until the sun emerged and bathed them in its vermilion rays and they faded with the light of day. It was a wooded, windy place, with broom and laurel clinging to the steep hillsides. It is easy to reach the underworld through this lake.

I missed Naples. From a distance of forty years, my memories of the city assume almost mythical form (and forms). A number of memories have faded, while others have proved to be seminal. If I were to attempt to convey a general impression and paint my own portrait of Naples at that time, it would – I think – be like holding up a lantern in a dormitory: the beam of light passes briefly over this or that recumbent form that lies there, snoring and asleep, the rest is silence, and the light is immediately turned off again. Or it is like a glimpse backstage at the marionette theatre at San Nazzaro, where the puppets hang, awaiting their next entrance, their arms hanging limply by their sides and their heads awry, a lifeless expression in their eyes. But nobody knows when or where that appearance will be. Perhaps the figures will end up not on stage at all but in crates and never be seen again. Among these hand-carved and -painted *fantoccini* hanging there on the wall were characters from the late *ottocento*, barons, *lazzaroni*, virtuous young maids from the people, wicked courtiers, policemen, countesses, monks, *camorristi*, clergymen, fishermen, mothers, convicts and market women. In a word, all that one needs to tell some tall story set in the underworld and *demi-monde* of early nineteenth-century Naples, a soap opera lasting twenty-four evenings, each evening an episode in the dramatic narrative, a new slice of life in three acts, ending on Christmas Eve – *Santissima Notte* – with a comforting Catholic finale, gilded angels, tinsel hair, the ox in the manger and people in and around the crib. Thus the destitute troupe of showmen would arrive for engagements with their patrons among the clergy. I looked at the ancient playscripts, including some handwritten ones for *Orlando furioso*, a standard work in the repertory of the southern Italian marionette theatre that was now in the grip of death. Although the profession of puppeteer had hitherto been well-regarded and respected as an honourable and artistic craft, there was now virtually no one to take any interest in it any longer, not even an institute keen to protect the region's folklore, while even the puppeteers' own children refused to carry on the family business. I asked them what sort of professions they had chosen instead: well, they said, office jobs basically, secretaries, reps. They sold me an Orlando, a cross-eyed Ruggiero and a sweet and blue-eyed Clorinda. (They now belong to my godson, Pierre-Dominique Ponnelle.) Perhaps the Naples I knew and loved no longer exists – perhaps it never existed, so that I have to conjure these memories from out of thin air. No, I do not have to do that. All I have to do is let one or other of these characters out of their boxes for a brief space of time. Take Tancredi and Clorinda, for instance: their tale – a transvestite tragedy – is part and parcel of the whole culture of Mediterranean sexuality, the artistic expression of an everyday occurrence that differs from the original only on points of detail (as a glance at the newspapers shows) – the difference really lies only in the social castes and classes: on the one hand, the crusading aristocracy, on the other the subproletariat in drag, offering itself for sale. This is something that southern men find unsettling and, hence, especially attractive; a quintessential sin, perhaps an old moral tradition dating back to the beginnings of history and to the time of the ancient Greeks? From Phoenicia, the home of Heliogabalus (who, according to Stefan George, 'gave himself to Caesar's mercenaries')? Or from the cultural customs of the predatory Saracens, who left their mark not only on the sexual mores but also on the architecture of Naples, her islands and the Amalfi coast in general? Naples gazes southwards towards Palermo, casting long shadows over Tunis and Tunisia, a city of astrologers, where mathematics and philosophy enjoyed princely, imperial patronage and ancient cultures met and mingled. The Neapolitans whom I remember all had one thing in common: originality. Each and every one of them had his own particular conception of life, his own ideas of good and evil (= beauty and ugliness), his own sense of humour and of comedy, tragedy and lyricism. With them, individualism was inborn, but it was also an acquired trait, inculcated by their free-thinkingly anti-authoritarian parents. One of the reasons why I had to escape from Naples was the social and cultural pessimism that was part of the local colour, a phenomenon as fashionable as it was natural, perhaps a throwback to the period of Spanish rule, a negative outlook that effectively discouraged the city's inhabitants from ever harbouring ambitions or making plans, still less from ever achieving anything. One of my favourite songs (and one that Ingeborg hated) has the refrain

> Vita, vita sbagliata!
> Ch'aggiu perduto,
> ch'aggiu lassata!

Roughly translatable as 'Life, botched life! A life I have lost and let slip away!', these words are then taken up in a carefree conclusion, dispelling these sombre insights and bringing us back to our starting point, to the restless, unthinking activity that is part of the daily round. It is the sort of idea one would find in an *opera buffa*, a delightful reversion to type, a Rossinian evasion of a kind that is found at deeply tragic moments in his *opere serie*, so that charm may win the day instead of the earthbound ungainliness of the *attaccabottoni* or *rompicoglioni*. For where does it say that art exists to encourage us to make life difficult for our neighbours and that this aggression is the *summum bonum*, the artist's noblest duty?

Giuseppina d'Avalos, the mother of my colleague, Francesco d'Avalos, was a wonderful person, a delicate-featured, energetic, lively, witty woman with beautiful round eyes like those of some Aragonese Arab. She was always very kind to me and helped me in various ways, including practical assistance with buying flowerpots for my large terrace and loaning me, free of charge, her own gardener to tend our roses. The d'Avalos family hailed from Aragon, but had come to Naples in the reign of Charles V and were members of the Society of Spanish Nobility in Naples, a society that shunned republicans and the bourgeoisie. Incredibly, the children of members of this society were forbidden to consort with such riff-raff. Every summer the family would go to Lucerne and Bayreuth. Twenty years ago, Francesco d'Avalos, who teaches composition in Naples and conducts Bruckner symphonies in London, inherited Luigi Vanvitelli's vast eighteenth-century palazzo in the Via dei Mille from his Uncle Fernando and now lives it up there. Needless to say, these aristocratic contacts in my private life had a tangible counterpart in the form of a colourful alternative world that had something fantastical about it, peopled, as it was, with mythical creatures such as Tritons, cyclopes, mermaids and also, of course, with Ingeborg's Illyrians, harbourside whores and fugitives. Emerald sea horses, corals, Pompeian phalluses, the evil eye, lovesick glances, Clorinda's wooden, unseeing eyes, Rinaldo's pointedly squinting eyes, the many Madonnas' porcelain eyes behind glass or in processions, arrogant, cold and heartlessly introspective, and the body of the embalmed Saint Clare laid out on her bier in the monastery church that bears her name and whose Spanish Baroque wooden carvings are outrageously over the top. Supplicants are invited to write petitions to her and attach them to her sarcophagus, ideally enclosing folding money to the tune of at least 5000 lire to cover the cost of postage. Only then will their requests be met. But one must take care, of course, not to ask for anything that cannot be granted. From a dark side aisle a Franciscan monk looks across, barely visible and as motionless as a waxwork. Three minutes away is the Piazza del Gesù, where from 16 to 24 October 1590 the gates of the Palazzo Venosa stood open, revealing the stairwell in which, closely guarded by Gesualdo's servants and worried by all the stray dogs of the neighbourhood, lay the bodies of Prince Carafa and Maria d'Avalos, the adulterous Princess Venosa. No one, including even the Vatican, has ever been able to forgive Gesualdo for the fact that, instead of doing the job himself, he had the lovers killed by his servants much as one would drown a litter of kittens or smoke out a nest of mice. That is why his music sounds so sinful and repentant: it has, as it were, to grant itself absolution. In this, it reminds me a little of Auden's sonnet, *The Composer*:

All the others translate: the painter sketches
A visible world to love or reject;
Rummaging into his living, the poet fetches
The images out that hurt and connect,

From Life to Art by painstaking adaption,
Relying on us to cover the rift;
Only your notes are pure contraption,
Only your song is an absolute gift.

Pour out your presence, a delight cascading
The falls of the knee and the weirs of the spine,
Our climate of silence and doubt invading;

You alone, alone, imaginary song,
Are unable to say an existence is wrong,
And pour out your forgiveness like a wine.

Naples, for me, also means the New Year pagan celebrations at which people are killed every year and one thinks that Vesuvius must have erupted and that the city is in flames, yet it is only the traditional firework display organized annually by each Neapolitan family with the help of one and a half million of their fellow citizens, a kind of collective exorcism of a particularly radical kind. And what can one say of the little matter of the blood plasma of Saint Januarius? Preserved in the city's cathedral, it liquefies once a year in the archbishop's hands and in full sight of many thousands of the faithful, who foregather on 19 September to pray and beg for the annual miracle that means that Naples will have a good year, without famine or fire, with fewer murders, fewer assassinations and other acts of violence, and with greater attentiveness and less corruption and less Neapolitan negativism.

Before the scene changes, I should first like to glance back briefly at the Naples of the late fifties and report on the local début of the great Maria Callas. Although she was already world-famous, she had always fought shy of appearing in Naples: the San Carlo was the home of her great rival, Renata Tebaldi, just as La Scala was Callas's theatre. It was enemy terrain. But one fine day the name of Maria Meneghini Callas appeared on the San Carlo playbill, and the evening duly arrived when the almost completely blind diva set foot on the enormous stage to the sounds of a cascading harp, a waifish figure as poor mad Lucy Ashton, another Fonteyn, sniffing the air, sensing the hostility of a crowd that was baying for blood and feeling an atmosphere so thick that it could be cut with a knife. She began her opening recitative, 'Ancor non giunse', followed by her first cavatina, 'Regnava nel silenzio', the difficult high notes and modulations of which were tantamount to a test flight, during which the house grew gradually quieter, holding its breath as the singer succeeded in imposing her own interpretation on her jaded, yet demanding listeners, implementing the vocal strategy that she used to master her innate and inbuilt vocal deficiencies, including what was later to become an increasingly audible guttural tremolo, overcoming them by means of her musicianship and intelligence, until audiences forgot that they existed. Her listeners could feel the effort involved and were all the better able, therefore, to appreciate and assess her achievement. In this way the singer captivated her public, one by one, men and women alike, turning them not into swine, as Circe once did, but into fans of Callas, Neapolitan lovers of music and music theatre who were won over by the diva's art and inspired by what they heard. I too was one of these people, although in my own case, my enthusiasm did not mean that I also had to be disloyal to Tebaldi. Indeed, the whole affair was not so important to me, since I had never been a fan in that sense. But Ingeborg, too, was fascinated by Callas's method and by her ability to portray human feelings, an ability that she owed to her highly gifted and extraordinary mentor, Luchino Visconti. I loved this audience for its readiness to fall under the spell of an artistic performance, to attend an event and grasp its importance, responding to the message and being able to express its delight and gratitude in so unmistakable a manner.

I often went to the Teatro San Ferdinando, which was run by Eduardo de Filippo, a great actor and dramatist who was well known for his performances as Pulcinella. I saw several productions of his works here, all of which, needless to say, included a starring role for their author, a taciturn, somehow Viennese and vaguely clownlike melancholic figure, but I also saw a number of works by one of his spiritual fathers, Edoardo Scarpetta, insanely funny pieces full of bitterness and misanthropy and with lots of wonderful roles. Two of the greatest Italian actresses, Puppella Maggio and Tina Pica, were members of his company, as was Eduardo's brother, Peppino, who wrote plays of his own but who was gradually to part company with his greater and more eminent brother. It was a theatre for the people run by a popular Chekhov or perhaps a latterday Nestroy, but altogether unique, with its own distinctive criteria, a distinctiveness due, not least, to the language in which these plays were performed. I was impressed by the force of a living tradition and by the simplicity and chaste elegance that it encapsulated and that clearly allowed it to depict even complex human relationships, without ever descending into kitsch or fustian or lewd jokes. Scarpetta's *Miseria e nobiltà* of 1888 is an out-and-out masterpiece of its kind. Performances of these unique pieces are among the most fascinating experiences of my years of apprenticeship in Naples, a period that came to an end with the beginning of the new decade.

I was no longer really turned on by Rome, by its noise and its cultural and social attractions. Indeed, I found myself forever being drawn back across the Alps by the magnetic appeal of the arts scene in Central Europe, but once I had found the house at Castel Gandolfo, there was no longer any question of my leaving Italy for good. I had rediscovered the place in the Castelli that had so much impressed me some ten years earlier and where I had felt so much at home. I gave up the flat in Rome, which had barely been used, and had the furniture brought to Castel Gandolfo. It was a decision that was to affect the whole of the rest of my life: Italy was to be the birthplace of all my works from now on, here in the light and airy *campagna*, and whenever I had had enough of my work and my hermit's existence, I could go to one of the great metropolises and gratify a rather more practical bent, conducting, staging my operas, teaching and generally enjoying myself.

At Castel Gandolfo, high above the Lago di Albano, I resumed work on my *Novae de infinito laudes*, a set of six songs of praise drawn from the world of philosophical treatises of the great sixteenth-century Nolan philosopher Giordano Bruno. The texts in question deal with the nature of the heavenly bodies and contain descriptions of all four elements, but always in an uncommonly figurative language in which even complex matters are expressed with a simplicity that is typical of the grandeur and majesty of the whole. I poured all my previous experience into the piece and took pains, once again, to obey only the strictest rules and apply the most rigorous standards: in 'La continua mutazione', for example, a glance at the score will show how the choral writing and brief ritornellos are strictly ordered – who nowadays can still do this sort of thing, I ask, and by 'this sort of thing' I mean not only the strict counterpoint and the polyphonic writing, each detail of which can be clearly heard, but also the whole musical expression and the manner in which the orchestral sound is organized in order to ensure that it makes its due effect. Of the cantata's last two movements, 'Sunrise' was somehow inspired by the descriptions of nature in Haydn's *Die Schöpfung* and passes without a break into the chorale-like final *lauda*. Both were written in Copenhagen during the winter of 1961/2 on afternoons when I was not rehearsing a production of *Elegie für junge Liebende*, which I was conducting, directing and designing myself (the latter with the help of Lila de Nobili's pupil, Fiorella Mariani). Folker Bohnet was free, and so he joined me there, practising voice exercises in our hotel room, studying the role of Hamlet, sometimes helping me a little at the rehearsals and trying to master Italian. On this occasion I was lucky with the opera, and the Copenhagen staging was revived, with immense success, at the 1962 Berlin Festival, when it was seen (as usual, with changes and improvements) at the Deutsche Oper in the Bismarckstraße. A large part in the success was played by Fischer-Dieskau, who had meanwhile grown into his part, and by Martha Mödl as Countess Kirchstetten. I recall that my set looked wonderful, not least because it was built and lit by the house's finest technicians. The production remained in the Deutsche Oper's repertory for many years and was also taken on tour to Brussels, Tokyo, Helsinki, Mexico City and Amsterdam, generally conducted by myself. The new intendant, Gustav Rudolf Sellner, became one of my staunchest supporters, and his assistant and later successor, Egon Seefehlner, proved no less enthusiastic in his encouragement. For both these men I feel only gratitude. It was thanks to them that West Berlin became my true artistic home at this time.

Meanwhile I had also started to appear on a regular basis – in other words, approximately once a season – with the Berlin Philharmonic. On almost every occasion it was my own works that I conducted, a programming decision that was welcomed and encouraged by both Karajan and his intendant, Wolfgang Stresemann. It also led to the first of several high points in the history of my liaison with the orchestra, when I was privileged to conduct my first five symphonies at two concerts at the new Philharmonie on 9 and 12 April 1964, the second of which also included the first performance of my new cantata, *Being Beauteous*, a setting of Rimbaud's poem of the same name from his cycle, *Les illuminations*. The soprano soloist on that occasion was Ingeborg Hallstein, who was joined by the orchestra's harpist, Fritz Helmis, and by four of its cellists, Eberhard Finke, Wolfgang Boettcher, Peter Steiner and Heinrich Majowski, who, between them, proved admirable midwives in bringing this new work into the world. And it was for Berlin that I wrote *Der junge Lord*, which received its first performance at the Deutsche Oper in the spring of 1965. But I am getting ahead of myself once again – the intervening years were to prove particularly eventful and need to be retold in some detail before we reach the mid-sixties.

It must have been during the early part of 1962 that I completed the score of the *Novae de infinito laudes* in Castel Gandolfo. Immediately afterwards I set to work on my Fifth Symphony, a commission from the New York Philharmonic that I finished in the course of the summer and that evokes the toccata-like animation of a large city like modern Rome, but it could just as well be New York, with its physical energy and dancing, its hectic pace and brutality. It harks back to the sound world of my *Novae de infinito laudes* and, as with the earlier piece, I privately referred to it as 'Renaissance music', fully conscious of what I meant by that. It is clear from the pieces I wrote at this time that new encounters had taken place. One such encounter, already mentioned, was with the musical world of Carlo Gesualdo and with the note of profound malaise that sounds throughout this music, burning its way into the listener's consciousness, while the other encounter was unhoped for and unexpected, nay, undesired and disruptive, a meeting with an ethereal son of New York, a creature of altogether exceptional beauty, so overwhelming as to cause me the greatest and stupidest difficulties of a private and emotional nature, causing the house of cards of my carefully ordered and happy private life to collapse with a resounding clatter.

In March 1963 I conducted a revised version of *König Hirsch* in Kassel. Now renamed *Il re cervo oder Die Irrfahrten der Wahrheit*, it was devised by Heinz von Cramer and me, with the aim of enabling the work to be staged in smaller houses. A reduced orchestral score had to be written and the daunting length of the original reduced from five to three and a half hours. Whole blocks of music were cut – including the second-act finale, which provided the material for my Fourth Symphony – and replaced by recitative. Cramer introduced a speaking role, the magician Cigolotti, who guides us through the story, a friend of all the good people and clowns, who in this new version have become alchemists. The production, directed by Hans Hartleb and designed by Ekkehard Grübler, was a great success, and the piece was later often revived elsewhere, notably in Zurich (with Ponnelle as director and me as conductor), in Munich under Dohnányi, and in Florence and Santa Fe. When the original version was finally seen in Stuttgart in 1985, it proved by no means as long or as tedious as had been feared. Conducted by Dennis Russell Davies, it was directed by Hans Hollmann and designed by Hans Hoffer, who came up with an ingenious solution to the problems of presenting the piece. It was clear what a qualitative difference there was between the two versions: *Il re cervo* is a compromise in which the white-hot inspiration of *König Hirsch* had been replaced by artificiality and interventionism.

As I have already mentioned, I conducted the first performance of *Novae de infinito laudes* in Venice on 24 April 1963. The chorus and orchestra of West German Radio, together with the four vocal soloists, Elisabeth Söderström, Kerstin Meyer, Peter Pears and Dietrich Fischer-Dieskau, and myself flew in the previous day from Cologne, where we had spent the previous two weeks rehearsing the piece and where we would give the German première the following evening. I almost died of stage fright, so, for me, the performance in Venice was a somewhat anxious occasion, but the evening as a whole was quite brilliant, by which I mean, first and foremost, the setting of the wonderful Teatro La Fenice, on whose stage the concert took place, and the sympathetic and *simpatico* audience. The first part of the programme consisted of the Italian première of Karl Amadeus Hartmann's beautiful, monumental Eighth Symphony, which I conducted in the presence of the composer.

But my conducting was still so highly strung and so concerned with the right notes and entries, with dynamics and with tempo relationships that I never really enjoyed the sensual pleasures of conducting – if such a sensation does indeed exist, it must be a wonderful feeling. I was never sufficiently well prepared. Learning scores was unspeakably tedious, and I invariably found myself thinking of other things. And even while conducting, in the middle of a concert, it was not unknown for my thoughts to wander – I was always terrified of such moments of distraction. As a conductor I was, and remain, an amateur, which is why I needed the very best orchestras, orchestras that were interested not in my stick technique but in the works that I asked to conduct. In this frame of mind, I appeared with some of the world's great orchestras and never made a fool of myself. But who can describe the torments of the sleepless nights during which I was plagued by a single all-consuming fear from which I could never escape. On one such occasion, in Vienna in 1978, I even suffered a heart attack. There was something inside me that forever fought against the perfectionism that might have made it possible for me to embrace the career of a conductor, with all its preordained phases – not that this was ever my intention. I conducted for two reasons: first, to perform my music as authoritatively as possible (or that, at least, was my aim) and, secondly, to get to know classical and contemporary composers, especially Mahler, in all their physicality. And in order to make music. And to make money. I have not conducted for a number of years. My hearing is no longer what it was, and I was increasingly afraid of stage fright, of hypersensitivity at rehearsals and of my own uncertainty and impatience. For weeks on either side of a concert I would be completely obsessed with it, which is no good: I need all my time for composing, before it is too late.

On 16 May 1963, a month after *Novae de infinito laudes*, my Fifth Symphony was unveiled in New York. It was the first time I had visited the city, which I found filled with African smells and animal passions. Everything seemed designed to ensure that Harlem, which in my own eyes is its beating heart and centre, was the most magnificent possible backdrop to the tragedies and enchantments that were played out within its walls and dilapidated tenements and among its degraded and humiliated inhabitants. It reminded me of lines from Ingeborg Bachmann's poem, 'Liebe: Dunkler Erdteil':

> The black king bares rapacious claws and, wide-
> Eyed, steers into their orbits ten pale moons
> And sets in train the tropical typhoons.
> The world sees you from a different side.

And

> Around the equator barriers fall.
> The panther alone is warmed by love's breath.
> He leaps across from the valley of death
> And rends heaven's hem with his paw withal.

But there was something else here, too, something like a wistful enslavement, as though I might find a cure for all the world's grief, here in 22nd Street. Bound up with this was a desire to change the colour of my skin and my psychological make-up in order to disappear among these people and escape from myself. My first visit to New York was notable for its romantic infatuation, its sense of Hoffmannesque illusion, but in spite of that – or, rather, precisely because of that – it was really quite fantastic. It was a new experience not to be able to sleep for sheer happiness – or was it simply jet lag? I had little time for musical matters: Bernstein, fortunately, needed little help in understanding my score. He said that he had noticed that it was clearly structured along systematic lines, but had not been able to work out what that system was. We left it at that. After the first rehearsal he invited me to go with him and watch him play squash – I thought I must have misheard. I also saw Rouben Ter-Arutunian again, who was doing splendidly in New York. He showed me the beauties of the city, where it was still possible to walk at night unarmed. On one occasion I had a couple of drinks (whisky sour) with Lenny at the Plaza bar. And I went with Aaron Copland to an official lunch, where I even delivered a short after-dinner speech, naturally in praise of New York City, the scene of my happiness and blind infatuation. William Schuman delivered a witty reply. I felt accepted and welcome. At that time there was still a lot of resentment – both spoken and unspoken – towards the Germans: the Second World War, after all, had ended less than twenty years earlier. For that reason I find it a little hard to understand that I should have delivered a paper – probably from one of my essays – at the Goethe-Institut that week, as a guest of Hans Egon Holthusen, and that I should have allowed myself to be seen with Friedelind Wagner in the box reserved for official guests at the Philharmonic Hall at the first performance of my Fifth Symphony. Although Friedelind Wagner's anti-Nazi credentials were not in question, there was something about her Aryan blondness that suggested guilt by association. Her presence was felt to be unfortunate. People were disappointed. 'You see,' they said, 'birds of a feather flock together whenever the going gets rough.' But the going was far from rough.

I had little time for such gossip in my present emotional state. Also I had to return straight home after the concert to write the music for Alain Resnais' *Muriel*, which I completed within a week, and then had to go to Paris to record the score in a studio in Boulogne. I had a wonderful time, not only with the silent, serious Resnais, but also with Delphine Seyrig and the producer Anatole Dauman. It was exciting, conducting with stopwatch in hand while the film was running in order to achieve perfect synchronization.

I then returned to Castel Gandolfo for a productive summer, sporadically interrupted by tempestuous storms of passion, the aftershocks of the events of recent months, like the explosions caused by dynamite packed within a confined space.

My feelings trailed along the ground. My heart lay exposed on the street. Composing was the only solution, I clung to it as a drowning man to a raft, writing one piece after another during these summer months, day in, day out: *Being Beauteous*, *Los caprichos*, a revised version of my First Symphony and *Ariosi*, a setting of love poems by Torquato Tasso for soprano, violin and orchestra that was first performed at the Edinburgh Festival on 23 August 1964 with Irmgard Seefried and Wolfgang Schneiderhan under the direction of Colin Davis. Thanks to its missing substantive, the second *Arioso* has an enigmatic quality to it:

No ha fiori il terreno
Come questo mi pare
Maraviglioso fior del vostro mare

A cui non fu mai pare
In ramo o'nprato ameno,
O pur di conca nel porporeo seno
Tra vaghi scogli e l'acque
Fra cui Venere bella in prima nacque.

Some time before that I had renewed contact with Jean Cocteau, years after my first visit to see him in 1953, when he was in Munich to stage his ballet *La dame et la licorne* at the Theater am Gärtnerplatz, for which he also created the *décor* and costumes. (On that occasion we had discussed a project involving *La voix humaine*, but happily nothing had come of it.) Folker Bohnet and I called on him at his apartment in the Palais-Royal on the day after the first performance in Paris of *Der Prinz von Homburg*, which he had attended with the Princesse de Polignac and Marie-Laure de Noailles. (On my way to the Théâtre Sarah Bernhardt, I bumped into Francis Poulenc carrying a little black leather suitcase: he was on his way, he explained, to see his chiropodist.) The embodiment of irresistible charm and wit, Cocteau received his visitors in a reception room lined with red satin, his manner reminiscent of a bygone age and suggesting a Proustian audience. It was impossible not to help wondering whether he had so much time for others because he no longer wrote himself or, if he did so, wrote very little. Had he turned instead to less demanding activities, such as ballets, painting ties, making films and producing frescoes? Munich's *maître de ballet*, Heinz Rosen, wanted to work with Cocteau again and invited me to write the music. The result was a desultory correspondence between the poet and me in which may be found some early sketches, fleeting but apt little images and finally the finished libretto for the ballet *Le fils de l'air*. Nothing came of it, I no longer know why – perhaps it was because of Cocteau's sudden death on 11 October 1963. All I remember is that I was unable or unwilling to make anything of the subject, or perhaps it was a mixture of the two. The whole affair was forgotten, and it was only recently that I rediscovered the typescript of *Le fils de l'air* among some yellowing papers. As I read through it, a few stray notes vibrated against my inner ear, so that, instead of returning it to the drawer, I wrote to Édouard Dermit, the *vitrier* in Cocteau's *Orphée*, in order to acquire the rights to the scenario, rights which, as it turned out, I had owned for the last thirty years. *Le fils de l'air ou L'enfant changé en jeune homme* deals with the Erlkönig motif, with temptation, seduction, enchantment and transformation. The ballet is based on a German-language poem, *Das Luftkind*, from a cycle that Cocteau wrote in 1934 for *Die Sammlung*, a journal published in Amsterdam by Klaus Mann, and that the poet recorded in French in 1935 in a longer and superior version. The whole libretto is conceived in terms of dance and cries out for a musical setting. But it would have to be set to spine-tingling music, music that could fragment and pass into natural sounds. A hurdy-gurdy, electric keyboards and the appalling din of fairground carousels would probably also be needed.

I warmed to the idea of being able to sit next to Édouard Dermit at the first performance of this drama about a spirit of the air: for years I looked forward to the prospect, it kept me going, and in my thoughts I wrote the music for Dermit's – the *vitrier*'s – ears alone, as though I wanted in this way to recall a period in my life that was long since past, to rediscover something that I had lost and to feel as young as I had done half a century earlier, when I first encountered Cocteau's *Orphée*. But in the event I had to attend the first night of *Le fils de l'air* on my own, without Édouard Dermit: on 15 May 1995 he stepped through the mirror into another world, in which he will remain for ever, discoverable only in thought. The ballet was premièred at the Schwetzingen Festival on 25 May 1997.

In mid-October 1963 Ingeborg Bachmann came to Castel Gandolfo. We had met up in Salzburg and set off towards Venice with Wenzel and a long-standing friend, Hubert Hilten, only to find ourselves late that evening driving through the Valle di Vaiònt, where a few days earlier a dam had burst, flooding the whole of the area and leaving some 1,800 dead. Speechless with horror, we gazed at the floodlit scene before us in which mud, wrecked cars and ruined houses stood out in unnatural brightness.

Ingeborg set to work on the opening scene of our comic opera, *Der junge Lord*. It was wonderful having her in the house. I had seen precious little of her in recent years, although I had sometimes been invited to her apartment in the Via Don Minsoni in Rome, where a Hollywood actor had lived until recently, Humphrey someone or other, a tenancy still clearly visible in the style in which it was decorated. Since around 1960 it had provided a home for Inge and Max Frisch. Frisch had gradually discovered Rome and enjoyed it in his own way, finding almost everything 'great', especially the snack bar on the first floor of the Café de Paris in the Via Veneto, which for him was urbane and chic and lively in a way that Zurich was not. Inge introduced him to Rome's literary world, but he spoke virtually no Italian and would suck at his pipe and stare, smiling with Swiss cunning, at this immoral, dubious foreign land that bristled with unpredictable sexual encounters of every conceivable kind and which he thought that he had long since understood. He felt, for example, that there were too many shower scenes in Visconti's *Rocco*. What else can one say? Life was not easy with 'the girl', as he called Inge, or so he told me one night over Irish whiskey. Whenever he heard her typing, he simply had to stop working, since he knew that its sound spelt quality and superiority. I, too, was always filled with feelings of quasi-religious awe whenever I heard Inge typing, be it in Naples, Castel Gandolfo or Marino, but it did not prevent me from working. Quite the opposite: it set me up and encouraged me to go on. And whenever Inge heard Max typing – he was notoriously hardworking – she would go off to the Café Greco or else to the hairdresser's and sit for hours under the dryer, reading glossy magazines. She had virtually stopped writing. Finally Herr Frisch made so bold as to run off with an even younger 'girl' (I once saw them together in the Via Condotti, he had his arm around her, like some prize possession, and was smoking his pipe, like Surabaya Johnny, you dog). The whole affair left Ingeborg desperately unhappy – for a time we even feared for her life, and from that day forth she was regularly ill.

After she had split up with Max Frisch, Fausto Moroni helped her to set herself up in a flat in Rome, in the Via Bocca di Leone. She also spent some time in Berlin on a grant from the Ford Foundation, a grant that was later awarded to Auden and also to me, so that, quite by chance, all three of us found ourselves in Berlin in the winter of 1964/5. All three of us, moreover, were living in the Grunewald: Auden was in the Hagenstraße, Inge on the Hasensprung and I myself only a few minutes away from her in the Trabener Straße, where I remained until the early summer of 1964, completing the whole of the opening act of *Der junge Lord*. 'But music is born by the lakeside, tossed off in a tearing hurry,' Ingeborg wrote in 1964 in *Ein Ort für Zufälle*, her deeply troubled dirge to Berlin. The second act of *Der junge Lord* was written in Castel Gandolfo, where I was largely thrown back on myself, although I sometimes drove out to the coast to spend a few hours unwinding at Sabaudia or visited the popular sulphur baths at Tivoli. On other occasions I would spend a wild evening in Rome, enjoying its nightlife's more dissolute delights. Folker had gone to South America with a German touring company, giving his Hamlet to the subcontinent's German colonies. I had said goodbye to him at the airport in Düsseldorf and now felt a certain emptiness, not least because the tour was to last rather more than a year. In the second act of *Der junge Lord*, the music slowly and not without good reason becomes somewhat blacker, after it has already become clear at the end of the opening act that there must be a certain ambiguity or something similar here.

I am particularly fond of the duet for Luise and Wilhelm in Scene Four, which takes place in the snow one night. Offstage we hear the crack of a whip and the screams of the ape being flayed, an ape whose existence is still unsuspected at this point in the story. The simple, true-hearted love of these two delightful young people is expressed in a folk-song-like style, a little reminiscent of Lortzing, a little of Mozart and Schubert (a number of musicologists have wrongly suggested Rossini, too), recalling the world of early German Romanticism, an ideal world, innocent and carefree, into which a tempest sweeps, bringing with it snow and pain and illusion, grim forebodings and blindness and truth, without the two of them being in the least aware of all this. The polyphonic writing that I had tried out in *Novae de infinito laudes* is now taken a stage further in antiphonal writing for the chorus. Dance and march rhythms predominate. The Hülsdorf-Gotha Municipal Band has been rehearsing the Janissary Chorus from *Die Entführung aus dem Serail* in order to welcome the distinguished foreigner (only a few days before I wrote this scene, Inge and I had attended a performance of Mozart's Singspiel at the Deutsche Oper in Berlin, conducted by Karl Böhm), while the children sing silly and/or malicious canons on genuine Austrian nursery rhymes. It all reminds one of folk dancing and salon dances. Only at the opera's dramatic high point, the rape scene, does the music suddenly switch to a virile Tempo di Madison unknown to the early *ottocento* but recalling Harlem instead. I like it when music dances: it can do so as well, or better, than anything or anyone else. In the kind of ballet that I like, the music itself seems to dance, and the dancers make music in turn. In *Der junge Lord*, I am particularly proud of the final scene or, rather, of the way in which it is structured – and how magnificently my librettist provided me with the necessary framework! It works. In spite of the steady increase in the number of voices deployed in this scene and in spite of the mounting sound pressure, everything remains audible, so the composition may be said to constitute a bulwark against the chaos that is all around and within us, driving us insane, at least until such time as we have learnt to exorcize it, taken it in hand and cut the Gordian knot. And it is art that allows us to do all this! Thus we cast out witches and devils by an act of conjuration. It was an attempt on both our parts to laugh at what we had suffered. We enjoyed a good laugh together. At some date – I no longer remember when – Inge moved out of her rooms in the Via Bocca de Leone and into a quieter and more beautiful flat in the beautiful Via Giulia, where fate overtook her in so terrible a fashion. She found it hard to write the libretto and was always tired, sickly and sad. Often, feigning strictness, I had to force her back to her desk, a strictness that we both found funny. But finally it was finished, a unified whole, written in a specifically literary German that was borrowed from early nineteenth-century novels, confessions and correspondence. The opera, it may be noted, ends with a curious, inverse allusion to the end of *Der Prinz von Homburg*, where the last two speeches read:

> **Homburg** No, tell me, is it a dream?
> **Kottwitz** A dream, what else?

In *Der junge Lord*, the corresponding lines are:

> **Wilhelm** You've been dreaming, a terrible dream.
> **Luise** It wasn't a dream.

And the townsfolk, duped, exclaim: 'It's an ape. It was the ape.' (For those many music lovers who know *Das Lied von der Erde*, this Mahlerian quotation and all that it stands for in the libretto do not need spelling out.) And, one last time, the ape calls out from the distance, citing Goethe's 'May the good spirit be kind to you'. But I like the fifth scene best of all, a scene that depicts the comic reception at Sir Edgar's home, together with the way in which luxury quickly decays and fashion falls from favour.

Here the music becomes highly artificial and comic – in my heartless and frivolous manner I had great fun with this scene. Comedy and satire are generally avoided today, not only because it is so difficult to strike the right note, but above all because most of our contemporaries lack the vocabulary necessary to avoid the feebleness of modern clichés and to produce and delineate comedy.

The first performance on 7 April 1965 was all that one associates with the idea of a triumphant success. From the stage, the sounds of acclaim on the part of the audience were every bit as powerful and demonstrative as the voices of dissent to which I had long since grown inured. We artistes are happy simply to be allowed on stage at all. Everything else – wages, assent, dissent – is altogether secondary. On the day after the final dress rehearsal, the Federal Bundestag was due to meet in West Berlin, a session designed as an act of provocation on the part of the West or, to be more precise, on the part of Ludwig Erhard's government. (In this context I remember bumping into the liberal politician, Erich Mende, in the lift at the Kempinski Hotel and almost speaking my mind on the subject.) The day before, fighter-bombers of the GDR's air force had flown low over the city, their supersonic booms clearly audible at the rehearsal of *Der junge Lord* at the Deutsche Oper. It was a political crisis that led several foreign friends of ours to cancel their visits to Berlin.

At the first-night party arranged by the West Berlin Senate, Paul Dessau and his wife, Ruth Berghaus, who had come over for the occasion from the East, were insulted by Senate secretaries and asked to leave. I had to intervene to ensure that good sense prevailed. But otherwise everything passed off wonderfully well, and the GDR's air force remained grounded from then on. Perhaps the Central Committee knew that I had a first night in the western half of the city. The show had turned out to be a huge success. In their style and sophistication, the stage-sets caught to perfection the mood of the libretto and the music, revealing a secret love for the object of the satire, a satire involving not victims, but human beings, the *dramatis personae* of comedy. As a whole, the work was both skilfully structured and warm-hearted, two qualities that made it unusual, not to say sensational, for its time. Everyone admired its perfection, but such perfection aroused suspicions, of course, since there was no longer any sign here of the chaos that was obligatory at this time: the self-confessions and self-accusations had taken on a life of their own. Where, it was asked, were the outbursts of primeval angst and despair? Stuckenschmidt's review was headed: 'Henze turns the clock back.' My initial reaction was not to read any further. Did people really think me capable of such a strong-man act, I wondered? Which clock did Stuckenschmidt mean? And how late was it anyway? In the hearts of so many people at this time there still existed this *esprit de corps* that demanded that every deviation from the officially prescribed rules and regulations that were dictated by curiously structuralist progressive thinking and that were applied to both life and art with equal rigour had to be denounced and punished without a moment's delay. But who was in charge of this organization? Who set the standards? Pierre? Or the frightful Heinrich Strobel? A kangaroo court? A central committee, a shady academy somewhere, in Darmstadt perhaps? No, that really was inconceivable. But why, in heaven's name, did people not slowly get used to seeing and accepting artistic objects for what they are, namely, as independent creatures with lives of their own? That would at least have been a beginning.

By the time that the Senate party was over, it was already late, but a dozen or so of us then went on to Wenzel's, including some of my friends from Rome, as well as Inge, Filippo and Christoph von Dohnányi, who had celebrated his début at the Deutsche Oper with this brilliantly rehearsed and conducted performance. We thought we were all wonderful and found each other immensely sympathetic.

Unfortunately, I cannot say that I myself felt particularly wonderful: my delight, which had turned to harmony and bliss when the aircraft arrived from Rome on the morning of the première, and my satisfaction at having found perfection and achieved a state of balance between deception and reality – this sense of delight was troubled by a new feeling that stirred within me, a feeling that Konrad Lorenz terms 'aggression' and that, in my own particular case, was principally turned – as always – against myself. It made me ill and withdrawn. I feared the worst, but I pulled myself together, smiled ingratiatingly and encouraged myself to carry on as though all was well. Yet the seeds of unhappiness were sown and were soon to bear their blighted harvest. The fruit of evil was reflected in the ageless, noiseless lakes of Upper Italy past which we drove on our silent way home.

7

My librettist had scored a palpable hit with *Der junge Lord* and, with the help of her royalties, was soon able to defray the not inconsiderable expense of replacing the whole of her wardrobe – with shoes to match, of course. The opera was recorded for the gramophone and for television and for a time was performed not only in West Berlin but in the eastern sector, too, where it was staged at the Komische Oper in a brilliant production by Joachim Herz. To date, it has been seen in more than fifty productions all over the world, including three in the United States, four in the German Democratic Republic and thirty-one in the Federal Republic. Composer, librettist and title were even mentioned in crosswords. In terms of its subject, the piece, alas, is as relevant as ever, although xenophobia is now so rife in Germany that it can no longer be combated with comedy or mockery. In the sixties, this was far less of a problem, so that light comedy may then have seemed a entirely suitable way of dealing with such an evil. Even so, it cannot be claimed that the Germans' attitude to foreigners is anything more than an incidental theme of *Der junge Lord*.

I had always been attracted by the idea of living off my work – and preferably living well off it, rather than being forever dependent on bursaries and grants. It has something to do with professional pride and with the need for independence. Advances from my publisher, which at some stage naturally have to be made good, and payments from the Society of Authors have always saved me from having to apply for government grants and the like. I have only ever begged on behalf of others, notably in the context of my various festivals, which are always devoted to works by my fellow composers. Unlike so many other artists, who have travelled the world with their works at the expense of the Goethe-Institut and similar organizations, my own affairs have always been managed in such a way that I have rarely had to tug my forelock at sponsors and yet still been able to pay my bills.

Life in the Castelli Romani appealed to me immensely. Indeed, it still appeals to me so much that, whenever I am away and however much I may be enjoying myself, I always feel very homesick and long to get back to my desk, to my garden and to my pets, and to the incomparable Italian sky. Even at that time, in the early sixties, I already knew that this was where I wanted to stay, and so I began to look around for some land (the little house in Castel Gandolfo where I was living was run down and the land on which it stood was not for sale). I found what I was looking for and paid for it with my fee from *Der junge Lord*. Unlike the house at nearby Castel Gandolfo, it did not overlook the lake, which has something sad and sinister about it, but lay amid vineyards below and to the west of Marino. It was an olive grove surrounded by high walls that were broken only by a baroque archway surmounted by a Latin inscription and the date '1710'. The gate itself was missing. I went inside and waded through the tall grass and corn poppies. It was a sizeable estate – several times larger than I had really intended to buy. I sat down in the shade of an olive tree and allowed the *genius loci* to weave its magic spell. At the northern end of the property stood five gigantic elms. Marino lies near the top of a hill not far from Cicero's Tusculum, beneath the extinct volcano of Monte Cavo, where the goddess Diana was worshipped in classical times. We were in the old *lepraia* of the Colonnas, one of Rome's leading houses. Even as late as the eighteenth century hares were still being raised here and released in the course of the autumn, when they were large enough to be brought down with bows and arrows fired by noble huntsmen on horseback, accompanied by greyhounds and whippets.

The years that I spent at Castel Gandolfo, from 1962 to 1966, are filled with some of my happiest memories. In Naples I had been obliged, much to my own discomfiture, to mix with what are called the 'right' people (in other words, lovers of music, and especially German music), whereas in Rome I did everything in my power to avoid all contact with such types, since I knew I would only be bored – just as I am today. I could not speak my mind and could not say what I wanted. One always had to hide one's true feelings in the absurdest possible ways and feign an interest in things that were not of the slightest concern. Sometimes, at parties, I was able to stand it no longer and simply got up and left. At that time it was still fairly easy to drive into town – and, once a week, to the garage for repairs to the beautiful Maserati that Folker had made me buy. The traffic still flowed freely, so that there was no difficulty in meeting people in town in the afternoon or evening or in inviting them out to the country. You could easily go to the theatre in the evening and did not need to spend hours searching in vain for a parking space. It had now also become much easier to see Luchino Visconti. His film *Rocco and his Brothers*, which had just been released, struck me as a remake of, or a sequel to, *La terra trema*, serious and powerful, and every bit as implacable as the people who have Rocco's fate and that of his millions of brothers in their hands. I also saw several of Luchino's new productions in the theatre, including a remarkable *Cherry Orchard*, a lavish *Don Carlos* and an unforgettable *Nozze di Figaro*, the most beautiful and intelligent staging of this opera that I have ever seen. Both were conducted by Giulini. The artistic director at that time was the young Massimo Bogianckino, who over several seasons succeeded in transforming the Teatro dell'Opera from the lethargic, ossified, provincial theatre that it has always tended to be into what was hailed – all too briefly – as Italy's leading opera house, with the finest repertory and casts. Little suspecting what he was doing, Bogianckino had given up his career as a pianist out of his love of the theatre and, at the time that I met him, was running the Accademia Filarmonica Romana, a kind of concert society founded by Rossini, where I conducted on a number of occasions. He later went to La Scala, then to the Paris Opéra, and latterly to Florence, where he even served as mayor for a time, an incumbency that ended in a serious heart attack but that did not deter him from returning to administration and running both the Teatro Comunale and the Maggio Musicale. Massimo Bogianckino has helped and encouraged me in not unimportant ways: wherever he has held office, it has always gone without saying that one or other of my works would invariably appear on the programme. Without him, my music, and in particular my music for the theatre, would still be largely unknown in Italy.

It was also in Rome in the 1960s that I became friendly with Elsa Morante, a petite and attractive woman of more or less my own age, with a serious, open face and beautiful, short-sighted eyes that forever betrayed her true feelings. She was a fighter by nature, someone who would tremble with emotion like the leaves of a mountain ash. When she spoke – and she spoke a great deal – her voice, which was normally a gentle contralto, would grow ever so slightly louder and acquire a suggestion of shrillness, a hint of the *hochdramatisch* soprano. By the time that I got to know her, she had long since separated from Alberto Moravia, whom she had married in 1941, and was internationally famous in her own right. I knew *L'isola di Arturo* and thought especially highly of her great novel, *Menzogna e sortilegio*: in other words, I already knew a little about her through her books, hence my initial shyness when, fighting back my curiosity, I first approached her, utterly terrified lest I say something inappropriate. At the time in question (1964/5), she was just getting over the death of Bill Morrow, a young American artist of whom she had been very fond and who, apparently under the influence of mescaline, had thrown himself from a window in New York. She particularly liked young people and just now had eyes only for Peter Hartman, a crazy Californian poet and composer of a somewhat obsessive bent. I conducted one of his orchestral works in Munich on 11 December 1964 as part of the musica viva series of concerts. It was called Adagio for Orchestra, a title that summed it up well. Elsa, of course, was in the audience.

Elsa also had time for Allan Midgette, a member of Andy Warhol's Factory, who had just been working in Italy as an actor on Bernardo Bertolucci's first film, *The Grim Reaper*. He looked just like his boss and was sometimes sent to replace him at vernissages and awards ceremonies in the southern states or on the West coast. Allan's red hair had to be permanently bleached so that it looked like Warhol's. He would have had no difficulty in opening his mouth and saying something appropriate on occasions of this kind, but since his boss only ever said 'Oh yes' or 'Oh no', no one needed to worry that the ruse would be detected. Allan was sweet – and a natural for the then fashionable part of a flower child. Apart from Bob Dylan, Elsa was especially fond of Pier Paolo Pasolini – it was through her that I, too, was later to get to know him. Pasolini's voice, soft and harassed, sounded like that of a man in a state of mental torment, a man who lived under the greatest pressure and who was engaged in a constant struggle. It reminded me somewhat of Luigi Nono's. He was short of stature, slenderly built, wiry and physically fit, with two weary eyes filled with a strange sense of isolation that peered out at you from behind black-rimmed glasses. A keen and lonely intellectuality was offset by his restless nocturnal search for happiness, for redemption in the suburbs, among the very people whose existence and problems were so central to his work.

These were the years of Pasolini's first films. On 22 November 1961 I went with Ingeborg Bachmann to the Piazza Barbarini, where his very first film, *Accattone*, was due to be shown. But Fascists had daubed the screen with ink, and the showing had to be cancelled. Elsa Morante chose the music not only for *Accattone* – which I consider Pasolini's finest film – but also for *The Gospel According to Saint Matthew*. In both cases it was music by Johann Sebastian Bach, a juxtaposition that allowed their messages and images to emerge with particular clarity and urgency. With his characteristic mixture of grim determination and self-denial, Pasolini lived in a state of feverish hyperactivity, not least as a journalist and as co-editor of Moravia's literary journal, *Nuovi argomenti*, repeatedly taking part in political discussions and constantly finding himself involved in petty disputes and litigation. Elsa, by contrast, remained within her self-appointed confines, which is not to say that politics was a matter of total indifference to her. She was interested in that aspect of politics that has to do with language, with human expression and its dignity in language, with the truth of the word and its reflection in class conflict and consciousness. She shared with Pasolini the same unfathomable, ethically and culturally justified hatred of the Italian bourgeoisie, a hatred and contempt that provide a key to understanding their way of thinking and that found their fullest and most frightening expression in Pasolini's final film, *Salò*.

There was someone else of importance who shared these sentiments, and that was the shy and silent *poète maudit*, Sandro Penna. I am certain that in no case was it merely a matter of taste that led to their vehement rejection of the brutalistic and Fascist *borghesía*, a class from which all three of them hailed, which is why they knew it so well. Far more was at stake here, to wit, the agitated concern that Italy's industrial revolution was on the point of destroying all the old cultural values that were rooted in the common people. They watched as their country was brutalized and Americanized, observed the loss of purity and sense of identity among the working classes and saw the death throes of an ancient, traditional culture. This gave them a sense of mission: each in his or her own way sought to draw their audiences' attention to the common, simple people and their culture and to remind the common people of their own distinctive features.

Elsa was used to people coming and pouring out their troubles to her – and that included me. Indeed, I did so with what can only be called increasing enthusiasm. We would talk on the telephone for hours. Once she came to spend Christmas at Castel Gandolfo (needless to say, there was no Christmas tree) and, as always, we would walk for miles by the lakeside and listen to music together. Mahler was her favourite composer. Mozart she regarded as the world's wisdom transmuted into music. I set her beautiful poem, 'Alibi', in my *Cantata della fiaba estrema*. It is a kind of love song – 'Only those who know love can understand, only to the lover does the world's diversity unfold its splendours, only to him is the house of its twofold mysteries opened: the mystery of grief and the mystery of joy' – but I am afraid that she did not like the setting when she heard it at its first performance in Zurich on 26 February 1965, when the conductor was

Paul Sacher and the soloist Ingeborg Hallstein, for whom the work was written. If I remember aright, Elsa thought that the music was not sufficiently impassioned and that the choice of a coloratura soprano as soloist was a miscalculation. In order for her to have liked it, the music would have had to be more dark-toned, to have been sung by a contralto and to have been filled with burning passion. I ought, she felt, to have forgone the fairy-tale element in the poem and dispensed with its childlike, playful qualities, but it was very much these qualities that had made possible the stylization already suggested by the poem. Perhaps she did not notice or understand the evangelical, cantata-like nature of my setting, but I did not feel like explaining my intentions to her after the event. The piece breathes a gentle, childlike atmosphere with its wholly unsensuous bucolic character – indeed, its lack of sensuality was something I thought particularly important. Central to it is an a cappella chorus – the first I had ever written and, as such, a fair example of what I was capable of achieving at that time. I wrote another choral work at this period, a setting of Ingeborg Bachmann's *Lieder von einer Insel*, which she had completed ten or more years earlier. It was scored for a chamber choir and small instrumental ensemble. I tried to add a few highlights to the songlike, understated simplicity of these poems and to reflect, confirm and clarify their message by adding a second voice to that of the poet herself.

Ingeborg wrote to me from Montigny-sur-Loing on 26 July 1965:

> I saw Günter Grass yesterday. He's travelling around, trying to drum up support for the Social Democrats and he'd so much like you to come to Bayreuth and share a platform with him, since Willy Brandt is turning out to be the only serious figure in the country. We spoke about it at length. And so I'm like a diplomat with limited powers, although I realize that, in spite of everything that's being said, this party simply *must* win the elections, so that people can go on living, otherwise the country will go to the dogs.

I wrote at once to Ingeborg and Grass, agreeing to go to Bayreuth and talk. She then wrote two more letters from Montigny, in both of which she agonized over whether she had done the right thing in summoning me to Bayreuth and inviting me to speak in support of Willy Brandt. She was now uncertain of the implications of such a move, an uncertainty due, not least, to the SPD's increasing willingness to compromise and adopt a pragmatic stance. She was afraid that I might fall into a trap and wrote: 'But I really do believe that our aspirations, our ideas and our demands must rise above day-to-day politics like a melody – in short, I remain incorrigible and believe that we must remain true to these ideas, even if no one else wants them, since one cannot exist without the insane belief that there is such a thing as an absolute, a belief for which Grass, for example, rebukes me.'

In her second letter, dated 13 August, she wrote: 'If you go to Bayreuth, I'd like to come, too. I'd come straight from here, and we might perhaps spend a couple of hours looking through your speech beforehand, since I really would like to help you – and I think I probably can. You can safely go some way *beyond* social democracy, that won't harm these waverers in the least.'

And so it came about that I sat down and wrote a speech that I took with me to Munich, where it was carefully edited by Ingeborg. I delivered it in Bayreuth – not in the Festspielhaus or the Villa Wahnfried, but in the Stadthalle – on the evening of 4 September 1965. In excerpted form, it ran as follows:

> Here in Bayreuth one becomes conscious of the dualism that is so typical of the Germans, of the vacillation between cosmopolitanism and national provincialism and, hence, of the whole difficulty that we face as a nation. In our country, the artist is often forced into the role of the court jester, so that there is a tendency to forget that it is artists in particular who, questioning, doubting and demanding [i.e. demanding a solution to intellectual and moral problems], are most deeply committed to their country. Think of Heinrich von Kleist, Georg Büchner, Heinrich Heine, Kurt Tucholsky and Heinrich and Thomas Mann. All of them held political views and harboured political desires; all of them loved their country; and all were afraid of the darker instincts that dwell within this nation, a nation so easily led astray as soon as the emotionalism is cheap enough, the political slogans aggressive enough to appeal to its permanently offended, subliminal instincts. All these men were misunderstood and isolated; they fought unsuccessfully and were driven away. In the majority of cases, their ideas bore fruit only many years after their deaths, and even then, it was more in the form of literary success than as a genuinely formative element.
>
> [. . .] Musicians are said to dream a lot and to tend to exaggerate and transfigure the things of this world, or at least to see them in the light of their own inner tensions. As they weave their contrapuntal textures out of loneliness and night, the emotions they normally express

are hatred and love. They give mankind a voice with which to sing, and in that way they, too, achieve materiality and can be called to account and made to feel responsible. Even if they cannot be expected to observe the quotidian world with the eyes of a union secretary, one must none the less accept that although their thinking is influenced by the familiar ritual of the musician's daily round, it is not thereby rendered incapable of concrete expression. If I speak to you here today, I do so by appealing to many other musicians, to other artists and individuals otherwise associated with art, all of whom would have something similar to say and who, like me, suffer on account of the state of things in Germany today, but who have no chance to express themselves publicly. [. . .]

It was with a very real sense of horror that we witnessed something which, in our innocence, we should never have thought possible: we saw the government in Bonn inviting Germany's nuclear families to finance Germany's nuclear weapons, fatal cudgels for future crusades. It was a relatively slow process that led to this demand, so that sheer terror at the idea could gradually grow and insinuate itself with every passing year. For quite a lot of young Germans, myself included, this development is little short of a disaster. Should we have spoken out straightaway? Many did indeed speak out, protesting and demonstrating. Others, including myself, simply went abroad. For the sake of my work and my own lucidity I went to another country. But from there I observe my native Germany with the inquisitiveness of a lover [a lover, I now feel, who was spurned], and I have learnt a great deal from Italian newspapers that finds little coverage in the German press but which inspires headlines there that keep our sense of horror in a state of constant ferment.

How am I supposed to explain to my Italian neighbours and friends such phenomena as the anti-Semitism in secondary schools and government departments, the old Nazis in the judiciary, the daubed swastikas, the embarrassing eloquence of Hans-Christoph Seebohm, the claims to power of Franz Josef Strauß, the Spiegel Affair, Erhard's condemnation of 'degenerate art', and so on? As a catalogue, it is as terrible as it is incomplete. Should I try to make light of it? Should I share the fears and worries of my Italian neighbours and friends? What should I say to my Jewish colleagues in New York and London when they ask me about these things? How am I to continue to fulfil the conditions enshrined in our country's constitution, conditions that

> I will not allow to be violated? This is the constitution of every democratically thinking, modern German who takes upon himself the burden of the past but who wishes to balance that burden with his sense of pride, a sense of national pride that can appeal to a new Germany, a Germany with an anti-militaristic younger generation not yet born at the time of Auschwitz, a Germany that has no desire to demand back regions that she lost through her historical guilt and which can be regained only by incurring yet further guilt, a Germany that demands no nuclear weapons for her army, a Germany that could show the world how national intelligence and the capacity for work may be directed upwards, not downwards again, where vindictiveness lurks with one of the most risible, absurd and offensive of all emotions: the racial arrogance that has enriched the German language with the word 'degenerate' [. . .].

Also present in the hall that evening were not only Willy Brandt and his wife, but also my ghost writer, Ingeborg Bachmann, as well as Günter Grass and his wife, the writer Reinhard Baumgart and his wife, the directors Fritz Kortner and Bernhard Wicki, the actress Agnes Fink and Karl Schiller, who later became minister of trade. It is said to have been an important evening.

It was thanks to Ingeborg's political concerns and to the political resolve of my new friends in Rome that I now began to take a greater and more regular interest in all that was going on in the outside world and to read the newspapers, even if only to have a vague understanding of what people were discussing in the trattoria in the evenings. My carefree years in Naples, when I lived out the adolescence which, for historical reasons, I had never known at home, were now definitively over. There were things in the world, I now realized, that affected me as much as the next man and which were far more important than I myself.

It was at this point that Ingeborg pressed into my hand a copy of Herbert Marcuse's *Eros and Civilization*. Doors sprang open. It became possible to see myself in a wider social context. My next book was Frantz Fanon's *The Wretched of the Earth*. It became clear to me that I knew far too little about the world – a place filled with impenetrable darkness in which, thoughtlessly and egocentrically, I had pursued my private pleasures as though my life were textured like some old French polyphonic motet: a cantus firmus in the baritone register inspired by the smallholder's dreary round, with a contrapuntal line on, say, the viola above it singing its melancholy strains; above them both, in a bright soprano register, the trumpet's strident blare signalling the author's urge to assert himself, while far below, in the contrabass clarinets and double basses, slept 'aggression', the urge for sexual oblivion which, like a pit for murderers and suicides, calls everything into question. But at the pitch of the alto saxophone was a kind of broken-down gallows humour from a film with Marlene Dietrich, forever repeating the words, 'Can't help myself, no one can help me'. Life and art had become interchangeable, so that it was no longer possible to say for certain what was part of real life and what belonged in my music.

In the autumn of 1964, immediately after completing my setting of Ingeborg Bachmann's motets and shortly after finishing *Der junge Lord*, I began work on *The Bassarids*. In order to attack this piece with the requisite *élan* and come to terms, both musically and psychologically, with all the personal experiences and acts of utter madness that I had committed in recent years, I felt as though I should like a little company and, with it, a reason for entering into a relationship with someone else, with all the tensions that that would involve. One sunny Sunday morning in Rome in November 1964, the gods were sufficiently well disposed to arrange just what I wanted. Hans Schmidt-Isserstedt (known to his German colleagues as 'der blanke Hans', an expression more normally used of the storm-tossed North Sea) had just conducted a performance of my *Trois pas des Tritons* at the Accademia di Santa Cecilia in Rome, and I was sitting alone in a crystal-encrusted bar in the Via Veneto, contentedly drinking a Beefeater Martini on the rocks, when it happened. Shivering slightly with the cold, wearing the green loden coat that characterized his class and frowning as always, Fate entered the room with a spring in his step and a condescending glance, and, with the unmistakable self-assurance of his caste (an assurance that can neither be imitated nor feigned and which one either has or has not), he made himself known: the highly unreliable muse of *The Bassarids* had entered the drama of my life. My depression and tiredness vanished in a trice, and I could get on with my opera. Only it wasn't as simple as that. My monastic life as a composer was once again undermined by a hedonistic component. The covert aim of the exercise was to furnish me with the feelings generally associated with love at its most tempestuous, from simple desire to the bitterness of jealousy (of which I could never get enough) and from tender veneration to a very real longing for death – feelings, in short, that had to be depicted in every bar of *The Bassarids*. Before they could be turned into music, I first had to experience these feelings myself – including Pentheus's obsessions. In that sense, I could hardly have been better provided for. It was winter, the little house was damp, and the electric stoves either gave of their best or gave out completely. I could have gone away – perhaps to see Wenzel in Berlin, where a welcoming fire was waiting, but no, I couldn't leave. I had to stay in Castel Gandolfo, waiting for the phone to ring. Sometimes it didn't ring for two or three days at a time, so that the days spent at my desk – days artificially drawn out – were followed by sleepless nights during which the 'Frère Jacques' motif from Mahler's First Symphony kept on going round and round, remorselessly, inside my head.

Ingeborg spent most of the winter in Berlin and so was unavailable to help me. On one occasion – it was March 1965 – the tiny house at Castel Gandolfo was snowed in for a week, making it impossible to get in or out. Trees came down under the exceptional weight of the snow. I felt an enormous tension vis-à-vis the outside world, besotted, as I was, with a single person – someone who, merely because of his beauty and perhaps because of his somewhat dubious or at least inscrutable character, had to act as a catalyst for sin, seduction, deception and promiscuity, someone in league with the Devil or with the god of wine, smiling the smile of the Bassarids and acting on behalf of a band of conspirators sent out to undermine my moral and intellectual well-being. Behind it all, I saw the ideology of the Roman bourgeoisie, an ideology nurtured on the unshakeable arrogance of the rich and on a total contempt for their fellow human beings already imbibed by their tiny offspring at the breast of their wet-nurses from Sardinia or the Abruzzi and reinforced by the potty-training of their prim Swiss nursemaids. Such people were not allowed to know what was going on – his parents, after all, would have been appalled, not least on account of the combatants' social incompatibility: this was another of the humiliations I had to endure. I knew now what Elsa Morante meant when she refused to have anything to do with the object of my great passion.

With the advent of spring, I left for Berlin and *Der junge Lord*, after which I travelled on to New York, where I made the most of my four weeks' leave of absence from the battle front, putting Italy and its Bassarids behind me, listening to Stokowski's public rehearsals and his first performance of Ives' Fourth Symphony on WNYC on 26 April 1965, rehearsing and conducting *Elegy for Young Lovers* at the old Juilliard School and finally returning to Stuttgart for the West German première of *Der junge Lord*, which I saw in the company of Ernst Bloch, who seemed much taken by the piece.

I then returned to Marino, only to find that, in spite of all my attempts to break free, I was still suffering from all my old feelings and that I was on the point of going completely mad. Once again I bundled my music together and flew to Berlin, where I spent the whole of the summer with Wenzel, writing not only the Intermezzo for *The Bassarids* but also a letter, breaking the whole thing off, and feeling utterly wretched, as though a tiny computer-driven instrument of torture were built into my solar plexus.

To turn Euripides' *Bacchae* into a modern music drama and give the piece the title of Aeschylus's lost *Bassarids* (= 'those who wear fox-skins') was Auden's idea, of course. He had first mentioned it at Glyndebourne during the summer of 1961, and I returned to his suggestion in 1963, when I received a commission from the Salzburg Festival to write an opera suited to the vast expanse of the Großes Festspielhaus stage. On this occasion there were no lengthy discussions – not only was the subject matter familiar, it also decreed the work's form. Both Auden and Kallman were keen that, as a relatively young German composer, I should learn to overcome my political and aesthetic aversions to Wagner's music, aversions bound up in no small measure with my many unfortunate experiences in the past. It was unclear to me why this should be so necessary, but I willingly agreed to their conditions and consented to attend a Wagner opera without walking out after only ten minutes – as Nono had done at my *Elegie*. The conditions under which I was to make good my promise were as auspicious as they were luxurious: I happened to be in Vienna at the very time that *Götterdämmerung* was being given at the State Opera, in a production directed and conducted by Karajan. He gave me the use of his private box, so that I was able to observe the proceedings in comparative comfort, and a fascinating experience it turned out to be: the conductor's composure, his superior manner and total control over his players and singers were certainly without equal. On stage it was so dark that only the spotlit figure of the conductor stood out from the all-pervading gloom. On my way to see him during the first interval I bumped into Adorno, with a copy of the thick green study score under his arm. During the second interval I had arranged to meet Chester Kallman in the bar – Auden had sent him along to keep an eye on me. According to the programme, the performance was due to end at around ten o'clock, and it was already half past ten. It seemed to go on for ever. Of course, I was perfectly capable of judging the wider significance of Wagner's music: as any fool can tell you, it is a summation of all Romantic experience, introducing new ideas, new perspectives and new proportions. And, I have to admit, it sounded wonderful – silky and heroic, ardent and full-throated, and extremely well written into the bargain. But I simply cannot abide this silly and self-regarding emotionalism, behind which it is impossible not to detect a neo-German mentality and ideology. There is the sense of an imperialist threat, of something militantly nationalistic, something disagreeably heterosexual and Aryan in all these rampant horn calls, this pseudo-Germanic *Stabreim*, these incessant chords of a seventh and all the insecure heroes and villains that people Wagner's librettos.

There was little real danger that I would explore Wagnerian techniques when writing *Die Bassariden*. In their libretto, my two authors called the piece an *opera seria*, which seemed to me to point the work in an entirely different direction, although even this suggestion I followed to only a limited extent and up to a certain point. The inclusion of individual numbers such as arias, choruses and ensembles notwithstanding, the opera as a whole is based on a four-part symphonic structure which, musically and formally, spans the great conflict of this human drama and thereby holds it together. I tried to show how the musical material associated with the god Dionysus slowly, insinuatingly, insidiously and, finally, with the most terrible brutality destroys Pentheus's monastically chaste world of sound, undermining it and, in the end, annihilating it utterly. I wanted to write a grand opera. But when the libretto arrived in Castel Gandolfo during the late summer of 1964, I felt only exhaustion, paralysis and discouragement, feelings no doubt made worse by the depression from which I suffered every autumn. Generally a week or two of tormenting inactivity, a wasted journey or a deadly boring hotel overlooking some beach or other was enough to drive me back to my desk, happy, penitent, grateful and in the very best of spirits.

As for the musical language of *Die Bassariden* – where exactly does it come from? And on what tradition is it based? After all, it is certainly not Wagner's compositional method that is taken up and developed here; for that, my piece is far too close to the older type of number opera. Still less can it be compared with Strauss – I really do not know what Stuckenschmidt can have been thinking of when he wrote after the Salzburg première in 1966 that Strauss had finally found his true successor here. I was especially annoyed at this, since Stuckenschmidt clearly thought that he was doing me a favour by defining my position in the *Frankfurter Allgemeine Zeitung*. It was an English colleague of his who unwittingly came much closer to the truth when he wrote somewhere (I was told this only recently) that my music sounded like 'Strauss turned sour'. That is a view that I can more easily accept. After all, the occasional late Romantic exuberance that is found in my works is not intended to be exuberance as such but its anachronistic opposite. A Mahlerian such as myself (and Mahler's influence is greater in the music of *Die Bassariden* than even in my Sixth, Seventh and Eighth Symphonies) cannot simultaneously summon up the same degree of enthusiasm for Richard Strauss. But one can show its negative aspects, can turn existing values upside-down and call them into question, just as everything in art must forever be re-examined and constantly called into question.

The artist must always work to improve his means of expression and, like every artist and artisan, strive for perfection. The successful work should be his life's ambition. Once he has managed to reformulate and refashion all his ideas about beauty and horror, hell and paradise and to express them in faultless, unique and matchless metaphors – only then may he perhaps retire, relieved, from the field of battle. But who can say when this point has been reached, if not the creative artist himself? My old friend Francis Bacon, whom I admired enormously and whom I miss very much, would still get up at seven every morning, even when he was eighty, and stand, as straight-backed as any soldier, in front of his canvas, struggling to come to terms with chaos and seeking to capture the fortuitous joy of perfection. I was not yet forty when I finished *Die Bassariden*. But, even if I had been able to spend longer on the work than circumstances permitted, I would have been unable to summon up any more emotional force or creative imagination than are already to be found in this piece.

The full score was completed on 28 September 1965, so that my publisher still had plenty of time to produce not only a vocal score for the singers to learn their roles but also the parts and a full orchestral score which, prepared by first-rate graphic artists, looked for all the world as though it had actually been printed. The first performance of the work had been fixed for 6 August 1966 in Salzburg. The director was Gustav Rudolf Sellner, the designer Filippo Sanjust and the conductor Christoph von Dohnányi – in other words, the same team as the one to which Ingeborg and I owed the success of *Der junge Lord*. Karajan had originally intended to mount the piece in Vienna, but this plan had had to be abandoned when it was discovered that he no longer had the time and that the resources of the Großes Festspielhaus were taken up by his new production of *Carmen*, including a television recording of the work. The only remaining possibility, suggested by Sellner, was to rehearse *Die Bassariden* in Berlin and bring the production, lock, stock and barrel, to Salzburg in time for the dress rehearsal. I went away to relax and unwind, stopping first in Agadir, where, on only the second day of my holiday, I dislocated my right arm in a stupid attempt to show off by diving from a five-metre board. From there I travelled to Marrakesh, where it never once stopped raining, and finally to Madrid for a highly eventful and somewhat dissolute weekend that I wish could have lasted longer, so surprisingly well did it go in its inconsequential, delightful, touching and pleasing way. But I had to return to Rome and conduct a concert with soloists from the Berlin Philharmonic: Elsa's cantata was one of the pieces on the programme, which consisted entirely of my own compositions.

In the meantime I had rented a small apartment in Rome, on the top floor of a house in the Via Sant'Andrea delle Fratte, since I would have to attend the opera house every day during the coming weeks and months in order to rehearse *Giovane Lord*, which was to receive its Italian première at the Teatro dell'Opera in November 1965. The production was entrusted to Virginio Puecher, while the sets and costumes were again designed by Filippo Sanjust – and once again they were magnificent, albeit completely different from the ones he had designed for Berlin only six months earlier, being somewhat cruder, more expressionistic, more eerie, no doubt a little more attuned to local expectations and to the Roman way of seeing things. I spent these autumn months feeling listless, disorientated and exhausted. I remember conducting Mahler's First Symphony with the Berlin Philharmonic and can still recall my inner emptiness, a kind of apathy that constantly plagued me, so that everything I touched or attempted to touch went wrong. It was a feeling that I was unable to shake off, not only on this pointless, dispiriting evening at the Philharmonie but also in my private dealings with my fellow human beings. Everything felt joyless and uninspired. Friends from Rome, including Fonteyn and Nureyev, attended the concert. Normally I would have been delighted by their presence, but how much rather would I have been elsewhere – ideally, nowhere at all – on that particular evening. How often I felt like this at that time! It would have been best if I could have stayed at home, unseen and unheard, until I had recovered my health and regained a sense of normality, and people would no longer have been bored in my presence and would no longer have needed to fear my company.

Since 1962 I had torn myself away from my desk at Castel Gandolfo and travelled to Salzburg seven times a year – in other words, once a month during term time – in order to take charge of a composition class at the town's Mozarteum. This appointment had been the idea of the director, Eberhard Preussner, to whom I had additional reason for being grateful in that it was he who had drawn the Salzburg Festival's attention to me and my works. I ran this class until 1967, but it gave me little pleasure. I simply did not know where to start, there was no method to my teaching, and all I could do was repeat and pass on to my students all I had learnt from Wolfgang Fortner twenty years earlier – techniques which, based on the achievements of the classical, contrapuntal Leipzig school, could be applied to contemporary music. The time had not yet come when I could regard my own compositional style as something worth passing on to others, so that I was able to restrict myself here to questions of general compositional technique and to the sort of problems raised by Classical Modernism in general and by my students in particular. I insisted on teaching my students individually. Among those who were later to devote themselves to full-time composition were Tona Scherchen (Hermann Scherchen's half-Chinese daughter), Stephen Douglas Burton (who came to Salzburg on an exchange programme from Oberlin College, Ohio), Henning Brauel from Hanover and Walter Haupt from Munich. Brauel and Burton later worked for me as assistants, conductors and arrangers, a collaboration that I repaid by conducting Brauel's music in London and Berlin and by giving the first performance of Burton's *Ode to a Nightingale* with the Berlin Philharmonic.

It was while I was in Salzburg for *Die Bassariden* in 1966 that I handed in my notice at the Mozarteum with effect from the following term – I no longer wanted to teach other people how to write music, but first wanted to learn to do so myself. I had no wish to establish a 'School of Henze' or to carve out an academic career for myself. The fact that I gave up such a well-paid job at a time of financial crisis in my life is a clear sign of the intolerable nature of the post or else of my general state of mind at that time. Perhaps it was also bound up with my earliest efforts to gain my independence. I felt a need to account for myself and my artistic activities. This may also explain why I prevailed upon Schott's to publish a selection of my miscellaneous prose writings in 1964 under the title *Essays*, a collection that also includes the public lecture that I delivered in Berlin's Kongreßhalle on 28 January 1963. Even today, this lecture remains no less important as a programme or statement of my position as an artist than my 1955 letter to Josef Rufer, a letter likewise included in the same volume of essays and its later editions, now retitled 'Music and Politics'.

In the meantime, the building work on my house at Marino, which had started early in 1963, was progressing, but twice had to be broken off for financial reasons during the years that followed. I kept visiting the site and inspecting it, paying the bills and worrying endlessly. What had I let myself in for? I was trying to break away from the Establishment, gain my freedom, cast off existing shackles and, with a new-found vigilance, travel light – and, at the same time, I was becoming increasingly bogged down in debts because of a piece of property. Where would it all end? And how was I to meet the difficulties bound up with my attempts to run a house that was far too big and expensive for my needs?

By a stroke of luck – or perhaps it was a conciliatory gesture from on high – it was at about this time that I met a young man from Forlì (where the forlana is still danced to this day), Fausto Ubaldo Moroni by name. Fausto looked like the son of a Byzantine prince as depicted in a Ravenna mosaic, or else like a peasant's son or a maritime adventurer. He spoke Romansh and, with his passionate love of good food and fine wines and of other sensual pleasures, evinced a unique lust for life. He had attended a performance of *Giovane Lord*, which was currently playing at the Teatro dell'Opera, and called on me a few days later in the Via Sant'Andrea delle Fratte, not least to confess that he had found it almost impossible to come to grips with my music. One day he came with me to Marino to take a look at the ruins at La Leprara. I noticed that he was familiar with administrative procedures and at the same time exceptionally practical. He had worked for an academic publishing house, La Nuova Italia, before becoming an art dealer and was now on the point of going to America to explore the opportunities for advancing his career and making his fortune there. But I also noticed that the building project at Marino and the problems associated with it were beginning to exercise a certain hold on him, so that I finally plucked up the courage to ask whether he might care to take over the running of the estate as a full-time job. He was initially appalled at the idea – he must have realized how hard the work would be and how much responsibility and pressure would be placed on him in consequence. It would involve a radical change of plan, a totally different lifestyle and working environment. Not only was the offer unexpected, it came from a wholly unfamiliar quarter. He got to know my friends, foremost among whom was Ingeborg, who was immediately taken by him, just as he was by her.

Fausto came with me to Berlin at the beginning of 1966. I stayed there for several months, helping Sellner and Sanjust on their production of *Die*

Bassariden, imposing myself on Wenzel and writing *Musen Siziliens* for the Singakademie in West Berlin. This last-named work was a commission requiring me to devise a choral style that could be mastered by amateur singers and is a setting of three excerpts from Virgil's *Eclogues* adapted by Franco Serpa, whom the reader will recall having met in chapter five, when he shook my hand after the ill-starred local première of *Boulevard Solitude* in Rome in 1954 and who now taught at the University of Trieste. The chance to see him again with a certain regularity was one of the few pleasures that Rome then had to afford in terms of human contact. He knew the Latin classics intimately and was also interested in music, so that he was able to familiarize me with the prosody and rhythmic peculiarities of my Virgilian original and to answer all my questions, most of which were of a philological or philosophical nature and stemmed from the lamentable gaps in my general education and from my lack of knowledge of Greek. He was able and trustworthy – in a word, what we would call 'serious'. For a joker and a madcap like me, he was a useful, not to say indispensably necessary, antidote.

On the day of our departure for Berlin, we were met at Rome's Fiumicino Airport by two young American pianists, Joseph Rollino and Paul Sheftel, who wanted to say goodbye. Unable to find sufficient work as a piano duet in Europe, they were on the point of returning to the United States in the hope of taking up teaching appointments there. They were brilliant pianists and delightful people, and I liked them both very much. During the flight to Berlin, I was suddenly struck by the idea of setting *Musen Siziliens* as a concerto for two pianos and offering it to Joseph Rollino and Paul Sheftel, both of whom loved Rome and were sad to have to leave Italy and return to their native New York. Such an approach would allow me to transfer technically demanding musical procedures from the chorus to the two solo instruments. The chorus is now supported by a standard Classical complement of wind instruments and takes the place of the string orchestra that would normally accompany the soloists.

I am well aware that, in its open espousal of traditional tonalities, *Musen Siziliens* is a borderline case and that a number of champions of modernism have found it hard to follow me down this particular road. Hans Heinz Stuckenschmidt is said to have remarked – and, indeed, may even have done so – that the piece contains a number of passages that can no longer be described as modern. As with *Der junge Lord*, there are also reminiscences of more conventional writing from the pen of a father figure such as Stravinsky, reminiscences that have encouraged progressives to turn up their noses at the piece. There are also echoes of Mozart and even of Berlioz, for whom I actually care very little. And there is also, in the third movement, a lengthy and direct quotation from Beethoven that has always been overlooked. Whether or not it was influenced by my source, the form of the piece is Classical, emphatically Classical. I cannot hear it often enough and often hum it to myself. There are sections that I know by heart, and for years I included it in my concert programmes, mostly with the Rollino–Sheftel duet. They had now been able, after all, to remain in their beautiful apartments in Rome, together with their wives and children. I particularly like the slow second movement, which has the same degree of grace and feeling that had initially endeared Virgil's poem to me and made me want to set it. I have long considered it the best possible sign that an artistic challenge has successfully been surmounted when private concerns and shortcomings have been excluded from the field of vision and are no longer evident, as though the author has made himself scarce. As for the opening fragment's pastoral character and the furious capers of the Silenus screaming for the young Hylas in the final movement, I have always associated them with the Castelli Romani, and I invariably feel as though I can see Moeris and Lycidas from the Ninth Eclogue approaching the city along the Appian Way to the North, as though the events in question are taking place today, at this very moment in time.

With the onset of spring we returned from Berlin to Marino. At the tender age of twenty-one, Fausto Moroni had decided to take over the running of my life and also, of course, to see that my villa was finished. He had got to know a little more about me and also learnt to understand the way I lived (an understanding that was due, perhaps, to the absence of any viable comparison) – and he seemed to like what he saw. From now on Fausto was to be one of the team, slowly feeling his way into a world that was so new to him, acquiring the necessary skills and learning to feel at home in it. With the passing years and decades, he played the part to perfection. In spite of our totally different cultural backgrounds, in spite of our disparate interests and temperaments, we may still be seen to this day, trotting along through the world together like two utterly inseparable friends.

I now had far more time to compose – the first sign of a change for the better. While in Berlin, I wrote and recorded the music for Volker Schlöndorff's splendid first film, *Der junge Törless*, and then returned to Castel Gandolfo, where I set about composing a double concerto for oboe, harp and string orchestra commissioned by Paul Sacher for Heinz and

Ursula Holliger. It was a work which again breathed the air of the Castelli Romani, where the summer light fell, as though of its own accord, upon a world which, if not exactly ideal (and in many ways much the worse for wear), was at the very least bearable: wounds seemed able to heal at last and sufferings to sink into oblivion. I still have fond memories of these weeks and months, when all seemed to be back on an even keel. On 16 May we travelled to Vienna and two days later attended the first performance of *Tancredi*, a ballet by Peter Csobádi using the music of *Pas d'action*, which had first been heard in Munich in 1952. My recollection of the evening is somewhat vague, perhaps because Nureyev's choreography, visibly indebted to Balanchine's Webern-based ballets, failed to hit the nail on the head. There had clearly been no collaboration between choreographer, designer, librettist and composer – but that, of course, is really quite normal today, is it not?

Several weeks later we travelled to Salzburg for *Die Bassariden*. As our passports were being checked on the train at the border, an Austrian customs official wished me well for the première. We stayed some distance outside Salzburg – under the same roof as Mirella Freni and her husband and Christoph von Dohnányi and his wife. We were all kept busy rehearsing, and what little time we had left was spent playing cards or walking in the woods and fields. We avoided the town, where the narrow streets were packed from morning till evening with gaudily dressed and deodorized crowds. I saw Strehler's famous staging of *Die Entführung aus dem Serail* at the Kleines Festspielhaus (a production now revived for the second or third time) and also attended a performance of Karajan's *Carmen*, a work which, to my own eyes and ears, is far better suited to the place where it was originally performed – the Salle Favart at the Opéra-Comique – than to the vast proportions of modern festival theatres. And I finally heard the Vienna Philharmonic, the sound of which I had so often had in my inner ear when writing my music for *Die Bassariden*, especially the score's more seductive passages. To hear them playing was a source of pleasure of a kind that I find very hard to describe but which I shall certainly never forget.

The production had been rehearsed in Berlin but fit fairly easily into the cinemascope dimensions of Salzburg's Großes Festspielhaus. It was a particularly attractive production from a visual point of view, with Visconti's artistry clearly reflected in his pupils' work. Sanjust and the director had stuck closely to the stage directions prescribed by Auden and Kallman, whereby the costumes in particular changed from scene to scene, evoking different periods when the trends and tendencies bound up with the opera's basic conflict had existed in real life. Dionysus, for example, first appears as a blasé adolescent wearing the open-necked shirt and tight-fitting trousers that might have been worn by Byron at a picnic in the Romagna. In the final scene, at his triumphant farewell, he arrives tarted up in the style of Beau Brummell with a complicated cravat, a monocle and a lorgnette. Pentheus looks like a medieval prince setting out on a pilgrimage. His mother, Agave, and his aunt, Autonoe, are elaborately dressed in the style of the Second Empire, with hairstyles to match; and the blind seer, Tiresias, is clad as an Anglican archdeacon. Various objections have been made to this dress-code, but all boil down to the criticism that such transformations either turn the work into an example of what the Germans call *Bildungstheater* – in other words, a play concerned with its characters' spiritual development (to which I can only ask, 'What's wrong with such a development, even if it occurs in the theatre?') – or that they reduce the unique effectiveness of the piece's one great, shocking act of cross-dressing, when Pentheus succumbs to Dionysus and, dressed in women's clothing, dances to his pipe; a charge that may have some truth to it. The libretto teems with cultural and historical ideas, with parallels and discoveries, of which only a fraction can be caught and grasped by the listener at any one time. It is one of those librettos that it is advisable to read and study in detail, even if only on account of the beauty of the language and the magnificence of the vision that unfolds on stage.

At the press conference in Salzburg chaired by Hans Heinz Stuckenschmidt, Auden got to his feet and, in a loud, firm voice, declared, in reply to a question about how he saw the characters: 'Dionysos ist ein Schwein.' The journalists, opera lovers and other interested parties who were present on that occasion were all as dumbstruck as I – I who had spent the last few years grappling with the god of pleasure and drugs and delving ever deeper into his musical world. And again the poet was right. That is my only recollection of that press conference. I saw little of the first-night audience, since *Die Bassariden* is played without a break, with the result that there was no interval during which members of the audience could saunter round the theatre in their long dresses, pearls and dinner jackets. Had anyone come at all, I wondered. The performance itself was excellent. Kerstin Meyer as Agave, Kostas Paskalis as Pentheus and Loren Driscoll (my 'Young Lord' from Berlin) as Dionysus were all magnificent. The vast chorus came from the Vienna State Opera and was beyond praise: under Walter Hagen-Groll they had mastered their music right down to the very last detail. The performance was followed by the usual first-night party, when I finally had a chance to see the various friends who had come to Salzburg for the occasion: Wenzel, Ludwig of Hesse and Aunt Peg, Sir William and Lady Walton, Fausto and Folker Bohnet. I had entered the auditorium with Ingeborg, who was dressed in what, for my own taste, was a somewhat over-spectacular number, and we had sat together, hand in hand, cold-heartedly letting the performance wash over us. She had come as a maenad and wore a pyjama suit of white crêpe de Chine, as prescribed by the world of Italian fashion at that time, her hair had been curled and stuck out at every conceivable angle, like that of Caravaggio's Medusa, while imitation drop pearls hung down from both her ears over her décolleté neckline.

The Salzburg staging of *Die Bassariden* was seen at the Deutsche Oper, Berlin, on 28 September 1966. On this occasion it was my mother who sat in Sellner's box, holding her eldest son's hand, but I have no idea whether she liked the work or not: whenever she was with me, she was always very hesitant to express her views on music. Yet I believe that she was really very proud of me and is said to have claimed that she could immediately recognize my music on the radio – apparently she used to say on such occasions: 'Listen, it's my boy's music.'

On the morning after the Salzburg première, even before it was properly light, I was already playing with my toes, sleeplessly but happily, and thinking fondly of the successful first night. Two days later I flew with the Waltons to Naples and spent a week with them, resting, on Ischia.

I should like to say a little more about my friendship with William Walton, since I have not yet described it in the detail that it deserves. I have already explained how our friendship deepened during the cold, wet Ischian winter of 1953/4, when I became something of a surrogate son in the Walton household. Our relations grew slightly more distant following my move to Naples, even though we often still met in the town either to talk or to go to the theatre together (generally we went to the San Carlo, of course), and I would occasionally spend a few days with them on their island. But when I moved to Rome and then to Castel Gandolfo, we saw one another only very infrequently. Yet, just as I travelled to London and La Scala for performances of *Troilus and Cressida*, so the Waltons came to Salzburg for *Die Bassariden* and to Rome in May 1971 for the first performance of *Natascha Ungeheuer*. (Had they also, I wonder, been in London for the première of *Ondine* in 1958?) Time and again my older colleague showed signs of his high regard for me, and his curiosity in respect of works so completely and utterly different from his own in terms of their conception and construction encouraged me not to deviate from the course that I had chosen. That I myself had certain difficulties with his own music, which he liked to play to me in the evening, was something which, I hope, he never noticed. They were *my* difficulties, not his – why should I have tormented or unsettled him by mentioning them?

There is a particular sort of English music – Elgar's, for example – that invariably and inevitably brought tears to William's eyes whenever he heard it. I was simply incapable of feeling the same. I can place Elgar historically. I understand the importance and distinctiveness of this music. Perhaps it is bound up with a particular kind of countryside and has something to do with the weather. Or with certain traditions. Undoubtedly it has something to do with language. There is something of the ritual of a high tea at the Savoy about it, a ritual whose meaning can never be fully grasped by a stranger. Rhythmically, everything is always very soft-edged, as though the composer were afraid of creating too physical an impression, in other words, of seeming ill-mannered or importunate. It is well-behaved music, the music of more or less polite society, a liberal, somewhat insular but eccentric variant of the society that must have been revealed to the young Walton in the shape of the Sitwells and their circle of friends. He had no reason, no occasion and no desire to reject, ignore or change this society. It seems to me that what he did do – and with immense skill and wit – was to introduce a very real zest into English music, a freshness of tone, a liveliness and urbanity that until then had been somewhat lacking.

I am indebted to William Walton for a number of important pieces of advice: even today, when writing for string instruments, I take care to avoid certain intervals that are likely to involve intonational traps for players with even the best technique, to which he drew my attention after reading through one of my scores. He himself had been alerted to the problem by his own unfortunate experiences in this field. On more than one occasion he discussed with me problems of balance between individual instrumental groups in today's (and yesterday's) orchestras. And it was he who, on seeing the autograph score of the first act of *König Hirsch* growing visibly out of hand, pointed out that it was bound to be exceptionally long and advised me to do something that I had not thought necessary before: to time each scene with a stopwatch in my hand and to tot up the resultant totals without turning a blind eye or seeking to fiddle the figures.

I always think that it would have been better for him if, towards the end of his life, he could have spent longer periods in London. He could have enjoyed great personal acclaim, and there is no doubt that his younger colleagues' working methods and ways of thinking would have interested and stimulated him. But he did not visit London, contenting himself, instead, with remaining on Ischia, reading old scores, listening to tape recordings and receiving all too infrequent visitors from the world of continental music. Finally, he too became an island. But I understood and loved him, loved his pride, his vulnerability, the metropolitan thrust of his orchestral music, the tender melodies of his solo concertos and, above all, William Walton the human being, in all his good-naturedness, generosity, the constancy of his emotions and his multifaceted sense of humour which, on a much deeper level, always seemed to me to be underscored by the barely audible undertow of a profoundly sorrowful elegy.

At the end of the week, Fausto came to take me back to Castel Gandolfo and my desk. I had rested a little, slept a lot, had gone swimming twice a day and had spent some delightful, quiet evenings with Su and William. But I still felt tired, and when I got home, my exhaustion was compounded by the sense of melancholy that always went with it. My heart was empty, my feelings atrophied. I wish I could have crept away into some dark corner, where I would be left undisturbed. But I was contractually committed to staying alive. Strange things were starting to happen to me. Perhaps I was beginning to notice that my solitary lifestyle, which was also bound up, of course, with my anti-German attitude of defiance, was unsuited to me in the longer term. I was too young and far from strong and mature enough to live the life of a hermit: after all, I had just turned forty and wanted to live life to the full. Perhaps I would one day succeed in resolving the conflict between 'learning' (that is, permanently experimenting and producing work, while locked away in my study, with no time to raise my eyes from my desk and to examine the waiting world outside) and 'living' (being with people, touching them out of a sense of curiosity to find out whether they are genuine, sleeping with them, exchanging ideas and feelings with them, and being indispensable to them). And, once again, I began to brood on my whole profession. It did not seem to me that my success was any justification for it. On the one hand, I was happy – who would not have been happy to have had six curtain calls at a first night in Salzburg before a capacity audience? – but, on the other, my prescient eastern Westphalian brain kept telling me that it was all based on a misunderstanding, on something that I would either have to sort out or else cultivate. I decided to try to sort it out – not overnight (it was far too complicated for that), but at least with immediate effect. As I have already noted, I resigned my teaching appointment in Salzburg and decided not to write anything more for the theatre for the present. My self-imposed abstinence was to last a good ten years, a period that leads me to think that I must have had a somewhat sceptical attitude to my ability to write abstract instrumental music and that I believed it necessary to gain some more experience in this field before definitively deciding that I was incapable of abstract musical thinking.

In the autumn of 1966 I wrote a concerto for Gary Karr, the American double-bass player, and at the same time tried to think only of music, not of people or sex. The piece was intended as music pure and simple, an exercise in musical form (at which point formalism inevitably raised its ugly head) and was premièred in my absence in Chicago on 2 November 1967, when the conductor was Jean Martinon. Early the following year Gary Karr and I recorded the piece in London. At that time it seemed completely unplayable from the soloist's point of view: with my permission, Gary Karr simplified a number of passages, and the Munich-based double-bass player and concert manager Georg Hörtnagel and I later prepared a published version that was slightly easier to perform. Finally, the Italian double-bass player Franco Petracchi prepared his own version (again with my permission), for his own private use, as it were. Today there are many young double-bass players who can perform the published version without batting an eyelid, thereby demonstrating that it is still possible – and always will be – to make technical progress and that technique, as a rule, develops in order to keep pace with the demands that are placed on it.

Throughout the autumn of 1966, Fausto and I would go almost daily to inspect the building site at La Leprara (as my property was called in the Marino dialect) and check that all was in order. To the sound of laughter on the part of the ostensibly enlightened, anti-clerical building workers, a Franciscan monk explored the area with his dowsing rod and in less than a quarter of an hour had found the spot where the house's future water supply was bubbling away underground, unaware of its imminent destiny. The laughter died on their lips as the water started to flow and shoot up from the ground like a fountain.

I was called away on business once again. My first port of call was Dresden, where, plagued by violent toothache, I conducted the Staatskapelle on 21 October 1966 in a programme comprising *Musen Siziliens*, *Being Beauteous* and my Fifth Symphony. Immediately after the concert, and with constant doses of pain-killing whisky, I betook myself to

Berlin and to the operating theatre of the city's dental clinic. My departure for Japan, where I was expected as composer, conductor, director and designer of my Berlin production of *Elegie für junge Liebende*, had to be postponed until things were more or less sorted out. For a few days it even looked as though I would have to cancel my visit. Kerstin Meyer was similarly detained (she was to sing the Second Lady in *Die Zauberflöte* and Countess Kirchstetten in *Elegy*), so we travelled together on the same flight from Hamburg, via Copenhagen and Anchorage, to Tokyo, both of us buried in our scores. None the less, we still had time to draw each other's attention to the constant succession of glorious sunsets and sunrises that could be seen through the aircraft windows.

Between our arrival in Tokyo and the first performance of *Elegie*, there was nothing for me to do but study, rehearse and recover from my jet lag. The crown prince had announced his intention of attending the first night, and so I had the honour of playing the Japanese national anthem with a unison string orchestra and the pleasure of conducting the German national anthem in Haydn's original version for string quartet. Dietrich Fischer-Dieskau was the star of the Tokyo opera season. In addition to his other major roles and a series of song recitals, he also sang Mittenhofer in *Elegie für junge Liebende* and once again ensured that the work was a huge success. He was quite magnificent in a part that seemed to be tailor-made for him.

Once the first performance was out of the way, I and my colleagues from the Deutsche Oper had a little free time to look round Tokyo and were able to spend our remaining evenings in the city's notorious night-clubs in the entertainments district of Shinyuku, which is said to be bigger than the whole of Nuremberg. Two more performances followed, both of which were recorded by Japanese television, so that an edited version could be broadcast nationwide. It went out at eight o'clock in the evening a week later as a thrilling black-and-white detective story with Japanese subtitles and more than a hint of expressionism – I watched it, astonished and impressed, in a hotel room in Kyoto. I was then able to spend several days exploring the country and trying to get to know more about the Japanese way of life. The people struck me as fascinating and mysterious. Some of them were very beautiful – like characters out of Resnais' *Hiroshima, mon amour* – and it was impossible not to be deeply touched by them. The Berlin technicians and administrators told me how impressed they were by the efficiency, modesty and politeness of their Japanese colleagues, who had been taken on to assist the company's resident staff.

Most of my time was spent with an attractive young woman of mixed Japanese and German extraction. Yurika by name, she was a granddaughter of Katia Mann's twin brother, the conductor Klaus Pringsheim, and played the oboe in the NHK Orchestra, but also enjoyed taking people like me to the theatre. We went several times to the old Kabuki-za and twice to the large new building that housed both kabuki and bunraku theatres and that was situated not far from the Imperial Palace. She not only interpreted for me but also tried to explain a little of what I was seeing. At the kabuki the audience was made up entirely of ordinary people with their pots of rice and what seemed like all their belongings, including babes in arms who never screamed but gurgled contentedly to themselves. They would squat in the auditorium for five or six hours on end, as quiet as mice, never averting their eyes from the stage, but following and understanding everything. The plays themselves, it may be added, draw upon popular, comparatively simple themes and on dramatic structures not dissimilar to those of Elizabethan drama.

At the old Noh theatre, in a space not much larger than the Munich Kammerspiele or one of London's smaller West-End theatres, the audience seemed to be made up exclusively of bespectacled philologists of somewhat ascetic appearance. During the intervals they would nervously sip their espresso coffee and consult the modern Japanese translations that were printed in the textbooks that they carried with them. Yurika and I had difficulty understanding what was going on – she, too, was unfamiliar with the medieval Japanese language in which Noh dramas are written – and so we did not stay for the whole afternoon or evening that the performance invariably lasted: everything happened too slowly for us, as though it were in slow motion, or even slower, so that the whole thing went on for five hours in all. Of course, that was how it was meant to be. We were *supposed* to lose our conventional western sense of time and be forced to think of it in a different way by entering into a totally different world in which this strange, but fascinating and stimulating form of theatrical ritual was enacted. I still have a lively recollection of many of the images and sounds that I saw and heard at these performances – it is as though they wanted me to take a lasting interest in them. But there could never be any question of that.

The famous kabuki actor Baiko Onoe had seen *Elegie für junge Liebende* and expressed a desire to meet me. He suggested that I might like to watch him putting on his costume and make-up, an invitation which, I was given to understand, was a sign of especial esteem. Be that as it may, it was a profoundly fascinating experience (I have reported on it in detail elsewhere, in the first edition of *Die englische Katze: Ein Arbeitstagebuch*). One evening Keita Asari, the director of the Nissei Theatre, where the Deutsche Oper's four-week season was taking place, took me and my amusing assistant, Winfried Bauernfeind, on a tour of Tokyo's low dives. Asari was himself a theatre director and told me a lot about the journalist, film actor, novelist and playwright, Yukio Mishima, with whom he had already worked on a number of occasions. Unfortunately, Mishima was then in New York, so I was unable to get to know him, but one rainy Sunday afternoon in Nagoya, Asari invited me to a performance of his production of Racine's *Phèdre* in Mishima's translation. Back in Tokyo, Japanese colleagues arranged a private performance of imperial court music, gagaku, for my benefit. Kyoto left a deep impression upon me, and I began to take an interest in Japanese culture, especially the visual arts – it was all so remote from us and from Europe. Perhaps that was why I found it so vastly appealing.

But I finally had to return to Marino and move into my new house. Approaching Rome from the south (we had stopped off in Cairo to refuel), I saw it below me as the aircraft flew over the Castelli Romani one bright November morning. A completely exhausted Fausto greeted me. The move was largely complete, but I had still arrived too soon, and it was not yet possible to use the technical amenities, so I was promptly sent away again. Immediately after the first performance of my Doppio Concerto in Zurich on 2 December, I spent a fortnight with Paul and Maja Sacher on the Schönenberg outside Basle, as I had often done in the past. Here, at last, I was able to rest a little. It was a house completely devoted to modern art, prime examples of which were to be seen not only inside on the walls but also outside as an integral part of the landscaped garden. But composers were also welcome. Now in his nineties, Paul Sacher is a conductor whose knowledge of art and music is based upon practical experience. He used to maintain two orchestras, the Basle Chamber Orchestra and the Zurich Collegium Musicum, both of which performed almost exclusively twentieth-century works. Among the pieces performed, generally under Sacher's own direction, were many which, commissioned and handsomely paid for by himself, have become internationally famous: I am thinking in particular of Strauss's *Metamorphosen*, Stravinsky's Concerto in D and three pieces by Bartók, his Divertimento, the Sonata for Two Pianos and Percussion, and the Music for Strings, Percussion and Celesta.

On my very first encounter with the Zurich Collegium Musicum in the spring of 1958 I had already become friendly with its leader, the delightful Australian violinist, Brenton Langbein, whom I admired as much as a fellow human being as I did as a musician. I later gave him a few lessons in composition, wrote my Second Violin Concerto for him and managed to persuade him to bring some of his friends and pupils to Montepulciano. He often performed the concerto, not only in Basle but also in London, Zurich, Australia and on record. Brenton also played an important role in Basle's musical life, a role that included a chair at the local conservatory. This dear friend died only recently – blown away like a handful of dust. By chance I myself was spared (to quote Brecht), and so I go on for as long as it is granted me to do so.

Let me return to a wintery Schönenberg, where I remember stumbling alone through the snowbound forests, completely wrapped up in my thoughts of Japan, the Buddha and the idea of Zen. But there was no one to talk to about it, and I did not even know how to formulate the questions that were lurking in my subconscious like hungry wild animals. I stayed calm and made myself slow down but still managed to fall into the trap of a kind of existential sadness, an all too familiar inability to speak and communicate of which experience tells me I must always be wary.

I returned home, weighed down with presents for La Leprara. Marino is a tiny market town that started life as a fortified castle and, as such, is typical of many small towns in Latium. Their principal produce, and the source of their staple economy, is wine and olive oil, although in Marino's case, there are also huge quarries producing a light porous volcanic rock known as peperino. My builders used almost exclusively local stone for my house, although all the floors were laid with *cotto toscano*, huge terracotta tiles from Siena that are originally brick-red in colour but which over the years acquire a wonderful patina, becoming darker and speckled until they look like old pigskin. The house is spacious and built in the style of a traditional (in other words, medieval or baroque) *casale* or country villa. It looks like a farmhouse, as it had to do if it was to conform to the – unfortunately generally far too lax – local planning laws. It stands in the middle of a beautiful olive grove – I had it built in a position where there were no existing trees and where, on the very day that building work began, the remains of the vaulted cellar of a Roman villa were discovered, together with its mosaics and walls and *opus reticulatum*. The building is centred around a large, patio-like hall, two storeys high, which functions as a meeting point for residents and guests, as a music room (in the past we also used to dance here, ushering in the New Year, for example) and as a space in which to hold working discussions with theatre people, administrators, performing artists, colleagues and pupils. For the first time in my life I was also able to enjoy the comforts of central heating and running water, the latter provided by our own private supply, pumped up hydraulically at a rate of thirteen litres a second. This central hall is flanked on both sides by self-contained guest rooms, including my own – except that, in my case, I also have a study with a balcony from which I can see what the weather is like over Grottaferrata to the east and over Ostia and the sea to the west. Sometimes I sit on the balcony, with a book, a sheet of music manuscript paper or a writing pad. Or I take out a pair of field glasses and watch the local wildlife, with its hoopoes, blackbirds, robins and wagtails.

There is a large cherrywood desk, made decades ago by Mario, a master carpenter from Albano, with an adjustable writing surface, drawers and pigeon-holes. Two smaller desks are reserved for less weighty concerns. Letters are written in the drawing room downstairs: the room upstairs is intended solely for music. If I want to try out on the piano what I have just written down, I have to get up and walk round the desk and across the room to my asthmatic Grotrian–Steinweg, which I brought with me from Naples, where I acquired and paid for it in 1957 – not without great difficulty. I now regard it as an old friend. It is still in the same position today, still taking up rather too much space, still ready to tell me, as soon as I press its keys, whether what I have heard in my mind's ear is any good or whether my work is sloppy. I often have it tuned. Whenever I work with the window open and even when I sing to myself while working, I never disturb a living soul either within the immediate neighbourhood or inside the house itself. The people are all completely unmusical and immune to all forms of noise. And so I spend most of my life in this upstairs studio, armed with electric pencil sharpeners, metronomes and stopwatches, suffering agonies of uncertainty and prey to the monsters that lie in wait for the moment of greatest weakness or inattentiveness to attack me and tear me apart.

Christmas 1966 arrived. The chimney no longer smoked, and the water supply was excellent. I celebrated with Ingeborg, Wenzel and two of Ingeborg's friends, the publisher Roberto Calasso and his wife, and the writer Fleur Jaeggy. The holiday was barely over when I received a call from Berlin: Dohnányi had been taken ill and was unable to conduct the performance of *Die Bassariden* on 3 January 1967. Would I take over? All that they could offer me was a complete run-through on the morning of the performance. I considered the matter briefly before agreeing. The New Year celebrations in Marino were cancelled and, instead, I found myself at Wenzel's in Berlin, frantically preparing a conducting score. At the morning's run-through we got no further than the end of the Intermezzo. What an adventure this was proving! The evening's performance also marked Edda Moser's début as Autonoe, a potentially hazardous appearance for which she had had no stage rehearsal but which fortunately passed off without incident.

Whenever experienced opera conductors stand in for one of their colleagues, they are normally helped not only by their knowledge of the piece (which they have generally helped to rehearse) but also by the habits of a lifetime of conducting, so that they are able to avoid disaster without any difficulty. But when someone like myself, who had never for a moment thought that he might one day have to conduct *Die Bassariden*, has to step in . . .! I was no doubt helped by the fact that I simply did not know where disaster might strike (what happens, for example, if A is not given her cue at B or if X fails to look at me when he has to be given his entry?). The chorus was no problem, since it was largely conducted from the wings by the admirable Walter Hagen-Groll. But the miracle happened, and, after a nervous first fifteen minutes involving a great deal of unnecessary gesticulating of a kind more associated with the concert hall, my heart stopped audibly pounding and I calmed down, forcing myself to gesture less wildly, restricting myself to only the most necessary physical activity and generally remaining seated, so that I finally began to enjoy myself, much as Baron Münchhausen must have done on his journey to the moon. I was expressing myself in my own language. All sense of fear evaporated and the whole thing passed off successfully. The feeling of heaviness that otherwise holds one down like a magnet had gone. It was just like one of those dreams in which you think you have learnt how to fly. I recall thinking that the music was very beautiful. The opera had been well rehearsed, so scarcely anything went wrong, and I had the feeling that, fired by their sense of solidarity and professionalism, soloists, chorus and orchestra were sharing my delight in this unforgettable evening. It ended with a small party at the home of Klaus Henneberg (who was then one of Sellner's assistants, but who is now based in Cologne, where he works as a writer, librettist and man of the theatre), during which I attempted to calm my nerves with far too much tobacco and red wine, resulting in a bad night, with difficulty in breathing, hypertonia and a racing pulse. Although long since over, the evening's performance continued to reverberate within my head. It had been a wonderful experience, but it had also involved me in excessive emotion. Once again, I had to call a doctor, who established that both my upper and lower tonicity values were far above the norm and that certain precautions would have to be taken to counter this life-threatening condition. I was told not to conduct and, at least in the short term, was glad to take this advice – but only in the short term. On 23 January I conducted the first performance of Ingeborg's *Lieder von einer Insel* at Selb in Franconia to mark Philipp Rosenthal's 100th Workers' Concert. The performers included members of the Berlin Philharmonic and the RIAS Chamber Chorus. But I realized that the doctor had been right after all, and that I would do well to abandon the concert tour that I had just begun and return to Marino to write my Second Piano Concerto.

This piece comprises three interconnected but clearly distinguished movements – the first slow, the second violently agitated and the third rhapsodical in character. The first part is lyrical, its linear writing characterized by strict counterpoint, pedal points and fermatas that reminded everyone (or at any rate me) of the sound of gagaku or at least of things Japanese: I was thinking, for example, of the smell of bamboo exuded by Japanese bodies or of a Pacific coastal landscape – a grey sea, grey sky and white-capped waves – and green tea that has a bitter taste and that keeps you awake at night. A face in the crowd. Its owner lowers his eyes when you look at him, everything is unspoken and remains so. Someone running along the visitors' terrace, waving his school cap, as the aeroplane taxis along the runway. But plans had already been made, contracts signed, only the bills had still to be settled. Life had to go on as before.

Work on my Second Piano Concerto proved difficult and I had to take myself in hand. Unless I am much mistaken, it was at this period that I developed my habit of not only singing, humming and howling what I had just written but also of talking to myself while working, swearing at myself and deriding my achievements. Never praising them. As though I were going beyond my own limitations when things had not worked out on the staves in front of me. Perhaps it is possible in this piece to see or hear the efforts that the music cost its creator. But is it not also possible to hear a new note here? Is it not something different that finds expression here? Would it be wrong to claim that this new music has something to do with King Pentheus, that it is connected with his sufferings and with his problems with the uncontrollable and inscrutable nature of the Bassarids?

What is the meaning behind this turmoil in the piece's second section, this incessant hammering and screaming and sense of desolation? From now on I was to write many such movements in which quick tempi are retained unbroken over lengthy periods, in spite of the changing content and shifting moods. The first time that anything like this occurs is in the third scene from Act Two of *König Hirsch*. Both the fast movements of my Seventh Symphony, which was written thirty years later, and the whole of the *Requiem* of 1992/3 are based on this principle of a fixed basic tempo. The third section of the Second Piano Concerto is cast in the form of a recitation or recitative: soloist and orchestra declaim Shakespeare's Sonnet no. 129, 'The expense of spirit in a waste of shame', as interpreted by the composer and as incorporated into his musical structures as a formative element, triggering outbursts of emotion and heralding private catastrophes. Yes, there is no doubt that it is an extension of the music of *Die Bassariden*. Even the duration of the piece – some three quarters of an hour – suggests that we are not dealing here with the usual concerto form but with an extended attempt to find an apt way of depicting new musical ideas.

During the early summer of 1967 I received a visit from my mother. She would sit in the shade in the garden at Marino beside her eldest son, sewing (even when visiting, she could not keep still, but always had to be doing something whenever others were working). She liked Fausto very much – indeed, she could not help but find him irresistible. I can no longer remember exactly when I completed my Second Piano Concerto, whether it was during the summer or not until the autumn, but I do recall driving with Fausto to attend the Vienna Festival and visiting Auden in the country. Although this was my third or fourth visit to Kirchstetten, I was again unable to find Auden's isolated farmhouse. Fausto asked why anyone as famous as Auden should live in such a dump and be so impossible to find. When we finally reached the garden gate, all that I needed to do by way of an answer was to point to Wystan sitting outside beneath a sunshade, reading from a volume of Goethe, like Saint Jerome in his hermit's cell, a picture of peace and otherworldiness – or was it, rather, that he was closer to the world in this way?

During the summer of 1967 I spent a few weeks as composer in residence at Dartmouth College, Hanover, New Hampshire, where the conductor Mario di Buonaventura had organized a festival and where I was required to attend rehearsals of some of my own orchestral and chamber works and in some cases even to conduct them myself; other works, finally, had to be analyzed with the help of a blackboard and projection equipment. Outside it was hot and humid, without a breath of wind. On a few occasions I went swimming in a peaty woodland lake with the New York artist Hal George. I also attended a great many parties held by the teaching staff and on one such occasion met Freya von Moltke, the widow of the freedom fighter. I talked a lot with old *émigrés* and also with Hal George, with whom I discussed my desperate state of mind, my sense of not being at home anywhere, of appearing not to fit and not knowing where to turn.

Every lunch-time the students would appear and stand bareheaded for an hour on the campus lawn beneath a pitiless midday sun, silently protesting at the escalation of the war in Vietnam. I was impressed and felt a growing interest in Vietnam, with the result that I read everything I could lay my hands on about the country and its history, a history that is one long tale of wars of liberation and independence. All the reports and information on its current situation I eagerly devoured. For the first time I saw and understood some of the links between imperialist policies and the unregulated nature of capital. I should add that this was the summer of the black riots in Newark and Syracuse. Following the Dartmouth College workshop, I travelled on to Santa Fe, New Mexico, to see the North American première of *Boulevard Solitude*. The theatre had burnt down and the production had been transferred overnight to a sports hall, yet, in spite of everything, these enterprising youngsters had knocked together a brilliant show with vaudeville costumes from Las Vegas, a show that they presented beneath pouring rain and with a typically American pioneering spirit and talent for improvisation. On the flight back, the person sitting next to me in the aeroplane drew my attention to the thick black clouds of smoke that lay beneath us over Washington, where I knew that men and women were fighting for their rights: they had had enough oppression and, refusing to tolerate it any longer, were finally rebelling. Years previously, I had been confronted with the world's misery in Harlem and, as a white man, had felt ashamed. I still feel shame to this day. I am on the side of the blacks. I prefer to be where there are no whites. Here I am moved and touched by all humanity, and I sense that there is a world which, unattainable to us Europeans, is free from sin, free from all those countless notions of Christian guilt and beatitude that make our lives a living hell and bar us from entering a world without sin by marring our feelings of pleasure.

It was already late summer or early autumn by the time I returned to Marino. I was in a bad way. I felt tired and depressed, as though plagued by some illness or fever or poison. Real life appeared to have passed me by. Everything was out of joint. A kind of nervous exhaustion was all that I could feel. Ingeborg came to stay, bringing with her her own clinical experiences in this regard and attempting to apply them to me and my own particular problems. She prescribed a strict regime of swimming and walking and kept a close eye on its implementation. Although it did not really help, it was a relief to be able to talk to someone whom I had long regarded as a sister and a friend, and I began to feel calmer, things settled down, and the circus horse was soon able to leap back into the ring, evidently cheered and refreshed.

I set to work on my next piece, an oratorio called *Das Floß der 'Medusa'* (The Raft of the 'Medusa'). Years previously my old friend Ernst Schnabel had mentioned his plans for a large-scale, full-length narrative cantata, and North German Radio now offered me a commission to set the text to music. The performance was scheduled to take place during the late autumn of 1968 in the Planten un Blomen Hall in Hamburg. The oratorio tells of the dramatic death throes and struggle for survival of a group of Third-World people after they have been abandoned to their fate on a raft off the West African coast by representatives of a heartless and thoughtless ruling caste. In its initial stages, it was still far from clear that Schnabel's draft contained allegorical features which, if developed, would reveal striking affinities with the present, notably with the struggles fought by the revolutionary movements of the day. I read Ernesto ('Che') Guevara's essay, 'Socialism and the New Man in Cuba', and his diaries from the years 1958/9, when he was fighting in the Sierra Maestra. I was especially impressed by the humanitarian and social commitment of these writings and jottings, a commitment that revealed an almost religious fervour. When it was announced on 10 October 1967 that Che Guevara had been taken prisoner by Cuban exiles acting as CIA agents in Bolivia and executed on the spot, the figure of the guerrilla leader and idol of thousands upon thousands of men and women all over the world merged with that of the hero of our piece, Jean-Charles, so that Schnabel and I decided – after reflecting long and hard on the matter – to turn the work into a sort of allegorical requiem for Che Guevara.

I had Théodore Géricault's magnificent painting, *The Raft of the 'Medusa'*, clearly in my mind's eye when I started work on the music. The pyramid-like pile of human figures in the painting, which is now in the Louvre in Paris, is surmounted by our hero, the mulatto Jean-Charles, waving a fragment of tattered red cloth at a boat that is seen sailing past in the distance and that signifies hope and perhaps also salvation – an idea present in our own piece from the very outset. The choral writing, which reveals the influence of the music of Bach's Passions, extends from pure declamation to aria and from pure aria to naturalistic human sounds, including whimpering and screaming – even the wailing of Arab women is audible here. Ernst Schnabel and I identified with the figures in Géricault's painting, not only in order to be able to deal artistically with the subject matter of the piece and in order to give credible expression to our shared experiences and fellow suffering but because we felt a sense of inner solidarity with these people and with their struggle.

The polyphonic style of writing that I had developed in such disparate works as *Novae de infinito laudes*, *Der junge Lord* and *Die Bassariden* now acquired a very real power and a realistic dimension: these were the voices of people thrown together, voices that rose to a scream or died away to a murmur and to silence. And it seemed to me (and this was something new in my writing) that the orchestral instruments, too, merely represent voices, singing and declamation by instrumental means. In other words, it is perfectly possible for instrumental music to be treated, entirely consciously, as an instrumental version of vocal music, as the music of wordless Greek choruses. Even before I encountered the Medusan theme, I had occasionally written for instruments as though I were writing roles for performers, as though the instrumentalists were actors reciting and interpreting texts, but with notes instead of lines. When faced with such a challenge, players are much more likely to respond to a piece on an intellectual level, since ideas are involved that they have to make an effort to grasp both artistically and interpretatively, ideas that go beyond merely reading and playing the notes. They have to think while playing. And the composer must want his performers to think when playing his works. I should also mention another of the influences exerted by Géricault's painting: its immense emotional power – a power that stems from French Classicism and, at the same time, leaves that Classicism far behind it – is so emphatic that it robs the viewer of all peace of mind by depicting these blacks and objects of compassion with an expressive beauty of a kind which, prior to Géricault, had been permitted only to heroes and martyrs, in other words, to figures from the world of mythology, including Christian myth. I avoided the mistake of using existing folk music or of inventing a new type of folk music of my own to portray these doomed figures but simply took my cue from Géricault: I saw them and, using my own artistic resources and drawing upon my own criteria, made them more beautiful and more noble in their suffering than the greatest heroes and gods in world history.

Ernst Schnabel included details from the *Medusa*'s logbook, thereby increasing the documentary character of our report. For the sake of clarity, these sections of the text are entrusted to a speaker who stands in the middle of the platform and introduces himself as Charon ferrying the souls of the dead across the River Styx. This clearly represents a return to, and revival of, the idea of a speaking role as used in Cocteau's libretto for *Oedipus rex*. A second figure of similar provenance is Madame La Mort from Cocteau's *Orphée*, sung by a soprano soloist positioned downstage left, in front of the string orchestra, which represents the underworld. With her siren singing she lures the combatants over to her side and to the side of the dead, where they will find peace and redemption. On the opposite side of the platform stands Jean-Charles (baritone), who conducts a form of higher dialogue with Death, whom he spurns and to whose blandishments he remains deaf. On the side of the living (initially full of people but by the end of the piece only a handful remain) we have a large number of wind instruments – instruments associated with the sound of breathing and of human voices, whereas the music of the underworld is sweet-toned, Renaissance-like string music. Italian is the language of the underworld, with sung quotations from the *Divine Comedy*.

The belligerence that we describe here presupposes, first and foremost, a refusal to give in, a determination not to fail, the converse of resignation. Such resistance constitutes our piece's ethical centre, investing it with its meaning and its message.

8

> Come hither, Bohemians one and all, seafarers, harbour whores and ships unanchored. Would you not be Bohemians, all you citizens of Illyria, Verona and Venice . . .
>
> . . . And though you err a hundred times,
> As I have erred and passed no tests,
> Yet have I passed them, now and then.
>
> Ingeborg Bachmann, 'Böhmen liegt am Meer', 1964

In the German colony in Rome no less than elsewhere, the news of the mass demonstrations against the Shah of Persia in Berlin on 2 June 1967 gave rise to heated debate, stirring up new feelings unknown until then among Germans. They marked, we felt, the beginning of the end of something, but of what we were not yet sure. What if it were the end of the status quo? The killing of a student demonstrator, Benno Ohnesorg, by an armed policeman, Heinz Kurras, in the underground car park beneath the Deutsche Oper on the very evening that Sellner's staging of *Die Zauberflöte* – a work which, as a product of the humanist Enlightenment, tells how two lovers attain to humanity and speaks of forgiveness, of goodness and tolerance – was taking place above them provoked immense indignation and disquiet far beyond the confines of Berlin and even of Germany itself. In his capacity as intendant of the Deutsche Oper (or 'Sing Sing' as the forbidding building in the Bismarckstraße is known to the local populace), Sellner dutifully welcomed the Shah and the Empress Farah Diba at the house's main glass doors and accompanied them to the royal box, where His Majesty – like his lady wife, bespattered with rotten fruit – was able to brood upon the indignities he had just suffered and ponder on the source of the hatred to which he had just been exposed in this totally alien land, while the company's resident soubrette and the evening's Pamina, Erika Köth from Darmstadt, sobbed uncontrollably in her dressing room. But the Shah was not alone in being surprised. A sea change was under way, and by the date of my next visit to Berlin, in the autumn of 1967 (I was hard at work on *Das Floß der 'Medusa'*), it was no longer possible to ignore it. Borders had been closed, consequences drawn, positions marked out. To my immense satisfaction, I noticed that questions were now being asked by the younger generation, by a national and international intelligentsia made up of young men and women and that many things were now being questioned, from bourgeois views on upbringing and modern education to the infallibility and ethical inviolability of teachers in schools and universities; from sexual repression to parliamentary democracy; and from the paternalistic thinking bound up with the denazification trials of the post-war period to the racism of these very same paternalistic figures, men sedulously hard-working but intellectually lazy.

It was at Hans Magnus Enzensberger's home in Friedenau that I got to know some of these young people – the 'ringleaders', as they were already starting to be called. Most of them were members of the Socialist League of German Students and included Christian Semler, Peter Schneider, Günter Amendt (a pupil of Adorno's from Frankfurt), Gastón Salvatore, Bahman Nirumand and Gretchen and Rudi Dutschke. For all their differing views, all their contrasting characters and varied social backgrounds, they all shared one idea and worked for a single goal, albeit one that still lay far in the future and was difficult to express, still harder to achieve. It was, however, no unrealizable Utopia but the vision of a society free from repression in which other criteria would obtain than those of productivity, success and the amassing of wealth and possessions. Instead, new values would be propagated, values such as social usefulness, the freedom to hold alternative views and the chance to develop one's own personality unhindered. These pioneers were severe on themselves. In their eyes, it was necessary to challenge the whole world order and ask the most basic questions about ourselves in the way in which the founders of any new religion do. Many were of the opinion – and they practised what they preached with militant fervour – that God should be brought down to earth by force in order to prove His existence. Indeed, there was something exclusive about them, a whiff of the catacombs and the confessional that one always finds with young and old believers.

Rudi Dutschke had been accepted, more or less unquestioningly, as the head of the whole school by the New Left in West Germany and Western Europe as a whole. For the many who were prepared to listen, his thoughts and ideas had something axiomatic about them, something that deserved to be taken entirely seriously. I liked him a lot and always enjoyed meeting him, listening to him and (not least) trying to answer his questions on matters relating to art as aptly and appositely as possible. In less than a year – through a tragic turn of events – we would have ample enough opportunity to continue the conversations that we had embarked upon in Berlin. He had something of a Protestant monk about him – it was no accident that he had been brought up in a Prussian parsonage in Brandenburg. He was an altruist who strove for inner perfection, an Alyosha Karamazov, bright and open in a way that I have never encountered with any other person to such a disarming extent: his fighting spirit and boldness were so completely convincing precisely because these qualities did not come naturally to him: he had to train himself to show them in order to be able to express his ideas in all their graphic intensity. One could see that it was not easy for him to do so. It was his love of his fellow humans, his inquisitiveness about these eggheads and about life in general that motivated him, giving him his charismatic force and charm and taking him so far out of himself that he was able, in all purity of heart, to play the part of the hero. And his eyes – the eyes of a Brandenburg Christian – flashed diabolically and bright laughter sprang from his lips as soon as he started to speak in his sociologist's and agitator's German.

One of Rudi's closest colleagues was the Chilean poet Gastón Salvatore, whom I also met at Enzensberger's house in the autumn of 1967 and who was studying at the Freie Universität in Berlin (I think his teachers were Helmut Gollwitzer and Jacob Taubes). He has always enjoyed the respect not only of people like me and of many other men and women with an interest in questions of culture but also of a man of Enzensberger's stature. With his head in the clouds, he was totally different from Rudi. His cultural background was that of Latin American poetry and of the anti-imperialist struggles in his native Chile and elsewhere on the South American continent, struggles that he had witnessed at first hand. He too was not lacking in courage and energy, he too had charisma and ideas, and he too was characterized by that curious flight of fancy that enabled these young intellectuals among my new circle of friends to avoid the thin ice of practical reality by systematically jumping over it. That they had to pay dearly for this ability, history was soon to relate.

Where was this flying boat heading in the middle of the night, with its passengers passionately engaged in overheated discussions? What was to become of these struggles? What were the German League of Socialist Students and extra-parliamentary opposition attempting to achieve? After all, the question of power had simply never been asked, and to have done so would, in any case, have ill consorted with the makeshift, improvisatory style of this opposition alliance. But a moral question had been asked, and it was this that was so hugely important, so novel and so utterly fascinating about the whole affair, something that affected society in general, from the worker to the industrialist and from the cleaning lady to the media tycoon. Now, at last, there were young Germans ready to rebel against a morally ossified system and a political culture that was bound to strike them as reactionary, mendacious and insufferable and that forced them to take an interest in the total overthrow of the present order and the existing system of values.

Gastón was a long-haired, heavily built and melancholic youth who reminded me of the crazed and long-suffering hero of Thomas Mann's short story, *Unordnung und frühes Leid*, and whose years in Berlin were a time of feverish activity. I saw him often and we became good friends. He took an altogether exceptional interest in everything related to art. I wanted him to tell me how, in his eyes, it was possible to reconcile modern art – this product of the bourgeoisie – with the Socialist Revolution and whether, within the new context, such art might simply cease to be bourgeois of its own inevitable accord. In the case of music, with its imputed lack of a linguistic dimension, it is particularly difficult to define what class it belongs to. Or is that perhaps not true? Gastón himself was none too sure: like me, he was attracted rather than repelled by the products of bourgeois art, just as one may be attracted by the comforts of western car manufacture and by the advantages of modern morphology. At that time I was still unaware that, from now on, I should have to scour the face of the earth in my search for a reliable answer to the question, 'What is revolutionary music?' Here, of course, one can work only with accurate and scientifically tested data, not in the flickering light of illusions. For what is at stake is an understanding of reality, which in turn is the herald of truth.

Gastón's political radicalism was fuelled by a vast inner fire like the flame that burns on an altar. Behind his consciously rough exterior was a sensitive, sentimental man, for whom life and love were as hard as writing poems in German. Throughout these hectic months, when he was hounded by the police, he continued to write his poems in the rooms of friends and strangers or else while banged up in prison, poems containing surprisingly beautiful passages but also, of course, not a little that was linguistically obscure and in need of remedial attention. I still have a whole pile of his manuscripts in my collection, moving testimony to the inner life of a young intellectual during these years, a man who was additionally a foreigner in

Germany but who spoke on behalf of an entire group with the voice of one who was hurt, the voice of anger and grief. My two settings of Gastón's texts, the cantatas *Versuch über Schweine* and *Natascha Ungeheuer*, may be seen as evidence of a friendship which, like old documentaries or newspaper cuttings, records and preserves the mood of those years in a callous and cold-blooded way.

Both pieces are set in Berlin, and both were written at the speed with which films are developed, thereby preserving a little of the actuality which, for purely technical reasons, is generally denied to an art like music, which takes time to be produced, so that it is mostly finished only when the event that inspired it has already faded from memory. Most of the time that I was not in Berlin, meeting people and engaging in lively discussion, I spent in Marino working on the score of *Das Floß der 'Medusa'*, my imagination fired by all that I had seen and heard in the city. (I kept having to phone Berlin and ask for the latest news.) At the same time, I felt unsettled by another new passion, an almost religious desire to return to Japan, a longing which, instead of becoming less intense, grew gradually more importunate, like some psychological need, a dream of another, alternative lifestyle and, as such, the very opposite of what I was doing at present or what I had done until now. How I wished that I could disappear prematurely and fade away in a kind of earthly paradise!

Have we not been here before? Was it not the same old story, exactly the same motivation as when I had first left German soil or first set foot in Harlem? Although it no doubt followed its own inner laws, this conflict was of my own making and certainly far from new. And it seemed to me – or perhaps this was wishful thinking – that it could be solved only by my living it out to the full, with all the human and practical difficulties involved.

In February 1968 the great Vietnam Conference was held in Berlin, an event that I myself helped to organize and that was attended by many people from abroad, including Italy, France, Scandinavia and the United States. Bishop Kurt Scharf, Professor Helmut Gollwitzer and I went to see the Minister of the Interior to ask him to lift the ban on the demonstration, since we feared that otherwise the result would be bloody confrontation. On the morning of Sunday, 18 February 1968 I joined five thousand other demonstrators and, arm in arm, we marched through the streets with Luigi Nono and the Communist painter Titina Maselli. Also present were Peter and Gunilla Weiss, Reinhard Lettau, Eduardo Arroyo and Carl Timner, Giangiacomo Feltrinelli and academics from Berlin and abroad, but otherwise there were very few artists. Gigi Nono felt that, instead of the slogans that we were shouting, whether improvised or hackneyed, it was time for new songs to ring forth from a thousand throats, songs to be newly written by revolutionary artists. Yes, I said, new songs would be nice, but what would happen to the spontaneity, and who would write the music and peddle it to the people? Who? Who would be prepared to take it on, who had the ability to write the words, words that had to be popular? Why did this not happen? Why did the avant-garde miss this opportunity to put in an appearance here in Berlin?

The conference's opening ceremony was held in the Great Hall of the Technische Universität, where the huge flag of the Vietnamese Liberation Front was unfurled. Both Titina and I were seized, not to say overwhelmed, by joy and solidarity. Our hearts beat wildly, and we felt that what we were doing was worthwhile and somehow important. Soldiers from the American occupation army burnt their military passbooks and called on others to desert. To disobey! Titina had discovered that *Lulu* was being given at the Deutsche Oper that evening, with Böhm conducting and an all- star cast, and she begged me to take her to see it. I saw to the tickets and accompanied her to the performance. But the world in which we had just been living with such all-consuming intensity had drawn us so far away from the worlds of fiction, opera and the theatre that we felt like visitors from another planet. We found ourselves growing impatient with the Dr Schöns, the Casti-Pianis and Schigolchs and with the sobbing music that misrepresented Wedekind's style. We had arrived late and were allowed to sit in Sellner's box, but within ten minutes we had left. Dietrich Fischer-Dieskau's gentlemanly Dr Schön was just groping the comically bestockinged calves of Evelyn Lear's Lulu in his absent-minded manner, while, serpent-like, she writhed and wriggled on a couch. We made our way back to the Technische Universität.

By Easter I had made good progress on *Das Floß der 'Medusa'*, but my nerves were still playing up. I was easily distracted and absent-minded and would suddenly feel weak and depressed. Something had to be done about it. Folker was free and so we were able to go away together to Beirut – at that time still a beautiful city – where we stayed with Aimée Kettaneh, the director of the Baalbek Festival, in a large house in the Arab part of the old town. Unfortunately, Aimée failed to appreciate the seriousness of the state that I was in (perhaps because I was always so polite?) and did not understand that I needed to be left alone and allowed to rest. Every lunch-time and evening she would introduce me to new faces from the diplomatic corps. If her guests had been looking forward to finding a brilliant conversationalist in me, these parties must have been a source of the gravest disappointment. We drove to Baalbek, where members of Aimée's festival staff were waiting to welcome us and escort us, taking care not to lose sight of me for even a single moment. I felt so awful that I spent most of my time in my hotel room. And it rained. It was here of all places (or perhaps it was not so incongruous, but the result of a happy accident) that I first read the *Communist Manifesto*. I was deeply shocked and thrown into a state of turmoil. Finally we escaped and returned to Beirut, where we moved into rooms at the Georges V, now a pile of rubble, and where I remained in bed for days, without moving and without speaking, flinching painfully at the slightest noise or light.

Then one morning I opened a newspaper to read that an attempt had been made on the life of Rudi Dutschke in Berlin. I took the next flight back to Rome and from there flew straight to Berlin. The German papers were full of Dutschke, one – the unspeakable *Bild-Zeitung* – with the banner headline: 'Red Rudi Swears Again'. Apart from the fact that Red Rudi never swore, it was at least good to know that he was still alive. Once in Berlin, I headed straight for the Great Hall of the Technische Universität, where a plenary session had been in progress since the previous day. Committees were being set up. Unexpectedly, I found myself on the platform, and before I knew what was happening, Hans Magnus Enzensberger, Wolfgang Neuss and I were deputed to see the controller of the Sender Freies Berlin and demand daily broadcasts for the extra-parliamentary opposition. We were not to leave until the times had been fixed. I seem to remember that the broadcasts were to last not minutes but hours and that they were to be on both radio and television. If our demands were not met, the station would be taken by storm. The controller, Franz Barsig, noted our request and understandably declined to commit himself. I said nothing, but left my two fellow committee members – especially the eloquent and aggressive Wolfgang Neuss – to do the talking, only wondering whether I was really awake or merely dreaming and what I was doing here in the first place. When we finally left the building, armed with a few vague explanations, including the controller's promise to appear before a kind of tribunal at the Technische Universität that afternoon in order to answer charges that he had too many right-wing employees on his staff, foremost among whom was a certain Matthias Walden, the police were already erecting barricades. But it soon became clear that, without Rudi, the whole point of the revolt had been lost from sight and was no longer understood. Within days, most of the committees had been disbanded as though of their own accord. All too prematurely, many of the protestors returned to their private lives, while others continued their work in the context of party politics, although a number chose the extreme step of going underground and opting for the armed struggle as the ultimate and loneliest consequence of the course that they had adopted.

Rudi was admitted to a clinic in Berne. His attacker, a young Bavarian Nazi by the name of Bachmann (!), had left him with serious brain damage. After several weeks in Berne, during which time he was fortunately treated by first-class doctors, he was finally declared fit to travel and, accompanied by a doctor and two nurses, secretly brought to Marino, where he stayed for a period of months. Daily lessons with his doctor helped him to learn to speak again and to regain the ability to make conceptual links between different words and ideas. He recovered with quite astonishing speed: it was as though the undamaged half of his brain was taking over the functions of the damaged half. All his needs were attended to, not least the calm and safety that the patient so urgently needed.

On 16 July, Fausto and I flew to Santa Fe to rehearse *The Bassarids*, which I was to conduct in a staging by Bodo Igesz, with designs by Rouben Ter-Arutunian. The chorus, made up of local students, was absolutely stupendous and never missed an entry, whether dancing, standing on their heads or clambering all over the sets. Walter Felsenstein would have wept with sheer delight. Every few days I would telephone Marino: yes, Rudi was doing well, his treatment was a success, there were no serious complications. And he had been joined by his wife Gretchen and by their first child, Hosea Che. After the final performance of *The Bassarids* (at the end of each, spectacular fires were lit on all the surrounding hillsides, marking a Bacchic solstice or signalling an *auto-da-fé*), a small private jet took us at dawn to Aspen, Colorado, where we flew through the famous canyons and spent a wet weekend performing some of my symphonies and chamber works, as well as my opera *A Country Doctor*, the last-named in a production by Madeleine Milhaud. We then flew on to New York, where we had booked cabins on the *Cristofero Colombo* to take us back to Naples, but a strike by the crew delayed our departure by three days, during which time there was nothing for us to do but see the Broadway production of *Hair* or freeze in ice-cold, air-conditioned cinemas: in keeping with tradition, we had already had the usual party and champagne on board ship and said goodbye to all our friends. Finally the ship's siren sounded and my first and last ocean voyage got under way. The people all appalled me, I preferred not to have to see anyone but to remain completely unnoticed and avoid all the usual customs observed on ships like this. I sat in my creaking, groaning cabin, staring in turn at a blank sheet of paper and out at the leaden sea – what was it that I had wanted to write and why was I making this crossing? It might have been to prepare the preliminary sketches for my Sixth Symphony – but I wrote not a single note.

On our third day at sea, a bored Fausto was leafing through some Italian newspapers and magazines that he had bought in New York when he discovered to our horror that they contained photographs of my house at Marino, the now far from secret hiding place of Germany's Public Enemy Number One, the dangerous and subversive Rudi Dutschke. We were on board ship, in the middle of the Atlantic, and in a state of panic. It was impossible to telephone Italy, but by the time that Fausto and I finally arrived in Rome, the hullabaloo that had been caused by German journalists had almost completely died down: some shit must have revealed where the patient was staying. The teams of television reporters, the helicopters and telephoto lenses had all disappeared after an eight-day siege. Rudi was waiting for us at the station, together with a contingent of a dozen or so *carabinieri* loitering discreetly in the background who accompanied us back to Marino, shadowing us and surrounding my house day and night for the coming weeks and months. They even had a direct telephone line to the Ministry of the Interior. Outside the house our every step was monitored. The *carabinieri* were even kind enough to run errands for us, buying cigarettes or posting letters for my guest, who would give them his autograph in return. They were friendliness itself and felt something akin to admiration for 'Rudi il Rosso'. La Leprara had become his headquarters, large numbers of guests would come and go, important visitors, or others who pretended to be important, but invariably at least twice as many as he could really bear. The Italian Left, especially those to the left of the Italian Communist Party, also put in an appearance. I would act as interpreter at their meetings, listening and trying in this way to form a picture of a world that seemed to me to be growing more and more complex and attempting to fathom all the contradictions, defeats and irreconcilabilities involved in political struggles.

The Vietnam War was still far from over and, on top of everything, we had heard on board the *Cristofero Colombo* that on 21 August troops from the Warsaw Pact countries had occupied Czechoslovakia, unleashing a moral and political disaster on the widest possible scale, dividing people and their opinions and alienating the sympathies of left-wing thinkers in the West to the way in which power was wielded in the Eastern Bloc countries and to the way in which Socialism was applied in practice. And Fidel Castro's eagerly awaited pronouncement on Prague proved a disappointment: to see the otherwise so unshakeable Cuban leader so willing to compromise in the face of one of the superpowers was really not at all easy. The fact that the reasons were obvious did not make it any simpler.

Meanwhile autumn had come. On 29 September a new centre for the arts was to be opened in Bielefeld in eastern Westphalia. The money for it had been put up by a custard-powder manufacturer by the name of Rudolf-August Oetker, who had also dug deep into his pocket to pay for a piece of music to celebrate the occasion – my Second Piano Concerto. Christoph Eschenbach had learnt the difficult solo part. The idea had come from Joachim Wolfgang von Moltke, the director of the new concert hall, whose sister-in-law, Freya, we had met in New Hampshire the previous summer. I had worked on the score with Eschenbach in the course of the spring and was already looking forward to the performance of the new piece when the appalling news reached me from Bielefeld: the sponsors wanted their museum to be named after one of the members of their own family, Richard Kaselowsky, an active and influential member of the SS, who had died in 1944. As soon as I arrived in Bielefeld, I was asked by both the old and the new Left to say and write something on the subject of this embarrassing affair. I responded by writing a short newspaper article about the phenomenon of new arts centres and the foundations that sponsored the arts, while also stressing the need for people to devote themselves meanwhile, as an alternative to such arts centres, to what would be their greatest artistic achievement of all – a world revolution.

I assume that by now the reader will have gained sufficient insight into my thinking as an artist and into my views of the affairs of this world to be able to accept a remark such as this without too much difficulty and certainly without choking on the sentiment. He or she will know by now what I have in mind when I speak of world revolution, will know what sort of a form it would take and why it is so necessary. Such readers will also know that, when I wrote my article, I cannot have meant only a cultural revolution, but also changes to the system, of which an equal distribution of worldly goods would have to be the first requirement. What I most certainly did not mean when I wrote these words in 1968 was international Stalinization or some such other horrific scenario. Be that as it may, my remarks unleashed a storm of righteous indignation and were reprinted in newspapers up and down the country, generally out of context, with the result that I was only half understood. I harmed myself and was harmed in return. At the first performance of my Second Piano Concerto on the morning of Sunday, 29 September, there was considerable applause and I was called back on to the platform several times, but my colleagues in the orchestra, who had all played very well, declined to share the applause with me, something I had never known before. I asked the conductor, Bernhard Conz, why they had behaved in this way. You've guessed: it was because of my world revolution, Herr Generalmusikdirektor Conz informed me.

I returned to Marino and to Rudi, who was visibly on the mend. Later that year he went to stay with the Feltrinellis on Lake Como, then moved on to London, only to be deported within a matter of months – not even Karl Marx had been treated in such a fashion. I saw him a few times in London and cooked spaghetti for him and his family, and Rudi accompanied me to rehearsals and on walks. The vice-chancellors of the University of Aarhus in Jutland then took him under their wing, offering him a lectureship and allowing him to live in safety and to lead a life more attuned to his physical condition.

In Marino I tried to work again, but this time it was really no good at all. As soon as I started to write, I invariably got a headache. My whole system was now in a mess, the thread had been lost. And so I went off for a break with Fausto, a week in enchanted Apulia, in an ancient tower, surrounded by the sea. I could have stayed there for weeks, sleeping away my cares, but I had to get back to the grindstone. My first destination was the Amsterdam Concertgebouw for my *Musen Siziliens* and Double Concerto, two pastoral works that I programmed with Mozart's 'Haffner' Symphony of 1782. It gave me enormous pleasure to make music with this full-toned body of players. Amsterdam in the autumn is a city of mists and rain, a place of faded gardens. For months I had been waiting in vain for a new beginning, for the motivation for a new work: most of all, I wanted to write a piece for large orchestra, that wonderful and resourceful instrument declared dead by the modernists of the day.

It was certainly high time that I wrote such a piece, since I had spent the last few years working principally, nay, almost exclusively, on vocal music and now needed to transfer the emotions derived from recent experiences to the technical context created by my work on *Die Bassariden*, my Second

Piano Concerto and *Das Floß der 'Medusa'*. In Marino a handful of sketches already lay on my desk, but I regarded them as unusable. I did not know where to go from here. And now, to make matters worse, there was the media's grotesque and foolish interest in my 'case'. As a Hamburg critic had so kindly put it many years before, I had scaled the greatest heights with *Der junge Lord*, with the result that there was now only one direction in which I could – and would have to – go. And fall I did. I sensed it from the type of questions that journalists started to put to me: aggressively worded, sceptical at best, also, of course, questioning my commitment, which, as I knew better than anyone, was still entirely intact. It was a commitment fired by the sense of euphoria that characterizes the beginner. There was much that I got wrong, and I simply did not understand enough to be treated as an authority, still less as a 'case'. I saw myself being forced in a direction that did not necessarily have to be mine but, at the same time, found myself incapable of distancing myself from a philosophy which, as a matter of principle and, as it were, subliminally, corresponded with all that I felt was both necessary and sensible if the human race was to have any future at all.

Amsterdam, delightful and magical, was followed by Hamburg, with its gloom and sleet, its waterways and cold. The rehearsals for *Das Floß der 'Medusa'* were exceptionally tiring, on top of which I found myself the helpless and defenceless victim of a media campaign that soon got out of hand. Its authors were a ghost writer who, also active as a composer, was ill-disposed towards me and a Hamburg-based journalist of ill repute who, between them, thought up a particularly effective trick as part of their campaign of vilification: a week before the first night they published a kind of *ta tzu-pao* – a Chinese wall poster denouncing a particular person – in a widely read magazine, attacking me as a private individual and also pillorying my music and the artistic ideas contained in the score of *Das Floß der 'Medusa'*, a work which, as yet unperformed, they could not possibly have known. There is no doubt that this attack was incompatible with the accepted practices of civilized music criticism, which no doubt helps to explain why it had such an explosive impact. Needless to say, the seriousness of my political commitment was once again called into question, since there was one thing that people could simply not understand: that someone who was not hard up but who had a roof over his head and contracts with an appreciative Establishment should want to become a spokesman for minorities, for the underprivileged and for opponents of the system. Also: anyone who wanted revolution would surely have to write revolutionary music. Something was not quite right. There must be something wrong with the equation. The fact that the music that was considered revolutionary by a radical minority in the mid-sixties could have been anything but revolutionary and that there were hundreds of different kinds of revolutionary thinking had not yet occurred to anyone. Today, as we sweep up the snows of yesteryear, we can see the cultural misunderstanding that obtained at that time for precisely what it was – stupid and arrogant – and we shake our heads in dismay. But at that date . . . how difficult it was to explain oneself, to find the right words and, above all, to deal with all the wrongs that had built up over the years.

The author, after all, is always the one who is least aware of the repercussions of his actions: certainly he knows less than his victims, that is to say, his readers and his listeners. During the rehearsals in Hamburg, I was invited to a discussion with a group of 'socialist music students', who wanted to talk about music and politics: all I remember – and my memory is still as vivid as though it were yesterday – is the aggression and malice with which I found myself faced. I could not explain it, could make no sense of such personal, *ad hominem* jibes. These people did not know the first thing about me. Who were their informants? And who had set them up to it? Until then, all my encounters with young people had passed off without animosity. This here was completely new and had all the charm of the unexpected and barely comprehensible.

The article by our two good-for-nothing journalists required a response. I telephoned Professor Adorno to ask if he would write to the newspapers: he declared his willingness to do so and even hinted that he liked the way in which I was developing as a composer and that he regarded us both as sharing common ground. But when he heard that Luigi Nono and Peter Weiss had also written letters, he changed his mind: he could not consort with Communists, he said, that was something that I must surely understand.

Some eight days before the first performance of *Das Floß der 'Medusa'* I gave an interview to two German journalists, at the end of which they asked me what I would do if there were to be any unpleasant scenes at the following Monday's concert. The question puzzled me greatly. Somehow it appeared as though the old tom-cat was in for it – was it the socialist music students and their mentors who were after me? As a result, the final week's rehearsals were accompanied by an additional sense of unease, quite apart from all the problems of ensuring that the huge choral and orchestral forces demanded by my score were fully under control. There was no time left to deal with journalists, with conjectures and mere suspicions and with all such similar nonsense. I had to concentrate and husband my resources, since I had an important concert to conduct.

A concert platform had been erected in Planten un Blomen, an enormous multi-purpose hall in Hamburg, where the sound technicians from Deutsche Grammophon had set up their recording equipment and spent the whole week making test recordings. Fortunately, they also recorded the final run-through – whether on the morning of the concert or the previous day I no longer recall. Even though this live recording has all the qualities of a rehearsal – the performers not giving their all, but saving themselves for the actual performance, the conducting, singing and playing all matter-of-fact and calculated – it remains the only record of the oratorio's planned première, since the concert itself notoriously never took place. This tape was then broadcast that evening in place of the performance that several regional radio stations had intended to broadcast live. What had happened?

I can describe this fateful evening only as I myself saw it, from my double perspective as composer and conductor. I have no difficulty in doing so, even though it is disagreeable for me to have to recall those terrible days in Hamburg. Moreover, I have never spoken or written about this affair until now, but at most have referred to it only in passing and only when obliged to do so. That has been all. Ernst Schnabel immediately wrote a short book on the subject, which readers can consult for themselves and see how the fiasco unfolded from my librettist's point of view. For me, of course, the whole affair looked somewhat different since I was not only attacked on a personal level, with my whole aesthetic as a composer called into question, but I was also the musical director responsible for the evening's performance. My memory of the occasion is dominated by the terrible feeling of being completely alone. Throughout this period, I felt as though I were cut off from the rest of humanity and utterly on my own.

There we were, waiting backstage – Charles Regnier (Charon), Edda Moser (Madame La Mort), Dietrich Fischer-Dieskau (the mulatto Jean-Charles) and I, ready to go on, but no one came to fetch us, even though it was already a few minutes past eight o'clock. Through a chink in the wall, we could see that something was wrong in the hall. People were standing around. Had there been problems with tickets? In the front row sat Rolf Liebermann, Peter Ustinov, Georg Solti, the radio controller and his programme directors, the Dessaus and the Schnabels. We had no idea what was happening. (Later we discovered that plain-clothes detectives were in the auditorium, keeping a look-out for rebellious-looking types – would that be my claque or my critics?) Since no one came to fetch us, the four of us decided to go out on to the platform on our own. After all, the power of music or, at least, the power of musicians might have been sufficient to restore a semblance of order. And so we set off, the soloists ahead of me, with the result that they were unaware of a man in grey detaining me and saying that if I did not remove the red flag that was then being unfurled on stage, I would be held responsible for the consequences. And, sure enough, someone had just attached a scrap of red material to my conductor's podium. There it was for all to see. In a flash I realized that it was important for my whole future as an artist and as a member of civilized society to react impeccably to this obvious provocation, however ridiculous it may have been. And so I told the man in grey, an employee of North German Radio by the name of Carsten Puttfarcken (or so he informed me), that I had no intention of following his instructions and continued on my way. I could also have said that I was there to conduct, not to keep the place clean. I mounted the podium and asked for silence in the hall, a request that was duly met, so that I raised my baton for the orchestra's first entry. It was then that I heard a chorus of voices, first *pianissimo*, then increasingly audible. Where was it coming from? I could scarcely believe my ears: it was coming from the platform. The ladies and gentlemen of the RIAS Chamber Choir that had come to Hamburg from Berlin to make up numbers and with whom I had often worked in the past on terms of perfect amity were chanting in unison: 'Get rid of the flag! Get rid of the flag!' I looked at them and waited, they looked back at me and continued their chanting. I looked at Fidi: what should I do? He shrugged his shoulders. Finally we signalled to each other through eye contact alone that it would be better if we left the platform. Which we did. The members of the RIAS Chamber Choir duly followed suit.

A violent off-stage discussion now broke out. The ladies and gentlemen of the chorus said that, however much they liked me, they could not bring themselves to appear on stage with the red flag, the very flag that fluttered from the Brandenburg Gate in Berlin. I said that one also fluttered from the Hamburg Town Hall and from the Schöneberg Town Hall in West Berlin, but no doubt that was not the same thing. By now, Fidi, too, was worked up and announced that this was the last time he would allow himself to be led up the garden path by me. I was so shocked by his remark that I forgot to ask when the previous occasion had been. And whatever did he mean? What garden path? But before I could think of an answer, Frau Moser broke in and threw her arms around me, exclaiming that, whatever happened, she would always stick by me. All this happened in the green room within a matter of seconds, while outside in the hall riot police were starting to launch their attack. That they were already on the scene was due to the fact that they had been stationed in an adjoining room since before the start of the concert, ready for action with their clubs and shields and riot gear. In other words, the organizers had clearly reckoned on trouble and asked for police protection as a precautionary measure. But why, I wondered, had Mr Plod entered the fray? I returned to the platform to find that the orchestra, too, had now left and, finding Charon's microphone, tried to protest at the fact that the police had been deployed, but even before I had finished the sentence, the microphone had been torn from my hand by a member of the constabulary. Meanwhile, at the front entrance, representatives of different schools of socialist thought were laying into each other with a will. There was total confusion, brute force was used, and a number of arrests were made. Ernst Schnabel may have been a former controller of North German Radio, but that did not stop him from being thrown through a plate-glass door by a representative of the forces of law and order and from being briefly locked up in a cell for opposing the state's authority. He had tried to stop the fighting. The red flag was torn to shreds. One thing that I did not see that evening and that I discovered only later from a photograph in the paper was a further poster attached to the conductor's desk on which someone had daubed the word 'Revolutionary', followed by a question mark. What was meant by this and what happened to the poster are questions that I have never been able to answer.

The concert was abandoned and, perturbed by all that had happened, people went their separate ways. It was still early. Paul Dessau and Georg Solti returned to their hotel to discuss the role of politics in the concert hall and music and society in general. I spent the evening with some acquaintances in Pöseldorf (one of Hamburg's more salubrious districts), in the same street as the one in which some old friends from the world of music lived – they were at home, I saw the lights on, and I knew that they knew where I was, but none of them made any effort to telephone or call round. Here we were joined not only by Ernst Schnabel, swathed in bandages as a result of his altercation with the plate-glass door and bailed out of prison by his lawyer, Kurt Groenewold, but also by Ernesto's lady friend, the sinister Sissi Plessen, togther with a number of acquaintances from Hamburg and three of my friends from Berlin, Gastón, Günter Amendt and Rainer

Esche, the last-named a schoolboy completely crazy about Lenny Bernstein and the revolution. All were talking excitedly at once, but none of them really knew what to say. As for myself, I recall only my silent composure, something like a personal kind of Zen that is famously capable of helping to make even physical suffering more bearable: it was not I that was being tormented. I was more worried about Fausto, who had taken the whole affair very badly and whose mistrust of the Germans, inculcuated in Italy, had unfortunately now been confirmed. He was in tears. The very next morning, as soon as it was light, he drove back to Italy, stopping only briefly for petrol, but refusing to get out of his car, refusing to eat or drink, refusing even to pee on German soil.

It was fortunate, I thought, that neither my mother nor Inge had come to Hamburg. I immediately rang them to reassure them, promising to explain the whole story as soon as I could. Princess Margaret of Hesse – Aunt Peg – had left a letter at my hotel, but I did not see it until the next morning, so that I did not know that she, too, had been in Hamburg. She wrote that artists exist to create beauty, since there is already more than enough ugliness in the world (and she was right, of course). The situation in which I had become caught up was particularly unpleasant, she wrote, but she wanted to assure me of her undiminished friendship. I wrote back to her, touched and grateful, saying that art is concerned, first and foremost, with truth, truth which is even more important and more beautiful than beauty: truth *is* beauty. During the years and decades that followed, our friendship never wavered, a friendship forged between an honest, witty, warm-hearted Scot and Christian and myself, the black sheep of the family and a pagan. It triumphed over all hostility and every attempt to poison it. There are friendships – and what would the world be without them? – that are so utterly exceptional that all shortcomings, character defects and differences between the two parties simply never impinge on their field of vision, or else one loves the weaknesses as part of the character, part of the friend whom one loves. There are friendships that are like love affairs, except that they last much longer.

While on the subject of friendship and loss, I must briefly report the sad news that relations between me and Elsa Morante had broken down irretrievably. It had happened at the beginning of the year and taken the form of a rather unpleasant scene of quite astonishing vehemence on the part of the intolerant Elsa. It took place in the street, not far from the Largo Goldoni on the Corso. It had just been raining. Car doors were slammed, steps receded into the distance. 'Siete dei totalitarii!', she called out from afar in her strident voice. I should add that, like Pasolini, Elsa was filled with mistrust of the student movement: both felt that the people involved were the sons of bourgeois parents, sons of the rich and of the Establishment who were motivated only by frustration and who carried on in such a way that the sons of the proletariat, who, because of their circumstances, were obliged to wear police uniforms and serve the forces of law and order, had no choice but to lay into them with their truncheons and fire tear gas at them. Pasolini bluntly expressed this point of view in a leading article published at the height of the student revolts, during the summer of 1968, when it appeared in a national weekly under the title 'I hate you students'. From now on, doors were to be constantly closed, as though of their own accord. And for the most part they were banged, rather than quietly shut.

At Easter I wrote to Elsa about the beautiful arioso 'Am Abend, da es kühle war' from the *St Matthew Passion*, reminding her of the dove of spiritual peace that returns with an olive leaf in its beak and expressing my desire to make my peace with her. Her answer was no. Rarely have I felt so sad. There was something devastating about her reply: a part of my life, a source of light and warmth had been taken away from me. I saw Elsa only once more, ten years later, during the summer of 1978, when she arrived one evening at Marino unannounced, with a group of our mutual friends, to surprise me on my birthday. I was just getting over a serious illness, was full of medicines and virtually incapable of communicating. I had reached a state of nervous exhaustion in which I was no longer capable of a single coherent sentence. All I could do was look at Elsa and listen: she was as witty and as anti-bourgeois as ever. But we no longer inhabited the same world, I had moved so far away from her in the meantime. And the saddest thing of all was that she now got on my nerves!

One after another I lost touch with various friends at this time, as though in a chain reaction. It was as if a crate of jumping jacks had suddenly caught fire. In a number of cases, however, the move was all to the good and could be welcomed as a sign that I had broken free from onerous obligations. But there were unfortunately other, important cases that made me feel like an outcast. Wenzel in Berlin and even Franco in Rome muttered warnings that their patience was running out; Ingeborg asked to talk things over with me and repeated her credo that no artist should ever allow other people to dictate what he should and should not do – but that was not what was involved just now.

I have no idea how much work the media must have done in generating so much stupidity, misunderstanding and hatred of my own poor self. Why, I wondered, was the whole world so convinced that it must have been I who had organized the Hamburg fiasco? According to Ernst Schnabel, there were more than one hundred newspaper articles that all levelled the same accusations. But when has an artist ever been known to prevent a performance of one of his own works from going ahead and to have engineered his own downfall? There is absolutely nothing that could have given rise to such a suspicion – as is now more or less accepted to be the case.

On the morning after the Hamburg débâcle, while Fausto was heading back to the Brenner Pass, I myself was bound for West Berlin, where I joined thousands of others in a demonstration against Hans Joachim Rehse, a former member of the German Supreme Court who had just been acquitted of membership of the National Socialist People's Court, an acquittal that had sparked a wave of indignation throughout the whole of the Federal Republic. It was said that the court had failed in its democratic duty by acquitting an individual who, as a judge in Nazi Germany, had clearly been implicated in a whole series of judicial murders and that, in acquitting him, the Berlin Court had effectively given its blessing to the institutionalized brutality committed by the National Socialists. That evening I met Peter Weiss, who, together with Wenzel (but without me), had been watching a programme on current affairs on television: fifteen minutes of moral and artistic outrage directed at the old tom-cat. That morning, the programme director of North German Radio, Franz Reinholz, had called a press conference, to which – be it noted in passing – I myself had not been invited and at which he played the tape of the final run-through of *Das Floß der 'Medusa'*, telling the journalists present that for the next ten years I was dead as far as the German musical scene was concerned. In the event, it turned out to be more than ten years. How right the prophetic Herr Reinholz was to be proved! At the same time a musicologist by the name of Heinz-Klaus Metzger opined in print that the fact that I had refused to conduct (I had done no such thing) was beside the point: only when orchestras refused to play my music would it be possible to speak of progress. I should also add that North German Radio initially tried to hold me responsible for the damage caused to the Planten un Blomen exhibition hall (in order to prepare the ground for their surprise attack, they began by sending an advance guard in the person of their barman, who wanted me to make good the loss of his interval receipts but whom I referred instead to the promoter), but they were soon forced to realize what a senseless exercise this would have been. At the time I thought the whole thing risible and shameful, unnecessary, mismanaged and mean. Time has done nothing to alter that opinion. The breach that I had expected and feared and that had come about in this scandalous, culpably negligent, highly discourteous and contemptuously inhuman way (albeit perhaps unavoidably, even if only to clear up a basic aesthetic misconception?) had started in a typically Teutonic manner – noisy, forceful and unpleasant.

I could, of course, have called a press conference of my own and explained things from my own perspective, but I wanted nothing more to do with journalists. And so I returned to Marino and began a musical setting of Gastón Salvatore's *Versuch über Schweine*, using the few sketches from my Sixth Symphony that I had noted down in the course of the summer. I had a concert with the English Chamber Orchestra in London the following February and used the occasion to toss off and publish a piece that reflected a whole new awareness of the age, a living topicality.

The piece was inspired less by my anger at the scandal surrounding *Das Floß der 'Medusa'* than by the personality of Gastón Salvatore and a (brief) encounter with the singer Roy Hart, an Australian guru based in London who played squash at his meditation centre, the Abraxas Club, in Hampstead and who was followed everywhere by a bevy of angry young women. He happened to be lecturing on the human voice in Amsterdam while I myself was in the city in the autumn of 1968, and he gave me a practical demonstration of his theory in the conductor's room at the Concertgebouw: according to Roy Hart, all of us used to have (and, indeed, still have) an additional octave both at the top and bottom of our voices and, hence, greater individuality, greater courage to stand up for our beliefs and more revolutionary zeal than we generally imagine that we possess. The loss of these two octaves is indicative of the extent to which we are repressed in the western world – not only Roy Hart and his lovely ladies but also all the rest of us. When these two octaves have been fully restored to the civilized world, then may God help the fickle, the petty bourgeois and the all too cautious!

Roy Hart was a guru, not a musician, and it was not easy for me to perform *Versuch über Schweine* or to record the work with him immediately afterwards, since he had difficulty counting time and reacting to his entries. He also had problems of intonation. The day that he spent in the recording studio was the worst he had ever known, he announced that evening, completely exhausted. But two good things did at least come of our encounter: from then on, Roy Hart was less contemptuous of musicians, whom he had hitherto regarded as an altogether conventional bunch of professionals, while I for my own part realized that, revolutionary ideals notwithstanding, it is safer to work with professionals. I had already chatted with Fidi on the subject of Roy Hart's theories and practices, but they had been of no interest at all to him. He felt no need to extend his range by a further two octaves, although he knew that it is a good thing for musicians to think from time to time about the curious relationship between sound and soul, content and language and about ways of deepening and improving these links.

The first performance of *Versuch über Schweine* (or *Essay on Pigs*, as it now became known) took place in the Queen Elizabeth Hall on the South Bank on 14 February 1969 and made a great impression not only on Gastón Salvatore's many admirers in the hall – astute students and staff from the London School of Economics – but also, I think, on my own friends and fans. Otto Klemperer came to the final rehearsal in his wheelchair, accompanied by his daughter, Lotte, but missed *Versuch über Schweine*, which was the piece that had interested him most. During a break in the rehearsal, he told me that he had recently seen Paul Dessau in Vienna. (Dessau had once been a conductor under Klemperer at the Hamburg Opera.) 'He spoke of the class struggle, just imagine – the class struggle! In Vienna!' In the evening, after the concert, Rudolf Nureyev came backstage, together with Margot Fonteyn, who said something along the lines of 'So now you, too, have taken to protesting'. Later that evening I met Peter Maxwell Davies in a pub in Hampstead and became friends with him for life. We saw each other often in the years that followed, exchanging scores and experiences and writing letters to each other. He came twice to Montepulciano, although not until many years later.

Five weeks after the London concert, on 21 March 1969, I arrived in Havana, where Hans Magnus Enzensberger had been instrumental in persuading the Cuban authorities to extend an invitation to me. Two weeks before that I had conducted Brahms's Fourth Symphony in Detroit (a dreadful place), Kansas City and St Louis – rugged art music, manly and dour and North German, sentimentally melancholic, filled with a sense of loss and renunciation. I asked to be paid in cash and, with the fee in my pocket, flew to Mexico City, where I spent the time waiting for my visa poring over Spanish books and newspapers in my hotel room for hours on end every day. There was plenty of time to study and think. I had visited

Mexico City with the Deutsche Oper only the previous autumn, when I had conducted *Elegie für junge Liebende* and, as a result, had got to know a few people whose telephone numbers I had been given by comrades in Berlin: artists and writers who kept me company and showed me the city and its environs. I was also introduced to some local musicians, including the delightful Manuel Enríquez and his wife, who threw a small party for me on the eve of my departure for Cuba, when I also met a whole group of other Mexican colleagues.

In the departure hall at Mexico City airport, my passport was stamped in red: 'Salido por Cuba.' And I was photographed by the Mexican police, once from the front and twice in profile (for the CIA, I was told), and I knew that from now on I would be registered as being on the other side of the social divide, someone who was subversive and dangerous, an opponent of the system. My in-flight reading consisted of a supplement to the daily paper, *Granma*, containing a speech by Fidel (as I had taken the liberty of calling my great contemporary, albeit only in conversations with myself and then only with a beating heart) that set forth many new ideas on educational reform, a not unrealistic plan that could perhaps have been realized, had there been no United States embargo and if the population as a whole had enjoyed a tolerable standard of living. Each citizen would have had the right to an education paid for by the state and would have ended up at university. But the state expected something in return; namely, practical help in agriculture, industry, the army, research or wherever people's knowledge and revolutionary enthusiasm could best be exploited. Essentially, it was Antonio Gramsci's belief that social divisions would disappear if professional differences were abolished. In his speech Fidel made no secret of the fact that great efforts would be needed if this humanitarian and revolutionary plan was to be brought any closer to realization, and I thought to myself: if it cannot even be achieved without difficulty on an island in Central America, what hope is there for the rest of the world? How were we to go on? What must happen to make the impossible possible? Would the Cubans achieve this goal?

Jesús Menéndez from the National Council for Culture was waiting for me at Havana Airport. On our journey into the city, I told him how much I wanted to get to know Cuban revolutionary music and its practitioners. I had brought with me a tape of *Das Floß der 'Medusa'*, my requiem for Che, which I wanted to play to my fellow musicians in order to have their opinion. Miguel Barnet was someone else to whom I wanted to be introduced. An ethnologist and poet, he had written a life of Esteban Montejo,

El Cimarrón, that I wanted to try to set to music. And there was so much that I wanted to see for myself, to hear and to learn about in this spontaneous, vibrant, revolutionary world. What sort of an approach did they have to art? What was expected of artists, what kind of involvement? Who or what was a revolutionary artist? It was largely to discover all this that I had come to visit Cuba.

During the weeks that followed I wrote down all that I read and heard and saw in a thick notebook, from which I shall sometimes have occasion to quote in the pages that follow. I spent my first evening in Havana with Hans Magnus Enzensberger and his Russian wife, Masha, walking along the coastal road, the Malecón, and catching up on the events of the last few weeks and months. Only the previous year Hans Magnus had resigned his professorship at the Center for Advanced Studies at Wesleyan University, a move accompanied by a spectacular gesture on his part and by an open letter explaining his reasons for resigning. He was now in Havana waiting to begin a series of lectures at the city's university, but the signal to begin showed no sign at all of coming. What he did not know at that time was that his negative stance towards the invasion of Czechoslovakia by troops from the Warsaw Pact was not shared by the revolutionary authorities in Cuba. The head of state had himself adopted a more or less positive attitude towards it. Instead of discussing the matter openly with their guest, the authorities simply prevented him from appearing in public. At the time of our evening stroll along the Malecón, none of us was aware of this, and Hans Magnus spent his time waiting, working, meeting fellow writers, expressing surprise and bewilderment, and waiting. During the summer he proudly spent four weeks working on a sugar plantation, before returning to Europe, disappointed, insulted and angered.

I did not wait to be introduced to Miguel Barnet by my colleagues from the National Council for Culture but simply consulted the local telephone directory and rang his number. An hour later we met in the foyer of my hotel, the Riviera, where sentimental American songs still oozed oleaginously from speakers set in the pink-coloured walls. We met virtually every day, generally at his tiny two-room apartment in Vedado. Only his manners revealed him to be the grandson of the president of the republic and suggested that his parents, who had remained in the country, had once been wealthy landowners. His flat contained not ancient pomp and splendour but living, colourful testimony to modern Cuba in the form of books and pictures, tape recordings and gramophone records. Miguel was all in favour of the revolution: he himself wanted and needed to change and so he had made the long journey from liberal young bourgeois to simple socialist scholar and poet who served his people with enthusiasm – which does not mean that, having successfully completed this metamorphosis, he was overcome by Brechtian bitterness. Far from it. His thoughts were filled with tropical sensuality, he loved flowers, beautiful women, sentimental ballads and zarzuelas. A white man who had been baptized a Catholic, he was a follower of the black Yoruba cult that had been brought to Cuba from the Congo. Miguel's ethnological studies were to be important to me when writing *El Cimarrón*. And it was he who, over the coming weeks, introduced me to a whole series of younger and older writers and artists, as well as to songwriters and singers, all of them kind-hearted souls, black and white alike, all animated and fired by optimism and by the experiments and endless imponderables of the revolutionary process.

I attended a rehearsal of the National Symphony Orchestra and introduced myself to its principal conductor. The orchestra was no longer the dazzling body of players that it must once have been under conductors like Erich Kleiber and Igor Markevich. But that was *antes*, before. *Después*, afterwards, most of the players had left, mainly for the United States, and had to be replaced by retired professionals, students and a number of string players from Bulgaria. I also attended the evening's concert, which included a performance of Shostakovich's Fifth Symphony under a female Soviet conductor. There were lots of young people in the hall, which was packed to the rafters, and their expectant enthusiasm clearly affected the orchestra, which sounded much better, much fresher and more human than it had at the morning's rehearsal.

Notes from my diary:

> 24 March 1969. With Enzensberger to view the Spanish Old Town. Most of the buildings in a sorry state and in urgent need of repair, looking as rundown as their counterparts in well-to-do but corrupt Palermo. A rickety sign bearing the word 'Nacionalizado' hangs over the closed shutters of the Chase Manhattan Bank. The shop windows are empty, rather as in Germany during the 'difficult years' between 1945 and 1948, also in Chinatown, where there are three Chinese cinemas instead. In the main modern residential quarter of Vedado there are hotels everywhere, apartment blocks and private villas that have been turned into boarding houses for thousands upon thousands of students. The street scene is dominated by children and adolescents,

> soldiers and students. Everywhere there is a feeling of youth, the sense of a new beginning.

A new world is coming into being, I thought, a world in which I felt as old as the whole of the moribund capitalist system – and yet I was not even fifty.

The Instituto Cubano de Arte y Industria Cinematográfica, whose musical director was the composer Leo Brouwer, published a brief manifesto to mark its tenth anniversary. Among its aims and intentions were:

> To seek a contemporary and renovatory ways of seeing things from a Cuban perspective
> To encourage revolutionary activity and freedom of creative expression
> To enrich and disseminate the culture of the cinema
> To educate a critical, discriminating, active and more complex audience.

I noted down a few of Fidel's remarks from an interview that he had given two years previously to the American journalist, Lee Lockwood. Lockwood had asked him: 'And what about the arts? Are attempts being made to teach the history of art and literature, together with their critique, from a Marxist standpoint?' To which Fidel replied:

> Until now we have had very few qualified people capable of even attempting to analyze artistic phenomena from a Marxist point of view. I think our basic concern must be to ensure that all forms of culture serve mankind and enable us to develop many different positive feelings. For me, the goal of art is not art, but the individual. Art should make people happier and better. I cannot conceive of any achievements of a cultural, scientific and artistic nature that find fulfilment only in themselves. Man alone is the realization of science and culture.

And the New Man of whom we dream – what does he look like? What is it that distinguishes him, what does he lack? Well, said Miguel, it was not yet entirely settled what the New Man would look like. He would be someone without bourgeois capitalist instincts: he would not want to own his fellow humans and their property, for example, he would not crave power and so on. The basis for the New Man lay in culture. Cuba's future, thought Miguel, belonged to an egalitarian society that would be largely inspired by artistic understanding.

Enzensberger, too, was a little unclear how to imagine the New Man. He would have to be selfless, that much was certain. Enzensberger told me that he had recently met a twenty-year-old Cuban youth who was completely convinced that he belonged to this new species, and ever since this encounter Enzensberger himself had thought that this new type of *uomo sociale* now existed and that he would henceforth exist in increasingly large numbers, as in China, as a kind of soldier of socialism. But, I said, everyone who takes an interest in the arts is immediately influenced by them in a deviant way: he is changed by them and becomes noticeably more sensitive, discovering within himself centres of individual conflict or at the very least beginning to develop such centres within himself. There could be nothing more terrible than a life or a world without this deviant element, nothing more desolate than a stage teeming only with so-called normality. That cannot be the meaning behind such a concept. I would have to continue asking questions and making enquiries of my own.

On 27 March, Enzensberger and I visited Esteban Montejo, El Cimarrón, a tall, slim, straight-backed man with dark brown leathery skin and a great love of Romeo y Julietas, one of the finest Havana cigars. Already over a hundred (or so it was said), he regaled us with wonderful and, for the most part, amusing tales not only from his past but also from the present. In 1895, while still a runaway slave, he had fought in the Battle of Mal Tiempo with a horde of naked *cimarrónes* armed with enormous knives, attacking and massacring the Spanish and thus helping Cuba to gain her independence. Now he sat on the VIP rostrum at military parades, weighed down with decorations, and was on first-name terms with Fidel. He was delighted to discover that I wanted to set his life to music, finding it somehow entirely appropriate. I made a note of his intonational patterns, with their complex modulations. He spoke of ghosts as though they really existed. His voice had an enormous compass, extending far beyond the absurd two octaves that are typical of us westerners.

I attended a rehearsal of a play by Aimé Césaire, *Patrice Lumumba*, with fantastic actors, especially the faunlike (white) protagonist. Among the people I had met on one of the previous evenings were Tomás Gutiérrez Alea, who had directed the film *Memories of Underdevelopment* (a film about the difficulties of living through the revolution without, however, taking part in it), and the thirty-five-year-old composer Carlos Fariñas, who worked at the National Library and wrote aleatory music. When I asked him what he understood by bourgeois music, he replied that the question was absurd and unworthy of an answer, or at least of one that could be printed: there was no such thing as 'bourgeois' music, said the *compañero*, just as there was no such thing as 'unbourgeois' or 'revolutionary' music. There was only the free artistic development of the individual and his or her chosen means of expression – all this, of course, as Fidel had already so aptly said, in the spirit of the revolution, in it, with it, not outside it and not directed against it.

The composer Harold Gramatges had spent a number of years as ambassador in Paris but now worked at the Casa de las Americas (Havana's America House prior to its political realignment). He championed a type of music intelligible to the 'people' and regretted the arrogance of those 'modern composers who flatter the snobs'. He was not a member of the Brouwer–Blanco–Fariñas group but something of a loner. (He was also somewhat older than they.) According to the notes that I made at the time, the most charming musician I have ever met, apart from Paul Dessau, was Jorge Berróa, whose ballet music, only recently drawn to my attention, was equally indebted to the worlds of folk music and modernism. It was Miguel Barnet who introduced us. A tall and portly mulatto, relaxed but intense in his manner, Berróa came to visit me, bringing with him his guitar and a number of his scores, including a dance piece on which he was currently working for the modern-dance company with which he must have been under permanent contract. He sang and played me his songs, some of which were good, a successful blend of folk music and modernism, but there were others in which the two elements simply did not gel – the difficulties began even with the notation. I tried to give him a few tips – I of all people!

I spent the first few days of April on the Isla de Pinos, the great Island of Youth on which the New Man was taking his first few tentative steps. The whole island had once resembled a jungle, so densely was it overgrown, but it had been cleared by thousands of youngsters and transformed into fertile plantations. Citrus fruit was cultivated, as were tobacco and rice. Artificial lakes had been dug and pastureland created. Not only was the New Man being reared here, so, too, was F1, a cross between a male zebu and a Holstein cow and, as such, well able to withstand the tropical climate. All these jobs were done voluntarily by young people and were described as *trabajo productivo*. Their schooling took place in the afternoon and evening and, if I understood correctly, included not only paramilitary training but also dancing, acting, singing and playing musical instruments.

According to my notebook, I felt 'very tired and bourgeois' at the end of my three-day stay on the Isla de Pinos and sensed that it was already all too late for me. Meanwhile, I had agreed with the members of the National Council that I would première my Sixth Symphony here in Havana rather than in Berlin or New York. The performance would take place very soon, before the end of the year. They promised to let me have as much rehearsal time as I needed. I agreed in principle and, indeed, was proud to do so, although I made it clear that I would first have to see whether the piece that we had in mind could be written in what little time remained.

In my pink-coloured, single room at the Hotel Riviera, where the lifts were guarded by armed militia and the guests were under strict instructions not to receive any visitors in their rooms (the counter-revolution lurked behind every corner and in the head of every stranger), I was able to feel my own isolation in all its depth and bitterness, as I stared down from the twelfth floor on to the Malecón, against the quay walls of which the Atlantic breakers were silently pounding. A handful of lorries and armoured vehicles rumbled noiselessly past, toylike reminders of a reality from which I was painfully excluded by more than the solid pane of glass in the window of my hotel for political refugees.

I also got to know the composer Juan Blanco, then forty-one years old and, with his electronically charged compositions, a member of the Cuban avant-garde. He refused to draw on autochthonous sources. His music, he said, served the revolution by expressing all its *violencia*, its primal force and power. He and his music affirmed and confirmed the revolution. He was a friend of Luigi Nono's. He said that electronic music in Cuba was different from everywhere else, since, unlike its non-Cuban counterparts, it drew its strength from the revolution. It represented upheaval, not evolution, Juan Blanco insisted.

On 4 April tapes of my *Medusa* and *Versuch* were played in rooms belonging to the Writers' Association. There were some fifty people present, composers, instrumentalists and writers. According to my notes, they seemed moved by both these pieces, especially by the oratorio. I found them 'kind and friendly'. The musicians thought it great that this music could tell its own story and that one could understand its origins and development. That, at least, was the reaction of the musicologist Odilio Urfé who, like the others, had heard my music for the first time that evening. Leo Brouwer, who was regarded as the leader of Cuba's avant-garde, knew a few of my pieces from his time as a student in New York.

Dutch, Chinese and Creole by extraction, Brouwer is an extraordinarily sensitive and delightful individual, a gifted composer and a highly resourceful instrumentalist.

With my suitcases bulging with new books and music, with tapes and photos and addresses, I flew back to Rome, via Madrid, on 16 April and was immediately struck down by shingles, followed by nervous spasms, sleeplessness and an immense desire to return to Cuba. I told no one that I was back. In Havana I had already sketched out the basic material for my new symphony, creating a twelve-note row and more or less deciding on the form – exactly as I had been in the habit of doing for some time past. One part of this process involved the use of that remarkable compositional technique of late medieval isorhythm to which Luigi Nono had drawn my attention in the 1950s and which I had subsequently interpreted, applied and evolved in my own particular way and for my own individual needs. In *Die Bassariden* there are even two contrastive types of rhythm, one for Pentheus (rhythms associated with march music, with two and four beats in a bar) and the other for that swine, Dionysus, whose rhythms are exclusively three in a bar – sicilianas, waltzes and sarabandes.

When I conceived my Sixth Symphony, I was not thinking of providing practical answers to the question that exercised me so intensely at that time; namely, the role of music in a revolutionary society. I have never felt competent to deal in universalities, but have always been mindful of my shortcomings and weaknesses. I could not have appeared in public with a new style, a new cast of mind and an unprecedented type of new music, still less could I have done so in Cuba. I told myself that it was best if, as always, I simply gave the audience what I myself imagined by music. And if I showed them how difficult things were for us, especially here in the West.

What was novel about this piece was the way in which it incorporated both contemporary and timeless folk music into its structure. I made the step from quotation to integration. Even the basic rhythm of my Sixth Symphony comes from the people (not my own, not least because we eastern Westphalians have no real rhythmic or dancelike qualities to show for ourselves): it was Jorge Berróa, an Afro-Cuban adherent of the Yoruba faith and a comrade of mine, who passed it on to me. It was as though a direct link were somehow trying to establish itself with my first visit to New York in 1963, when my Fifth Symphony had received its first performance and I had had my first seminal experience of Harlem. My Sixth, a

1 HWH's paternal grandmother, Helene Henze

2 HWH's maternal grandfather, Karl Geldmacher

3 HWH with brother Gerhard (left), Bielefeld, 1932

4 HWH's mother, 1930

5 HWH's father

6 HWH in the army, 1944

7 Deutsches Jungvolk, Dünne.
(HWH far right)

8 L. TO R. René Leibowitz, HWH, Peter Stadlen, Darmstadt, 1948

9 Benjamin Britten and HWH, London, c. 1958

10 L. TO R. Luchino Visconti (director), Dick Sanders (choreographer), Jean Babilée, HWH, Renzo Vespignani, in front of the Städtische Oper, (première of *Maratona*), Berlin, 24 September 1957

11 L. TO R. Pierre Boulez, Rudolf Alberth, Olivier Messiaen, HWH, Paris, 1956

12 L. TO R. Margot Fonteyn, Frederick Ashton, HWH, première of *Ondine,* Covent Garden, 27 October 1958

13 HWH, Ischia, 1953

14 HWH and Elsa Morante at a rehearsal for *Cantata della fiaba estrema,* Rome, c. 1965

15 Ingeborg Bachmann and HWH at the dress rehearsal of *Der junge Lord*, April 1965

16 Fausto Moroni, 1967

17 Election campaign for Willy Brandt. BACK ROW L. TO R. Bernhard Wicki (film director), Fritz Kortner (actor and director), HWH, Günter Grass, Willy Brandt, Karl Schiller (mayor of West Berlin, later Minister of Finance in the Brandt government). FRONT ROW L. TO R. Frau Agnes Wicki, Ingeborg Bachmann, Frau Rut Brandt

82 Telegramm **Deutsche Bundespost**

aus West Hollywood Calif 19 20 429p

Datum 21.5.61 Uhrzeit 1045

Aufgenommen Platz durch

Amt **Schwetzingen**

=LT= Wystan Auden
Chester Kallman
Hans Henze
Schloßplatz Postfach 159
Festspiele
Schwetzingen

All good things come in threes

Stravinsky

Für dienstliche Rückfragen

18 Telegram from Igor Stravinsky to W. H. Auden, Chester Kallman and HWH, for the première of *Elegie für junge Liebende*, Schwetzingen, 20 May 1961

19 L. TO R. G. R. Sellner (producer of *Die Bassariden*), W. H. Auden, HWH, Salzburg, 1966

20 HWH with the cast of the world première of *Pollicino*, Montepulciano, 1980

21 L. TO R. Peter Maxwell Davies, HWH, Harrison Birtwistle, London

22 HWH and Simon Rattle, rehearsing with the CBSO, Aldeburgh, 1986

23 HWH and Oliver Knussen, 1997

Lutheran, Protestant symphony, has a pagan body: its pulse and blood are black. This is due to the rhythms of the music, which can be interpreted from a mythological point of view as a means of expression on the part of the Africans who were once brought to Cuba against their will and who made their homes there. Such music remains as irrepressible and as vital as ever. I made these rhythms my own: I wanted them to permeate the whole piece and ensure that all the individual voices were part of the overall texture. I also wrote for two orchestras that were intended to be in constant contact with each other, permanently interrelated. Otherwise, I am unaware of any influence of modern Cuban music. No, what really attracted me were the psychedelic colours on the posters, the greens and orange and the gaudy red, together with noises whose effects left their mark on my feelings and music. Two contemporary songs became part of the process of integration to which I have already referred: one is Vietnamese and first appears on page 24 of the study score, at rehearsal letter E. It is called 'Nhu'ng ánh sao dem' (Stars in the Night) and is taken from a songbook of the Vietnamese Liberation Front, while the other was written in gaol by the popular Greek composer Mikis Theodorakis, who was thrown into prison by his country's Fascist military dictators.

I had already orchestrated Theodorakis's hymn to freedom some two years earlier and, in a recording by Christoph von Dohnányi and the West German Radio Orchestra, it was broadcast several times, with an accompanying message from me as a declaration of solidarity on my part. Also in 1967, the Korean composer Isang Yun was abducted from Berlin with a number of other South Koreans and smuggled out of the country through a West German airport. On his return to Korea, he was accused of left-wing tendencies and high treason and tortured while in prison. It was out of solidarity for Theodorakis and Isang Yun that Paul Dessau, the President of the West Berlin Academy of Arts, Boris Blacher, and I suggested to our colleagues at the academy that we might be able to save our two fellow composers, whose very lives were in danger, if we lost no time in making them ordinary, corresponding or honorary members. The suggestion was turned down by a majority vote on the grounds of quality and political neutrality. Blacher informed me by telegram and at the same time advised me not to draw any 'serious conclusions' from this negative outcome, advice that naturally encouraged me to draw such conclusions at once. A short time later I became a corresponding member of the corresponding Academy in East Berlin.

In May 1969 I was obliged to break off work on my new symphony in order to rehearse and conduct *Il re cervo* at the Stadttheater in Zurich, although the interruption was not, in fact, unwelcome. Distracted by the intensity of the rehearsals, I did not have to think about my symphony for a while, or about music and revolution. Jean-Pierre Ponnelle staged the piece with the most incredible skill and energy. I felt happy and contented: we were finally able to work together again. And the elder was in blossom, as also was the lilac. The production opened on 31 May, when a leaflet attacking my music and its author was handed out at the main entrance to the theatre. Written by the aforementioned Heinz-Klaus Metzger, it was dedicated – God alone knows why – to Zurich's student population. A few of Metzger's henchmen even managed to penetrate the theatre and find their way into rooms normally inaccessible to ordinary mortals, where they regaled the ladies and gentlemen of the chorus and orchestra with their onanistic musings. But it made no difference, no one sang or played any better or worse as a result, and it in no way affected the quality of the performance – yet it left me wondering how far certain people are prepared to go in their misguided sense of mission. It was curiously impressive, in the way that men like Savonarola and Dr Goebbels were impressive.

I spent the whole of the summer in Marino, working on my symphony, with only a handful of visitors to distract me: Ernst Schnabel, Gastón Salvatore, Michelangelo Antonioni, the artist Titina Maselli and her brother Citto, who made films, the painter Renzo Vespignani, Ingeborg and other young friends from Rome and Berlin all looked in from time to time. I often saw the Cuban writer Carlos Franqui, who had settled in Italy with his family after having fallen out with Fidel, his erstwhile comrade-in-arms from the Sierra Maestra. Antonioni wanted to make a film about the state of the world in the wake of the events of 1968 and about the way in which these events had left their mark on, and been taken up by, left-wing intellectuals in western Europe. Gastón was to be his scriptwriter. On another occasion I received a visit from Herbert Marcuse, who had delivered a lecture that very afternoon at the Teatro Eliso, when Daniel Cohn-Bendit had attacked him from the higher reaches of the auditorium, disrupting him and disturbing him to such an extent that he had finally walked offstage. It was now the height of fashion to boo our spiritual fathers off the stage: Adorno, too, had to endure such treatment on several occasions at the universities of Frankfurt and Berlin. And at the start of one of Boulez's concerts in Berlin, a member of the Red Guard had leapt up on to the stage at the Philharmonie and begun to recite from Mao's Red

Book, with the result that the conductor was unable to start the concert and had to wait until two men had felled the intruder and physically removed him from the hall. Only then could the music begin.

At some point during the summer I telegraphed to Jesús Menéndez in Havana:

> Compañero, my Sinfonía no. 6 is making good progress, and so I can now report that it will be available for its first performance in Cuba towards the end of the autumn. For various technical reasons I cannot arrive before the beginning of November. You should know that the piece will last about forty minutes and that lots of rehearsals will be required. I should very much like to remain in Cuba for a while after the concert, in order to visit Santiago and other towns and to get to know the works of the revolution. I should also like to work on *El Cimarrón* during my visit and for this purpose need to study Afro-Cuban vocal music in some depth. I shall bring the orchestral parts of the symphony with me.

I think that when I wrote this I must have been working on the middle section of the symphony. In the opening movement, I had experimented with classical German sonata form or, to be more precise, had tried out the effectiveness of this dialectic form in a contemporary socio-cultural context, whereas in the second I allowed myself to bid a brief farewell to the basic heroism of the whole and to turn, instead, to the inner and most intimate world of the Cuban soul, setting the theses and antitheses of lines of poetry from 'Fé de erratas' (Proof Corrections) by Miguel Barnet, a poet deeply shaken by the pain of love. But instead of a single voice crying out in its lonely despair, we hear not one but two full orchestras, from within which madness and the end of a human relationship that has been destroyed as though in a shipwreck demand a hearing before the world's tribunal. I followed the poem's ever-changing moods, having more time than Miguel's words and ideas to allow the music to take on physical form with these various states of mind, states all too familiar to myself and to all our brothers.

Ay, Miguel!

In the final movement, the basic rhythms are systematically exploited to the point where they finally explode, an explosion that has long been expected and that takes the form of a cheerless dance of joy, with the percussion instruments intruding upon the free handling of the rhythmic cantus firmus of the Cuban national dance, the *son*, and bursting out as though in carnival mood or in an act of liberation. Folk music and art music embrace here. The finale was meant to sound triumphant, affirmative and life-enhancing, which is why I made things so hard for myself when writing it. Typically German, I guess. There is a fugal texture divided between the two orchestras, a kind of double fugue that is difficult to bring out in performance, since I was so determined to be strict with myself, to the point at which the rules gained the upper hand and took away the initiative from me as the composer. In other words, at the very moment at which the music could have breathed and sung of freedom and joy, there was, for me, only an empirical and theoretical notion of concepts and new forms of expression, new metaphors for this new, socialist kind of joy and freedom: but since I myself was not a revolutionary and since I was to take part in the Cuban revolution only briefly and as a visitor, I could really do no more than make an entirely personal contribution to the extraordinary changes that were taking place here and taking place, moreover, in the name of humanity and human dignity. And I was able to show in my music how deeply this new and modern revolution had affected me as a person.

And, at the same time, to show how remote from the world of Cuba are my music, my history and my tradition. The piece inevitably expresses all the torment, oppressiveness and difficulty that prevented me from breathing properly and acquiring – or reacquiring – the sense of certainty without which man can neither live nor die. I think that listeners will be able to sense this and, to a certain extent, empathize with the effort that went into creating this score. I wanted to provide answers, but also, of course, I wanted my music to change and move on, while at the same time wanting to include a large number of the achievements of western 'bourgeois' compositional techniques (including, for example, my own) within this process of transformation or self-improvement, so that they would not be lost to me and my listeners and readers, for it is on such achievements that my whole art is based: it is they that constitute my spiritual homeland.

9
Excerpts from my diaries, Cuba, 1969/70

Havana, 8 November 1969

Fausto and I arrived in Havana late in the evening after a nineteen-hour flight on board an old Viscount belonging to Cubana Aviación. We came from Madrid and flew via Gander, Newfoundland, where we had to spend three hours in an unserviced part of the airfield isolated from passengers on other airlines. Six hours later, we were met at Havana airport by two ladies from the National Council for Culture and by my colleague Juan Blanco (whom we were able to congratulate on his recent marriage – his seventh). The three of them then brought us to the apartment that has been rented for us and introduced us to the *conserje*. It is a large flat on the tenth floor of a thirty-storey block called Focsa in the centre of the residential quarter of Vedado, commanding a view of the sea, the legendary Hotel Nacional and neighbouring high-rise buildings, the majority of which date from the Batista years and are built in the North American style of the period.

Early the following morning there was a ring at the doorbell (we have no telephone), and who should be standing outside but Jorge Berróa, beaming from ear to ear. As soon as he noticed that I had learnt a sprinkling of Spanish in the meantime, there was no holding him back as he explored the whole compass of Creole phonology, plunging right down to the lowest notes of his range and soaring right up to the top, then back to the bottom again, as he told me about everything that exercised him in his singsong tone of voice. He had been in Prague since we had last met, but he had not enjoyed his visit (his expression darkened as he spoke about it), since he had suffered discrimination and racism there. He said that the same sort of thing also happens in Cuba, where blacks are rarely found in top positions, even though at least half the population is black. There is even an offshoot of the Black Power movement here (you occasionally see the words 'Poder Negro' sprayed on walls) and there is a tendency for such people to assert themselves culturally in a way that seeks to distance them from both Christianity and Socialism and that could well end up with them turning their backs on the world of the whites and of the white-led revolution in general.

Jorge spends a few hours helping me to ink in the notes in the rather pale photocopy of my score. Later Carlos Fariñas drops by. I was hoping to perform his new piece at my concert, but it's not finished yet. There were delays with my own orchestral parts and this, coupled with the fact that I arrived a week later than agreed, means that we now have only fourteen out of a planned total of twenty-eight rehearsals. The conductor Manolo Duchezne Cuzán, with whom I shall be jointly conducting the symphony (it is conceived for two orchestras positioned side by side), arrives to discuss the situation. Leo Brouwer appears with the score of his new piece, *Exaedros*, which consists of a handful of pages covered in graphic notation. This piece, too, I have agreed to conduct. He explains what is involved: the orchestra is divided into a (random) number of groups, each comprising six players and each distinguished as far as possible from the others in terms of its instrumental composition. Conductor and instrumentalists all have the same score and the same graphic symbols in front of them – crescendo markings, dots and strokes and written instructions and suggestions – all of which must be converted into pitches, intervals and performance techniques selected by the players themselves. In consequence, the players have to pay even more attention than usual to each other and avoid conventional sequences and intervals, especially major and minor thirds and octaves. Juan Blanco will figure as co-author of this piece, since it is he who will provide the electronic ritornellos that are to be included between the individual sections. After our meeting, Duchezne and I drive round the darkened city, delivering the parts of my Sixth Symphony to the members of the National Orchestra who, I know, will not find them easy to play. Juan Blanco will play the electric organ and Leo Brouwer the guitar part. Later that evening, Fausto and I go on a tour of our *barrio*. It is Saturday. There are queues everywhere, outside bars and restaurants, outside the famous ice-cream parlour, the Coppelia, and outside the *posadas* – hotels that can be rented by the hour and that are used by young married couples with no home of their own. They have all made an effort to look their best, especially the girls. The couples walk hand in hand.

A wooden pavilion has been erected on Fifth Avenue in which a light show plays after dark, a kind of psychedelic circus act with pop-art colours accompanied by Rolf Liebermann's *Concert des échanges* amplified over loudspeakers and played on a continuous loop – Liebermann himself will probably never know of this highly effective, albeit unplanned use of his score and will certainly find no trace of it on his annual royalty statements:

here they do not believe in old-fashioned authors' rights. An enormous yellow electric sun rises from below, while yellow electric clouds move in from the right to frame a brown Mona Lisa that pulsates in the electric light. In the upper left-hand corner of the background, blue and white bulbs pulsate. Everywhere there are plywood and cardboard cut-outs that closer inspection reveals to represent brightly painted children and young girls waving the Cuban flag. From out of the background, the Star of Cuba fitfully emerges, pulsating electrically in blue and white, growing larger and larger until its points finally extend to cover the whole of the pavilion's plywood proscenium arch. And the words ¡¡¡LOS 10 MILLIONES VAN!!! pulsate in changing colours to the rhythm of Swiss electronic music, referring to the record harvest of ten million tonnes of sugar cane that is to be achieved this year, the year of the *esfuerzo decisivo*, a combined and decisive effort on the part of the whole of the population that has remained behind on the island, an effort that the country must and *will* make in order that it may finally break free from the economic difficulties that are due, not least, to the total blockade on the part of the Americans and their allies (including the Federal Republic).

We enter the pavilion along lurching pathways edged with neon strips that flicker yellow and red and involuntarily become caught up in the repetitive, kadeidoscopic show, our shadows standing out against the sun and rising up the walls, only to disappear as they are engulfed in the penumbra of the pavilion's ceiling. We find ourselves in a large room, where the scene is suddenly totally different – an exhibition organized by the Comitato de la Defensa de la Revolución and documenting the activities of the counter-revolution in papers, photographs, films and a large number of impounded weapons, including American incendiary bombs, rubber dinghies and diving suits.

Miguel shows us the German edition of his documentary novel, *El Cimarrón*, which has just been published, together with the Cuban edition of his *Canción de Rachel*, which he hopes that Enzensberger and I might perhaps turn into a kind of mime show with music, but music that would have to be a collage of material from the worlds of operetta and sentimental ballads. In writing *Canción*, Miguel has adopted exactly the same approach as that used in his *El Cimarrón*, spending a whole year talking to the elderly Amalia Vorg, a star of the old Cuban nightclubs whose stage name was Rachel, using a tape recorder to take notes on her extraordinarily animated and complicated life, later putting all the material collected in this way into some kind of order and giving it the form of a documentary novel. Like *El Cimarrón*, *Canción de Rachel* is both a work of literature and a socio-ethnological study, a study in which art (or cabaret as a form of art) is to be seen as a mirror held up to a corrupt and bankrupt world that may or may not be a thing of the past. It is no accident that Rachel expresses herself in a flat and foolishly frivolous bordello slang.

During the afternoon we receive a visit from Manolo Duchezne, who has now looked at the score of my Sixth Symphony and, to my relief, suggests postponing the concert until the 24th. The Russian pianist Lyubov Timofeyeva (dubbed 'La Soviética' by Manolo) is scheduled to perform Prokofiev's Third Piano Concerto that evening, a piece that is notoriously very long. Manolo suggests that he himself should accompany her, that I should conduct the first performance of Leo Brouwer's *Exaedros* during the first half of the concert and that we should both conduct my symphony as the second part of the programme. We shall now have enough rehearsals, the first of which is tomorrow morning at the Teatro Chaplin and is due to last four hours.

11 November

The rehearsal started late. I sat on a wall overlooking the sea and waited for the players to arrive. I could have stayed there much longer, watching the waves as they pounded the pier, instead of which work called. Finally we got under way. We worked for an hour. The brass sound out of tune, as in a southern Italian opera house, while the string tone is thin – but I already knew this from the concert I attended last spring, so I have no reason to be astonished now. Well, my Sixth is harder than Shostakovich. After the first hour we drew up a plan for sectional rehearsals: in the course of the coming days we'll work individually with the woodwind, brass, percussion and so on. The strings, I may add, cannot play in time either. Needless to say, the aleatory passages work best, here there is nothing to rehearse. The piccolo trumpet is played by an ancient and charming mulatto by the name of Quiñones, the alto flute by a young white man, the saxophone by a *chino*. The actual rehearsal is straightforward, since they are all so inquisitive and obliging, and their concentration never falters. During the breaks, most of the players remain in their seats, marking up their parts and practising different fingerings.

12 November

In the evening to one of the studios at Radio Liberación, where five young composers, all of them around twenty years of age, play me tapes of their work. They're studying with a North American musician, Frederick Smith, who came to Cuba in the third year of the Revolution. I almost fell asleep during the last piece, not because of the music, but because it had been a long day. I was afraid they might have noticed, but fortunately they didn't. Afterwards, in the street, I continued to talk at length with these young composers from a new world. The most gifted of them seems to me to be Carlos Malcolm, a fireball with a Black Power haircut and almond-shaped eyes. Must make more effort to give a proper answer to complicated questions. They want to commandeer me for the whole three months of my visit. They say that whenever other composers have come, they have generally been snapped up by the older generation. This time it is their turn. I wonder who the older generation is. Presumably Leo Brouwer and Carlos Fariñas, both of whom are barely thirty.

13 November

The whole of the Teatro Chaplin has been taken over by groups of musicians, all rehearsing their parts. While I myself work with the winds, I can hear various string groups in other rooms. Each one of them has met under its sectional leader. On the top floor Duchezne is working with Orchestra I. During the afternoon I work in an upstairs room, the fourth wall of which is open to the street, First Avenue. Occasionally one hears and sees a group of schoolchildren walking past, the girls performing a kind of dance step. They sing a song about Vietnam. Sometimes they are drowned out by the roar of jet fighters – are they Cuban or American fighter-bombers stationed at Guantánamo?

In the evening we are visited by the poet Heberto Padilla, who is currently in the news. The criticism levelled at his volume of poetry, *Fuera del juego*, by the Writers' Union and, indirectly, at the international jury of the Casa de las Américas that has just awarded him first prize has not been easy for him to accept. In particular, it has been poems such as 'Advice to a Lady' and 'Farewell to the Bishops' (in other words, the very ones that I like best and that I want to set to music) that have caused the greatest offence and been branded counter-revolutionary. I was suddenly reminded of the fact that last week, shortly before we left for Cuba, Carlos Franqui had said to me in Rome: 'What a pity that you're going to Cuba only now that Stalinism is beginning to gain ground.' Padilla has lost his job as a university librarian and doesn't know how he'll survive. His is a classic example of the confusions that can arise when artists and their work are judged by political standards. Padilla's confrontation with his colleagues, some of whom hold positions of political power, is not yet over, and it is said that it will be continued in other branches of art.

15 November
Manolo and Orchestra I play me the first movement. It's already going very well. I'm still slogging away with my violins. It's particularly hot today. We've propped open the door at the back of the stage. It looks out over the sea. There are times when I'd like to jump straight down from my conductor's podium into the cool and refreshing water, but I remain cheerful, while possessing my soul in patience and working on intonation and rhythmic precision. Leo Brouwer wanders through the building with a wild expression in his eyes, followed by clouds of cigar smoke, going from one rehearsal to the next, helping out, offering advice and correcting mistakes. He is losing days of his own work. A young soldier is sitting in my dressing room, talking on the phone to his girlfriend at considerable length. He has placed his sub-machine gun on my score. I hope it leaves a speck of oil.

16 November
String rehearsals finished. Players take their parts home with them. In the afternoon, Leo Brouwer, the kindest and most sensitive of them all. He tells me about himself: he's not yet thirty but has already been married twice. His father is a millionaire and lives in the States. Leo, too, could live there if he wanted to and make a career for himself not only as a composer but also as a guitarist – he was still only twenty when he gave his first concert in New York. Yet he remains here, without convertible currency and without a car, but with lots of work, teaching and writing 'utility music' of every description. We discuss the programme of a concert that Ben Britten has organized for him at Aldeburgh during the summer of 1970. He has several interesting ideas for it: it is intended as an overview of the history of Cuban music and will include a parallel account of political developments in Cuba.

We then return to the rehearsal and work on Leo's *Exaedros*, setting up six orchestral groups, each consisting of six players, apart from the sixth group, which comprises the grand piano, on which I myself have to play and improvise six-part harmonies. Each group will include a keyboard instrument. Leo knows the players very well, so we choose them on the strength of their musical abilities, intelligence and amiability, since the work as a whole will boil down to a communal creative act. The first group will include an electrically amplified harpsichord and a number of percussion instruments all played by Leo himself.

One disadvantage of our apartment in the Habitación Focsa is that there's no telephone, quite apart from the noise from the street, which I'm having difficulty getting used to. In order to call anyone, you have to walk down a five-hundred-metre long corridor, wait up to five minutes for a lift, go down to the ground floor and use the telephone in the entrance hall, where there are generally already several people queuing. Visitors necessarily arrive unannounced and interrupt me at my work. At around ten in the evening we received a visit from Heberto P. and his wife, the writer Belkis Cuza Malé, together with the writer Furé Rogelio Martínez. Since yesterday it has been overcast and stormy, the wind howls incessantly, making the corridors of the *edificio* resonate like organ pipes. The light is a greyish white, the windows caked with sea salt and dust. Feel slightly *afraid*.

18 November

We've worked through the first and second part of the symphony with Orchestra II and played it through without breaking down. It went quite well. Manolo is afraid that we won't be able to do *Exaedros* since too much time is being taken up with the symphony. We have a meeting to discuss this at five o'clock today. The electric organ was repaired and tested during this morning's rehearsal, when the occasional thunderclap was heard to break out from it. Conversely, it's not always easy to hear the few *pianissimo* passages in my score because of the sea pounding amorously against the rear wall of the theatre. Artists from the Leipzig Opera have arrived, accompanied by the head of the Central Committee of the (East) German Socialist Party, with the result that all the drivers from the National Council for Culture are now to be seen wearing collar and tie. Merciful heavens! A Soviet army minister is likewise here on an official visit and spent the whole of yesterday symbolically cutting sugar cane. Even Leo and Manolo are wearing ties, since some people from UNESCO have also arrived.

21 November

Yesterday evening we visited the legendary dancer Alicia Alonso, who returned to Cuba a few years after the *triunfo de la rebelión* in order to build up the National Ballet with her husband Fernando and the latter's brother, Alberto. It can now be numbered as one of the best in the world. Art tags along behind the Revolution, all three of them say, it simply cannot keep pace with it.

Today we called together the groups involved in Leo's *Exaedros* and explained to the players that, like all games, this is a piece where the rules must be followed to the letter, otherwise there will be only chaos and no sense to it all. We then made a start: the feeling that emerged was one of immense enjoyment, a sense of freedom, for the players, too, who grew more and more relaxed as the morning wore on, producing increasingly interesting combinations of sounds. The order in which the groups enter and the ways in which they combine and overlap are all left to the conductor – while I'm conducting, I have to think ahead, imagining new colours in new combinations, yet there is always an element of surprise. We play through several versions. At certain points in the score there are fermatas lasting between fifteen and twenty seconds, during which six, twenty-four or sixty players improvise in a totally random way. These are the passages that the players enjoy most, although some of them thought up 'cadenzas' during the morning and noted them down. There's nothing we can do about this and so we leave things as they are.

22 November

Rehearsal for both orchestras on stage at the Lorca (as the old opera house is now called). It is here that the concert will be held in three days' time. It turns out that two conductors have difficulty agreeing and, above all, are incapable of maintaining the same metre and beat. We are in eye contact, I try to follow Manolo's beat, since he is the more experienced and has a firm, regular beat, whereas I keep allowing the tempo to fluctuate agogically – a polite way of saying that I'm incapable of staying in time. We're constantly adrift, not least because he cannot hear Orchestra II and I cannot hear Orchestra I. The idea of doing the piece with two conductors had occurred to me on the flight here, but the score isn't antiphonal and was in fact conceived, in essence, for only one conductor. Tomorrow we'll try it with only one, which I expect will be me. I'm all on edge and can't get to sleep. Today there's a howling gale again. Stage fright. I wish it were all over!

23 November

This morning I conducted on my own. (I spent the whole night studying the music of Orchestra I.) There were no problems, it all seems more straightforward. The strings of Manolo's group are better rehearsed. (He'd given me the 'better' players, while he'd worked with the younger ones from the rear desks; they've been practising like mad and can now produce the sort of sound that reminds me of some of the leading Western orchestras.)

26 November

The final rehearsal the day before yesterday was far from easy. The loudspeakers kept shutting off. I scarcely slept this afternoon but spent the time studying *Exaedros* and the score of my symphony. Then went downstairs, where a car was waiting with 'La Soviética', who seemed somehow offended. At the theatre I waited in the corridor, since 'La Soviética' and I have to share a dressing room. She finally appears in a wig and evening dress, whereupon Manolo, Leo and I commandeer the room. The whole proceedings are being recorded for television, and the lights add to the heat and discomfort. The concert begins at nine o'clock with Prokofiev's Third Piano Concerto, which seems to go on for hours, after which the frightful Frau Timofeyeva plays several inordinately distended encores by Chopin, so that the programme, already far too long, is now extended by a further twenty minutes. When does the last tram leave? A further fifteen minutes are needed to rearrange the platform for *Exaedros*. During this time the audience is allowed out. We're then ready for Leo's piece. The house is packed to bursting point. *Exaedros* goes like clockwork. Melodies, chords and colours are created that it would be almost impossible to invent or write down. The piece flashes and sparkles, is witty and sad by turns, then fades away, lost for ever, like some passing natural phenomenon or fleeting dream. Another break is needed to rearrange the platform. The *habaneros* in the hall seize the chance to read my programme note:

> Symphony No. 6: two orchestral groups are positioned side by side. Each instrument (or each smaller group of instruments) is related to an instrument (or group of instruments) in the opposing orchestra. The relationship may be based on echo, canon, inversion, variation, substitution or reinforcement. The result is a network of lines that pass to and fro between the instrumental groupings.
>
> The work is divided into three major sections, which are played

> without a break: the first consists of the exposition, with a number of blocks of sound of the most varied nature juxtaposed with one another, colliding with each other in the course of the piece and, in the process, becoming impregnated with the characteristic qualities of the neighbouring blocks, so that they are palpably and continually transformed. In the second section, seven different ideas are presented in succession, each of which is transformed in turn into its opposite or at least into something different: light becomes dark, what had been colourless acquires colour, the tranquil becomes restless, the beautiful fatal. The third section is a sequence of fugal episodes interpolated with brief interludes. Here, too, the material says something different at each new appearance, expressing the opposite of what it had said before or contradicting the other episodes; by being worn down in this way, the material acquires a new identity, an identity that becomes clear and assumes a tangible reality towards the end of the piece.

I take my courage in both hands and throw myself into the fray, placing my trust in Maruja, the orchestra's diminutive leader, in the *chino*, in Leo, who plays the guitar and the banjo, in Bistros, whose violin is fitted with a contact microphone, and in Oreste, the double-bass player – they are all quite brilliant. We do not break down. Things that were still problematical at the final rehearsal pass off without trouble at this evening's performance. This is the first time I've conducted the long second movement, with all its fermatas, tears and sighs, without having to stop for corrections. The whole thing strikes me as very short, though it lasts more than forty minutes. To my amazement, I don't make a single mistake. I'm completely absorbed by the performance and by the unfolding textures of the piece – my difficult, polyphonic tribute to, and expression of solidarity with, the modern Cuba that I love so much. We pull through and reach the thrusting fanfares of the final movement, followed by endless applause, shouting and stamping, and we are all very proud of each other and return home with lots of people, and Fausto makes a wonderful Italo-Cuban *maccheronata*, and there's beer and rum till four in the morning. I then sleep badly and spend the 25th writing letters.

Last Sunday I attended an initiation rite of the Yoruba cult with relatives of one of the music students, Carlos Malcolm. It took place in one of the shanties at the edge of the city. The drums, three in number, were 'warmed up' (as they call it) from early morning onwards. Old men ceaselessly beat out symbolic rhythms, not merely inviting the gods to appear but sending for them in person. A narrow room, filled to bursting with dancers who are pressed so close together that they are unable to move from the spot but can only bob up and down. On the white walls, photographs of Che, Fidel and the national hero, José Martí, look down disapprovingly on this retrogressive demonic celebration. It takes several hours before the hypnotic drumbeat, growing ever louder and more insistent, finally conjures up a god or goddess (all tastes are catered for here): they come flying in and at once take possession of one or other of the mediums' bodies. And the medium screams and howls, rolls on the ground, foaming at the mouth, trying to beat down the walls with his head and escape. It takes several people to hold the man down and clip him round the head. There's a wonderful atmosphere, everyone's happy and in party mood. And now a young man starts to leap round the drums: some divinity or other has entered him, too. Perhaps it is Changó, the god of war, or Babalu Ayé, whose invocatory rhythms will later accompany and protect El Cimarrón on his lonely flight. The possessed youth dances out of control, growing convulsive as he screams and raves. He, too, finally has to be held, calmed down and led away. The same thing happens again and again in the course of the hours that follow. Carlos explains the presence of several extremely tall and effeminate-looking beaux, who, clearly treated as high-ranking individuals and guests of honour, represent an important element in the matriarchal Yoruba cult: all gods are both man and woman in one and the selfsame person. Women come first in the human hierarchy, with homosexual men and women ranked above heterosexuals in the natural order of things.

27 November

Leo says that, as a result of the 1959 Revolution, artists are now confronted for the first time with two fundamental issues: first, there is absolute creative freedom, since in Cuba no one needs to make any artistic compromises as a result of economic problems and doesn't have to make concessions to any rules or formulas or patrons, be they Koussevitzky or Stalin, and, secondly, they have to face up to their audiences, who have to be convinced, won over and inspired.

Visit Moreno Fraginals, a sociologist who is working on a multi-volume history of Cuba. He points out that Barnet's *Cimarrón* should be seen as an account of someone who is no longer part of a whole and who no longer fits into the world of men. Two problems torment El Cimarrón:

first, his permanent sylvan solitude (in which a highly individual sexual fantasy necessarily arises) and, secondly, fear of the deep sense of social disillusionment that awaits him when slavery is abolished and he can return to live among his fellow human beings as a 'free man'.

2 December

The papers are full of reports of the massacre at Sou My Lai. Vietnam is Cuba's closest ally, so that indignation and human sympathy are particularly pronounced here. Whenever I meet Vietnamese residents in the hallway or in the lift, I feel embarrassed at the fact that I so obviously belong to the 'civilized world'. Downstairs in the lobby, there is a little girl in front of me in the queue to use the telephone. She shows me her exercise book, on the cover of which have been printed the words:

> The peoples of Latin America feel no hostility to any other nation. They extend their hands in brotherhood to the inhabitants of the United States and entreat them to resist the repressive policies of imperialistic monopolies.

4 December

Yesterday afternoon, while it was still light, I walked round the old town with Jorge Berróa and saw some of the beautiful old buildings, Spanish colonial style, lots of wood carvings, staircases in inner courtyards, balconies, carriage entrances. The Calle de la Reina is *Jugendstil*. Beneath the arcades in the square in front of the Capitol, I listened to a woman singing popular Spanish songs.

Worked on a viola concerto to be called *Compases para preguntas ensimismadas* (Questions Asked of One's Soul). I admit that every musical situation develops from a previous one, but still don't know how it will end. Here my plans and prefabricated parameters are of no more value than an empty canvas. You have to be prepared for surprises. It has even been known for me to be struck by odd notes in the street, notes that fit into no set but that I used even so or, rather, that I used in spite of that, since they tied in with my idea of *musica impura*. Melody picked up in passing and retained. Sometimes you write something down that sounds familiar simply because you like it, because it moves you or because it describes a particular moment in your life, perhaps in your childhood. It's no longer possible to be more precise, only the notes have remained, the image behind them has gone out of focus. It is borne on the breeze, and so

I retain it. Perhaps this explains the narrative element in my music, the retelling of an old story that refuses to be forgotten.

6 December

Alicia Alonso says that her country is like a crystal. Everything that happens in it is clearly visible from the outside. You can see the heart beating and watch the central nervous system functioning. Sometimes they are overcome by a sense of fear that all this openness might one day leave them vulnerable.

With Leo and the songwriter Sergio Vitier to the ICAIC to hear pieces by Brouwer's students, but it is Saturday, everywhere is closed. We go to Miguel's, since he lives nearby. But his tape recorder is broken, and so there's nothing we can do there either. Someone has the idea of going back to my place. Although I don't have a tape recorder, I do at least have some rum and can even rustle up some soup. (Fausto has gone dancing at the Nacional.) The result is a party that lasts until early the next morning. We are joined around midnight by Sergio's wife, Sareska, who has left their children asleep at home. I am given a long and illuminating lecture on the characteristics of the *son*, with everyone growing increasingly high on the music examples that they sing and play (rum glasses, cutlery and pencils are all pressed into service as percussion instruments). Sergio has just returned from a tour of remote areas of the Sierra Maestra, where he has performed for the *campesinos*, people who had never previously heard music like this and who, according to Sergio, were extraordinarily interested and attracted by it all.

7 December

At seven o'clock this morning by car to Varadero on the coast. The National Council for Culture has placed a room at our disposal – it's my first holiday for years.

It's overcast and damp, making me think that I'm on the Wannsee in Berlin, an impression heightened by the predominant style of architecture, a sort of neo-Romanesque, and by the tall conifers. A sad Sunday: on the radio some glum piece for cello and piano by Shostakovich. I can't stand cello sonatas, this impossible combination of banging and scraping, helplessness and pathos, with the piano's silvery cascades of notes paying not the slightest heed to the desperate actions of the cello as it scrapes away in its tartly tormented fashion. I try to find another station and suddenly have the smug, bass voice of an American newsreader in the room, presumably from Radio Miami. I switch off at once, startled and offended.

Varadero, 10 December

This morning I sketched out the first number of *El Cimarrón*, with the indescribably awestruck feeling that I've taken a step into uncharted territory. The vocalists' part has only a single line in this sketch, indicating its middle register. The notes are added at varying distances above and below this line, and it is left to the singer to determine their pitch: for this, the singer will make only limited concessions to the conventions of functional harmony. (When shall we reach the point where the conventions of aleatory music will have to be avoided here? Has that time already come?) Be that as it may, this first piece, which bears the unassuming title 'The World', treats the vocalist as co-author, a fellow artist who creatively and inventively chooses the notes to go with his words. The rhythms are equally free. At least as far as the vocal part is concerned, they will emerge naturally and meaningfully from the manner in which the text is recited.

Enzensberger translated fifteen passages from Miguel's novel for me last summer, arranging them as a kind of (song) cycle for music, in prose. I brought this with me, of course, and it has provided the basis for all the experiments and voyages of discovery that I have been engaged in for some time – certainly not just since this morning. We plan to rehearse *El Cimarrón* in Marino during the summer and then give the first performance immediately afterwards at Aldeburgh. It's Ben Britten to whom we owe the opportunity to give this first performance: about a year ago, shortly after the *Medusa* scandal, he told me in London that he and his festival would welcome me with open arms at any time, if ever I had problems launching a new piece. When the idea of writing *El Cimarrón* began to take shape, I told him all about it and by return of post received an invitation to perform the piece for him and to do so, moreover, extremely soon: on 22 June 1970.

It's intended as a piece of instrumental theatre – but what will it look like in detail? I'll have to find out gradually. What I have in mind is an easily transportable street theatre, a kind of agitprop, but only indirectly related to the issues of the day. At the end of January 1969, at the rehearsals for a concert in Chicago (with the Chicago Symphony Orchestra) I saw and heard the percussionist Stomu Yamash'ta, who showed me a number of old Japanese percussion instruments, telling me all about them and demonstrating the sort of sounds they produce. I'd never heard anything like it before. Perhaps it was this encounter that first gave me the idea for a new kind of theatre piece. Yes, maybe that's how it was. For *El Cimarrón*, I'd need not only a singer and a percussionist but also two instrumentalists, one of whom would be a flautist who needed to be prepared to play a whole series of secondary instruments, principally, of course, several other flutes and pipes (also folk instruments). I had already got Karlheinz Zöller lined up for this. Zöller was the principal flautist with the Berlin Philharmonic and was known for his great love of music and experimentation. I had also brought Bruno Bartolozzi's *New Sounds for Woodwind* with me and consulted it from time to time. I experimented with triple and quadruple harmonics and whistling noises, which I hoped would sound like the final death rattle of a wind band. And in order to have a string instrument, something reliable and well suited to bringing out the harmonies, I also included a guitar, so that Leo Brouwer's contribution became an important element in the creative process. Instead of lying around on the beach for a week, as we had planned, Fausto and I returned to town after only two days, so that I could show Leo what I had come up with so far. Excited, enthusiastic, and not unhappy.

The expectant and ambitious illusion that one can invent a second reality for oneself by working for the theatre and achieve a sense of security in a state of utter helplessness . . . Work for the theatre strikes me as a pretext, a reason for realizing such pipe dreams. We're not far here from the child playing with puppets – later it was ballet that promised elation and ecstasy, then opera, where the music audibly issues from the performers' bodies. We rebuke our dreams, but they return, like old desires. When, and in what circumstances, will we be able to live in harmony with the world? What sort of compromises would it demand or make unnecessary, what restrictions or freedoms? And how temporary will it have to be to enable us to bear the inescapable knowledge that it involves an act of sacrifice, an act of submission, whatever form that act may take? How final can something be when freedom becomes a reality and, hence, when reality no longer has to be a thing of dreams and a means by which we may escape?

Havana, 14 December

Completed second number of *El Cimarrón* yesterday. Esteban recounts his childhood. Flute and guitar have been silent until now. Only when there is mention of the Spanish plantation owners who spend all day at table eating, while the *negritos* have to stand there shooing away the flies, do these two instruments enter. The result is a kind of habanera, something disgusting and sticky like fly-papers, something sentimental and unpleasant.

In the evening to the theatre for a new version of the Orpheus legend by the Conjunto Folklórico Nacional, *Orfeo antillano*, choreographed by Ramiro Guerra and with music adapted from carnival congas and a Yoruba rite by Leo Brouwer and Pierre Henry. This particular Orpheus lives on the dividing line between two different periods, the abruptly changing circumstances necessitating quick decisions. Bound to his primitive origins and to the religious roots of his former life as a slave, he is caught up in a disruptive adventure that turns him into life's anti-hero and destroys him. The myth ends with a glimmer of hope as another Orpheus takes up the drum (not, in this case, a lyre) and, with an open smile and new, firm dance steps, ushers in the carnival. There are parallels with Marcuse's view of Orpheus, with Orpheus's death as a symbol of the death of art.

This morning I went with Miguel Barnet to see Mendive, a local artist and member of the Yoruba cult, who lost his foot two years ago in a tramway accident. His house is full of relatives, as well as chickens, parrots, dogs, a monkey and, in the backyard, the obligatory brightly coloured Yoruba peacock. Some of his paintings are on wood, others are done in tempera. They lie somewhere between those of the Douanier Rousseau and those of Werner Gilles, not that he knows either man's work. But there is nothing amateurish about the *naïveté* of his style. Their symbolism is unencoded, their colours strong and expressive, not to say loud. Gods and humans appear together in all his pictures. One can see his parents with Changó (the god of virility and master of fire and drums and, hence, of music, too) sitting at a table, spooning up *polenta*. Mendive himself can be seen in a large triptych, leaning on a crutch, at the end of a line of kinsmen, friends and gods. The central panel, entitled 'Men and Women', shows its subjects running around, stretching, sleeping and screwing and murdering one another. At the bottom, the same size as the strip at the top, is a depiction of Mendive's accident: Oyá, Changó's companion and the goddess of death, graveyards, burials, lightning and bats, is seen pushing our host out of the moving tram. Another picture shows Babalu Ayé, the goddess of diseases who tends the sick and injured, preventing red-necked vultures from tearing at the bleeding wounds of leprosy victims. At the bottom of the picture is a row of cripples, the dominating colour a disgustingly cloying bluish white. Oyá and the national hero José Martí are seen picking flowers for Che in Paradise. He is already covered in them, and all three seem to be asleep or to be dreaming. At all events, their eyes are closed. A large panel shows fourteen different ways of making love, the various partners including a butterfly, elephant, snake and vulture, while another painting depicts the god of hunting, Ochósi, a wild sorcerer, flying through the air, with mortals riding above and below him, wielding machetes and flaunting enormous erections. They are watched by Changó, who is now shown wearing a crown on his head, while Mendive's aunt bathes the wound on his stump. Suns have eyes and sometimes rise beneath the fields, humans can shin straight up house walls in a horizontal plane, dogs walk on their heads, and a peacock swims towards Ochún, the goddess of love and rivers, leaving behind it a spumy-white crest on the waves.

21 December

Just returned from working on the land. We spent a week at Ceiba del Agua in the province of Havana, where there are huge fields reclaimed from the jungle and now used, in the main, to cultivate citrus fruit and coffee, kilometre upon kilometre of plantations, most of which have been laid out and maintained by orchestral musicians, actors, ballet dancers and members of the Academy of Sciences, the National Library and ICAIC: *el trabajo productivo*. We planted the whole of one freshly cleared field with young citrus bushes and fumigated the underground colonies of the *bibiyagua*, a termite-like insect that can strip the leaves off the plants in the course of a single night. It was hard work under a hot sun from six till twelve and again from two till six. But good fun. We lived in windowless thatched huts. At night it was bitterly cold. There are English irrigation plants and Soviet and Italian tractors. We were covered in red sand dust when we got back to the city late last night.

One of Miguel Barnet's friends, Rogelio Rodríguez, has been telling me about himself and his life: as a young lad he was one of a group of *negritos* who would dive into the harbour in search of coins thrown into the water by tourists. Later he earned his living from drugs and prostitution. An illegitimate child, he had white brothers and sisters. He keeps coming back to this point, it seems as though he was treated as a second-class citizen even by the family that adopted him. In 1959 he joined the army only days after the white-led *triunfo de la rebelión*; he was present at the Battle of the Bay of Pigs and later spent years in Escambray fighting the counter-revolutionaries. He sounds almost to be singing when he speaks, his language is as florid and colourful as Mendive's paintings. He has scars from knife wounds and operations. Once he saved the life of a badly wounded enemy soldier by means of a direct blood transfusion from arm to arm. Everything he says makes it sound as though he has had a difficult life, but, as Esteban Montejo – El Cimarrón – says, it is not sad, because it is nothing more nor less than the truth.

Yesterday evening I had a meeting with the composers' collective, a branch of UNEAC (Unión de los Escritores y Artistas Cubanos), of which all the country's composers are members. I had the impression that some of the older musicians would like to see the avant-garde as an expression of Western capitalist decadence and that they want me to agree with them and to say something to this effect. I sidestepped the issue and tried to say something along the lines that we know that artists are concerned with longing, and it is this longing, this burning desire that sometimes raises their work to the level of art. Whenever this sense of longing falters, the beauty of the resultant works is compromised. Depending on the artist and upon his ambience and natural bent, this longing has been called Jesus, redemption, fraternity, escape, death, revolution and Paradise. It continues to seek and find new names, but ultimately it amounts to only one thing: freedom and fresh air and the end of inadequacy, slavery and oppression. It is freedom from existential fear, from the achievement principle, from superstition and from all the loneliness and despair bound up with all these things.

23 December

Lots of visitors: not only friends who were with us at the *campo* but also Leo, who shows me new performance techniques on the guitar and new ways of producing different sounds on it, some of which will undoubtedly find their way into *El Cimarrón*. He plays through everything I've written so far for his instrument, trying to make the impossible possible, so that I won't have to make too many changes. He knows some wonderful *ponticello* and legato effects and an amazing variety of uses for vibrato. I've sketched out the fourth number, 'Flight'. It contains the first theatrical elements: the pig of an overseer has his face smashed in (I hate him because I recognize in him the German corporals and tormentors from my youth and take my revenge accordingly) and involves the singer and protagonist dropping a heavy iron chain on to a metal plate. The Calabran *scacciapensieri* – a jew's harp played by the flautist – makes a whimpering sound that describes, of course, the pain felt by the overseer as he sees stars. Esteban says with immense satisfaction: 'He's got what he deserved.' He then runs off, followed by the shouting and whistling of his pursuers. Their music notated only in the form of graphic symbols, the percussionist and guitarist, who likewise now turns his hand to the percussion department, accompany El Cimarrón on his flight into freedom, his *cimarronería.*

26 December

The streets are empty, many of the *habaneros* have left the city to bring in the sugar harvest. In order not to feel like wastrels, Fausto and I are spending half of each day working in a canned-food factory, so that *El Cimarrón* is now relegated to the afternoons and evenings. There is only a limited bus service – eighty per cent of the drivers are working on the plantations. But no fewer than three new plays are scheduled to open on 2 January, and the members of an experimental theatre group have just arrived from Mexico. The chansonnier and pianist Bola de Nieve gives a concert in the packed Lorca Theatre. It is hot during the daytime. There is a whiff of war in the air. On the front page of all the papers is a strongly worded warning from the army about saboteurs and counter-revolutionaries. Another group of them landed a few days ago (with United States Army equipment), but they were rounded up and shot. Spent yesterday evening with Saul Gelin (ICAIC), who has a collection of Cuban art nouveau and Bauhaus furniture and some good modern Cuban paintings on his walls, including two Portocarreros. Rogelio has gone off to the plantations with the rest of his department. In my thoughts I make him the protagonist of the fifth movement of *El Cimarrón*, 'The Forest', where we learn that Esteban found happiness here for the first time in his life, discovering a sense of calm, remote from other people, in a world filled with new experiences amongst plants and mysterious trees and noises.

A letter from Enzensberger:

> NEWS FROM BERLIN: party squabbles music-induced highs bombings causes of sadness east berlin idylls millilitre culs-de-sac hashish-induced images video stories
> AN ENTIRELY ORDINARY MAELSTROM
> and on the department-store escalators people fight for their gifts for the festive day
> LIES HAVE BECOME SO CONFUSED WITH THE TRUTH THAT WE NO LONGER KNOW WHETHER WE'RE DEVOURING THE ONE OR THE OTHER

In my viola concerto, *Compases*, the texture of voices and lines is growing increasingly dense. I'll have to find a solution during the next few days or else call a halt or change it. A unit of soldiers is living in the penthouse of our *habitación*. In the flat next to us is a student from Las Villas who sits by the open window practising his accordion. A Vietnamese woman gives the porters Christmas presents even though both Christmas and the New Year have been cancelled this year; people don't even say 'felicidades', it's all been postponed until July, by which time the ten million tonnes will have been harvested. A honey-coloured full moon rises over the Hotel Nacional even though it is broad daylight, loudspeaker vans drive past blaring out newly written rumbas with words about the sugar harvest. A few days ago the National Council for Culture gave a cocktail party for me in a magnificent state-owned villa. (It reminded me somewhat of Rome and of Arroyo's painting, *The Last Days of Pompeii*, which shows General Franco, Queen Fabiola and others, painted like whores, wandering among the palaces as they wait to be engulfed by the streams of lava.) The feeling of a Roman party was in fact mitigated by the presence of heavily armed soldiers at the gate and in the grounds – as though to remind us that the Revolution is not yet over but that it is constantly under threat. Royal palms, statues, sub-machine guns, Sèvres porcelain, servants dressed in white serving Scotch on the rocks to erstwhile *campesinos*, ballerinas, secret police, members of the avant-garde. The only people who are noticeably uneasy about the unusual interior décor are the few who can still remember the people who lived here *antes* (when it would never have entered their heads to set foot in such a house): namely, the sugar millionaires who bought their aristocratic titles. General Franco, King Baudouin, President Salazar and their kind all stayed here. The Philharmonic Orchestra used to play at garden parties, and it is said that the marquesa was a generous woman, although it is not quite clear whether this is meant as praise or censure. Leo is wearing a tie. Even here in the grounds of the villa there are arguments over modernism. I'm getting used to rum. There's nothing that Alberto Alonso would like more than to talk to me all day about his plans for a ballet. He has the idea of writing a sequence about, for example, repression, insurrection, change, friction, conflict, despair, construction and triumph. It could contain realistic elements and work with a background of concrete sounds, he says, but also with filmed episodes, short titles, moods that overlap, synchronicity and clearly visible and audible (that is to say, glaring) contradictions.

28 December

A *comparsa* is playing in the street beneath our windows, lots of percussion and trumpets, strident and cheerful. More and more people arrive and soon there are over a hundred. We can see straw hats, brightly coloured clothes, people with suitcases and bags on their shoulders. The traffic comes to a standstill, the street fills up and people start to dance. Those not dancing play percussion. After an hour, the music suddenly stops, *camiones* arrive, the people clamber aboard, and off they all go to the sugar harvest – the *zafra*.

30 December

Spent the morning loading crates at the factory and in the afternoon worked on the fair copy of 'Flight'. In the evening we had visitors: Sareska Vitier, Heberto Padilla and his wife Belkis and Alberto Mora, who is still very young and who used to be a friend of El Che. He was, and possibly still is, Minister of Industry. Also present were Miguel, the folksinger Martínez Furé and a beautiful mulatto by the name of Nancy Morejon. She is a colleague of Fariñas and writes magical poems. It looked as though another literary party – a *tertulia de criollos* – was about to break out, when we were all taken off to the National Theatre, where a large audience had foregathered and where a three-hour discussion developed: can music express anything? Is there music that expresses nothing? Even music that sets out to express nothing cannot help doing so – or is that not true? Some of the speakers drew attention to Webern's poetics and to comments by the late Stravinsky. It was said that music can be seen as a receptacle for human states of mind and that empirical research not only *could* but *should* be undertaken into the meaning, substance and origins of such emotions.

31 December

Detailed working out of 'Flight' and part of 'The Forest' as far as the pseudo-*son*, which I've revised once again and rendered more unfamiliar, without, I hope, making it totally unrecognizable. I've explored the guitar's highest register, while in the case of the bass flute I've written the part very low. Between them is heard a marimba that has to be struck with soft sticks. The bass flute makes its first appearance in 'The Forest', after El Cimarrón has made good his escape. For the flight improvisations I have notated a passage for piccolo as a fixed point for the others, a sort of latter-day cantus firmus. We also hear the panting and terrified screams of the running Cimarrón, screams that later turn into shouts of joy. His arrival in the forest and the growing sense of calm are also part of this improvised section.

1 January 1970
We celebrate the New Year with Alberto Mora in Miramar: *guerrilleros*, people from the theatre, writers. Open windows giving on to the garden, where crickets chirrup and mosquitoes come buzzing into the room. Huge library. No one feels the need to create the sort of fuss normally associated with New Year's Eve, but at the stroke of midnight we embrace and there is a genuine feeling of friendship, after which the conversation continues, as affable and earnest as before.

3 January
In the bus this morning, on our way to work, I observed the faces of the *habaneros*. Beautiful, serious, betraying a very real sensitivity. An old female mulatto, all wrinkled. A nurse, standing at the bus stop, smoking a cigar and going on and on at a child. I long to be part of this people: all that is sad and different seems to be far more normal and more bearable here than it is elsewhere. One feels affection, as though there were invisible threads between people. Perhaps it is due to the constant threat from outside, so that people stick together better in their desire to survive the conflicts and deprivations.

Miguel is sorry that Enzensberger has omitted the story of the dead slaves from his version of *El Cimarrón*: these slaves were spirited away from Cuba by Congolese magicians riding on broomsticks and in five seconds flat taken to the Azores, where they find peace – although not really Africa, they already feel much closer there to their homeland and, as such, far, far away from Cuba. The next morning they continue their journey home, to the West African coast, where they remain for ever more.

5 January
Jorge B. has returned from working in the fields and so we make a start on the Spanish version of *El Cimarrón*. Enzenberger's poetic version has to be translated into Spanish, taking Barnet's original as our starting point, although we'll be able to use only odd words from it. This afternoon, Rogelio returns unexpectedly from the *zafra*. He has a high temperature: he cut his hand on a thorn of the sacred but poisonous ceiba – a tree originally from Africa. He was in Flor de Sagua (where Esteban Montejo grew up as a slave) and brings me a book, poems by Nicolás Guillén.

6 January
Fidel is tearing round the country, visiting the *campos* from morning till

evening and talking to the people there. Miguel's friends, Caita and Sergio Vitier, met him last week on a vegetable plantation and chatted with him. It is cold, with a howling wind. You can hear the breakers beating against the Malecón.

Poor-quality rum is dispiriting. The popular poet and composer, Rogelio Martínez Furé, drops in and embraces his namesake as though they were brothers. He's a wonderful singer and a fabulous musician. He says that there are hundreds of African songs here. He adapts the melodic material to suit his own particular ends, producing a delicate musculature of forms and falling into foreign scales, with rhythms that have a narcotic effect and that are impossible to write down. Cuba opens up here like some nocturnal flower. Martínez beats out unheard-of rhythms with his hands, bending and turning the whole of his body, hiding his face, leaping up and taking odd dance steps. At the same time, a young writer in the adjoining room is reading Nietzsche to his wife in a loud Spanish voice.

9 January
The black tom-cat that follows our corpulent comrade, Jorge Berróa, everywhere, while remaining invisible to the majority of people, paraded through the room this lunchtime under my very eyes. Fausto was also there to see it look at us briefly and condescendingly, before disappearing again only a few seconds later. *Un sortilegio, una brujería criolla.*

10 January
All fears and worries vanish when you go out again after being cooped up for two days with only your books and music and find yourself in a crowd of people, all of whom are happy and noisy and high-spirited and likeable and intelligent in their cosmopolitan way. You feel safe with them, as though you're in good hands; all petty niggles and sense of isolation are suddenly forgotten.

11 January
Miguel B. tells me about a reception for members of the Pen Club at Abidjan on the Ivory Coast in 1967, when blacks wearing Louis XVI wigs greeted the guests' arrival with fanfares, and long tables laden with choice dishes were roped off from the crowd that stood behind it, begging: 'Monsieur, s'il vous plaît.' Miguel and Pierre Gorin borrowed a knife from one of the policemen on guard and cut the ropes. It caused an enormous scandal, both poets were declared *personae non gratae* and had to leave the country.

12 January
Fidel interrupts a television programme to express his concern at the delays to the *zafra* caused by the heavy rainfall.

I've caught flu. The devastating effects of poor-quality rum: an immediate headache and, with it, hypersensitivity to the dark, an oppressive blackness that you can suddenly see effortlessly entering the room through every crack. Miguel casts a spell, muttering enchantments to stop my fits of depression, which assail me every evening. It's only in the dark that I feel depressed – during the daytime there's no problem.

Rogelio reads me poems by Guillén, including, for example, 'Pequeña oda a un negro boxeador cubano', which begins:

> Tus guantes
> puestos en la punta de tu cuerpo de ardilla,
> y el punch de tu sonrisa.
> El Norte es fiero y rudo, boxeador.
> Ese mismo Broadway,
> [. . .]
> que unta de asombro su boca de melón
> ante tus puños explosivos
> y tus actuales zapatos de charol;
> ese mismo Broadway,
> es el que estira su hocico con una enorme lengua húmeda
> para lamer glotonamente
> toda la sangre de nuestro cañaveral
> [. . .]

Or 'Mi chiquita':

> La chiquita que yo tengo
> tan negra come é,
> no la cambio po ninguna,
> po ninguna otra mujé
> [. . .]

14 January
Plans for the second part of *El Cimarrón*: more songlike and 'entertaining', more like an illustrated broadsheet. In the first part we're dealing with remote prehistory, in the second with more recent history, with examples of what it was like at the time when the country was underdeveloped: injustice, bad habits, priests, superstition, the lack of any real prospects. But there will also be mention of disquiet, women, rebellion and the idea of struggle.

Fausto and I go to UNEAC, where the abstract painter, Salvador Corratgé, is holding an exhibition to mark the centenary of Lenin's birth, *Fragmentos de una sinfonía*. An article in the catalogue claims that the road from the image to music, as taken, for example, by Mussorgsky and Stravinsky, has here been reversed: Corratgé proceeds from music to the image. Some of his drawings do indeed look like music that could actually be played, just as music sometimes reminds one of paintings. A tape recording of my Sixth Symphony is being played continuously in the exhibition hall. I wonder why the artist has brought out only these lines and dots and not all the things that were undoubtedly more important to me: clenched fists, screams, love, distant landscapes, dancing, a shipwreck and victory.

16 January
In an essay on Barnet's *novela testimonio*, I read: 'Tradition is made up of all man's spiritual and intellectual possessions. A nation without traditions is like a tree without leaves. A nation without memories is a worthless nation.' That's a bit like Auden's 'People who aren't interested in their history don't believe in their future.'

17 January
Tomorrow the second of the ten million tonnes of sugar was due to have been harvested, but it will be difficult, since it's pouring down again. The official party newspaper, *Granma*, reports that 1,885,582 tonnes had been brought in between the start of production and seven o'clock yesterday evening. Other news: the war in Biafra is over, Gowon has invited U Thant to visit the country. Tonnes of food are being shipped to the famine-stricken areas. Joseph Yablonsky, head of the United States miners' unions, has been murdered. A sensational interview in Santiago in Chile: thirty questions to a Tupamaro. Every day there are reports of clashes between freedom fighters and the forces of repression in the whole of Latin America. There are fatalities every day. Wave of arrests in Venezuela. More than one hundred 'subversive elements' have been arrested there. More student unrest in Mexico. In Guatemala the chief of police has been shot in the street. In Tucumán, Argentina, several people were seriously injured when the police cleared workers from the Escalada textile factory. In Santo Domingo, guerrilla activity has led the authorities to proclaim a state of emergency in the province of Barahona. In La Paz, students have occupied the radio station and are reading out revolutionary texts over the

airwaves. In Rio, two more people were killed yesterday by a Fascist 'death squad'.

18 January
Humid, streets in darkness, state of siege. Sometimes, during daylight hours, you can see United States warships on the horizon, as tiny as toys, far out at sea.

Have almost finished 'Friendliness' in Part Two, was able to work undisturbed all day. Each time my concentration falters or I feel unwell, I immediately leave my study, look out of the window and peel an orange. I've tried to reduce the music to very simple formulas and intervals in order to achieve something restful and definitive-sounding, something that reflects my present state of inner calm.

19 January
This morning I sketched the end of *El Cimarrón*. It's called 'The Knife'. The music returns to its archaic beginnings. The guitar is played with a bow, as at the start, and changes positions, playing tremolos and glissandos. 'The Clergy', 'Friendliness' and 'The Knife' are all calm as numbers, so that it's now time for some livelier tempos, and I also need to introduce some new ideas. So far I've avoided all manner of 'thematic writing': nothing is repeated, nothing developed, and there are not really even any allusions to older forms (except to dance music). No isorhythm, no kind of serialism. Instead, there's occasionally the suggestion of new and idiosyncratic links entering the musical texture, as though borne along on the wind.

First sketch for the *son*, 'Women'.

This afternoon we had a *tertulia de criollos* lasting several hours. Jorge Berróa has finished the Spanish version of the first part of *El Cimarrón*. Leo calls round in the evening and we go through those parts of the second half that are already completed. A long sequence of double octaves in 'The Knife' sounds strange and unprecedented, bringing a whole new colour to the guitar part right at the very end. In 'Friendliness', the melody is in the guitar's soprano register. The result is a bitter-sweet mood, rather like a mixture of Cuba and the Castelli Romani.

Leo says that the *son* is a way of seeing the world, a form of life, a perfume, a temperature, something climatic, physical and, for that very reason, also something mental. Leo says that the *son* is very close to the music of Webern. Perhaps that's a very slight exaggeration.

22 January
Unfortunately it turns out that, in order to be in Rome in time for the European première of my Sixth on 7 February, we have to leave here on the 29th of this month, in other words, next Thursday. That means that *El Cimarrón* can only be sketched here and that the instrumentation of Part Two will have to wait until Marino. Also, several unavoidable *tertulias* will now have to be arranged without any further delay.

26 January
Alberto Alonso has had yet another new idea for a dance piece: the stage is a box lined with grey paper. Inside it are people swathed in white, their various costumes recalling classical fools. Faces painted white. A series of delineations of 'rien ne va plus' and of attempts to break free, between them an ever-increasing number of policemen, enemies and spies, all acting out a 'journey to Jerusalem', a game that ends in a furious power struggle in the course of which arms, legs and heads fly through the air. But the fools (in other words, those who are pure at heart, the believers and the non-pragmatists) have still not abandoned their roles and continue to make every attempt to play their old lyrical games; but it's no good – we get bogged down, can make no progress, as in a bad dream. At the height of their despair, the fools destroy the box in which they appear to be trapped, making holes in the walls and tearing their fools' apparel to shreds.

Finished the vocal part of *El Cimarrón*, but the instrumental part still contains only verbal instructions. Berróa and his black cat bring us the Spanish version of the *son*, *Las mujeres*.

27 January
Miguel has written a long poem on my Sixth. It starts:

> El Teatro se desploma en un alud
> de astillas invisibles. Una a una las columnas van perdiendo
> su vieja dignidad. El Teatro es ya un buque anclado en sombras
> que se dispone a alcanzar su enorme transparencia.
> Un arco de fuego se desliza en medio del escenario
> come en un delicado lienzo japonés.
> Los gorriones revolotean en sus nidos de polvo
> y los ángeles del techo belle époque escapan horrorizados
> al contrapunto y la flautas [. . .]

Which might be translated more or less as follows:

The theatre collapses in a cloud
Of invisible shards. One by one, the columns lose
Their ancient dignity. Already the theatre's a vessel that is anchored in the shade
And that slowly assumes its tremendous transparency.
A rainbow of fire glides centre-stage
As if on a delicate Japanese canvas.
The sparrows flutter in their nests of dust,
And the angels on the *belle époque* ceiling flee in horror
From the counterpoint and flutes [. . .]

Miguel also gave me a genuine, personally signed photograph of Amalia Vorg, La Cubana, the Rachel of the 1920s. All day long we had visitors coming to say goodbye. Some of Fausto's delightful friends whom he has got to know while helping out at the factory. The minister Alberto Mora throws a farewell party. A UNEAC meeting has been hurriedly convened for tomorrow. Visited Heberto Padilla and wandered around the town for a while with him; it was overcast, with a heaviness in the air only occasionally broken by gusts of cooling wind. Observe the people. Sometimes I'd like to do nothing more than ask one or other of them why it is that he is so beautiful. Yes, I'm sure he could tell a tale or two about centuries of Paradise, about slavery and mob rule, about *cimarronería*, the literacy campaign of the 1960s and of growing consciousness.

A woman wearing perfect make-up and a two-piece suit walks down the Rampa, a carbine on her shoulders, on her way to do guard duty. *Macheteros*, students with books, Carlos Marx. Ancient blacks outside their front doors, sitting in rocking chairs and silently enjoying what remains of their decolonization. A queue outside a cinema that is showing Glauber Rocha's *Antonio das mortes*, the uncut version. Children – the great hope of the Revolution – march across the street in groups. Lorries rumble by.

The aeroplane from Cubana Aviación shudders as it flies over La Villas in the direction of Martinique. We're two days on (*chaleco salvavidas debajo del asiento*). Pretty stewardesses carry the emigrants' sickbags to the toilet, but their usual smile is noticeably absent. All our friends had gathered at the airport, only Rogelio was missing, since he was cutting sugar cane in the remote region of Las Villas. It was very hot. No time left to buy any rum. At the airport, Sareska kept repeating 'No dejar de volver' and cried a little into her crumpled handkerchief.

Yesterday's UNEAC meeting was nothing special but intended only to say goodbye to me. We sat in the garden, the Corratgé exhibition was still going on inside, and the Sixth still being played on its permanent loop. Outside we couldn't hear it, instead there was the sound of the crickets and the scent of the trees. In the afternoon another rehearsal of Alonso's ballet *El güije* (The Water Goblin) at the Lorca, with a *musique concrète* score by Juan Blanco. As so often (or always?) with electronic or concrete music, the choreography looks a bit lost, clutching desperately at recognizable, identifiable elements in the waves of sound. But it's not just that: it's the physical absence of players in the pit, the lack of concentrated physical interaction between stage and orchestra, an absence that strikes one all the more painfully when the sound is mechanically reproduced. With stagings involving electronic music, whether of ballet or other works, the gestural element always seems unfocused, creating a mood that owes everything to the lack of clarity, a sort of groundless shudder. It is a kind of theatre that pretends it is on intimate terms with transcendental matters, a theatre that can do everything and that has a suitable formula ready for every human state. Nothing seems absolutely necessary, with the result that it is slick and predictable. The *corps de ballet*, consisting largely of members of the Cubanacán School, is perfectly drilled and, in that respect, most clearly comparable, perhaps, to the Copenhagen Ballet. I spot one elegant youth in the group, Muñiz, a young Communist, who was my boss in the country – it was under his command that I worked in the citrus plantations.

Leo has recorded a tape of Elizabethan music for Magnus, the other side is taken up by Miguel singing Cuban songs from the Roaring Twenties. This morning we passed through Revolution Square on our way to the airport, driving through rundown suburbs and slums.

A neon sign was flashing on and off: 'The armed struggle is the road to freedom.'

10

As long as vanity
Still desecrates your eye,
Your time is not yet nigh.

As long as you still stand
On public platforms and
Are seen, no joy's at hand.

For only he who'd free
Himself from pride and be
Brought low his God shall see.

Franz Werfel, 'Amore', from *Wir sind* (1914)

And so we were back in Europe. In our enthusiasm we had almost forgotten what capitalism was like, but everything was just as we had left it: the large numbers of flashy cars, the full shop windows, the empty trousers and full pockets, joylessness everywhere, and cold and fog. For days we told no one that we were back. I saw only Bruno Maderna, whom I collected from his hotel and accompanied to the first rehearsal of my Sixth. He had no queries about the piece, and there was not a single question mark in his conducting score. On our way to the Foro Italico, where the RAI Orchestra was based until its disbandment in 1994, he fell asleep in the taxi. I was growing a little concerned about my symphony's future well-being but fortunately soon had to admit that my fears were unfounded: the conductor knew the piece. He praised it, or at least was kind enough to pretend that he was praising me for spending the whole of my time running around in the orchestra – which I did only because I had just learnt how difficult the piece is and that there is never enough time to get to know it properly. I also marked up the parts, something which, Bruno told me, made his job somewhat easier.

Hidden away from the world in Marino, I finished not only Part Two of

El Cimarrón but also *Compases*, after which I conducted a couple of concerts and then began to prepare for the summer and for the arrival of my *cimarronistas*. On 31 May 1970 I conducted Leo Brouwer's *Sonograma II* at the Komische Oper in Berlin. Brouwer himself had flown into Schönefeld the day before, bringing with him his guitar, some letters for me and six bottles of genuine Cuban rum. There were flowers and curtain calls aplenty for him, and after a delightful evening with Dessau and Matthus, the two of us drove over to the West. Leo loved it – it was all so glitzy and relaxed and colourful, with a surfeit of everything. Only the large number of cars initially caused him a certain apprehension and claustrophobia. The next day we flew to Rome and, thence, to Marino, where Stomu Yamash'ta and Karlheinz Zöller had already arrived and where an elaborate array of percussion instruments had been set up in the large music room. Most of the instruments had been hired, but Stomu had brought some of the others with him. The twelve chromatically tuned tom-toms that are needed in the piece and that I had had specially made in Germany were brought one night by sleeper by one of our obliging supporters, Renate Praetorius, who had been working for me for a time as my secretary in Munich.

The weeks that followed were a time of sheer enjoyment, full of new discoveries. There was so much for us all to learn. The four members of the team, William Pearson, Karlheinz Zöller, Leo Brouwer and Stomu Yamash'ta, turned out to be an ideal combination, and the left-wing intellectual's luxury villa proved for the first time to be a suitable place for rehearsing such a piece in cloistral seclusion. Although they hailed from four different parts of the world and came from differing cultural backgrounds, these four musicians none the less had one thing in common: they understood a great deal about music and loved their work. The rehearsals invariably lasted all day, since Zöller, a strict and self-critical taskmaster, insisted that they should and refused to let up until everything was exactly as it ought to be. I spent the whole day with them. In this way, we worked together on the style of the performance, discovering or inventing formulas and means of expression for what, for each and every one of us, was a novel way of playing and performing. Stomu was one of the wittiest kids I have ever known, fairly Americanized and, as a result, free from the usual Japanese reserve, a state of affairs that made his remarks so genuinely funny. A brilliant imp. In spite of all possible cultural and philosophical reserves, Leo tried to emulate him, no doubt because he was also a little jealous that he could achieve relatively little with his understated guitar, at least when compared to this Far Eastern showman, who would leap around like a cat – or, rather, like a Bengal tiger – through his jungle of idiophones, timpani, drums and gongs and thunder-sheets.

All four of them stayed at the house and were worshipped by the domestic staff. There was nothing to do but work on *El Cimarrón* and polish it until it shone like a jewel in all its Creole colours. I was more than pleased and satisfied with the result, and we were all a little sad when the rehearsals came to an end and we had to set off on our journey northwards.

At the instigation of my old friend from Berlin, the eccentric Peter Adam, who was now making films for the BBC, the Cuban ambassador in London, Alba Griñan, organized a private concert at her ambassador's flat in Knightsbridge at which the star turn was undoubtedly Leo and Stomu, who served notice of their sensational, not to say subversive, gifts on their respective solo instruments, regaling an invited audience that also included some left-wing English artists – even then an endangered species. We had agreed with Ben Britten that the first performance of *El Cimarrón* would be accompanied by a kind of showcase of new Cuban music. The Manson Ensemble, a group of young soloists from the Royal Academy under Paul Patterson, were invited to present the programme, the first part of which was devoted to two established composers from the eighteenth and nineteenth centuries, Esteban Salas y Castro and Manuel Saumell, followed by two important members of the older generation, José Ardévol and Amadeo Roldán. Following the interval there were three works by modern Cuban composers, Carlos Fariñas, Héctor Angulo and Leo Brouwer. There was also a showing of the film *Memories of Underdevelopment* mentioned in an earlier chapter and a lecture entitled 'Cuba Today' by the distinguished literary critic and Latinist, J. M. Cohen.

El Cimarrón left a powerful impression on its Aldeburgh audience. With the sympathetic assistance of the director Colin Graham, we were able to finish rehearsing the piece in the Maltings at Snape under first-class conditions in terms of both sound and lighting. After the performance, Britten came backstage, congratulated my soloists most warmly and patted me on the shoulder, lightly and without condescension. Even then he was already showing signs of the illness that was to kill him in 1976. I dedicated my Fifth String Quartet to his memory.

Our *Cimarrón* ensemble remained together, virtually without a break, until the autumn, appearing at festivals in Spoleto, Munich, Edinburgh, Berlin and Avignon. We gave three performances at the Cloître des

Célestins in Avignon, where I spent an exceptionally turbulent few days, gratifying my curiosity about life in general and about people and myself in particular with a whole series of new cultural stimuli (and horrors). At each performance there was such a rush for tickets at the beleaguered entrance to the cloisters that the police were obliged to intervene, and the festival director, Jean Vilar, had to promise the furious crowd that he would mount a further six performances at the following summer's festival. For the first performance, I myself designed the lighting. We started after sunset. The background was provided by the dormitory façade of a barracks for recruits that was beguiling from more than a merely architectural point of view, for from every window leant a young Frenchman, each more or less the same age as my first immortal beloved of 1948; in other words, more or less the age of Fassbinder's Querelle. Resting their classical heads on their elbows and revealing their short-sleeved army vests, these big kids listened to the work of a man who, I hardly need add, wanted, above all, to speak to people like himself in order to show them that he, too, knows exactly what it is like to be a recruit, to be quartered in barracks and punished. I also saw Vilar's production of a French translation of Edward Bond's *Early Morning* at this time – my first exposure to one of Bond's works on stage.

Throughout the whole of our stay in Avignon a hot sirocco blew across the town, setting our nerves on edge. I was happy to escape to Scotland for a production of *Elegy for Young Lovers* for the Edinburgh Festival on which I began work in late July or early August. The blocking rehearsals were held at Scottish Opera's rehearsal rooms in Glasgow. My set designer was Ralph Koltai, and the costumes were designed and realized by Fausto Moroni. The conductor was Alexander Gibson, Scottish Opera's artistic director. The festival director, Peter Diamand, had programmed not only *Elegy* but also several other new pieces from my pen: I conducted my Sixth Symphony, *Versuch über Schweine* and Leo Brouwer's *Exaedros*, and there were several performances of *El Cimarrón*, all with the original cast.

During the summer, while Fausto and I were already in Glasgow, Leo returned to Marino, where he used my music room to prepare a fixed version of *Exaedros* for full orchestra, a version that required two conductors, Leo and me, and also a solo percussionist, who, needless to say, was Stomu. We performed this version with the Berlin Philharmonic on 3 October 1970 in Hans Scharoun's wonderful new Philharmonie. For the second part of the concert I again conducted my Sixth.

*

A brief political flashback: by the end of 1969 it had become clear that the *gran zafra* had failed in Cuba and that it would never have been possible to harvest ten million tonnes of sugar since not enough cane had been planted. Embittered, Fidel told the masses in the Plaza de la Revolución that they would do well to depose him, whereupon they all shouted back: 'No! No! Fidel! Fidel!' Sareska wrote to tell me this, as did Rogelio and the others. They were all profoundly impressed and showed their solidarity. But nothing now came of the planned economic recovery, and Cuba became more dependent by the day on its great friend and ally, the open-handed Soviet Union. Soviet influence and Soviet advisers were everywhere, not only in politics and finance, but also in the arts and, above all, in the police force and spy network. Whenever they spoke in private, Cubans would switch on the radio or turn on the tap, so as not to be heard by the Soviet bugs. Visitors from abroad likewise felt uneasy at this oppressive East German syndrome, with its combination of fear of the police, uncertainty, intimidation, the presentiment of a certain lawlessness and the feeling of being at the mercy of others. Although I refused to share such sentimental feelings, I could not close my eyes to the reality of the situation: on one occasion, for example, I saw a man being bundled into a car on the Rampa in broad daylight, without a single protest on the part of the numerous passers-by: no one wrote down the number of the vehicle or ran after it or anything of the kind. They simply went on their way, an expressionless look in their eyes, pretending that they had seen nothing. I did exactly the same myself. The lives of all private citizens were kept under constant surveillance by a Comitato de la Difensa de la Revolución, a block-warden system just like the one that had once thrived in Nazi Germany. Who was visiting whom? Who was shirking voluntary agricultural work on Sundays? Who was sleeping with whom? And who was complaining about shortages of footwear, clothes and food? Who was telling jokes against the system? Who had the nerve to stand up and be counted as a *conflictivo* or dissident and openly express his opinions? Who was disinclined to be a part of the masses? Who wanted to escape and was prevented from doing so? And even as I write these lines I am reminded of the fact that there were indeed concentration camps for gays, although Feltrinelli and Sartre are said to have succeeded years ago in persuading the *jefe* to abolish these medieval monstrosities.

It was difficult for me to acknowledge the existence of this very real aspect of Caribbean socialism without speaking out about it. Willing and able only to argue the matter with myself, I had to suppress the boundless and bitter disappointment inspired by Cuban and, indeed, all other forms of existing social reality, a disappointment that rested very much on the imprecise nature of my own ideas about private and idealistic (and perhaps also illusory) freedom. I blamed myself and my bourgeois, liberal prejudices for my inability to see the lawless aspects of the Revolution as necessary stages on the road to freedom and for the lack of intellectual insight and consistency of approach that would have allowed me to have applauded them unconditionally.

On 20 March 1971 Heberto Padilla and his wife, Belkis Cuza Malé, were arrested in Havana. At the same time, their flat was seized and seals placed on the door and windows: it was to be reallocated to others. In other words, sentence was passed even as the accused were still leafing through the charge sheet. They were accused of high treason: in prose and verse Padilla had had the nerve to criticize the system and the Revolution that meant everything in the world to him. In Paris, *Le Monde* organized and published a petition to Castro in which, no doubt at the instigation of Carlos Franqui, the spirit of the Sierra Maestra and the Revolution's early ideals (foremost among which was freedom of thought) were invoked and Padilla's release demanded. Among the signatories were Sartre, Simone de Beauvoir and a large number of Latin American and European writers, sociologists and philosophers, including Pasolini, Moravia, Elsa Morante, Enzensberger, the Rome Manifesto group (led by Luigi Pintor and Rossana Rossanda), Luigi Nono and myself. A few weeks later it was reported by the Prensa Latina news agency that plain-clothes officials in Havana had personally invited every member of the country's Writers' and Artists' Union to its headquarters (thereby ensuring that no one skived off) in order to hear Padilla read out a confession. Prensa Latina reported that on several occasions the poet's voice failed him, a circumstance that it ascribed to the exceptional heat and to the failure of the building's air-conditioning system. Padilla publicly thanked the political police for their 'friendly and courteous treatment' and for the 'stimulating discussions' that had made it possible for him to see the error of his ways, a lapse due both to his constitutional inability to transcend his essentially bourgeois, egotistical nature, with its propensity for irony, and to his having consorted with 'counter-revolutionaries' and 'CIA agents' such as Enzensberger, the Franco-Polish writer, K. S. Karol, and the French agrarian scientist René Dumont (amongst whose luggage the manuscript of one of Padilla's novels, already rejected by the censor, had been found as he was leaving the country). I, who knew and valued Padilla for his wit, his courage to stand up for his beliefs, his critical grasp of the aims of the Revolution and his honesty, intelligence and love of the truth, suffered from this humiliation as though it were my own. According to the press agency, Heberto had also admitted in the course of his recantation that his interlocutors had succeeded in making it clear to him that politics and poetry must never mix and that this experience had taught him that in future he should treat only the genuine themes of poetry, namely, the beauty of women and trees, the countryside and the songs and legends of his people. He now found himself in his native Havana without work, without a roof over his head, shunned by people who had once been his friends and robbed of the manuscript of his novel. When he was released from prison, his friend Miguel Barnet went to collect him, a simple, spontaneous act of friendship that was in itself sufficient to ensure that Miguel, too, was ostracized and that for the next seven years not a single one of his books or a line of his poetry appeared in print in Cuba. An eyewitness of these events, the writer Reinaldo Arenas describes in his autobiography *Before Night Falls* not only the humiliations to which his fellow writer was subjected but also the shaming spectacle of the self-accusations of every nature that other novelists and poets now felt obliged to undergo as though in some chain reaction. The land was filled with the sound of artists beating their counter-revolutionary breasts.

I think it was Edward Kennedy who, in the course of a private meeting with Castro, later obtained permission for Padilla to leave the country. Since 1981 Heberto has lived in the United States, where he has taught at Princeton and rather been forgotten. His friend and admirer, the young Minister of Finance, Alberto Mora, shot himself. Leo Brouwer's wife, a much-loved pop star, slashed her wrists in 1971 while her husband was on a concert tour of Europe, and one of Che's sisters threw herself from an upper floor of the Habitación Focsa. Among others who played an extremely important part in the Revolution and who later took their own lives were Celia Sánchez and Haydée Santamaría, both of whom had served Fidel and fought alongside him at the time of the attack on the Moncada barracks in Santiago. Even Osvaldo Dórticos, who became President of the Senate in 1959 only to be ousted by Castro in 1976, committed suicide in 1983. And no one ever seems to know the reason why or, if they do, they never let on. And what can one say about the show trial of the popular General Ochóa and his colleagues, who were accused of drug trafficking and similar offences for which there was never a shred of evidence and who, physically and morally sapped by Russian-style injections and by humiliations of every kind meted out before the eyes of thousands of television viewers, were reduced to remorseful and penitent zombies? The news that all three had been executed on the morning after sentence had been passed did much to undermine my remaining faith in the Cuban experiment. A philanthropic autocrat suddenly seemed to have been replaced by a bloodthirsty murderer – how is one to cope with that? How is one to bear it? How is a nation to survive such events? Should one regard the whole vast experiment as a failure? Might it turn out to have been a mistake, an error, a knavish trick or an attempt to achieve the sort of Utopia that it is unreasonable to expect of mere mortals? Was it a tragedy? It would be terrible if that were so, for it would mean that a final bastion of dialectical materialism had fallen. Yet I do believe that the achievements of the Cuban Revolution are irreversible, since they are the achievements of six million individuals. May the gods – or, rather, may all rational and energetic men and women – ensure that the results of this extraordinary social experiment are not lost and swept away by the maelstrom of general regression that is so sadly typical of the end of this terrible century.

On 6 April 1971 Stravinsky died in New York. He was buried in Venice on the 15th, but I was unable to attend the service, since Leo was due to fly in from Cuba late that morning and I had to await his arrival. Instead I watched the service on television. Leo arrived in Marino at the very moment that the gondolas bearing the coffin and mourners were making their way to the cemetery on the island of San Michele. He brought with him letters, good wishes and news. He had visited Rogelio, who was still out in the country, and had disturbing things to tell us about the Padilla affair. We were about to sit down to eat when the telephone rang. It was for Leo. It was not an especially long conversation – just enough for Leo to turn deathly pale and to start to blub quietly to himself. The call was from his ministry in Havana, ordering him to leave my house at once and avoid all contact with people who, like me, had signed the telegram asking for clemency to be shown to Heberto Padilla. He was to report to his embassy in Rome without delay.

In the event, there *was* a delay, since Leo stayed the night in Marino and it was not until the next day that he set off back to Rome. This was not the last time that I saw him. Less than a year later, on 18 March 1972, he was again our guest in Marino, and again he brought with him good wishes and letters. But with that all communication unexpectedly ended. A few months later I happened to pick up a Rome newspaper one day and read that he had given a concert there the previous evening. He must have been acting on instructions: like Brecht's yea-sayer, he must have broken off all contact out of a sense of obligation. Now it was my turn to blub quietly to myself. I have said nothing about all of these things for more than two decades.

All those who signed the telegram to the *jefe* asking for clemency for Heberto Padilla were later declared *personae non gratae*. This was the only reply ever given to the appeal that had been made by a large section of the international intelligentsia with an interest in socialism on Cuba. A few weeks later, at the end of a visit to Chile, in the course of which he had seen Allende in person, Luigi Nono applied for a visa to visit Cuba. His application was turned down. He, too, had signed the notorious telegram, he too – an *onorevole* of the Italian Parliament and more than just a comrade – was now *persona non grata*. He told me so himself, on the telephone, following his return to Europe. He had discussed the affair with comrades in Chile, he went on, and the Cuban embassy had let it be known that he would not be refused entry if he were to publish an apology in the Chilean party newspaper, a self-critique that would then be reprinted in its Cuban equivalent and in the relevant international press. I asked him what he had done. He said he had written an apology (it was published first in Chile and then in Cuba) and had duly been given a visa. *Voilà un homme nouveau!* I was flabbergasted. 'And how was it in Cuba?' I asked. He filled me in, adding that he had also met Heberto Padilla. 'And how is he then?' I enquired, trembling inwardly. To which Gigi replied: 'Do you know, I have the impression that the man's an opportunist.' Those were his very words. 'I'm sorry?' I said. And he repeated: 'An opportunist.' At that, I hung up without another word. That's exactly how it was. That's how sad it was. And that was that.

I spent the autumn and winter of 1970/1 rather aimlessly travelling around, conducting, and writing a piece of platform theatre, *Der langwierige Weg in die Wohnung der Natascha Ungeheuer*, a 'show for seventeen performers' (to give it its subtitle) to words by Gastón Salvatore. First performed at the Teatro Olimpico in Rome on 17 May 1971, it was written for William Pearson, Stomu Yamash'ta, Peter Maxwell Davies's Fires of London, the Philip Jones Brass Ensemble and Gunter Hampel's Cologne-based Free Jazz Group, all of them good friends of mine and all of them first-class musicians. I myself not only conducted the performance but was also responsible for the semi-staged production. The score included an electronic component in the form of individual voices and street noises that I had recorded myself in Berlin. The tapes were prepared in the recording studio at the Technische Universität in Berlin, where my assistant was the actor Dieter Schidor, who was better known in the German-speaking world for his portrayals of criminals on television and who I think I must have met at around this time in Munich, an entertaining, highly intelligent and troubled individual who went on to make a name for himself as a film producer, not least of Fassbinder's *Querelle*. Natasha Ungeheuer is not intended to be the Berlin artist of the same name. Or perhaps she is. At all events, I did not know her at that time (later I bought a number of her paintings), and Gastón, too, had yet to meet her when he used her name. He knew only that an invitation to visit Natascha Ungeheuer in Kreuzberg was somehow 'in' among left-wing students of the time and seen as something of a privilege. Our own piece is a kind of latter-day *Berliner Requiem* and is about a young man who sets off for Kreuzberg in search of Natascha Ungeheuer and her eponymous apartment, a sphinx who may be induced to tell people what is to happen to them. Or perhaps she is Utopia personified. Yet Natascha Ungeheuer's apartment in this *fantasía* may also be no more than a whisky bar or simply a cosy, depoliticized garden of delights full of clouds of hashish smoke. Our hero does not reach his destination: but, although he does not find the place, he hears in his head the sirenlike voice of Comrade Natascha, who, far from welcoming and accommodating, reels off a list of objections to him. Attempts to renew his bourgeois connections prove a failure. It is a lonely show that our hero stages. It flatters me to think that the West Berlin of 1970/1 is easy to recognize in my gaudy colours and montages. There is the same coldness and harshness, the same implacability and cheerlessness that can overcome and overwhelm one in this great, sad city, a 'grey city by the sea', as the artist Werner Heldt used to call it. I knew – and know – all this from my own experiences of Berlin, experiences which, albeit long since past, were fraught with bitterness, temptations and terrors.

And now I wrote what I called my Second Violin Concerto. If I remember aright, the idea for this piece came to me following the final rehearsal for my Viola Concerto, *Compases para preguntas ensimismadas* (the title is by Gastón Salvatore and means, literally, 'metres for questions absorbed in self-contemplation'), which received its first performance in Basle on 11 February 1971. Paul Sacher had commissioned the piece for a young Japanese viola player, Hirofumi Fukai. It was wonderfully well played. When Sacher asked me after the final rehearsal what we should do next, I suggested a violin concerto, not least because his utterly delightful leader, Brenton Langbein, happened to be sitting next to us with his glass of whisky and I had always wanted to write something for him. I was attracted by a new poem by Enzensberger which, although not about the beauty of women and trees, none the less had a very real charm. It was about Baron Münchhausen and Kurt Gödel's crystal-clear but annihilating theorem: 'In every sufficiently complex system propositions can be formulated that are neither verifiable nor refutable within that system, unless the system itself is inconsistent.'

In a way, this theorem may be seen to justify the attempts of an inveterate liar like Baron Münchhausen to pull himself and his horse out of a swamp by tugging at his own hair. This poem of Enzensberger's has a jocular, mordant tone to it, and I felt that I could reflect that in my music. I turned it into a kind of music theatre (how could it be otherwise!) and reproduced the poem piecemeal. It was meant to be spoken on tape, with the music anticipating and concentrating the spoken word, reflecting upon it and reconstructing its contents, animated by Enzensberger's gloss on Gödel's theorem and by my idea of offering a musical account of Münchhausen's futile and desperate actions. Meanwhile, the actions of the soloist – fiddling away in the face of time and of the world and humanity's laws of gravity – are designed to be comical and also somewhat touching, perhaps on account of the hint of clownishness that they contain. Can one pull oneself out of the mud by one's hair with the help of music? Heaven and earth shall pass away, but shall music not pass away? The violinist enters. He is late and hurries through the auditorium, his coat tails flailing behind him, the orchestra having already started. He finally reaches the platform but cannot begin: something keeps happening in the music, something different, something unexpected, that prevents him, the soloist, from entering. But at last the moment arrives – he shoves his instrument under his chin and begins to play, only to start talking after the first few notes, reciting the theorem quoted above while at the same time accompanying himself on his fiddle. It is a frightening piece, precisely because it is so amusing – sheer pessimism. And it is very much this that makes it so frightening: in its mathematical irrefutability it tells only the truth; namely, that certainty = inconsistency.

After the first few performances I realized that the effectiveness of the poem was reduced and that the words tended, in consequence, to fall flat when delivered by a disembodied voice over a loudspeaker: in other words, the text needed to be clearly articulated and properly understood.

As a result, I revised the piece, so that the baritone, whom I imagine as a dead ringer for Papageno, now comes on stage and addresses the audience directly, declaiming the text in a mixture of Sprechgesang and chanson. Following this revision, the tapes now contain only violin music transformed by a computer into curious splashes of colour and ethereal sounds, music with which the soloist, in his guise as Baron Münchhausen, accompanies himself from time to time. They are echoes of, and canons on, his own successions of notes. Otherwise there is nothing. The orchestra falls silent. The man is now completely alone in the world. Brenton Langbein played the piece quite brilliantly at its first performance in Basle on 2 November 1972 under Paul Sacher, bringing wit and verve to roles that an instrumentalist is not normally required to assume. It saddened me deeply to learn that he had returned to the happy hunting grounds of his native Australia in 1995. He had taken such infinite pains to be kind, bringing so much love to his work with his young string ensemble, The Chamber Musicians; to his activities as leader of the Zurich Collegium Musicum and his teaching duties at the Basle Conservatory; to his concert tours with the pianist Maureen Jones and, finally, to the Barossa Festival that he ran in Adelaide in South Australia.

After completing my Second Violin Concerto, I turned to *Heliogabalus imperator*, an allegory in music inspired by my reading of Artaud's *Héliogabale, ou L'anarchiste couronné*. Like the concerto, it constitutes a curious reflection on my experiences in Cuba – rather as though I were still trying to come to terms with those experiences. The result is a series of cinematic, circus-like images of Rome as the city might have looked and sounded to Cecil B. De Mille. In my mind's eye I saw the magnificent, spec tacular entry of the sixteen-year-old emperor and god and imagined his provocatively androgynous appearance and behaviour, which were soon to prove a slap in the cretinous face for all of Rome's customs and conventions. Elected emperor *per acclamationem* by the Roman army on the Phoenician plains, El Algabal – 'he who has come down from the mountain' – had come to lead a cultural revolution and found a new religion. Sixty oxen drew the enormous moonstone phallus that the strange youth had brought with him from his home in Asia Minor, fully intending to unite it with the popular moon goddess, Juno, who was held in high regard by the Romans, an aim befitting her godlike station and, as such, entirely reasonable. At the front of the triumphal procession, ecstatic Arab children danced to the strident strains of barbarian music. A cloud of gold dust hung in the air. All morals and manners were progressively overthrown. One conventional virtue after another was systematically violated. Concepts such as magnanimity and dignity were scorned. The Antichrist had taken on human form. All sexual inhibitions were overcome. Happiness was something quite new in Rome. But this could not go on, could not be allowed to continue, law and order had to be restored as soon as possible, which is why His Majesty was murdered in only the third year of his reign. I took over the garish pop-art colours from my earlier pieces and reused them in a succession of images that inevitably contain elements of a spectacle, producing all the noise, vulgarity, showiness and bestiality so typical of Romans, then and now. In this I imitated the artist Renzo Vespignani, whose cycle on 'Fascism of 1972–1975' was exhibited in 1976 not only in Bologna and Bonn but also at the Kunstamt in Kreuzberg in Berlin. There is no doubt that these aggressive images left their mark on my music. Contrasted with this are the episodes in my score in which we meet the calumnified sun-god alone: here, finally, the purity and awesomeness of a character wholly imbued with a very real sense of his mission is revealed for all to see and hear. Towards the end of the allegory we follow the Praetorian Guard, characterized by snatches of German and American march music, as it pursues its beloved boss through the night-shrouded gardens between the Capitol and Tiber, their swords and daggers drawn, their halberds lowered, until they can attack him and hack him limb from limb – there they all lie now, his blood-soaked remains. Nothing more is left of this demigod and revolutionary who had tried to transform a wilderness totally paralyzed by decrees and bad habits into a veritable oasis, a Paradise on earth.

Heliogabalus received its first performance in Chicago on 16 November 1972 under the direction of Sir Georg Solti. Fausto and I tagged along with the conductor and his orchestra and also heard the piece in Washington and New York. Later, when I myself had to grapple with the technical problems involved in rehearsing and conducting this score (problems bound up with my clumsy aleatory notation), I prepared a new version that can virtually be sight-read like any normal piece and that needs few explanations and introductory remarks in rehearsal. (It could be said that, using traditional notation, I gave fixed form to one of the countless versions implicit in the original's aleatory material.)

I spent the summer of 1972 working on a television opera, or would it be better described as a vaudeville? Or a zarzuela? Or an operetta? *La*

Cubana was commissioned from Enzensberger and me by New York's NET Opera. It was originally to have been called *Ay, Rachel*, but since no one was ever sure how to pronounce the name Rachel, which differs in every language, and since it does not sound especially attractive however it is pronounced, we decided on the alternative title – one that is unfortunately rather vague and fails to hit the nail on the head. The text on which the piece is based was freely adapted from Miguel Barnet's *Canción de Rachel.* It suggested a radio play, which Enzensberger had already finished and which needed only to be adapted to the new medium of television. The musical and artistic director of NET Opera was the conductor Peter Hermann Adler. It was he who had commissioned and produced Stravinsky's *The Flood* and he, too, who invited Balanchine to stage *The Magic Flute* in an English translation by Auden and Kallman. I shall later have more to say about the production of *La Cubana*. But first the music had to be written, and that was to prove far from easy. I had to ensure that what I was writing was a genuine television opera: in other words, all the right ingredients had to be included, and the genre's potential and limitations correctly assessed. It was not to be a film but, rather, an artistic fantasy in video format. I had just started work on the score when Rouben Ter-Arutunian arrived in Marino to discuss the dramaturgy of the whole and agree on a performing style so that image and sound would be in perfect accord. Not until the piece was already in production was I to have a chance to meet the director, Kirk Browning, and to come to blows with him.

The story of *La Cubana* is as follows: Rachel, an ageing *chansonnière* and madam, is sitting in her tiny flat in Havana, surrounded by souvenirs, old clothes and frippery, and thinking of the past. She begins to tell the story of her life, first to her servant and then to a series of visitors, most of whom are as old as herself. At the start of the piece we hear the sound of shooting and uproar in the distance: Fidel and his followers have just arrived in the city. It is 1 January 1959. But our protagonist is unimpressed. Five times her narrative develops into a radiophonic or cinematic flashback in which we meet Rachel first as a very young rumba dancer; then (clearly recognizable) as one of the streetwalkers who work for and drool over the handsome pimp, Yarini; then as a circus performer; next as a music-hall singer; and finally as an ageing star about to step down from the limelight. In each of these flashbacks, Rachel has to be played by a younger singer who grows older with each passing scene, a difficulty that Enzensberger and I overcame only recently by revising the work: in the new version, a pocket-sized *La Cubana*, there is only one performer who operates on both levels. The flashbacks no longer involve elaborate scene-changes but are acted out by the elderly Rachel and her circle of friends in her plushly furnished salon.

I made life difficult for myself with *La Cubana*. Apart from my attempts to handle realism in *Maratona* and my fondness for Berlin cabaret songs of the 1920s, I had never really been interested in light music or dance music and now had to get to know this art form in detail. (Ever since the endless hours spent in the ballet rehearsal room at the theatre in Bielefeld after the war, I had simply closed my ears to such music.) Vulgarity cannot be depicted by vulgar means, whereas ambiguity, for example, can be illustrated by using ambiguous devices. Rachel's lies must be unmasked by the music, just as the mendacities in the music have to be exposed by Rachel. Another difficulty lay in the fact that I found Rachel unsympathetic as a character. I was unable to feel any affection for her but thought her as stupid and tedious as she was, in fact, in real life. In consequence, the music had, as it were, to learn to disregard itself whenever it was accompanying one of her chansons or tangos. I listened to Latin American light music and particularly enjoyed Carmen Miranda, the 'Brazilian Fireball' (with her light voice and attractive Portuguese accent, I found her by far the best of these *chansonnières*), and I think that her vocal style must have influenced that of my main character, certainly in the Alhambra Tango and the song 'Illusion'. On the other hand, there is virtually no Afro-Cuban folk music in our piece: it appears only in the circus scene, at the entrance of El Cimarrón and his comrades-in-arms. When the music falls silent, El Cimarrón delivers himself of his speech and drums can be heard outside, lots of drums, playing Yoruba music at various distances and differing volumes. The same music is heard again, but this time very loud, very close, in the final scene, when the people pour out into the street, the pornographic operetta house goes bankrupt and Rachel's favourite song is drowned out by the noise of a street battle. In our baleful zarzuela, the world of art is revealed as a second-rate nightclub, artistry as the kitsch associated with tarts.

Throughout the time that I was working on this score and grappling with all these difficulties, my thoughts were often elsewhere, my heart weighed down with sadness. The events that took place in Cuba in 1971 left me profoundly affected. I felt personally offended by them and was unable and unwilling even to consider ways of remedying or correcting the situation, least of all now that it had turned out that a public apology or the like would have had to be the price of my return to Cuba and the chance to see my friends there. A revolution like that was not for people like me. What does a rebel do when he sees himself forced to submit? To do one's duty as a rebel and obey one's basic law of disobedience, one must become a *disidente* as a matter of course. In a word, one must rebel.

In Europe, too, I had long since given up pestering those of my friends and old acquaintances from the past, from *antes*, who had not already broken with me of their own accord. I lived in the knowledge that I had become *persona non grata* for the world in general. Not only in artistic circles but elsewhere, too, I aroused a feeling of indignation – I who had abandoned the Establishment, after it had famously helped to establish me. I was the one who was busily sawing away at the branch on which not only I myself but all other artists, too, were sitting. Even from a distance I could still make out at least some of the malicious remarks that were being muttered about me not just in the world of art but also in the real world – my character was impugned and spiteful comments were made about the way in which I had changed, both politically and morally. Even on their own, these mutterings were more than enough for my already severely strained nerves.

If I append a brief and incomplete account of all the unpleasantness associated with my sawing through the branch on which we were sitting, I do so not in order to complain or because I covet a martyr's crown, but simply for the sake of a well-ordered narrative. During these and subsequent years my income fell by half. My (German) record company did not renew its exclusive contract with me. It was said – and the reader can believe this or not – that, as the result of my political commitment, the quality of my works had suffered so much that the company could no longer take the responsibility for releasing them. I also had a lot of trouble with my publishers, who had looked after me in such a paternalistic and friendly way for more than thirty years – in the case of one particular dispute, I was convinced that the parting of the ways had come. It was one Sunday lunch-time in Frankfurt. We could not reach an agreement. Outside in the street a large and noisy demonstration marking the death, on hunger strike, of one of the members of the Red Army Faction, Holger Meins, was making its way past the building; 'a small minority', commented one of the participants in our discussion. Only a short time previously there had been a scandal when a Frankfurt daily paper had published details of negotiations that were still in progress between Schott's and me, negotiations that involved my publisher making available a little more space in the company's various journals in order to create a small forum in which politically committed composers in both Germany and the rest of Europe could write about their new works and ideas. I was already in contact with the musicologist Carl Dahlhaus, who was editor-in-chief of Schott's various journals, and had talked to him about the possibilities of opening them up to left-wing views. He even called on me in Marino to discuss the matter. Thanks, however, to the extraordinary but effective interference of outside journalists, it now became more difficult, if not impossible, to continue what one Darmstadt journalist had the effrontery to call my 'attempt at blackmail'. In the event, we found a less than ideal solution to the problem of establishing a forum for non-conformist ideas by founding a series of publications under the title *Neue Aspekte der musikalischen Ästhetik*, the publishing costs of which were generously shared by Schott's.

In the midst of all these upheavals and problems, my only hope was to bury myself in my work. I completed the score of *La Cubana*, then took a break from composing and, as usual, travelled around, conducting and, on this occasion, making some recordings for English record companies. Then, at the beginning of 1973, I made a start on *Voices*, a setting of twenty-two songs.

This collection was intended as a contribution to the political art song. With the exception of a single poem by Heinrich Heine (a highly personal product of its age), all are based on texts by twentieth-century poets, from Ho Chi Minh to Heberto Padilla, from Giuseppe Ungaretti to the voices of black America, and from Brecht to F. C. Delius. Each song has its own instrumental accompaniment. I wrote them for the London Sinfonietta, a full-length 'Song of the Earth' (as it was called at the time), rather than for the sort of amateur choirs and other non-professional groups with whom I had occasionally worked in the past only to make the appalling discovery that they are incapable of singing or staying in time. In consequence, all twenty-two of these songs place often extreme artistic demands on their performers. *Voices* is music for the concert hall, but it is also a confessional work. Each of the twenty-two numbers reflects my sympathies, thoughts and experiences at that time. My own presence lurks behind each of these poems, including No. 21, 'Schluß', by the former Communist Michaelis Katsaros, who had grown weary of his Communism and, above all, of himself. And I am especially fond of the epilogue, a poem from an ancient

Colombian flower festival translated into German by Hans Magnus Enzensberger that is sometimes omitted in performance since it speaks lightly and dreamily of love and, in its curious, unsettling way, adopts a festive, playful tone to tell of happiness. The Sinfonietta soloists had to strike gongs and musical glasses and metallophones here, as in an Inca fairy tale or in Tibet: its meditative manner reminds one of the atmosphere of a temple, but at the same time there is a slight tendency for it to parody the flower-power culture (already past its sell-by date by then), a circumstance that encouraged a number of my sterner critics to speak of recidivist leanings. This 'Flower Festival' was sketched on a single summer morning in Marino, leaping almost unbidden off the page and needing no further revisions of a structural, serial or moralistic nature.

The voices of the title are those of young and old artists whose work is politically committed. These people are concerned with their fellow human beings, with the contemporary human condition within the world around them and with all the problems of race and class in which they themselves often seem fated to be embroiled. For each of these statements I had to devise music appropriate to its contents and to its author's cultural background. It was a question, therefore, of ignoring my own stylistic habits as far as I could and of unearthing new and unexpected objects, rather after the fashion of the old mannerists and parodists. In this way – in other words, in the course of my searches and voyages of discovery – I expanded my vocabulary and hit upon new forms and formal possibilities. My vocal style, too, acquired rather greater variety and flexibility.

In December 1972, before setting to work on *Voices*, I went to New York to help to prepare for *La Cubana*. As a project, it suffered from the outset from the fact that the directors at NET were firmly resolved to render the piece as harmless as possible and subvert its original aims, removing even the slightest mordancy and producing a piece that we no longer recognized as our own – and all without consulting us. I have never known anything like it. It was bowdlerized, subjected to swingeing cuts, misunderstood and mistranslated, without my being able to do a thing about it – it all happened overnight, as though of its own accord. It was in the nature of the beast. Every day I would telephone Enzensberger in the sleepy Berlin suburb of Friedenau (he himself could not come since he had vowed never to set foot in the States as long as the Vietnam War was still being fought), pouring out my troubles and asking him for his advice. I consulted lawyers and considered packing my bags and leaving – but we are brought up to believe that it is wrong to abandon our children. In the event, I stayed and watched in dismay as this bastard son of mine grew into someone I no longer recognized, but as soon as the music and video recordings were finished, I flew back to Italy, saddened, concerned and completely worn out.

But now there was Marino and Christmas. We had visitors, including, as always, dear, kind Inge and friends from Rome – Franco Serpa, Renzo Vespignani and Titina Maselli. We wined and dined and made music. As soon as the festive season was over, I rearranged my music room and acquired some better shelving with more space for my books and music. At the same time, I began to cast round for the right form for *Voices*. I remember once thinking that all the songs should deal with the artist's conflicts in his contradictory universe and with his problems with the real world, but then it seemed to me more important to strike a positive note and to keep a look-out for suitable texts. The first to be set was Heberto Padilla's 'Los poetas cubanos ya no sueñan', followed by Ho Chi Minh's 'Prison Song' and then, I think, by Heine's 'Heimkehr' – each poem was chosen on the basis of what the previous one had produced and expressed. Only slowly did the overall picture emerge, and there is no doubt that current events and personal experiences played a crucial role in every new decision.

It was winter and I was again suffering from the kind of nervous exhaustion from which it always seemed impossible to escape. Was it the inexorable ageing process or was it the result of working such long hours? I read Caudwell's *Illusion and Reality* and was so impressed by the clarity and precision of its author's thoughts (he had been killed in the Spanish Civil War) that I wrote a long letter on the subject to Edward Bond. For him, too, Caudwell's writings were a discovery.

It was Volker Schlöndorff who had introduced me to Bond in London the previous year. Bond had praised my music in a letter to Volker and expressed an interest in working with me. Our first meeting took place in a Japanese bistro just off Wigmore Street in the autumn of 1972. I asked him to provide me with a multi-dimensional libretto based on Marlowe's *Edward II*, describing how I myself imagined it would look and pointing out that my musical conception had been strongly influenced by two innovatory theatre productions, Luca Ronconi's *Orlando furioso* and Ariane Mnouchkine's *1792*. Bond listened to everything I had to say but then, some time later, wrote back to report that he could make no headway with *Edward II* and would like to suggest another subject instead. I swallowed hard and read the script that he had enclosed, a loose sequence of scenes filled with the actions of war: the first part took place on a battlefield, the second in a madhouse. I thought of Goya's *The Disasters of War*. Suspecting the horrors that lay ahead, I swallowed hard again and showed the draft to Ronconi and his designer, Pier Luigi Pizzi, both of whom I wanted to work with me on staging the new piece.

I recall an evening in Marino when we discussed the positioning of the three orchestral groupings in three different playing areas, together with the function of the music in such a context and the nature of the venue itself: an opera house or a hangar? It was immensely important to decide these points, since without an answer to them, I simply could not begin. We held frequent meetings, Ronconi, Pizzi and I, and in mid-February I drew up a sketch, listing the order of the scenes and the individual events that unfold simultaneously on stage, writing a synopsis for every scene and compiling a list of questions for Bond, including questions raised by Pizzi and Ronconi (neither of whom felt comfortable with the 'romantic' form of the draft). All of these points I was able to put to Bond in person at a meeting in Vienna on 28 January, in the middle of a blizzard, on the day after the first performance of his production of *Lear* at the Burgtheater.

Following the première (I did not particularly enjoy the production, which seemed rather slow and leaden and as crude as the play itself), Edward and Elisabeth Bond (a schoolfriend of Ingeborg Bachmann's from Carinthia) and I went to dine at the Hofburg with the eighty-two-year-old Helene Thimig. The widow of Max Reinhardt, Frau Thimig occupied a lavishly furnished apartment, suffered from insomnia and, in her extraordinarily animated manner, was still chatting with Edward about his production at three o'clock the next morning. I spent the whole of the following day with Bond, fearlessly informing him of my worries concerning our plans. Bond was ready to make cuts and to countenance additions, and at certain points he had no difficulty altering this or that in accordance with my wishes, but there was clearly a certain cultural difference between the way we both thought and felt, a difference that seemed to amount to a point of principle and that could not just be ignored. It could be seen only as a challenge. It became difficult when, as was sometimes to happen, Bond stopped speaking and averted his gaze, the glass in his spectacles momentarily catching the light and obscuring his friendly blue eyes. His brow would then furrow a little and his whole face would seem to scowl and assume an increasingly hostile expression, as though he had been overcome by some sense of inner horror. It is impossible to conceive of deeper silences: there was something terrible about them; no one seemed to have the courage to break them, apart from his loyal wife, herself a writer and former theatre critic who loved her Edward dearly and understood him. She had a way of dealing with these minute-long silences and of breaking the spell, a gift that she exercised on this particular day, too, with all its difficulties and its very real tests of nerve. There was always a pot of tea or a bite to eat to separate the combatants. There were two or three occasions in the course of that day when we reached the point of saying that we could not go on, that we did not understand one another and that we would have to abandon the project. That evening I returned to my hotel, lugubriously drunk on Edward's excellent Chianti, and spent a restless night. Although I was due to leave the next morning, I first had to give three interviews on my future plans with Bond. (One of them I chanced to hear two hours later over the loudspeakers in the restaurant at Schwechat Airport.) In all of them I made it clear that we were working on a book, the contents of which could not be revealed in its present state. In fact, Edward and I had finally agreed that he would write a new version in which at least some of my wishes and ideas would be implemented. I returned to Marino and to the wintery bleakness and desolation of my displeasure, and threw myself into my work, perhaps with somewhat more patience and, I think, also with somewhat more confidence than before, in order that my music – my little mad world theatre with all its Baroque *concetti* and illusions – might sound as humanly approachable as possible. And I awaited Edward's new draft.

On 29 March 1973 I saw and heard an excellent production of *The Young Lord* at the New York City Opera, conducted by Julius Rudel and directed by Sarah Caldwell, and the following morning attended a private preview of *La Cubana*, which had been completed during the intervening months. I found it tiresome, ridiculous, embarrassing and untrue to the original. No wonder that the director had removed his name from the credits. The choreographer at least had the grace to apologize to me in person: the whole thing, he said, had simply been 'fucked up'. Even Rouben's hand-painted sets and costumes looked pale and insipid – just like the music, which the sound engineers had edited and emasculated to the point where it was no longer recognizably my own. Once again I wondered whether to seek legal redress and prevent the film from being shown, but who can ever afford to pay the costs of such a case, to say nothing of the attorney's fees? And so one leaves things as they are, promising oneself only that never again will one allow oneself to be taken for a ride in this way – a promise that one keeps only until the next unimaginable occasion. Throughout my stay in New York I repeatedly found myself at loggerheads with the people that I met there, always on political grounds, I felt constantly annoyed and could agree with nothing and no one, least of all with myself. On a couple of occasions I went with Lorca Massine to the Saturday evening shindigs held on Upper West Side by Cuban exiles, the young men wearing ties and Elvis quiffs, the girls all tarted up in petticoats, while their mothers sat at the edge of the dance floor, watching closely and counting the number of times that José invited their Celia to dance. I went to hear how razor-sharp these Cuban big bands played their sexy rumbas and cha-chas in these echoing halls. It was erotic and powerful, and it went right through you.

I then spent a few days in Paris, where I saw the Solti–Strehler *Nozze di Figaro* at Versailles, visited old friends and, together with Titina Maselli, queued with schoolchildren and tourists to pay a courtesy call on Géricault at the Louvre. London was my next port of call. Here I met Peter Zinovieff to discuss the electronic sounds that I wanted to include in my new piece, which was already going through my mind: a dance drama with the title *Tristan*. I had recently met the choreographer John Cranko, who had built up a wonderful company in Stuttgart. If I remember aright, it was he who suggested attempting a *Tristan* dance trilogy together. I was again in London in May, this time to conduct the British premières of my Viola Concerto, *Compases*, and my Second Violin Concerto with Michael Vyner's Sinfonietta. On this occasion, I remained in the capital long enough to meet a number of interesting new friends, foremost among whom were Peter Maxwell Davies, Harrison Birtwistle and Peter Zinovieff. I spent an entertaining and convivial evening with William Walton. And, together with John Tooley, the general administrator of Covent Garden, I attended the first night of Edward Bond's *The Sea* at the Royal Court Theatre in Sloane Square. By now I had in my pocket a commission to write an opera for Covent Garden and had announced that Bond was working on a libretto for me. Bond himself had come to my Sinfonietta concert and told me that he had liked my music very much, to which I was able to reply that, for my own part, I was now very pleased with his new libretto, which had arrived in Marino in the meantime. So far we had not had much luck with the title. *Privates* was impossible. *The Chorus* was good, but open to misunderstanding. *The General* was no less misleading. My own suggestion, *In the Colonies*, was rejected on the grounds that such a title might give the impression that, by shifting the action to the former colonies, we were trying to distract attention from the horrors that were taking place in our own part of the world. It was here, after all, that the war was being fought, here within our own four walls. Then suddenly Bond announced that he had decided to call the piece *We Come to the River* and that he was prepared to fight tooth and nail for this title. At the same time – it was now June 1973 – I decided how the three orchestral groupings would be constituted.

By the summer of 1973 I had finally completed the last of the twenty-two numbers of *Voices*, rounding off the collection with 'Roses and Revolution' and arranging them in the order in which they were later to see the light of day. There now followed a brief lull, which I shall fill in by regaling the reader with a few details necessary to understand the links between all these different events. First, we need to go back to the summer of 1972, when I spent some weeks in London with Peter Zinovieff, preparing the first tapes for *Tristan* in his electronic studio in Putney. I began by writing down and recording the basic material: for the opening episode, 'Tristan's Lament', I wrote a six-minute fantasy for early instruments based on a medieval Florentine *Lamento di Tristano*. The well-known early music specialist, David Munrow, recorded these various takes for me, one after the other, to produce the most wonderful polyphonic texture. We then took each of these takes in turn and transformed the archaic instrumental sound into a magically hollow-sounding web of sexless, frigid computer music.

We adopted a similar procedure with the second electronic passage, for which I had already prepared a score for six-part percussion that was recorded in Zinovieff's studio by myself, Zinovieff, and my assistant on this project, Geoffrey King, a delightful and talented pupil of Peter Maxwell Davies, all three of us throwing ourselves with wild-eyed enthusiasm into the task of producing these lunatic sounds as we let off steam like so many brilliant brutalists. To produce this percussive pandemonium, we belaboured the strings of Zinovieff's piano with tennis balls, walking sticks, riding crops and so on and, by transforming both this and a piano-roll version of Chopin's Funeral March into electronic music, were able to instil a great deal of energy into the piece. But *Tristan* was still in its infancy. With the exception of the material needed for the prepared tapes, I had still not written a note – what I was aiming to do was to create three electronic episodes upon whose carpet-like textures I would be able to construct my instrumental music at some later date, probably not for another twelve months, rather as though I were working to the sort of fixed rules associated, for example, with a basso continuo. In short, it was another attempt to approach an unknown goal, to push back the bounds of experience, another attempt to get round myself, not only to prove myself wrong but also, I hoped, to break free from myself and from all my conventions and in that way to take a further step forward. There is nothing that I find as repellent as routine, no one who is as anti-artistic as the creature of routine.

The third of the three electronic sections was the finale of the whole work: for this, the opening bars of the Prelude to Act Three of Wagner's music drama were to be subjected to a series of transformations. Peter was tinkering with it one evening after I had already returned to my hotel, where he suddenly called me up, summoning me back to Putney without delay. I set off at once. It was almost midnight when I got back to Putney from Piccadilly, but it was still quite light – it was one of those remarkably moving and unsettling summer nights that have something elegiac about them and that (as far as I know) one finds only in England. Peter and his beautiful wife, Victoria, were sitting in his software studio, listening, deeply stirred, as his computer kept on pouring out new and fascinating information on the harmonic nature of Wagner's musical idea, on its instrumentation and the particular qualities of the instruments used by the Master, and on the dynamics and the intensity of the vibrato employed by the orchestra. Peter and Victoria were weeping copiously, and for good reason: here was information technology at its most seductive. It was overwhelming. What a basso continuo had fallen into my hands! I felt only admiration and affection for Peter, this astute mathematician, composer, computer scientist, poet and eccentric, and have always retained the fondest memories of the time that I spent in Putney, where his state-of-the-art studio was part of his detached family house.

The doors of his studio gave on to his garden, at the end of which ran the Thames. At low tide, youngsters in wellington boots and armed with metal detectors would wade through the mud, looking for Roman coins. I spent most of the time in the garden with Zinovieff's children, the beautiful, freckled, red-haired Zofka; the silent, red-haired Leo; and little Kolinka, five years old, dark-haired and with bright blue and red speckles on his cheeks, one of the first children to have been born in Great Britain after only a seven-month pregnancy and to have survived. We played croquet and they told me about themselves and about their friends and their likes and dislikes. They worshipped their parents. It was probably during the course of this week, while we were working on *Tristan*, that we had the idea of including the sound of a human voice on tape, telling of Isolde's *Liebestod*. And what a stroke of luck that we had little Kolinka there, for no one could have done it better than this innocent child with his Putney accent. From time to time Peter would call me into his studio from the garden in order to show me what he had done in his attempts to come closer to my ideas. Mostly I was immediately satisfied – the main thing was that I did not have to stay too long surrounded by all this meaningless and unloved software but could return outside and admire the children's paintings: they were in the throes of creating a title page for a collection of sixty-two songs that I ought to have written during my stay (from 18 to 28 June) and on which Peter had encouraged me to work so that I would not get bored while he was tinkering with my *Tristan* tapes. The title page shows a circular volcanic crater filled with blue water, with the volcano itself above it, then a hill with a castle and flag, a peacock and a trumpet, all of them pictorial representations of my descriptions of Marino, the place where they were to spend their forthcoming summer holidays – a vision of things to come.

To have the Zinovieffs in Marino was a source of immense enjoyment. We were determined that it should be a holiday for us all, and so we played *boccia*, badminton, croquet and the piano, went to the coast and visited the other Castelli: Palestrina, Tivoli and Bomarzo. Cats, dogs, goats and birds of every description made a deep impression upon all the children, who spent much of their time with these animals. I wish the whole family could have stayed with us for ever.

We were all shocked to learn that John Cranko, whom I had met in Venice in May to discuss our plans for *Tristan*, had died suddenly on 26 June 1973 on the flight back from a tour of America, with the result that nothing could come of our *Tristan* trilogy. I decided, therefore, to use the existing material, which currently consisted of no more than the sketches for a piano piece and the tapes that had been prepared in London, and to develop it according to my own criteria. The London Symphony Orchestra wanted a new piece and so I proposed *Tristan*, which was now subtitled 'Preludes for piano, tapes and orchestra'. (Initially I had thought of 'Rounds' as a subtitle and description of the piece.) The first prelude was worked out in Marino on 17 July, when I also noted down an overall design for the piece, a design that was later to prove definitive when it came to the work as a whole. I spent a wonderful summer, listening to the three electronic *Tristan* episodes every day and on each occasion writing down the new sounds, the lines and traces, backlights and counterweights, the intensities and colours that took shape in my imagination above the ornamental background of the carpet of electronic sounds. But for the present this was all no more than a game, perhaps only a way of passing the time. Nothing else was particularly important to me any longer now that our house had been blessed for a while by the presence of a *spirito benigno*, a kindly spirit that brought a little rest to my poor, tormented soul and at the same time enabled new ideas, thoughts and moral concepts to come flooding in through the doors that lay wide open.

The spirit in question was the Japanese sculptor and designer, Yoichi Ohira, the son of an old friend from Tokyo, Akira Ohira, who spent the summer with us in Marino before moving on to Venice in the autumn and taking up his place at the Academy of Fine Arts, for which he had been awarded an Italian government scholarship. Initially, he had difficulty getting used to Europe, but since we treated our guest like royalty (which he found to be only right), he soon got used to Marino and its reverential inhabitants, at the same time recreating his own native country in our midst, a Japanese enclave in the heart of our brutally barbarous western world. He had started to learn Italian as soon as his father had given him permission to travel, and he was already making rapid progress, but for a time we largely spoke English together. He already had his own idea of the world, of the significance of work and love, of the various Japanese virtues, all of them of porcelain-like purity and transparency and all expressed in Japanese ideograms, and it was an effort for him to translate this Asiatic understanding of the world into western idioms, into a language that was so difficult for him to understand precisely because of its simplicity. It turned out that, for him, the greatest thing in life was to turn liquid glass into self-contained forms with his own hands and using only his own breath in the manner of a pair of bellows. He had already worked as an apprentice at the Yamaha Glass Factory in Chiba, a suburb of Tokyo, where he had been paid a pittance in pursuit of his goal. But his dream, his goal in life, was to go to Venice and work in a glasshouse on Murano, becoming an artist by watching others, by sheer hard work and by submitting to the will of his teachers.

Yoichi Ohira has now reached that goal. After completing his course as a draughtsman and sculptor at the Academy *summa cum laude*, he did indeed spend many years earning his living as a simple worker on Murano and, by dint of his courtesy, modesty and a great deal of patience, won the respect of the Venetian art world and glass industry. Today he creates the most beautiful forms and colours for famous Venetian firms. But the months that he spent in Marino during the spring and summer of 1973 were a time when everything still seemed new and strange to him. He often felt very alone, like a bird that had fallen out of its nest – as he himself expressed it. Although we did what we could to make his homesickness a little less unbearable, it often overwhelmed him, and although he tried to conceal it steadfastly and masterfully, there were times when, all his good intentions notwithstanding, it would break through and express itself in tears and anger. And it did so whenever the world collapsed around him and whenever we – insensitive Westerners that we were – had failed yet again to pay proper attention and had made mistakes, committed some act of thoughtlessness or shown a want of tact.

His linguistic limitations and initial unfortunate experiences had naturally left Yoichi feeling a little uncertain and mistrustful in his dealings with the Christian cannibals whom he encountered at every turn. I acted as considerately as I could, since I wanted us all to prove worthy of the privilege that his presence meant to our household. Yoichi was entrusted to my care, and I wanted him to feel safe and self-confident as he settled down in Europe. I particularly recall the eighteenth of June, a red-letter day when I showed our Buddhist agnostic the abbey church at Fossanova and he was deeply moved by nave's sublime Gothic architecture. I do not suppose that he had ever seen such a building before, perhaps never even imagined that one could exist. We often went to the coast, of course, generally to Sabaudia, where Pasolini, Moravia, Laura Betti, the painter Lorenzo Tornabuoni and others had their large summer villas, but generally we remained at La Leprara, where there was always so much to do and to learn.

The cicadas' concerti grossi began on 1 July, marking midsummer. Peter Zinovieff looked in on us once again and we celebrated in style, dining in the cool Roman cellar that we had discovered in the vineyard only a few years previously and restored to working order. Ingeborg was also there – since our birthdays fell only six days apart, we mostly celebrated them together. She was a little *distraite*, something that I had noticed on frequent occasions in the course of our recent meetings. She seemed to have even more difficulty than usual in finishing a sentence or in listening to what other people were saying. It was the tablets. I told her how sorry I was. She thanked me and said that she had decided to kick the habit and was going to spend the whole summer at Badgastein. I offered to accompany her to the station, but she thanked me again and said it was all taken care of.

It was also at around this time that Franco Serpa brought three hedgehogs from Todi for our little tract of woodland. And I made the first sketches for the orchestral music for *Tristan.* James Gibson and the conductor David Atherton, who was then still on the staff at Covent Garden, dropped in and asked me to draw up a list of the singers required in *We Come to the River*, a subject to which I had not yet given any thought. We also discussed the instrumentalists, and the idea was mooted of using the Sinfonietta rather than Covent Garden's own orchestra, an idea that was subsequently taken up. I had put *We Come to the River* on the back burner and for the present could hear only *Tristan*, a full-bodied, sensual symphonic score. As a result, it was virtually impossible for me to talk about the opera.

I slept impatiently, dreaming foolish dreams in German: a few dear old friends expressed their views on *La Cubana*, opining that the text could never be set to music. One of them advised me to publish the score as a mere curiosity in twenty years' time. On 30 July I completed the fair copy of the full score of 'Tristan's Lament', the first orchestral section of the piece, then flew to East Berlin for the International Youth Festival.

There I saw Luigi Nono, Nicolás Guillén, Heiner Müller, Peter Weiss and Rolf Hochhuth at the Academy's opening reception. Television, *Das Neue Deutschland*, radio. Went on a walkabout with Maxim Dessau in the crowded city. Felt a festive, optimistic atmosphere in the air. Was delighted to meet Alicia Alonso among the crowd. She was wearing a pink denim suit. She said: 'You've put on weight.' 'How can you tell?' I asked. 'You were almost blind when we last met.' (She had had an operation and her eyesight had been partially restored.) 'I could recognize outlines even then,' she replied. I spent an evening with Ruth Zechlin at Siegfried and Helga Matthus's dacha on the Stolzenhagener See. It was bright, with not a trace of a breeze.

By Saturday, 6 August, I was back in Marino, where the sirocco had started to blow with a vengeance. I felt feverish and exhausted, perhaps partly in reaction to the days I had spent in Berlin. Memories of faces and voices kept popping up like snapshots. Perhaps my encounter with the reality of East Berlin had been a little too violent for my late bourgeois sensitivities. There were certain things that I needed to come to terms with. I felt out of sorts, was afraid of the unexpected and of shocks of every kind. I sketched the second of the piano pieces for *Tristan*, spent the August holiday – the *ferragosto* – in the Ciociaria and, together with Yoichi and

Fausto, picnicked at Genazzano in a silvery *uliveto* on lush red earth with Titina Maselli and her wonderful old Communist mother, the universally admired Elena. Everything at this time was mysteriously *sotto voce*. I got as far as 'Tristan's Folly' with my sketches (or 'Tristan's Flagellation', as I still called it at this time) and around 20 August returned to London to make recordings with the Sinfonietta for an English record company. Among the works we set down were *Apollo et Hyazinthus* and the *Wiegenlied der Mutter Gottes*, both of which date from the same period, reminding me of the time that I had spent in Göttingen a quarter of a century earlier. As one of his first official duties following his appointment as general administrator of the Sadler's Wells Opera (soon to be renamed the English National Opera), George Harewood had decided to mount a production of *The Bassarids* and engaged me as its conductor and director. I sat through an act of *The Twilight of the Gods* at the London Coliseum, a vast barn of a building in the Edwardian style that had been the company's home since 1968.

Tazeena Firth and Timothy O'Brien, who had been recommended to me by Lord Harewood to design the sets and costumes for *The Bassarids*, visited me at Marino and we spent two weeks working together on the production. At the end of that period we had two promising stage models that our two designers cleverly constructed, one for Thebes, the other for the scenes on Mount Cytheron. A few days later, another model appeared, this time for the Intermezzo, a Freudian bordello, its colours and lighting presaging the catastrophe on the sacred mount. I thought about reinstrumenting the Intermezzo and scoring it for Dionysian string instruments alone, especially harpsichord and mandolin, in order to set it off as far as possible from the orchestral sound of the main part of the opera and mark it out as something different, a clear interpolation. (In the exposition to the main part of the work, the guitar had already been heard in the god's first aria.)

Meanwhile, my brother Jürgen had furnished a small apartment for Yoichi on the second floor of a block of workers' flats in the vicinity of San Giacomo a l'Orio, a typically Venetian part of the city, with its *rio*, bridge, *sottoportico* and little garden with a pomegranate tree. Jürgen then came to Marino to work on his set model for *River*. Luca Ronconi had withdrawn from the production since Covent Garden had declared itself unable to meet his request to remove all the existing seating from the stalls in order for Mr Ronconi to use it as his principal acting area. Anxious to compromise, I had taken the matter into my own hands and, in doing so, shouldered a heavy burden of responsibility. But since my musical ideas were closely bound up with the drama as set forth in the libretto, it seemed to make sense for me to plan the production myself both in my own head and with the help of a set model even as the music was taking shape. As a result, I had Jürgen's model beside me in my music room from the end of September onwards, waiting for the day when I could finish *Tristan* and turn to the novel experiment represented by *We Come to the River*. I could already hear this new music in my mind's ear, could see and smell it, whereas in the case of *Tristan*, I was having to grope my way forward like a blind man, especially, of course, in the piano and orchestral episodes that still had to be written over the electronic continuo. I made only very slow progress.

At eleven o'clock on the evening of 11 September, Italian television reported that the Chilean president, Salvador Allende, had been arrested in Santiago and was believed to have committed suicide. More details began to emerge very shortly: the government palace had been attacked and flames were seen leaping from the building. It was now said that the state president, a sub-machine gun in his hand, had fallen in a hail of bullets fired at him by storm-troopers. An illegal right-wing military putsch had brought an end to Allende's socialist experiment. A reign of terror was established in its place. Even today I can still feel the weight of the depression that overcame me on hearing this news. It is hard to speak of this and of the other terrible events that were to put a permanent end to my radiant, carefree summer.

On 29 September, Wystan Auden died in Vienna. I read about it in the newspaper. In accordance with his wishes, he was buried not in New York or Oxford but in Kirchstetten. With what fondness I recalled our final meeting. It must have been the summer of 1972. Much as I worshipped Auden and regarded him as my friend, I had tended to avoid both him and Chester Kallman in recent years, since I was afraid of their sarcasm and especially Auden's infamous lectures and sermons which, given my own political development, I was not prepared – or strong enough – to endure. When a Victorian music scholar telephoned me one day in London and said that Wystan was staying with him and that it was mad that we had not seen each other, I agreed to drop by the next morning, but only on condition that Wystan did not try to talk politics. I shall never forget that morning, which I spent in Bryanston Square, dazzled not just by the sun streaming in through the windows but, above all, by the magic and charm of Auden's conversation. Slowly and systematically working his way through the contents of a bottle of vodka diluted with orange juice, he gradually grew more animated, as, too, did his conversation. But 'conversation' is hardly the word for an extempore two-hour disquisition on the weather, a discourse that ravished my ear, with excursuses into the dangers of direct exposure to sunlight and the lack of chlorophyll in the epidermis of whites ('After all, we are no trees,' he said) and the beneficial effects of fog on the English psyche. In this way, my great friend spent the whole morning avoiding all personal questions and also, of course, all reference to politics. When he had to leave and catch his train to Oxford, I hugged him with an enthusiasm bordering on love, so much had I missed him in the meantime. Who could ever have imagined that this would be our final meeting?

I spent these late September days in Marino, working on *Tristan*. There were also wildly animated discussions on music and politics with Michael Vyner and the pianist Paul Crossley. News arrived of the funeral of Pablo Neruda in Santiago, at which thousands sang the Internationale. Fascists destroyed Neruda's house in Valparaiso, together with the Inca artefacts that it had contained. Books were burnt. Six union leaders were shot. Thousands of political prisoners were herded together in the football stadium in Santiago and 'tried' one after the other. I had just completed 'Tristan's Folly' – my 'flagellation' – and ended it with a terrible scream on the part of the whole of the orchestra, turning Isolde's deathly cry from the third act of Wagner's opera into a shrill and metallic expression of horror.

11

> What is so terrible about death is that it brings the very real pain of the end but not the end itself.
>
> Franz Kafka, *Das vierte Oktavheft*

Friday, 28 September 1973 was a clear blue day in early autumn. It started well: as usual there was work to be done, visitors came and went, and the mood was comparatively cheerful. But late that evening the telephone rang. It was Sergei, a good friend of Ingeborg's. He sounded on edge and his voice, which I knew very well, struck a profoundly serious note – I suspected at once that something had happened. Sergei had received a call from one of Ingeborg's former housekeepers who had discovered by chance – from the *portiere* at the *palazzo* in the Via Giulia – that three days earlier the *signora* had been taken to the San Camillo Hospital suffering from serious burns and was now lying unconscious in an oxygen tent. It was said that she had fallen asleep with a lighted cigarette and, following the accident, had telephoned Maria, an old friend, to ask for bandages and ointment for burns. Maria had duly gone to the Via Giulia and immediately called the emergency services, since it was clear to her that the *signora* needed hospital treatment. A German secretary was asked to inform Ingeborg's sister in Carinthia and to run a couple of errands but – she said – she had had to swear to the strictest secrecy. And so it was only several days later that Ingeborg's friends in Rome, including myself, found out about the accident. None of us in fact had known she was in the city. She had said goodbye, then gone off into the mountains for a rest-cure, saying that she might later go on to Vienna and travel around a bit. I immediately called her sister in the Via Giulia to find out more, but she did not really know who I was and her reply was guarded and monosyllabic. She had not been able to see Ingeborg and knew only what the doctors had said. She was crying. I, too, cried all night long, as the news, in all its seriousness, slowly began to sink in and a boundless sense of horror overwhelmed me.

The next morning I drove to the clinic to try to find out more and was shattered by what I discovered. It was all far worse than we had been told: she was suffering from forty per cent burns. The doctors had just performed a tracheotomy in order to help her breathing. She was still unconscious but was not in pain since her nerve ends, too, had been burnt, or so I was told. During the days and weeks that followed, other friends of Ingeborg arrived in Rome from Vienna, Paris, St Moritz and Milan – we met in the corridors of the San Camillo Hospital. I spent the whole of this period in a somnambulatory state, unable to sleep and unable to work, except for purely mechanical jobs such as drawing bar-lines and copying. All I could do was to wait and hope.

One day there was said to have been a slight improvement. They were preparing to operate and remove burnt tissue to prevent the build-up of toxins that were threatening to prevent her organism from functioning. Franco Serpa organized a blood-donor session among his students. The doctors expressed concern: further surgery would be necessary. A few days later it was announced that they were unable to operate after all, since the patient was too weak. No one had thought it necessary to draw the doctors' attention to the patient's drug dependency, and there are many people alive today who think that it may perhaps have been withdrawal symptoms that precipitated the end. But no one knew what medicines she had been taking or what effect they had.

Grape harvest. October sun. Swarms of wasps buzzing all round the house, so that we had to shut ourselves in. One morning I met Pierre Evrard, a Parisian friend of Inge's, at the clinic. He was standing by the window, looking out into empty space, tears streaming down his cheeks. It was possible to talk to Ingeborg through an intercom and call out to her, and on one occasion the night nurse assured me that she had replied 'yes' in a loud, firm voice. Later, one Sunday evening, the same sympathetic and forbearing nurse let Fausto and me into the isolation ward – we had to wear face masks and protective coats. Suddenly we saw before us a scene of devastation and finally realized the full extent of the disaster. Fausto tried to push me away, but it was too late, I had seen everything and rushed out, screaming loudly, in a state of indescribable despair. She died on Wednesday, 17 October 1973, at six o'clock in the morning. Her next of kin were not in favour of burying her in the Protestant Cemetery in the Via Caio Cestio. There would have been space for her there between Shelley and Keats and it would have been in keeping with her own wishes – after all, she had never really wanted to leave a country that she had described in one of her poems as her 'first-born land'.

I felt utterly weary: death seemed to hang over everything I saw and heard and thought. One Sunday – it may have been 28 October – I tried to write the piano prelude that leads into the epilogue of *Tristan*, but after only a short space of time I had to stop. I went to Venice. Yellowing maple leaves floated on the canal, with a glassy October sky overhead. Not even work and self-discipline helped to silence the voices of fear and guilt that pursued and tormented me – so much so, indeed, that I was on the point of cracking up completely. I ran outside and spent hours walking through the dark, cold streets. I made an appointment to see Michele Risso, who practised as a psychoanalyst in Rome. I was obliged to see him many times in the course of the next few years – or perhaps it would be truer to say that I had the privilege of seeing him. But first I had to go to New York, taking my illness with me. Even here it continued to torment me and was clearly not confined to any one particular place. My head was in a constant turmoil, a feeling that could change at any moment to impotence or violence, so that I lived in fear of myself. On 18 November I conducted my Viola Concerto, *Compases*, at a *conversazione* at the Town Hall. The soloist was Walter Trampler. I also heard Solti conduct Mahler's Sixth but found it hard to stay to the end – this was the piece that Ingeborg and I had listened to only recently in Marino, when it had disturbed her deeply: she said that things are expressed in this music that cannot be said in verse, it was all a question of words. I heard the Concord String Quartet playing Carter and conceived the idea of writing a set of quartets for these four young performers. I then flew to London to meet Edward Bond and my brother Jürgen and to discuss with them the set model for *We Come to the River*. I also spoke to Covent Garden's general administrator, John Tooley, to ask for a year's deferral: I should have been working on the opera for months, instead of finishing off *Tristan*. I then travelled to Berlin to visit Wenzel and to discuss with the intendant of the Berlin Philharmonic, Wolfgang Stresemann, the possibility of my making a comeback as a guest conductor: my fiftieth birthday seemed an opportune moment.

By early December I was back in a cold and grey Marino. Pierre Evrard, Fausto and I went to the *questura* in Rome to institute legal proceedings for murder against person or persons unknown. Our grounds for suspicion were duly minuted. No one can be so terribly injured by a piece of burning material. Time and time again we met mutual friends and asked ourselves why Ingeborg had not telephoned on her return from

Badgastein. Or perhaps she had not gone away at all but had remained in the city all the time. Such an idea was by no means out of the question, given her habit of cultivating her private relationships individually and in strict isolation and her refusal to allow others to meddle in her life. I thought with a shudder of the end of *Malina*:

> Steps, Malina's steps, as before, steps that grew quieter, the quietest of steps. Standing still. No alarm, no sirens. No one comes to help. No ambulance, no police. It is a very old, a very solid wall from which no one can fall, that no one can break down, from which no sound can be heard.
>
> It was murder.

Meanwhile winter had come and the new year had begun. I made various notes and plans for a book – it was neither the first nor the last time I was to do so. It was to have been an analysis of Fascism – I wanted to show the links between the objective aspects of this view of the world (including art) and its impact on the individual (in other words, personal experiences would also be included). It would contain thoughts on the concept of freedom and new aspects of the aesthetics and practice of music. I also planned some draft proposals for a new type of music teaching appropriate to the modern age, but it was not to be a political pamphlet or a list of decrees. My aim was to take Pablo Neruda's idea of a *poesía impura* and apply it to music. And I also thought about my life, which really only existed on paper: real life had been sidelined by an alternative reality in the form of my work as a composer, a reality that was threatening to repress its authentic rival with totalitarian ruthlessness. Real life was being restructured, reinterpreted, rethought and turned into music. I realized that until now my life had been entirely geared to producing works of music, even if appearances generally suggested otherwise: chance occurrences and chaos appeared to predominate. But life as a whole involves tenderness, violent aversions, idiosyncrasies, injuries and a sense of devastation.

As in psychiatry, so too in art a study of the past, including the primordial states of creative consciousness, should be an indivisible part of the working process – it would then be a systematic exploration or rediscovery and activation of the artist's own psychological primordial states. We are used to treating music as a language but should now try to find out more about its peculiarities, to understand the mythic element that it contains, shed light on its mystery and, at the same time, prevent the linguistic element from being further marginalized and dehumanized: instead, we need to reinforce this linguistic aspect, make it accessible and useful and see it as a necessary extension of human awareness and of man's expressive abilities.

On 4 January 1974 I conducted the first performance of *Voices* at the Queen Elizabeth Hall on London's South Bank. The tenor soloist was Paul Sperry from New York, while the contralto songs were sung by Rose Taylor, who was also from the United States. The London Sinfonietta was on excellent form. The players all had to perform on subsidiary instruments (generally percussion) and to mime the theatrical episodes such as 'Vermutung über Hessen', 'The Electric Cop' and 'Prison Song', and the male members of the ensemble additionally formed the excellent a cappella chorus in 'The Worker'. A great success for the singers and the ensemble, it was broadcast live by the BBC and later recorded. Michael Vyner was radiant. There was a party after the performance, and among those present, to my great delight, were Max Davies and Harry Birtwistle. Also the ever-youthful Peter Adam, whom we last saw standing on the platform at the Gare du Nord in Paris with a red rose in his hand before abandoning him to his fate – a fate that mercifully was far from unbearable. Not that it should be inferred from this that we had not seen each other in the meantime. Quite the opposite. Kindness itself, Peter was brought up by Jewish parents in Zehlendorf near Berlin and in 1958 moved to London, later taking British nationality. Whenever I was in London, I generally looked him up at his elegant apartment in Earls Terrace, off Kensington High Street, an apartment in which Victorian England rubbed shoulders with Prussia. He was always immensely patient and forbearing with my difficult and wearisome habits. He knows all my works and has made at least two full-length documentaries about me. As a film and television director, he is responsible for some extremely beautiful and important films, including one on Lotte Lenya, two on Visconti, one on Lillian Hellman and a series, *Architecture at the Crossroad*. More recently, he has devoted most of his time to researching and documenting Nazi art, in the process of which he has made some fascinating and remarkable discoveries.

It is almost half a century since Peter sat at my feet in the Hotel Gît-le-cœur in Paris, reading to me from Genet's prose. Although no longer as slim and lithe as he was then, he remains at heart an innocent eighteen-year-old youth from Berlin, still firmly believing in human virtues. It cannot have been easy for him to have made his mark as an immigrant in a foreign country and especially in an environment teeming with inscrutable powers and influences such as those that obtained – and still obtain – at the BBC. His private life, too, was unhappy, filled, as it was, with tragedy, renunciation and sacrifice. It could well be set to music (primarily in a minor tonality) as a great hymn to human trust and dependability. By a happy coincidence, Peter's twin sister, Renate, arrived in Rome some twenty years ago with a friend of mine, the art historian Matthias Winner and their two sons, Boguslav and Jonas. By no means as fair-haired as her Prussian twin, but as dark as the shadow of a gardenia, she speaks with a strong upper-class Berlin accent and has a permanently witty, knowing expression in her eyes. We occasionally meet to trade our thoughts on the absent Peter and exchange the latest news about him. The older one grows, the more beautiful, important and dependable old friendships invariably become.

Within two weeks of the first performance of *Voices* I was back in Italy, where, a year later than intended and with a sense of great trepidation, I completed a sketch of the opening of *We Come to the River*. But my body feigned tiredness and weakness, a state of affairs undoubtedly due to my fear of the intellectual, emotional and physical effort that lay ahead. After a few uneventful days I had again taken myself in hand and within the space of a single morning I established the whole basis for the work and decided on the style in which it would be written. I felt that I was safely berthed, felt patient and attentive, as I needed to be, with none of the earlier tedium and tension. Many recent experiences, including those gleaned in the field of composition, were to find expression in the new piece. Everything that I had tried out in my Sixth Symphony, in *El Cimarrón*, the Second Violin Concerto and *Natascha Ungeheuer*, to say nothing of *La Cubana*, was now to have a chance to unfold within a single arching paragraph of polyphonic writing that was bound up with the action in an extraordinary way and that actively engaged with that action. Stage and orchestra(s) were to merge to form a single entity of a kind never previously known. The instrumentalists would play in their normal uniforms – white tie and tails – in the middle of the battlefield, on the place of execution, at the Emperor's picnic, during the execution and at the official ceremony. I wanted my music to be as human and as real as possible. The omniscient organ plays at a drumhead court martial. At the end of Part One, the death of the Old Woman in the river's eddying currents, her grandchild in her arms, is depicted by means of a sort of centrifugal music that passes from orchestra to orchestra, encircling the stage like a whirlwind and overlapping canonically. Improvisation, too, is used for both functional and dramaturgical ends, notably in the scene in the madhouse in Part Two and in the great solo scene for the Drummer.

I completed the opening scene at the end of January 1974. Sleep came easily now, and there began a period of immense productivity, when I no longer knew whether I was asleep or dreaming. Meanwhile I continued to see Michele Risso on a regular basis: it was marvellous slowly to find a way back and escape from the labyrinth of emotions by taking hold of Ariadne's thread of memory and feeling it pass through my fingers. Apart from Yoichi's weekend visits, I allowed myself no distractions so that my powers of concentration would not be impaired. I suffered from stomach cramps at memories of my father, memories that rose unceasingly to the surface from oblivion's vast black pool.

Outside could be heard the sound of rifles – huntsmen shooting songbirds. It was cold and foggy again. I consumed a disturbing amount of tablets and pills – sedatives, sleeping pills, painkillers and blood-pressure tablets – but in spite of that I felt well. Edward sent a new and better version of Part Two that reflected virtually all the suggestions that I had made in Vienna when we had last met to discuss the project. I was delighted to discover that I had learnt to express my opinions openly and steadfastly. Now there was only music and me. Michele thought that my music was probably the only thing at which I regarded myself as in any way competent and in which I found myself bearable.

Winter melancholy in Venice. Work on Scene Three, with its occasional verses for the bourgeois girl, Rachel (unrelated to the protagonist of *La Cubana*), and on a German version of all that I have composed so far. Write something about the Chilean group Inti Illimani. And a song about Chile for Dieter Süverkrüp that he will sing in Düsseldorf at a solidarity concert. Mid-March: Jean-Pierre Ponnelle's staging of *Boulevard Solitude* in Munich, my disappointment at a production designed to curry favour with the Establishment – nothing remains of the lyrical immorality, rebelliousness and artifice that is second nature to this piece and that we felt and shared when we first worked on it together. Then to London to work on the production of *The Bassarids* with the O'Briens and to rehearse *Voices*. Tour Italy with this last-named piece: Milan, Turin, Naples. Early April back in Marino: a rain-sodden Easter. Take out mortgage with Banca Agricola in Marino to pay off debts. Read *Brothers Karamazov* for the first time. Lay off wine for several weeks. On 8 May conduct German première of *Voices* at the Kleines Haus in Wiesbaden (where I had once worked), this time in the absence of the borough treasurer, Heinrich Roos, but in the presence of a largely young, attentive and enthusiastic audience. Stay on for a few days in Germany and make formal representations to my publisher in the hope of obtaining greater left-wing coverage. Things not looking too bad: new editors on various journals express an interest in my ideas and concepts. Back to Italy, Venice, Marino and work. First steps towards joining Italian Communist Party.

Scene Four evolves, the *Grundgestalt* of a rhythm that can later be used isorhythmically. The general administrator of the Württemberg Staatstheater, Hans Peter Doll, comes to inform me that his theatre – in other words, Doll himself – intends to stage a whole series of my works over the coming years. It takes a while for the news to sink in, but when it does I am pleased, immensely pleased. It is a productive time, with a general feeling of energy and euphoria, as though life has just begun. Lines, *Hauptstimmen*, variations, serial technique. I have already written three scenes, 'Fatigue', 'Execution' and 'Battlefield', that take place simultaneously, and have orchestrated the military march that is to be played on stage by a real army band at the start of Scene Four.

Immersed in work on *River*, between six and ten hours a day, my mood changing as the piece itself changes, but in fine physical shape. Early July with Glen Tetley to Paris to tape my *Tristan* music at the Opéra. It is the first time that I have heard the music on instruments. The pianist is Georges Pludermacher, the conductor Marius Constant. Satisfaction at the new quality of these sounds. I feel I am on the right path, that I am penetrating the soul of music and entering a world of ghosts. Fly to London for three days of meetings with the O'Briens and also with my musical assistant, Mark Elder, and my production assistant, Christopher de Souza, to discuss preparations for *The Bassarids*. Then back to Marino. The 'actions' of *We Come to the River* – both on stage and in the music – are tried out with the help of our model, we time each scene, and the various events that take place simultaneously on stage are all carefully and systematically weighed up, one against the other.

One Sunday we drive out to Cuma, where there is not a breath of wind and the only sound – as always – is the booming of the sea far beneath us. I long to settle here and write a string quartet or the like. With my old-fashioned German feel for such things, I sense the religious aura of these Greek ruins (razed to the ground by the Christians) and am deeply moved by the greyness of the volcanic ash and by the laurel green of these last, silent witnesses. I show Yoichi the Greek sculptures in the National Museum at Naples, emblems of the concept of beauty espoused by European culture, and in the evening we arrive at Ravello, high above the sheer Amalfi cliffs. I am tense and terrified of having an accident while driving. I find it impossible to pull myself together and spend a restless night, tossing and turning in bed and wondering whether to telephone Fausto and ask him to come and drive us home. When I finally get to sleep, I suffer drug-induced hallucinations until I finally discover why: I am afraid of the psychological strain involved in setting to music the death of the Young Woman in *We Come to the River* and, even more, the subsequent murder of the Old Woman and her grandchild. Half asleep, I hear the voice of my mother, Grete, and feel myself shaking all over.

On 27 August I flew back to London for the stage and orchestral rehearsals of *The Bassarids*. The production was rehearsed in a wonderful old warehouse, Camperdown House, in the East End, at the north-western end of Commercial Road. The building was situated in the middle of a busy roundabout, and through its huge windows we could see a cemetery and tiny church on rising ground on the other side of the road. Here spindly, wraithlike meths drinkers had established a colony and from time to time could be seen cavorting among the tombstones, poor sinners worshipping a vengeful Dionysus. I spent whole days and weeks at Camperdown House, rehearsing with my singers, dancers and chorus, interrupted only by sessions with the orchestra and by interviews (for the *Observer* colour supplement, the BBC, *The Times* and, eventually, all the other London papers). On 2 October, I braved the pouring rain to attend Auden's memorial service in Westminster Abbey at which lilac-clad choirboys sang a Haydn Mass in Latin in memory of the late poet. The prayers and sermon were all about sin and sinners, about vice and forgiveness, and were followed by a service in Poets' Corner, during which a stone was laid in Auden's memory. I also saw Chester Kallman, but only in the distance, surrounded by a group of Auden's relatives. I had to get straight back to the rehearsal studio.

Fausto and I had rented a small flat in Grosvenor Street, in Mayfair, but I could enjoy its amenities only at night and on the few free days allowed me by my dual responsibilities as director and conductor. But English objectivity and correctness, together with the professionalism of my fellow artists and technicians, meant that, however thin and shrunken I may have looked, I was still able to feel triumphant when I appeared on the stage of the sold-out English National Opera at the end of the first night of *The Bassarids* on 10 October 1974 and, happy and even proud, thanked not only the managing director, Lord Harewood, but also my singers: Katherine Pring (Agave), Josephine Barstow (Autonoe), Gregory Dempsey

(Dionysus, the stranger) and Norman Welsby (Pentheus). After the show, Lord Harewood gave us all a magnificent supper and made a delightful speech.

Ten days later the London Symphony Orchestra under Colin Davis gave the first performance of *Tristan* at the Royal Festival Hall. The pianist was Homero Francesch. Davis did not like the piece and had not even felt the need to discuss it with me, but had none the less discovered or at least decided that it was an example of its composer's 'fantastic sense of humour'. This was the only thing he had to tell me, apart from the fact that he had refused to use a stopwatch in those sections of the score involving electronic effects, a use essential to ensure that the orchestra is in sync with the tape. Predictably, the two elements fell apart at the evening's performance, functioning – meaninglessly – as two completely separate elements. We were not able to try out the electronic equipment until the morning of the concert, and it had to be dismantled immediately after the wholly inadequate final rehearsal, since the Communist Party of Great Britain had hired the hall for an afternoon function. As a result, we were unable to experiment with the balance or to undertake any repairs (at the evening's performance a number of the loudspeakers began to emit an unpleasant, high-pitched squeal, driving several members of the audience to take refuge in headlong flight). *Tristan*, then, was a failure and, as such, a great disappointment not only for me but also for the painfully embarrassed Peter Zinovieff. Yet the piece's fortunes were not fatally impaired and, its initial failure notwithstanding, it eventually found a niche for itself on London's musical scene.

I spent a weekend with Edward and Elisabeth Bond at their house at Great Wilbraham near Cambridge, where we discussed the title of our opera and plans for further collaborations.

On the evening of the fourth performance of *The Bassarids*, on 31 October 1974, I had already taken my place in the orchestra pit and was waiting for my cue to start – we were already several minutes late – when I was asked to go up on stage and meet a three-man strike committee. I was told that the stage technicians were stopping work in support of the company's workshops, whose demands for higher overtime rates had not been met – or at least not yet been met. I asked for a cigarette and consulted those responsible for the smooth running of the show to find out whether we should try to perform the piece without technical help; in other words, without stage lighting and without any scene changes. Meanwhile, on the other side of the curtain, we could hear the audience growing audibly restless. We decided to go ahead and got as far as the Intermezzo, which involved the first change of scene: the sets were duly lowered, but there was no one there able or willing to support them and fix them to the stage floor, with the result that the main curtain now had to be lowered and the lights came up in the auditorium. There were renewed shouts of protest, louder and more vocal than before, while the theatre slowly emptied. I did not return home but went with the singers and some of my fellow artists to a party that had been planned some time previously. Their cheerfulness helped for a time to overcome the sense of shock and disappointment that we all felt, and it was only during the days that followed that we were able to judge the full extent of the misfortune that we had suffered.

The strike was settled, and the remaining performances were conducted by the excellent Mark Elder, so that I was finally able to follow my production from the darkened auditorium. I then moved on to Paris, where Glen Tetley's version of *Tristan* was unveiled at the Palais Garnier on 13 November. The title roles were danced by Rudolf Nureyev (who did not care for Tetley's choreography) and Carolyn Carlson. By 24 November I was back in Marino, where I tried to resume work on Scene Seven of *We Come to the River* and immersed myself in some of my earlier scores, including the Three Symphonic Studies (in a revised version), *Lieder von einer Insel*, *Fünf neapolitanische Lieder*, a handful of juvenilia such as the Concertino for piano and winds, the early Villon madrigals and the concert aria *Der Vorwurf* (later discarded), all of which I rehearsed for the BBC in mid-December and performed at two concerts in the corporation's Maida Vale studios for a circle of friends that had in the meantime grown considerably. I spent the next three weeks, including Christmas and the New Year, skiing with friends at St Moritz but within a few days of arriving had cracked two of my ribs, with the result that I used the time, instead, to work on a lecture, 'The Artist as Bourgeois Hero', with which I was to introduce the forthcoming staging of *Elegy for Young Lovers* in Stuttgart (in my old Scottish Opera production). In turn, this staging was to inaugurate the Staatstheater's cycle of my works. I also received a visit from Volker Schlöndorff, who wanted me to write the music for his film version of *Katharina Blum*.

By early January 1975 I was back in Marino, where I laid off alcohol completely and got on with Scene Seven. By the 15th I was on the road again, this time to Stuttgart, where I delivered my lecture prior to Scottish Opera's visiting production of *Elegy* and met the set designer Axel

Manthey with a view to collaborating with him at a later date. Then back home again: bright light, deep blue, gold. A cloistered existence, lenten diet, *senza vino*. Still working on Scene Seven, slow progress, a difficult scene, and I harbour the greatest ambitions for the piece. Polyphony becomes visible, a theatrical happening, music incarnate: the expressive abilities of the instrumentalists and singers are challenged in an unusual, novel way, life and art interact and interpenetrate with each other. I etch and paint my own Goyaesque disasters of war in strict counterpoint and dream only of compositional matters. In my dreams I hear a new wind quintet and also details of a new piece for the London Symphony Orchestra, to which I give the title *Pompes funèbres* (I had just read Genet's novel). I visit Vespignani in Bracciano and he shows me part of a cycle of paintings on Fascism on which he is currently working – garish, ironic, cold-bloodedly accusatory images. I see parallels – or attempt to see parallels – with my own way of dealing in my music with the semiotic language of the bourgeois world. The stylistic devices of our time are wrenched out of that time and directed against it, the tables are turned in such a way that the work itself becomes a weapon as though in consequence of some show of spiritual strength.

In his preface to Paul Morand's *Tendres stocks*, Proust has something curious to say under the heading 'Remarks on Style': 'Style must be renewed by each new author since it is based not on observance of some classical model but on the moment at which the writer identifies with his theme.'

During the night of 9/10 February I noted down an idea for the beginning of a guitar sonata to be called *Royal Winter Music* – a reference to Gloucester's 'winter of discontent'. Romeo and Juliet would also be involved, as would Oberon, Ophelia, Ariel and Touchstone. In mid-February I was delighted to receive a visit from Hans Magnus Enzensberger, who stayed for several days, during which time we talked endlessly about art and its relationship to history. What matters is not to have recourse to the past but to reach inside oneself and listen to one's own inner voice. It is in one's own psyche, one's own history, I told the great thinker, that the preconditions for our archetypal forms of consciousness are all to be found. They are our private history, but in their infinite variety they become identical with the history of our civilization. Magnus helped me with my essays on *Natascha Ungeheuer* and *Tristan* and even claimed to like them.

On Easter Monday I flew to Frankfurt for rehearsals for a production of

Die Bassariden at the Städtische Bühnen. The production – identical to the one seen in London – opened on 11 May under the musical direction of Klauspeter Seibel. By the 14th I was happy to be back in Marino, although my most pressing concern was now the film score for Volker Schlöndorff and *Katharina Blum*. With the help of Henning Brauel, I managed to complete this by 21 May and eight days later recorded the entire score in Munich. Schlöndorff was pleased. On 28 May, at the Gärtneroper, I saw a failed attempt to stage *La Cubana* and found it hard to conceal my disappointment. By contrast, the following evening brought an entertaining party at Marianne Koch's house on Lake Starnberg, where Fausto, Yoichi and I were joined by her son, Gregor Freund, and also by Peter Hamm, Schlöndorff and Margarethe von Trotta. Even today I can still hear in my mind's ear the popping of the white-wine corks and the noise of the rain pouring down outside. On 4 June I travelled to Florence for the Italian *prima* of *Das Floß der 'Medusa'* at the Maggio Musicale. The singers, chorus and orchestra from the Nuremberg Städtische Oper under Hans Gierster all acquitted themselves admirably.

On 7 June I met a young philosopher from Gütersloh, Jens Brockmeier, and was immediately struck by his kindness, an impression that the passing years have done nothing to alter. Our meeting took place in Rome, where, as good fortune would have it, he was planning to stay for some time, so that we were able to see each other as often as we wanted – as, indeed, we did, comparing and exchanging ideas with avaricious enthusiasm. I opened his eyes and ears to the world of Monteverdi, while he, for his part, knew all that there was to know about the Tuscan city republics of the Renaissance, to say nothing of the Enlightenment and 'Karlemann', as so many comrades from West Berlin called the great German economist and class enemy, Karl Marx. I had spent the last two years tinkering away, fairly helplessly, at an edition of my older and newer writings, when it suddenly occurred to me to ask him to take over the task, to look through the existing material and to edit what seemed to him usable. He agreed, with the result that at a stroke I was freed from a time-consuming and laborious chore. Fausto, Titina, Jens and I then travelled to Bologna for the official opening of a large exhibition devoted to Vespignani's work at the National Gallery of Modern Art. On our way there we made a detour to visit a small mountain town in southern Tuscany by the name of Montepulciano, where I had been invited to preside over a festival planned for later that year, an invitation that I had in fact already turned down.

It was around midday when we arrived. The sun was beating down implacably on a large and treeless piazza, dust was swirling everywhere and the wind was playing absent-mindedly with a handful of unpaid bills, as an old peasant woman, dressed only in black, scurried away round the corner: high noon in Montepulciano. We clambered out of the car, dragged ourselves up the steep alleyways, often threatening to lose our foothold, and gazed in awe at the astonishing architecture of the town's Renaissance *palazzi*, which stood there as though uninhabited. We stopped for a snack and, for the first time in my life, I drank a *vino nobile*, a profoundly impressive experience. We then continued on our journey, and I thought no more of this silent mountain fastness surmounted – remarkably yet gratifyingly – by a red flag, the same red flag that continues to this day to flutter from town-hall spires in practically every remote mountain town and village in Tuscany and Umbria. At the time in question, 1975, the recent municipal elections had brought the Italian Communist Party to power with an overwhelming majority. On 17 May, Fausto and I had joined a quarter of a million other people in the Piazza San Giovanni in Rome for a great celebration at which Enrico Berlinguer spoke and Severino Gazzelloni played Bach on his flute. For me, it was like a second coming, the birth of modern Italy, the holy land of *resistenza* and *neorealismo*, the land of the anti-Fascist intelligentsia, the land of Gramsci, of sound common sense, of intellectual openness and cultural wisdom. On the morning after the launch of the Vespignani exhibition in Bologna, we drove to Fausto's part of the country. Here, too, were red flags on all the old towers, just as there were in Sant'Arcangelo di Romagna, the attractive position and architecture of which were currently being captured by means of tempera and canvas by a man looking like an English landscape painter. I peered over his shoulder and noted with some bemusement that he had not included the red flag.

My work was slowly progressing. Among our visitors were my brother Jürgen and David Pountney, who was to be my production assistant on next year's première of *We Come to the River*. Another interruption was a production of *El Cimarrón* that I had undertaken to give with British performers, in English, at the Proms at the Round House in Camden Town. After the show I went for a meal with Edward Bond in Hampstead and did what I could to persuade him to write a ballet for me and the Stuttgart dance company. A young and amusing Costa Rican by the name of Gastón Fournier Facio came to the rehearsals of *El Cimarrón*, bringing with him a group of equally shrewd and inquisitive fellow Costa Ricans, all the same age as he and all students at Sussex University. It was to be the start of a great friendship, about which I shall have rather more to say in due course.

On 15 August I began Scene Ten of *We Come to the River*, the Emperor's Buddha narration. It starts with a fanned-out variant of the chords associated with the Emperor's toast in Scene Three. The girls' singing is simple and folklike in a vaguely Schubertian way, but accompanied by iridescent chords. The entire scene is meant to have its own distinctive harmonic language, a language at odds with the musical mood of the rest of the work. It blossoms with Parsifalian luxuriance, revelling in orientalisms, not least on the level of timbre, when we hear the sounds of the *angklung*, a kind of Burmese bamboo organ, the pentatonically tuned tubes of which produce driplike, tapping sounds. I created the role of the Drummer specially for the piece (chiefly in order to be able to use the spectacular Stomu Yamash'ta in my production): like a jester or joker he keeps having to play new roles and instruments and is used again here, this time dressed as a musician from the imperial Indian court. For me, the story about the Buddha is like a deadly poisonous plant, a seductively destructive *fleur du mal.*

The pile of pieces that make up a mosaic is slowly reduced as the mosaic itself ineluctably falls into place. An unfinished work means tormenting uncertainty and a latent psychological and physical worry that the artist will never complete it.

I set to work on the terrible eleventh scene in which the General is straitjacketed and murdered. Entirely within the convention of the piece I had recourse to extreme instrumental effects, conjuring up key *Gestalten* such as chord combinations, themes and timbres from Part One and treating them like ghosts, thereby creating conceptual links between the musical textures and the developing drama. The two murderers are coloratura tenors (*buffi*). To a brass accompaniment, they enter via Stage III, which is set upstage of the other two, and move downstage at seven-second intervals. The brass writing continues as the two killers reach Stage II to the sound of string glissandos, which likewise continue after they have reached Stage I, at which point we hear the sounds of a mouth organ that appear to come from a western, yet I wrote this passage feeling chilled to the marrow.

Towards the end of August I spent two days in Montepulciano, meeting the mayor, town councillors and some of the local townspeople with an interest in the arts, trying to find out more about existing structures, especially the school system, and about what was lacking and what was needed in the population's cultural life. The younger members of the town council were all very keen that the population should play a creative and active role in the festival that they had in mind. This was the most important point of all and one that would later constitute the principal difference between this particular institution and other music and theatre festivals.

I continued to make progress on my opera and by early September Scene Eleven was finished in full score. When the terrible General is blinded by the two *bravi* in the most terrible manner imaginable, the same organ plays the same music as that which had been heard in Part One when the General had sentenced the Deserter to death. I created new combinations of notes based on the principal intervals associated with his victims – the Second Soldier, the Deserter and the women. This same material also provided a theme for the final chorus and new harmonies for what I call a 'Hymn to (Ernst Bloch's) Hope'. But the music is still oppressive, still nightmare-like: the sun cannot rise and the music cannot begin to blossom until the madmen remove the General and usher in a new age. I completed the sketches on 15 September and immediately felt very tired. A state of nervous confusion followed, in which figures from the past rose up, unbidden. They were not, however, ghosts but willing spirits ready to help in times of defeat and defencelessness. I suffered from chest pains. In the mirror a stranger stared back at me, bloated and ugly, with tiny, staring eyes and mottled cheeks.

I completed the full score at four o'clock in the morning on 19 September. Fausto was present, having sat up, waiting to see me place the last double bar-line and date at the end of the final page. At midday I flew to Amsterdam and from there went straight to Ochtrup on the Dutch–German border, where my mother was lying in hospital, already visibly marked by her illness. She told me about the terrible ordeals that she had already had to go through. The diagnosis was incorrect, she thought, with the result that the treatment was not only wrong but making things worse. The next morning, my brother Jochen and the doctor in charge of the case took me to one side and told me that it had become clear three days ago that our mother's cancer was inoperable but that she herself was either unaware of the fact or else she refused to acknowledge it. I saw her again the next day and made sure that she was not unduly taxed by talking or by asking questions and generally getting worked up as she had done throughout the whole of her life on account of her children. I told her that I had finished the opera, explained how I had felt when writing it – needless to say, I said that I had felt good – and told her that I was now going to spend a couple of weeks on the Cretan coast, trying to sort myself out and to relax and recover. I said that I would visit her again soon. Shortly after that, she was allowed home, a move that somehow encouraged her to think that she was fully recovered.

Yoichi came with me to Crete. We stayed very close to the beach and could go swimming at any time. I slept for hours on end, day and night, a deep sleep unvisited by dreams. I remember the scent of the pine trees, the mountain villages and sweet wine. On a number of occasions I burst into tears, weeping loudly and uncontrollably and worrying that my schizophrenia was becoming worse. Each day I would telephone my mother, who was now back at home in Salzuflen. From time to time I thought vaguely of the string quartets that I was planning to write: one of them would be a single-movement work, another would be traditional in form, a third built up on the note row of the martyrs in *We Come to the River*.

The newspapers reported that five revolutionaries had been shot in Madrid. They were said to have sung as they faced the firing squad. We travelled around the Peloponnesus and I showed Yoichi Delphi, Mycenae and Olympia. By 5 October we were back in Marino, where Fausto had arranged a kind of harvest festival to mark the completion of both the grape harvest and the opera. Friends came and helped us to celebrate. I then returned to Salzuflen to see my mother and to calm and reassure her. I conducted a concert in Zurich in a state of somnambulatory depression, a feeling that affected everyone around me.

Later that month there was the first – week-long – meeting of a composers' collective whose members – Fabio Vacchi, Luca Lombardi, Wilhelm Zobel, Thomas Jahn, Nils Hoffmann, Richard Blackford, Peter Maxwell Davies, Wolfgang Florey and I – were interested in writing an anti-smog opera. We met in Montepulciano and worked on improving the libretto, for which we still had no name, although we had already abandoned the title of the first draft, *Michel und Rosi*. Not until many years later was it called *Der heiße Ofen* and staged at the Staatstheater in Kassel. We wrote the basic material and divided it among us. All the ideas made available in this way could be used, with the exception of one's own, which could be worked up only by the other participants. Max Davies proved a mine of good ideas. We managed to do most of the work there and then. Although this week in Montepulciano was overshadowed by my mother's final illness, it was also a chance to get to know other members of the local community, including a formal meeting in the town hall with around fifty representatives of various cultural organizations and spokesmen and -women of the individual districts that make up the town and that have had their own distinctive names from time immemorial: Cagnano, Collazzi, Gracciano, Le Coste, Poggiolo, San Donato, Talosa and Voltaia. These were not easy people to deal with, but nor were they wholly unresponsive to the outsider and his plans, plans which had in the meantime received the full approval of the council and the support of the major, Francesco Colajanni. Colajanni even came with me when I went to the local primary and secondary schools to talk about music. He thought that I should move and come and live and teach among the Poliziani. My impressions were mixed. The people here speak a harsh-sounding language, in part petty bourgeois, in part uncouth. I was hesitant to go any further down this particular *strada vicinale* – perhaps I already suspected the scale of the difficulties that lay ahead. To which of my Italian colleagues could I pass on the responsibility? At the same time, however, I was motivated by the idea that as an artist I should make myself socially useful and, indeed, devise some stratagem to keep the Grim Reaper at bay.

I began work on my Third String Quartet, my first since 1951. It was meant to be autumnal music and to express a sense of growing old, feelings of suffering – self-inflicted suffering – as well as love and death, but it was also to be calm and tolerant and resigned. A golden red piece with an ice-cold sky behind it, beneath falling leaves. Unfortunately, I was overcome by feelings of weakness, feverishness and defeatism and unable to go on with the piece. I tried studying the full score of Mahler's Second Symphony. The olive harvest began. By November I was feeling better and was able to work on the Third Quartet. I then flew to Stuttgart for performances of Mahler's Second with the Stuttgart Opera Orchestra in the city's Liederhalle on 16 and 17 November.

Resurrection. Each of my evenings in Stuttgart was given over to working sessions, including one at which the extraordinary Axel Manthey showed me his highly original set model for *Boulevard Solitude*, which he proceeded to explain to me in detail. Towards the end of the month I conducted the Rome Radio Orchestra in performances of my Doppio Concerto and *Heliogabalus imperator* – the culmination of a week of agonizing rehearsals with a collection of indifferent, not to say, refractory musicians with not a glimmer of interest in what they were doing. I thought fondly of the great civilized orchestras of Germany, Great Britain and the United States and had to take a tranquillizer before and after each rehearsal. I grew annoyed with myself at the waste of time and made up my mind never again to conduct this orchestra, which, in the event, was later disbanded.

In late November and early December I visited my mother in Salzuflen, and one Sunday lunch-time all six of us children took her to an expensive restaurant. She looked particularly beautiful and dignified, wore an elegant dress and had had her grey hair dyed. Her hands trembled a little. My brothers and sisters all pretended to be cheerful and happy, but it was clear from looking at them that they found it difficult to suppress the desire to burst into tears. On my return to Marino, I resumed work on my Third Quartet. For a time it was simply a succession of ideas, each one inspired by its predecessor. I felt no need for a recapitulation or anything similar. Perhaps, I thought briefly, I could regard the whole single-movement piece as an example of the sort of discourse that requires no reference to the past and never needs to repeat itself. But within a week all that I had written so far had turned out to be an exposition and, as such, the starting point for all manner of developments and interrelationships. Only the autumnal mood was to continue uninterrupted throughout the whole of the movement's four-part writing. Since Julian Bream was planning to visit me in mid-December, I also sketched out three sections of his sonata, 'Oberon', 'Ophelia' and 'Romeo and Juliet'. But before that, there was the first important meeting for everyone involved in the first Cantiere at Montepulciano.

After a weekend in rain-sodden Venice, I flew back to Rome. Among the crowd, wearing a worker's cap, was Luigi Nono – we ignored one another. Julian Bream arrived at Marino and rehearsed the first number of my *Royal Winter Music*. I told him that I was not going to ask for a fee but that, in return, he must agree to give a course in guitar playing – for Italians only and without remuneration – at the first Cantiere Internazionale d'Arte, as the festival at Montepulciano was to be called: a construction site for the arts, a shipyard and a workshop. The fees paid by the participants on the course were all to go to the commune's department of culture. Julian also had to give a solo recital, which he did indeed do on 1 August 1976 in the packed Tempio de San Biagio, in the presence of Sir William and Lady Walton, who were officially greeted by the cultural bolshevist of a mayor and regaled by a performance of Walton's own *Bagatelles*, a piece for solo guitar dedicated to the performer. Julian had agreed to my conditions, albeit with a bad grace, so eager was he to have my *Royal Winter Music*. Our aim of making an additional and substantial contribution to the guitar repertory played a part in his decision. Julian said: 'What the Hammerklavier Sonata is to pianists and the keyboard repertory, the *Royal Winter Music* must be to the guitar.' He wanted to explore the innermost essence of the instrument with me and see it become the most colourful and fascinating of our time. No doubt he also remembered his time as a student at the Royal Academy of Music, when it had been forbidden to enter the venerable building with a guitar under one's arm. In Marino we worked hard together. Julian is a wonderful instrumentalist, he sings and conjures up hundreds of heart-rending sounds from his old Italian guitar. He speaks with a Cockney accent, which I have always found hugely amusing. Unfortunately, he was unable to come with me to Montepulciano the next day, as agreed, and to give a free concert for the town's young people at the Istituto di Musica, although the fault was not his, but Alitalia's. He was replaced by a Japanese flautist, Tone Takahashi, playing Bach, Rossini and Berio. Meanwhile, I myself addressed a large and young audience about music and its social significance. The town hall informed me that all my proposals had been accepted – it would have surprised me had it been otherwise. Marino and Montepulciano are some two hundred kilometres apart, a distance that I would now be covering at frequent intervals, in all weathers, including perhaps even brilliant sunshine. My mother was now staying with my sister, Margitta, and her husband, Gabriel Saour, and their two well-behaved and delightful children, Markus and Yussuf. We spoke to each other every day by telephone. My sister kept reassuring me. I became more and more immersed in my quartet and its permanent four-part writing, fully resolved not to introduce any radical changes in terms of pitch or tempo. Lots of *piano* and legato, a meditative state had to be achieved, a circling of planets whose steady motion was somehow maintained, or perhaps it was only my intuition. Yet there were times when I thought that I should abandon my plans to compose quartets and not write another note for the whole of the next twelve months.

My sister Margitta telephoned to say that Mother was in a bad way, but that I was not to come, since the sudden and unexpected visit would only alarm her. The doctor suggested that I should go for New Year's Eve – my father's birthday – and so my mother was told that this was the reason for my visit. I booked my flight. Again I tried to express my fears and grief in the four obbligato voices of my string quartet. I also drafted a sketch for 'Ariel'. And I drove to Florence and Montepulciano for meetings with directors and conductors. I had just returned when Margitta rang: Mother had taken a turn for the worse. It was only to be expected, of course, an inevitability that I could have foreseen long ago, and yet the news still affected me deeply. The next morning I flew to Hanover, where I was collected by my brother-in-law, Gabriel. Snow was already falling heavily as we climbed out of the car in Salzuflen late that afternoon and my brothers and sisters came slowly out of the house, one by one. I knew at once what had happened: Mother had died an hour earlier, the doctor was still there. He wrote out the papers, offered his condolences and left. He did not say 'Happy New Year', although it was already 1976. It all happened so long ago, and yet the sight of my poor, dead mother is etched in my memory for ever. It caused the same unrestrained grief as I had felt on Ingeborg's death only a little over a year previously – or feelings virtually identical to those that I had felt on that occasion. It is an archetypal feeling of loss and irretrievability, mixed with remorse and regret, that opens up in the individual's consciousness like a vast, gaping wound, a volcanic crater, like the end of the world. My brothers and sisters and I sat there weeping uncontrollably, for hours on end. For us all, it was the end of the most important human relationship in our lives. I stayed with them for a few days, but then had to go to Bonn to take the rehearsals for a concert that I was conducting there on 9 January 1976. Before the concert itself I returned to Salzuflen for the funeral at the Senne Cemetery (of this, too, I have unhappy memories), then went back to Bonn, taking my two half-Arab nephews with me in order not to feel completely abandoned. And so, together with their parents, they heard me conduct *Heliogabalus imperator*, Mozart's 'Coronation' Concerto played by Homero Francesch, and the ballet music from *Idomeneo*. I then drove to Stuttgart and began the blocking rehearsals for *Boulevard Solitude*. I had also brought a little work with me and spent each evening working on an adaptation of Paisiello's *Don Chisciotte* for Montepulciano, a task that had recently fallen to me when the Florentine artists originally entrusted with it withdrew from the undertaking. Henning Brauel realized the score both for a small ensemble similar in size to the forces used in *Pierrot lunaire* and also for wind band. I had additionally brought with me my unfinished Third String Quartet and sketches for the *Royal Winter Music*. Fausto and I stayed at a frightful hotel outside the town. The hideous furniture and the view of an endless expanse of Württemberg fields covered only in snowdrifts, puddles of water and a handful of crows did nothing to raise our spirits.

It was a difficult time, in spite of the interesting work in the theatre. Axel Manthey's sets left their mark upon the production. The singers were all excellent, Manon was played by the famous Sylvia Geszty, Armand by

Rüdiger Wohlers, Lescaut by Wolfgang Schöne. The *corps de ballet* included a bright, thin and pallid youth by the name of Billy Forsythe. Egon Madsen was in charge of the choreography, which was economical and discreet. I had asked for Dennis Russell Davies to take control of the musical side of things, and he duly arrived from St Paul, Minnesota, making a deep impression on all involved in the production. It was his first engagement in a German opera house. Rudi Dutschke also looked in and we spent a whole day together, including lunch at the local Mövenpick Restaurant, where people stared at us throughout the whole meal. Things were going well for him. Sinopoli, too, called in on me and told me about the way in which history was being falsified in Darmstadt, by which he meant the new – or by then not really so very new – view of Webern as the starting point of a cold and inexpressive serialism (a serialism which in 1976 none the less still implied the only way to the light for certain individual composers). The production of *Boulevard Solitude* opened on 12 February, a staging that I thought was wholly successful and practically flawless and which was right royally applauded. The proofs of *Music and Politics* arrived. A young, anorexic and macrobiotic composer by the name of Francis Pinto had joined me in the meantime, having telephoned me from Los Angeles some months previously to ask whether he could study with me. I had refused to commit myself but turned up for a rehearsal one day at the theatre in Stuttgart to find him sitting on a box of props, with the result that since then I had been teaching him in odd moments between rehearsals and during my own working hours. I got him to act as my assistant, to make copies, write out short scores and the like. He followed me back to Italy, where he found a small house in Castel Gandolfo overlooking the lake and prepared his solitary meals there, while busying himself with his studies in counterpoint.

12

If you force the tone, the fifths will go.
German proverb

I spent most of March 1976 in South Australia as a guest of the Adelaide Festival, conducting concerts of works by Mozart and myself and rehearsing a production of *El Cimarrón* with a group of young Australian artists. The protagonist was Lyndon Terracini, who was to appear in Montepulciano a few months later as Sancho Panza in *Don Chisciotte*.

I have few recollections of Australia, although I do remember working on the sketches of my string quartets on what seemed like an endless flight and being asked by graceless reporters on my arrival whether I had come to bring revolution to the colony and which dissident groups I intended to meet. On a more pleasant note, I recall the hospitality of the premier of South Australia, Don Dunstan. I also visited the writer Geoffrey Dutton on his farm, met several Australian colleagues and on a couple of occasions threw myself – unenthusiastically and in the company of my Australian manager, James Murdoch – into the cold Great Australian Bight. But I have the impression that I spent most of my time in my hotel room, suffering from sleeping disorders and homesickness, which suggests that I did not much care for the country. Whenever I looked out of the window, I saw a park in which a handful of grey-faced Aborigines were working, looking like shades from Hades or like ghosts from a play by Bond, spindly and transparent, as though they might at any moment become invisible and vanish into thin air. The whites – originally mainly criminals who were deported to Australia from 1788 onwards in order to serve out their sentences and at the same time win new territories for the Crown – had for centuries nothing better to do than exterminate the indigenous population. At that time they were all still simple-minded Puritan butchers and Christian louts, although all this has naturally changed since then.

Not even the colours and light of Australia struck me as especially attractive: there was something slightly false and unnatural about them, they were garish and badly matched. I worked on my Third Quartet and thought about my mother, to whom I dedicated the piece as though she might still have been alive to hear it. Every day I telephoned either Montepulciano or Marino and in that way discovered that Luchino Visconti had died in Rome on 17 March. He had suffered a stroke some two years earlier and, semi-paralyzed and white-haired, had directed his last film, *The Innocent*, from a wheelchair, and it seems that he no longer had the strength to fight off a flu-like viral infection. There was no one in Adelaide to whom I could talk about him and his death, so I had to keep my feelings to myself. At all events, there can have been no one down under who had known such an exceptional person as Luchino or who had even seen such a man.

I stared at the whitewashed ceiling of my hotel room and projected on to it images from Luca's films – the nondescript yet mysterious villa in Essen, where the young industrialist and future millionaire, Helmut Berger, guards his unspeakable sexual secrets; the storm-troopers' armoured scout cars which, to the sound of a deep-toned pedal point, approach in the grey light of dawn; the yellow uniforms, red armbands and flags with a white centre for the swastika; Alida Valli and Farley Granger in the granary on the Serpieri estates (a study in base instincts, cowardice, bribery, lust and deceit); and the Countess Serpieri's drive by coach to Verona, where death and destruction await her; and her dusty journey through the thick of battle. The picnic scene from *The Leopard* also came to mind, with the saddle-horses being exercised in the background, while in the foreground the family settles down around a beautifully laid-out tablecloth to enjoy an elegant snack. The middle-class Claudia Cardinale gets her young prince in the person of Alain Delon – an excellent match. Castles, Sicilian mountains, meadows and valleys. Ludwig II and Josef Kainz on the king's private steamer on Lake Chiem. Voices calling out in the night, torches on the lakeside and in the waters of Lake Starnberg. The sufferings of Dr von Gudden and His Majesty. A shot of the Grand Hôtel des Bains on the Lido in Venice. The dark and semi-derelict guest house on the Po in summer, where Clara Calamai and Massimo Girotti kill the man who would have come between them and their inevitably boundless adulterous happiness. Massimo meets a strange, nonconformist character in Ancona and together they think of hitch-hiking, but nothing comes of the plan. Female figures dressed in black like Arab women on the rocky coastline at Aci Trezza, gazing out at the sea as it pounds the foot of the cliffs beneath them. An austere and medieval world of work is depicted here, a world that is unfamiliar to us but which has something fascinating about it precisely because it is still intact. Yet already we sense that it will soon be destroyed as a result of our social conditions: a culture that is frail and weak with age will all too soon be lost.

I recall that these films were generally heavily cut when shown in the cinema. The scissor-wielding producers knew no mercy and had no qualms about cutting ninety minutes from *The Leopard* and almost seventy from *Ludwig*. Today these films may be seen uncut, with the result that it has long been clear that only in this way does Visconti's style, with his idiosyncratic treatment of time, of individual detail and character development, achieve its proper effect. I am reminded of the countless occasions when he suffered at not being able to get his way with his sponsors and at having to release his films in a form that was not the one that he himself had intended.

By now I left my Australian hotel room only to fulfil my contractual commitments, most of which had to be performed in the evenings and which also entailed an eight-day stay in Sydney, while I waited with apathetic impatience for my return flight on 28 March. Meanwhile I thought of Luchino, whom I could not imagine dead, but only as the intellectually stimulating individual whom I had known and valued for his weaknesses and virtues and idiosyncrasies. I saw him as guard of honour at Palmiro Togliatti's funeral, saw him at rehearsals in the theatre or enjoying a Sunday excursion, saw him out walking or breakfasting on the Appian Way. In my inner ear I heard his husky bass voice, with its strong Lombardy accent, heard the colourful insults drawn from the rich vocabulary of the Roman proletariat that he favoured while he was working. On one occasion, at the start of a press conference in Venice, I heard him tell the assembled journalists that if they insisted on asking 'mindless questions', 'all hell' would break loose. That is the sort of man he was. He seemed to me to have an exceptional understanding of art. What trouble I went to in my attempts to be acknowledged by him and to learn from him – to learn, for example, from his great love of Italy and of the Italian culture that he had made so much his own and to which he felt called upon to add. I often used to visit him in search of advice on artistic and private matters, and on each occasion the advice that I received, although quite unexpected, was always of practical use. But all this was now over: the world was becoming increasingly empty – four important people, including the most important of all to me, had all been taken away within such a short space of time.

I thought of the post-war years, of my mother and of eastern Westphalia. I remembered going to a nearby fair one Sunday evening as the sun was beginning to set and my younger brothers and sisters were swept along on the merry-go-round with its brightly coloured electric lights to the frightful throbbing of a hurdy-gurdy and its infernally jarring and jolting staccato, beneath the unfeeling, unseeing eyes of Moorish princes and pink, fish-tailed mermaids who never once deigned to look at you and who never smiled but had nothing better to do with their time than go round and round in circles, shrugging their shoulders or beating a drum with their stiff lower arms. While my brothers and sisters were enjoying themselves, my mother consulted a fortune-teller, doing everything possible to find out whether her husband – our father – might soon return home. I waited for her outside the tent.

Even today I still catch myself thinking that I must ring my mother simply to find out how things are going and what my little nephews, Yussuf and Markus, are up to (she was always so fond of their company) or to tell her about some insane or comical incident in my life. The truth I largely hid from her. Her own life had not been easy, yet she had borne it all with great heroism. 'Our father' – as we children called him, perhaps not altogether without irony – *pater noster* had not returned home at the end of the war and we were never able to discover how and where he had met his end – or where his end had met him, poor, benighted, party member Franz Henze. All we managed to establish was that he had been a member of the German units that had taken part in the great offensive in Poland in March 1945 and that had been massacred or taken prisoner by the advancing Soviet divisions. (A few had sought refuge on the *Kraft durch Freude* steamers moored in Danzig harbour only to be torpedoed and sunk by the victorious powers.) Our mother had long hoped that our missing father would one day return through some magical garden gate, so that ever since the war had ended, her private life had consisted solely of waiting. Her children had caused her worries enough and continued to do so decades later, regardless of whether they had flown the parental nest or still lived within reachable distance. Her letters were wonderfully written, full of great detail, and always ended with some evangelical blessing. She was proud of me, and I always tried to live up to her high expectations. In that sense there was a parallel with Ingeborg, who was likewise very demanding, so that I had always seen it as the main challenge of my life and of our friendship – a friendship that by the end could no longer be made to work – to meet her demands. In Ingeborg's case, the fact that our friendship atrophied was also bound up on a deeper level with my political development. Should I not have taken far more trouble with her for precisely that reason, especially when things began to go wrong for her and the drugs that she was taking placed a barrier between us and made it more difficult to exchange ideas? And why did she not telephone *me*, but some maid or other, when disaster struck in Rome? Did she not want to trouble her friends, or did she hope that the whole affair was not so serious and that it could easily be hushed up? How lonely she must have been in her despair in the grey light of dawn on 26 September 1973, in her insane distress and in the horror of her suffering.

It was not in Hofmannsthal's metres that I now thought of transience and death, of loss and the snuffing out of human life, but in the embittered prose of a man who sees that he is growing old, that nothing is as it was, that he must change the way he lives and behaves and that he is now, of course, on his own. My music, too, would reflect this new attitude to life, this new awareness of death and the need to resist death, a need which, in turn, meant working harder than ever. By this, I also meant that death of the spirit that we artists have been called upon to resist from time immemorial. I thought: it is not enough merely to reflect the age in which we live. If existence, work and our efforts in general are to have any meaning today, we have to go a stage further and not forget or feel despair – we must share our gifts with *everyone*.

In the case of Montepulciano, I imagined something like a people's academy for the arts, which I reckoned also included handicrafts and the performing arts. This little mountain fastness with its marvellously taciturn and minatory architecture, this dull and God-forsaken place at the back of beyond, where the snow piles high in winter and from which the young people of the town are all desperately keen to escape, since there is not even a cinema to entertain them – I now wanted to turn it into an exciting workshop that no one would want to flee any longer and which the world would find so attractive that Montepulciano would become an internationally recognized centre for applied teaching, a model of modern, democratic training and practice in the arts, a school of practical theory. All the townspeople would profit from this development, quite apart from the economic benefits. I had already been working on this project for several months, had spent at least half my time on it and managed to find a number of young artists who were sufficiently impressed by the idea to offer their services, free of charge, so that we might realize these plans.

But even today I have still not managed to do what I hoped to achieve at that time and I do not think that I shall ever be able to do so. Neither I nor my fellow workers ever succeeded in fully breaking down the resistance that we had to face at every step, not least because the members of the town council with whom I had to deal and who were largely iron-willed Young Communists were unpopular with the commune's older inhabitants. There were never enough resources for the task of building up the project, in addition to which I was always seen as an outsider, a foreigner, which not only hurt me deeply but also made it harder to obtain state funding. I hoped that my successor, the intelligent and highly gifted composer and man of the theatre, Giorgio Battistelli, would have more success than I ever did, not only on a financial level but in matters of artistic policy too, yet even he had to admit defeat when he resigned as artistic director in the autumn of 1996. It is impossible to predict what will happen to the arts in Italy under the Second Republic. Will things improve? Will Montepulciano suddenly receive lots more money? Or will it simply be destroyed with a single stroke of the pen, perhaps on account of its old Communist background? Nothing can be ruled out. In 1976 my optimism was accompanied by an almost pathological, feverish excitement: after all, I was determined to realize this great project, it meant everything to me. My love of teaching had undoubtedly given me a decisive impulse, but even more important was the idea of making myself *useful* as a teacher – albeit one who still had much to learn – and of serving the (Italian) people in order to fend off loneliness and death. At no point in our existence did our programmes contain anything that might have contradicted these aims. We were friendly, welcoming and considerate: no one was to be given the impression of needing to be taught. The local population with whom we had to deal and for whose sake we were making all these efforts was to be drawn imperceptibly into our sway and sense the magic aura exuded by art in all its manifestations: without realizing it, they were to fall into the Muses' snare. That, at least, was our intention.

My Australian fee allowed me to acquire a Jaguar Mark 4 (export model), which even today continues to get me from place to place. I worked on my Fourth String Quartet and at Easter wrote the curious second movement, an Adagio containing fragments of a pavane by William Byrd: a modern ruined landscape dotted with creepers, acanthus and dreary evergreens.

*

At the end of April I conducted a performance of *Voices* with the Sinfonietta in London and on several occasions saw Gastón Fournier, whose charm and enthusiasm for the arts were as irrepressible as ever. At the beginning of May, my new assistant, Helen Grob, and I went to Brighton, where I conducted some works by Mozart and a number of my own pieces as part of the Brighton Festival. I also spoke about the Cantiere at Sussex University and one evening, anonymously and unannounced, improvised on the piano at a performance of Stroheim's silent classic, *Greed*, in one of the local cinemas. It had been Ingeborg's favourite film. I had been able to watch it earlier that day and had made a few notes, which I then worked up into an outline score, a musical crib that I and my partner, the percussionist Gary Kettel, were able to use at the evening's performance, when we both had enormous fun. I then spent a weekend with Julian Bream in Dorset, working on the *Royal Winter Music*, slowly, laboriously, effortfully, and also jotted down some ideas for the third movement of my Fourth String Quartet. Meanwhile, Fausto had bought an attractive little house in Knightsbridge, after which we returned to Italy. In mid-May *Il re cervo* (the chamber version of *König Hirsch*) was performed in Florence, conducted by Bruno Bartoletti, directed by Roberto Guicciardini and wonderfully designed by Pier Luigi Samaritani. There followed a pilgrimage to Montepulciano, where I conducted and analyzed Mozart's A major Symphony, K186a with a small regional orchestra at the municipal theatre and told the audience a little about the Cantiere Internazionale d'Arte that was currently being set up in the town.

Much to our delight, a pair of hoopoes – Ugo Foscolo's bird of death – had established themselves in the grounds at La Leprara. From now on the pair would return punctually every year at the onset of spring and honour us with their shy presence, a presence detectable only by their monotonous but bright trisyllabic call in a high tenor register, *u-pu-pa*, or by their occasional darting flight past the house, when we would glimpse their bright, black-and-white-barred wings and tail feathers that flashed in the summer sun. Their visit would end after *ferragosto*, when they would fly south in the company of the three or four of their young that had grown to maturity during the months they were with us.

The rehearsals for *We Come to the River* were held in London's East End, in a former cinema known at that time as the London Opera Centre. It was around here that Jack the Ripper had gone about his misogynistic business almost a century previously. By 1976, this part of the London docklands was virtually deserted, filled with unused warehouses and winding alleys of the kind familiar from detective stories and films. Here and there you would stumble across a solitary pub with real people inside and wonder why they were there and where they had come from. My splendid assistant, David Pountney, who has since become famous as a brilliant opera director in his own right, knew this part of London well and, not without pride, showed me the whole of the dockland area, a vast expanse that conveyed a vague but powerful impression of the greatness and worldwide importance of Great Britain as a trading nation. We spent the whole of the next few weeks at the Centre, plagued by the heatwave that affected England in June and July 1976. Indeed, the heat was so intense that at the *Sitzproben* the men from the Sinfonietta stripped to the waist, exposing their pale, sweating bodies. We then decamped to Covent Garden. Here, too, there was no air-conditioning. The piece's three playing areas, each with its own instrumental group, were arranged in such a way that Stage I and its orchestra were positioned over the covered orchestra pit, Stage II was downstage right (from the actors' point of view), and Stage III was further upstage, with the musicians placed on a rostrum some three feet high. Unfortunately, a number of acoustical problems came to light when we started the final rehearsals. Orchestra II was badly positioned: the sound disappeared into the wings or was lost in the flies, reaching the auditorium with less than half its true potential. We tried various solutions in an attempt to overcome the problem, but had negligible success. It also turned out that members of the audience sitting to the right of the stage could not hear Orchestra III, with the result that the intended blend of voices, lines and colours did not really come off. I was against amplifying the sound electronically, since I feared additional complications and did not want to spoil the woodcut-like simplicity of the whole. In any case, there was no time for any experiments. The rehearsal schedule had been haggled over and worked out in advance right down to the final second, so no more changes were possible.

On 1 July I turned fifty: during the morning's rehearsal – we were working on Scene Five at the time – singers and orchestra suddenly stopped and, instead of the mindless victory anthem *Hail, Liberator* that is heard at this point in score, they broke into a rendition of the (equally awful) Anglo-American *Happy Birthday*. I was very touched by their gesture, thanked them via the theatre's tannoy, told them how much I loved them all and could we start again at figure 9? At midday Helen, Yoichi and I were joined by Freddy Ashton and John Tooley and together we went off to a

French restaurant just off Kensington High Street, where we celebrated in style. In the evening we returned to Covent Garden to see Fred's wonderful new ballet, *A Month in the Country*, based on Turgenev's short story of the same name and with a score taken from Chopin's early Mozart Variations. There was champagne and a light supper in the private room immediately behind our box. There are several such rooms here, all of which – like those at San Carlo in Naples and La Scala, Milan – recall an age when evenings at the opera were largely spent in the private rooms of other families and of representatives of the Establishment. Whenever an important aria came up, the usher would inform the box holders, who would step through into the box and, still chewing their food and with their napkins held to their mouths, listen briefly to the music, so that they would later be able to talk about it in the salons that they frequented.

The first Covent Garden Opera was built in 1732 and burnt down in 1808. It was immediately rebuilt but burnt down again in 1855, after which it acquired the form that it still has today, a form designed to meet the demands and what was then the new style of Italian opera. It was wonderful for me to return to this house after an absence of eighteen years, albeit on this occasion not with a para-romantic fairy-tale ballet but with an anti-plutocratic theatre piece. My brother's simple structures of rough-hewn timber looked good in the house's red plush, creating a stage picture that appeared at first sight to have been purpose-built to resemble a chess-board, thus ushering the spectator straight into the world of our opera's draughtsman-like, ornament-free style and rules.

On the morning of the first performance – 12 July 1976 – I found a card in our letter-box in Knightsbridge on which were written the words 'Good luck for you tonight, your neighbours'. I had not even realized that they knew me, they were so discreet, these neighbours, but the next morning I dropped by to thank them and in that way got to know them. Fausto and our friend Maureen McNally Giroux (who was singing the role of the Duchess in *Don Chisciotte* in Montepulciano and for whom I was later to write *El rey de Harlem*) had slipped away from preparations for the first Cantiere for twenty-four hours, so that we were all able to go to the opening night together. It was still light outside when it began, and even during the interval there was a golden glow in the sky. I spent the interval in the Crush Bar with Freddy Ashton and his nephew, Anthony Russell Roberts. They were impressed, they said – especially by the end of the act, with its sense of panic and the curlews' cries of alarm. The house was completely sold out, I saw lots of familiar faces, including ones from abroad, and waved to Kerstin Meyer and Elisabeth Söderström in the distance. During the second half there was a sudden burst of heckling, which proved to emanate from the film-maker Ken Russell, who left the theatre fulminating against the piece – evidently he had not liked it one little bit. There were also expressions of disapproval at the end of the performance, but fortunately the demonstrations of support prevailed, and the later performances all played to full houses. The whole company and I celebrated the evening's success in the foyer afterwards, a lavish celebration that unfortunately marked the end of our work together, the white-hot intensity of which seemed even to have affected the weather.

Later that evening, a small group of close friends gathered at Fausto's house in Knightsbridge, where we celebrated and drank until daybreak. Fausto, Helen and Maureen then caught the early flight back to Pisa, while Yoichi and I remained in London for a few more days. I still had a concert to conduct on 14 July as part of the City of London Festival. Held at London's oldest church, St Bartholomew-the-Great, it included Bach's motet *Jesu meine Freude* and the first performance of my 1975 arrangement of Carissimi's *Jephte* for four vocal soloists (Jane Manning, Sarah Walker, Philip Langridge and Stephen Roberts), four flutes, four percussion instruments and four plucked instruments. I dedicated the concert to all who had worked with me on *River*.

The next day we flew to Pisa. The driver, who had been sent to collect me by the local authority at Montepulciano, had instructions to use only country roads in order to avoid the expense of the motorway toll, but I was more than happy to fall in with this idea, since there is always something agreeable and relaxing about a leisurely tour of Tuscany. We stopped for a break at the roadside and drank red wine in the green grass, arriving in Montepulciano just in time for me to take the first stage rehearsal for *Don Chisciotte* at eight o'clock that evening. It was held on a wooden platform erected in the Piazza Grande on the basis of instructions and drawings by our set designer, the Venetian painter, Giovanni Soccol. Every day from now on I worked on this platform, surrounded by cars and buses, until the production was ready or, rather, until it was less than half ready and the first Cantiere Internazionale could open with it on 1 August 1976.

No, I have no wish to weary my readers by repeating the whole of the Montepulciano saga here. I have often described how the Cantiere was set up and how it progressed – there are articles on it in *Music and Politics*, in my writings on the aesthetics of new music and, not least, in my working diary for 1978 to 1982, *Die englische Katze*, which contains a detailed account of the fifth festival in the summer of 1980, a festival that was to be the last that I ran for a number of years. Instead, I should prefer to try to colour in the background against which my life and work were to unfold between 1976 and 1980. Often enough my private life would become inseparable from artistic considerations, and there were certainly times when it seemed as though I and my music existed solely for the benefit of the Cantiere at Montepulciano.

At the second Cantiere in 1977 an important ethnomusicological event took place in the piazza in the form of *Villan d'un contadino*, an account of local agricultural work retold and recalled by amateur writers from the region and accompanied by songs, choruses and wind music from the Orcia valley and surrounding area. A large number of amateur musicians and singers were involved, and the result was an opportunity to get to know some extremely interesting musical traditions. In the same piazza we performed the *Fabula di Orfeo* by the fifteenth-century Tuscan poet and humanist Angelo Ambrogini ('Il Poliziano'). And in the theatre we staged an early piece by Paul Dessau, *Orpheus und der Bürgermeister*, and Milhaud's *Les malheurs d'Orphée*. The concerts, too, were dominated by the Orpheus theme, with a dozen or so first performances and a revival of Rossini's cantata *Il pianto dell'Armonia sulla morte di Orfeo*. The third Cantiere (which I was not able to attend) was called 'La Spagna, la Follia, la Passione' and featured Classical and modern Spanish works: Cristobal Halffter conducted his own *Requiem por la libertad imaginada*, Giuseppe Sinopoli conducted works by Luis de Pablo, and José Ramón Encinár played two pieces of his own and Nono's *Y su sangre ya viene cantando*. In the theatre there was Falla's *La vida breve* and my own *Aria de la folía espagñola* in a production by William Forsythe, while the cloisters of St Agnes's Church were the setting for a performance of a piece by the Dutch composer, Jochem Slothouwer, based on Calderón's *El mayor encanto, amor* and performed by the Cambridge University Choir.

The fourth Cantiere was presented under the title 'La Banda e la Danza, la Chiesa e il Circo' and was memorable, not least, for the fact that it rarely stopped raining. On this occasion we did not use the municipal theatre, since we did not want to hold up the building work planned for that summer, although in the event – or, rather, needless to say – the work in question did not take place. I staged *Die Dreigroschenoper* in a bakingly hot circus tent, Sinopoli conducted Mahler at St Blaise's, and a full-scale ballet – a comico-heroic *ballet d'action* entitled *I muti di Portici* – was performed in the piazza by young soloists and students from Stuttgart and Berlin. The scenario, freely based on Eugène Scribe, was by Giuseppe di Leva and was choreographed and directed by Jörg Schmalz from the Deutsche Oper, Berlin. The wind bands of Abbadia San Salvatore, Siena, San Quirico d'Orcia and Montepulciano itself (the last-named conducted by myself and made up largely of members of the Cantiere orchestra) took turns to play works in their regular repertory that they already knew by heart. Among the pieces that it fell to my lot to conduct was the overture to Verdi's *Giovanna d'Arco*, which I performed with tremendous pleasure. And the excellent Grimethorpe Colliery Band, one of the best miners' bands from Yorkshire, conducted by Elgar Howarth, was also stationed in Montepulciano, where it gave a concert at St Blaise's including works by older and more recent English composers such as Farnaby, Byrd, Holst, Grainger and Elgar, and ending with the Triumphal March from *Aida*. They later visited some of the neighbouring towns and were particularly warmly received by the people of Abbadia San Salvatore, miners like themselves, albeit unemployed following the closure of the local mercury mines. The fourth Cantiere ended with a gala performance of Monteverdi's Vespers of 1610 conducted by Dennis Russell Davies.

At the very first festival in 1976, all manner of unforeseeable events occurred: singers refused to work with certain conductors, and composers followed suit. The local population objected to the anarchical mores and customs of a group of young mime artists from Milan who descended on us out of the blue at the very moment when it emerged that the local amateur artists were not taking their work sufficiently seriously and were skiving off rehearsals. The Australian clown, Mark Fornaux, took charge of these *enfants terribles*, instructing them all in both dance and mime. They had their work cut out, since they not only had to mime the part of shepherds, townsfolk and peasants in *Don Chisciotte* but also had to appear as the chorus in *Il turco in Italia* and play the leading roles in *Tradimenti*, a collaborative venture by Peter Maxwell Davies and the director Memè Perlini. On the final day of the festival, the municipal authorities refused to reimburse their travelling expenses since a number of them had no return tickets or something similar, whereupon the understandably furious actors occupied the theatre and prevented the second of only two performances of *Il turco in Italia* from taking place. The first festival ended with this extraordinarily unpleasant scene, a total débâcle at which the Tuscan audience and Lombardy mime artists hurled abuse and threats at each other, while I myself remained outside in the foyer, begging the *carabinieri* not to intervene. But as sure as night follows day, the left-wing junta and their musical stooges could now expect to be heaped with scorn and contempt.

Late in the afternoon of this all too memorable day, a sizeable number of the local townspeople had already got terribly worked up at Memè Perlini's *Tradimenti*, a monster spectacle that had taken place in all the classrooms and corridors of their plainly furnished secondary modern school and that comprised strange and silent goings-on accompanied by unbelievably shrill-sounding music from the reverberant stone stairwell written, moreover, by a foreigner – Peter (now Sir Peter) Maxwell Davies – and bound to confuse the untutored ear. The events in question were unrelated to one another and depicted highly paranoid scenes from provincial life. The work as a whole was profoundly shocking, a uniquely brilliant and carefully calculated act of provocation that regrettably destroyed what little sympathy our work might otherwise have won for itself. Questions were raised in the Tuscan parliament by the right-wing opposition, and the Christian Democrats stuck protest posters on walls erected in the early sixteenth century by Antonio Sangallo the Elder (or possibly the Younger). The whole affair became a political issue, and open conflict broke out in the form of a latter-day *Kulturkampf*. Here it was again, then, this all too fraught relationship between poetry and politics, reality and art!

In the autumn of 1976 my comrades in Montepulciano brought me my Italian Communist Party membership card, number 1744458, Federazione di Siena. My preparations and planning for the second Cantiere were rather better organized than they had been for the first – not that this meant that things became any easier. Riccardo Chailly insisted on being allowed to conduct Verdi's *I masnadieri* (based on Schiller's *Die Räuber*), but for this we needed to excavate an orchestra pit under the stage. Quite incredibly, the local planning department agreed to this and gave the go-ahead for work to begin without waiting for permission from the ministry responsible for listed buildings. Four weeks before the first night, there was still a hole in the ground where the stage should have been. The builders had come up against a large rock, the highest point of which was where the conductor's podium ought to have been. We were fortunate in being able to call on the services of Carlo Diappi, the Milan designer who was responsible for the costumes for *I masnadieri* and whose solution, far from being a makeshift, proved ideal. The orchestra sat on wooden steps that descended progressively into the pit, with the strings at the top and the winds on ground level. The production was to have been the work of Pier

Luigi Pizzi, but, on seeing the building delays in the theatre, he wrote to me to withdraw, saying that he was not in the habit of working between buckets of whitewash and piles of mortar, as a result of which I took over as director myself, deriving enormous pleasure from the task. In Hiroyuki Toyota, an assistant of the Venetian architect Carlo Spada, I found an inventive designer: since we had absolutely no money, we used grain sacks, tastefully stitched together, as five wonderful sets and a front curtain, into which blue and white ropes were woven by the dextrous hands of the wives of our bass and tenor soloists. Toyota's sets were stylish and distinguished. Here and there it was still possible to read the words 'Consorzio agrario, Provincia di Siena' on the sacking, discreetly drawing the public's attention to our extreme material poverty. And it looked wonderful. The stage floor and orchestra pit were finished just in time, and only occasionally did a pneumatic drill provide an obbligato accompaniment to Verdi's cabalettas. On one occasion Pietro Ingrao, the Communist president of the Chamber of Deputies, dropped in from Rome and, accompanied by proud members of the Montepulciano town council, inspected the preparations for the festival, including the building work in the theatre. 'E questo qui è il nostro Henze,' they said, pointing at me, and my heart beat wildly with delight, but I did not let it show. At ten o'clock on the morning of 23 July 1977, the entire Cantiere orchestra assembled punctually in the theatre to rehearse *I masnadieri*, which was due to open eight days later. Riccardo Chailly raised his baton for the overture's *fortissimo* opening chord, and the sound welled up from our novel mystic abyss, powerful, beautiful and full-bodied. The local building workers and I were crouched in the boxes, playing the part of acousticians, moving around the auditorium, listening carefully, and testing and approving the sound, unable to contain our delight. This was the occasion when I received an even greater compliment from my *compagni* than the one recently bestowed during Pietro Ingrao's visit. This time, however, it was dry and sincere in the true Tuscan fashion: 'Henze, until now we'd all thought of you as a *cretino*.'

At this second Cantiere I particularly enjoyed working with Richard Marlow's Cambridge University Chamber Choir, whose student members not only had to sing and perform the parts of brigands, sutlers and whores in *I masnadieri* but also had to represent fire and tempest. To work with them was sheer joy. And how intelligent and well brought up they were! Apprised of the town's political tensions, they suggested the idea of singing Mass in the local churches, with the result that virtually every day they gave first-class well-sung performances of unaccompanied Italian, German and English works, although only, of course, for the duration of the 'Communist' Cantiere. During the afternoon, the young ladies of the choir could be seen in their pink, light blue or white dresses, wearing their broad-brimmed sunhats or carrying parasols and wandering over the hills, while busily learning their parts from *I masnadieri*. In later years, too, we were to enjoy the visits of these civilized young students. If everyone had been as agreeable as they were, life in Montepulciano would certainly have been much easier. During the second Cantiere (and it was by no means the last time that this happened), we had to deal with the threat of a strike on the part of the orchestra, a body of players that was made up, for the most part, of heterogeneous elements drawn from all over Europe and that objected to the fact that in one of the modern works in that year's repertory the violas were required to play tremolando for ten whole minutes, a performance instruction deemed to be exploitative and repressive and to betray a lamentable lack of solidarity. I asked the mayor, Francesco Colajanni, to take part in the discussion, and it was he, not I, who succeeded in calming the rebellious spirits in our midst, with the result that I did not need to draw their attention to the hour-long tremolos in Wagner or to give free and destructive rein to my all too volatile temper. The fact that attendance was wholly voluntary naturally gave every participant the right to say what he or she felt, and they were free to use that right as much or as little as they wanted. They could also wander off or absent themselves from rehearsals without so much as a by-your-leave, or they could suddenly yield to the urge to visit some distant beloved and disappear at dead of night, never to be seen again, taking their instrument and music with them. On one occasion a singer caused a performance to be cancelled simply because he had received some bad reviews and felt offended. But it was also possible, in the case of open-air performances, to expose the lacquer of one's priceless Amati to the damp night air or to the first sudden drops of summer rain, and that, indeed, is what happened whenever circumstances required it. Members of German state orchestras such as those from Stuttgart and Bamberg were deployed as transport workers. Together with his guitar and circle of listeners, Julian Bream similarly once got wet late one evening on the pavement outside the café on the piazza, although on this occasion the water was thrown down at him by a sleepy local philistine.

It was clear that a great deal of work still had to be done before we could interest the provincial Poliziani in music as a means of expression and communication – it had not struck them hitherto as in any way interesting or important in their lives. Music and its hangers-on were a source of deep suspicion: they saw in us a sinful band of travellers who sang a siren song, and they wanted nothing to do with it. Radio and television were quite sufficient for them, and these could be switched on and off at will.

A local schoolteacher and pillar of the artistic community, Mariano Fresta, said to me only recently: 'If I want to hear music, I don't need concerts – I simply buy a CD.' People had not left their houses at night since the winter of 1464, when Benedetto Ambrogini, the father of Il Poliziano, had been killed in a feud and young Angelo, still a mere boy, had escaped from his murderers beneath the woollen skirts of a fleeing nurse. Raised in Florence, he became famous – and popular – as a classical philologist at the local University, adding to his reputation as court poet to Lorenzo de' Medici, acting as the latter's political adviser and never again setting foot in unwelcoming Montepulciano. People did not seek each other's company but were sceptical, taciturn and suspicious. It struck me that only young people could bring light to this benighted world. Somehow they had to be mobilized and taught a love of music: music teachers had to be won over.

Gastón Fournier Facio, who had in the meantime taken his doctorate in musicology and sociology at Sussex University, was immensely fond of Montepulciano. He had participated in the first two Cantieri in various capacities, working as production assistant, dramaturge, waiter, chorister, stage hand and mime and although he was due to return to his native Costa Rica, he was delighted to be offered accommodation in Montepulciano and to be invited to work with the townspeople as *animatore culturale* from now on – and, it was hoped, for many years to come. He achieved the most brilliant results: it is to Gastón Fournier Facio's credit that real progress could finally be made up there on the mountain. The townspeople recently thanked him by giving him a medal. He remained until 1982, when he failed to turn down an offer from the Teatro Comunale in Florence and duly took up an appointment in which, with mounting success, he displayed his exceptional qualities not only as an expert on music but also as a diplomat, skilled organizer and irresistibly charming individual. (Since 1995 he has worked for the National Academy of Santa Cecilia in Rome.) He retained his flat in Montepulciano for a further four years, commuting between the town and Florence and remaining in charge of the Cantieri until 1986. When he first arrived in Montepulciano by bus from Chiusi on 2 January 1979, it was snowing heavily. He dragged his pile of books through the deep snow that covered the steep main street and moved into his small cold flat, quickly taking in hand his task of promoting art in both theory and practice, championing the constructive potential of music and music-making and enabling us finally to breathe a sigh of relief and harbour something approaching hope that one day a new reality would perhaps come to pass in the town. Modest to the point of self-denial, Gastón set about his pioneering work with realistic resolve and a genuine love of his work. He consulted a number of pupils of Boris Porena, who all worked as *animatori culturali* in Monteluco in the north of Latium, and asked them to cooperate with him, taking over some of their newer pedagogical practices and building up a group of very young instrumentalists – mostly children – with whom he studied monophonic and polyphonic music, before slowly and cautiously tackling increasingly ambitious pieces.

This new group called itself the Concentus Politianus and first appeared in public at the end of the third Cantiere – not, however, on the concert platform but in the guise of a brightly coloured paper dragon that wound its way through the streets and alleys of its culturally impoverished native town, clattering and piping and thereby inviting interest in the incredible things that were to happen. The following year two recorder players from the Concentus joined forces with Gidon Kremer to perform Bach's Fourth Brandenburg Concerto under Cristobal Halffter's direction in St Blaise's Church. Both players, Giampiero Allegro and Luca Vanneschi, remained in Montepulciano and studied music, taking part in the Cantiere courses and becoming important figures on the local cultural scene. As a result, Montepulciano can once again boast a decent *banda*. By 1981 the Istituto di Musica had eighty students on its books, and the Concentus Politianus had become the heart and soul of Montepulciano's musical life.

During the years that followed, things continued to develop in a thoroughly gratifying manner, even after Gastón's departure. My former pupils, David Graham and, later, Detlev Glanert, lived and taught there for many years, and today there are a number of young people in Montepulciano who are amateur composers – I hope that they will long continue to compose, instructed and encouraged by my Italian successors, of whom not only I myself but others too expect only the highest achievements and results.

Time and again the cultural life of Montepulciano has been beset by crisis after crisis – and always for the same stupid reasons, namely, the perpetual lack of resources and the resultant need for the festival organizers to have to go a-begging, year in, year out, and to grovel before ministers. On one occasion I was summoned to the Ministry of the Arts in Florence at eight o'clock in the morning in order to plead my case for more money. While I described the difficulties facing us, the minister read the morning's papers, and when I stopped speaking because it seemed pointless to go on, he said 'Parla, parla!', and so I went on talking, while he continued to read the day's leading articles – but I did, none the less, receive a little more money. From year to year we lived in a state of uncertainty, unable to make any definite arrangements. I invariably bore it all with a certain stubborn and dogged enthusiasm – after all, I saw it as my political duty, I was doing what I had to do and fulfilling a commission. If it had ever been at all disagreeable, I should scarcely have done it. And I always went to Party meetings and told my comrades exactly what we were planning to do in pursuit of our artistic and didactic ends, and I listened carefully to what they had to say. I set great store by the need for us to get along together for as long as was possible, without any misunderstandings. After all, it was the first time in my whole life that I had been able and willing to feel that I really belonged somewhere – it was a completely new and unusual experience. There was also a slight sense of unease, not least because of the novelty of the situation, but the overriding feeling was one of pride. My life, I thought with relief, was now to gain some inner and outer order. The feeling that I belonged to this humanistically enlightened, democratic and cosmopolitan organization gave me a sense of security and provided a form of protection – against calumny and spite, for example. A thoroughly respectable person, I now belonged to a thoroughly respectable party – attacks no longer needed to be quite so senseless and so random as before. I felt at ease with myself.

Among the works that were centred on the Orpheus myth and performed at the 1977 Cantiere was my own solo sonata *Tirsi, Mopso, Aristeo* – the piece takes its title from the names of the three sexy clowns that launch Il Poliziano's play, the first non-Christian *rappresentazione sacra* of our age. Dedicated to the violinist Jenny Abel, my sonata is a triptych of portraits – I drew and photographed these three lads from Montepulciano, whistling, laughing and joking as they saunter through the stubble, until one of them, Aristeo, spies the nymph Eurydice and sets off in pursuit, his unambiguous intentions reflected in the tempo of the music. Just as Eurydice reaches the haven of the forest, she is bitten by a tiny grey and murderous viper, an emissary from hell: she screams and at the very same moment Aristeo, too, still more than half a kilometre from the object of his desire, lets out a piercing scream. A great moment!

Jenny Abel played the piece with great passion and beauty on 10 August 1977, after which I drove to nearby Pienza to watch the young people of Montepulciano acting and dancing in Stravinsky's *Histoire du soldat* in the town's Piazza Piccolomini. The libretto had been rewritten by Carlo Pasquini and some of his young friends from Montepulciano and was now an oppressive mix of Nietzsche, Marcuse and Freud, but none of this seemed to matter: their message was so insistent and their work so intense that it was impossible to hold it against them. And they performed it exactly as Stravinsky and Ramuz wanted, in various hostelry gardens and in small squares in the surrounding area. The music was splendidly played by British performers of their own age. We adopted a similar practice with a number of our other concert programmes and with plays that were specially rewritten for this decentralized approach. Among examples of the latter was *Il Mongomo a lapislazzuli* by the Hamburg group, Hinz & Kunst, who came to Montepulciano almost every year and who were among the most loyal and reliable of the Cantieristi. At the time in question, their members were Wolfgang Florey (cello), Hedwig Florey (piano), Thomas Jahn (trombone), Bernhard Asche (clarinet and saxophone), Peter Wulfert and Matthias Kaul (percussion) and Horst Huhn (trumpet). They were all completely committed to the basic idea behind the Cantieri, which is perhaps why they were all particularly popular with local audiences.

I found it interesting to see what effect the absence of a fee had on the artists' morale and the state of their nerves. The result was a feeling of equality; we were – and knew ourselves to be – united in a common cause. Inevitably, not all my friends and acquaintances could be persuaded to share this feeling – their curiosity could simply never be whetted – but many of them accepted it and had a good time, not least because of the chance that it gave them to flex their pedagogical muscles. Italian, German and British television companies and radio stations also helped every year by means of co-productions. Particularly helpful and imaginative was the support of WDR's third television channel, whose head of department was a long-standing friend, Manfred Gräter, who did not think it excessive to come to Montepulciano every year and to finance and film a production. There were also private sponsors who contributed greater and lesser amounts: every summer, for example, the German firm of Ibach would send five grand pianos from Schwelm in Westphalia to Montepulciano and back; and the Teatro Comunale in Florence and La Scala helped through their workshops and through the loan of various objects, without in any way compromising the character of our festival or destroying its *arte povera* style. I really ought to have moved to Montepulciano and, oblivious to everything else, have spent the whole of each day teaching hundreds of wonderful and highly intelligent children and giving them a basic education in the arts, thereby not only serving the people but also gratifying my own pedagogical ambitions. The fact that I did not do so and, unlike such great men as Mao and Fidel, did not renounce all bourgeois luxury (including my private life and my left-wing intellectual ideas) was not a mistake, as it later turned out, but proved to have been intuitively correct, deriving, as it did, from the instinct for survival. Like Jacopo del Pecora, a stranger from enemy Siena at the end of the fourteenth century, I should otherwise have been butchered by the Poliziani in the Piazza Grande, then roasted and consumed and my innards thrown to the commune's many stray dogs. I have many bitter memories of Montepulciano. Much later I made the mistake of returning to the town in response to endless entreaties from various quarters, including the Communist Party, in order to rescue the sinking ship. But this was still many years off. Let us first return to 1979/80.

The great leap forward in the cultural life of the young people of Montepulciano took place during the months of rehearsals leading up to the first performance of *Pollicino* on 2 August 1980. The previous autumn the children from the Concentus had asked me to write an opera for them and I had, of course, agreed: here was an opportunity to extend the course of studies of my young charges and steer them towards a concrete goal in the form of a public performance – a veritable ordeal by fire. In short, I had to write a piece that could be taught in school and that was suitable for children who had only just begun to read music and who could produce only a few notes on their recorders and on other instruments from Carl Orff's *Schulwerk*. Curiously enough, it gave me enormous pleasure to write music for children of such limited abilities, although it was by no means easy to ensure that the music itself was easy. I wrote parts for solo violin and piano that could really only be mastered by more advanced players or by members of the teaching staff: in these sections, the composer himself is heard *in propria persona*, until the weakly wailing tone of the *flauti dolci* and the clatter of Carl Orff's instruments once again fills the air. With the successful launch of *Pollicino*, I saw my task as ended: there was now music in the little town, there were now musicians in the form of children both keen and able to sing. More than seventy of them took part in the performance, and almost all of them have remained loyal to music or to the theatre in one way or another or have at least continued to take an interest in the arts. Once we had achieved this, I could retire. In 1980 I handed over the running of the future Cantieri to Gastón and to Jan Latham-Koenig, who had conducted the first performances of *Pollicino*.

I was able to relax only briefly at the end of the first Cantiere in the autumn of 1976, for I then had to set off again on my travels, first to Bonn, where I spent the daytime working on a production of *Elegie für junge Liebende* and where I devoted the evenings to orchestrating a mezzo-soprano version of Wagner's Wesendonk Lieder, then to Berlin, where the Concord Quartet gave the first performance of my Third String Quartet on 12 September and where I conducted a number of my own works with the Berlin Philharmonic on the 10th and again on the 19th. And there was also a further attempt to stage *La Cubana*, this time in Wuppertal. It was not until 16 October that I finally returned from a joyless fatherland and was able to work in peace on my Fifth String Quartet, but the month of November brought further disruptions in the form of preparations for the second Cantiere, including visits to Leipzig and Berlin.

On the evening of 13 November 1976, the dissident writer and singer Wolf Biermann – at that time still a citizen of the Democratic Republic – gave a concert in Cologne that was highly critical of the GDR and that was broadcast on West German television. On the 16th he was refused re-entry to the GDR, a decision that was to have serious repercussions in numerous quarters. The following Saturday evening I conducted a performance of *Voices* in Leipzig's packed town hall (the performance was enthusiastically received and released only a short time later on the Eterna label with Roswitha Trexler, Jochen Vogt and members of the Leipzig Radio Orchestra), and the next day we all drove to Berlin to repeat the piece at the Komische Oper at eleven o'clock in the morning. It gives me no pleasure to report what happened next. We arrived to find Paul Dessau waiting at the stage door in the company of the acting Minister of Culture, Klaus Höpcke. Paul had aged visibly since we had last met and the rims of his eyes were red. We said hello and they told me that they would not be attending the concert and that they were now leaving. I did not ask them why, but soon – perhaps it was later that morning – discovered that, one by one, my colleagues in East Berlin had all been asked not to attend my concert. It may have had something to do with the public letter of protest at the treatment of Wolf Biermann to which artists and writers throughout the world were currently putting their names. Perhaps it was feared that a concert by a West German artist with left-wing views might be seen as a suitable platform for a demonstration on the part of sympathetic colleagues or the like. Yes, Paul had himself telephoned our friends and colleagues and advised them to follow instructions and stay at home. The hall was empty, with no more than a handful of strangers in it. My music and the texts that I had set suddenly sounded subversive and dangerous (as, indeed, they were, featuring, as they did, poems by Padilla, Heine, Enzensberger and Brecht). But they went unheard. Even the courtesies normally extended by the management of the Komische Oper were more honoured in the breach than in the observance, and the concert was no sooner over than our hosts beat a hasty retreat. At Checkpoint Charlie, Fausto's passport photograph, which had been stuck in at a slight angle, aroused mistrust and resulted in our car and luggage being searched for hours. 'You'll not get any further today,' said the officer on duty. I was too proud and too angry to tell him that I had just given two tiring concerts in his country and that all I wanted to do now was to go home. When we were finally allowed to cross over into the West, I swore that from that day forth I would never again set foot in the GDR. It is entirely possible, of course, that there was no causal connection between the boycott of our concert and the sort of harassment that we suffered on passing through customs, but I was oddly affected by the whole affair and felt both insulted and incensed.

I spent Christmas on St Lucia in the West Indies, sketching out my Violin Sonata and completing my Fifth String Quartet, and with the New Year set off on another concert tour, this time to Stockholm and Nuremberg (where I conducted Mahler's Third), followed by a five-week stay in gloomy Franconia, once again rehearsing *Elegie für junge Liebende*. Between these commitments came a series of visits to Amsterdam.

It was in Amsterdam – normally an especially delightful city – that an encounter took place at a party that was slowly but surely to knock the old tom-cat for six. Love overwhelmed him like some terrible disaster or natural catastrophe. The *Aria de la folía espagñola* that dates from this time is merely a brief shorthand account of what he then felt, and the same is true of *Il Vitalino raddoppiato* for violin and chamber orchestra, on which he worked, for the most part, in planes and at makeshift desks. And yet it was impossible for him at that time to find the means to express the very real shock that he felt at the coldness with which he set about betraying and abandoning a fellow human being. He had to start to lead a double life, to be secretive, to conceal the truth and to lie. He felt a sense of humiliation but at the same time an addictive obsession and a very real curiosity: everything was different, the world was no longer the same, he learnt to see it from a different perspective, it tasted different, felt different, made a different noise. He could not be held back but once again had to destroy everything that got in his way, everything that bound him to the good things in life, he had to remove it and wreck it. The conflict lasted throughout the whole of 1977 and led to repeated scenes and complications that it still fills him with the deepest shame and remorse to recall. Even now, memories of this period continue to haunt me virtually every day, like ghosts or bereavements or black-and-white films that have lost none of their terrible intensity, none of their stabbing immediacy.

Among other experiences at this time was that of artistic failure. In March 1977 I travelled to Hamburg to conduct a new production of *Die Zauberflöte* directed by Götz Friedrich and designed by the Viennese Fantastic Realist, Ernst Fuchs. At the first orchestral rehearsal I noticed that the sound was dull and monochromatic but did not know how to improve it. I came up against a wall of animosity – was it a distant echo, perhaps, of the events surrounding the first performance of *Das Floß der 'Medusa'*? I was blacklisted. At each rehearsal there were different players and it was not until the final week that a leader arrived. I asked the house's principal conductor, Horst Stein, to attend a rehearsal, which he duly did, commenting afterwards: 'They clearly don't want to play for you.' The orchestral manager, Ernst Schönfelder, told me that the band would perform Mozart's music note-perfect on the first night, but no more than that. At the final orchestral rehearsal, six Japanese viola players from the local conservatory turned up at the stage door and asked the way to the orchestra pit, at which point I sent Helen Grob to administration to inform the intendant, August Everding, that I was withdrawing from the production. In keeping with time-honoured custom, he came to see me at my hotel in an attempt to talk me round, but my mind was firmly made up. As a result, and in accordance with his contract, the general music director, Herr Stein (who had spent the whole time secretly rehearsing with the real State Opera Orchestra in preparation for a concert tour), had to take over on the first night and conduct an ensemble made up of neighbours, pensioners and students, although they played no better for him than they had done for me – they were simply incapable of playing any better.

I then went to Stuttgart to direct a production, in German, of *We Come to the River* – or *Wir erreichen den Fluß*, as it had now become known. I had a good time there, one that I still recall with great fondness, not least because I got on so well with Axel Manthey and Dennis Russell Davies and also with the singers – Irmgard Stadler, Elke Estlinbaum, Grace Hoffman, Siegfried Jerusalem, Kimmo Lappalainen, Günter Reich and Wolfgang Schöne. On 25 May – the evening of the dress rehearsal – my Fourth and Fifth String Quartets were premièred in Schwetzingen, and so I was unable to attend. The production of *Wir erreichen den Fluß* was a great success and reinforced my friendly ties with the Staatstheater and its general administrator, Hans Peter Doll, as well as with the director, Wolfram Schwinger, and with the house's principal conductor, Dennis Russell Davies.

Fausto had found a small flat at the upper end of the Sonnenbergstraße, where the city ends and woodland begins. It was already mid-April, but the woods were still a silvery brown, with no trace of green. Only in the Swabian gardens were the first fruit trees starting to blossom, recalling more pleasant memories of a childhood and adolescence spent in eastern Westphalia. During my free hours I worked on *Vitalino*, which is also bound up with such memories, of course, with lilac bushes and one's very first blushes and sense of fright. At the end of April, Gudrun Ensslin, Andreas Baader and Jan-Carl Raspe were sentenced to life imprisonment at Stammheim, and the *Stuttgarter Zeitung* spoke of the 'swamp of sympathizers' that still had to be drained. At Whitsuntide, Helen and I flew to Prague, where I conducted Mozart and *Heliogabalus imperator* in Smetana Hall, the very same hall as the one in which, as a little German soldier, I had heard an all-Dvořák programme with the Czech Philharmonic in January 1945. I dreamt that Yoichi's body had been hidden among the granules that covered the floor of Axel Manthey's sets for *Wir erreichen den Fluß*, but that heavy rain the next morning would uncover it and wash it all away. From Prague I flew to Amsterdam for three days and nights of intense emotion, darkness, cold, raptus, rain and terror.

My next piece of work for the Württemberg Staatstheater was to be the dance drama *Orpheus*, a work that I had already discussed some time earlier with the ballet administration. It was I who had suggested the subject matter (no doubt inspired, in part, by my work on Il Poliziano), and I wanted Edward Bond to work on the project with me and elaborate it in keeping with his own ideas. The basic concept had come to me at dawn on the morning following that party in Amsterdam in the autumn of 1976 when I looked out of my hotel-room window and discovered a solitary grey heron perched on a post in the Amstel. This bird would also feature in Bond's later poems on the Orpheus legend.

The complications to my private life were to continue to plague me throughout the second Cantiere and by the autumn had developed into a veritable illness that required the use of drugs and medicine as part of a kill-or-cure remedy. I spent part of September in St Paul, Minnesota, as a guest of the local Chamber Orchestra and its conductor, Dennis Davies. Here I learnt and conducted Beethoven's Second Symphony and also conducted a couple of my own works – the Second Violin Concerto and *Compases*. Autumn was already in the air when we went for a picnic with the Davies family on the banks of the Mississippi and were preyed on by swarms of midges. I also began work on what was to be my first volume of aesthetics and spoke at various colleges, mainly on new music and the theatre. And Dennis gave the first performance of my *Aria de la folía* on 17 September. I also went for long walks, enjoying the Indian summer, and telephoned Amsterdam daily. Yoichi spent the vacation in Marino, working on his sculptures. At the end of October I flew to Berlin, where I premièred Wolfgang Rihm's *Lichtzwang* with the Philharmonic and conducted my Second Piano Concerto, with Paul Crossley as the soloist, then travelled to Paris for a concert in the half-empty Athenée including *Aria de la folía* and *Compases*. I also went to St Denis to see TSE, a group of actors from Argentina, performing Roberto de Arias's production of *Peines de cœur d'une chatte anglaise*, a piece by Geneviève Serrault based on a short prose work by Balzac. The images, forms and colours of the production became lodged in my brain and soon would not leave me in peace, although I did not know this at the time. I was then thinking almost exclusively of instrumental music, a preoccupation no doubt inspired by my works for violin, by my quartets and brief wind symphony, *L'autunno*, and by my work with Julian Bream and Dennis Davies.

To that extent, it was only natural for me to conceive of *Orpheus* as a *ballet d'action*, with gestures and steps on stage replacing the usual singers and with the orchestra taking over the melodic *Hauptstimmen* and *Nebenstimmen*. And in order for me to accompany the story, it was necessary to observe and continue the narrative in the way that the chorus does in Greek drama. It was during the autumn of 1975, during my second visit to Greece, that such an idea first entered my head, late one afternoon at Delphi, as I sat on the amphitheatre steps and thought of Inge and my terminally ill mother, and of Eurydice, of her death, her time in the underworld and of the endless pain that Orpheus suffers and articulates. As I was thinking these thoughts, a few notes registered on my inner ear. I can still hear them today, percussive and strident, stabbing and signal-like, and although I no longer know what they mean, I noted them down at the time and introduced them into the Apollo sections of my ballet like the briefest of snapshots, just as I heard them in 1975, as penetrating as flashes of lightning, in order to highlight the entrances of Apollo, a divine but cruel and cunning potentate – Apollo as a figure who is capable of robbing us of our lives, of denying our happiness and extinguishing love. Much of my grief at that time found its way into this score, but this in itself was not sufficient: I had to penetrate still deeper into this world of darkness, obeying the orders of a strange inner voice that sent me into the firing line of my wretchedness, unswervingly, like a soldier on the front. On 17 November, while returning from Amsterdam to Rome, I wrote down in a notebook that this whole problem – this *casus belli* – existed only so as to ensure that my *Orpheus* was as ravishingly beautiful as possible: I should lavish all my strength on it, so that an alternative world might be created within me. Resistance! At the end of November I travelled to Madrid to meet some Spanish colleagues who wanted to come to Montepulciano in 1978, following up this visit with similar missions to Zurich and Stuttgart, where I also saw William Forsythe to discuss his participation in the third Cantiere and to assemble a small company for it.

Christmas and the New Year were spent in London, but in different company from previously – a symptom of the extent of my infatuation. It was an anxious time. Occasionally there was an atmosphere of false joviality. My conflict expressed itself more clearly than ever: I was unable and unwilling to decide between the bottomless pit and paradise – both at once were impossible, it was as simple and as difficult as that. Nor was it by any means the first time in my life that it had been as simple and difficult as this, so impossible, so unforgivable and so indispensable, except that on this occasion it was already very late in the day – people of my own age simply never figured in the personal ads in *Time Out*.

On New Year's Eve I suffered my first, painful heart attack. I had been in Cambridge on 22 December and had discussed my wishes and ideas concerning *Orpheus* with Edward and tried to explain to him why I wanted him to treat this subject. His first draft arrived in London on the morning of 11 January. I read it in the taxi on the way to Hampstead, where the recording of *Voices* was due to take place, and I immediately telephoned Edward to tell him how much I liked it. A few days later we met in London to discuss the next stage in the process, after which I had to return to the Continent.

In early February, the blocking rehearsals for my production of *Die Zauberflöte* began in Stuttgart. And Edward's finished manuscript of *Orpheus* arrived, a great poem full of apocalyptic images and visions, of which only a selection would have to be treated – unless, that is, a film were made of it. But even then there would have been too much. Hans van Manen had been offered the job of choreographing the work but showed no interest in it (it would have been his first full-length ballet), and so it was tempting to take the risk of entrusting its realization to a member of the Stuttgart company, the young and talented, but inexperienced, William Forsythe, who announced that he would give his eye-teeth to work with a living composer.

I spent the first weekend in February alone in Stuttgart writing *Five Scenes from the Snow Country* for the Japanese marimba player, Michiko Takahashi, and in mid-February travelled to Zurich for a *conversazione* with an analysis and performance of *Tristan* in the Tonhalle. Meanwhile, work was progressing on *Die Zauberflöte* in Stuttgart. I see from my working diary that what I was looking for was neoclassicism, stylistic consistency and a draughtsman-like approach to the opera's process of humanization, the whole integrated into a kind of Jacobin Masonic ritual and resembling a Brechtian Lehrstück. The sun of wisdom and nobility was to bathe everything in its rays in Pier Luigi Pizzi's glittering, Palladian *palazzo* courtyard. The priests wore elegant everyday clothes, and it was no accident that the costumes were tailored by Tirelli of Rome. It looked like an Italian opera of the late *settecento*, somewhat inflexible perhaps, somewhat cold, not very amusing, but at least consistent. There was none of the warmth of the popular theatre, there was nothing circus-like about it. Instead, it had the not inconsiderable merit that music played the predominant role, with everything else merely serving that end and underscoring this earthly music of the spheres. And Pizzi's temple ('made in Italy') was so solidly built that the production could be revived a decade later and still look as spanking new as ever.

My next port of call was Vienna, where I was due to give a concert with the Austrian Radio Orchestra, but on the eve of the first rehearsal on 12 April, events at last caught up with me and after hours of terrible anxiety, pain, breathing difficulties and mortal anguish, I finally found the courage to call the sneeringly offhand night porter at the Hotel Imperial where I was staying (the place is no longer run as a state concern, as it was then, but has since been privatized and is now in Italian hands) and asked him to call a doctor. The doctor duly came and called the emergency services.

Helen came with me to the emergency department. My strongest memory of that charcoal-grey dawn was of the house walls in the narrow streets through which we passed on our way to the hospital: there was something quite chilling about them, as though we were already in the kingdom of the dead.

13

> 'What a pity,' said Karl. It was the first disappointment that he had suffered in this whole undertaking. 'I once knew an angel.'
>
> Frank Kafka, *Das Naturtheater von Oklahoma*

I was referred to Karl Fellinger, the cardiac consultant at Vienna's Rudolfinum Hospital, and remained with him for several weeks until Fausto was allowed to take me home to a steamily tropical Marino, although it was still only the middle of May. I tried to get on with *Orpheus* and sat on my balcony, gazing out helplessly into the northern sky and looking for the aeroplane that would bring Barnaby Priest to Marino. Barnaby was to work with me on the music for the ballet.

My illness – you could call it an industrial accident – had left me physically weak and extraordinarily over-sensitive. My capacity for work was much reduced. My doctors refused to allow me to go to Montepulciano. During the months that followed, I worked on *Orpheus* each morning but soon became tired and suffered from panic attacks, breaking down almost daily. But work was my only salvation. During the afternoon, Barnaby and I would work on the fair copy of the full score and in that way we managed to build up a rhythm. The orchestra associated with Orpheus and Eurydice is made up solely of strings, while Apollo – the ruling figure – is represented by a wind ensemble that also includes cymbals and all manner of bells. The writing for the strings I would describe as humanistic and introspective, while the wind music is imperious, resplendent and cold-hearted.

Throughout the summer and autumn I had regular sessions with Michele Risso, until I finally succeeded in breaking free from the fatal ties that had led me astray for so long, casting their magic spell on me and driving me to despair. Yet – to borrow an image from Bond – it needed a surgeon's knife to achieve this end. I found myself alone in a new and uncharted country, on a plateau so cold as to cut right through me. In the distance lay a mountain range, snow glittered on its peaks, and on the other side a steel-grey sea created a natural barrier and cut off all means of escape. It was here that life and its resultant encounters with reality, here that its confrontations and challenges had to be fought out and met. I felt weak and naked in the face of the music for *Orpheus*. There was such sadness in the world, I could not even express it in words, it seemed to me, let alone in musical sounds.

Orpheus's opening aria was written to the sound of pealing thunder. A few days later I jotted down an initial solo for the harpsichord, Eurydice's principal instrument, followed by the first *pas de deux* for Orpheus and his sweetheart. I wanted to write something more beautiful than life. I went outside before it was light and listened to the nightingales. On 10 June – the day of the new moon – I finished the opening scene. Meanwhile, Edward had had two meetings with Billy Forsythe at Great Wilbraham and telephoned me to dictate some of the changes that had emerged in the course of their discussions.

A piano solo for Scene Two, accompanied by six horns. Worked on the programme booklet for Montepulciano. On 29 June, in the gazebo, I began Eurydice's death and on 1 July Orpheus's second aria. I cut the pages of the last two volumes of the Gallimard edition of *A la recherche du temps perdu* and started to study them in detail. Took my first walk since the Viennese débâcle in the company of Yoichi and Barnaby. Fausto and Helen had gone to Montepulciano for the third Cantiere.

I began the third scene. What a world of darkness! I could now give a fair description of the kingdom of the dead. At night the barking of the neighbours' dogs went right through me. In the morning things were worse again. Black flags, bells tolling. On 3 August Gidon Kremer gave the first performance of *Il Vitalino raddoppiato* in Salzburg, and we listened to it on the radio. In early August, Billy Forsythe called in to hear what I had written so far. The sirocco ravaged the garden, and I made a start on the third of Orpheus's arias – the end of Act One was in sight.

> *Dream: five underground streams, clear, fast-flowing water, in pipes, natural riverbeds, i can see all five, am myself in one of these streams, don't know where i'm going, begin to resist and stand up in the stream and call out, louder and louder and increasingly insistent, i start to cry.*

Michele Risso tells me that what repulses me was made for me.

One beautiful and peaceful September evening – all the windows and doors were open, Wenzel and his son, Wolfram, had arrived from Berlin and Fausto had long since returned from Montepulciano – we were just sitting down to supper when half a dozen masked men burst in, waving guns, which they kept pointed at us while they robbed us of all that we had. We were so shocked by the experience that during the days that followed we seriously wondered whether in future it would not be better to have nothing further to do with such an unsafe part of the world. I thought it simpler to take rather better precautions in future and forget the whole affair. None the less, I lost four days' work while the bone in my nose, which had been cracked by the barrel of a pistol, was operated on. But after that I went straight back to *Orpheus*.

> Dreamt of *two groups of people arguing with each other, workmen, separated by a barrier. i heard them saying that peaceful solutions should be reached by thinking about them, in that way people would be happier. and i heard the pope giving orders to the effect that wherever there was a contradiction – in other words, a hole in the structure – the crack had to be covered over immediately with crimson velvet.*

At the end of September I started work on Orpheus's Great Aria in Act Two, into which I incorporated a number of ritornellos from the parallel passage in Monteverdi's *L'Orfeo*. Or should I say, rather, that Monteverdi's music represented the solid surface that my own work could use as a launch pad or springboard, just as a boat pushes off from dry land? The result was the Great Adagio that I had wanted to write for so long. And then it was the turn of the terrible scene in the Underworld in which Hades and Persephone fight like vultures over the fairest of all the shades in hell, Eurydice. I wrote it as an organ piece, which I called *Toccata senza fuga*, and had the impression that the whole horror of the past year's experiences had once again found expression here in particularly concentrated form.

> Nightmare: *Party offices in Milan. swastikas, i'm to be tortured, they're about to start, a priest in white is already there. i went there of my own free will.*

In October a delegation from Montepulciano arrived to discuss the following year's Cantiere. I suggested a folk music festival with lots of new folk music. I travelled to Florence for a ministerial meeting and worked on the Mad Scene in the train; it later got out of hand and had to be shortened.

Opposite me in the train sat a young worker interested in music: his name was Speranza – Hope. The minister agreed to a small increase in our grant for the fourth Cantiere. In early November I flew to London and worked with the Ardittis on my three new quartets, which they introduced to South Bank audiences on the 12th. The evening's programme was rounded off by a performance of my solo sonata, *Tirsi, Mopso, Aristeo*, again played by Jenny Abel. On 10 December I completed the score of *Orpheus* in London, an event that Fausto marked with a wonderful party at his house in Knightsbridge. By Christmas we were back in Marino, where I started work on a sonata for the Scottish viola player, Garth Knox. Saturn entered the Tropic of Cancer, which made me think that things would now get better. And I told Michele Risso that 1979 would be the year of the great *rilancio* of my birth sign, Cancer. Never again would we want to experience all we had been through in 1978.

On 1 January 1979 I began the slow section of my viola sonata and a few days later found myself in Stuttgart, where I inspected Axel Manthey's set model for *Orpheus* and met Billy Forsythe and Jens Brockmeier, whose services had been enlisted as dramaturge. It was twenty degrees below zero. I thought of my next piece, *El rey de Harlem*, which I wanted to start the following week and which I imagined as something exceptionally savage, colourful, tender and rampantly tropical. In mid-January I completed the viola sonata in London and during a raging gale went for a brisk march through Hyde Park with Michael Vyner. Meanwhile, Edward had started to write the libretto for *The English Cat*. I held out the sketches of *Royal Winter Music II* to Julian Bream as a bait that I hoped would persuade him to come to Montepulciano that summer and not only première it in the Pieve di Pienza but also present a popular concert at St Blaise's. Deep snow in London. I did not feel too good.

Early March – first orchestral rehearsals for *Orpheus* in Stuttgart. First night on 17th a brilliant success. London, work on *Royal Winter Music II*. Thinking of setting some of Bond's Orpheus poems for unaccompanied chorus. Early April write 'Mad Lady Macbeth', jot down first sketches of *El rey de Harlem* and study Mahler's Fifth. Think about *La Cubana*, which in its original version for television does not work in the theatre. My work makes only slow progress, moving along various furrows. Rogelio writes from Havana, complaining that he never receives any letters. All manner of preparations for fourth Cantiere. End of April with Mahler and Bournemouth Symphony Orchestra in Bristol, Bournemouth and Exeter, where I slipped on the freshly polished podium, but conducted Mahler's

Fifth to the end – with cracked bones in my right hand. Not until some hours later did the pain begin to set in. Eight days later, in Berlin, I conducted *Aria de la folía* and *Vitalino* with Gidon Kremer and the Philharmonic. Visited Paul Dessau, who had grown wizened and almost blind, led him by the hand through his garden. Looked at his score of *Leonce und Lena*, humming and beating time. Jens Brockmeier introduced me to Hans-Ulrich Treichel, a student of German literature and a secret poet who, like us, comes from eastern Westphalia. He trotted through Friedenau in tennis shoes and jeans, reminding me of a young stallion. Or perhaps it was more like an awakening colt.

The Berlin Philharmonic offered me a commission to write a new symphony, my seventh. In mid-May I devised some strenuous activities for Montepulciano and drove to Milan to hire a circus tent for my production of *Die Dreigroschenoper* – or *L'opera da tre soldi*, as it now became. Made little progress on *El rey*. On 22 May, Fascists in Rome poured petrol over a sleeping Somali in the Piazza Navona and set him alight. The Compagni di Piazza Navona collected money to give him a decent burial – a burial more beautiful than his life. Or so it said on the cardboard memorial plaques surrounding the scene of the crime, which was itself a sea of flowers. In spite of all their formal and atmospheric differences, there is a growing sense of harmonic affinity not only between *Orpheus* and *El rey* (it is no accident that García Lorca's Harlem is also a hell) but also with my three new quartets. Am I perhaps evolving some new means of expression? As long as it remains open and free from routine.

Attack the a cappella choruses with great gusto. Early June in London, where I succeed in raising funds for Montepulciano: Granada Television will finance and film the visit by the Grimethorpe Colliery Band. Sybaritic days spent beneath chestnut trees in flower, red and white hawthorn, lilac and peonies, but I feel to be growing older and dying. Can't accept it. How often I should like to hold on to what I feel – mostly it is things bound up with a certain painful enthusiasm. But I fail to do so. Moods come and go with a speed that makes it impossible to write them down and hold on to them. *Fotografieren verboten.*

Back in Marino. The *Cat* libretto had arrived, I read it to the assembled household. It had turned out quite different from the story recounted by Geneviève Serrault and was far more witty, far more relevant in terms of social criticism. It could have been subtitled *L'argent fait tout* – 'Money Rules the World'. It was no longer a fairy-tale play but a Victorian comedy of manners. Although much too long, it was beautiful and entertaining and reminded me of popular English art from the early Victorian era. I would have to keep this aspect in mind and find a suitable style for it. The libretto was exactly what I wanted, only much better, and showed once again how much of my work and my life Edward understands. It was as though we had always been together. Unfortunately about half of his uproariously rhymed songs and couplets had to be cut.

Went to Florence again in mid-June to fight for more money for Montepulciano, threatened to resign, got what we needed. Studied Beethoven's Diabelli Variations with amazement and admiration. Finished the short score of *El rey* on 14 June. Saw Lindsay Kemp in his own show, *Flowers*, in Rome. Bought a zither for Minette, my new protagonist. Thought of English folk-songs. Some time previously, the director of the Cologne Academy of Music, Franz Müller-Heuser, had asked me whether I would like to teach at his institution and set up a new course in composition. And Michael Hampe, the intendant of the Cologne Opera, was also trying to persuade me to reset Monteverdi's *Il ritorno d'Ulisse in patria*, using the existing material which consists only of the vocal lines and the continuo part in a copyist's hand. Couldn't imagine making much of it at this juncture.

I then jotted down the first sketches for *Barcarola*, a commission from Gerd Albrecht and the Zurich Tonhalle Orchestra: it is all about crossing the Styx. Charon's call is brought to life in the form of a trumpet fanfare. The piece will include several variants of this call and convey the feeling of a rondo. Don't know what the overall form will look like, intend to proceed piece by piece, associatively, without any plan, following feeling and intuition alone. Quote the 'Eton Boating Song' from one of the male-voice choruses in *We Come to the River*. The barcarole itself will be entrusted to a solo viola. Instead of variations, I mean to write counterproposals, increasingly fiery and impassioned; it will be like a great tempest. Recall the final lines of Ingeborg Bachmann's *Lieder von einer Insel*:

A great fire will come,
A flood will come over the earth.
We shall all be witnesses.

On 2 July I flew to Berlin for Paul Dessau's funeral and stayed at his house in Zeuthen near Königs Wusterhausen. In the evening I heard a blackbird, but the reply was very faint, its partner was so far away. Kaddish. *Barcarola* begins with a low, fortissimo D flat, the German note name,

Des, recalling my colleague's memory. His dog, Sasso, wandered through the garden, howling quietly. His children, Peter and Eva, came from the United States, Lotte Klemperer from Zurich. I went off on my own for a walk through the Brandenburg Forest, with its sea of purple loosestrife. The cemetery at Dorotheenstadt, the silent mourners. Wind in the oak trees. Paul's urn buried beside Fichte, Hegel, Schinkel, Bonhoeffer, Brecht, Heinrich Mann and Anna Seghers. On the way home I wrote in my notebook:

> *GDR – is the unease that i regularly feel when i stay there perhaps unfounded? is it all due only to western propaganda in the wake of the cold war? am i afraid of the punitive justice of the people i see in the streets, dejected and unsmiling, with their briefcases and nylon garments, they look depressed and seem so unfriendly. i'm very much reminded of the war years, when everyone was afraid of informers, afraid of deviants – perhaps it is this, maybe it is this parallel that made me feel so sad.*

Utterly exhausted and alone in Marino, wrapped up in the secret of my mortal anxieties, with no sense of desire, at the end of a tiring phase that would be followed by an even more tiring one. On 9 July I began work on the populistic fourth Cantiere, in which over one hundred townsfolk from Montepulciano were actively involved, young and old alike. By *ferragosto* I was back in Marino, shaking with exhaustion. I took a look at the sketches for *Barcarola* – but the earliest ones already struck me as the work of a stranger. I felt discouraged, but then moved on to the more recent passages, the livelier ones, and thought how wonderful it would be if something new and different were to come along and lift me out of this stylistic impasse and give me some new ideas. Gastón Fournier dropped by with his group of schoolchildren from Montepulciano and we spent the day celebrating, and I thought, these young people are the best thing about Montepulciano, they are our only hope. I wrote a brief solo for double bass, *S. Biagio 9 agosto ore 12.07*.

Over-exertion, physical discomfort. Black clouds trouble me. Have been working without a break since March. How is the barcarole to end? It cannot end in the kingdom of the dead, since at present I know what goes on there only from allegories. Perhaps there would have to be the sound of twittering and chirruping, as of birds and cicadas, certainly it would have to pass by in a strangely open way, with nothing more to see but only to hear, even if only because one has closed one's eyes. The musical shapes of the introduction will keep on reappearing in constantly changing forms, like memories transmuted with the passage of time, fading away or becoming distorted, while Charon's skiff continues to battle upstream, struggling to cross the river.

Michele Risso thinks that Ulysses set out again from Ithaca shortly after his *ritorno*. Shift of tempo in the barcarole, music full of anger and a literally infernal din. Longing for German forests and shade and for a break from this endless drudgery. To Bonn, thence to Brühl, for a state banquet in honour of the president of Italy, Sandro Pertini, who, as he indicated in his after-dinner speech, was going to the Flossenbürg concentration camp the next morning to visit his brother's grave. For my own part, I spent the morning walking in the ancient forest of Ardenne, but – alas – without meeting any of those strange, early Romantic visionaries of 1623 such as Touchstone or the fair Rosalind or even Audrey and William. On my return to Marino, I wrote a piece for Herbert Marcuse's memorial service at La Jolla, California. Giuseppe di Leva's libretto for *Pollicino* arrives and proves to be still closely modelled on Collodi's original. Michele Risso reads it and, aghast at the story's immoral and unpedagogical ending, suggests rewriting it to provide a positive, optimistic finale: instead of insidiously murdering and robbing the Man-Eater and returning home with the spoils, so that their dear parents now show them more affection and will presumably no longer expose them in the forest, the children break free from their terrible mothers and fathers, found a commune, smoke dope and grow tomatoes.

It is now late September and the bird-hunting season is upon us. We have to shut in our doves to prevent them from being shot. There is a constant noise of rifles going off, spent cartridges and shot are everywhere. I write a brief cello solo, *Paul Dessau*, that is intended to serve as a cantus firmus for a communal piece by Dessau's friends and pupils. At the beginning of October I pay another visit to Montepulciano. The fifth Cantiere is to be a festival of youth music and, at least for the present, to be my last contribution to the cultural life of this little mountain town.

Pollicino: di Leva spoke to the children of some of his friends and made a note of their theories and views on the subject of parental love and life, as well as parental loyalty (!). He also consulted a number of students of myth, especially Bruno Bettelheim, to whose writings I myself was finally alerted thanks to di Leva and this new composition. At the end of October our first volume of aesthetics was launched at the Frankfurt Book Fair, while the first notes of *Pollicino* were being written in Marino, allowing me to immerse myself gratefully in simple music under the pretext of introducing the next generation to the world of contemporary music. I kept trying to remind myself what it was like for me as a child and, later, as an adolescent to discover new music and to be so affected – so *bouleversé* – by it. What was it that had enchanted me with its magic spell and drawn me into its sway?

I wrote a schmaltzy, saccharine number for Pollicino's mother. I see her lack of resolve in defending her children as a weakness, a sign of sentimentality, a tendency towards kitsch. In other words, I use a musico-dramatic device to show kitsch as anti-social. Muster up all my reserves of banality to write a song about lying, a song, moreover, that attempts to do justice not just to the sentimental side of Pollicino's mum but also to her alcoholic binges. While *Pollicino* is still in its early stages and with a deadline for my realization of Monteverdi's *Ritorno* hanging over my head, I can already feel the music of *The English Cat* impatiently clamouring for Hinze the tom-cat's attention.

I lacked for nothing, I told myself. By the end of November I was hard at work among the creature comforts of London and by mid-December was able to send off Scenes Six and Seven of *Pollicino* to my publisher in Mainz; Scenes Nine and Ten were to follow by the end of the month. In all, *Pollicino* has twelve scenes. The new year – 1980 – had begun and by now I was in Copenhagen for a round of concerts. Here I got to know the *guldsmed* Torben Hardenberg and heard and saw some young Danish musicians at the Conservatory, including Hans Abrahamsen and his strangely affecting *Winternacht* for chamber ensemble. A few days later I was back in London for a visit to the Old Vic with Edward and Elisabeth Bond, whom I took to see *Peines de cœur d'une chatte anglaise* performed by TSE. Afterwards Edward went backstage to congratulate the actors. I was brooding on the idea of a more reflective type of music – pieces that would turn out completely *sui generis*. Now that the whole of the score of *Pollicino* had been sent off to Schott's, I was happy to be allowed to write for clarinets again, instead of for recorders. Meanwhile, Riccardo Chailly and Julian Bream had withdrawn from the fifth Cantiere.

In mid-March I jotted down the first sketches for *The English Cat* – with feelings of pleasure and contentment. Edward telephoned me in Marino and advised me, when writing the music, to think less of Gilbert and Sullivan and more of Mozart. The piece's harmonic language emerged in the course of composition, a combination of counterpoint and crystalline chords which, as the basic material of a set of variations, would be placed at the disposal of the villain, Arnold Plaice, and of the other members of the Royal Society for the Protection of Rats. I recalled the Diabelli Variations. At the end of March, while working on the finale of the opening scene, I noted that I had written twenty-two minutes of music in fourteen days. Entertaining, diverting and quietly enjoyable.

Ten thousand political refugees in the Peruvian embassy in Havana. On 22 April I hear Gerd Albrecht conduct *Barcarola* in Zurich. The audience demands to hear the last movement again. Prior to that, I had been in Witten on the Ruhr, my mother's birthplace, where I heard Garth Knox and Jan Latham-Koenig play my new viola sonata, after which Maureen McNally Giroux and my friends Hinz & Kunst performed *El rey de Harlem* under the baton of Spiros Argiris. Prescribed medicine for high blood pressure. Would so much like to do nothing but compose. In Marino, the May breeze brushes over our fields. In the middle of the month, Cubans flee the island in their thousands. I have to ask for a further year to complete *The English Cat*. At the beginning of June I start work on Scene Two, the night-time serenade on the rooftops of Knightsbridge. In mid-June I suffer a circulatory collapse and need to take a break. On 9 July Fausto drives to Montepulciano with clenched teeth and tears in his eyes. I remain behind in Marino for a few days. Grief gnaws at my thoughts.

The fifth Cantiere, from 25 July to 10 August 1980, was an outright success. I could not have wished for a better way of saying goodbye to a post for which I had such mixed feelings. I still recall the first night of *Pollicino* as vividly as if it were yesterday – the excitement in the packed hall, the atmosphere of a great family celebration, the ethereal, fresh-sounding voices of the *bambini*, the *gravitas* of the amateur actors who played the parts of grown-ups and the irresistible magic of Pollicino and Clotilda, the one-eyed Man-Eater's daughter who is helplessly in love with him. It gave me particular pleasure to write a little opera in which two wonderful Tuscan folk melodies that were no longer sung in the Orcia Valley and elsewhere in southern Tuscany found their way back into the world of Montepulciano's folk music. Long after the performance was over, we could still hear groups of young people wandering through the town and singing these songs at the tops of their voices. The second ends with the words:

Orchi, orche, maghi, streghe,
lupi non ci spaventan più.
Primavera è arrivata,
tratteniamola quaggiù.

(Monsters male and female, wizards and witches and wolves can frighten us no longer. Spring has arrived. Let us hold on to it.)

The Tölz Boys' Choir sang Bach cantatas and performed Purcell's *Dido and Aeneas*. And Billy Forsythe choreographed Thomas Jahn's ballet, *Peccato che sía una sgualdrina* in the Piazza Grande, a choreographic *tour de force* based on John Ford's incest tragedy, *'Tis Pity She's a Whore*, and danced by the youngest members of the Stuttgart State Ballet and by amateur dancers from Montepulciano. The performance went down well with the townspeople and their guests, especially the younger ones among them – even today, they still talk about it. There was also a series of concerts featuring works by the young Mozart, and Yoichi exhibited his sculptures. For me, the whole occasion had something final about it, but I was not in the least bit sad.

On 10 September I wrote to the mayor to tender my resignation and, as though to confirm me in my resolve, immediately resumed work on Scene Two of *The English Cat*. Michele Risso was ill. I accepted the position of honorary artistic director of the Accademia Filarmonica in Rome and almost immediately regretted my decision, since it meant having to go into town at least twice a week and spend hours sitting on a committee with Signore Panni and Pavolini, discussing concert programmes, savings, lock-outs and, above all, constant infringements in matters of artistic direction. I finished Scene Two of *The English Cat* on 12 October, a scene of moon and stars, with the lonely and thoroughly confused Minette alone on the tiles.

. . . such facility is almost irresponsible! my hand can scarcely follow my ideas . . . occult forces are at work. my desk has become too small, my powers of imagination are intense, i feel free from sin and contented. i must be ill, since writing has recently become such an enjoyable occupation. my senses hum like a beehive.

On 28 November a terrible earthquake in Irpinia causes immense panic and loss of human life. Write Minette's entrance in Scene Three. Early December to London for the English edition of my collection of writings,

Music and Politics. Christmas at Marino. At the end of the year I visited Michele Risso in hospital: his voice was weak as he spoke of the horrors of the leukaemia from which he was suffering.

At the beginning of January 1981 I conducted a number of my own compositions in Zurich and Basle. By mid-January I was back in Marino, working on the finale of Scene Three and, hence, on the end of Act One.

> *21 January: two days ago sketched out first part of finale, yesterday Puff's recitative, and immediately started part two, working on it till midday, also the postlude, and adding the harmonies. during the afternoon added the voices, too. i needed some more lines for Babette, Edward rings back half an hour after my cry for help and dictates the additional passages down the telephone.*

Nordic, Gothic enchantment in Copenhagen, to the beating of the Olympian wings of Purcell's 'Hail, bright Cecilia' and the singing of swans as they fly past our fifth-floor windows. In February, Fausto and I spent two weeks on the freezing-cold Portuguese island of Madeira, where my Aunt Leni from Braunschweig had fetched up in 1937 on board the *Kraft durch Freude* steamer, the *Wilhelm Gustloff*, and where it now did nothing but rain and snow. Here I not only jotted down my first ideas for my Monteverdi arrangement but also wrote the second subject of my Seventh Symphony, a theme that I later took over, almost unchanged, into the orchestral score.

Late March: final *couplets* of Scene Five completed in Marino. Read Marguerite Yourcenar's book about Yukio Mishima and began to work more seriously on the Monteverdi project. Also read Genet's *Miracle de la rose*. Torben Hardenberg visited Rome and made me a most welcome present of a young, female whippet, Tania by name, that was intended to keep me company from now on. After briefly thinking the matter over, she declared her willingness to do so. I fell helplessly in love with her.

> Dreamt *of a packed theatre, where Hinz & Kunst performed with white animal heads on their bodies and a member of the audience put his arm round me and said 'that's honesty for you!' i found it embarrassing and was glad to wake up*. My cheeks were flushed, but with despair, not shame.

Greek Orthodox antiphons in the Saint Nilus Monastery at Grottaferrata. I read to Torben from *The Selfish Giant* and *The Nightingale and the Rose*. Completed the prologue of *Ritorno*. Large orchestra. Choirs of trumpets and trombones. A large, modern continuo group that also includes electric guitars, banjo, harps, celesta, grand piano and the like. Folk instruments such as the accordion are reserved for the common people – the servants, swineherd and nurse. Towards the end of April everything gets worse again, and a period of deep depression follows.

Mid-May, another earthquake; we have to sleep out of doors. Are the police surrounding the house? Michele says 'Dio non esiste'. Whitish, lurid light. Whistling wind. *Pollicino* was shown on Italian television, and I was told that all the children from Montepulciano had watched themselves, after which they and their parents had paraded through the piazza. On 27 May I completed the fair copy of the first act of *Cat*. Permanent mood swings depending solely on the success or failure of my work. Also, the sirocco was blowing again, and at night, during a storm, I looked out of the window and, to my horror, saw an enormous, sinister red half-moon above the hill to the right of Marino. It had a threatening halo, a circle of light that boded no good. Michele says that if we were Catholic, he would say that I should pray for him. I shall lose my dearest and closest friend, someone who knows me better than I know myself, and I shall be more lonely than ever. I went to Cologne to spend a week with my students. By 6 June I was back in Marino. Fausto fetched me from the airport and said that there was bad news. I knew at once: Michele. He had been buried the previous day at Bracciano. According to Fausto, there were more than one hundred young people present, schoolfriends of Michele's son, their arms filled with flowers. No priest, but the widow of his friend and colleague, Franco Basaglia, spoke, as did the father of a patient. On the telephone, Ursula Risso told me that from now on he would guide us from within.

the birds' busy piping and calling among the scented flowers, but everything seems to tell only of grief and fragmentation. in the morning formal analysis of the scene in Genet in which Harcamone is executed, in the evening i plan out the form of the music from start to finish.
10 June: musical portrait of Harcamone as a childish double murderer, 1st subject. to Bracciano to visit Michele's grave, promised to hold out to the bitter end. Resistenza sempre! *called on Ursula.*
19 June: weather cool today, wrote 2 bars. 'Miracle' will not be a proper solo concerto, more of a Brandenburg.
21 June: make slow progress on clar. piece. drunk every evening.
22 June: seismic shock. double *of air in 'Miracle'.*

> 24 *June:* Ulisse – *draft Penelope's monologue as far as first outburst.*
> *27 June: nightmares about police. Monteverdi: concertante oboe for Penelope. yesterday memorable for unexpected burst of energy and the heady thrill of Monteverdi's harmonies.*
> *Sunday: dream in which a woman reads my palm and says i have 7 years to live. another 7 years in my lonely prison, immured within the high walls that cut off the elderly from the world, alone with my strife-torn, fragmented feelings, which i can discuss with no one now that Michele is dead.*

Occasionally the earth would tremble, my bed and desk would wobble and books would fall from the shelves. Gusts of howling wind, police sirens. Smell of sulphur in the air.

> Fall of the four officials in *Miracle*, la fête foraine – *even if i want to depict things that are ugly, evil and negative, it still turns out somehow classical, 'beautiful' – i'd have to have recourse to extra-musical devices in order to produce something genuinely ugly, but that's of no interest to me. i have to let my sense of style prevail and follow my intuition.*

Edward sent his revisions for Act Two of *The English Cat*. I read John Nathan's life of Mishima and began Ulysses' monologue, 'Dormo ancora?'. Every day, 8–9 hours' work. *in the morning the meadows wet with dew*. Fly to London on 19 August for rehearsals with Sinfonietta, Fourth String Quartet and wind symphony, *L'autunno. no longer feel the depressive tension of recent months. I can see:* in Marino we have been living in a state of perpetual fear, night and day. Unpleasant memories of it, feelings of irritability, evil, hostility, opposition. The Sinfonietta's concert took place on the morning of 22 August in the Queen's Hall in Edinburgh, and the next day we left the city for a week-long stay with Gaia and William Mostyn-Owen and their children at Comrie in Perthshire, a week of exquisite calm in the heart of completely unspoilt countryside, with pheasants, hares, ancient trees, amazing herons, fast-flowing streams and waterfalls. I lay down beneath a tree and immediately fell asleep. On the Sunday, Fausto and I had spent a wonderful time exploring Edinburgh, starting with the Princes Street Gardens, where we watched the entrants preparing for the annual bagpipe competition: dressed in their various distinctive tartans, they had come from all over Scotland and were now assembling in groups for the competition that was to take place later in the day. It was here that they warmed their instruments and tuned up, producing an open fifth as a double pedal point, a humming, buzzing, nasal sound that seems to issue from times long past. To move around among these pipers and approach a new group of players while the sound of the one that we had just left grew quieter and the strains of a dozen other pipers at greater or lesser distances filled the air with their silvery sounds was a source of genuine pleasure.

We spent the afternoon on the beach at Portobello, a resort popular with Edinburgh's ordinary citizens, who could be seen taking the late summer air, half-baring their deathly pale bodies and disporting themselves in the freezing Firth of Forth. There were also beer and bingo halls, merry-go-rounds, fortune-tellers and acrobats. I liked it here, I was moved, I felt at home and thought of the people from my petty bourgeois childhood, thoughts that sprang, not least, from the fact that this was my first free day for a very long time and because I did not have to work or to be in hot and dangerous Marino.

At the beginning of September I travelled to Wales with the Sinfonietta for a workshop at the Welsh College of Music and Drama at St Donat's Castle. The workshop lasted several days and revolved around preparations for a revival of *Voices*, which we then went on to perform in Frankfurt on the 12th to open the first season of concerts at the Alte Oper.

By the 15th I was back in Marino and with the house to myself, alone with my work and with unpleasant memories of the previous summer, memories that were so difficult to come to terms with and forget. On 3 October I wrote my romantic horn introduction to Ulysses' 'Io Greco son', and a few days later – *the october sun seduces me* – the slow bass clarinet section in my setting of Genet. I enter *les maisons des amours dangereuses, Pasoliniland.*

> *the 4 officials set off.*
> *17 October: read Mishima's* Decay of the Angels, *with background music provided by John Coltrane and John Clark.*
> *19 October: march of the 4 murderers in* Miracle. *'o fortunato Ulisse' transposed to E major. plan out in my imagination the drummer's music in* Miracle. *i live for* Miracle, *sleeping, eating, loving, it's work that counts. like the cabinetmaker or smith. pasting, cutting, discarding, transplanting. obeying one's own inner laws, putting up no resistance.*

today i have to play the part of a smith and drive wedges into a lengthy horizontal flood of tears.
26 October: still 'automatic writing' in Miracle. *Dance suite.*
27 October: The Tearing to Shreds of the Rose.
Anti-American peace demonstrations in London, Brussels, Paris and Bonn.

I completed the sketches for *Miracle*, then flew to Rome and from there travelled on to the Styrian town of Mürzzuschlag, where my colleagues from Hinz & Kunst were awaiting Maureen and me for a performance of *El rey de Harlem*. The idea for this concert – and it was to have notable repercussions – had come from my old friend, the cellist Wolfgang Florey. Many years previously, while driving from St Pölten to Italy, I had stopped off in Mürzzuschlag to fill up the car with petrol and stretch my legs and had noticed a plaque near the petrol station announcing that Brahms had spent a couple of summers in the town and written his Fourth Symphony there. But it was not really this that persuaded me to call in again later. Following the performance of *El rey* and a panel discussion that also included the general administrator of the Styrian Autumn Festival, Peter Vujica, I was taken to one side by a small group of young people who wanted to make it clear to me that it was they – the young and unemployed workers of the area – rather than the good burghers of Mürzzuschlag who represented local cultural interests or, rather, local cultural needs. They felt as though they had been sidelined and forgotten. They demanded culture and wanted people to be aware of them and their problem. They wanted to judge and portray life in their own particular way, even if in doing so they risked offending the cultural representatives of this nodal point on their country's railway network – a sort of Austrian Clapham Junction. Was I prepared to help them? I was.

During the weeks and months that followed I commuted regularly between Rome and Mürzzuschlag in order to work with these youngsters. Together we created a story which, grounded in real life, dealt with the cares and complications of the world of work and of those who were no longer in employment. The state-owned, high-grade steel works that had once seemed to guarantee a livelihood for many local people had all just been closed in the Mürz Valley. In our own piece, this became the starting point of a consciously exaggerated account of a local action group whose activities culminate in blockading the motorway and flooding the valley. The government's solution to the problem was to put all the strikers in a rocket and despatch them to the moon, where they were able to establish a society run entirely along their own lines. Or something like that. It was all very bitter and sarcastic. We dramatized the story, wrote song texts in rhyme, learnt how to set them to music and gradually and very cautiously abandoned the clichés of rock music, replacing them with home-grown produce. The result took the form of a rock opera, *Sperrstund* (the title means 'Closing Time'), and, together with a whole series of other events, was staged the following year in a room at one of the local pubs on the occasion of the Mürz Valley Music Workshop, as my initiative had now been called. My pupils from Cologne were also involved in the project, composing music and organizing and taking part in the performances. The whole exercise revolved around topical issues in Styria's history and art. Preoccupied with these new themes and challenges, I returned to Marino, whistling a snatch of a tune that was later to find a home for itself in my music for *The English Cat*, as the upper line on the celesta that accompanies the final villanella for the mouse, Louise, in the epilogue to the opera.

> Marino, 30 October. *This morning had the idea of basing one of the movements of the Seventh Symphony on Pierre Bertaux' reports from the Autenrieth Clinic in Tübingen, where Hölderlin was immured in 1806/7 and made to see reason by means of drugs and torture. perhaps like an arsenal of musical shapes shaken about in constantly changing patterns. there's also something Piranesian about it all, a wicked, evil 'scherzo' with a scream, shrill laughter, trembling, pathos.*

I finished the full score of *Le miracle de la rose* on 16 November.

> *Crystal-clear day, the peaks and ravines of the Abruzzi, the nearby olive trees and cypresses stand out from the overall picture like isolated phenomena, providing it with contours, shadows, lots of green. the stonework of the walls and old archways seems to expand in the sun.*

At the end of November I conducted a number of concerts of my own pieces in Chicago and at the end was asked by the director of the Symphony Orchestra's artistic administration, Peter Jonas, to extend my stay and take over a concert from an ailing Erich Leinsdorf. I agreed and went to New York, where there was more to amuse me than in Chicago and where I set to work studying my programme: my own *Quattro poemi*, Mozart's Piano Concerto, K488 and the 'Eroica' Symphony, which I conducted with great satisfaction in Chicago's Orchestra Hall on 11, 12, 13 and 14 December. I had already conducted the 'Eroica' in the Rhineland and in Edinburgh and had developed a very real affinity with a musical language that throws light on both present and future with staggering clarity. At each reacquaintance with the piece I had to reimmerse myself in the score and re-examine its every detail in order to fathom its secrets and see how I could best impart to my audience the multiple meanings inherent in symphonic writing of this order. For players who were used, on the whole, to working with jet-setting star conductors, it seemed not uninteresting to follow me down this path and to see for themselves how every evening the same pieces would strike me afresh and turn out differently as I noticed or discovered new aspects of them in the course of the performance. It was all a lot of fun.

By Christmas, I was back in a grey and windswept Marino, where I finally started work on my long-planned a cappella song cycle, *Orpheus behind the Wire*. Bond wrote a poem especially for it that relates to the occasion for which I composed the piece, namely, a protest concert held at the Academy in Cologne and organized by AIDA – an international organization for the defence of persecuted artists throughout the world. It was directed at the Argentine military government, which sanctioned kidnapping, torture and murder, and included first performances of pieces by Juan Allende-Blin, Dieter Schnebel, Jürg Baur, Wilhelm Killmayer, Johannes Fritsch, Joachim Blume, Tilo Medek, Charles Amirkhanian, Luigi Nono, Wolfgang Rihm, Thomas Jahn, Hans-Jürgen von Bose, Manfred Trojahn and Eric Stokes. It was also a gesture of solidarity on behalf of the wives and mothers who assembled every day outside the government offices in Buenos Aires to demand information about their missing husbands and sons, the *desaparecidos* – the men who had disappeared. We now know that most of them never came back – they died, or were liquidated, or were thrown into the sea from aeroplanes while still alive.

Throughout the whole of 1982 I continued to work on my reconstruction of *Ulisse* – and I use the term 'reconstruction' advisedly, since this, after all, was what my work was all about. The number of orchestral players that I used was more or less the same as that which is known to have been available to the Teatro di SS Giovanni e Paolo in 1640, when there had been around ten continuo instruments. I tried to imagine the sounds of the *Ulisse* orchestra at the time of its first performance playing music which, far from sounding sterilely scholarly, was pure yet impassioned, permeated, as it was, with the most subtle emotions of the human soul. Once again I found myself working under pressure of time – just like

Monteverdi, who spent his whole life complaining about such pressures – and became physically ill with exhaustion.

At the beginning of February, Fausto and I were invited by Gastón Fournier Facio's parents to visit them at their home in San José, Costa Rica, from where we moved on to Sacramento, a 2,500-metre-high mountain ten miles to the north of the capital, where we spent a couple of weeks, and from there to Tambor on the Pacific coast, with its farm and some four hundred zebus that were herded along the shoreline by cowboys every morning. There were reptiles here, too, and a tree full of monkeys. It was so hot that only at dusk and dawn could I go out without my straw hat on. I also had to spend nine or ten hours a day wrestling with Claudio, but I still had time and leisure enough to go for long walks on the beach or to swim in the sea, while the pelicans looked down with an expression of tragic bewilderment. By 17 February – Fausto's birthday – I had completed the recognition scene between Ulysses and Telemachus, and by 1 March had reached Penelope's final aria, 'Illustratevi o cieli', where it turned out that our heroine's obbligato instruments were wonderfully well suited to the four-part writing of Monteverdi's ritornellos, which I interpreted not only as the solution of a puzzle – rather like a game of solitaire in which no cards are left over at the end – but also as a belated acknowledgement by Monteverdi himself that I had been on the right lines from the very beginning.

trembling with exhaustion, flew from San José. stopover in Havana. Peeped out from the transit lounge. Not much to see, it was night, everyone was asleep in Havana. Only the customs officials were there, now wearing the yellowish-green uniforms of the GDR police. Some of my closest friends lived here, but I wasn't allowed to see them, simply because I wasn't able or willing or allowed to pay the price of the abject apology that would have entitled me to a visa.

> *Cuban emigrants on the plane to Madrid. try to engage them in conversation and find out more about the mass exodus in the harbour at Mariel – terrible: for every refugee there were four convicts. 125,000 people have left.*
> *head feels empty, little sense of emotion. no longer motivated, sucked dry, robbed of everything I've got, fit to drop.*
> *Marino, 4 March. improvise in the early evening, sounds that could lead back from Claudio to* Cat *(and to me) and may already have done so in fact.*

> *12 March. musica viva in Munich. conducted* Orpheus *suite and* Barcarola *(house sold out, lots of young people), while conducting felt like an old bird flying from all injustice (and from itself).*

On 25 March conducted the Berlin Philharmonic in performances of *Nachtstücke und Arien* and *Barcarola*, together with two pieces by Hans Abrahamsen, *Stratifications* and *Nacht und Trompeten*, the last-named a world première. Also visited Ernst Schnabel, who cut a sorry figure, semi-paralyzed, it was heart-breaking to see him. Went with Torben Hardenberg to see the film set for *Querelle de Brest*; it was the last day of filming. No one knew that it was also to be the last day of filming in the life of its director, Rainer Werner Fassbinder. My eccentric friend Dieter was there – it was he who had invited us to go along and watch. He was playing the part of an ordinary seaman who was to be murdered by Querelle and was also financing the whole production, presumably with bank loans. I did not ask how or why. It was his life: it was what entertained and amused him.

Back in Marino, I began work on Act Two of *The English Cat* in early April, slowly reacquainting myself with its style by rereading Act One. Suffered from headaches every day. Worked in the garden, spent Easter walking round the lake with Yoichi. He had been working on a new sculpture, a glassy wave of steel breaking against a black moonstone. I studied the diary that the Mürz Valley worker–poet, Walter Buchebner, had kept during his final illness. (It was Buchebner who gave his name to the Mürzzuschlag Society for the Arts.) Also read Karl Kraus's account of the case of another inhabitant of Mürzzuschlag, a local government officer by the name of Franz Hervay: so it was true, after all, that in 1904 the regional and, later, the national press had taken Hervay's wife to task for being Jewish, accusing her of adultery and pillorying her with such spitefulness and malice that Hervay had felt that he had no alternative but to take his own life. I planned to suggest that the Society for the Arts should take up this story at the next Mürz Valley Music Workshop and use it as the basis of a joint production involving the whole population and drawing on both music and theatre, but in the event the idea was rejected out of hand.

I spent a long weekend there during the second half of April, writing poetry and music with the young *fauves* in the cellar of the local elementary school. Some outstanding assistants had been placed at my disposal, including Harri Huber from Vienna and, an extremely important contributor, the lyric poet Hubert Höllmüller – Hölm – who was studying forestry and whom I still see occasionally today. I then went to Wolfsgarten to see dear old Aunt Peg and to rest a little. Thence to Cologne, which I left this year with the feeling that I was not such a bad teacher after all.

> *we worked on the middle section of a piano piece by H., breathless involvement of whole class. it was a bit like a father repairing his son's bicycle or taking over his electric train set. it was an exciting time, I've never been as good or worked with such concentration.*

On the other hand, I was now so exhausted – as always, hypertension was the worrying symptom – that medical help had become unavoidable. My blood pressure was lowered in Zurich, and my weight reduced. Sleep was also prescribed. Over the main entrance to the clinic were inscribed the words 'Medicus minister non magister naturae', a sentiment that I thought could so aptly be applied to musicians, too, and especially to composers.

Early in May we had a wonderful visit from Miguel Barnet. Fausto telephoned me in Zurich to say that he was waiting for me in Marino; I could hardly believe it. What pleasure I felt! I couldn't wait to get back to Marino. *everything should be less baroque, simpler, lighter.* Completely run down and at his wits' end, Miguelito told us a lot, but not, I think, everything. I had the impression that he was holding himself back. He had brought letters with him, together with an audio cassette of good wishes from our mutual friends and poems by Rogelio Rodríguez. Miguel tried to give me an idea of the present situation in Cuba. It wasn't rosy. It looked as though things were not working out. There was a shortage of everything, including foreign currency. The blockade by the capitalist camp was working like a dream. The New Man was still nowhere in sight. Miguel himself was still not a member of the island's only political party and continued to be isolated, but he was respected and even loved by the many people who knew him. Following his visit to Europe, he would return to his native land and continue to defend his rights *in situ* and in person.

We drove to Rostock and, together with Hans Magnus Enzensberger and Helen, spent eight days there as guests of the Städtisches Theater and its general administrator, Anselm Perten. Here we saw and heard the seventieth performance of an exciting production of *El Cimarrón* that had already left a deep impression on audiences in Mozambique and Angola, or so the actors assured us. We also saw *La Cubana*, heard *Vitalino* and attended a performance of *Undine* danced by a ballerina from one of the Warsaw Pact countries. Miguelito and I spent an hour one morning on the beach at Warnemünde, smoking pot on a bench in the shade of the birches and pine trees that looked out over the gently lapping waters of the Baltic Sea and dreaming of Changó, Yemayá and the drums.

A shadow was cast over this mood of carefree relaxation: Peter Weiss had died on 10 May 1982, and the sense of grief was particularly palpable in Rostock. It was here that Anselm Perten had championed Weiss's plays with particular attentiveness, and Weiss had attended all their first nights. I wrote to Gunilla in Stockholm. Never before had I met a man as sensitive as Peter, nor one as willing to take such risks and make such efforts. I admired his industry and meticulousness. His *Aesthetics of Resistance* is without doubt one of the best introductions for creative artists, whether they are interested in ethics or not. I recommend this work to my students and friends as a volume worth studying closely. How I wish I could have worked with Peter Weiss. We had once spoken of writing something for the young people of Montepulciano; and at an even earlier date, when my plans to set his first work for the theatre, *Die Versicherung*, had come to nothing, he had said that it did not matter and that it might in any case be better for us to collaborate on something new. Unfortunately, this was as far as we ever got.

On 26 May the brilliant clarinettist Antony Pay played and conducted the first performance of *Le miracle de la rose* in London and scored an enormous success with it. *Tout Londres* was there. I, too, liked what I heard – I thought that the music was wickedly glitzy and dazzling (an impression perhaps due, in some measure, to the humming and buzzing in my ears) and discovered Vespignani-like colours in it, especially those of his new *notturni* of the Roman underworld. The Bonds, too, liked it, as did the Brendels, the Hemmingses and the Pountneys. The Falklands War was then at its height, and the Argentinians had just sunk the British munitions ship, the *Sir Galahad*, with a French Exocet missile. Unemployed youths from the inner cities were queuing up to kill and be killed.

Early June: composing a source of pure joy. *yesterday I again twice felt the pleasure of total concentration like a gift from heaven.* I am both Tom and Minette, depending on the mood I'm in, and at other times I'm Tom's and Minette's boyfriend, who knows everything about them both and constantly blurts it out.

In mid-June there was a major concert at the Academy in Cologne, with twelve new works by members of my composition class broadcast on the radio. Puffed up with pride, they continued to work on their a cappella Buchebner project for the forthcoming Mürzzuschlag festival. At the beginning of July, I had a week-long season of concerts at the Barbican Centre in the City of London, where I conducted a number of my own works as well as some Classical pieces – Mozart and Weber, all dashed off with very few rehearsals, though I recall with particular pleasure a lively performance of Schubert's 'Great' C major Symphony. Dinner with William and Susana Walton at the Savoy. My friend had just turned eighty and was having problems with his eyes.

During the second half of June I had been Visiting Lecturer at the Fondazione Chigiana, where I was expected to enlighten young composers from various western countries and introduce them to the rudiments of music, a pedagogic aim that is, of course, well-nigh impossible to achieve in so short a space of time. To my dismay, my pupils from Cologne, whom I had taken with me to Siena, were not allowed to sit in on my lectures, and so I taught them on my free mornings and evenings at my hotel, an exercise attended by far more sympathy and success than my official duties were.

During August, Harrison Birtwistle placed at my disposal his house on the Inner Hebridean island of Raasey, and I spent a pleasantly quiet and productive time there in the company of my brooding fellow Westphalian, Jens Brockmeier. Whenever we were not working, we would go for long walks on the island, which was covered in heather and in yellow and purple rhododendron bushes that grew wild. Until the middle of the nineteenth century, Raasey had been fertile pasture and arable land, but the Industrial Revolution had brought with it a vast increase in the need for wool, which in turn had led to the introduction of the black-face sheep from Africa, a creature that remains grateful to its creator even in freezing temperatures and deep snow and without a roof over its woolly head, positively drooling over heather and rhododendron shrubs, with the result that huge numbers were introduced into the Highlands and islands, a move preceded by what is euphemistically described by cultural historians as 'highland clearances', when the crofters and their families were dispossessed and driven into the industrialized towns and cities, where they eked out a living as workers, the avant-garde of the later proletariat and of press-ganged cannon fodder. Others emigrated to America or even to Australia. The villages had long since fallen into disrepair, and Jens and I would occasionally stumble upon ancient, ruined houses, silent witnesses to a bygone tragedy. And black-face sheep grazed everywhere.

The light on Raasey was impressive. Whipped up by the constant wind, the sea reflected cloud formations that could change from the densest of thunder-black masses to silver-grey layers transfixed by thin pencils of light. Or a cavalcade of celestial wild horses rushed past, as though in a whirl of white smoke. Filtered sunlight and moonbeams struck the waters of these Hebridean islands and were caught up and refracted in a hundred different facets, sparkling and flashing to dramatic effect. Sometimes several different types of weather would all come along at once: while a cloudless evening service was being celebrated in the west, dark blue storm clouds would gather in the east – a storm was already brewing there, bringing psychedelic darkness to the island at five in the afternoon. In the south we would have a heron-grey drizzle applied with the lightest of brush strokes, while in the north was an almost Italianate opaline green, with funny little pink clouds that recalled nothing so much as a theatrical backdrop by Tiepolo and that disappeared into the distance, dancing and skipping as though centrifugally driven.

At ground level it was windy and cold. I had to go looking for firewood on the beach and would return with flotsam and jetsam that we were indeed able to burn – it reminded me of the past and of the time that I had spent with Fausto in Apulia at the end of the sixties. Our food was frugal, but the wine cellar more than satisfactory. A couple of crates of the finest vintage that had arrived from the mainland were left waiting for collection at the jetty of the strictly Presbyterian island, unrecognized and, therefore, unclaimed for fourteen days. Jens had to leave at the end of the month and was replaced by Hans-Ulrich Treichel. At that date neither he nor I knew that one day he would reach the same high level in my estimation and respect as that already occupied by the likes of Auden, Bachmann and Bond.

Back in Marino, work on fair copy of Scene Four of *Cat* that was sketched out in Scotland. Work on set-design, write out Scene Five. Mid-October, in Stuttgart for *Tristan* – Wagner's (Prelude and *Liebestod*) and my own – with the excellent Radio Orchestra. End of October in Mürzzuschlag, Buchebner choruses, satirical rock opera *Sperrstund*. All Saints' Day in Marino. The sirocco leaves us on edge. Have to ask Edward to make further cuts. Start work on Scene Six and, with it, a period of intense productivity during which music continues to obsess me at night and in my dreams. Nothing else seems important any longer. I think this piece must have something to do with the musical fantasies of my childhood and with traumatic encounters with humans and animals.

Dream about a tall derelict building. Jens, Uli and i climb up it on the outside (taking care not to look down!), accompanied by music by Brahms. at the top, clinging to a wobbly pedestal, we managed to enter through a sliding window. what we found was somehow connected with Montepulciano or some other God-forsaken mountain village. and there was a river, or the sea, in which i bathed for a while, until two frightful Italian women came swimming up between water lilies: they wanted to speak to me about certain matters relating to art. At that point i woke up with a start.

I had already begun work on Scene Six when I completed the fair copy of Scene Five on 28 December (it deals with the divorce proceedings between Minette and Lord Puff and the sensation caused when Tom is exposed as the counsel for the defence and is miraculously saved). Sketched interlude between Scenes Six and Seven, which I had already planned out in writing. It is to ooze passion and be called 'Courante', a title bound up, on the one hand, with a visual idea of the tubes and pipes through which London's sewage is discharged with enormous force into the Thames and, on the other, with William Byrd's Coranto, which I allow to come to the surface out of this flood of water – the same flood of water that will soon carry poor dead Minette out into the North Sea.

Once I have finished the opera, I shall reward myself by driving to Styria and going on long walks with the co-author of *Sperrstund*, Hubert Höllmüller, who tells me that he wants to show me the mountains of his native Austria.

On New Year's Eve I wrote Babette's entrance in Scene Six and on New Year's Day began the great trio for Minette (in a sack), Babette and Tom (on the point of falling in love again at first sight). Rang Uli Treichel to ask him how he would feel if, like Tom in *Cat*, he was suddenly not the poorest but the richest man in England (or, in his case, Germany), rich enough to pay Minette's (or, in his case, Ulrike's) divorce costs and take the girl home with him. He said that there was no doubt he would think himself one of the happiest men alive – and at a stroke I knew how the music could continue, what music must sound like when someone like Tom or Uli is happy.

In my search for the feeling of happiness that comes from a sense of Mozartian lightness, I started to suffer at night from hypertension and the fear of death. I read Elsa Morante's recently published work, *Aracoeli*, a wordy and poetic text that I found profoundly hard-going. By the end of January – *deeply confused and under some strain* – I had sketched as far as the beginning of the seventh and final scene. I now asked my former pupil, David Graham, to join me, and it was he who instrumented the short scores of the last two scenes. It was still not the end of the month and I already had Tom's murder under my belt and had finished the RSPR's final ensemble, 'In cases of this sort we charge enormous fees'. The children's tune that I had jotted down in Vienna over twelve months previously was now incorporated into the opera's closing words:

Louise I have become a mouse again
I'll steal the milk and rob the grain
My teeth are sharp and I can bite
I'll give the ladies such a fright
They'll stand upon their chairs and yell
I'll be a little fiend from hell
Screech! Screech!

This conclusion is preceded by what I can describe only as the very opposite of a love duet. In it, Minette appears to the dying Tom rather as the angel appears to the Christian convert, King Agramante, in *Orlando furioso*, as he lies dying. In combining and interweaving the intervals of the note rows associated with Minette and Tom, I promised myself that, *in its poetic way*, the music would *produce different and new harmonic results*.

By 31 January 1983 the opera was finished. Off to Styria! But on the Semmering Pass and in the southern part of the Mürz Valley it snowed incessantly, and all that could be seen of the mountains of Hölm's native Styria were the wooded foothills, and even these were snowbound. Long walks were out of the question, and so I flew straight to Berlin to talk to the set designer Jakob Niedermeier about working with me on my production of *The English Cat*. I also saw Jens and Uli and said hello to Peter Schneider. I stayed in the apartment in the Königsallee that Wenzel always placed at his visitors' disposal and it was here that I wrote 'Three Auden Songs' for Aunt Peg's seventieth birthday. At the end of February, to Cologne, then to London, where I had a good time at Fausto's and was able to rest a little and take myself in hand. Took the train to Cambridge and listened to the rhythms of the British Rail carriages from a musical standpoint, weighing up their potential use as the basic material for a planned Seventh Symphony. Pleasant weekend with Edward and Elisabeth, relaxed conversations and a long walk.

At the end of March I conducted a couple of my own works with the

Munich Philharmonic, *Tristan* and *Barcarola*, and by Easter I was back in Marino, where I was overcome by a sense of profound exhaustion, with hypertension, headaches and eye strain. In mid-April I was admitted to a clinic in Stuttgart for an operation on my sinuses. The senior consultant refused to allow me to start the blocking rehearsals for *Cat*. Finally I was allowed home and went straight to the theatre to make a start on the production. Three times a week I had to return to the hospital as an out-patient and have them continue to fiddle with my sinuses. Work suffered, and I was unable to get a grip on the situation. Scenographically and sartorially, too, we were still a long way behindhand and were to remain so right up to the opening night. Even on the musical side, there was a feeling of apprehensiveness. Indeed, a kind of joylessness settled over the whole undertaking – perhaps it emanated from me, because I was so under the weather, chock-a-block as I was with beta-blockers and antibiotics. I wondered if it would not have been better to postpone the first night, but, once set in motion, the machine could no longer be stopped, everything had to run its course. And run its course it did.

Most of all, I liked to wander off into the park at Schwetzingen, especially after it had rained, which it did a lot that May. Day and night, I would go there and listen as Nature breathed more deeply and the nightingales and frogs would sing and croak, and the mosquitoes buzzed like mad things. Or I would walk with the Bonds along the banks of an overgrown tributary of the Rhine, where there were large numbers of waterfowl and other strange birds that Edward was able to name without exception, recognizing them by the way in which they beat their wings, by the colour of their plumage or by their various types of call.

As the first night drew closer – it had been fixed for 2 June – so tensions increased, not least with our poet (which drove me to the brink of despair). The Schloßtheater has only 466 seats, the majority of which were filled with journalists, although there were also friends and sympathetic colleagues, family members from far and wide and, of course, regular visitors to the Schwetzingen Festival. It all passed off well enough, but I remained unhappy. Why hadn't someone else directed it, I thought, someone who was fit and healthy, someone with the necessary skill for the difficult task of directing an *opera buffa*? Someone capable of persuading opera singers to act and, above all, not someone like me, who was still too close to the only recently completed piece and incapable, therefore, of standing back from his work with the requisite critical and interpretative distance. Unfortunately, there was far too little contact on this occasion between

Dennis Davies and me – only rarely did the overworked general music director appear at the blocking rehearsals. No one knew – or so it seemed – in what stylistic and socio-critical direction the show was meant to be moving. At the first complete run-through, our poet – who had only just come to Schwetzingen – called all the singers together and explained to them that they represented the bourgeoisie, at which point the soprano singing the mouse, Louise, piped up: 'Me too?' – 'No, not you, of course,' replied the poet. 'You represent the proletariat.' So now we all knew where we stood and could finally get on with the show.

From a present-day perspective and at a distance of more than ten years, it has become clear to me that the music for *The English Cat* follows on naturally from that of my Montepulciano children's opera. It is, as it were, a *Pollicino* for grown-ups. It consists of lots of little songs – perhaps there are simply too many of them: Edward has such a tremendous facility for producing rhymes that everything was thrown in regardless. A scene is over, the *dramatis personae* prepare to leave and the audience is already looking forward to what happens next, when the characters tend to be struck by a further thought, a moral which, in their own view and in that of the poet, they feel the most pressing need to get off their furry chests as fast as possible.

In a diary that I kept while working on the music and which has since been published, I tried to show how and whence the individual ideas came together, arriving – as it were – on a wing and a prayer, and what I was thinking of at the time that I caught them up and wrote them down. Of Beethoven, for example. It is the music of masks: we, the listeners, are not required to know when the masks are removed and whether they are removed in the interests of the truth or merely for the sake of a change of mask. The truth of the matter is that I am not familiar with the music of grisettes from Paris cabarets, I invent such music and that is what I call it, but on no other authority save that which we ourselves, as creative artists craving approval, have laid claim to from time immemorial. It is Struwwelpeter's music, the music of a terrible bogeyman, as cold as the east wind whistling down from the Kahlenberg: it is the sound of Pomerania ravaged by fire, the sound of abandoned souls, robbed of their parents and children, silently weeping their floods of bitter tears. In this opera, it seems to me, major tonalities sound somehow more despairing than the comforting minor traditionally associated with gloom.

I tell of a fairy-tale capital, a cold, wet, overcast London peopled with ghosts and with figments of a lively imagination, where Father Brown and

Charles Dickens and Sacheverell Sitwell meet at midnight on a foggy Hampstead Heath and pass the time of day, a city of clubs and slums and so many people that it is easy to lose one's bearings; easy, too, to lose sight of all the criteria necessary to distinguish a Cherubino from a sex killer or a sister of mercy from a good-time girl. The setting, from which we, as authors, repeatedly stand back and which is forever on the point of disappearing, is a small West End theatre, reeking of gin, with threadbare crimson plush (of course) and a management that can afford no more than a handful of – admittedly highly gifted – musicians and a very limited number of no less brilliant singers, unreal figures with their trills and roulades, their vocal gymnastics and acrobatic turns. It is not my own heart that beats so fearfully against my ribcage, but that of Minette, my country cousin who, in a curious way, quits this life as a virgin precisely because she is so innocent and unsuspecting. For her boyfriend, Tom the alley cat, I had several real-life models on which I could draw, among them the black poet Anthony Mussala and his white colleague Uli Treichel and, as a result, had a greater body of evidence at my disposal, evidence that afforded a concrete starting point. And, needless to say, I imagined – nay, fervently hoped – that, like Tieck's tom-cat, Hinze, I too might possess an animal soul, so that, as though armed with some golden master key, I might reach the spiritual centre of my own music for *The English Cat*. A place where everything is allowed, because everything is pure. Where people still think of melody as a viable means of artistic expression. Where we break free from convention and chuck it all in, raise the mask and say exactly how things are, how we are and how we feel. And then replace the mask, so that the comedy can continue.

At the first performance in Schwetzingen, the piece was given without cuts and lasted 155 minutes, which struck people as rather long, a feeling that was shared, I think, by both Edward and myself. This may have been due to the shortcomings of the production, for which I myself was to blame. Later, I tried out several shorter versions, but was never entirely happy with any of them. It seems to me that there is still something not quite right. Perhaps it is the oft-noted and -regretted difference between English and German comedy that produces this disjunction. Or else the music is quite simply empty and misconceived, having slipped from my control. If the music fails to communicate itself to the sympathetic listener, then cuts would make no difference. It is like playing with a sick doll. I do not know what to do – as I write these lines, I can feel only the faintest glimmer of a hope that someone may one day turn up, some intellectual and musical director, who will find a way of approaching this piece and of bringing out the real character and style of a work that both Bond and I originally intended should be a folk opera pure and simple.

I returned to Marino and slept soundly for the first time in months. By now it was summer, with all its advantages and pleasures. At the end of June, we received a visitor: a magician by the name of Hächi Büm Büm presented himself on our doorstep.

14

The summer and autumn of 1983 passed off relatively peacefully. In July, Fausto accompanied me to Tanglewood for the summer school founded in 1940 by Serge Koussevitzky and still run by the Boston Symphony Orchestra. Tanglewood, where I had been signed up to teach composition for the whole of the 1983 festival, lies some 120 miles to the west of Boston in the middle of an area of woodland known as The Berkshires and overlooks Lake Mahkeenac (also called Stockbridge Bowl). The lakeside and surrounding countryside belong to the orchestra, which takes up residence here each summer and gives at least two major concerts a week under the direction of some star conductor. Audiences arrive in their thousands from miles around, and the vast majority listen to the music over loudspeakers while picnicking by candlelight on the rolling meadows. Bottles of champagne are uncorked *sotto voce* and the diners hand each other vol-au-vents, smoked meat and home-made delicacies to the strains of Debussy, Berlioz and Beethoven. In 1983 the concert hall itself – 'The Shed' – was still very simple, yet functional: there were no side walls, and swallows nested on the left above the first violins and on the right above the basses, darting in and out as though borne aloft, twittering, on the waves of symphonic sound. The fledgeling swallows used to make most noise during early Classical works. The eight-week festival has always been financed solely by private sponsors and concert receipts, and from the outset it has had the character of an academy, a character that continues to distinguish it to this day. A dozen young composers from all over the world come here every year to study, as do young conductors, singers and instrumentalists, all chosen by an international jury according to the strictest standards. In turn, these instrumentalists form an orchestra that meets at least once a day, and also form many mixed ensembles that rehearse mainly modern pieces, including ones written by the young composers who are present. In 1983 the conducting class was taken jointly by Seiji Ozawa and by Koussevitzky's great discovery, Leonard Bernstein, who, as such, was a product of Tanglewood, while the chamber-music class was entrusted to the famous violinist, Louis Krasner, who had given the first performances of the violin concertos of Berg and Schoenberg. I liked to attend these classes, as I found it extremely instructive and stimulating for a practising composer like myself to see how performing artists – our interpreters – come to terms technically with the products of our imagination. The members of the student orchestra were coached by the likes of Lenny, Seiji and Olly (Oliver Knussen) and by the end of the course had generally reached a degree of precision and unanimity that persuaded their listeners that they had been performing together for years.

We stayed in a large wooden house at the edge of the forest near Lee, a hamlet consisting of little more than a handful of buildings half an hour's car ride away from the campus. In fact, it was a glorified, two-storey hunting lodge with open hearths and bearskin rugs that seemed a trifle unnecessary, given the soaring, searing summer temperatures. All the pictures on the walls and every conceivable piece of crockery and kitchenware, including napkins and cutlery, were inscribed with portraits and the insignia of George Washington – the proud result of the owner's lifelong enthusiasm as a collector of such memorabilia. Racoons and skunks prowled the woods and hamlets, plundering dustbins and unlocked kitchens. At first light, red deer would appear in the mist-shrouded meadow and breakfast by the brook. As I watched them, I thought of Hächi Büm Büm and his funny name. (Where does it come from? Is it early Celtic, as spoken by the mythical Merlin?) I thought of this remote, mysterious and impish fellow, to whom we shall often have occasion to return, and I thought, too, of the pelicans, before reapplying myself to the tasks in hand, finally completing my a cappella choruses, *Orpheus behind the Wire*, reading some books on Johann Sebastian Bach, giving private lessons for the fellowship-holders and young composers entrusted to my care, lecturing twice a week and attending rehearsals and concerts. The student orchestra was conducted on this occasion by Gunther Schuller and at the end of the course played my Sixth Symphony as though to remind me that certain passages needed to be rewritten and others to be reworked and that this task still remained to be done. Not until December 1994, more than ten years later, did I finally get round to doing so – it was Ingo Metzmacher and the Munich Philharmonic who, keen-eared and keen-hearted, gave the first performance of what was effectively a new composition, in which passages originally left to the performers to improvise were now written out in full. The result I found deeply satisfying.

From Tanglewood we flew to San Francisco for the Cabrillo Festival which, founded by Lou Harrison in 1962, takes place every summer in Santa Cruz and the surrounding area – it was here, at the whitewashed mission of Dolores de San Juan Bautista, that Alfred Hitchcock filmed parts of *Vertigo* in 1957. Here, too, Dennis Russell Davies conducted my *Barcarola*, and I too wielded a baton on a couple of other occasions, albeit at other venues. The regular rhythm of work was agreeably interrupted by automobile excusions into the interior and along the magnificent coastline. Everything seemed so easy and yet so unfathomable. A mild morning breeze was blowing in from the Pacific as a guitarist from Oakland, David Tanenbaum, played me the whole of the *Royal Winter Music*, a performance so intelligent and affectionate that I was moved to write a piece especially for him a few years later, my *Ode an eine Äolsharfe*. The good people of Santa Cruz County had joined forces with local firms to enable them to give the United States première of *Pollicino* with Hispanic, black and pale-faced children, directed by Rhoda Levine and conducted by Dennis himself. They all had a whale of a time.

At some point I had to return to Europe and to Marino, where I explored some new themes, at least to the extent that it was not a question of taking up certain old themes again, themes which, like a pedal point or a cantus firmus or basso continuo, have accompanied me throughout my life. On 17 September I again conducted the Berlin Philharmonic – on the programme on this occasion was the première of a piece for brass, *Sonata per otto ottoni*, together with *Cinque piccoli concerti* from *The English Cat* and *Heliogabalus imperator*. The following evening I went with Jens Brockmeier and Uli Treichel to the Ellis Bar in the Skalitzer Straße in Berlin, where I enjoyed myself every bit as much as I had done thirty years earlier. For reasons that he did not understand but that invariably made him blush slightly, Uli kept finding himself on the receiving end of free rounds of brandy.

In the autumn of 1983 the angelic figure of Hächi Büm Büm entered my life with foolhardy bravery, taking upon himself the difficult task of watching over me and keeping me company, albeit only in my thoughts and at a distance. From now on, an extraordinary presence was to accompany me and my work, investing it with a delightful tension, high expectations and even with a certain curiosity about what the future might offer.

Rather like Comrade Berroa's black cat in chapter nine, Hächi Büm Büm is generally invisible, but, bidden or unbidden, he is invariably there in a trice, only to disappear again the moment you look up from your book. Perhaps he was never there. He is virtually immaterial, more a figment of the imagination, a train of thought, an outburst of emotion, a mood or some extraordinarily disorderly state of mind.

> No! No little puppet he (don't snigger!),
> But just a beautiful fictional figure . . .

On 29 September I drove to Taverna di Montecolombo for the burial of Fausto's eighty-seven-year-old father, Don Mario, a wonderful *romagnolo* of late nineteteenth-century archaic peasant stock, with finely chiselled features inherited by his sons and with immense expertise in the fields of viticulture and olive-growing. He had come to Marino every year to superintend the olive harvest and grape-pressing. When his end was at hand – and dying, for him, was no easy matter – his sons had shared his bed with him in time-honoured fashion and held their father in their arms as he slowly slipped away.

Throughout the journey there and back, I could not get out of my head the opening movement of my new symphony – my seventh – not a single note of which had yet been written down.

> 14 October: *every day since my return* [from Hamburg, where I gave a talk on Bach on the 7th and received the Bach Prize, and from Cologne, where I had had one of my regular meetings with my composition class] *spent a few hours in the morning working on the symph., have found a form that reflects HBB's ideas. keep the music light, continue to strike a note of blissful happiness, express the joy that the october light brings with it.*

I had a brief distraction in the form of three puppet plays for Montepulciano to words by Uli. For each piece, I wrote a little song for the young members of the Concentus Politianus. Also a fairy chorus, with accompaniment for three psalteries. All four contributions were conceived as basic material for the town's young composers-to-be, which they could use *ad libitum* under the supervision of their teacher, David Graham. The return journey along the old Via Cassia was memorable not only for the magical autumnal light in which the whole scene was bathed, but also for the Perugino that we saw in Città della Pieve.

> *18 October: a third of the 1st movement is now down on paper. HBB has devised a note row that i can introduce into the movement's tex-*

tures as a third distinctive element. i'd like to try to sketch out the whole of the movement in advance. i know that it is intended to be a pyramid and that there will the sense of a gradual ascent, also in terms of pitch. rhythmic energies have been developed, and there are already almost too many melodic ideas.

the autumnal brownish-gold of the beginning could become brighter as the shadows disappear.

each section is a variation on something that has gone before it, thereby changing its underlying shape.

the opening movement is a dance, a Deutscher, a Swabian dance, an allemande.

November spent in London; made good progress on the symphony, although it was not until the beginning of January of the following year that the first movement was finished in short score. As it developed, this pastoral allemande gained in momentum, until by early December *the planets were skipping and dancing* at its second great climax.

At Christmas, Uli arrives in Marino and reads me the draft of a libretto. Our piece is intended to be a German opera and to treat a German problem that became increasingly acute in 1968 and in its immediate aftermath; namely, the problem of the Münster Anabaptists and rebaptism. It is about revolution, longings, dreams, about the death of death and about immortality.

it is full of images and feelings that concern us – and, of course, there is a lot of talk about failure. at present, the book still strikes me as a little too understated and too cautious, seems not to draw on all the available resources, but to need more lyricism, more expression and excitement.

On 8 February 1984 *La chatte anglaise* received its first performance at the Opéra-Comique in Paris and, according to Helen, was a great success with audiences and critics alike. (There were seven perfomances in all.) Two pages in *Le monde*. I had a great time at the rehearsals and enjoyed meeting not only journalistic researchers (an opportunity to polish my French!) but also the Bertaux, the Bogianckinos, Aunt Peg, our mutual friend, the kind and witty Beatrix von Hohenlohe, Titina Maselli and, last but not least, Charlotte Aillaud, the mother of the painter and set designer, Gilles Aillaud. There was a gala supper after the first performance at the Louis XIV on the Boulevard St-Denis.

*

On 17 February we celebrated Fausto's birthday at Marino. By way of a surprise, children from Montepulciano performed a serenata with a number of older and newer pieces, together with a serenade by David Graham. *on monday that funny little man, the old magician Hächi Büm Büm, put in an appearance.* I was sitting at my score, my head fit to burst. Absurdly high blood pressure, no one knows the medical reason for it. I say it is the psyche, deep injuries, rootless unrest, *after all, I am cut off from my fellow creatures.* It was not until March that I was finally able to make a start on the second movement of the symphony. On 14 March I conducted my Wagner–Henze programme with the Orchestre de Paris at the Salle Pleyel. A young local pianist, Pierre-Laurent Aimard, played the solo part in *Tristan.* After the concert, Pierre Bertaux gave me some more details about the methods used at the Autenrieth Clinic at Tübingen, details that he had not included in his book and that helped to explain how the excitable Hölderlin had been forcibly reduced to silence in 1806.

> Marino, late March: *last night tormented by the same recurring dream: no matter what i do, i fail to complete a drawing showing the three dimensions of my work on* River: *real life, its scenic component and the music. by day, conversely, i make good progress on the second movement of the symph. deep shadows are cast over the soul of this music.*

From time to time I help out in the garden, doing odd jobs of a strictly subordinate – and, therefore, all the more welcome – nature. We have planted a young olive tree – it is still only fifty years old. Work quietly and conscientiously on the full score. Soulscape. Epilogue for bass and contrabass clarinet, a variant on the oboe duet from the opening. Also solemn interjections on the woodwind and brass in other registers, interjections derived from material from before the oboe duet and revealing a certain harmonic beauty. Went on five-kilometre walk with Uli through verdure-clad vineyards. Wonderful trip to Morocco at Easter. HBB sits at the steering wheel, his wings neatly folded, and acts as our guide. The Atlantic air is like paradise. A stork's nest on nearly every roof-top. Not a breath of wind as we travel over a sun-baked plateau and in the evening reach Fès, the Middle Ages, an awe-inspiring experience, a foreign culture sinisterly associated in my mind with fairy tales and primeval fears. The uptown tanners and dyers remind me of Hades and of the leather-shirted boilermen at the crematorium in the Central Cemetery at Lichtenberg in Berlin, their bare arms caked with greasy, coal-black soot. On the brightly coloured hills beyond the city walls, young men in white caftans can be seen reading as they take the fresh Easter air, sauntering along and sometimes stopping for a moment to mark a particular passage in their books: it turns out that they are students elegantly preparing for their university examinations (at home or in their student hostels it would no doubt be too crowded and too noisy) and presumably studying and learning all the important rules and ideas set forth in the Koran. On we go. In Marrakesh the tourist gains the impression that he is not allowed to stand still or wander around and that it is only right that he is forever assailed, accosted and importuned. You feel somehow out of place here. You wish you were somewhere else. In the mountains, for example, by the snowline. Majestic scenery, crystalline air, light and cool. Delicate shades of arboreal blossom against the darker stonework. Water from melting snow plunging down in torrents. And in the evening toads can be heard calling in the gardens of the famous Mammounia Hotel.

Peter Vujica from the Styrian Autumn Festival had rung me while I was still in Paris to suggest that I might like to transfer my didactic experiments from the Mürz Valley to western Styria and to a little town by the name of Deutschlandsberg (stressed, please, on the second syllable), where Barbara Faulend-Klauser, the director of the local school of music, was awaiting me with open arms. And so, immediately after my return from Morocco, I drove to Deutschlandsberg, taking with me a sociologist from Stuttgart, Michael Kerstan, who was especially interested in ways of educating people in the arts and in breathing cultural life into towns and cities. Here we joined up with one of my former pupils, Gerd Kühr from Klagenfurt, and looked over the place, meeting local music lovers and receiving an account of the population's cultural needs and wishes. They were all wildly enthusiastic about the idea and wasted no time in proposing a couple of projects that could be realized in time for the forthcoming festival: the people from the 'theatre centre' wanted to stage a great spectacle with fireworks and music; and the cellist Heinrich Schiff was keen to hold a workshop with the school of music's chamber orchestra, a body of players which, largely made up of strings, consisted of pupils and staff from the school. The result of our collaborative efforts was to be a popular piece telling of the delights and worries of the local population both past and present. And on 24 April four children from Landsberg began their first attempts at composition at the school of music, under the watchful eyes of myself and Gerd Kühr. The results were so encouraging that we decided to continue with the experiment: the youngsters would come to Marino after Easter for an intensive course to further their education.

On the evening of 1 May, I completed the full score of the second movement of my symphony in a hotel room in Cologne – never before had I known music of such darkness nor been able to capture it in writing with so great a degree of intensity.

> Dream: *Pierre Bertaux and his wife (Danielle Laroche-Bouvy) help me with a difficult passage in the symphony. (for the 3rd movement) have the idea of generating and combining several heterogeneous cells that keep on appearing and colliding with each other, rather in the manner of a rondo, but in different forms. also there is the very naïve Bruegelesque or Piranesian presence of sinister gadgets, instruments of torture of a kind recently described to me by Pierre in Paris. can be cold-hearted about it, and am determined to be so, in order not to become too personally involved.*

By 8 May I was back in Marino and had made a start on the first of these infernal machines.

> *already have a sense of spinning, a kind of toccata-like recitative and also a song, a folksong and popular number that could turn into Hölderlin's screams, louder and louder and ever more terrifying, until they finally break off.*

30° in the shade. Fear of earthquakes. White light. 13 May: another fairly powerful tremor in southern Latium and the Campagna – 27,000 people have been left homeless. On the 19th I completed the sketches of the third movement. And on the 31st, profoundly moved, I performed *Tristan* with the New York Philharmonic and the extraordinary Emanuel Ax at the piano. As soon as I got back from New York, the children from Landsberg arrived, accompanied by their delightful director of studies, and learnt to make the first connections between one note and the next, a learning process that involved not only playing the music but also playing games. They sat apart in the garden, humming and listening to themselves, thinking and making corrections. Gerd Kühr and I would walk round, stopping at each of the children from time to time and, wherever required, offering our advice and practical help. At midday and again in the evening, the results were collected and performed in front of the whole of the group for constructive individual and collective criticism.

At the end of June I met Alain Resnais in Paris and discussed with him the music for his new film, *L'amour à mort* (a kind of take on the Orpheus myth set in the present – the woman follows her dead lover into the hereafter). I watched the film mute on the editing bench and made a note of Alain's wishes. Thought the film very beautiful and moving. In early July there began a more settled period in Santa Fe, New Mexico, where I was able to complete the fair copy of the third movement of the symphony and write and instrument the whole of the fourth. We lived in the middle of the Pueblo in one of those comfortable American houses furnished in the Indian fashion; there was shade and a garden, and it was quiet – we could leave the doors and windows open and breathe the high-altitude air 7000 feet above sea level. Our host, the director of Santa Fe Opera, John Crosby, had placed a piano at my disposal and so I was able to work for eight or nine hours a day on the symphony, while above me, nearer the mountains (and not far from Los Alamos and its atom bombs), the American première of *We Come to the River* was being rehearsed with Dennis Russell Davies and Alfred Kirchner. The production opened on 28 July and left, I think, a fairly deep impression.

That my memories of these weeks in Santa Fe are as vivid as they are specific is due, I think, not only to the effort involved in such concentrated work that absorbed me to the point where I seemed to enter a trance-like state, but also to a combination of mental and physical circumstances of which I was a prisoner and that seemed, in one way or another, to place extreme demands on me, while in a different time warp, parallel to it but not in sync with it, my music – my actual and principal *raison d'être* – continued to be written.

I ruined my birthday party by throwing a series of tantrums, demanding examples and proof of my alleged lack of love. While sparklers burnt outside in the garden, I sat indoors reading the final volume of Virginia Woolf's diaries – ideal material for an invalid incapable of sleeping from sheer exhaustion and resistant to any impulse to make his peace or to derive any pleasure from scenes of reconciliation. Together with Fausto, I drove out to see Red Indian settlements to the west. Watched a vulture as it soared majestically into the air with a fat rattlesnake held tightly in its talons. And we came to the river – the Rio Grande – only to find that it is no grander or wider here than the Weser at home in the Porta Westfalica. Tired, but twitching with a real love of life. A new moon above wonderful clouds, a golden red horizon, with Hächi B.B. sitting on a telegraph wire diagonally opposite the house where we were staying and twittering a serenade. At first light we were woken by noisy crows, blue jays and turtledoves recalling the terrible state of abandonment, finality and damnation. Walked hand in hand down Canyon Road in the evening. During the daytime worked on my symphony, inspired by Hölderlin's lovely swans as they dip their heads in the sacramentally sobering water, an ideal image of redemption and harmony.

On Saturday, 28 July, I noted in my diary that at eight o'clock the previous evening the final notes were entered into the score ('in the wind the flags are jangling'), that my Seventh Symphony was finished, that we celebrated the occasion at the 'Rancho encantado' with Maureen, Claude, their daughter, Jocelyn, and her boyfried, Tom, and that I was surprised that I was still alive.

In early August I recorded the soundtrack of *L'amour à mort* in London and in the middle of the month conducted the excellent Scottish Chamber Orchestra at the Edinburgh Festival in performances of my own *Aria de la folía española*, Haydn's Symphony No. 105 and a concert aria, *Abendland*, by one of my students from Cologne, the American composer, Jeffrey Cotton. At the end of the month I flew from London to Berlin, where I stayed with Wenzel and spent several hours at a working meeting with Uli, by the end of which I think that neither of us felt that we were on the right lines with the Anabaptist idea. By early September I was back in Marino. I cancelled concerts. Was unable to work. Had difficulty proofreading the first galleys of the first part of my Seventh Symphony. Mid-October, travelled to Deutschlandsberg for the first Youth Music Festival, a five-day programme of performances of older and newer works at the centre of which was, on the one hand, Heinrich Schiff's orchestra workshop and, on the other, performances of four pieces by first-time composers from our own workshop. The whole affair was a huge and outright success with music lovers of all ages from this small market town in western Styria.

By 17 October 1984, I was back in Marino and had started work on my *Liebeslieder* for cello and orchestra. My basic aim in writing this piece was to compose a set of songs without words or, to be more accurate, to follow up an idea that I had already tried out with my students, namely, to analyze poetry and to give appropriate musical expression to the formal and figurative criteria that might possibly emerge in this way. In other words, a poetic formal model would be turned into a musical formal model; and musical shapes would have to be found to correspond to this or that poetic object or idea, to this or that image or emotion or figure or effect. I have always considered this method to be both instructive and stimulating (well, it was I, after all, who devised it) and have drawn upon it for decades in the context of my own work. Indeed, I had just done so in the finale of my Seventh Symphony when I set Hölderlin's *Hälfte des Lebens* for symphony orchestra. But even in my First Cello Concerto (*Ode to the West Wind*) from the early fifties a relationship had already been established with the poetic word – the very title of the piece refers to Shelley's eponymous cycle of sonnets. At that date I was still keen that this relationship should be spelt out in the printed score, but in the case of the *Liebeslieder* I preferred to draw a veil over the names of my collaborators (all of them excellent poets), so that listeners should not feel obliged to keep looking for parallels between poetic and musical expression, but should simply follow the music. Only later, as the music reverberates in their inner ear and its message continues to echo within them should they begin to appreciate the links between the two and understand how they are related.

The piece was to be free from unnecessary flourishes, but it was also intended to be free from the drama and darkness of my Seventh Symphony. Only the beautiful aspects of love, the blissful, heart-warming and rare moments of emotional calm were to find expression here.

My Seventh Symphony received its first performance at the hands of the orchestra that had commissioned it – the Berlin Philharmonic – on 1 December 1984, when it was conducted with *élan* and expressive power by Gianluigi Gelmetti, whom I had observed and admired in recent years as principal conductor of the RAI Symphony Orchestra and, later, at the Rome Opera. *black grief, gaping chasms, a bottomless pit.* I trembled and shook throughout the rehearsals and performance. Felt admiration and gratitude for the orchestra. *the applause went on for 12 mins.* Under Gelmetti, the piece lasted forty-six minutes. (When I conducted it myself in Cleveland in 1985, it took 35′ 52″.)

I wish I could have stayed longer in Berlin, this sprawling, crackling, solidly frozen city that creaked at every joint. I called on Götz Friedrich, who had invited Uli and me to write the German opera that was refusing to make any progress. Was the subject matter to blame? (Somehow or other, the Münster of the Anabaptists was to be linked on a cerebral level with a besieged town of today, but not in too obvious a manner.) Had we finally realized that we were getting bogged down in speculation and cultivating a false artificiality that lacked both nitrogen and oxygen?

Finally I was able to take a break, and so I set off for Cyprus, where it is said to be quite glorious, even in December, or so I was assured by the travel writer of the *Observer*. A week at the deserted Hotel Forest Park high up in the rain clouds. One could walk for miles if well wrapped up in scarves and woollies, and it was even possible to trudge through the snow and pine-scented forests to the monastery at Phini. At sea level, there are three lakes near the airport at Nicosia, and all were completely covered with wild swans awaiting the end of the cold spell that was currently affecting their destination in Asia Minor. (The meteorological abilities of Siberian swans are evidently far superior to those of British weather forecasters.) It was wonderful to see them caught in the sun's first rays on the morning of my departure. At that very moment, a wedge of them flew past in a majestic V-formation, silent, alien and strange.

Cyprus had proved a wash-out, but I was reluctant to return to Marino, since I can never be there with a good conscience and not be working. But as I had a doctor's certificate, I decided to spend Christmas and the New Year with Peter Adam at La Garde-Freinet in Provence. Here the sun was shining, and I was able to chat with Peter and his friends – matters of no moment and unrelated to music – and eventually began to calm down a little. On 5 January 1985 I decided to telephone Götz Friedrich in Berlin and call off the opera, at least for now. Uli and I had to come up with some new ideas. I felt that a load had been taken off my mind. I taught my composition class in Cologne, stopped off for a working visit in Deutschlandsberg and by the 13th was back in Marino, looking forward to writing a new piece, on which I set to work with a will. Uli looked in and I told him that, as far as I was concerned, the Anabaptists were dead. I talked to him about myths and fairy tales, and also about the need for a proper dramatic conflict, at which point Uli fainted. Fausto caught him as he fell and buffeted his cheeks, while I brought vinegar and a sponge. Uli opened his eyes and the first thing that he asked was whether I now wanted something completely different. I told him that, well, it all needed more passion or, not to put too fine a point on it, it needed some passion, full stop. In short, it needed a plot. And I wanted it to be somehow mythical, with various dimensions of time and space. Then, feeling slightly feverish, I withdrew.

On 8 March 1985, following the final rehearsal of my Seventh Symphony in Munich's Herkulessaal, I was invited to have lunch with Jürgen Kolbe, who advised the city on artistic matters and whose other guests included Elisabeth Hartmann, Marianne Koch and two local councillors, Irmgard Mager and Franz Forchheimer. I found myself sitting next to the art historian Hans-Georg Berger, who had an excellent record organizing festivals. Kolbe was keen to interest me in running some kind of music-theatre festival – it was to be left to me to devise what sort of a festival it was to be and to define its contents. I thought the matter over only briefly before saying that, yes, I would think it over – I first wanted to reflect on its form and content and also on the possible cultural and political uses of such an institution, but it was not long before I submitted an outline proposal in which I pointed out that there were already opportunities for young composers in the recital room and concert hall, but that such composers were rarely heard in the opera house. The reason for this, I went on, was principally because young composers were put off writing operas: they were remote from the theatre and the world, a remoteness that was due, in turn, to indifference to new names on the part of opera-house administrators, to a lack of encouragement and to the hegemony of the older generation of composers, all of which 'forced composers of the younger generation to abandon all hope of working in the music theatre, at least for the foreseeable future, even though such work is crucial for their artistic development, not least because it brings them into contact with a non-specialized but no less demanding audience'. And I wrote: 'In Munich, there would be an opportunity to remedy this situation.'

I suggested that in the course of an approximately four-week festival, between four and six new works – all commissioned by the city of Munich – should be rehearsed and performed there. Such a festival should take place every two years and be called a 'Biennale'. And I went on:

> In addition to new commissions, existing examples of contemporary theatre music, previously unperformed in Munich, could also be presented, in the form of guest performances or local productions, in concert or semi-staged performances and in unusual venues such as sports halls, tents or even the open air. They should be works which, in terms of their writing, point in the direction of the newer types of music theatre and that may be regarded as their spiritual precursors. In parallel with these activities – and, as it were, in the manner of an urban Montepulciano – other forms of music theatre should be devised and worked out, not only in the rooms of the Gasteig, but elsewhere, too, allowing amateur groups from all possible social backgrounds, including, not least, those from national and cultural minorities, to articulate their feelings in keeping with the democratic aims of the whole undertaking, for our intention, first and foremost, is to educate and win over

a new, lively and critical public and to open up new music to these audiences.

On 31 May, my students at the Academy in Cologne proudly presented a concert of their works in the school's main concert hall, followed by a delightful party to which we had also invited our performers, some fifty in number. The following morning it was so hot in the school that we went off to the park and worked on the shaded bank of a pond. In the afternoon, my students took me to the airport, and I left them with the feeling that these young people were on genuinely friendly terms and keen to cooperate with one another: they were not motivated by envy or nastiness. As always, it was my wish that the students entrusted to my care should learn to show good manners not only on a professional level but also in their daily lives and in their dealings with the rest of the world – in other words, they should behave better than I, for example, had done.

I spent a day in Swabia, in the calm of the countryside, feeling at home and yet not at home, a feeling that I like, even though it leaves me on edge. But such a calm and relaxing evening out of doors, among chestnut trees, peonies, swallows and Swabians, such an excellent Swabian wine, such southern German Whitsun light against an economically applied background of silvery gold – the sort of light that one really knows what to make of – it all seemed so familiar, so natural and so innocent!

I then spent another four weeks in Santa Fe before returning home in the middle of July. I stayed in the same house as I had done the previous summer, completing the *Liebeslieder* in full score and listening in the evening to a blackbird singing – Hächi Büm Büm again – as it grew dark, and a starry heaven, like a painted backdrop by Karl Friedrich Schinkel, unfolded above the New Mexico desert. I attended only very few of the rehearsals for *The English Cat* in a witty but not very musical production by the New York quick-change artist and comedian, Charles Ludlam, who was cutting his teeth as an opera director on this particularly complex piece. The conductor was George Manahan, who achieved translucent textures with his well-rehearsed musicians.

I started to think about a fandango that I had promised to write for Daniel Barenboim and the Orchestre de Paris and that was to be based on the famous harpsichord fandango by the eighteenth-century composer Antonio Soler, who, as *maestro de capilla* to the Spanish court, had taught the Infante Gabriel.

*

Felsenreitschule, Salzburg, 16 August 1985: first night of *Il ritorno d'Ulisse in patria* in a visually ravishing staging directed by Michael Hampe and designed by Mauro Pagano. It was Hampe who had had the idea of entrusting me with this reconstruction of Monteverdi's work and whose adaptation of the libretto (virtually indistinguishable from the original) was so familiar to me from our many working sessions that it had become my guiding principle. Both he and Pagano had paid tribute in their production to the age of the baroque – that same age that stubbornly demands its due from all who use the Felsenreitschule as a venue for their work, with the result that it looked magnificent, to the immense delight of the audience. Even I myself was amused by it all. It was also very well sung, with a cast that included Kathleen Kuhlmann and Thomas Allen, together with Ann Murray, Robert Tear, Alejandro Ramírez and James King. I had already attended a week of orchestral rehearsals in Vienna during the early summer, conducted by Jeffrey Tate – I had hurried to the city in order to be able to intervene promptly in the event of wrong notes and other misunderstandings, but my presence proved wholly unnecessary, since the orchestral parts were as good as free from error. And I was deeply affected, first with relief and then by the Apollonian beauty of the orchestral sounds conjured up by the conductor, seeming to raise Monteverdi's music out of its shadowy existence as a fading manuscript in a copyist's hand in Vienna's State Library and into the light of the Aegean, where it now sparkled and shone, warming the world with its aureole and with the halo of the Odysseus legend.

As for the opera's staging, I had in fact imagined an austere island kingdom (as a young man, I had, after all, seen Ithaca slip past in the morning light), and was expecting to see the austerely simple, frugal Peloponnese of today recreated on the Salzburg stage, or perhaps something similar to the ancient Islamic island kingdom of Pate in the Indian Ocean. But in Salzburg, the swineherd had become a baroque shepherd, which simply did not suit the music – the music that I had written for faithful old Eumaeus was porcine, not pastoral, in tone. Ulysses and Eumaeus were to have sat on an upturned trough and sung a song together, as in Monteverdi, but this number was cut in Salzburg. In the recognition scene between Ulysses and Telemachus in the finale to Act One, the two men were unable to embrace properly, as demanded by Homer, Monteverdi and the circumstances in which they find themselves, since they were both encased in Roman armour, complete with ornately plumed helmets. And in Act Two, there is a wonderful passage in Badoaro's libretto –

'Wasteland: Mercury is seen accompanying the dead suitors into the afterlife' – which Monteverdi, no doubt in his capacity as a theatre director under pressure to score a success and with an eye on box-office receipts, had cut with the remark 'this scene is omitted as too melancholic in tone', but which I had taken it upon myself to reintroduce with the aid of one of his wonderful choral madrigals, scored for large string orchestra. Although the music was retained, the main curtain remained lowered, concealing from the audience's view what I had imagined would be a Daliesque desert with a procession of shades following a wing-footed youth with a black floppy hat and golden staff who disappears into the distance upstage. But otherwise everything was fine. Minerva and Telemachus really did enter in an airship and Neptune rose up out of the sea in the most spectacular manner imaginable. It was a visual treat, and the festival audience fêted us all accordingly. We had to give endless press conferences and introductory lectures and interviews. Jeffrey Tate's record company organized a banquet at a delightful guest house just outside the town, where I sat beneath an apple tree, surrounded by friends, filled with a warm glow of pleasure and enjoying the cool evening air and the very real success of our Monteverdian adventure.

The next morning I flew to Copenhagen to visit Torben Hardenberg. We drove past Karen Blixen's house to Gurre and, after searching on our own and making enquiries of a countrywoman on a bicycle, succeeded in finding King Valdemar's ruined castle. We teetered along the foundation walls, which were only partially overgrown and which reminded us of those at Mycenae or Tusculum, and listened to the wild wood doves cooing in the trees, while in our inner ear we could hear the musical sounds that Arnold Schoenberg had conjured up nearly ninety years earlier in his setting of Jens Peter Jacobsen's poem about Gurre. How well they suited each other! Even the song of the goblin-like Klaus made sense in its powerfully hedonistic manner here in the summer wind and tall grass – and yet, as far as I know, Schoenberg was never in Denmark and, even if he was, he can hardly have visited the then unknown Gurre. Even the Danes who live there know next to nothing about Valdemar, or about Schoenberg and the Wood Dove – another example of the Hächi Büm Büm Syndrome, a syndrome which was, as it were, a fascinating guide and, as such, just right for someone as anxious as I was to escape from a state of permanent tension. How to achieve this I did not know, but blindly followed the rhythm of my vacillating feelings.

Took the night ferry to Oslo, where there was a general air of melancholy, and left the Munch Museum feeling completely shattered. The next day I flew to Tromsö, one of the country's northernmost mailboat stations, and spent the Sunday morning sheltering beneath an umbrella and restlessly wandering round the apparently deserted and rainswept little town – was there no human life here at all? Somewhere bells could be heard ringing. A figure came towards me, and it was only when he was already quite close that I saw that half of his face was missing beneath his sailor's cap. Late that evening – it was pitch-black and squally – I boarded the mailboat and settled down in my tiny cabin. Not until the next morning was I finally able to appreciate the Norwegian landscape, with its fondness for blue skies and bright sunlight. I sat on deck with a book in my hand, but it remained firmly shut throughout virtually the whole of the voyage, so keen was I not to avert my eyes for a moment from these inviolable cliffs, which remind us of our human limitations and at the same time convey an impression of timelessness and vastness. How well I can understand Wittgenstein's wish to withdraw into this world as often as he was able. I have no recollection of reading anything during these days on board the mailboat or of speaking to any of the passengers but feel that I spent the whole time looking. Each day the boat would stop at one of its ports of call, a tiny harbour town, where goods and equipment were loaded and unloaded, offering the passengers a good opportunity to wander round and stretch their legs. It was, I think, on the very first day that I took advantage of this and visited Risöyhamm, wandering pensively round the deserted hamlet, enchanted by the northern vegetation, with its wild roses and purple loosestrife, and, without realizing it, moving further and further away from the harbour. Indeed, I could have gone on walking for ever, exploring the empty interior, but suddenly an inner voice – perhaps it was Hächi's – suggested that I look at my watch. Breathlessly, I rushed back to the pier, just in time to see my snow-white mailboat disappearing round the distant wall of the fiord. I was almost a little disappointed to find a lorry driver willing to take me to the next port at Sortland. Or, rather, he dropped me off some distance from Sortland in order to continue his journey to Narvik, leaving me to cross the Sortland Bridge that spans the whole of the Sortland Sound. I set off walking, with the wind whistling all around me and the bridge shuddering beneath my feet. I was still walking uphill as a strange sense of calm overcame me in my despondency, and I suddenly felt like following an impulse and drawing the irresistible conclusion: it seemed to me the most natural thing in the world to throw myself over the parapet – nothing could have been simpler or easier. But at that very moment I heard a child's voice shouting to make itself heard above the wind and, looking up, saw a young boy, freckled and red-headed, who had got down from his bicycle and was pushing it along beside him, while talking incessantly at me in Norwegian so that I was not even able to tell him that I did not understand a word that he was saying. Once we had reached *terra firma*, he jumped back on his bike and, ringing his bell, peddled off into the distance. I returned on board ship – no one had noticed anything. I had not been missed for a moment.

At the beginning of September I spent nearly a week in Southampton, at the music festival run by the remarkable Simon Bainbridge. The Ardittis played my Fourth and Fifth String Quartets, and on 12 September the great Oliver Knussen conducted *Tristan* with the Bournemouth Symphony Orchestra and with Ian Brown as the sensitive soloist. It was the first time that the piece had been performed in Great Britain since its première in 1974. I held a seminar for composers and also attended the first performance of *Orpheus behind the Wire* with the BBC Singers under John Alldis, their singing as delicate and razor-sharp, as responsive and as appealing as anyone could wish. I was a happy man! You could hear everything. It was an experience that I urgently needed if I was to continue with my polyphonic writing, in which I had to be on permanent guard not to overload the textures and provide too much information. My harmonic writing – or whatever one wants to call it (in other words, whatever emerges vertically as chordal textures from the horizontally developing lines) – was a single *espressivo*, a systematic and expressionistically knowing handling of chromaticism aimed at reaching my listeners' psyche and stimulating it at exactly the right point. It was for this reason that these harmonic progressions and other devices, with their indebtedness to German Classicism, had to be made clear and easy to follow in whatever ways I was able to achieve.

Oliver Knussen's ancestors were all Vikings, huge strapping fellows who used to hurl boulders at their enemies and at each other in much the same way that their highly sensitive and sophisticated descendant nowadays does with the musical sounds that he writes himself or conjures up from other composers' scores like a legendary smith whose furnace flashes and glows like fireworks. Whenever we embrace, I have to stand on a chair if I am to make do with more than his navel and want to implant a kiss on his bearded cheek. Olly is one of the few people in the world of composers who is interested not only in the works and lives of his younger colleagues and contemporaries but also in the visual arts, so the range of possible topics of conversation is vastly increased. I enjoy listening to his music and would be delighted if he would stop doing everything else and write some more of the same, even more beautiful and exciting than before. But he is an exceptionally fine conductor with a well-tuned ear and brilliant stick technique, in addition to which he enjoys conducting and is loath to give it up. His readings are full of drama and violent contrasts, with surging tempi, toughness and sheer ferocity. The composers whose music Olly takes to heart have every reason to be grateful for his support but always suffer from something of a guilty conscience, since, as a result of his encouragement, he no longer has as much time for composition.

At the performance of *Tristan* in Southampton, I was visited out of the blue by Kolinka Zinovieff – who as a child had provided the voice that we had used to describe Isolde's transfiguration. He was now nineteen, with a baritone voice, a handsome, well-educated youth, who had brought his delightful father, Peter, with him. It was good to see him again. He had long since moved out of London and now lived rather cut off from the world, a state of affairs to which he is very well suited. And of course I met Michael Vyner in London. He was as amusing and as busy as ever, and, as always, full of plans. In particular, he wanted to present a series of semi-staged performances of *Elegy for Young Lovers* with the Sinfonietta and then take the production on tour the following year.

I spent part of October in Cologne. *yesterday busy with the vampires, in the evening fed and watered them à la turque. people from Alsfeld, initial plans.* The 'people from Alsfeld' in Upper Hesse were a group of music lovers headed by Messrs Köhler and Kramer, who had asked whether I might like to organize something along the lines of Montepulciano for them. I had to say no, but suggested that our composition class from Cologne might write something practical for them in the near future, so that all of their fellow inhabitants who were able to sing and play a musical instrument would be able to take part. The following month I visited the town with my students and found an attractive rural community with half-timbered houses, where, in spite of the heavy rain, we were able to take a good look round and talk to the mayor and the townspeople about this excellent idea. We were thinking of some kind of music theatre, a scenic cantata, ideally something to do with the history of Alsfeld and its culture. *Could it be about nature, the seasons, agriculture, a celebration of animals, in praise of pets or something similar, an agnus dei?* I thought this could be an exciting challenge for my young composers – to write the music for an opera for amateur musicians and then to rehearse it with them in person.

While still in Salzburg I had received a letter from the mayor of Gütersloh, Karl Ernst Strothmann, asking me whether, on the occasion of my sixtieth birthday the following year, I might return for a few days to the town in which I had been born. His letter had touched me: it made me think how a person must feel after spending decades crossing a dangerous, sun-baked desert and suddenly finding himself, breathless, in the shade of tall trees and sinking down on a cool, mossy bed. I had written back, and duly stopped off in Gütersloh on 3 October, on my way to Cologne, when I had got to know not only Herr Strothmann but also the town clerk, Otto Wixforth, and the local cultural officer, Bernhard Cordes, and his assistant, Klaus Klein, who appears to have been the driving force behind the whole affair. I entered my name in the city's visitors' book, and we discussed what arrangements might be made, both musically and culturally, to mark my *ritorno*. It would have to be something substantial, although at present no one knew in detail of what it might consist.

The second Youth Festival in Deutschlandsberg took place between 14 and 27 October 1987 and proved a great success. Like the first, it began with a concert of new works for young performers – students from the local music school – and, as before, was extremely well played. These Landsberg years saw the composition of a splendid collection of eminently playable and artistically worthwhile pieces suitable for performance in schools. Among their composers were Hans Abrahamsen, Volker Blumenthaler, Thomas Donecker, Lorenzo Ferrero, Detlev Glanert, Gerd Kühr, David Lang, Wolfgang Rihm, Oliver Trötschel and Mark-Anthony Turnage. The performance at the 'theatre centre' included a bonfire, a torchlight procession beneath a cold full moon and a powerful, austere piece of theatre by the Berlin choreographer, Gerhard Bohner, to the accompaniment of music by my counterpoint teacher, the baroque composer Johann Joseph Fux, who had been born near the Styrian city of Graz in 1660. It was played by members of the Landsberg wind band and intercut with eruptive passages on percussion composed and directed by another of my students from Cologne, Stefan Hakenberg, who was concealed behind the hedges that surround the Landsberg football pitch where the alfresco performance took place, beside the River Laßnitz that hurried on its way, adding to the cool of the night. It was here on its banks, legend has it, that Schubert conceived *Die Forelle*, although one hopes that on that occasion the temperature was rather more tolerable. I provided the somewhat small audience with rubber boots and mulled wine. Amusingly staged by Birgitta Trommler and colourfully designed by local children under the guidance of the excellent Hans Hoffer, the communal opera, *Robert der Teufel*, was enthusiastically received. Every wall in the hall was covered with murals showing scenes and views of the opera. Elfriede Jelinek had organized a little workshop for the children, and some of the poems that they wrote about *Robert* were taken over into the piece. One, I remember, ran 'The Landsberghausen poacher shot / A goat that didn't deserve what it got'; another was 'The robbers rob the woods of their green / And kill the flowers with their poison gas'. The young amateur composers – Hansjörg Arndt, Max Koch, Hartmut Kleindienst, Daniel Kügerl, Olga Neuwirth, Viktor Rieß and Arno Steinwider – were speechless at the unexpected impact of their communal composition.

In Marino, meanwhile, the new wine was fermenting in its vats.

Have reached the second climax of *Fandango*. Keep thinking of Goya's fandango dancer, the village idiot. Wherever I turn, I see the world around me fragmenting, with objects breaking free from each other as a result of centrifugal force and becoming the pieces of a mosaic or kaleidoscope. A visit from Dieter Schidor leaves me unsettled and concerned. The bogeyman, as I call him, has visibly aged and is a total wreck. I hide my dismay and listen to one tale of psychological horror after another. It is now the end of November.

Last Wednesday morning, 27 November, I attended the funeral of Elsa Morante at the Church of Santa Maria on the Piazza del Popolo (the name has nothing to do with the people or plebs but is named after the poplar tree, the *pioppo*). There was a large crowd both inside and outside the building, and many people were in tears. After the service, the coffin was borne outside and the onlookers burst into applause to pay their last respects as the black wooden box was loaded into a black limousine that was immediately swallowed up by the midday traffic in the Via del Babuino. Our friendship had ended abruptly some twenty years earlier. *the moon is vertically overhead. clean, dry winter air.*

In mid-December I came across Mörike's wonderful ode *An eine Äolsharfe* and suddenly knew not only what I would call my guitar concerto but also what its form would be: structurally, it will take as its starting point Mörike's poetry, which will play a role not just in the opening movement but in the other movements, too. (For a performance at the Frankfurt

Festival in 1986 I wrote a report minuting the genesis of the piece as a whole.) I also found another poem, the impassioned *An Hermann*, which I decided to use in the final movement. Continued to search for suitable material for the *rapt tone* that I had in mind. Completed a string introduction to the ode. Hächi Büm Büm and Mörike's Swabia are now my only contacts with the world – the world of German emotion. On 27 December a terrorist attack on the Leonardo da Vinci Airport in Rome left sixteen people dead.

> 29 December. Dream *about a college in the United States, only it had beautiful old houses like those in Havana. i lose my way, try to find Fausto, meet students and enter their rooms, where they are sleeping in positions that look to be carved by Canova in marble. a girl implies that Yiddish is the preferred language here, and i tell her that i'm too old to learn it. she showed me the way to my building, but i was unable to find it, more and more obstacles got in the way, and the whole thing turned increasingly into a labyrinth, and it became harder and harder to place one foot in front of the other.*

1986. While reading Mörike's (really rather silly) libretto for *Die Regenbrüder* (set to music by the director of music of the court in Stuttgart, Ignaz Lachner), I had the idea of using Theodor Storm's *Regentrude* as the subject matter for the Alsfeld project *and other fairy tales, myths and animal stories?*

On 8 January, I and my English publisher, Sally Groves, arranged a meeting in London between the young English composer Mark-Anthony Turnage (recommended to me by Olly Knussen) and the dramatist, actor and director Steven Berkoff. We wanted to obtain Berkoff's permission to use his play *Greek*, which Turnage was very keen to set to music. Turnage was more or less the first composer that I was to suggest to the Munich authorities as someone whom they should commission to write an opera for the Biennale. At the end of January I went to a concert in the Munich Hofbräukeller with members of the city's arts advisory committee and heard Turkish and Bavarian folk music. At a meeting in Jürgen Kolbe's office, I was reintroduced to Sergiu Celibidache, who kissed me on both cheeks and promised to place both himself and his orchestra at my disposal for the first Biennale in May 1988. I refrained from asking him about the Two-part Inventions in G that I had written in Berlin during the winter of 1950. I also managed to persuade Bavarian Radio to act as co-producer and spoke about the Biennale's programme and aims at a public meeting of the arts advisory committee. At the same time I suggested that commissions be offered to Adriana Hölszky and Gerd Kühr, whom I introduced to the playwright Franz Xaver Kroetz in the hope that their resultant collaboration might have an air of Alpine mysticism to it. And, finally, I asked Wolfgang von Schweinitz to explain what he and D. E. Sattler were planning to do with *Patmos* and the Apocalypse of St John the Divine. I was delighted at the overwhelming cordiality that I encountered at every turn in Munich.

In early February I met Ruth Berghaus and her designer Hans-Dieter Schaal in Paris to discover how far they had already moved away from me and Edward Bond in their plans for *Orpheus* in Vienna – very far indeed, it transpired. And, at the same time, I was able to hear Barenboim and the Orchestre de Paris give the first performance of *Fandango*.

Back in a snow-covered Marino, I wrote the Scherzo of my guitar concerto, a setting of Mörike's *An Philomele*, and at the end of the month flew to London for a European Broadcasting Union concert from a packed St John's, Smith Square, where I conducted *Miracle* and *Being Beauteous*. I also met the conductor Simon Rattle, who wanted to ask me about my Seventh Symphony and *Barcarola* and who had kind things to say to me about how he had cried during *We Come to the River* at Covent Garden. As he was leaving, he said how happy he was to be able to play my beautiful music. The Royal Academy of Music offered me a teaching post – an International Chair in Composition – which I accepted. At the sold-out Queen Elizabeth Hall, I conducted the Sinfonietta's semi-staged production of *Elegy*, while suffering from a slight bout of influenza, then flew to New York, where I met various people interested in a co-production of Harry Partch's *Revelation in the Courthouse Park* at the Biennale and also heard *The English Cat* at the Manhattan School. Heddy Baum, the widow of the co-founder of the New York City Ballet, Morton Baum, and a patron of the arts in her own right, gave a cocktail party at which I met a quite unbelievable number of old friends. My Third, Fourth and Fifth String Quartets were performed by the Concord String Quartet in the Merkin Concert Hall – magical performances. Claude and Maureen Giroux organized a private concert with David Tanenbaum and the *Royal Winter Music*; and I took tea with my young colleague, David Lang, at the 'Pierre'.

I returned home at Easter to find the house full of young musicians from Deutschlandsberg, together with their director. We worked together on a new project: as I made it abundantly clear to Frau Faulend-Klauser, this was to be my Landsberg swan-song, a multimedia show that we planned to perform in the old ruined castle above the present town. Here, each of the four young amateur composers from Landsberg would have his own space, with its own special ambience, in which to realize his ideas. On the day of my departure the previous autumn, the director – kindness itself – had done everything in her power to persuade me to return the following year, and, although I was keen to get back to Marino, to my hermit's existence and my music, I gave her my word that I would indeed come back: I was dazzled by the morning sunlight, by my love of life and by the indescribable charm of the golden yellow vineyards of western Styria and its warmly welcoming beech woods.

I can hear Hächi Büm Büm whistling and humming alluringly from the telegraph wire opposite, and the message of the medium is to go home, home, home, to come home and write. I set *Frage und Antwort*, which deals with the same sort of serious psychoanalytical matters that I had asked one of my Alsfeld students, Thomas Donecker, to examine at more or less the same time in a series of a cappella settings of this and other Mörike poems. Sung by the local choir, they will be part of the *Regentrude* opera. The Americans bomb Tripoli and Benghazi, killing hundreds of people. At the end of April, following a terrible heat wave, I conduct four performances of my Seventh Symphony with the Munich Philharmonic at the new Gasteig Hall. Here, too, several older members of the audiences (and also, to my consternation, a number of younger couples) slip out of the hall after each movement, an exodus that seems to have become something of a tradition at performances of this piece.

Aunt Peg remained in the city the whole time that I was there, attending all my concerts and even sitting in on my composition classes (I had brought my students with me from Cologne for a few days). We were concerned at that time with creating or completing a number of brief, self-contained scenes that the students had to select, cut down to size and adapt in order to produce something effective from a musical and dramatic point of view. Among the problems that they had to solve was that of devising cinematographic and musical forms for scenes such as Hamlet's sword entering Polonius's bloated body or the effects of the poison as it makes its insidious way through Luise Miller's veins or to find convincing ways of showing a whale singing or finding the right sound to describe a visitor from beyond the grave suddenly arriving in one's room. They had an opportunity to see and hear the cycle performed by the Hamburg group of L'Art pour l'Art (the artists formerly known as Hinz &

Kunst), who formed part of the m(or)ass of my sympathizers. We were invited to present the whole show at the Évian Festival in May.

It was not until 11 May that I arrived in Évian-les-Bains – right up until the last minute I had hoped to get rid of the feverish sinusitis that had been plaguing me, but in vain: on the flight from Rome to Geneva the buzzing in my ears reached the point where they ceased to perform their rightful function, and I remained in this state for the whole of the next few days, able to hear my students' music only in the far-off distance. Finally I went to see an ear specialist – a pleasant enough fellow, who professed to a love of music and who lived in nearby Thonon-les-Bains. He asked me what I thought of Boulez's music and, without waiting for an answer, perforated my left eardrum, repeating the process on the right-hand side while asking me what I felt about the sound world of Olivier Messiaen. Now I could hear nothing at all and was not allowed to fly, but had to return to Marino by car – which in itself I did not mind, since it gave me my first opportunity to see Aosta and its beautiful valley in spring. On the tender green shoots that peeped up from the rice fields on the border between Piedmont and Lombardy lay the poisonous dust of Chernobyl.

In Marino it was 32°C. In Rome, Dr Scuri diagnosed a serious loss of hearing. A fifty per cent loss. I wrote the middle section of *An Hermann* using Dionysus's note row from *The Bassarids* (I can no longer remember why), while feeling infinitely miserable and forlorn and thinking that this would be the last piece of music that I ever wrote. *my life hangs by a silken thread called Hächi Büm Büm*. Then, at the beginning of June, Professor Ehrenberger of the Vienna University Clinic operated on me, an operation designed to prevent any further trouble, at least for the foreseeable future. I conducted my Seventh Symphony with the Vienna Radio Orchestra in the Vienna Konzerthaus, then flew to England and the Aldeburgh Festival, where I heard Simon Rattle conduct *Barcarola* and took part in a panel discussion with Oliver Knussen, who, together with Rattle and Murray Perahia, had become part of the festival's artistic directorate. I performed *Musen Siziliens* with the young ladies and gentlemen of the Cambridge University Music Society and was delighted by the excellent piano playing of Marie McClahan and Edmund Forey. I also went for a walk by the sea with Aunt Peg and our friend, Tittu, through brackish meadows, stumbling and sliding over pebbles on the beach, admiring the large number of local birds and sleeping badly, since it never really got dark as it does in Marino. After hearing a rehearsal of *Miracle* under Olly, I flew to Vienna to see Ruth Berghaus's production of *Orpheus*, superbly conducted by Ulf

Schirmer and euphoniously played by the Vienna Philharmonic. At the dress rehearsal I was still not certain whether I liked what I saw, but, as the first night drew closer, my memories of the rehearsal began to fill me with a very real curiosity to see the performance itself, which duly cast its spell on me and left me deeply moved. The audience, too, seemed genuinely affected, and there were ovations at the end, especially for dear Ruth, who, unused to such acclaim, was correspondingly radiant.

I spent the next day working with the children in Landsberg and in the evening drove out to Heiligenstadt to introduce Ruth Berghaus to my colleague Wolfgang von Schweinitz so that they could discuss their collaboration on *Patmos* for the Munich Biennale. Then it was back to London, but this time with my students from Cologne, who spent a whole week in the city with their old teacher, attending classes by day and, in the evening, visiting the theatre or concert hall. They heard Isaac Stern give the London première of Peter Maxwell Davies's Violin Concerto at the Festival Hall and saw Harrison Birtwistle's highly impressive *Mask of Orpheus* at the English National Opera. There were also a number of new works, including some of their own, performed at Pierre Audi's Almeida Festival in Islington.

The whole of 1986 was spent travelling and living out of suitcases: although there were brief, occasional breaks in Marino or Wolfsgarten, I was away more often than not. At the end of July I found myself in Warwick, where the BBC filmed my Seventh Symphony with Simon Rattle and his excellent orchestra, the City of Birmingham Symphony. On 25 July they played the piece at the Proms in London, an unforgettable evening for me, which was followed by three ethereal weeks at Aunt Peg's summer home in the Engadine. We were joined there by Uli Treichel, since I had a new idea that I wanted to put to him after our earlier attempts at mythological subjects had failed to make any progress. (At the time of writing we have still not got any further with this idea, and I do not know if and when we shall have the time or inclination to take any further interest in it.) Only recently, during the spring of 1986, while discussing with Olly a number of themes and questions relating to music theatre, I had got talking about Yukio Mishima and his novel, *Gogo no eiko* (more familiar in English under the title *The Sailor Who Fell from Grace with the Sea*). I kept coming back to it, imagining the events from Mishima's novella in dramatized form. The original is a great and tragic love story of classical, not to say, archaic proportions. It is set in the present day, in modern Yokohama, among completely normal people like you and me; 'he' is a sailor, a ship's officer in the Japanese merchant navy, while 'she' is a beautiful, rich young widow (presumably a war widow). The two of them naturally fall in love in the usual middle-class manner, hence his banal desire to resign his commission and marry her. Opposed to his plans is Fusako's thirteen-year-old son, Noboru, the intensity of whose feelings, with their mixture of hatred and contempt, is the result of his adolescent immaturity. From this stems the work's underlying conflict, which acquires its particular piquancy by virtue of the fact that our little grammar schoolboy is a member of a secret society comprising a handful of spoilt and highly charged children, all of them seemingly model pupils but constituting a puerile gang that is a danger to society, so that one inevitably fears the worst. It struck me that the story of Fusako and Ryuji contains curious parallels to the tale of Odysseus and Penelope – it was as though I had no choice but to retell this story about a homecoming, except that on this occasion it was an unheroic, negative and profoundly pessimistic modern reading.

Mishima's novel contains allusions to French culture at every turn: apart from the boutique that is run by Fusako, there is a French restaurant, where the first tête-à-tête between the two of them takes place; also Fusako's apartment is furnished in the style of Louis XIV and her claret-coloured kimono is trimmed with Breton lace. You might think you were in a Japanese Paris or a Parisian Japan, or, indeed, in the theatre, at a neoclassical French tragedy by Corneille or Racine, the sort of piece which, with its stately tempi and solemn metres, was modelled on the great plays of ancient Greece. It was very much this kind of theatre that interested Mishima, not least because he thought he could see in it certain affinities with Noh and kabuki. For weeks on end, Uli and I sat on a bench beneath the chestnut tree beside Aunt Peg's tea house in Tarasp, tossing ideas to and fro, until we finally had a basic plan, no, more than that – a workable outline or scenario in the form of an attractive sequence of scenes.

We said goodbye, and I moved on to the Alte Oper in Frankfurt, where the intendant, Rudolf Sailer, and his artistic adviser, Dieter Rexroth, had organized a great festival of my music. I stayed in the Taunus Mountains and travelled in and out each day, bowing profusely each night to express my gratitude. The festival began with a vast *ricevimento* in the foyer of the Alte Oper at which Wolfgang Rihm had some kind things to say about me and I was privileged to shake hands with hundreds of people from the world of German music. On 29 August, two days after its first performance in Lucerne, David Tanenbaum and Ensemble Modern gave the

German première of *An eine Äolsharfe* under the baton of Bernhard Klee. And the gifted violinist, Thomas Zehetmair, played my Second Violin Concerto. There was also a performance of *El Cimarrón* with Allan Evans and members of Ensemble Modern. I myself conducted the London production of *Elegy for Young Lovers*, and the Junge Deutsche Philharmonie performed my Seventh Symphony. Ingo Metzmacher conducted *Voices* with Nancy Shade, John Potter and Ensemble Modern, and in the Mozartsaal there was a performance of an enchanting, completely apolitical, abstract and modern *opera buffa* by the name of *The English Cat*, directed by Ian Strasfogel, designed by Hans Hoffer and conducted by David Shallon, with the excellent young members of the German Chamber Philharmonic. Even *Das Floß der 'Medusa'* was performed, in a co-production between the Alte Oper and Austrian and Hesse Radio.

But I was happy when it was all over. So much of the Taunus, so many people, so much Henze – it was beyond a joke. And certainly it was a source of anything but unadulterated pleasure: as a composer, one generally hears only what one has failed to bring off, here a passage that went wrong (and that one may repeatedly have forgotten to correct), there a grey area, an omission, a sense of failure, an example of compromise. And I still found myself bobbing up and down, bowing my thanks to audiences, this time in Turin, which had organised its own festival of my music – the Seventh Symphony, *The English Cat*, *Medusa*, *El rey de Harlem* and *Miracle de la rose*, together with a round-table discussion involving Messrs Vlad, Mila, D'Amico, Serpa and Restagno and performances of a number of chamber works. During the daytime, meanwhile, there were the first white truffles of the Piedmontese season to be had in the surrounding hills.

I then had to go to Munich to rescue the Biennale, which had embarked on a programme of cuts. Together with Jürgen Kolbe, I went to see the mayor, the city treasurer and party whips and left the town hall with friendly reassurances and the certainty – shared by Jürgen Kolbe – that at least part of the organizational costs would not be met or, if they were, then they would have to be paid by me personally. As a result, I spent a not inconsiderable part of the following weeks and months and years shouldering an additional burden of responsibility and enjoying the dubious pleasure of going cap in hand to bankers and other well-to-do members of a social class that was totally alien to me and whose representatives soon turned out to be less than open-handed, not least, perhaps, because what I wanted was still not so easy to describe. Sometimes I was successful – certainly more so than the professional fund-raisers whom we had employed in recent years and who had failed to raise a single penny. But I cannot deny that I regularly shrank each time that I was helped out of my coat on – for example – the executive floor of the Deutsche Bank's skyscraper in Frankfurt and heard an inner voice – perhaps it was Hächi Büm Büm's – asking insistently and offendedly what I was actually doing there.

Then came the week in Gütersloh to which I have already alluded in the opening pages of this book: here I gave a talk in which I told people all about myself and reported on all that I had done in the last sixty years (omitting certain details, of course) and, at the same time, gradually got to know a little more about my fellow Westphalians. From time to time I found it necessary to blow my nose. All my relations turned up and I met a number of new nephews and nieces and heard details of family histories about which I had had no inkling. Olly came with the BBC Philharmonic Orchestra and (as in Cologne and Frankfurt) there were performances of the *Orpheus* choruses, *Tristan* and *Laudes*, while the London Sinfonietta played *Miracle*, *Rey* and *Elegy*, the last-named with me as conductor. Ensemble Modern performed *El Cimarrón*, and Jens Brockmeier and Hans-Ulrich Treichel read from their philosophical and poetic writings. The performances were well attended and the audiences gratifyingly attentive. I was asked not to leave it another sixty years before my next visit.

Berlin was my next port of call. Here I visited Thomas Brasch in the hope of persuading him to work with Adriana Hölszky on a piece for the Munich Biennale (nothing came of the idea) and attended a concert performance, in English, of *The Bassarids* at the Philharmonie, wonderfully conducted by Gerd Albrecht and sung by an all-star cast including Karan Armstrong, Kenneth Riegel, Andreas Schmidt, Robert Tear and Ortrun Wenkel, with the combined choirs of RIAS Berlin and South German Radio. Brilliantly played by the Berlin Radio Symphony Orchestra, this performance broke the oppressive spell on the score, and in the course of the years that followed there were to be many more performances of the opera, both in the theatre and in the concert hall, interpreting and elucidating the work in countless different ways. At my own suggestion, the performance in Berlin omitted the Intermezzo, thereby making the opera around twenty minutes shorter and, at the same time, considerably increasing the dramatic tension and allowing listeners a clearer insight into the form and nature of the great central Adagio that is the seduction scene between Dionysus and Pentheus. In this way, my somewhat disrespectful attitude towards my two librettists was proved to have been correct. The

Intermezzo has likewise been omitted from more recent stagings of the opera, where it has been replaced by a brief scene that I had already had in mind when drafting this episode in Castel Gandolfo during the early sixties, since I had never believed in the dramaturgical need for the Intermezzo – a need of which neither Wystan Auden nor Chester Kallman was in any way convinced. Like them, I considered it a literary, rather than a theatrical, device and one, moreover, that stood out from the measured Euripidean directness of the main plot through its volubility and campness. What is needed here is a distorted vision of horror lasting only a few seconds and glimpsed as though in a mirror, reflecting the sexual ideas that terrify and threaten the prurient Pentheus, as in a series of flashlit photographs, and explaining the reasons why he hates the Dionysian element or at least what he, Pentheus, imagines as such. Directors should – indeed, *must* – devise some really quite violent and shocking images for this. While working on *Idomeneo* in Munich, Mozart once wrote to his father, who, although left at home in Salzburg, continued to follow his son's dramaturgical thinking:

> Tell me, don't you think that the speech of the subterranean voice is too long? Consider it carefully. Picture to yourself the theatre, and remember that the voice must be terrifying – must penetrate – that the audience must believe that it really exists. Well, how can this effect be produced if the speech is too long, for in this case the listeners will become more and more convinced that it means nothing. If the speech of the Ghost in *Hamlet* were not so long, it would be far more effective.

On the morning after the epiphany of the revitalized *Bassy* (or *Becky*, as the two librettists and I used to call *The Bassarids* in private), I flew to Graz and from there drove to Landsberg for a final fond farewell. The larches in the pine forests, the vine leaves in the vineyards and the beeches around the ruined castle (the site of the hermit's cell familiar from our communal opera, *Robert der Teufel*, and also the spot where the Laßnitz, cascading down the hillside, reaches a more level tract of land) were once again clad in magnificent autumn colours. A few wisps of mist and the powerful smell of rotting grapes and fresh mushrooms filled the air. I spent every day working with my Cologne students on the Alsfeld project and, together, we continued to tinker with the scenario, working on the libretto and thinking further about it. (The salons at Alban Berg's villa at Trahütten were placed at our disposal for lessons.) I looked in on the rehearsals for our multi-media show and was delighted by what I saw and heard: it had turned out to be quite magical thanks to the efforts of the director, Ian Strasfogel, and his assistant, Michael Kerstan (who had in the meantime also taken over the running of the festival office, as well as editing the programme booklets): it was every bit as beautiful and as strange as I had imagined it. Uli's libretto worked well and contained dreamlike scenes, including a monologue for Icarus as he wanders, blindfold, through the defoliated forest to the sound of distant horns and rushing water.

The audience entered the ruined castle over a wooden bridge – beneath them, in the moat, a herd of goats grazed like so many bastardized minotaurs, munching away and ushering in the spectacle with their bells tuned to the Phrygian scale. Almost at once a melancholy wind serenade emerged from the right and, as the spectators proceeded on their way, up and down the many steps through various rooms and different levels, their eyes and ears were met by changing impressions, both aural and visual, overlapping and complementing one another, both close at hand and further away – here was the song of the captive maiden and a vision of her Rapunzel-like hair, there the wild dances of the bull-like, minotaurean monster and the liberator's heroic lays. From the castle battlements, trumpets rang forth across western Styria and as far as the nearby Croatian border, proclaiming to the world that the beast that had fallen in our midst had now been slain and that a new age was about to dawn, the age of pure and ideal youth. At the school of music we also heard a number of new and attractive pieces suitable for performance in schools. I said goodbye to all these delightful people and promised the Styrian Autumn Festival that I would continue to support Deutschlandsberg, while at the same time recommending Gerd Kühr as my successor.

In mid-November, Ronald Freed, the president of European American Music Publishers in Valley Forge, Pennsylvania, wrote to ICM, the New York agents of Mishima's widow, Yoko, and obtained permission for me to set *Gogo no eiko* to music.

> *perhaps i'll be able to break free in this piece from all that i've written so far. i imagine the individual scenes as dovetailed together, each with a constant tempo (or the opposite), regardless of the events taking place on stage and with a specific group of instruments for each scene. this is already suggested by the book and its basic structure. i'd like to*

start on the preliminary work during the next few days. feel a different person, no longer tired. every day more and more thoughts about the piece.

Spent a few strenuous days in Cologne with the kids there. They are starting to outgrow me. Each of them now has a specific contribution to make to the Alsfeld *Regentrude*: one of them will write the fireworks music (for Alsfeld's trumpeters), another the water music (for the fire-brigade band), a third the songs for Trude, a fourth those of the two lovers (scored for the Alsfeld Chamber Orchestra incorporating the 1977 Mandolin Club) and a fifth the musical interludes, which will comprise unaccompanied settings of Mörike songs for the Alsfeld Singers. We worked on the basic material together, producing musical portraits of Maren, Andres and Regentrude which all the participants could use as material for their own individual variations. I showed the students how to create new musical shapes on the basis of even the briefest cells, as was now necessary with this type of class work. And we had to keep it simple and write music that amateurs could sing and play, so that they would get some pleasure from rehearsing it and performing it together. These young composers were thus faced with a whole series of socio-political challenges.

Read Henry Scott Stokes' life of Mishima. As a person, M. remains an enigma (as, indeed, he no doubt was). Unfortunate that he held right-wing views or at least appeared to do so. I feel a whistling and seething around me and within me, like new wine in a vat: my Mishima music is under way. Am bent on change. A polecat wrought havoc in the dovecote during the night of 1/2 December. On the 15th I gave a concert with Ensemble Modern in the Villa Pignatelli in Naples (I recognized people in the hall whom I had not seen in decades and said hello to them), and my old friend and colleague Francesco d'Avalos afterwards gave a great dinner for the whole company in his three-storey *palazzo* in the Via dei Mille. The following morning I showed the members of the Ensemble the old Spanish quarter, the monastery of Santa Chiara, the venerable Conservatorio San Pietro a Majella and the excavation sites in the Via Costantinopoli, where the old Greek city had once been and which are now filled with filth and refuse.

On the 12th and 13th, I had been in Cologne for the first performances of my *Liebeslieder* with Heinrich Schiff, David Shallon and the West German Radio Orchestra and of the *Kleine Elegien* for Renaissance instruments performed by Andrew Parrott and his Taverner Players. I also looked in at the Academy to see how the music for *Regentrude* was progressing and heard a very young student in the conducting class, Markus Stenz, conducting my Second Symphony with the student orchestra. My colleagues found that they could get on well with him, and so I signed him up on the spot as musical director of our Alsfeld opera.

Cold winter in Marino. Yoko Mishima in distant Tokyo wants the operatic version to stick closer to the original title, *Gogo no eiko*, than existing translations for the cinema and for books. Instead of *The Sailor Who Fell from Grace with the Sea*, she would prefer something like *Taking the Ship in Tow in the Late Afternoon* or *Pilot Services in the Late Afternoon* or even *The Launch*.

> *i find this piece really quite eerie and know that i'll never want to take sides but must remain as indifferent as the sea. this is an approach completely unlike anything i've tried before (and the opposite of what i keep impressing on my students). i'd like to get away from my previous approach and branch out in another direction – the direction of natural sounds? the form not symphonic but cyclical, epic.*

1987: Spent the beginning of the year painting miniature watercolours of scenes from the opera and tinkering with the libretto with Uli. Began work on the score on 2 March, starting with Part One, 'Summer'. *it must be different, novel, beautiful – not for nothing did I hear so many of my own works last year and discovered what i should stop doing & what i should keep a look-out for*. Uli has also completed the second part of the libretto, *but why am i so agitated when composing? my whole body is affected by it and out of control. is there nothing that can be done about it? today i must keep calm and sit up straight while writing.*

14 March. Fair copy of Scene One: Fusako has put her thirteen-year-old son, Noboru, to bed and locked the door to stop him from sloping off during the night and meeting his classmates. We then see her undress, while sonny boy watches her secretly through a hole in the wall. Cantilenas. The beginning of Scene Two will be in F sharp minor or major, dazzled by so much sunlight, as mother and son are shown round the magnificent, ultramodern freighter, the *Rakuyo-Maru*, in the port at Yokohama and get to know the second officer, Ryuji Tsukazaki.

The first interlude depicts one of Noboru's dreams: he dreams about the *Rakuyo-Maru*, which he will be shown round the following morning, also about his beautiful, naked mother, whom he secretly watches every evening, and, finally, self-discipline, toughness and the school friends who so impress him.

I slowly feel my way into the opera's motoric rhythms and harmonic language.

Yesterday I heard two beautiful pieces from Gesualdo's Fifth Book of Madrigals on the radio.

> Early May. *helped in the garden, encountered 2 grass snakes, saw the hoopoe, heard the cuckoo, the energy of the world and of the earth. how the grass overcomes gravity and strives towards heaven. how time can be told from the growth of an iris. – wanted to phone someone in my search for artistic support and encouragement, but couldn't think of anyone.*

Played over Scene Two on the piano, concentrating and distancing myself from it, made some improvements, gained an overall impression, found it *gentle, feminine, even Parisian, a sickly violet, tonal, decadent, as it were*, as indeed it ought to be – for how else could I describe and depict Mme Fusako Kuroda's emotional world in music? Although I had fully intended to remain morally and mentally objective, it was important to me that listeners should be affected by Fusako and that they should always be able to recognize her and her emotions from her music, just as one must always be able to recognize Ryuji from *his* tone colours, progressions and rhythms, while the protagonist, Noboru, should be instantly identifiable by the pounding ostinatos of *his* music, which is designed to remind the listener of piano studies à la Clementi and Czerny before rising to the hallucinatory excesses of the final bars of the score. I kept thinking that I must adopt a 'Parisian' style of writing, especially for Fusako, and when I asked myself when I actually meant by that, it turned out that it was anything from Rameau to Dukas and Debussy that is not silly and/or banal. I made up my mind to change direction at least from the first scene with the boys (in other words, Scene Five) and introduce some basic new ideas not only harmonically but also structurally – ideas already implicit, in part, in Noboru's initial music.

Mid-June found me sitting bolt upright at my desk and working on the full score of the interlude between Scenes Two and Three, an episode developed out of the saxophone melody from the musette, the *galant* conclusion to Scene Two, at the point where Fusako invites the young seaman out to dinner, naturally at a French restaurant, where the food – she promises – is excellent. The result is a storm tide or what the Second

Gentleman, in Act Two, Scene One of *Othello*, describes as an 'enchafèd flood':

> I never did like molestation view
> On the enchafèd flood.

I described some seven or nine waves breaking. One of my pupils, Detlev Glanert, who, I maintain, was born not in Berlin but on an island in the North Sea, drew my attention to the fact that, during a storm, it is the seventh (or is it the ninth?) wave that is always the highest and most powerful and that the moment of calm after it has broken is the best one for pouring a can of oil on the troubled waters, before jumping in after it and dog-paddling smartly towards the lifeboat. I wrote these seven breakers into my score. I had hoped that Yoko Mishima's New York agents would accept *The Enchafèd Flood* as the English title, not only because it is so beautiful but also because Auden had used it in a wonderful three-part lecture that he delivered at the University of Virginia in 1949, *The Enchafèd Flood, or The Romantic Iconography of the Sea*, each part of which – 'The Sea and the Desert', 'The Stone and the Shell' and 'Ishmael – Don Quixote' – had dealt with the nature of Romanticism by concentrating on the treatment of a single theme, namely, the sea. But ICM rejected it on the grounds that the word 'enchafèd' is no longer used in colloquial American (and, indeed, may never have been so used). I began work on Scene Three on 12 July: Fusako and Ryuji enjoy the evening air in a park overlooking the brightly lit harbour. It is a moment that marks the onset of love and, with it, the betrayal of the sea.

> *jap. orch. in short score means something quiet, delicate – but no chinoiserie or orientalisms.*
>
> *terrible fear of devastation, a dying cedar in the garden, deaths in the animal world – i can't bear to look, not least when i think that it's me who did all this, me who is to blame. 4 aug. third scene of meer finished. it needs to be lighter, more flexible, less static. 7 aug. have written a sarabande that i think i shall now have to sublimate and transform by treating it cubistically. it begins when Ryuji kisses Fusako for the first time. in other words, the sarabande comes between scenes three and four, during the scene-change, or else it is the prelude to scene four.*
>
> *must break down the music and atomize it.*

It looks as though the five sections that make up Scene Four will be five variations on the sarabande. The whole scene is a trio, with Ryuji and Fusako making love while Norobu lies in his room and watches them. Or, to be more precise, it is made up of three inner monologues. Am no longer under pressure of time now that I have asked Berlin to postpone the first performance by a year. Continued to hammer away at the sarabande a couple more times yesterday. Have acquired a dog whistle, with which I have occasionally succeeded in silencing the barking and howling of the neighbours' dogs, a racket in which our own superior beasts naturally and thoughtfully refrain from joining and which I find as insufferable as car engines and noisy people. My first thought on waking up is always the opera. There seems to be no greater problem in the world than the third interlude. I complete it in full score in mid-August and once again find myself trembling with exhaustion. By the end of the month I am finally able to start on Scene Four. The variations turn out to be light and lascivious, as is only to be expected, given the harmonic writing in the sarabande. What pleasure I feel when everything sounds right and logical and when one has the curious, but eerie feeling that the music is writing itself.

During September and October I took a break and embarked on a series of tours to do with my work, and it was not until the end of November that I was able to get back to Marino and to my desk. *i don't yet know exactly what the next scenes in the opera will sound like, yet i'm already thinking of a chamber work, an eighth symph. for the Sinfonietta, something that lasts a whole evening.* On 29 December I noted that on the previous morning I had had some success with Scene Five and that I had set the ringleader's first speech and couplet:

> *'No father, no mother will ever do what we ourselves can't do. A word is burnt into the flesh of their world, that word is "impossible". Never forget, Number Three* [*i.e.,* Noboru], *that it is us and no one else who can remove all trace of such a word.'*
>
> *instead of a recitative for the ringleader, i now have a 3rd element, four-part writing, sombre, negative, for the lower woodwind. couplet: variation on Noboru's music over a chord of A flat major with the fifth, G flat/D flat, in the bass, a pedal point, increasing the sense of tension. can tinker with it all day and draw on all 3 elements:*
>
> 1. *the instinctive savagery of early adolescence*
> 2. *instinctive evil*
> 3. *instinctive playfulness and boyishness*

> *1988. 2. 1. the most important thing this year will be the opera. once scene five is finished, i'll have a third of it in the can. if the gods keep me fit and sane, i can complete it in 1989 and it could be staged at the end of 1990.*

Sometimes I would begin the day by looking through, or playing over, an entire section or even a whole scene, as though to take the music's pulse. The existing section of Scene Five seemed to me to be fast-moving, bizarre and eerie, in spite of – or precisely because of – the fact that it is just like a musical box. I tried to describe the abrupt changes of mood within this young boy's heart, these sudden shifts of emotion and states of mind extending from the precocious to the infantile, from the dimly instinctive to the prematurely mature.

By early March I had reached the interlude between Scenes Five and Six, a dark-toned repetition of what I would describe as the schoolboy gang's Credo:

> *'The real danger is life itself, the beating of our hearts is dangerous, the wind in the trees, the dirt on our shoes, it is dangerous to wake up in the morning and to look at the clouds in the sky.'*

Early May: music for scene-change completed. Still fast tempi and semiquaver figurations. May have found a way that will allow me to adopt a measured tempo for the next scene – Scene Six: if so, it will be the first time in the opera. Keep waking up at night and allowing my thoughts to revolve round the music, listening and understanding the energies that it contains.

By the end of June the first Munich Biennale – our International Festival of New Music Theatre – was over, and I was able to resume work on Scene Six: Ryuji is alone, late one afternoon, in the park from Scene Three. He is in love and unhappy at the thought that his ship will soon be sailing again. He encounters the gang of schoolboys, and Noboru remains with him, so that Ryuji can tell him all about distant lands and people. Have written the first section of the seaman's monologue and am starting to gain a clearer idea of the second section. The music will develop out of harbour noises. Ryuji's song (a kind of folk-song or sea shanty) is something of a portrait of him in his baritonal and noble but ordinary sentimentality. I am enjoying composing (no wonder, after such a long period away from my desk), the music pours out of me as though of its own free will, and I shall be happy to observe its progress. Scene Six is based on the harmonic material from Ryuji's first entrance in Scene Two.

I recall my sense of well-being at the thought that there would be no further interruptions until the piece was finished. Uneasy calm, calm unease. As before, composing seems the most wonderful thing in the world, a privilege. It should involve no groaning or suffering, but should flow along uninterruptedly and be wonderfully developed, full of beautiful sounds and the virgin territory of artificial paradises. By the middle of July the full score of Scene Six was already on the stocks, while I was still tinkering with the short score of the middle section of the scene. The prelude to Scene Seven, on which I shall be working next, will deal with Fusako and Ryuji, while the prelude to Scene Eight will probably have to describe the entrance of the young 'samurai'.

> *Marino, 16 september. yesterday wrote the first Fusako variation in scene seven. it's the scene in which they say goodbye. worked my way through the whole of the existing score, trying to hear and understand everything as it will actually sound (i'd already forgotten a few things).*

During the days that followed, there were other passages, too, that succeeded, leaving me with a reckless feeling of euphoria. It is sometimes a little frightening to lean too far out of the window that overlooks the *terra incognita* of the emotions. Keep shaking my head in disbelief that the notes seem to finish up in the right place as though of their own accord. Most unsettling. The following day I began work on the trio for Fusako, Noboru and Ryuji, it went like a dream. Spent a whole night thinking only of the music, in a kind of half-sleep. Work has become an epicurean escapade of positively criminal proportions. But there are also times when I think that I shall never complete this piece, at any moment I may fall ill, and everything will go to waste. I allow the music to pursue its course, following the direction that it has chosen for itself. Scene Seven is dominated by dark colours (lighter ones enter when Fusako is singing), also natural sounds, above all, the mewing of seagulls. We are outside, it is open-air music, not chamber music, but harbour music, with dark undercurrents, bass notes, anchors, infinite melodies. The music of Noboru's piano studies develops and matures and has now assimilated the novel features first heard in the earlier trio, acquiring greater richness – especially harmonically – as a result.

At the end of October I returned from another foreign trip and, tired and subdued, trotted along the shores of the Lago di Albano. My work once again became very difficult, my biggest problem being the instrumentation of the final chord in Scene Seven, with the ship's siren on board the *Rakuyo-Maru*, which I had to try to convey in the music over five whole bars. Oh yes, and I also had to go back to see the ear specialist.

I sketched Scene Eight during the second half of November, but hardly knew how I had achieved it and, instead of being pleased, simply lay there motionless, hoping that the feelings of anxiety that had seized hold of me would not gain the upper hand. The act ends abruptly as the gang of Japanese acolytes prepares for Noboru to kill a kitten as a ritual test of his courage. At the moment of execution, there is a flash that dazzles the appalled spectator, followed by the interval, with champagne and smoked salmon sandwiches.

The thirteenth of December is dedicated to Saint Lucy of Syracuse, and young olive trees and piglets are sold in the market at Marino. North wind and new moon. I was keen to make an immediate start on the second part of the opera, and it was not long before I was able to do so, but Uli Treichel first had to write some additional lines of text, and a monologue had to be turned into a duet. The music of the opening scene of Part Two ('Winter' – it is the New Year and sunrise, so that an offer of marriage can be made) had to project a middle-class sense of heterosexual happiness and do so with such clarity that between thirty and ninety per cent of the audience would be able to empathize with it. It was a scene that had to teeter on the verge of kitsch.

1989. I hope I may never stop imagining new and different music, cruder, harsher music that resembles a landscape and admits of horizons and a feeling of distance. Each of the six scenes in Part Two must be differently instrumented, and the vocal lines must be treated in varying ways.

I keep catching myself committing the error of imagining future pieces in fairly concrete ways, instead of working on the task in hand and devoting all – and I mean *all* – my energies to the present preoccupation: it is a way of putting off decisions.

If you are lucky, you can keep the outside world at bay and fill your mind with music and technical matters: only in this way is life in any way bearable. Within a few days I had already sketched the whole of Scene Nine and begun to spend the afternoons working on the full score. On 12 February I made a note of the fact that I now knew what the music for the adolescents must sound like and that it had to be the principal concern in Act Two, and full of magnanimity . . .

. . . and the fact that love essentially ends with the promise of marriage in scene nine since it has nothing more to offer that could be expressed in musical terms except through parody or artificial tedium.

By the end of February I had completed the fair copy of Scene Nine in full score and had begun work on the interlude between Scenes Nine and Ten. Had the feeling that the new ideas that had struck me in recent weeks could now find expression. *this is also the moment at which the piece's peripeteia occurs*: the act of betrayal has now taken place. Ryuji the seaman has deceived, betrayed and sold out on his boat, the sea *and* Noboru, who had worshipped him until now.

I could hear the music growing wilder, and within a few days had sketched out this major interlude in short score, writing out all the layers and voices in full. There is a real sense of fury here that reflects not the premarital pleasures of Fusako and her husband, who has now resigned his commission, but, rather, the raging sea itself. I imagine that I shall be able to sketch out the whole of Scene Ten during the coming days, with its mustering of these young nihilists, who cannot get over their disappointment at the sailor whom they once revered and who is an ancient symbol of male honour and of identity with the world. They feel nothing but scorn and contempt for the traitor, and the scene ends with a foreboding of the catastrophe to come. The full score of Scene Ten was sent off to my publisher on 4 May.

Eight days later, the prelude and beginning of Scene Eleven were in hand, an Adagio for strings that unfolds independently of the action taking place on stage and that is conducted in Sprechgesang. (It is a painful scene in which Noboru's voyeurism is discovered and he is beaten and humiliated.) The sketches for this section were completed on 19 May, the fair copy on 4 June. In mid-May I wrote to Messrs Friedrich, Hoffer and Stenz, who were communally in charge of the production:

> In principle and at bottom, the music aims to be a metaphor for the betrayed and raging sea, a natural force more powerful than the passionate and carnal, if somewhat pedestrian, love between Fusako and Ryuji, as powerful as Noboru's jealousy and as the immature and cold-hearted feelings towards the world on the part of the ringleader and his associates. It is about elemental phenomena, including the seasons and temperatures. As a result, the colours mentioned by Mishima (together with the references to colours, all of which have been taken over into the libretto) have a huge symbolic role to play, just as certain gestures

and turns of phrase, as well as the position of the sun and moon, are intended to suggest particular things and states: sometimes such symbolism may strike us as a little naïve (or too direct), but I still think that it should be taken over without question, from the red kimono (which in kabuki indicates the desire to kill or similar passions bound up with love) to the blood-red sunset or sunrise (hence my idea of showing the planets and their movements as though they were some imperturbable and wonderfully beautiful clockwork mechanism) and from the blood-red glove lining to the green flag beneath the leaden sky of a hot and humid summer in a Japanese port. Grand opera on a lavish scale in a ritual style yet to be devised. [. . .] I think it is necessary to bear in mind that the piece has no moral in the western sense. Things happen because they are fated to happen, i.e. as though by chance and in nature. We should not judge, should not apply any western or Christian criteria. The piece shows how people meet and what the consequences of those meetings are. Every woman can identify with Fusako, every man with Ryuji, and each and every one of us with the novice who happens to fall in with a ringleader at college and to be taken up into his gang of boyish, almost infantile, but precocious classmates. It is important that these lads behave like normal or, rather, abnormally gifted college boys, we must be able to like them, in particular we must be able to sympathize with Noboru, who is the main character in the opera [. . .]. In staging the work, we must beware of making things too easy for ourselves and the audience. They are no perverts or skinheads or rockers, but sensitive, wounded creatures, old before their time, beautiful and puristic in an infantile way. As the result, as it were, of the unfortunate accident of a cerebral dysfunction, their games suddenly become horribly real. But they are no criminals. Something happens to them. An intellectual adventure that goes too far and gets out of hand. They overstep the mark. At all events, Noboru and the ringleader and the three other lads are more interesting than the ship's second officer and the owner of the boutique. [. . .] Each scene has, in the main, a single tempo, a single pulse that is maintained throughout that scene. The music that links these scenes and that covers the scene-changes takes the form of preludes and postludes. The music is in a constant state of flux and agitation, but such a hectic pace should not be replicated on stage. *Au contraire!* I imagine the singers' range of movements to be relatively economical and kabuki-like. The result should be a sense of opposites, of counterpoint and counterpositions.

On 19 June I began work on the prelude to Scene Twelve. In keeping with my plans, it was a variant of a section from the previous scene, but now scored for full orchestra, not just strings. And on the morning of the 29th I started Scene Twelve itself.

> *in the evening i followed an impulse that i had felt repeatedly yesterday and sketched the first part of scene thirteen, Fusako's aria, and in that way gained an insight into scene fourteen, the great ending – now i know what has to be done. must bear the following points in mind:*
>
> 1. *Ryuji's basic material must be used, fermented and poisoned*
> 2. musique concrète *with harbour and building-site noises*
> 3. *raise the keyboard music to a pitch of explosive intensity*
> 4. *full version of the sea shanty*
>
> *Fusako is becoming very beautiful*
> *monday is the new moon*

By *ferragosto* the sketches of Scene Thirteen were complete.

> *20 august. it appals me to act in such a self-indulgent way. and yet i feel a warm glow of satisfaction whenever i produce something beautiful. i completed the last 20 bars at my desk two days ago, the final 5–6 are linked to the opera's basic row and lead to a totally logical ending – i didn't need to alter a single note, or so it appeared as i played it through to myself,*

but in the course of the days that followed I kept getting out the music again, reworking it, changing it and improving it until I finally felt able to move on to the fair copy. Sent off the full score in early September and then set off for Gütersloh, where I planned to spend the coming weeks. On my way there, I noted that I would now have to address myself to Scene Fourteen, which begins with Uli's description of harbour noises, a scene of ravaged desolation.

Did not bring the earlier scenes with me to Gütersloh, but only the basic rows, so that I would not be tempted to reuse any of the existing material. I know that the music associated with the children and with the piano studies now has to acquire a note of menace and that it must bristle with bayonets. By the middle of the month I had sketched out the vocal ensemble with which the opera ends, and on 23 September I wrote in my notebook:

> still can't believe the opera is finished.

This detailed account of the genesis of *Das verratene Meer* has prevented me from mentioning the other activities that got in the way of my work on the score, interrupting it, delaying it and making it much more difficult but sometimes also lending it extra urgency. In order to list them all in turn, we unfortunately have to return once again to January 1987, when Uli was in Marino and working with me on the libretto of *Das verratene Meer*, and we were visited by Dieter Schidor, desperately depressed at the loss of his New Zealand boyfriend, Mike. I then went to Munich on Biennale business and on 9 January held a *conversazione* at the Vienna Konzerthaus, where I analyzed and performed my *Ode an eine Äolsharfe* with David Tanenbaum and members of the ORF Orchestra, after which I left for London, to teach at the Royal Academy and to rehearse *An eine Äolsharfe* with the Sinfonietta.

I felt that I would soon reach the point at which I could start work on my Japanese music drama, with its theme of destructive jealousy. In my dreams I identified with the character of Kioyuki in Mishima's *Sea of Fertility*. On 27 January I introduced the twenty-six-year-old Mark-Anthony Turnage to the octogenarian Francis Bacon, with whom my fellow composer wanted to discuss the designs for his first opera for the Munich Biennale. Of course, there was no question that anything would come of this, since Francis did not work in the theatre on principle and did not even design posters or the like. But he was very sweet to Mark and we lunched in lordly style with vast amounts of the most expensive Chianti at Cecconi's in Burlington Gardens, off Piccadilly, after which we had the privilege of accompanying him to Muriel's, a club for drinkers in Soho, where we moved on to champagne. My young colleague was ill for three days.

A blackbird, Hächi Büm Büm, sang from the roof-top in London's crystalline air, while a wintery sun shone overhead and Uli wrote to me from Berlin on the subject of our newly planned music drama. Among the things that he had to say was:

> the contest between the ruler (culture, civilization, power, etc.) and the Minotaur is a primeval one that has lasted since the dawn of history and that we can take for granted, an 'eternal conflict' that we tune into at a particular point in time. Against this background, I find Gide's interpretation of the Minotaur in *Thésée* both interesting and correct, the interpretation of the Minotaur or, rather, the world of the Minotaur not just as a world of death and destruction but also as a

seductive world of pleasure and enjoyment. And the labyrinth is seen as a place from which it is not only no longer possible to escape but from which we no longer *want* to escape, once we are inside it. The Minotaur is no doubt a destructive force but also an archaic, even naïve, cross-border figure (as drawn by Picasso), and his world is a world of naïve and terrible pleasure and sin that has not yet been shoehorned into the neat, geometrical arrangement of Oedipal compulsions and obsessions, as has happened, for example, with the Phaedra conflict. To love and to devour is still one and the same for the Minotaur, in other words, he simply does not know the difference between them, just as he does not know the difference between sleeping and waking, the conscious and the unconscious, the animal and the human, etc. It is this that makes him so attractive to all those who have moved on culturally, who are 'fully human' and who wrestle with the Minotaur. But to wrestle with the Minotaur, this great passion of the ruler, is also tantamount to seeking out the Minotaur and *going to him.*

can't help thinking of Francis B., his intensity, his seclusion, an existence that involves nothing but work, well, and muriel's, and John. feel almost the same kind of pleasure and dedication: would like to get back to Marino and my desk as soon as possible.

18. again thought of F.B. what's the reason? i think it's the aura of his strength and refusal to compromise. his determination to do only what is necessary to produce his paintings.

19. powerful presence of F.B. at night, inspiring me, urging me on and encouraging me. incitement. will write to him.

8 March. in Marino played piano duets with Salvatore Sciarrino.

15. Dream: *arrive with my mother at Francis's house by the sea, on looking closer i see that it's Turner's, then Sebastiano del Piombo's vision of San Marco as a setting for 'The Death of Adonis', with the grieving Venus in the foreground.*

Spent the last few days of March in Munich, pursuing sponsors, then flew to Berlin for a concert with Gerd Albrecht, who dissects and performs my *Barcarola*. Peter Schneider reads me his and Aras Ören's libretto for *Leyla und Medjnun*, a classical Islamic love story set in Asia Minor, the musical setting of which I have entrusted to my former pupil, Detlev Glanert, for the first Munich Biennale. Among the instruments will be an *'ūd*, to be played by Mehmet Yesilcay. My friends, Ulrich and Jo Eckhardt, take me to the Kreuzberg home of the painter Natascha Ungeheuer, and I buy a painting, *Waiting Room*, showing lots of people waiting, almost all of whom look sad and as though tormented by cares and homesickness and wanderlust and for whom the tiny flame of hope seems almost to have been extinguished. I later hung it in the music-cum-reception room in my Munich apartment and sat my visitors beneath it, so that, throughout their stay, I could always look at the people in the picture and thus be able to avert my eyes from time to time from my guest.

> 3/4 April (Marino) *spent yesterday morning working on the instrumentation, very difficult to get back into the music, extremely highly strung, on the verge of despair. want to sort out the Biennale as quickly as possible and delegate responsibility.*

Marino, 25 April 1987. Day of national celebration, 43rd anniversary of liberation from Nazi Fascism.

9 May. Back to Cologne, great deal of effort involved there, listless, and freezing all the time. Have to go begging for Munich. Read Feuchtwanger's *Erfolg* with great interest.

> *6 June. airport Cologne 2 tiring weeks. conversazione with Aeolsharfe at the Academy, Tanenbaum, Ensemble Modern, Glanert's transcriptions of Isaac and Schütz, Biennale problems. wish i didn't have to devote so much of my time to the rest of the world.*

Glorious Whitsuntide at Marino. On 9 June I attend the Italian *prima* of *Ritorno* in Florence, where I meet Iris Wagner and attempt to lure her to Munich for the Biennale, but she is committed to Berlin. Read *Billy Budd* for the first time. Back in Munich, changes to team of collaborators. The rent on one of the halls is extremely high, and I have to guarantee it out of my own pocket, but we cannot manage without the Kongreßsaal in the Deutsches Museum, especially since we have just lost another hall, the Alabamahalle to the north of the city centre: it will be pulled down exactly a week before the start of the Biennale. I had already found myself confronted with such unexpected and curious eventualities on a number of previous occasions, which had frequently given rise to the impression – due, perhaps, to my reading of Feuchtwanger – that here in Munich, to the north of the Alps, I am having to deal not only with sympathizers but also with enemies and that there are countercurrents and suchlike here, of a kind that life all too often throws up. Many is the time that I have been advised by various people to be on my guard: Munich is said to be a dangerous place. I find this hard to believe: my mind positively refuses to operate on the level of intrigue. I remain in Marino until the end of August and see that the only thing that really interests me is the wish to come as close as possible to perfection in my work as a composer. And I crouch even lower over the score of my opera.

In August the Frankfurt production of *The English Cat* was seen in Edinburgh, although my own presence in the city was bound up, rather, with the desire to speak to the Lord Mayor about the possibility of an artistic exchange programme with Munich, with which Edinburgh is twinned. I also visited Ian Barr in order to persuade him to help finance next year's visiting performances of Turnage's *Greek* and, finally, went to arrange this visit with the festival authorities. I then travelled to London and went to 7 Reece Mews, barely a stone's throw from Fausto's, where Francis B. lived, and placed a fan letter in the black letter-box of the pitch-black door. Also spoke with the viola player Garth Knox, who by now was spending most of his time in Paris, playing with the Ensemble InterContemporain, and whom I invited to join a small orchestra made up only of friends that would perform in Gütersloh the following year. I also discussed the idea with Peter Sheppard, a violinist from the Royal Academy. Worked on a speech that I was to give in Berlin in the autumn, *Channels, Gorges, Surfaces* – it was intended as a kind of musical prose, a spoken sonata, and it was to deal in a coded way with my private relations with Berlin.

One Sunday afternoon, Fausto and I drove out to Windsor with Michael Vyner and went for a boat trip on the Thames. It was hazy between the poplars and ash trees, a little grey and overcast but not at all cold, as we slowly chugged along upstream in the direction of Oxford, unable to get over the sight of the green fields that lined the increasingly narrow and restful river. Anglers sat on the reed-grown banks, smoking their pipes and allowing the good Lord to believe that all was well with His world. Around us lay typical English gardens in which sat typically English families in brightly coloured summer clothes rivalling the dahlias and roses in their gaily gaudy hues, while drinking tea and offering their neighbours a slice of home-made cake. At one point we saw a heron, which looked up at us for a moment, then went back to its fishing. It was a world that seemed alien to us, curious, not made for the likes of us, but the delightful impression that it created, the feeling that it was a weekend and that people were relaxing and clearly enjoying themselves, left us, too, feeling fairly calm and contented. Michael was unusually quiet, I can still remember the gentle melancholy surrounding him that warm, late-summer day. He was not normally given to thoughtful silences.

It was only later that it struck me that the conversation had turned not on music and the world of music, as it normally did, but on private matters and memories, generally from much earlier in our lives and including, therefore, the beginnings of our friendship. How young we were when we were young. What foolish things we said and did, however well-intentioned we may have been at the time, even if it was not always possible to explain to people exactly what we meant, since we lacked the words to do so. Yes, and how frivolous and yet how sophisticated we had been during those carefree years in the late fifties and early sixties when we had all been as happy as sandboys and could not get our fill of adventures, conquests and sleepless nights. We now talked about these follies as though we were discussing events and people that we had barely known in person. And there were other stories, too, from the time before we became friends, stories from Michael's past, from his Jewish family in Yorkshire, and it became possible to appreciate the Russian background that had so clearly shaped him, with his violent – not to say, excessive – mood swings, his declarations of love and hatred, his passions and his rhapsodical manner of expressing the vehemence of these feelings. And the way he spoke was not Yorkshire English, as I had long assumed, but Yorkshire Russian. Michael was much easier to understand if one kept this aspect in mind whenever one was dealing with him. It was important never to lose sight of this folkloristic background if one wanted fully to enjoy the pleasure of knowing and working with such an exceptional person as he was.

We sat on the bank for a while after the sun had set, silently regaling ourselves with a bottle of Scotch. A gentle whimpering filled the twilit gloom like a quarter-tone vibrato on the E string. Later I thought that the whole of the day had been like this, as though Michael had been wanting to get something important off his chest but had finally been unable to make up his mind to say it.

In London, Francis B. showed me his new triptych *A las cinco de la tarde* after Federico García Lorca, which I found very beautiful: the central panel showed a bull, a fearsome black Minotaur in the company of one of those Furies that are so often found in Bacon's work and that look like quotations from Hieronymus Bosch, demonic figures of fate. To the left and right were blooded *matadores*. I told him how impressive I found it, but he said, sorrowfully and in an attempt to dampen my enthusiasm, that it had not turned out as natural as he had intended.

He was very demanding. Once he said: 'The whole world hates me and I've no friends!' I retorted: 'But how can that be when you're revered by the whole world as if you were' – I was searching for a comparison and came up with the wrong one – 'as if you were Leonardo da Vinci?' To which Francis replied, grumbling: 'But *he* wasn't at all a good painter.'

Spectacular storms in Marino to mark the end of the summer, moments of apathy and inability to work. Fausto is not particularly well again; for years he has been suffering from depression, it comes and goes and sometimes seems almost to have past before returning to torment him with all the greater violence. I feel so desperately sorry for him, not least because there is nothing that anyone can do except offer him words of encouragement, but it is of little use, one cannot get through to the patient. As long as we never lose hope! This was, as it were, a second basso continuo – or a soprano continuo – that stole along above and beneath the cantus firmus of our lives, influencing the form that those lives took and affecting all our decisions, our inability to accept invitations and the various concessions that we had to make.

Can't think of anything except Dieter Schidor's suicide in Munich. I visited him last Monday evening as he lay dying in the hospital on the right bank of the Isar. He could no longer speak. We were told that he had wanted to avoid the humiliations and horrors of an Aids-related death. Tubes and transfusions. He was already fading away, but he looked beautiful, as if transfigured, smiling, as though he was finally fairly content, even happy. Two days later I woke up very early, curiously startled and sad and was on the point of going straight to the hospital when the phone rang: he had passed away in the night.

The days that followed were a time of anguish, the nights of sleepless torment. I went begging on behalf of the Biennale, then had to go to Alsfeld, where I saw and heard what my boys from Cologne had achieved in the meantime. Pleasantly surprised. Scene followed scene with a real sense of rhythm, while pulsating with lightness and life. There were no *longueurs* and no people failing to pull their weight. They must have rehearsed intensively, since everything sounded so plausible and as though self-evident, with a natural grace to it. You might almost think that the music had been written here in the fields and stables and orchards of Upper Hesse. The two wind bands, positioned antiphonally, vied in brilliance and volume, while the sound of the Alsfeld Chamber Orchestra and Singers, together with that of the local Mandolin, Recorder and Guitar Clubs, was all the more delicate and subtle in comparison, allowing listeners to appreciate the dramaturgical expediency of these divisions by virtue of the contrasts between them. There was never any impression of makeshift solutions, no sense of compromise or superfluity. It was clear from the final rehearsals that they were well organized and had been working to a plan: having set up a proper operational headquarters, all my young colleagues had been detailed to particular jobs and had to help out and make themselves useful as répétiteurs, copyists, errand boys, stage managers, assistant directors and musical assistants. Michael Kerstan and his designer, the Frankfurt-based scenographer, Hermann Haindl, had come up with a linear, impressively simple production for the young professional singers from the summer school at Bad Orb, a number of whom had never appeared on stage before and not had to perform modern music from memory. But here, too, it had proved possible to avoid the impression of effort or that the singers were out of their depth. Particularly amusing was the good-humoured finale with its local folk dances and rounds (of a kind that I had never seen before). The whole affair passed off more successfully than anyone had dared hope, and the locals – some two hundred and fifty Alsfelders had taken part – were at least as proud and pleased as we were. We had achieved what the class had set out to do.

At the final rehearsals I had, of course, observed the young conductor, Markus Stenz. It had struck me that he approached his work with a thoughtfulness and *savoir-faire* that communicated themselves to all the singers and musicians, resulting in a general sense of self-confidence and encouraging each and every member of the company to believe that he or she was utterly irreplaceable and of the very highest quality. A sense of calm prevailed at these rehearsals, people paid attention and took the trouble to meet the conductor's expectations, so that he would beam with satisfaction. And I said to myself – and also to young Markus himself after the first night – that here was a man who was born to be a conductor: everything that was needed was here – a good ear, charisma, the sense of realism that people with a talent for organizing things possess as a matter of course, and the gift of being able to work and rehearse in a rational and matter-of-fact manner. I decided to encourage him and help him, which in the first instance meant finding opportunities that would allow him to try out his gifts without exposing himself to undue dangers in the process – until such time as the doors of the world's great concert halls and opera houses would be opened up to him.

22–29 Sept. Taormina

gardens sea at night etna

can't sleep because of Dieter

plagued by thoughts of Munich

valium

drive into the depressing interior: seems to be in a permanent state of siege

heavily armed police everywhere, jeeps and cross-country vehicles, people shy, uncommunicative, the streets empty after dark

Castiglione di Sicilia, *above the terrible Francavilla, a mountain town built on Graeco-Norman foundations that gives the impression of a ghost town.*

lava, black fire on the hills.

the coasts scandalously impoverished

sirocco so hot you think it's burning

Syracuse: filth and devastation

hours of torment in the traffic in Catania

hell on earth

On Sunday, 4 October 1987, at 11.30 in the morning, I read my paper on *Channels, Gorges, Surfaces: Sonata in Prose* in the Renaissance-Theater in Berlin within the framework of a series of lectures designed to mark the five-hundredth anniversary of the founding of the city. Afterwards dined with Ulrich and Jo Eckhardt, also Natascha Ungeheuer and Johannes Schenk, a poet with a hat. In the evening attended the first performance of Wolfgang Rihm's *Oedipus*: positive impressions of the music, power, imagination. Real sense of style.

On 15 October heard a wonderful performance of my Seventh Symphony in Boston under Ozawa. Visited Harvard. On the journey from Boston to New York, Ron Freed reverently pointed out the house in Lowell, Massachusetts, where Bette Davis had been born, also the vast forests of scarlet maple and the Witches' Museum at Salem, Massachusetts, where a young witch, her face contorted with hatred, slammed the door in our faces with a furious cackle. In New York I could not resist the temptation to attend two further performances of my Seventh Symphony at Carnegie Hall and to mix with people at the main entrance, at the evening box office, observing the flourishing black market in tickets and finding myself infected by the general excitement that precedes a concert like this in New York, especially when there is a visiting orchestra such as the

Boston Symphony that performs in New York only once or twice a year.

On Tuesday, 3 November 1987, I held a press conference in Munich to discuss the Biennale and, at the same time, announced the 1988 programme. In the course of my travels as a mendicant, I even visited Regensburg and the badly heated, fortified palace of the Princes of Thurn und Taxis, where I was dismissed by His Serene Highness in a particularly uncouth and condescending manner even before I was able to say my piece about the Biennale and entreat his gracious help. Although Spanish court ceremonial prevailed at table (the servants were woodcutters dressed up as lackeys), there was no fire in the grate and so I caught a chill, which is the main reason why even today I continue to be annoyed with myself for ever having called on this arrogant, rouged and painted prince. Jürgen Kolbe was against my going from the outset.

In mid-November, a week at the Royal Academy in London.

Michael Vyner is very ill.
8th symph.: 1 chamber-orchestra work to last a whole evening
(neo-brandenburg concertos)
9th symph.: das 7. Kreuz –

Start a new address book in order to avoid stumbling at every turn across the names of dead and exiled friends.

Marino, 25 December. Christmas. Fausto has decorated the Church of the Madonna del Sasso, while three heathens look on during Mass and Communion: Yoichi, Ian Strasfogel and I. We then go to a cantina to play cards and celebrate Christmas beneath a photograph, in a somewhat dusty wooden frame, of Comrade Stalin, who, uniformed and bemedalled, stares down at us, without batting an eyelid, uncomprehending and unforgiving.

1988.

1 January. *yesterday at midnight F. lit a bonfire in the garden, Y. had made 20 witches out of straw, paper and laurel twigs: on the stroke of 12, each of the twenty guests was allowed to burn his or her witch, the witch of fear, the witch of jealousy, of pain etc. the witch that i burnt represented all the trouble that i've had to put up with in Munich – away with all these frightful disruptions and their attendant persecution mania!*

London, 25 January. yesterday 20th anniversary of Sinfonietta at Festival Hall. Michael V. spoke, looked very ill. last week with Francis

> *B., John and Fausto. Francis suffered an attack of asthma that began with violent scenes of jealousy in the street, it was all quite wild and even a little terrifying. at eighty!*

Spent a week in February as visiting lecturer at Basle Conservatory. Wide awake at night, worrying about Munich. *Mun. in the distance. every day and every hour more unpleasant and more disagreeable. should i fight back or give it all up?*

In mid-March my music was played every evening for a whole week at the Royal Academy, and I had to be there all the time, even at rehearsals. I felt ill, and finally suffered a kind of breakdown brought on by overwork and worry, and after Easter had to escape to a clinic, where I spent two weeks being stuffed full of the worst possible pills until I was scarcely able to write or read or speak any longer. I stopped taking them as soon as I was discharged and immediately began to feel better, so that I was able to travel to Berlin at the end of April to discuss *Das verratene Meer* with Götz Friedrich and Hans Hoffer (we talked about its style and about what it means and its social relevance) and to discover that a date had been fixed for the opening night: 28 April 1990, in other words, exactly two years hence.

In the garden at Marino I heard the wings of the hoopoe whizzing gently past my ear. Went for walks with Uli Treichel, in the course of which we fantasized endlessly about operatic myth and mythic opera.

> Still, all has gone *smoothly from start to finish, and we now have a basic structure with genuine ideas and also a novel form. the angels* [of which my readers will not yet have heard, I think] *overlap, stand to one side, report and proclaim things, but always wrong, always erroneously*
>
> *the buffo scenes in blank verse, the angels elevated prose*
> *discussed the main action today (this is where the problem lies)*
> *how will the buffo episodes fit into the main action?*
> *bring up the music from the depths, where it lies buried beneath so many other things, submerged. archaeology*
> *solemn. demands slow speeds*

On 10 May 1988 Fausto and I saw the revival of Ashton's *Ondine* at Covent Garden. The Royal Ballet had put the piece to one side long before Fonteyn had stopped dancing, while awaiting a new ballerina for this difficult, legendary role. Now two young dancers had arrived on the scene simultaneously and had both grown into the role together – Maria

Almeida and Cynthia Harvey. Money from a French sponsor had made it possible to remake many of the costumes (the old ones were unusable), although Lila's personal touch was missing, with the result that they clashed rather badly with the few that had survived and also with the scenery, the patina on which was no longer the one that the designer herself had applied with her own fair hand. It was also clear that thirty years previously lighting techniques had been different: the stage was less brightly lit then, and not even old Freddy, who knew all the tricks of the trade, was able to recreate the lighting effects of 1958. But, apart from these few shortcomings, the production left a deep impression on me – until now I had seen it only from the orchestra pit, of course, and in the cinema: I particularly liked the basically manneristic approach, and was pleased to note the combined effect of the three different elements of dance, colour and music. I was moved to see how, as a choreographer, Ashton had reacted to my music in 1958 – it must have sounded so new to him! – but it seemed to me that he had understood its essential qualities and that the answers that he had provided were beautiful, correct and apt. And I was pleased to see and hear how much trouble the composer had taken in meeting the demands that were placed on him and in ensuring a sense of variety and a rainbow range of emotions from melancholy and pain to lyricism, fairy-tale magic and the eerily supernatural.

15

In the early summer of 1988, only a few weeks after the first Munich Biennale (more on which in a moment), we returned to Tanglewood – 'we' being Fausto and I. It was my second visit. On this occasion we stayed in a large, wooden house in the middle of the forest at Richmond, Massachusetts. Close by, you could occasionally hear the hooting of the old express train – the Housatonic Railroad – a polyphonic chord that reminded me of the siren in the port at Yokohama calling the faithless Ryuji back on board. I was responsible for ten students, who looked in on me at regular intervals for individual tuition and with whom I also gave two or three seminars on *lieder* writing, at the end of which each of the ten participants regaled us with a regular German song. In addition, I conducted the United States première of my *Liebeslieder* (magically played by the cellist, Yo-Yo Ma); sat in the meadows, incognito, with twelve thousand other listeners to hear a performance of my Seventh Symphony; flew to New York and spoke to the choreographer, Bill T. Jones, about a piece for the Munich Biennale; got on with my opera; and was impressed by Elliott Carter's powerful and grandiose music.

It was in Tanglewood that I heard of the death of Jean-Pierre Ponnelle. It was difficult for me to take it in: he had always been as strong as an ox, so full of life and energy, and so young – I had always regarded him as a son! (The world keeps growing emptier and more alien: the stage designer Axel Manthey has just been taken from us, and in the early summer of 1993 my first Cimarrón, Billy Pearson, died, a man to whom I had been bound by so many ties of sympathy and by memories both happy and sad.)

On 24 August I found myself in the village church at Yaxley, Suffolk, for the funeral of Frederick Ashton, another sad occasion at which I met a number of old acquaintances, from Ninette de Valois and John Tooley to Fred's sister, Edith, and Alexander Grant. Michael Somes read the lesson but had to break off in tears. Back in London, I conducted a promenade concert at the Albert Hall, the culmination of a week of tiring orchestral rehearsals and involving a performance of *Liebeslieder* with the cellist Alexander Baillie and scenes and arias from *Ritorno* with soloists from the 1985 Salzburg Festival.

And I also saw Michael Vyner. The news concerning his health was not good: he could barely stand up, and his voice, now thin and quavery, had risen considerably in pitch. He had to support himself by holding on to things and no longer had the strength to tone down his complaints or control his expressions of pain. Someone had to be with him all the time now.

Back in Marino I received a deputation of ladies from Montepulciano, who were at a loss as to what they should do, but there was nothing that I could do to advise them. There was talk of disbanding the Cantieri. It seemed that no answer had been found to the underlying problems that continued to beset the festival, not only on an organizational and financial level but, above all, in terms of the place's artistic policy.

Markus Stenz came and helped me revise the orchestral score of *Elegy*, before conducting a concert performance of the new version at the Teatro La Fenice in Venice on 28 October 1988. It was sung in the original language with an international cast. I heard it on the radio in Marino and found it excellent, not least on account of the improvements to the orchestral writing that I had just made. By the morning of 29 November, I was back in London for Frederick Ashton's memorial service in a freezing cold Westminster Abbey, where I conducted the Andante from Mozart's Piano Concerto, K467 with the pianist Philip Gammon – it was apparently Fred's favourite piece. Among those who spoke were the artistic director of the Royal Ballet (and the new Palemon in *Ondine*), Anthony Dowell, who read something by Proust. Some four thousand people came to the service, including older and younger members of the royal family and a large number of personalities from London's artistic and theatrical world. Afterwards we joined lots of other people at a nearby pub, warmed our frozen limbs and drank a few gin and tonics 'to Fred' . . .

In mid-January 1989 – I had still not found a way of beginning Act Two of *Meer* – Fausto and I set off on a somewhat adventurous visit to Belize on Guatemala's Atlantic coast. Here, in a world like something out of a novel by Robert Louis Stevenson, we spent two weeks living on a sand dune called Caye Caulker situated far out in the Atlantic, with only a handful of palm trees to bear the brunt of the endless storms, while not far away lay a vast coral reef against which the ocean pounded unceasingly, roaring and foaming and booming like the bass notes of an organ. Our host, Don Pedro, and Fausto between them made me a desk from old crates, which I even used on occasion, writing long letters in the shade, setting Uli's *Drei Lieder über den Schnee* and from time to time sinking into a kind of deep sleep. No one could touch me here, we were in a nature reserve whose other inhabitants I found fascinating in the extreme. To go diving and meet a manatee with its offspring is the sort of thing that you could not even do in the Maximilianstraße in Munich. And shoals of brightly coloured fish – I was reminded of the first chapter of Lorenz's *On Aggression* – surrounded you in these waters, which were lit from above by the sun, but which grew dark and uncertain the deeper you went, filled, as they were, with electric rays from Schiller's ballad, *Der Taucher*, and with sharks and other murderous types from the world of myth and real life. There were also the most amazing waterbirds here, white herons, flamingos, humming-birds and marabou storks. I watched the pelicans circling overhead, then suddenly plunging seawards, into the water, head first, like bombs, and almost immediately shooting back up to the surface with a fish in their dredger-like bills. Don Pedro tells us that while the female pelican brings up her young, the male is responsible for feeding them all and brings back the fish he has caught to their nest in the depths of the forest of mangroves. But on days when the sea is rough and the swell is running high, so the surface is no longer clear, the pelican is unable to see any fish on to which to swoop down – he circles around and wanders further and further afield in his search for food, then flutters back to the nest and consoles his wife and offspring, before flying off again, albeit only by way of experiment and with little hope of success. If, on the second day, the water is still as turbid, the female opens her breast and, as she dies, she feeds her young with her own insides. And if, on the third day, the sea remains as impenetrable, the baby pelicans begin to starve, and their father flies off on his own into the middle of the mangrove thicket and hangs himself as though in some ancient Greek tragedy. On one occasion we crossed over to the mainland and sailed up one of the rivers as far as the Maya temples at Altun Ha, spending a whole day in a world remote from civilization but rank with vegetation and in forests filled with remarkable little foxes, racoons and wild cats. Several decades late, I finally set foot in the places that I had read about as a schoolboy and discovered that all that we had been told at that time was actually true and did indeed exist in real life.

At the beginning of July, Michael Vyner and his friend and carer, Colin Perry, arrived in Marino for a week-long visit. He had come to say goodbye – 'it is finished,' he told us – but we refused to listen and spoke instead about the future, making elaborate plans for the Sinfonietta in the East End, for my Eighth Symphony as a cycle of movements lasting an entire evening, for an experimental studio for young composers and so on. Every hour, both by day and by night, Michael had to take a large tablet. He had no reserves of energy left to withstand the attacks of shock-like anxiety that overcame him, the sudden outbursts of crying or the exaggerated reactions of every kind – only the emotions of delight and calm were denied him. He would suffer from sudden attacks of pain of such violent intensity that he would run screaming to his room. The outward signs of his illness were already clearly visible by now. Such is the misery that exists in this world.

Hypersensitive as he is, Fausto found it difficult to cope with the situation, and I was afraid that he would not be able to last out the week, but he put on a brave face and showed no reaction, but behaved in an altogether calm and considerate manner. Yet this was a particularly bad year for him, so much so, in fact, that I was seriously concerned for him. *Dalla sua pace la mia dipende* – my own peace of mind has always depended on his, just as *his* peace of mind depends upon mine: everything that happens to one of us, be it good or bad, affects the other twice or thrice as much. We try to ward off evil and hold it at bay through general attentiveness and other more practical measures or else merely by saying what it is that causes us disquiet or makes us feel so concerned for the other's well-being. As a small boy, Fausto was known in his local dialect as *Marott ad Brardon* – the little Moor of grandfather Berardo. (I still have a photograph of him from that period, with his parents' home – destroyed by the German armed forces shortly before the armistice – in the background.) He now talks to plants and trees and flowers and animals as though they were people, addressing them in a particularly strange-sounding accent to which his charges respond with vigorous growth, quite literally blossoming and striving towards the warming light or cooling shade depending upon their predisposition or predilection and needs. They blossom and bloom and thrive in countless shades of green, from the light-transmissive linden leaf to deep copper sulphate, moleskin and laurel black. The year takes us with it in a circle, to quote Thomas Mann, and we are happy to allow it to do so, patiently waiting for the new day to dawn or for evening to fall and quizzically lying in wait for the elves or the lunar eclipse and the darkness that always brings with it quite different types of blackness and light – rarely is any of them the same as before. We scarcely need to discuss these things, as each of us already knows what the other thinks and intends to say, what he feels and wants, and this is true, of course, not only of the times of day and the seasons and of the world of flora and fauna, but also of what I might call the aura of the fellow human beings who set foot in our house and whom, like it or not, we meet in the course of our travels, people who can still be regarded as peripheral, passing figures who have their exits and their entrances, like messengers bringing news from the outback, from border territories, with new stories in their panniers, comic tales about courtesans, incredible love songs and heroic lays.

I spent September 1989 in Gütersloh, a visit already mentioned in the opening pages of this book. It was here that I completed the sketches of *Meer* in total peace and quiet, while a party of young English singers and instrumentalists and a number of young German directors worked on *The English Cat*, the former under the guidance of Elisabeth Söderström and Markus Stenz. On a few occasions, I made music with the Parnassus Ensemble under its leader Peter Sheppard – the group had given an excellent performance of *Il matrimonio segreto* in Montepulciano the previous summer. It was all enormous fun, and we got on well together. The following year I directed another production of *The English Cat* with the same performers, a surrealistic and, at the same time, romantic staging that I also conducted, first at Montepulciano and then at the BBC's Henze Festival at the Guildhall School of Music and Drama at the beginning of 1991. The production was later filmed by Bavarian Television for a nationwide broadcast. It was to thank Peter Sheppard for his outstanding work in Montepulciano that I wrote my Five Nocturnes, which he played at his London début in May 1990. Manfred Gräter was buried in Cologne, Wenzel in Berlin. Brian Michaels' Gütersloh production of *The English Cat* was shown at Berlin's Hebbel-Theater on 7 October. I attended the performance and was delighted by the lively, audible reaction on the part of the metropolitan audience. I loved Berlin as much as the young musicians from London. From there I hurried to Marino to write begging letters for Montepulciano and Munich, while the earth trembled, the Berlin Wall fell and I set about preparing the fair copy of *Das verratene Meer*.

With the completion of *Das verratene Meer*, a phase in my life was over. Of course, daily, public life went on as before: eight days later, for example, I conducted the Berlin Philharmonic and in mid-December looked in on Götz Friedrich's fascinating production of *Die Bassariden* in Stuttgart and busied myself with plans for the second Biennale, but I was inwardly exhausted, and the process of ageing made itself felt not only in a whole series of physical disorders but also in the need for rest and seclusion. More than once, the difficulties involved in preparing for the first Biennale had been more than I could take, although it had become clear as soon as the festival got under way that the gods were smiling on our enterprise: there were full houses and approval and applause in plenty, and the impression arose – if not universal, it was at least shared by many competent observers as well as by my fellow workers and me – that we had found a formula capable of providing at least a few answers to some of the more pressing questions about the need to nurture a new generation of artists and about the future of both the music theatre in particular and of artistic and musical communication in general. In the course of the first four festivals (they took place every other year), we did indeed succeed in engaging the interest of a fair number of talented young artists and in winning them back to the theatre – a medium that was no longer familiar to them and that they had previously found inaccessible. By performing works based on this often quite unexpected and surprising experience, we were able to open up the way to a creative future for them.

One of my principal aims was to explore and develop a new way of performing and staging works of music that were less costly to mount and more easily transportable. This aim had previously been achieved only in the rarest cases – in street theatre, for example – and yet, although our own administration is as efficient and cost-effective as possible and although we need neither choruses of elephants nor a resident ballet, it still remains a little too cumbersome, too top-heavy, too slow and too expensive. I also encouraged the setting up of a school of puppetry, with the result that at each festival there have been the most wonderful and exciting contributions to a new kind of theatre in which music, space and gesture alone have created the atmosphere and conveyed the sense of the piece without recourse to the sung or spoken word. Unfortunately, the performances of new works – for the most part, well-funded municipal commissions – were always crammed into such a short space of time that, in spite of full houses, the great Munich public was never really able to get a look-in. And often enough the artistic director was unable to influence the character and quality of co-productions and equally often had cause to regret that he none the less had no choice but to put his name to them. With the passage of time this regret became more and more pronounced, finally leading to a sense of embitterment and the decision to introduce changes to our means of production, to slow down the rate at which new works were mounted and to ensure that, in future, commissions were presented individually and that the artistic direction of the Biennale as a whole remained in the hands of a composer. In short, he was keen that the direction of the festival be handed on to a younger person, his highly respected colleague, the then intendant of the Hamburg State Opera, Peter Ruzicka, who – he knew – would develop his ideas in appropriate ways and take steps to ensure that the festival was placed on a proper institutionalized footing, a situation that would almost certainly be achieved by the time the fifth Biennale took place in 1996. From then on, there would be an eight- to ten-day Biennale season every six months, at which no more than two stage works and a puppet play or the like would be performed. In this way it will be possible to give the productions all the attention that they deserve and restore them to the limelight, a limelight of which they have been deprived by the excessive number of alternative attractions on offer. Only through its lasting presence can an idea gain a foothold in the community. By dividing the Biennale programmes over shorter seasons, we have virtually created a kind of 'Municipal Opera House for Modern Music', a goal towards which the municipal department responsible for the arts, together with the city's mayors and governing bodies and I myself, have been working for many years. The Munich Biennale has become a great international point of reference for everyone involved in new music and especially for young composers who are interested in the theatre as a medium. It is a composers' festival and, at the same time, a place where one can work creatively and innovatively at one of the most beautiful and important forms of communication known to civilization.

I should add, perhaps, that it has never been particularly easy to find young people whose ability to write for the theatre was obvious from their previous, largely instrumental output. Talent is as rare as ever. Many people imagine that they can write music, but their ability melts away like wax when exposed to the glaring light of harsh reality. In consequence, every commission involves a certain risk – however good the preconditions, however favourable the points of departure and however careful the calculations, everything can still go wrong and end in unmitigated disaster, just as, conversely, everything may go according to plan and result in an outright success.

As a cultural centre, Munich – by which I mean its audiences, atmosphere, culture and history – is a phenomenon that I regard with the helpless fascination of the disadvantaged North German, while sharing the resigned admiration of the cheated Italian. I examine it closely and realize that this is not my own capital, but that of another country, the country of Bavaria. It has a fairy-tale history and folk traditions that are unique and, in spite of all its eccentricities, it still remains genuine and true and not in the least artificial. This is no doubt bound up, in part, with linguistic conditions, with the geographical situation and with the local – Catholic – religion, the practices and consequences of which may be clearly seen and felt wherever one looks, certainly more so than in any other European country with the possible exceptions of Ireland, Catholic Westphalia and the Vatican State. Religious observance is strict, yet refined, with the locals taking their cue in both word and deed from Rome, while also admitting of rustic delights such as the white-gold *putti* of the unrepressive Baroque, to say nothing of maypoles, cardinals and mysteries, all of them institutions of which the confessional seems to me by far the most important and most basic. For me, Munich is a foreign country and will undoubtedly always remain so, although I have many pleasant memories of the place, on both an artistic and personal level, and know a whole number of extremely kind and interesting people there, especially young people from the world of music and the theatre. What I like best are the educated middle-class audiences and the many individuals – largely from the sciences and fine arts – who have a genuine understanding of art and whom it has always been my greatest wish to interest in my work.

With the members of the Munich Philharmonic, the Radio Orchestra and the Staatskapelle I enjoy a cordial working relationship based on mutual respect and friendship, a circumstance that would in itself be sufficient to endear me to the city. But it is neither this alone, nor my work for the Biennale, nor the successes that I have enjoyed here that fascinates me about the place. What attracts me, rather, is not only the atmosphere of a capital city and royal seat, but also the tempo, energy and progressive nature of its urban social policies and the feeling that one is part of a modern, democratically functioning system on whose achievements and reassurances one can rely. There are also, I find, fewer signs of xenophobia than elsewhere – people have learnt their lesson from history, learnt to feel a permanent sense of shame at the unforgivable actions of a number of their former fellow citizens and realized that they must never let up in their determination to prevent such rabble from returning to their streets. The people of Munich and, indeed, the Bavarians in general are very much predestined to play this part and, no doubt as a result, are a little more tolerant of those who hold differing views and beliefs than certain representatives of other Germanic tribes – or am I completely wrong? Is there something that I have overlooked? I admit that, because it is only ever on business that I visit the place, I have never really had time to pay as much attention as I ought to have done to what the good people of Munich get up to during the daytime and at night – committees, rehearsals, discussions, letter-writing and the like have invariably got in my way. And so my impressions are probably a little superficial and ephemeral, yet it has not escaped my notice, for example, that even Munich has a problem with people sleeping rough. I see the homeless camped out under the bridges whenever I walk along the banks of the Isar and thus remain in some sort of tenuous contact with real life. Sometimes I follow one or other of the two raging torrents that flow through the city, the Östlicher Stadtgrabenbach and the Großer Ammerbach, both of which disappear underground near the Muffathalle, rushing inaudibly along beneath the Isar, before reappearing in all their icy splendour and power in the English Garden, immediately behind the Museum of Art – known to the locals as the Veal Sausage Palace. When the weather is fine, the English Garden is full of good-humoured sun-worshippers of both sexes sprawled out on the grass, and I sit on a bench and watch them a little, trying not to feel sad and envious but to delight in their youth and rejoice in the future. Near the Muffathalle is an island of pebbles opposite the dam and people even sunbathe nude here during the daytime and light fires at night, holding impromptu barbecues in an atmosphere which, cosy and romantic and civilized, breathes a spirit of total peace. On one occasion I peeped down from the Mariannenbrücke on one such tiny group and heard someone playing a guitar (very respectably, too, I may add), unaware that the bald Peeping Tom above him was the composer of the *Royal Winter Music*.

In Munich and, indeed, in Bavaria as a whole, the natives reveal a particular – not to say, extraordinary – predilection for boiled and salted meat. The legs and heads of pigs, horses and cows are consumed in considerable quantities; and the restaurants are packed with gourmandizers gorging themselves on lungs and digestive and reproductive organs that have been boiled until they have lost all their taste, then delightfully disguised with the aroma of herbs and spices. Newcomers go to elaborate and often inelegant lengths in their hopeless attempts to conform, not least in the area of *haute couture*, where there are specialist shops selling inordinately expensive Bavarian paraphernalia of every conceivable kind, from hat decorations made from the hair of a chamois to coshes, and from dirndls suitable for first nights at the opera to riding whips, lederhosen, calico and horn buttons.

What I like most about Munich is the way in which the horse-chestnut trees and white hawthorn are reflected in the river in spring and their lower branches are forced down into the water by the sheer weight of their flowers so that it cools and cradles them. The perfume of the trees in blossom at Nymphenburg and Schleißheim recalls fond memories of my own distant past, with its picnics and walks. Sometimes one shivers in the sunshine. One needs only to keep on walking in a straight line to find oneself very quickly in open countryside, on a high plateau, with its arable land and its farmers and their gleaming and well-groomed domesticated animals, all of which are electrically served and milked. And, not far from the site of the Dachau concentration camp, one can even steal into the forest and, with the hair on one's neck on end, encounter wild animals which, timid and easily frightened, go in fear of their lives and run away at the sight of us humans, such is their insane and yet wholly justified fear of us.

Most of all, I would like to remain with these animals here in a forest like this and clamber up some tall tree like Calvino's *barone rampante* and never have to answer another question.

Meanwhile, I had sent off the full score of *Das verratene Meer* at the end of 1989. My exhaustion dragged on into 1990, although I did what I could to meet all the many commitments that I had taken upon myself, including a residency with the Berlin Philharmonic and at the Wissenschaftskolleg in the late autumn of that year, a responsibility which, flattered, I had thoughtlessly accepted only to quit Berlin within a matter of weeks: I could not work there, everything was too old and, at the same time, too new and I did not understand – or refused to see – why I could not work in Marino at least as well, if not better, at my old familiar desk and with my old familiar books and music and instruments.

And Berlin had changed a lot in the meantime, now that neither Wenzel nor Paul was there any longer: a whole era had come to an end. The Wall had fallen and, with it, the GDR and, finally, the whole of the socialist Eastern Bloc. A gaping gash cut right across Berlin, running along the line where the border had been and the Wall had once stood and where, for decades, the inhabitants of the city and their compatriots from outside Berlin had been kept apart in order to encourage the growth of two fundamentally different forms of cultural, moral and social behaviour, the contradictions between which now constitute a serious human problem and, as such, a powerful obstacle in the way of intellectual and social reunification. I found the arrogance of the West Germans painful and insufferable: they behaved like victors, treating their fellow-countrymen from the new *Länder* as inferior beings and as a defeated nation. People had completely forgotten that it was they – the inhabitants of the new *Länder* – who for forty years had paid the heaviest price for Hitler and atoned for the Second World War, while the West Germans had been helped out by the Marshall Plan and hence by the free-market economy of capitalism. It was also forgotten – or swept under the carpet of people's bad consciences – that the GDR had not only been an Eastern Bloc country with a repressive police system and spy network, but that it had also had at its disposal a large number of first-class, well-subsidized theatres and orchestras and that it had paid special attention to the need to educate young people in the arts, while its schools and universities had produced many great writers, doctors and scientists. That there are fears and reservations on both sides is something that I find both natural and more than justified. Perhaps it needs more than one generation for the wound to cicatrize and for the breeding-grounds of hubris and shame to vanish beneath the showy steel façades of a more forward-looking twenty-first century.

My final concert and, I think, my last appearance as a conductor was with the Berlin Philharmonic in a series of performances in the orchestra's smaller concert hall between 2 and 5 October 1991, when I conducted works by Dittersdorf and Haydn, together with my own Three Dithyrambs and First Symphony. At the rehearsals for this last-named piece I was able to make some improvements to the orchestration, improvements that were duly entered in the score and orchestral parts.

During the early part of 1990 I took out an old preprint of my *Concerto per il Marigny* and had just started to expand it and make changes to it in different coloured crayons when I received a call from Covent Garden: the Royal Opera was organizing a memorial concert for Michael Vyner and was soliciting contributions from Berio, Birtwistle, Górecki, Knussen, Maxwell Davies, Osborne, Takemitsu and myself, all of them new pieces that would be performed by Olly and the Sinfonietta. I accepted the invitation without a moment's hesitation and, as soon as I had done so, knew what it was that I had to do with my old *Concerto per il Marigny*: it would serve as the basic material for a cyclical work, lasting an entire evening, that I had been planning for years, a large-scale, non-vocal *Requiem* in the form of nine movements for concertante instruments, with the piano and trumpet playing an especially important role from a formal and dramaturgical point of view. It would be an epitaph for Michael Vyner, a full-length piece, music about a particular friendship, about life and suffering, about hope and love and fate. The first movement, performed at Covent Garden on 6 May 1990, is called 'Introitus: Requiem' and on closer examination proves to be a much-improved and much-revised version of the former, fragmentary *Concerto per il Marigny*, now worked out in every last detail. As piano soloist I imagined Paul Crossley, who had been Michael's lifelong friend and colleague and who had now taken over from him as the orchestra's artistic director. The music of these piano solos expresses something of the private background described above, as well as the shared memories bound up with that background, memories that stretch back over several decades and that are full of enchantment and blessed with understanding. Paul knew all this and could express his own feelings on the matter in playing of powerful instrumental eloquence. It was inevitable that I should keep thinking of Michael while working on the score, since my music for this *Requiem* expresses my own developing involvement with the dead and dying and also with horror *tout court*.

On the morning of 11 May 1990 I found myself standing, dry-throated, in the island cemetery of San Michele in Venice, as Luigi Nono was carried to his final resting place. As with Paul Dessau in the early summer of 1979, there was nothing more that could be said. The only sound was the wind in the trees and the twittering of the birds. By the evening I was already back in Munich for the first performance of *The Mother of Three Sons*, a Biennale commission, at the Deutsches Theater. At the end of the second Biennale, I returned to Marino and wrote a triptych for piano quintet, something of a feet-finding exercise from which more music was later to be taken over into the *Requiem* and specifically into the 'Dies irae', the 'Ave verum' and the 'Lux aeterna'. The Day of Wrath is not necessarily or exclusively about the Last Judgement, but could also be the worst day in a person's life or the sum total of such days, when everything of value and substance collapses around you and everything that could once have offered you guidance and support is lost for ever. In the 'Ave verum corpus' I wonder if it was the image of a beautiful human body covered with Hölderlin's freckles and with ultramodern sores that inspired me to write this music, or was it, rather, the sight of a medieval German or Baconesque *pietà*, the tenderness of a man's final moments and the sense of farewell and departure? I no longer know what it was – I expect it was a combination of various impressions and insights, all of which came together here. And the light everlasting of which we hear in the other movement has nothing to do with the world of transcendency but refers to the light of day in its constant and endless interplay of phenomena and colours and atmospheres, the sparkle and glitter of silent sheet lightning on a summer's night and the redemptive, heart-warming sunlight of Marino.

For the Agnus Dei, which was the second section of the *Requiem* to be written after the opening Introit and which is scored for piano and small string orchestra alone, I took over the pastoral rhythm from the Agnus Dei in Beethoven's *Missa solemnis*, giving it virtually the status of a quotation, even though I was in fact thinking of the sheep pastures on the old Appian Way, of the local shepherds and their music, and of the ways in which living creatures are ritualistically or mechanically killed on hallowed ground and in the abattoirs and torture chambers of this world. In the 'Rex tremendae' we hear the voice of a ruler or commander relayed through the trumpet's amplifying bell in what seems to be an agitated, fanatically incendiary speech delivered in a rasping, peremptory tone and using a vocabulary which, vulgar to the point of sounding comical, is aggressively petty bourgeois. When the speaker stops to clear his throat or to allow the effect of his words to sink in, we hear the sounds of pleasure and approbation on the part of the downtrodden populace, sounds murmured with smoochy enjoyment.

This tone is mirrored in the 'Tuba mirum', which dates from the summer of 1992 and which was the last part of the *Requiem* to be written: it is intended as a concentrate of vulgar music, in which the sounds of childhood terrors are juxtaposed and superimposed on memories of marching songs and hymns, together with popular hits and moments of meanness and drunkenness. The sounds of Leni Riefenstahl's Nazi Nuremberg assault our ear with the speed of flashlight photographs, the trumpeters exude crass stupidity in the moronic major tonality of conformists and fellow-travellers. It is brass music of the worst possible kind, music that I want to chill the listener to the marrow. People must be made to realize that the language of these monsters is still in daily use, poisoning our hearts and dragging the concepts of dignity, intellectual beauty and aesthetic idealism through the quagmire of commonality and self-sufficiency.

Above and beyond all this, the piece is also designed to place very special demands on the skills of its instrumentalists. Whereas Masses for the Dead normally rely for their effectiveness, at least in part, on the human voice and their Latin words, it is now the instrumentalists who are entrusted with that task: they are expected to *think* the words and assume the function of the singers, empathizing with that role and imitating it on their instruments. One might say that in this work my theory and my ideal of the interchangeability of vocal and instrumental music has found its most extensive realization to date. The 'Lacrimosa' is a portrait of a suffering, weeping individual and, as such, a further example of this particular development in my style. We do not know the reasons for the man's weeping, do not know the nature of the pain that arises from the musical textures necessary to depict it. All that we can do is follow the course that is taken by this weeping and grieving, emotions depicted by a solo trumpeter with assistance from all the other performers, swelling, abating, welling up once again and finally breaking off for ever with an expression of utter despair. In the final Sanctus I have written parts for two additional *trombettieri* positioned in the main body of the hall, where they take up the solo trumpeter's music and echo it in canon, a musical gesture borrowed – of course – from the church music of the baroque and intended as a way of raising the roof and revealing a Tiepolesque sky in order that a little of its sempiternal light may descend upon this benighted world, while the attendant mood is that of a Protestant Whitsun festival or Catholic Epiphany or some other manifestation of divine or artistic comfort that involves the transcendent presence of archangels and cherubim.

My *Requiem* is a secular, multicultural piece, an act of brotherly love that was written 'in memoriam Michael Vyner', whose name does duty for all the many other people in the world who have died before their time and whose sufferings and passing are mourned in my music. Yet the work is not only about this one specific form of suffering, it also speaks of other pains, of abandonment, of the death of friendship, of breaches of faith and trust, of loneliness and also of (the vain) hope (of peace, peace of mind, calm and mental equilibrium) and of the longing to be with people who have abandoned us and whom we would like to have followed into the unknown other world, a world which, in all likelihood, does not in fact exist, at least not for the eyes of us poor mortals. Ghostly apparitions in music and poetry, events enacted in the world of our imagination, chance occurrences and dreams can sometimes give us the fleeting impression that an afterlife exists and that we ourselves are awaited there at some later date – whether we shall be welcomed with red-hot pincers or with myrrh and *vino nobile* is not clear – but doubts repeatedly assert themselves in the form of anxious inner voices and in the speechless fear of eternal, terrible darkness, of nothingness and of an end to all existence.

In writing the *Requiem*, I had solved my *Marigny* complex and brought to an end a chapter in the history of my oeuvre. Virtually all the movements were performed in isolation in London and Tokyo before the piece was given complete on 24 February 1993 in a live broadcast from the Philharmonic Hall in Cologne. The heart-rending Ensemble Modern was conducted by that highly gifted and supremely qualified musical fireball, Ingo Metzmacher, while the soloists were the trumpeter Håkan Hardenberger and the pianist Ueli Wiget, both of whom were outstanding and to both of whom I am bound by bonds of eternal friendship. Oliver Knussen conducted the British première at the Proms on 5 September, with Paul Crossley at the piano. It was a sunny Sunday morning, and the members of the London Sinfonietta and many of our mutual friends and acquaintances went for a picnic afterwards beneath the oaks in Kensington Gardens directly opposite the Albert Hall. It was John Drummond, an unusually witty and widely read individual, who, as head of music at the BBC and director of the Promenade Concerts, had programmed the performance of the *Requiem*, just as he had earlier programmed the spectacular British première of my Seventh Symphony on 25 July 1986 and, later, that of the Eighth on 4 August 1995, both with the City of Birmingham Symphony Orchestra under Simon Rattle. And it was he, too, who organized a ten-concert festival of my music at the Barbican Centre in 1991.

The *Requiem* soon became a repertory piece that other modern groups such as the Dutch ASKO and Schoenberg Ensembles, the Paris Ensemble InterContemporain and the Zurich Collegium Novum were able to take on tour with them. On 11 July 1995 I was moved beyond words to hear it performed by Sian Edwards and Ensemble Modern in St Mark's, Venice, and it has even been heard in Moscow, where a performance was given in the Great Hall at the Conservatory on 11 May 1995 to mark not only the fiftieth anniversary of the end of the war, but also the overthrow of two Fascist regimes and the outbreak of the cold war between two of the most fundamentally divergent schools of thought in recent European history – a period that is now perhaps gone for ever. And it also celebrated the peace of 1945 and the pax of 1995. Finally, Markus Stenz, the new principal conductor and artistic director of the London Sinfonietta, opened his first London season with the work on 27 November 1994.

In the autumn of 1992, in a state of relative peace and with feelings verging on happiness, I wrote the final movement of my Eighth Symphony. The idea for the work had come to me the previous summer in Amsterdam, where, having completed the 'Tuba mirum', I had fled to escape from the lion's mouth of an Italian August and where I had spoken to Jan van Vlijmen of the Holland Festival about a co-production of Robert Zuidam's opera, *Patty Hearst* (later renamed *FREEZE*) for the fourth Biennale. I also met the composer himself on more than one occasion, dined with him, listened to tapes of his wild orchestral studies and walked with him on the beach at Zandvoort in a pleasantly refreshing headwind. The rest of the time I spent in my hotel room or, by preference, at a coffee house, thinking about my Eighth Symphony.

Amsterdam, 24 August 1992. *01.30 p.m. Café Américain, Leidseplein. have reread Midsummer Night's Dream and marked three passages, Oberon's travelling instructions to Puck, the love scenes between Titania and Bottom and Puck's peroration, if we shadows have offended. it should be possible to produce a very neat three-movement symphony on the basis of these three incidents or situations or moods, symph. no. 8, very light-footed and full of tunes.*

orchestration 2/2/2/2 4/2/2/1

strings perc. harp keyboard instr.

ideas come and go very quickly, issuing forth from the bodies of Oberon (i.e., me), Tit and Bot (what sort of a duet will that *be?!), who are likewise naturally embodied by me – and Puck, too, of course, sorry, when he addresses his audience, just as much as i wish to do.*

harmonies to be less dense: use eight- and sixteen-foot metres. 1st movement with constantly changing patterns of light and no repeats.

if i were to write the epilogue first, it would contain the THEME *or a number of themes and harmonies that could then be subjected to several variations in the first and second sections (rapidly changing images: the one that Oberon describes is identical to the one that Puck, returning with the magic flower in his hand, actually sees on his forty-minute journey round the earth – a journey that modern man would nowadays take only seven or eight minutes to complete), and also a comic minor variation, or this and a chaconne, enabling me to write a dance form, something wide-ranging, not something restrictively elliptical or whatever, but a songlike, horizontal development of the scene between Tit and Bot. enormous contrasts. great possibilities.*

on 1st movement: this girdle (of vines, or at least ivy) that Puck intends to put round about the earth can be made visible, i mean its rotating movement. must think how this can be achieved. i like the idea of starting with the final movement.

the second movement will be the longest, the centre. the 1st movement its prologue, the 3rd its epilogue.

try to restrict your material and stay as simple as possible.
8th symph. with the new moon.

Hans-Ulrich Treichel and I had continued with our plans and deliberations for a mythological opera and had even made some progress and exchanged one protagonist for another, but the fish was still refusing to bite, and I was still plagued by doubts and suspicions concerning the credibility and attractiveness of our heroines and heroes. The intendant of the Bavarian State Opera, Peter Jonas, had been waiting for an opera from me for a number of years and, having already pencilled a date in his huge diary for the 1996/7 season, was beside himself with joy when I was finally able to provide him with concrete dates and a title and subtitle, which I did at the end of my summer travels, following detailed and careful discussions with Uli in Berlin.

How had we arrived at *Venus und Adonis*? As I write these lines today, on 7 February 1995, I can already describe it all in the past tense, since the music has all been written, having been completed in full score in September 1994. The date of the first night was fixed: 11 January 1997. It was to be directed by Pierre Audi, designed by Chloé Obolensky and conducted by Markus Stenz. Just as the spirit world of Shakespeare's *Dream* breathed life into my Eighth Symphony (to which we shall return in a moment), so the opera was to be a summation of random daily occurrences, encounters with reality and the emotions of a rapidly ageing old man, thus producing the form that developed out of my heteromorphous material in the course of a leisurely genesis. If I remember aright, it began many years ago when I was invited by the astute and charming director of the Berlin Biennale, Heike Hoffmann, to write something for the famous a cappella group, The King's Singers, and I had said that I would think it over. Well, I continued to think it over and began to imagine a piece of vocal music, gently flowing along and sounding like a string ensemble, a sound which at that time still floated around aimlessly in space, with no particular place to go. Fate then found me in Barcelona, where I saw a small dance group recommended to me by José Udaeta: amongst the fandangos and malagueñas and flamencos were a few pieces that were totally unrelated to the zapateados of Valencia and to the clattering castanets of tap-dancers from Madrid or to the Arab rhythms and melismas that characterize the bastardized folk dances and music of Andalusia. Here was something altogether different, something with its own distinctive charisma, calm and ceremonial, restrained, more austere than academic classical ballet and danced on silent shoes: this was the classical Basque bolero, a Celtic dance, and hence not dissimilar to Irish, Scottish and Breton dances.

Even as a young man in Paris, at a performance by Pilar Lopez, I still remember being captivated by the marionette-like charm and objectively stylized grace of the classical bolero, and had felt a sharp pain in my heart every time that I had seen it since then. It was exactly the same on this particular summer morning in the Valribera dance studio in Barcelona.

A few hours later I flew on to Berlin and went straight to see my poet in order to tell him what had happened in Barcelona and on the flight to Berlin, when, on my right, the snow-capped peaks of the Pyrenees had sparkled in the sun and, on my left, the mechanical rhythms of this classical bolero had continued to obsess me, humming and seething and fermenting and interrupted only by my thoughts of the flowing polyphony of human voices, a reaction I imagined was due to the overpowering need that I felt to develop the musical textures of my unaccompanied choruses, *Orpheus behind the Wire*, of 1983. Was this suite of vocal ensembles perhaps to acquire a sense of cyclical and thematic cohesion, much as its predecessor, the *Orpheus* songs, had done?

It was at this juncture that I recalled Shakespeare's verse romance, *Venus and Adonis*, and imagined in my mind's eye a stage action in which the bolero (a sequence of scenes, a suite of boleros) would fulfil a number of essential dramaturgical functions. It would be a dance drama performed in a marionette-like style, an ancient ritual that would show what happens between Venus, Adonis and, later and inevitably, Mars in both Shakespeare and the myth. To the accompaniment of these measured dance steps and gestures, all manner of inexpressible passions would seethe and boil and rage in my seven boleros, passions of which music alone is empowered to speak, certainly not the bolero dancers, inexpressive outer husks and masks of Venus, Adonis and Mars and of the nag and stallion and death-dealing boar. Six shepherds (two sopranos, alto, tenor, baritone and bass) would sit in the trees, observing events and commenting upon them, until everything collapses like a pack of cards.

The main character is a woman, an opera singer, the Prima Donna, a diva (soprano). She has been engaged to sing the dance songs in a ballet, *Venus und Adonis* (loosely based on Shakespeare), a practice often encountered in baroque operas. An anonymous baritone and a young tenor by the name of Clemente also find themselves on stage with her for the same contractual reasons. Trouble must have started brewing during the very first rehearsals: at all events, we become aware during the opening scene between the Prima Donna and the Baritone (like all the dialogue scenes, it is headed 'Recitative') that all is not well and that their marital or, rather, extramarital harmony is threatened by a more than passing disturbance. What develops is a frightening psychological drama: as in *Das verratene Meer*, we are dealing with an erotic eternal triangle that threatens the very lives of its three participants, except that on this occasion it is not a gang of unhinged milksops that puts an end to the affair, but the injured party himself, the Baritone, who rages with jealousy like a real wild boar and who stabs the young tenor, while on the stage above them the wild boar (Mars in disguise) tears Adonis limb from limb. The music that follows is music of the stars or planets, as Adonis soars through space on his way to his lover and mother, Venus, uniting with her for ever in death.

The preliminary studies for *Venus und Adonis* and the elaboration of the libretto took place while I was still working on my Eighth Symphony. As planned, I began with the symphony's final movement on 28 September 1992 and by 10 October (*tempests, floods, thunderstorms*) was already able to note that the sketches for it were complete, that I had had few problems with it and that it had given me enormous pleasure to write such 'insane light music'. There were no particular private reasons why I should have felt such a sense of well-being. I immediately made a start on the full score. The result is a great hymn, not an envoi, no, not that, but rather a placatory gesture, a belated explanation, as in Shakespeare: it is a peace accord, an act of reconciliation, a declaration of brotherly love (for myself, too), and the accompanying gesture is made by someone who loves and longs for a state of calm. By early November I had completed the third movement and now began to sketch the first in London and to develop it, as planned, from the music of the third. How I did so can be seen from the score. The first stage of the operation was to compose Puck's garland as he encircles the earth and it flutters after him: he starts in the west in the middle register (middle C), at the Equator, then travels in an anticlockwise direction and reaches the South Pole at the end of the first quarter of the time available for the completion of his journey; here are the lowest notes that the modern symphony orchestra can offer. Then, still travelling at the same speed, he reaches the East Pole – in other words, the Equatorial middle register – after which he dashes up to the North Pole as the icicles crunch in the highest register of the modern orchestra and Amor shoots his arrow at the soft underbelly of the moon, before Puck and his girdle return to their starting point. I hardly need to mention that, musically speaking, the girdle completes the second half of its journey in retrograde in order to represent by purely objective means the idea of curvature and the impression of a return from the opposite direction. Once the girdle was finished, I set about drafting an aria-like *Hauptstimme* in which the semiquaver movement of the girdle appears to have been reduced to an accompanying role and treated as an accompanying figure: this *Hauptstimme*, of course, is entrusted to the baritone voice of Oberon, who gives his instructions to the attentive and observant Puck and prescribes the route that the latter must take. Specific images in this speech are carried over into the music: at the very end of the movement, for example, on page 46 of the study score, the magic flower that Puck brings back with him from the other side of the world bursts into blossom and begins to fill the air with all its perfumed sweetness.

The middle section of the triptych depicts everything or, at least, some of the things that cannot be seen on midsummer night, but that can only be felt and tasted and heard and smelt. It has much to do with the blandishments of Eros, its aberrations and excesses, its wild passions and animistic animality. In concrete terms, it deals in the first instance with Titania, the queen of the fairies, and with her charm and musical accomplishments: think only of the curves of her swan-white body as painted by Henry Fuseli or of the look in Victoria Zinovieff's eyes or in those of the young Joana Maria Gorvin, of delicacy and delight, and the thrill of pleasure that one feels when intoxication in the form of Oberon's ear drops opens the way to uninhibited and unbounded behaviour and one forgets what an elfin queen may or may not do. And Titania naturally lusts after the kitchen staff and knows exactly what to look for down there, such is her fondness for earthiness and bestiality, for this elvish plain fare, the warmth of the stable and for genitalia of all shapes and sizes – not just those of Bottom the weaver but especially of the ass, of course – only as the lady of the house and as a fairy she is not allowed to show it. But the music reveals all, and does so, moreover, in a quite unmistakable manner, suggesting that not only Titania herself is having a great time tonight, so, too, of course, is Bottom, except that he is unable to express himself in such finely turned and well-honed prose – no attempt has been made so far to press into his hands a couple of string instruments with which to serenade his bride. No, Bottom expresses himself in the main through asinine whinnying and braying, with a concertante trombone as his *Hauptstimme*. But other wind instruments – brass and wood – add their voices, producing a whole chorus of good-naturedly good-humoured men and their four-legged equivalents, whom we watch as they go about their favourite activity as though it were some innocent sporting pastime. As a result, the whole movement has something of the character of a concerto cast fairly loosely in rondo form. I wrote it during the early months of 1993 and had still not finished it when I fell while playing ball with Tania's daughter, Arabella, at Easter and broke my right hand – my writing hand. It was all most unfortunate – I was so looking forward to hearing the piece as planned in Boston in the fall (this hope was also bound up with certain ideas and experiments relating to the sound world of *Venus und Adonis*), with the result that I had to train myself to write with my left hand in order to be able to finish the second movement and for a time had to call for help on two young assistants: Roderick Watkins, who worked on the full score of the first movement, and Jan Müller-Wieland, who transcribed a number of passages from the second movement that I had already completed in the form of individual sketches and who continued to work for me until such time as I was able to write with my left hand and sketch out and score the ending of this movement – the whole of the witty and well-constructed stretta – without any need for outside help, a task I accomplished left-handedly and not without a certain sense of pride.

The rehearsals and performances of the Eighth Symphony were held in Boston during early October 1993 and proved a particularly happy experience for me. While the harbour and bay outside the concert hall glinted in the Atlantic sun, the violins and trumpets inside glistened and gleamed with no less radiance: it all sounded bright and clear, full of warmth and love, and I was delighted with everything, including everything that the conductor and orchestra and audience had to say about the piece. Once again, there was proper contact between conductor, orchestra and me, indeed, it now seemed to have become self-evident. Seiji Ozawa's excellent assistant, Thomas Dausgaard, sat next to me at the rehearsals and noted down my remarks concerning dynamics, balance, expression and tempi, remarks that related, for the most part, to the need to ensure that the *Hauptstimmen* were clearly audible (without a knowledge of these, our listeners would have been left helpless and clueless). During breaks in the rehearsals I would discuss these points with the maestro, whereupon the librarian would make all the necessary changes and additions not only to the conductor's score but also to the orchestral parts. Dear Fausto was especially taken by Boston – socially, too: we had such good friends here, not just colleagues but also acquaintances, most of whom hailed, of course, from the world of music (with Tanglewood as a common background), although others travelled down specially from New York – Maureen and Claude, Tania León, David Lang, Ron Freed, Toshiro Saruya (have I forgotten anyone?), all of whom came to say hello to Fausto and the old man. On one occasion, Marti Epstein and her boyfriend threw a dinner party for us at their attractive studio in Brookline, to which they also invited a number of young and talented people from Boston (*these young people are so fascinating in all that they think and feel and in their spirit of enquiry!*). We got our own back on our final evening at a famous Indian restaurant that was licensed to sell alcohol and that had an excellent wine list.

It was very important for me to hear my Eighth Symphony: after all, it is like a curtain that goes up on a new action.

> *am satisfied that we've gone a stage beyond the Requiem. completely different feelings are present here, and it is now clear how i shall go on from here, i.e. what the music of 'Venus und Adonis' will sound like.*

What the opera would sound like, I had in fact known since the middle of July, since I had already started on it by that date. I had first of all been struck by the idea of dividing the orchestra into three (in keeping with tradition, the three resultant groups would be positioned in the pit, rather than in the wings or in the foyer of the Bavarian Nationaltheater), with a Venus orchestra (to the audience's left), a Mars orchestra (to the audience's right) and an Adonis orchestra (in the middle). All three contain the same number of strings, but otherwise everything possible has been done to ensure that each of these three participants in the conflict retains its own distinctive character or at least to create the basic conditions for such a characterization. The young tenor, Clemente, who lends his voice to Adonis, the shepherd and huntsman – who is represented in turn by a silent actor or dancer – is joined by oboes and horns in his pastorales and hunting music, the sound of which can be further brightened by means of a celesta and light percussion instruments. The Baritone is an unexceptional individual, an ageing actor who specializes in heroic roles and whose part is not doubled by a dancer (at least not until towards the end, when, in the irrational blindness of his jealousy, Mars takes over this function and role in the form of a wild boar, thereby implying that from the very beginning Mars has had an invisible hand in the whole affair and dominated the feelings of Herr X from first to last). In warlike passages, he is accompanied by trumpets, which often add their concertante voices more than a whole octave above his own vocal line, while in his fairly frequent sentimental passages, he is joined by clarinets and even by a concertante piano, which contrasts, as it were, with the harp, an instrument that is bound to feature in Venus's court orchestra. Flutes accompany the coloratura writing for the *divina*, while trombones, more than two whole octaves beneath her soprano register, underscore her mythical origins. When the Prima Donna is alone on stage, only the Venus orchestra is heard, and the same is true of the other two characters. When all three appear together (as happens increasingly often in the course of the piece), all three orchestras play at once, each with its own music. I imagine something intensely polyphonic, something that proliferates and grows and blows this way and that, calmly and at will.

> *21 July 1993. 11.00 a.m. wrote beautiful row yesterday, sketched about 50% of the prelude, impassioned music. expanded it today and finished it off, wanted to write it out in full score straightaway, but then saw that it will be better and simpler and, ultimately, quicker if i start again at the beginning with the short score.*
>
> *musica sontuosa*
>
> *first shepherds' chorus will emerge from the g sharp minor ending of the prelude (tomorrow)*
>
> *invent as you go*

A summer without Montepulciano! A year without the Biennale! By early August I was already well embarked on the first 'Recitative' between the Prima Donna and the Baritone and, having felt the need for a few extra instruments, had given Venus an additional alto saxophone as well as a tuba, while Mars had gained a bass trumpet for a number of the concertante *Nebenstimmen* that accompany the main vocal lines.

> *today, too, had a good morning, serious and solemn and nat. V and A are no neoclassical heroes but modern figures with psych. problems, modern living human beings and neurotics like you and me*

At the same time I was preoccupied with two lectures that I had agreed to deliver at the University of Zurich in September (and which I later conflated as a single essay, *The Language of Music and Artistic Invention*, for a fifth volume of aesthetics, *Myth and Music*, on which I am currently working). An entry dated 8 August in my working diary for *Venus* includes a plan for organizing and structuring the first bolero, Adonis's entrance music and his first dance song. Later, too, I repeatedly made a note of these preliminary plans, rather as in a logbook: one can then go back and see how a particular idea worked out quite differently from the way it was originally intended and how it finally turned out, a kind of second sight or third ear that allows me to intervene and change the direction of the music.

Markus Stenz, whom I had asked to conduct the first performance of the work, came to visit us for a few days and took a look at the orchestral plan. After some hesitation, I also allowed him the occasional glimpse of the short score. There were also frequent telephone calls to Uli T. in Berlin, whom I had to ask for additional lines and other alterations. We were for ever changing things, chiefly adding new passages to clarify certain nuances or to make the meaning clearer and to add some extra depth, although often enough it was simply for the sake of a particular rhythm or a single note or emotion. It was now exactly a year since Uli had written his first outline of the opera. For my own part, I was slowly becoming more confident in my handling of my three orchestras.

Tarasp, 21 August 1993. really must think of my work a little, but only what is to come, not retrospectively. the whole thing is meant to proceed virtually without a plan, virtually without a plan, one thing should develop spontaneously out of another (with the process of development guided and conditioned by the form of the libretto). these recitatives will be very colourful and sinewy, triply autobiographical, as it were, i'm also very pleased to be using Valéry's theorem which we're just trying out here and which states that when there are no more words to express our feelings, music takes over and the person in question or the person so affected bursts into song or, as in V & A, possibly even into dance.

Marino, early September. There will be seven bolero-like dance numbers in *Venus und Adonis*, each of which will have to perform a particular dramaturgical and narrative function. Uli still has to write monologues for all three singers. The music for the Prima Donna (Venus) will turn out increasingly like an ice-cold, white, glittering star observed from the sort of proximity that one sees and feels at the Equator. The planet Mars is reddish gold there, as though on fire – Adonis, by contrast, exists only in the mind. Perhaps he is a little like young Gulchenrouz in Beckford's *Vathek*.

3 totally different characters and types of music. the whole thing artificial and baroque. a baroque entertainment.

New wine is fermenting in the beautiful old wooden vats, you have only to place your ear to the walls to hear this mythical, Eros-laden music rumbling ominously and think of Persephone and of the voices and atmosphere in the underworld – and of eternity, divine violence and the meaning of ecstasy.

The traditional wine-growing festival at La Leprara in Marino generally takes place on the first Sunday of the month after the grape harvest has been gathered in, but in 1993 it had to be postponed to 17 October as a result of our visit to Boston and various other *contretemps*. On this occasion it marked a whole series of anniversaries: first, there was my arrival in Italy forty years earlier, then there was the thirtieth anniversary of the Henze–Moroni non-aggression pact and, finally, the forthcoming fiftieth birthday celebrations of Fausto himself, an event duly marked at the latter's request.

Various colleagues and friends, most of them younger than ourselves, came to Marino for the occasion, mainly from Italy, but also from America and Great Britain, as well as a few kind souls from the German colony. The pianists Moritz Eggert and Martin Zehn from Munich were also there and played Debussy's *En blanc et noir* and Stravinsky's Concerto. At lunch-time there was a baroque repast for some seventy people outside in the *cortile* by the wine cellars, over which hung a grey and cooling blanket of clouds. It was really only now that the leaves were beginning to turn yellow and red in the vineyards. The swallows were making their final preparations for their journey south and foregathering on the telegraph wires diagonally opposite our house, waiting to follow the family of hoopoes, who had set off long before them. The breasts of the robins and wagtails gleamed in the autumn light, as, too, did the sensual curves of ripe pomegranates, quinces, mulberries and the fruit of the *giuggiolo*, the jujube tree, while upstairs in my workroom, every surface was covered with sheets of manuscript paper, sketches, fair copies, abstracts, photocopies, metronomes and stopwatches: *Venus und Adonis* was now on the stocks.

Every day I would be struck by new ideas and continue to work on the score, composing, combining and constructing its network of notes from morning till evening and even working upon it at night in my dreams. My thoughts revolved around the opera unceasingly and obsessively, around its form and style and sound. The writer has to put himself in the position of his characters, feel his way into their psyches and their problems, he has to live the drama, experience the characters' jealousy for himself and suffer the complications of this eternal triangle, if necessary summoning them up from his memory. He must come out of his shell, express his innermost self and yield up everything he possesses. At the end – in other words, when the work is actually finished in full score (I imagined that it would be towards the end of 1995, although in the event I was able to put the finishing touches to the score on 9 September) – all that would be left of me would be an exhausted, tired old husk with a mind that was sensitive to noise and a body sensitive to pain and a wholly justified need for a couple of glasses of the new year's wine.

Such an idyllic, secluded existence, within the protecting embrace of castle-like walls, is not only possible but has actually come to pass. And all the while, other people starve and go in fear of their lives, bereft of all hope, on a massive scale, threatened by viruses, problems of identity and the generational divide. There is a lack of ideas, of medicine, of humanitarian concerns and brotherly love. History seems to have stopped in its tracks and to consist only of relapses and recidivism, relapses into the barbarism of military conflict, of racism and exploitation of the weak. As the twentieth century draws to a jangling close, we see all around us the pitiful failure of one of the first great attempts to improve the human condition and the conditions in which we live; in other words, to change mankind in order that we may aspire to a higher, superior level of coexistence. Nineteenth-century philosophers and economists, mainly from Germany, had pointed the way forward and laid the theoretical foundations of socialism. But this is as far as we got. The theory has lost none of its beauty and significance, even if reality and the actual state of the world have overtaken and undermined it and even if it seems to have been proved completely wrong by all the obvious signs of catastrophic failure and collapse. Perhaps insufficient attention has been paid to the theory, perhaps people overlooked this or that point when they set out in their subversive ways to put these ideas into practice. Or perhaps it was simply not a good time to do what it said in the textbooks, perhaps circumstances did not allow it – circumstances that include two world wars; Fascism; poverty; underdevelopment; the effortful round of human existence; our old bad habits like our need for freedom, the instinctive, rebellious, unbridled element within us; our reproductive and murderous urges; and the lively comings and goings of our sympathies, passions and idiosyncrasies. The chill wind of transience ruffles our best intentions.

And it is now October 1995. Another year has passed. My psychodrama on the subject of sexual jealousy is finished, and the 164-page manuscript score has long since been sent off to Germany. With it has gone my cast of characters, my Prima Donna (Venus), my jack of all trades (the Heldenbariton Mars), and the young singer (Clemente–Adonis). And I have fished out the short score of a seven-movement symphony that I had partly sketched out last winter and have spent the last few weeks slowly redirecting my thoughts from the opulent, sensual world of opera to another plane of awareness and emotion. My early, bleak experiences of my own country demand to be addressed and explored in this new choral symphony, a work that is, in short, an act of direct confrontation. Hans-Ulrich Treichel visited me recently to discuss textual details of its seven movements, each of which deals with the horrors and disasters described by Anna Seghers in her novel, *Das siebte Kreuz*, and with the fate of young German anti-Fascists during the early years of the Fascists' reign of terror. We identify with our fellow-countrymen and -women of that time and raise a new monument to them, the forgotten heroes of the Resistance. And I recall the fears and pain of my childhood and youth – they become landscapes, a land of mists and topsoil, from which I derive the backdrop of sound against which the tremendous stirrings and movements of the persecuted and the persecutors will have to be depicted and in which human nature merges with our environment, an environment to which we are exposed like a hare to a pack of hounds, fatally, tragically entangled, condemned by fate, with no hope of escape. And I have a deadline: the Berlin Philharmonic and Berlin Radio Choir will give the first performance on 11 September 1997 under the direction of Ingo Metzmacher.

At the moment, however, it is still possible to rest a little, to look back, to put things in order, to take deep breaths and to squint into the sun.

18 october. 2.00 p.m. sitting on balcony, in the top left-hand corner, almost vertically above me is Helios, to the left of me, at head height, a broad reddish gold strip to the south-west, the sea, my old ears are warmed and caressed, my old knee unbends. there is a smell of fermenting grapes in the air, also ivy in flower surrounded by a swarm of honey bees. cyclamen and meadow saffron from eastern Westphalia glisten in the bushes.

the silence creates a sense of distance, as though there were still cicadas here or as though it were already possible to hear the protractedly plaintive cries of the crickets in the evening.

yet it is probably deathly quiet outside – or is there perhaps some sound after all? only a few enemy aircraft in the sky, distant thunder.

but the land lies peaceful and proud and impressive here, Italy, the world.

Index